Human Intelligence

Human Intelligence is the most comprehensive, current, and readable textbook on human intelligence available today. Written by leading experts in the field, the text includes IQ-test-based, biological, cognitive, cultural, and systems-based perspectives. It also addresses genetic and environmental influences, extremes of intelligence, group differences, lifespan development, the relationship of intelligence to other psychological attributes, and educational interventions.

Specific pedagogical features make the text ideal for teaching. Introductions briefly preview what is to come in each chapter. Key terms and concepts are bolded and defined in the text as they are introduced and also found in a glossary at the end of the book. Chapter summaries highlight major points of each chapter, and "Comprehension and Reflection" questions help students check their understanding of the material they have just read. Each chapter also includes a "Focus on Contemporary Research" box that describes in vivid detail the chapter author's current research. A rich program of tables, figures, photos, and samples from research tools throughout helps students understand the material in a concrete way.

Robert J. Sternberg is Professor of Human Development at Cornell University, USA. He is also Honorary Professor of Psychology at Heidelberg University, Germany, and was previously IBM Professor of Psychology and Education at Yale University, USA. He has won the William James and James McKeen Cattell Awards from the Association for Psychological Science, and the Grawemeyer Award in Psychology.

Human Intelligence

An Introduction

Edited by

Robert J. Sternberg

Cornell University, New York

CAMBRIDGE
UNIVERSITY PRESS

CAMBRIDGE
UNIVERSITY PRESS

University Printing House, Cambridge CB2 8BS, United Kingdom

One Liberty Plaza, 20th Floor, New York, NY 10006, USA

477 Williamstown Road, Port Melbourne, VIC 3207, Australia

314–321, 3rd Floor, Plot 3, Splendor Forum, Jasola District Centre, New Delhi – 110025, India

79 Anson Road, #06-04/06, Singapore 079906

Cambridge University Press is part of the University of Cambridge.

It furthers the University's mission by disseminating knowledge in the pursuit of
education, learning, and research at the highest international levels of excellence.

www.cambridge.org
Information on this title: www.cambridge.org/9781108703864
DOI: 10.1017/9781108610636

First published 2020

Printed in Singapore by Markono Print Media Pte Ltd

A catalogue record for this publication is available from the British Library.

Library of Congress Cataloging-in-Publication Data
Names: Sternberg, Robert J., editor.
Title: Human intelligence : an introduction / edited by Robert J. Sternberg, Cornell University,
    New York.
Description: 1 [edition]. | New York : Cambridge University Press, 2019. | Includes bibliographical
    references and index.
Identifiers: LCCN 2019010798 | ISBN 9781108703864 (pbk. : alk. paper)
Subjects: LCSH: Intellect. | Thought and thinking.
Classification: LCC BF431 .H796 2019 | DDC 153.9–dc23
LC record available at https://lccn.loc.gov/2019010798

ISBN 978-1-108-70386-4 Paperback

Brief Contents

Contents

    Richard E. Mayer
    Learning Strategies   443
        Generative Learning Processes   444
        Generative Learning Strategies   445
    Cognitive Processing Skills   448
        Computer Games   449
    *Focus on Contemporary Research: Richard E. Mayer's Work
    on Computer Games for Learning*   451
        Brain-Training Games   452
    Transferable Knowledge   454
        Instructional Methods for Producing Transferable Knowledge   457
        Principles for Designing Multimedia Lessons   461
    Conclusion   462
    Chapter Summary   462
    Key Terms   463
    Comprehension and Reflection Questions   463
    References   463

    Glossary   467
    Index   481

Contributors

JEFFREY A. DAHLKE
University of Minnesota

COLIN G. DEYOUNG
University of Minnesota

VICTOR J. ELLINGSEN
United States Department of Defense

JULIAN G. ELLIOTT
Durham University

RANDALL W. ENGLE
Georgia Tech

JAMES R. FLYNN
University of Otago

ELENA L. GRIGORENKO
University of Houston, Baylor College of Medicine

RICHARD J. HAIER
University of California, Irvine

DIANE F. HALPERN
Claremont-McKenna College

CHRISTOPHER HERTZOG
Georgia Tech

TOMOE KANAYA
Claremont-McKenna College

ALAN S. KAUFMAN
Yale University

JAMES C. KAUFMAN
University of Connecticut

RICHARD E. MAYER
University of California, Santa Barbara

WILMA C. RESING
Leiden University

PAUL R. SACKETT
University of Minnesota

W. JOEL SCHNEIDER
Temple University

OREN R. SHEWACH
University of Minnesota

ROBERT J. STERNBERG
Cornell University

MEI TAN
University of Houston

Preface

Some people are better at some things than others; some of those people who are better are better not only at some things, but at lots of things. The study of intelligence evolved in part to try to explain these individual differences. As time has gone by, the field of human intelligence has addressed many other questions as well. But this problem of accounting for individual differences in performance that seem at least in part based on "mental abilities" has driven the field ever since its beginning. *Human Intelligence: An Introduction* offers an up-to-date survey of the latest knowledge about intelligence by the very researchers who have been at the forefront of this investigation. It provides students with a thorough yet accessible account of this research by looking at the big questions about intelligence that have persisted over the years.

Organization and Pedagogy

The 16 chapters of this text are divided into four parts. Part I, "Introduction," consists of Chapters 1, 2, and 3, setting the stage and defining important terms, questions, and approaches. Part II, "Approaches to Studying Intelligence," includes Chapters 4 through 8 and covers the major psychological schools of thought used to examine human intelligence. Where there is disagreement in the field about the importance or relevance of one theory compared to another, the authors present various sides with evidence but without partisanship.

Chapters 9 through 11 comprise Part III, "Theories on the Development of Intelligence." These chapters explore in greater depth the theories used to explain intelligence. Chapters 12 to 16 make up Part IV, "Applications of Intelligence Research." These chapters offer some wider applications of human intelligence in research and education. Chapter 16, in particular, will give students a sense of how intelligence research can broadly apply across many societal interests.

The chapters in the text are all written by experts in those particular areas, thus arming readers with the most current and well-informed scholarship about this topic. Chapters are written to be accessible to undergraduates and graduate students taking a course on human intelligence, human abilities, cognitive abilities, or a related topic for the first time. The chapters all follow a similar format, beginning with a brief introduction, with key terms defined where they are first introduced, and figures and tables integrated where they can provide additional context and illustration. At the end of every chapter, a Chapter Summary, list of the Key Terms, "Comprehension and Reflection Questions," and list of References used in the chapter give students both the pedagogical handles they need to fully grasp the chapter content and also the means to further investigate their own areas of interest. A glossary of all the terms and definitions is included at the end of the book.

Every chapter also contains a box titled "Focus on Contemporary Research." These boxes are meant to give students a sense of how the research in the specific area has unfolded, along with some insights that might spark their interest for additional study. The boxes generally focus on a chapter author's own research directions and often include the topics of research that are considered most cutting-edge today.

PART I
Introduction

1 What Is Intelligence and What Are the Big Questions about It?

ROBERT J. STERNBERG

Some people are better at some things than others; some of those people who are better are better not only at some things, but at lots of things. The study of intelligence evolved in part to try to explain these individual differences. As time has gone by, the field of human intelligence has addressed many other questions as well. But this question of accounting for individual differences in performance that seem at least in part based on "mental abilities" has driven the field ever since its beginning.

What Is Intelligence?

What is intelligence, exactly? There is no one definition that has garnered universal acceptance, but over the last 100 years, intelligence has been defined in some of these ways:

> It seems to us that in intelligence there is a fundamental faculty, the alteration or the lack of which is of the utmost importance for practical life. This faculty is judgment, otherwise called good sense, practical sense, initiative, the faculty of adapting one's self to circumstances. (Binet & Simon, 1916, pp. 42-43)

> Intelligence is the aggregate or global capacity of the individual to act purposefully, to think rationally and to deal effectively with his environment. (Wechsler, 1940, pp. 444-445)

> Individuals differ from one another in their intelligence – their ability to understand complex ideas, to adapt effectively to the environment, to learn from experience, to engage in various forms of reasoning, to make good decisions, and to solve problems. Although these individual differences can be substantial, they are never entirely consistent: A given person's intellectual performance will vary on different occasions, in different domains, as judged by different criteria. Concepts of "intelligence" are attempts to clarify and organize this complex set of phenomena. (Neisser et al., 1996, p. 77)

Although these definitions differ somewhat, they share the idea that **intelligence** involves the ability to learn new concepts, to form judgments with those concepts, and to solve problems based on those concepts (see also Sternberg, 1997; Sternberg & Hedlund, 2002). Intelligence differentiates people according to the kinds and difficulties of mental tasks they can perform to meet their adaptive needs. Intelligence also can be viewed at a species level, comparing, say, humans to other species such as monkeys or dogs. Such comparisons are extremely challenging, however. They tend to be made in terms of skills that are adaptive for humans or skills that humans imagine are adaptive for the other animals. For example, a dog's idea of an intelligent dog owner may differ from the dog owner's idea!

Some Big Questions about Intelligence

There is no universal agreement about which questions are most important to understanding intelligence, but there are some big questions that have persisted over the years. Some of these questions have been answered by different types of research over time and some are still in the process of being addressed. We will highlight these questions here and then spend the rest of the book delving more deeply into each of them.

Is There Such a Thing as Intelligence?

How did people come up with a construct such as intelligence anyway? Where did the concept come from? Intelligence was recognized in some form by the ancient philosophers. For example, Plato, who made his major contributions in the fourth century BC, had a great deal to say about intelligence. One aspect of intelligence that he wrote about is the ability to learn. In Plato's *Republic* Book 5, Socrates asks Glaucon:

> When you spoke of a nature gifted or not gifted in any respect, did you mean to say that one man will acquire a thing easily, another with difficulty; a little learning will lead the one to discover a great deal; whereas the other, after much study and application, no sooner learns than he forgets; or again did you mean, that the one has a body which is a good servant to his mind, while the body of the other is a hindrance to him? – Would not these be the sort of differences which distinguish the man gifted by nature from the one who is ungifted? (*Great Books of the Western World*, 1987, 5, 359)

Glaucon agrees with Socrates that his observations are correct. Socrates further demonstrates to Glaucon that part of human intelligence is the love of learning and knowledge; truthfulness and unwillingness to accept falsehoods, and indeed, love of the truth.

Love of truth today more likely might be classified as wisdom than as intelligence (see Sternberg & Jordan, 2005), but the idea that people can infer the truth and distinguish it from falsehood is very much alive in the notion of inductive reasoning as a key part of intelligence, ranging back to Charles Spearman (1923) and continuing with modern theories of intelligence (Sternberg, 2018).

In another work by Plato, the *Theaetetus*, the boy Theaetetus imagines that there exists in the mind of man a block of wax, which is of different sizes in different men. The blocks of wax can also differ in hardness, moistness, and purity. In this dialogue, Socrates suggests that when the wax is pure and clear and sufficiently deep, the mind will easily learn and retain and will not be subject to confusion. It only will think things that are true, and because the impressions in the wax are clear, they will be quickly distributed into their proper places on the block of wax. But when the wax is muddy or impure or very soft or very hard, there will be defects of the intellect. People whose wax is soft will be good at learning but apt to forget. People whose wax is hard will be slow to learn but will retain what they learn. People whose wax is shaggy or rugged or gritty, or whose wax has an admixture of earth or dung, will have only indistinct impressions. Those with hard wax will have the same, because there will be no depth to the thoughts. If the wax is too soft, the impressions will be indistinct, because they can be easily confused or remolded (*Great Books of the Western World*, 1987, 7, 540).

Plato's theory, as expressed in the dialogue, is a rather primitive metaphor of mind. But scientists still speak of brains as modifiable in varying degrees (Haier, 2017), and although they may not think of the brain as a ball of wax, they have simply replaced that concept with more modern biology, recognizing the roles of neurons, synapses, and interconnectivity in place of Plato's wax.

Aristotle, the third giant of Greek philosophy after Socrates and Plato, also had some fairly sophisticated views on the nature of intelligence. Aristotle lived in the fourth century BC. In the *Posterior Analytics* Book 1, he conceived of intelligence in terms of "quick wit":

> Quick wit is a faculty of hitting upon the middle term instantaneously. It would be exemplified by a man who saw that the moon has a bright side always turned towards the sun, and quickly grasped the cause of this, namely that she borrows her light from him; or observes somebody in conversation with a man of wealth and defined that he was borrowing money, or that the friendship of these people sprang from a common enmity. In all these instances he has seen the major and minor terms and then grasped the causes, the middle terms. (*Great Books of the Western World*, 1987, 8, 122)

Aristotle essentially was recognizing the importance of deductive reasoning to intelligence. Indeed, syllogisms of the form "All men are mortal. Socrates is a man. Therefore, Socrates is mortal" are referred to as Aristotelian syllogisms. In the early form of Louis Thurstone's (1938) theory of intelligence, deductive reasoning was identified as a factor, although it later was subsumed under other factors. And modern information-processing work has recognized deductive reasoning as an important part of intelligence (e.g., Sternberg, Guyote, & Turner, 1980; Sternberg & Weil, 1980). Aristotle's discussion of the conversation with the man of wealth also shows a sensitivity to the concept of social intelligence

(Kihlstrom & Cantor, 2011; Sternberg & Smith, 1985) or what Gardner (2011) calls "interpersonal intelligence."

So the concept of intelligence has a long history. One might wonder if we need it. But as long as people differ in their skills in solving real-world problems, people will invent a concept like intelligence, whether they call it "intelligence" or "aptitude" or "ability" or something else. In other words, one cannot say for certain that there is any one thing in the brain that constitutes intelligence, although some theorists believe there most likely is (Deary, 2000; Jensen, 1998; Spearman, 1927). But functionally, when people engage in tasks and solve problems, and when they differ in how well they do at them, there always will be a need for some concept like intelligence, whatever it may be called. And moreover, because different species also differ in what they can accomplish, the concept of intelligence seems to serve an evolutionary purpose as well as an individual-differences one (Jerison, 1982; Zentall, in press).

Is Intelligence a Single Thing or Many Things?

Scholars studying intelligence have had diverging views regarding whether intelligence is a single entity or a multifaceted one (Sternberg & Grigorenko, 2002). A major early twentieth-century theorist, Charles Spearman (1927), believed that intelligence has multiple facets, but that a single one, which he referred to as **general intelligence** (or *g*), predominates. Louis Thurstone (1938) disagreed, suggesting seven aspects to intelligence, all of which he believed to be important. To this day, psychologists disagree as to whether intelligence is predominantly one thing (Gottfredson, 1997) or many (Gardner, 2011; Sternberg, 1985a, 1985b, 1986). Many contemporary theorists somewhat bypass the issue, suggesting that intelligence can be understood hierarchically, with a general intelligence factor at the top of a hierarchy of abilities and more specific abilities at successive levels below that (e.g., Carroll, 1993; see Walrath, Willis, Dumont, & Kaufman, in press).

Figure 1.1 shows a schematic of Spearman's, Thurstone's, and Carroll's theories of intelligence. Note that each theory proposes not only somewhat different abilities, but also different structures for those abilities in the mind. Chapter 2 describes in more detail how psychologists have defined general intelligence and introduces the major approaches used to study intelligence.

Is Intelligence the Same Thing in All Places and at All Times?

Many theorists of intelligence have studied intelligence as though it is an entity the nature of which transcends time and space. In other words, they believe that it is the same thing, regardless of time and place. Most theories of intelligence have been constructed on the basis of the notion that intelligence is a thing that is unchanging across time and space.

Western cross-cultural researchers in much of the twentieth century believed that intelligence is the same everywhere, so they translated standard intelligence tests

Spearman's Theory of General Intelligence

General ability is supplemented by specific abilities, each representing a single test

g

_St_

Thurstone's Theory of Primary Mental Abilities

Seven primary mental abilities all at the same "group factor" level

| Verbal Comprehension | Verbal Fluency | Numerical | Memory | Inductive Reasoning | Spatial | Perceptual Speed |

Carroll's Hierarchical Theory

Mental abilities at three levels of a hierarchy

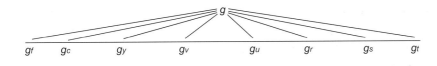

gf gc gy gv gu gr gs gt

Figure 1.1 Hierarchical models of intelligence. Spearman believed that the most important aspect of intelligence was a single entity, general intelligence, or *g*. Thurstone believed that there are seven primary mental abilities, all of roughly equal importance. Carroll and other hierarchical theorists suggested that abilities can be arranged in hierarchical form. Different hierarchical theorists have proposed somewhat different hierarchies, but all their models have in common that they postulate differing levels of generality of abilities.

and then used them in non-Western cultures. Typically (but not always!), people in these other cultures did worse on the tests to the extent that the cultures diverged from the norms of Western Civilization. The traditional view was that people in these other cultures (or subcultures) just were not as bright as Westerners. Some psychologists still hold this view. A different viewpoint (Greenfield, 1997; Rogoff, 2003; Sternberg, 2004) holds that, to be fair, the tests need to be tailored to the real-life adaptive demands of a particular culture. Chapter 7 discusses these cultural approaches to intelligence in depth. For example, children in some cultures may be unfamiliar with the kinds of stimuli and the knowledge required to do well on a standard Western test of intelligence. At the same time, many Westerners might be unfamiliar, today, with the hunting, fishing, and gathering skills needed for adaptation elsewhere. Knowing what plants to eat and not eat, and which animals were dangerous and which ones were not, would have been important for daily survival in some cultures. In times past, the technological skills that are so important in today's world would have been irrelevant, but hunting skills might have meant the difference between surviving and perishing. Perhaps intelligence, as we know it today, predicts practical adaptive kinds of knowledge and skills, but it is hard to say just how good the prediction is.

Have Levels of Intelligence Changed over Time?

Psychologists used to believe that levels of intelligence have remained fixed over time, at least in the modern day. After all, the average IQ (intelligence quotient) is 100; it is 100 now and was 100 a century ago and still will be 100 a century from now. Indeed, one of the things every first-year psychology student learns is that the average IQ is 100.

But James Flynn (2011) looked more deeply into this presupposition and found it to be true only in the most superficial sense. On the one hand, it is true that the average IQ always has been and probably always will be 100. But what he realized is that, because test publishers create new norms (conversions of *raw scores*, or numbers of items answered correctly, to IQs) every so often, 100 at any given time does not have to mean exactly the same thing as 100 at a different point in time.

In fact, as you will learn in Chapter 10, average IQs have changed over time. They have risen substantially – as much as 30 points during the twentieth century – meaning that an IQ of 100 in the year 1900 was the equivalent of only about 70 in the year 2000. Thus, we cannot assume that levels of intelligence always remain the same. And because evolution does not operate, at least for humans, on a time scale of 100 years, we can conclude that environment somehow must play an important role in affecting people's level of intelligence. Intelligence changes in response to the demands of the environment – when those demands on intellect increase, intelligence can rise; when those demands decrease, intelligence can fall (Flynn, 2011).

Is There a Best Way to Study Intelligence?

Scholars sometimes hope that there will be one *best* way to study scientific phenomena, whether the phenomenon is intelligence or anything else. In the early twentieth century, most psychologists studying intelligence used complex statistics to derive and test their theories. (Chapters 2, 3, and 4 explore the science of measuring intelligence.) In the latter part of that century, many psychologists instead turned to trying to understand the mental processes underlying particular abilities, such as verbal or mathematical ability. Other psychologists used cultural methods to understand intelligence, and still others biological methods. There is no one "right" or "best" way to study intelligence. Each method tells us things about intelligence that other methods may miss. If one wants to understand how the brain is related to intelligence, a biological approach (as described in Chapter 6) is almost certainly best. If one wants to understand the mental processing underlying intelligence, a cognitive approach is best. (Cognitive approaches are covered in Chapter 5.) If one wants to understand intelligence by looking at extreme groups, an approach is best that emphasizes intelligence toward the top and bottom of the intelligence scales. (Chapter 12 explores the extremes of intelligence.) And if one wants to understand how intelligence manifests itself differently across cultures, one may instead choose cultural methods for one's investigations, as described in Chapter 7.

Is There a Best Test of Intelligence?

There are a variety of tests of intelligence, and these are explored in Chapters 2 and 4. Most of these tests are chronicled in the *Buros' Mental Measurements Yearbook*. By far, the two most widely used tests are the series by David Wechsler (2008) and the Stanford-Binet (Roid, 2003), which are described in later chapters. A nonverbal test called the Raven Progressive Matrices (Raven, Raven, & Court, 2003) also is widely used. But of course, widespread use does not necessarily translate into "best."

If one is talking about intelligence as it is commonly operationalized in standardized tests, the Wechsler and Stanford-Binet are probably good choices. But at another level, it is not clear that the exact choice of test matters all that much. The reason is that almost all these tests measure more or less the same thing, general intelligence plus some other related factors. So it often does not make a great difference which test is chosen, given that most of them correlate rather highly with each other.

When most of the early tests of intelligence were created, they were not closely tied to any particular theories of intelligence. Today, many intelligence tests yield subscores based on one or another theory of intelligence, often Carroll's (1993) three-tiered theory, which has three levels of mental abilities (and is described in detail later).

Some test users would prefer tests based on other ideas, such as expanding measurement of intelligence to include creative and practical as well as analytical skills (e.g., Sternberg, 2018). Although such assessments exist (e.g., Sternberg, 2018), they are not ready for prime time in terms of measuring individual intelligence. It may be some years before viable alternatives are available. Figure 1.2 shows examples of what items measuring analytical, creative, and practical skills might look like.

A question one might want to ask before choosing a particular test is exactly why one wishes to measure someone's intelligence. Although intelligence testing used to be fairly commonplace, especially in schools, it is much less common today. Schools typically no longer routinely test the intelligence of their students, although they may do so for special program placements, such as for entry into a gifted program or a program for students with intellectual challenges or disabilities.

Analytical

1. What number comes next in the following series?

2, 5, 9,14,20,_____   a. 25, b. 26, c. 27, d. 28

2. In the morning, the BLEN arose on the horizon.

What does BLEN mean? a. sun, b. moon, c. asteroid, d. water

3. What is your favorite book? Why is it your favorite book? What are its strengths and weaknesses?

Creative

1. Suppose Germany had won World War II. What would the world be like today?

2. Draw an advertisement for asparagus.

3. Write a story with the title "Beyond the Edge."

Practical

1. How might you convince a friend to help you move from one place to another?

2. If you wanted a teacher to write the best possible letter of recommendation for you, what might you say to the teacher?

3. What kinds of clues might you use to figure out whether someone is lying to you?

Figure 1.2 Examples of items measuring analytical, creative, and practical skills

But even in these cases, it often is not clear why an intelligence test is needed in addition to, much less instead of, tests of achievement in targeted areas (Spear-Swerling & Sternberg, 1994).

In sum, there probably is no one "best" test, but there are many tests available – verbal, nonverbal, a combination of verbal and nonverbal, performance based among them – that can suit a fairly wide variety of needs. At the same time, it is important to remember that the tests all represent, whether openly or not, particular conceptions of intelligence, and they are only as good as the particular conception of intelligence and its applicability to the individuals being tested.

Is Intelligence Heritable?

In the twentieth century, as you will learn later, some psychologists were preoccupied – perhaps, in some cases, obsessed – with the heritability of intelligence.

Heritability refers to the proportion of variation in intelligence among individuals that is due to genetic effects (Plomin et al., 2012). In other words, when one looks at variations in intelligence among people, what proportion of it is a result of genes? But fixating on the heritability of intelligence may not be such a great idea. Heritability is not some fixed number waiting to be discovered. Heritability depends on many factors, especially the range of genetic variation and environmental variation in a population of people of interest. For reasons that we explore in Chapter 9, heritability tends to be higher when the range of environments is more narrow and lower when the range of environments is broader. Similarly, heritability is higher when the range of genes related to intelligence is more variable and lower when the range of genes related to intelligence is reduced. The details, at this point, are not important. What is important is to realize that there is no one fixed number that represents how heritable intelligence is. Moreover, how heritable intelligence is also will depend on how one measures intelligence. The early search for a "true" heritability of intelligence was misguided.

There is one more important fact to understand. Heritability is not the same as a trait's being fixed or unmodifiable. Levels of a trait can be modifiable, even highly modifiable, even when heritability is high. Height is a good example. Height is highly heritable (with a heritability of about .9 on a 0–1 scale) in a typical Western population, yet heights are highly modifiable, having increased very substantially from even the beginning of the twentieth century until today. When I was growing up in the latter part of the twentieth century, most of us young men were taller than our fathers. As we saw, levels of intelligence also increased during the twentieth century, but the increase told us nothing about heritability. Heritability is a mechanism of transmission of traits from one generation to another, but levels of traits can vary as a function of nutrition, availability of good medical care, and other factors.

Table 1.1 illustrates how a trait, height, can be highly heritable yet highly modifiable.

Can Intelligence Be Increased (or Decreased)?

Intelligence is at least somewhat modifiable (Ceci, 1996; Feuerstein, 1980; Nickerson, 2011; Detterman & Sternberg, 1982; Jaeggi et al., 2008). That is, with good education and good parental investment, parents and teachers can raise their children's intelligence. (Chapter 16 explores the relationship of intelligence and education.) Probably the best way to raise intelligence, at least for children, is just to go to school, and preferably a good school. It also helps greatly to have parents who care about developing their children's intellectual skills.

At the same time, there is no evidence that it is possible, in large number of cases, to obtain huge increases in people's intelligence. The differences one gets through excellent education are observable but they are not astronomical. Programs that

Table 1.1 Note how a trait, height, can be highly heritable yet highly modifiable. In this hypothetical situation the heritability of height is 1.00 (100%) because the correlation between the heights of parents and their children is perfect (1.00). Yet the children are on average 2 inches taller than their parents, presumably because the children grew up in a better environment that promoted physical growth.

	Average height of parents	Average height of children
Case 1	5'10"	6'00"
Case 2	5'4"	5'6"
Case 3	5'7"	5'9"
Case 4	5'3"	5'5"
Case 5	5'8"	5'10"

claim to perform miracles in raising people's intelligence are probably selling a contemporary brand of snake oil. A reasonable goal is to help people reach their full level of potential, rather than to become overnight geniuses.

Intelligence also can be decreased. Head injuries are a major cause of decreases in intelligence, when the brain is affected in a way that impairs learning, memory, or reasoning. Strokes also can affect intelligence, as can diseases of advancing age, such as various kinds of dementia, including Alzheimer's disease. In some ways, intelligence is like a muscle. When we exercise it more, we tend to increase it, and when we fail to use it, it begins to deteriorate.

Kohn and Schooler (1978) found that those in challenging jobs tended best to maintain their intelligence as adults. Exercising also appears to help people maintain their level of intelligence (Tomporowski et al., 2008). A challenge for maintaining one's level of intelligence can occur when someone retires and simply sits down and watches television a lot of the time, failing to exercise their intelligence.

Are There Sex Differences in Intelligence?

Sex differences in intelligence have been documented (Halpern, Beninger, & Straight, 2011), but as you will learn in Chapter 13, most of these differences pertain to particular patterns of abilities rather than overall levels of intelligence. For example, men, on average, excel on mental-rotation tasks – tasks that require a person mentally to rotate objects in his or her head. Women excel, on average, in some verbal and perceptual-speed tasks. There are other differences as well. On average, men have larger brains, but women often have better connections between the functioning of the left and right hemispheres of the brain. Perhaps because of sex-linked traits, men tend to show more variation than women in a variety of traits. There are more men than women both at the very low end of the intelligence spectrum and at the very high end. But on average, men and women are pretty much capable of doing the same tasks, if they set their minds to them!

Are There Racial/Cultural/Ethnic Differences in Intelligence?

There are many racial and ethnic-group differences in measured intelligence, as discussed later in the book. Chapter 7 on cultural approaches and Chapter 13 on group differences discuss these ethnic-group differences in detail. What is most interesting, from a psychological point of view, is understanding why these differences exist. Sometimes, the differences may be a function of the kinds of skills that parents and teachers encourage (see Focus on Contemporary Research box). Because parents in different groups have different conceptions of what it means for a child to be intelligent, and because most parents want their children to grow up to be reasonably intelligent, parents raise their children in ways that in part reflect their own implicit theories, or folk conceptions of intelligence. But those folk conceptions may or may not match what IQ tests measure. They also may differentially well represent the actual demands of adaptation to the environment.

FOCUS ON CONTEMPORARY RESEARCH: OKAGAKI AND STERNBERG'S WORK ON PARENTS' AND TEACHERS' BELIEFS AS THEY RELATE TO CHILDREN'S SCHOOL PERFORMANCE

As noted in this chapter, different racial, ethnic, and cultural groups can have different conceptions of what it means to be intelligent. Okagaki and Sternberg (1993) found that members of different ethnic groups living in San Jose, California, had rather different conceptions of what it means to be intelligent. The researchers asked parents of European American, Latino-American, and Asian American parents what they meant by having an intelligent child. In other words, how would intelligence manifest itself in the behavior of their children, and what kinds of skills would these adults want to develop in order to maximize the intelligence of the children under their care? The parents of the various groups had somewhat different conceptions of what it means for a child to be intelligent. For example, Latino parents of schoolchildren tended to emphasize the importance of social-competence skills in their conceptions of intelligence, whereas Asian American parents tended rather heavily to emphasize the importance of cognitive skills. European American parents also emphasized cognitive skills more. Teachers, representing the dominant culture of the school and, to some extent, what society values, emphasized cognitive rather than social-competence skills. There thus was a match between the conceptions of intelligence of the European American and Asian American parents and the children's teachers. There was something of a mismatch between the conceptions of the Latino-American parents and the teachers. The rank order of children's performance for various groups' performance (including subgroups within the Latino and Asian groups) could be predicted perfectly by the extent to which their parents shared their children's teachers' conception of intelligence. Put another way, teachers tended more to reward those children who were socialized into a view of intelligence that happened to correspond to the teachers' own conceptions of intelligence.

The message of this study is perhaps broader than that of conceptions of parents and teachers in one city in California. Parents have an idea of what it means to be smarter; so do teachers. To the extent that the parental conceptions match the teachers' conceptions, the teachers are more likely to view the children as smart.

Does Intelligence Decrease in Old Age?

This is another complex question that defies a simple answer, and Chapter 11 delves into lifespan theories and research. Intelligence certainly can decrease in old age, especially in cases of dementia and of various kinds of hardening of the arteries in the brain. But the picture is more complicated than that. As mentioned earlier, exercising the brain can help preserve intelligence. And different aspects of intelligence show different patterns. Fluid intelligence, the ability to handle novel kinds of tasks and stimuli, tends to increase into the 20s or even 30s, and then, on average, begins to show a slow but continual decline. The rate of decline varies enormously across individuals. Crystallized abilities, or the abilities represented by general information and vocabulary skills, tend to increase into later years, as late as the 60s or even 70s. They also begin to show a decline, but much later in life than fluid abilities (Hertzog, 2011). Moreover, older individuals often can excel in relatively domain-specific kinds of expertise – the kinds of expertise that they build up over a lifetime of work in a career or even in the context of their families. These kinds of expertise can be maintained at very high levels. Essentially, people of more advanced age may end up compensating for some decline in fluid abilities by their increases in crystallized abilities and task-specific domain expertise.

Does Intelligence Predict Success in Life as Well as in School?

In a nutshell, intelligence has predictive value across a wide range of domains (Deary & Whalley, 2008). Intelligence, or at least, IQ, predicts not only academic success, but also health, longevity, job success, marital success, and many other variables. Its greatest predictive power is for academic achievement, but without question the range of things which it predicts is large – some might think surprisingly large. Chapter 14 explores these ideas in depth.

This predictive power of intelligence is also complex. Part of the prediction is almost certainly due to the fact that the kinds of knowledge-based and analytical skills one needs to succeed on an intelligence test overlap with the kinds of knowledge and analytical skills one needs to be successful in school and in jobs (Sternberg, 1985b). But a further factor is operative as well. Society uses a variety of kinds of tests to create a rank-ordering of individuals. Many of these tests, such as standardized tests for measuring school achievement and for college admissions, indirectly measure IQ. People who test better are allowed to progress further in society's system, which represents a funnel that is wide on the bottom but narrow at the top. So the very fact that one does better on various kinds of standardized tests may help one advance in education and in society. In the study of intelligence, as in other areas, exact causal relations are difficult to estimate. That said, IQ does predict many different kinds of performance, and hence has been useful at least in some societies in predicting future outcomes (Deary & Whalley, 2008).

Are IQ Tests Inherently Biased?

Ever since IQ tests were invented, there has been some criticism that the tests are biased in favor of some groups and against other groups. The evidence for this claim has never been altogether clear. Most studies have shown that IQ tests predict about equally well for different groups, and that, if anything, they may overpredict for some of those groups against which the tests have been considered biased. In other words, those groups may do better on the IQ tests than their achievement would lead one to have expected (Valencia & Suzuki, 2000).

At the same time, there may be a more systemic bias that traditional methods of detecting bias do not pick up. This is bias that is found not just in the predictor, but also in the criterion. If the evaluation of real-world task performance of people represents a bias favoring those who do well on IQ tests, the tests may show a bias that statistical tests miss. For example, if evaluators of children's school achieve-ment tend to be biased against certain groups in evaluating the work of members of those groups, then it is quite possible that the correlation between the tests and measures of performance will be higher because the evaluators mark down people whom they expect to have low IQs, regardless of the level of those people's actual performance (Valencia & Suzuki, 2000). Moreover, Steele and Aronson (1995) and many others have shown that members of groups that have implicit stereotypes that they are poor at certain kinds of skills may do worse on tests of these skills because they believe that members of their particular group (racial, ethnic, gender, or whatever) are not the kinds of people who do well in those kinds of performance. In effect, they create a self-fulfilling prophecy against themselves. The bias of IQ testing is discussed in Chapter 7 on cultural approaches to intelligence and Chapter 13 on group differences.

What Is the Relationship of Intelligence to Other Psychological Constructs, Such as Creativity and Personality?

Intelligence is related to other constructs, and Chapter 15 discusses these associ-ations. Researchers generally agree that creativity requires some substantial level of intelligence (Niu & Sternberg, 2003). The reason is that part of **creativity** is not only coming up with new ideas, but also judging whether the ideas are good ones. Personality traits, such as openness to experience, also seem to bear some relation to intelligence. Research relating intelligence to other constructs helps us all understand both what intelligence is and what it is not.

Are Machines Becoming More Intelligent than Humans?

Machines are becoming better at doing what machines do best, which is to think algorithmically. Jobs that can be done by using algorithms – paths in solving well-defined problems that have well-defined solutions – are likely to begin to disappear in the future. But jobs requiring judgment – how to care for a child or a spouse or another loved one; how to teach young people to make wise judgments; how to expand one's business so that it thrives rather than tanks – are likely to retain their importance and be done best, as they always have been, by humans. So it all depends on what you mean by intelligence, and according to usual conceptions, machines tend to excel in well-defined algorithmic tasks whereas humans tend to excel in ill-defined tasks where there is no clear discernible path to solution.

CONCLUSION

Intelligence is one of the most important psychological constructs for psychologists, educators, and laypersons to understand. Much of contemporary society revolves around identifying people's intelligence, whether for school placements, hiring people for jobs, or selecting romantic partners. People can and do develop their intelligence, in school but also through life experiences. Although intelligence often is thought of as a single thing, most intelligence theorists believe there is more to intelligence than just a single IQ or measure of general ability. Many questions remain unanswered about intelligence, but often, asking the right questions and addressing those questions in scientifically defensible ways is at least as important as coming up with answers, many of which later will prove to be incomplete at best, and wrong at worst.

CHAPTER SUMMARY

Intelligence is the ability to understand complex ideas, to adapt effectively to the environment, to learn from experience, to engage in various forms of reasoning, to make good decisions, and to solve problems. Although people may disagree as to whether the concept of intelligence is a useful one, if the concept of intelligence did not exist, people probably would invent some similar construct to account, at some level, for why some people are better learners, reasoners, decision makers, and problem solvers than others. As discussed in depth in Chapter 4, there appears to be a quite general intellectual ability, g. Below g in a hierarchy are narrower abilities, such as fluid intelligence, used to handle relatively novel stimuli, and crystallized intelligence, which comprises one's organized knowledge base. There are probably some aspects of intelligence that are common across different places and times – such as the ability to formulate strategies for solving problems – but there also are less generalized skills that can be essential to intelligence in different cultures or at different times. As a simple example, reading skills were, and are, not part of intelligence in preliterate societies.

IQs have risen substantially since the beginning of the twentieth century. In some places, however, this rise has leveled off, and in other places, declines in IQs have started to take place (Bratsberg & Rogeberg, 2018). Presumably, the increases in the twentieth century are in part related to more challenging environments that have brought out greater intellectual skills, much as more challenging physical environments bring out greater physical skills.

There is no one best way to study intelligence, any more than there is any one best test of intelligence. How one best studies intelligence depends on the questions one wishes to answer, and how one tests intelligence depends in part on what one wishes to know about a person's intellectual performance. That said, most intelligence tests measure general intelligence (g) plus other related factors.

Intelligence is heritable to some degree, although the degree depends on the variability of genes and environments at a given time and place. Heritability increases as genetic variation increases and environmental variation decreases. Intelligence can and is increased by experiences that challenge the intellect, most notably, schooling. However, at this time, psychologists and educators do not know how to bring about massive changes in individual people's intelligence.

There are sex differences in averaged patterns of intelligence but such differences have not been demonstrated in averaged levels of intelligence. In particular, men tend to excel in mental-rotation skills, women in some verbal as well as perceptual skills. There also are differences in intelligence as measured by IQ tests across ethnicities, socially defined races, and cultures, but the applicability of intelligence tests may be greater among some groups than among others. For example, children in some cultures need to be taught hunting and gathering skills, which are highly relevant to their environmental adaptation, whereas children in other cultures may have little or no use for such skills.

Some aspects of intelligence, in particular, the ability to think quickly and flexibly, may show some declines with advancing years, but other aspects of intelligence – word knowledge and specialized expertise – often tend to hold steady or even increase until very advanced ages. Intelligence predicts success in many aspects of life. The greatest predictive validity of an intelligence test is to other intelligence tests and, almost equally, to tests of academic achievement.

Intelligence tests are not inherently biased; what can be biased is the *use* of these tests. Psychologists and others need to interpret them in context, taking into account as well as possible each tested individual's background and environmental context. Intelligence is related to other constructs, such as creativity. Some level of intelligence is necessary for creativity but not sufficient for it to manifest itself. Intelligence is also related to aspects of personality, especially openness to experience.

Machines can excel over humans in algorithmic tasks but are challenged in tasks requiring sophisticated judgment and understanding of human nature. There probably always will be jobs for those who have high levels of learning, reasoning, decision making, and problem solving skills – in other words, who have high intelligence.

KEY TERMS

creativity • general intelligence (*g*) • heritability • intelligence

COMPREHENSION AND REFLECTION QUESTIONS

1. What do you believe to be the definition of intelligence?
2. How, if at all, could one determine whether a definition of intelligence is correct?
3. What might be some reasons why IQs around the world increased during the twentieth century?
4. Can the same test, translated from one language to another, appropriately be used to measure intelligence for people in different cultures? Why or why not?
5. What do you think it would mean for computers to be more intelligent than humans?

References

Binet, A., & Simon, T. (1916). *The development of intelligence in children* (E. S. Kite, trans.). Baltimore, MD: Williams & Wilkins.

Bratsberg, B., & Rogeberg, O. (2018). Flynn effect and its reversal are both environmentally caused. *Proceedings of the National Academy of Sciences*, https://doi.org/10.1073/pnas.1718793115

Carroll, J. B. (1993). *Human cognitive abilities: A survey of factor-analytic studies.* New York: Cambridge University Press.

Ceci, S. J. (1996). *On intelligence…more or less: A bioecological treatise on intellectual development* (expanded). Cambridge, MA: Harvard University Press.

Deary, I. J. (2000). *Looking down on human intelligence: From psychometrics to the human brain.* Oxford: Oxford University Press.

Deary, I. J., & Whalley, L. J. (2008). *A lifetime of intelligence.* Washington, DC: American Psychological Association.

Dell'Amore, C. (2014). Species Extinction Happening 1,000 Times Faster Because of Humans? *National Geographic.* Retrieved from http://news.nationalgeographic.com/news/2014/05/140529-conservation-science-animals-species-endangered-extinction/

Detterman, D. K., & Sternberg, R. J. (eds.). (1982). *How and how much can intelligence be increased?* Norwood, NJ: Ablex.

Feuerstein, R. (1980). *Instrumental enrichment: An intervention program for cognitive modi ability.* Baltimore, MD: University Park Press.

Flynn, J. R. (2011). Secular changes in intelligence. In R. J. Sternberg & S. B. Kaufman (eds.), *Cambridge handbook of intelligence* (pp. 647-665). New York: Cambridge University Press.

Gardner, H. (2011). *Frames of mind: The theory of multiple intelligences.* New York: Basic Books.

Gottfredson, L. S. (1997). Why *g* matters: The complexity of everyday life. *Intelligence*, 24(1), 79–132.

Greenfield, P. M. (1997). You can't take it with you: Why abilities assessments don't cross cultures. *American Psychologist*, *52*, 1115–1124.

Guyote, M. J., & Sternberg, R. J. (1981). A transitive-chain theory of syllogistic reasoning. *Cognitive Psychology*, *13*, 461–525.

Haier, R. J. (2017). *The neuroscience of intelligence.* New York: Cambridge University Press.

Halpern, D. F., Beninger, A. S., & Straight, C. A. (2011). Sex differences in intelligence. In R. J. Sternberg & S. B. Kaufman (eds.), *Cambridge handbook of intelligence* (pp. 253-272). New York: Cambridge University Press.

Hertzog, C. (2011). Intelligence in adulthood. In R. J. Sternberg & S. B. Kaufman (eds.), *Cambridge handbook of intelligence* (pp. 174-190). New York: Cambridge University Press.

Jaeggi, S. M., Buschkuehl, M., Jonides, J., & Perrig, W. J. (2008). Improving fluid intelligence with training on working memory. *Proceedings of the National Academy of Sciences*, *105*, 6829-6833.

Jensen, A. R. (1998). *The general factor.* Westport, CT: Greenwood/Praeger.

Jerison, H. J. (1982). The evolution of intelligence. In R. J. Sternberg (ed.), *Handbook of human intelligence* (pp. 216-244). New York: Cambridge University Press.

Jerison, H. J. (2000). The evolution of intelligence. In R. J. Sternberg (ed.), *Handbook of intelligence* (pp. 216-244). New York: Cambridge University Press.

Kihlstrom, J. F., & Cantor, N. (2011). Social intelligence. In R. J. Sternberg & S. B. Kaufman (eds.), *Cambridge handbook of intelligence* (pp. 564-581). New York: Cambridge University Press.

Kohn, M. L., & Schooler, C. (1978). The reciprocal effects of the substantive complexity of work and intellectual flexibility: A longitudinal assessment. *American Journal of Sociology, 84*(1), 24-52.

Neisser, U., Boodoo, G., Bouchard, T. J., Boykin, W. A., & Brody, N., Ceci, S. J., Halpern, D. F., Loehlin, J. C., Perloff, R., Sternberg, R. J., & Urbina, S. (1996). Intelligence: Knowns and unknowns. *American Psychologist, 51*(2), 77–101.

Nickerson, R. S. (2011). Developing intelligence through instruction. In R. J. Sternberg & S. B. Kaufman (eds.), *Cambridge handbook of intelligence* (pp. 107-129). New York: Cambridge University Press.

Niu, W., & Sternberg, R. J. (2003). Societal and school influences on student creativity: The case of China. *Psychology in the Schools, 40*(1), 103–114.

Okagaki, L., & Sternberg, R. J. (1993). Parental beliefs and children's school performance. *Child Development, 64*(1), 36–56.

Plomin, R., DeFries, J., Knopik, V. S., & Neiderhiser, J. M. (2012). *Behavioral genetics* (6th ed.). New York: Worth.

Raven, J., Raven, J. C., & Court, J. H. (2003, updated 2004) *Manual for Raven's Progressive Matrices and Vocabulary Scales.* San Antonio, TX: Harcourt Assessment.

Rogoff, B. (2003). *The cultural nature of human development.* New York: Oxford University Press.

Roid, G. H. (2003). *Stanford-Binet Intelligence Scales* (5th ed.). Itasca, IL: Riverside Publishing.

Spear–Swerling, L., & Sternberg, R. J. (1994). The road not taken: An integrative theoretical model of reading disability. *Journal of Learning Disabilities, 27*(2), 91–103.

Spearman, C. (1923). *The nature of "intelligence" and the principles of cognition.* London: Macmillan.

Spearman, C. (1927). *The abilities of man.* New York: Macmillan.

Steele, C. M., & Aronson, J. (1995). Stereotype threat and the intellectual performance of African Americans. *Journal of Personality and Social Psychology: Attitudes and Social Cognition, 69*, 797-811.

Sternberg, R. J. (ed.). (1985a). *Human abilities: An information-processing approach.* San Francisco: Freeman.

Sternberg, R. J. (1985b). Human intelligence: The model is the message. *Science, 230*, 1111–1118.

Sternberg, R. J. (1986). Inside intelligence. *American Scientist, 74*, 137–143.

Sternberg, R. J. (1997). What does it mean to be smart? *Educational Leadership, 54*(6), 20–24.

Sternberg, R. J. (2004). Culture and intelligence. *American Psychologist, 59*(5), 325–338.

Sternberg, R. J. (2018). Successful intelligence in theory, research, and practice. In R. J. Sternberg (ed.), *The nature of human intelligence* (pp. 308-321). New York: Cambridge University Press.

Sternberg, R. J., & Grigorenko, E. L. (eds.). (2002). *The general factor of intelligence: How general is it?* Mahwah, NJ: Lawrence Erlbaum Associates.

Sternberg, R. J., Guyote, M. J., & Turner, M. E. (1980). Deductive reasoning. In R. E. Snow, P. A. Federico, & W. E. Montague (eds.), *Aptitude, learning, and instruction: Cognitive process analyses of aptitude* (vol. 1, pp. 219–245). Hillsdale, NJ: Lawrence Erlbaum Associates.

Sternberg, R. J., & Hedlund, J. (2002). Practical intelligence, *g*, and work psychology. *Human Performance 15*(1/2), 143–160.

Sternberg, R. J., & Jordan, J. (eds.) (2005). *Handbook of wisdom: Psychological perspectives.* New York: Cambridge University Press.

Sternberg, R. J., & Smith, C. (1985). Social intelligence and decoding skills in nonverbal communication. *Social Cognition, 2,* 168–192.

Sternberg, R. J., & Weil, E. M. (1980). An aptitude–strategy interaction in linear syllogistic reasoning. *Journal of Educational Psychology, 72,* 226–234.

Thurstone, L. L. (1938). *Primary mental abilities.* Chicago: University of Chicago Press.

Tomporowski, P. D., Davis, C. L., Miller, P. H., & Naglieri, J. A. (2008). Exercise and children's intelligence, cognitive, and academic achievement. *Educational Psychology Review, 20,* 111-131.

Valencia, R. R., & Suzuki, L. A. (2000). *Intelligence testing and minority students.* Thousand Oaks, CA: Sage.

Walrath, R., Willis, J. O., Dumont, R., & Kaufman, A. S. (in press). Factor-analytic models of intelligence. In R. J. Sternberg (ed.), *Cambridge handbook of intelligence* (2nd edn.). New York: Cambridge University Press.

Wechsler, D. (1940). Non-intellective factors in general intelligence. *Psychological Bulletin, 37,* 444-445.

Wechsler, D. (2008). *Wechsler Adult Intelligence Scale* (4th edn.). Hoboken, NJ: Pearson.

Zentall, T. (in press). Animal intelligence. In R. J. Sternberg (ed.), *Cambridge handbook of intelligence* (2nd edn.). New York: Cambridge University Press.

2 | Approaches to Understanding Human Intelligence

ROBERT J. STERNBERG

Scholars have taken several different approaches in their study of intelligence. A grounding in these approaches and how they differ is useful in order to understand theory, research, and practice related to intelligence (Sternberg, 1985c, 1986, 1990, in press). In this chapter I provide a comparative overview of these approaches; each of them will be described in later chapters in more detail.

Psychometric Approaches

One of the oldest scientific approaches to understanding intelligence is the set of approaches called **psychometric approaches**, all of which seek to understand intelligence through the statistical analysis of scores on tests alleged to measure intelligence. These approaches are called "psychometric" because they are *psycho*logically based, and because they emphasize measurement, or *metric*s. They have also been called "geographic approaches" (Sternberg, 1990) because they seek, in a sense, to map the mind. In psychometric approaches, psychologists (or other qualified individuals) will administer to examinees a test that has been shown to measure intelligence (at least according to some theoretical accounts of intelligence). The examinees answer as many questions as they can. After the examinees complete the tests, the tests are scored and the data analyzed.

Types of Psychometric Tests

There are two kinds of psychometric tests given: individual tests and group tests. *Individual intelligence tests* are given to individual people – that is, to one person at a time. *Group intelligence tests* are given to groups of people – that is, to multiple people at one time. Generally, individual tests are viewed as providing more accurate and sensitive measurements of intelligence than group tests. With individual testing, examiners can be sensitive to individual needs or quirks during testing, and can qualitatively as well as quantitatively appraise the individual being tested.

Both kinds of tests typically can yield several kinds of scores. The **IQ**, or **intelligence quotient,** is a number representing the intellectual performance of a given individual relative to other individuals. Originally, IQs were computed according to the formula

$$IQ = (\text{Mental Age} / \text{Chronological Age}) \times 100$$

The idea was that **mental age** represented the intellectual age level in years at which a given person performed, **chronological age** represented physical age in years, and the quotient represented the extent to which the person was either above or below (or, in a few cases, exactly) at the intellectual level that would be expected of someone of his or her chronological age. Today, IQs are usually computed on the basis of a different kind of score, called a percentile.

Figure 2.1 illustrates the relationship between mental age and chronological age, showing how three different 8-year-old children have different IQs, based on their different mental ages.

A **percentile** represents the percentage of people tested whose score one exceeds. So an average IQ would place an individual in the 50th percentile, meaning that one's score is higher than 50 percent of the other people taking the test (and also lower than 50 percent of the other people). A percentile of 75 would mean one's score exceeds the scores of 75 percent of the other people taking the test. Percentiles can be converted into IQs (or vice versa) through a conversion process based on the properties of normal distributions. In *normal distributions*, most scores are near the middle of the distribution of scores, and then tail off rapidly at first, and then gradually. (Details of normal distributions are beyond the scope of this text but are covered in introductory-statistics courses.) IQs typically have a mean of 100 and a standard deviation of 15, meaning that roughly 68 percent of the test-takers fall between an IQ of 85 and 115, and roughly 95 percent of test-takers fall between an IQ of 70 and 130. Almost everyone – 99.7 percent of people – falls between IQs of 55 and 145.

Figure 2.2 shows how percentiles work, illustrating where children stand who are in the 25th, 50th, and 75th percentiles of intelligence.

As you learned in Chapter 1, in psychometric approaches, some psychologists seek to understand the particular intellectual abilities that underlie **general intelligence**, or **g**, which is usually defined as a wide-ranging intellectual ability at the core of much (some would say all) mental performance (Sternberg & Grigorenko, 2002b). (There also are psychologists who question the existence of a general intelligence.) We will consider these abilities in more detail in later chapters, but examples include **verbal ability**, or one's ability with words, and **reasoning ability**, or one's ability to draw reasonable conclusions from data. These abilities are identified through a statistical technique called **factor analysis** (described in detail in Chapter 4), which seeks to uncover the mental abilities, such as verbal and reasoning abilities, into which test scores can be classified.

Over the years, various ideas have sprung up about what constitutes an exceptionally high or low IQ. Sometimes people with very high scores, perhaps over

8-year-old boy   **Mental age of 6-year-old**

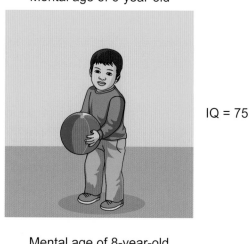

IQ = 75

8-year-old girl   **Mental age of 8-year-old**

IQ = 100

8-year-old boy   **Mental age of 10-year-old**

IQ = 125

Figure 2.1 Graphic representation of mental ages versus chronological ages. The 8-year-old boy in the top panel is below average in intelligence. His mental age of 6 means that his intellectual performance is equivalent to that of an average 6-year-old. He has an IQ of 75. The 8-year-old girl in the center is average in intelligence. Her mental age of 8 means that her intellectual performance is equivalent to that of an average 8-year-old. She has an IQ of 100. The 8-year-old boy in the bottom panel is above average in intelligence. His mental age of 10 means that his intellectual performance is that of an average 10-year-old. He has an IQ of 125.

**Students who score
BELOW our student**   **Students who score
ABOVE our student**

Jill scores in the 25th percentile

Matt scores in the 50th percentile

Sue scores in the 75th percentile

Figure 2.2 Graphic representation of scores in the 25th, 50th, and 75th percentiles

130 or so, are labeled as *gifted* (Sternberg, 1981a), whereas other people with very low scores, perhaps under 70 or so, are labeled as *intellectually challenged* or, in older and, today, much less currently used terms, *mentally retarded* or *intellectually deficient*. The exact cutoffs for the use of these terms differ across time and place, and usually other criteria besides IQ are (and should be) used to make these determinations.

Using Psychometric Approaches to Understand Intelligence

There have been many different uses of psychometric approaches to understanding intelligence. Charles Spearman (1927) proposed the theory that there is a general intelligence that is common to all intellectual tasks, and specific factors relevant to each individual test of intelligence. Louis Thurstone (1938) proposed there are multiple factors of intelligence, which he called *primary mental abilities,* such as verbal comprehension ability and numerical ability. John B. Carroll (1993) was one of several theorists who integrated these concepts, proposing a hierarchical model that allowed general intelligence at the top level of the hierarchy and then more specific abilities at each successive level further down in the three levels of his proposed hierarchy. We will discuss these theories in greater detail in Chapter 4.

Advantages and Disadvantages of Psychometric Approaches

A strength of psychometric approaches is that they enable psychologists or others to measure the mental abilities of large numbers of people with some degree of precision. Scores on intelligence tests have been found to be predictive of performance on many kinds of tasks, especially but not limited to academic ones. A weakness of psychometric approaches is that they do not tell us much about the mental processes underlying intelligence, or about the cultural context in which intelligence may need to be understood. A second possible weakness is proliferation of factors. It is not clear how many really important factors there are.

Cognitive Approaches

Cognitive approaches seek to understand intelligence in terms of elementary information processes underlying intelligence, the mental structures and representations upon which those processes act, and the strategies into which the components combine (Sternberg, 1981b).

   Cognitive approaches go back at least to the work of Newell, Shaw, and Simon (1957, 1958), who devised two computer programs, Logic Theorist and General Problem Solver, that could solve complex problems. The big idea underlying these programs was that it is possible to specify, in great detail, the processes computers use to solve intellectual problems, and so it presumably is possible as well to specify the processes humans use. Soon thereafter, Miller, Galanter, and Pribram (1960) proposed that plans in human behavior could be understood in terms of what they called "TOTEs," or "Test-Operate-Test-Exit" sequences. An individual first tests where they are in a plan and how far they are from their goal; then the individual operates to reduce the difference between where they are and where they wish to go. Then the individual tests again to see whether they are closer to the goal, and how further still to reduce the difference between where they are and the goal. And the individual keeps going through this sequence until they reach their goal and are ready to exit. For a simple example, suppose a light bulb goes out in your house. You first hypothesize that perhaps the bulb came loose. You operate by trying to turn the bulb tighter, and then you test: The light bulb still does not work. Now you hypothesize that maybe the light bulb has burned out. You operate by taking out the bulb and putting in a new one and then test: The new light bulb works. Your work is done. Figure 2.3 shows how the TOTE works.

Cognitive approaches were available but had not yet been applied directly to the study of intelligence when Lee Cronbach (1957) spoke of the difficulty psychologists had in bridging the gap between experimental-cognitive psychology and the traditional differential approach to intelligence. But it would be some years after Cronbach's plea for an integration of experimental psychology and the study of individual differences before proposed solutions started to appear as to how to accomplish this integration.

Specific Cognitive Approaches

Earl Hunt (Hunt, 1980; Hunt, Frost, & Lunneborg, 1973; Hunt, Lunneborg, & Lewis, 1975) proposed what he called a *cognitive correlates* approach to studying the relationship between intelligence and cognition – one would study typical cognitive tasks, such as the time an individual takes in naming a letter, and then look at the correlation between that time and scores on psychometric tests. In this way, Hunt thought, one could understand the basic cognitive building blocks of intelligence.

Sternberg later proposed an alternative *cognitive components* approach (Sternberg, 1977, 1983, 1985b), whereby intelligence could be understood in terms of components not of simple tasks, like identifying whether two letters are the same as each other, but rather more complex tasks similar to those that appear on intelligence tests, such as analogies or syllogistic reasoning. The approach was also applied to intellectual giftedness (Sternberg, 1981a) and intellectual challenges (Sternberg, 1984).

A third, *cognitive-training* approach was later utilized by Micheline Chi and Robert Glaser (see, e.g., Chi, Glaser, & Farr, 1988), among others. It involved an attempt to understand the basic information-processing components of intelligence by looking at what mental processes were trainable in task performance, and by comparing experts and novices in how they solved problems.

More recent work related to cognitive approaches to understanding intelligence has focused on working memory (e.g., Shipstead, Harrison, & Engle, 2016), various

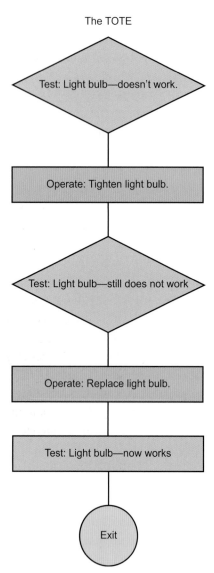

Figure 2.3 Illustration of how a TOTE works. The TOTE is a simple representation of how cognitive approaches to intelligence work. They follow processes of intelligence from the beginning to the end of a problem.

measures of mental speed (see Deary, 2000), and many other topics. This work will be described in later chapters.

Advantages and Disadvantages of Cognitive Approaches

Cognitive approaches seemed, when they were first used, to be an answer to the ever proliferating numbers of factors being put forth by psychometric theorists. At the time, the most notable psychometric proliferator was probably Guilford (1967, 1988), who early in his career proposed 120 factors of intelligence but by the end of his career had increased the total number of proposed factors in his theory to 150 and then to 180. But in fact, the cognitive approach has had some of the same problems as the psychometric approach. Just as factors can be subdivided endlessly, so can processes be endlessly subdivided. For example, one can speak of "encoding" stimuli (figuring out what the stimuli say), but certainly there are many sub-processes involved in figuring out what a stimulus is. And there may be individual differences in how these processes are executed (Hickendorff et al., 2010; Sternberg & Weil, 1980).

Cognitive theorists have even argued among themselves as to what constitutes a true information-processing theory. Some early theorists, such as Newell, Shaw, and Simon (1958) and Newell and Simon (1972), viewed their computer programs themselves as theories. This made for extreme specificity in a theory, but perhaps to a fault. Would one really want to argue that even changing a line of code in a computer program resulted in a new theory, or even a serious variant of the original theory? And how general were these theories anyway? A computer program might be able to solve a given type of problem or perform a particular kind of task, but usually it would not have much generalization beyond the problem or task. Designating a program as a theory results in at least two criteria for good theories perhaps going by the wayside – parsimony and generalizability. Other theorists, such as Schank (1972) and Anderson (2015), have viewed computer programs as operationalizations, and imperfect ones at that, of theories. That is, they do not view the programs as theories, per se, but rather as ways of putting theories into practice.

Biological Approaches

Biologically based approaches seek to understand intelligence in terms of the functioning of the brain. Because our understanding of the brain is still rather rudimentary, biological approaches are largely works in process. But some of them have come quite far (see, e.g., Haier, 2017). Many of the theories emanating from this work tend to be based on one or more of five types of data.

Models Based on Behavior-Genetic and Molecular-Genetic Data

The first kind of data is of two subtypes – behavior-genetic and molecular-genetic data (see Plomin, DeFries, Kopik, & Neiderhiser, 2012). These models typically use psychometrically derived theories to determine the structure of intelligence. That is, they are not models of structure or process but rather of the origins and development of intelligence. In the past, genetic and environmental factors were viewed as somehow opposed to each other. Researchers investigating genetic and environmental effects on intelligence use a construct called heritability. **Heritability,** as we learned in Chapter 1, refers to the proportion of variation in intelligence among individuals that is due to genetic effects. It is more specifically defined as the ratio of genetic variation in a trait to phenotypic (observable) variation in that trait. Theorists such as Jensen (1998) and Kamin (1974) saw their respective roles as arguing either for the higher (Jensen) or lower (Kamin) heritability of intelligence as defined by IQ. Hans Eysenck and Leon Kamin even wrote a book together that expressed their debating positions on higher or lower heritability (Eysenck & Kamin, 1981). Those arguing for higher heritability, such as Eysenck and Jensen, believed the heritability of IQ to be around .80, whereas those at the other extreme such as Kamin questioned whether there was any heritability at all. A consensus estimate was around .50 (Mandelman & Grigorenko, 2011).

The debate was not one of the more productive ones in the history of psychology. For one thing, the debate falsely assumed that genetics and environment work in opposition to, rather than in coordination, with each other. Today, there is good reason to believe that gene–environment covariation is extremely important, and it is hard to assign such covariation effects to either genes or the environment since they work in coordination (Flynn, 2016). For another thing, as Herrnstein (1973) pointed out, there is no single true heritability of intelligence or of anything else. Because heritability is determined as a ratio of genetic to phenotypic variance, the level of the ratio will depend on the amount of variation there is in a given gene pool or in a particular set of environments. Where genetic variance is low – in genetic pools that are largely homogeneous – the effect of the environment will have to be relatively high. Where environmental variance is low – in environments where everyone, say, has a poor or a good environment – heritability will have to be relatively high. These conclusions are deductively true – that is, they have to be correct because they are a function of the mathematics of the situation.

Eric Turkheimer and his colleagues (Turkheimer et al., 2003) showed that the situation is even more complex, in that the heritability of intelligence appears to vary with social class. In particular, lower social class is associated with lower heritability of intelligence, presumably because there is more variability in the environments of individuals from lower socioeconomic status (SES) than is found for individuals of higher socioeconomic status. The fact that SES affects heritability of intelligence suggests, of course, that there probably are other variables that affect heritability as well. The bottom line is that simply looking for some "true" value of heritability seems to be a fruitless search. Understanding the mechanisms aside from variability that affect heritability, however, seems like an entirely worthwhile pursuit.

Models Based on Data Obtained Through Brain Scans

A second path to understanding the biology of intelligence is via brain-scanning mechanisms, such as PET scanning and fMRI analysis. Some of the earliest pioneers of this method, such as Richard Haier et al. (1992a, 1992b), used PET scans to measure glucose consumption in the brain while subjects performed complex tasks, such as the computer game *Tetris*. One might have expected that the more intellectually able subjects would become deeply involved in the game and show higher levels of glucose consumption; however, the opposite was true. The more intellectually able subjects showed lower levels of glucose consumption, presumably because they found the tasks easy and did not have to work very hard on them. For more difficult tasks, the pattern was reversed, presumably because the less able subjects gave up and the more intellectually able ones worked hard to solve the problems.

More recent studies have used functional magnetic resonance imaging (fMRI) – a way of viewing the brain – to isolate portions of the brain involved in particular tasks. As a result of PET and fMRI analysis, Haier and Jung (2007; Jung & Haier, 2007) proposed a new theory of intelligence, parieto-frontal integration theory (P-FIT). This theory, described in more detail in Chapter 6, argues that the most important parts of the brain for the development and execution of intelligence are in the frontal and parietal lobes. Some of the relevant areas are in the left hemisphere, others in both hemispheres. The theory emphasizes the importance of the integration of the different parts of the brain in producing intelligence. This theory, in a sense, is opposite to Howard Gardner's (2011), which emphasizes the modularity of the various aspects of intelligence.

Figure 2.4 shows the lobes of the brain. The frontal and parietal lobes of the brain are where much of intelligence is theorized by P-FIT theory to reside.

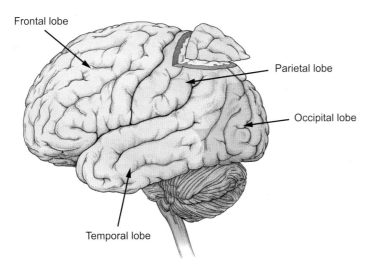

Figure 2.4 The lobes of the brain. The frontal and parietal lobes of the brain are primarily responsible for individual differences in intelligence, according to P-FIT theory.

Models Based on Data Specific to Patients with Brain Damage

A third type of data is the specific use of patients with various kinds of brain damage, such as HM (now known to be Henry Molaison), who had a bilateral medial temporal lobectomy in the hope of mitigating symptoms of epilepsy. As a result, HM lost most of his ability to acquire new information. Thus, he could remember much of what happened in his past, but he could not form new memories. Many of the early brain-based theories of intelligence relied heavily on knowledge gained from such patients (e.g., Gazzaniga, 1970; Levy, Trevarthen, & Sperry, 1972). These theories represent pioneering early work on brain-based theories of intelligence. The advantage of such theories was that it was possible to study what effects specific lesions had on intellectual functioning. At the same time, the methodologies raised some challenging questions. First, brain-damaged patients are scarcely typical – they are very different from most other people – and it has never been clear how generalizable results from these patients are to other individuals. Second, to the extent that intelligence depends upon interconnections among various brain systems, these patients are not the best individuals to study, because their brain interconnections are disrupted. One's conclusion may or may not generalize to normal brains. Third, the numbers of cases (N's) in studies of brain-damaged patients tend to be extremely small, leading to questions about how generalizable the results can be.

Models Based on Data Related to Head or Brain Size

A fourth method has been somewhat superficial but nevertheless popular among some investigators, namely, studying head size or brain size (Pietschnig et al., 2015; Witelson, Beresh, & Kigar, 2006). There seems to be little doubt that there is a correlation between brain size and intelligence, as well as between brain integrity and intelligence. The larger question is what to make of the correlation. For example, is a larger brain a cause of greater intelligence, an effect of greater intelligence, or both? In what specific areas does size matter? It appears that greater interconnectivity between hemispheres can compensate in some degree for lesser size (Gur et al., 1999). How much do size and interconnectivity actually matter, and to what extent can they trade off? At the very least, the technology has come a long way since people were simply measuring head size, as they did in earlier centuries.

Models Based on Electrophysiological Data

A fifth approach has been to use electrophysiological data. Electrodes are generally attached to a person's skull, and evoked potentials or EEGs are measured while subjects are at rest or while they are performing some task. The idea in this approach is usually to examine patterns in the electrophysiological data. One then can combine the data into one or more scores and next relate the patterns or scores to measures that are believed to assess intelligence, such as the Wechsler Adult

Intelligence Scales or the Raven Progressive Matrices (Neubauer et al., 1995). Such studies have revealed interesting aspects of performance, including the relevance of particular event-related potentials (such as P300) to alertness in task performance.

Advantages and Disadvantages of Biological Approaches

Biological approaches have the advantage that they help pinpoint areas of the brain associated with various intellectual abilities. Often, multiple interacting areas are associated with a single ability. The approaches also can help identify the mechanisms by which these abilities manifest themselves. But abilities always operate in particular sociocultural and other environmental contexts. So a full understanding of intelligence requires understanding of those contexts as well as the understanding of the brain. For example, taking precautions to protect oneself against malaria may be highly adaptive in one locale, and a waste of time in another. How intelligence manifests itself in daily life requires understanding beyond the brain.

Developmental Approaches

Developmental approaches seek to understand intelligence in terms of its development over time. One way to look at development is from the inside of the person, outward. This approach is due primarily to the Swiss psychologist Jean Piaget, although Piaget was influenced by others, such as James Mark Baldwin. Piaget referred to his own approach to theorizing as "genetic epistemological," reflecting its joint influence by biology and philosophy. Others, notably Vygotsky, have looked at development from the outside, inward. We will look at each of these approaches below.

Piaget's Theory of Development from the Inside, Outward

Although Piaget's theory is multifaceted, the theory as it applies to intelligence has two main parts (Piaget, 1972). One part is the theory of equilibration, according to which the absorption of new information is accomplished by a dynamic equilibrium between two complementary processes, **assimilation** (adapting one's cognitive structures to the environment) and **accommodation** (changing one's cognitive structures in response to the demands of the environment). The other part of the theory is the account of periods of development, beginning with a sensorimotor period (the first stage of cognitive development, occurring in the first two years of life) and ending with a formal-operational period (the stage at which a child can use abstract thinking to solve a problem). Piaget's theory has been enormously influential in developmental psychology and psychology in general, although today it has been superseded, at least in parts, by more modern cognitive theories (see Goswami, 2013).

Piaget's theory draws heavily on formal logic and other aspects of the philosophy of knowledge. As a result, it sometimes has been viewed as a theory of competence rather than of performance, describing the formal structures that underlie development rather than the way these structures are put into practice. In general, Piaget tended to overestimate the ages at which children first could accomplish cognitive tasks.

Theories Based on Development from the Outside, Inward

A second developmental approach owes as much to Lev Vygotsky (1978) as the inside-outward approach does to Piaget. Whereas Piaget tended to view intelligence as moving from the inside toward the outside, Vygotsky viewed it as moving from the outside toward the inside. As children develop, they internalize – they make a part of themselves – the social processes they observe in the environment. The outside-inward approach, therefore, zeroes in on how socialization processes affect the development of intelligence.

The outside-inward approach is a fairly popular one today in developmental psychology, perhaps partly in reaction to Piaget. It is also certainly due in large part to the field's regard for the importance of enculturation and socialization processes to the young. That said, there exists nothing even resembling a complete theory of intelligence that is based on the outside-inward approach. The closest is the theory of Reuven Feuerstein (1979), the late Israeli psychologist, who believed that human intelligence is fully modifiable. However, his theory is more one of cognitive modifiability than of intelligence per se.

Vygotsky emphasized the notion of a **zone of proximal development**, according to which learning occurs best with guidance from an experienced teacher at a level just beyond that at which an individual feels comfortable. The idea is that, with intervention, people can learn things they could never learn themselves. Intelligence is measured via *dynamic testing*. This section draws on descriptions of how dynamic testing differs from static testing (Grigorenko & Sternberg, 1998; Sternberg & Grigorenko, 2002a).

Conventional tests of intelligence are based on a model of **static testing**. In this model, an examinee takes a test and later receives a test score. With **dynamic testing**, individuals are tested and inferences are made about their abilities as with static testing; but unlike static testing, children are given some kind of helpful feedback in order to assist them in improving their performance. Vygotsky (1978) suggested that children's ability to profit from the guided instruction they received during the testing session might serve as an index of children's zone of proximal development, an indicator of the difference between their developed abilities and their latent capacities. Thus, testing and instruction are viewed as being of a single piece rather than as being distinct processes. This integration makes good sense in terms of traditional definitions viewing intelligence as, in part, the ability to learn. A dynamic test rather directly measures processes of learning in the context of testing rather than measuring these processes only indirectly as the products of past learning. Such measurement of learning processes is especially important in situations in which not all children have had equal opportunities to learn in the past.

Figure 2.5 schematically illustrates the difference between static and dynamic testing. In static testing, one simply takes a test and receives a score. In dynamic testing, one typically takes a pretest, then receives instruction relevant to performance on the pretest, and then takes a posttest to see how much one has learned from the instruction.

Vygotsky's approach, although useful, is rather vaguely specified. Psychologists are still trying to work out its implications. Vygotsky died at age 37, and so he never had a chance fully to work out the implications of his theory.

Anthropological Approaches

Adherents to anthropological approaches view intelligence as, at least in part, a cultural invention (Berry, 1974; Berry & Irvine, 1986; Sternberg, 2004). According to this view, intelligence is a somewhat different thing from one culture to another, because the knowledge and skills it takes to adapt to one culture will be quite different from those needed to adapt to another. Thus we may learn relatively little about the intelligence of one culture from studying intelligence in another culture, and indeed, our attempts to transfer knowledge actually may be harmful, because we may make generalizations that are likely not to be correct. From an anthropological point of view, the best example of this negative transfer may be IQ testing, by which a test that is developed and standardized in one culture is then carried directly over into another culture, with a translation that may not even adequately convey the meanings of the items to the individuals in the new culture.

John Berry is a radical cultural relativist, believing that there is not necessarily anything in common in the nature of intelligence across cultures. Not all adherents of the anthropological view are radical cultural relativists like John Berry, but all of them believe that in order fully to understand intelligence within a culture, one needs to study that culture in its own right and not assume that generalization can be made from one culture to another.

Figure 2.6 shows an example of a problem from an indigenous intelligence test. It is easy for many rural Kenyan children who live in communities where parasitic illnesses are omnipresent. Can you solve the problem?

Advantages of Anthropological Approaches

Anthropological approaches, which view intelligence in terms of the external world, not just the internal world of the individual, provide a needed counterbalance to the psychometric, cognitive, and biological approaches. So whereas Haier (2017) argued

Static test

Individual takes test

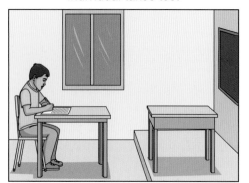

Individual gets test score

Dynamic test

Individual takes pretest

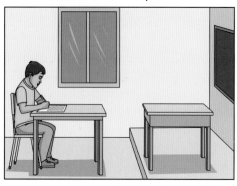

Individual receives
relevant instruction

Individual takes posttest

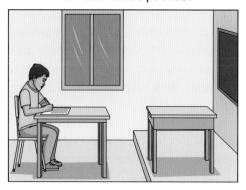

Individual gets test score

Figure 2.5 The difference between static and dynamic testing typically resides in whether students receive just a test or, instead, receive a pretest, relevant instruction, and then a posttest.

1. "A small child in your family has homa. She has a sore throat, headache, and fever. She

has been sick for 3 days. Which of the following five Yadh nyaluo (Luo herbal

medicines) can treat homa?

i. Chamama. Take the leaf and fito (sniff medicine up the nose to sneeze out illness).

ii. Kaladali. Take the leaves, drink, and fito.

iii. Obuo. Take the leaves and fito.

iv. Ogaka. Take the roots, pound, and drink.

v. Ahundo. Take the leaves and fito."

In this item, Options 1 and 2 represent common treatments for homa, Option 3

represents a rare treatment, Option 4 represents a treatment that is not used for homa

and Option 5 represents an imaginary (nonexistent) herb. Thus Options 1–3 were scored

as correct answers. If Option 5 (the false-positive) was chosen, a penalty of –3 points

was applied.

Figure 2.6 Test item and analysis from an indigenous intelligence test relevant to rural Kenyan children (from Sternberg et al., 2001)

that intelligence is entirely biological, those who believe in the anthropological approach might say that cognitive processes have some biological origins, but that how intelligence is displayed can vary widely from one culture to another.

Disadvantages of Anthropological Approaches

A first possible problem with anthropological approaches is that they can put too much emphasis on the role of culture. Intelligence probably represents some interaction of biology with culture. It is not clear that either a purely biological or a purely cultural viewpoint is as enlightening as some kind of integration of the two.

A second possible problem is that we do not have good theories of context, at least as it applies to intelligence. Context may well matter for the manifestation of intelligence, but we have nothing with the precision of the factor models in order to say just how these effects come about or even what exactly they are.

A third problem is that if intelligence is really so different from one culture to another, the implication is that any model may be painfully culturally specific. There have been attempts to remedy this apparent difficulty. For example, Sternberg (2004) has argued that the mental processes that underlie intelligence – things like recognizing the existence of a problem, defining the problem, formulating a strategy to solve the problem, representing information about the problem, etc. – are universal, the ways in which these processes are manifested in the environment, and the ways in which they are best tested, can differ radically from one culture to another. According to this view, some things are common, others are not, and part of understanding intelligence is understanding what is specific and what is not.

Systems Approaches

Systems approaches are perhaps the vaguest of all of the approaches that have been described. "Systems theories" are considered those theories that seek to understand intelligence in terms of multiple systems of intelligence or even multiple intelligences (Gardner, 2011; Sternberg, 2003). These theories are more complex, in some respects, than theories in the past generally have been, although probably no more complex than P-FIT theory. One goal of these theories is to understand intelligence in a way that transcends a single approach and that combines aspects of at least several of the approaches that have been considered above.

The dangers inherent in systems theories are not readily dismissed. For example, Gardner's theory of multiple intelligences was first presented in 1983 (Gardner, 1983). It argues that intelligence is not a single thing, but rather that there are multiple independent intelligences, such as linguistic, logical–mathematical, bodily–kinesthetic, and musical. But as yet there is no adequate empirical test or set of tests that provides solid empirical support for its main claims – that intelligence is modular, that there are eight multiple intelligences, and that the various intelligences are uncorrelated with each other. On the contrary, the existing evidence suggests that these claims are questionable (Haier, 2017; Visser, Ashton, & Vernon, 2006).

Sternberg's theory of successful intelligence (Sternberg, 2003) maintains that intelligence comprises the analytical skills measured by IQ tests, but also creative, practical, and wisdom-based skills. Although much evidence has been collected in favor of this theory, some would question whether elements such as creative, practical, and wisdom-based skills should be included in the definition of intelligence (Hunt, 2010). Hunt, among others (see Sternberg & Kaufman, 2011), also considers the general factor of intelligence (g) to be more powerful than the theory of successful intelligence implies. So one might argue that systems theories, in attempting to be more encompassing, may go too far in stretching the concept of intelligence. In large part, whether one thinks so depends on the approach to intelligence that underlies one's thinking about intelligence. Systems theories also are broad but when one looks broadly, one sometimes misses important local details. See Focus on Contemporary Research box for a description of this research.

FOCUS ON CONTEMPORARY RESEARCH: ROBERT J. STERNBERG'S WORK ON PRACTICAL INTELLIGENCE

The various approaches described in this chapter were combined in a study done in Tanzania (Sternberg et al., 2002). My collaborators and I administered tests to 358 schoolchildren. These children were between the ages of 11 and 13 years in a rural village near Bagamoyo, a town on the eastern coast of Tanzania. The tests included a form-board classification test (which is a kind of sorting task), a linear-syllogisms test (requiring children to infer logical relations between stimuli), and a Twenty Questions Test ("Find a Figure"). All of these kinds of items measure skills required on standardized tests of intelligence. For instance, a linear-syllogisms test might tell the participant that one individual is shorter than a second; that the second is shorter than the third; and then ask which is tallest. However, the different kinds of tests were administered dynamically rather than statically (see Vygotsky, 1978).

Dynamic testing, as described earlier in this chapter, is like conventional static testing in that individuals are assessed and inferences are made about their abilities. But dynamic tests differ in that the individuals are provided with some kind of feedback to help them improve their performance and the underlying skills on which this performance is based. Vygotsky (1978) argued that the individuals' ability to profit from the guided instruction of dynamic testing could serve as a measure of children's zone of proximal development – the difference between their developed abilities and their latent capacities. In other words, testing and instruction are viewed as being of one integrated piece rather than as being two distinct processes. A dynamic test directly measures processes of learning in the context of testing rather than measuring these learning processes indirectly as the result of past learning. Dynamic measurement is especially important when not all children being tested have had equal opportunities to learn in the past.

In the assessments in Tanzania, children were first given the ability tests. Experimental-group children were then given an intervention to help them understand how to solve the test problems; control-group children were not given any such intervention. The intervention involved a brief period of instruction in which children were able to learn skills that were relevant to helping them improve their scores. For example, in the Twenty Questions tasks, children would be taught how a single true–false question could be used to cut the number of possible correct solutions drastically. As an example, "Is it alive?" would be effective as a question, but "Is it a ball?" would not be. Then all children – experimental and control – were retested. Because the total time for instruction was under an hour, one would not expect the children to demonstrate dramatic gains. Nevertheless, on average, the gains from pretest to posttest in the experimental group were statistically significant. Moreover, those gains in performance were significantly greater than the gains in the control group. Thus, dynamic testing benefited those in the experimental group because it familiarized them with the basics of the testing situation and the tasks involved in it.

In the control group, the correlations between pretest and posttest scores were high – generally at the .8 level. This means that pretest scores were highly predictive of posttest scores. One would expect a high correlation because there was no intervention. Hence, the retesting was largely a measure of alternate-forms reliability, where one gives two different versions of a test to see if they measure the same thing. More important, however, scores on the pretest in the experimental group showed only weak although statistically significant correlations (at the .3 level) with scores on the posttest. These correlations were significantly lower than those in the control group. These results suggested that dynamic testing had a strong effect on which students did well and which students did less well. The dynamic tests also proved to be better predictors of scores on other kinds of cognitive tests than were the static tests. These results showed that for this population of children, which was unfamiliar with cognitive tests, dynamic tests were distinctly advantageous.

Note: This chapter draws on Sternberg et al. (2002).

CONCLUSION

This chapter has reviewed the primary approaches for understanding human intelligence. Battles among intelligence researchers have either been between competing theories within approaches, or equally often, between advocates for different approaches. Some researchers appear to believe that there is a "correct" or most basic approach. But the approaches are largely complementary, rather than contradictory.

Here is the problem: One can call into question and even disconfirm theories generated within an approach but there is no way of disconfirming an approach. Approaches are not right or wrong, but more or less useful for particular purposes. If someone is committed to an approach, over time that someone may come to believe that the approach really is somehow the "right" one, even though it is just one of many possible windows in the world of intelligence (or anything else).

Approaches are like languages: They are different ways of expressing ideas. And even languages can employ different symbol systems, such as those that use the Latin alphabet, or the Chinese hanzi symbol system of Chinese and some other Asian languages, or the gestural symbols of American Sign Language, or the Cyrillic alphabet of Russian, or simply the only vaguely specifiable code of the nonverbal communication we all use with each other. There is no single "correct" symbol system. Each can be useful for somewhat different purposes. So is it with approaches to intelligence. There is no one "right" one, although different ones can be more useful for different purposes. If we want to understand the role of the brain in intelligence, we might turn to biological approaches, but if we want to understand the role of culture, anthropological approaches will be more useful. We maximize our learning about human intelligence when we recognize that the approach that serves us best is the one that best serves our theoretical and research purposes, and combining approaches – even mixing them – sometimes is best of all.

CHAPTER SUMMARY

There are a number of different approaches to studying intelligence. Psychometric approaches involve administering psychometric tests to individuals and then analyzing patterns of correlations, or relationship among the tests. Factor analysis is used to try to identify the basic abilities underlying intelligence. Early theories viewed the ideas of general intelligence as conflicting with group factors, such as verbal and numerical abilities. Today, most psychometric theories are hierarchical, viewing general intelligence (g) at the top, and more specific abilities at successively lower levels of the hierarchy.

Cognitive approaches seek to identify the basic information-processing components underlying intelligence. They also seek to understand the mental representations upon which the components act, as well as the strategies into which the components combine. Historically, three major approaches have been the *cognitive-correlates*, *cognitive-components*, and *cognitive-training* approaches. Today, many users of these approaches seek to understand the role of working memory in intelligence, as well as the role of cognitive speed of processing.

Biological approaches seek to understand intelligence in terms of the structures and functions of the brain and the central nervous system. In what parts of the brain do various kinds of abilities originate at the biological level? These approaches provide unique understanding of the biological correlates of many of the things people do in their everyday lives. They have helped us understand that much of cognitive ability is distributed – originating in many parts of the brain rather than just one.

Developmental approaches can be from the inside, outward, or from the outside, inward. Piaget is best known for the former approach. In Piaget's theory, development is largely maturational – children develop according to a biological program, and environment has relatively little effect. In contrast, in Vygotsky's outside-inward approach, development is largely through socialization – one internalizes what one sees in the environment and it becomes part of oneself.

Cultural approaches view intelligence as at least partly an invention. Cultures decide what they believe are important skills for adaptation, and then label them as "intelligent." Different cultures may decide on different skills. What one culture views as important – say, hunting or fishing or gathering, or solving verbal or mathematical problems – another may view as unimportant. The cultural approach is not at odds with other approaches. The basic factors or processes of cognition are still there. What differs from one culture to another is whether those factors or processes are labeled as important to intelligence.

Finally, systems approaches view intelligence as part of a large system of cognitive and possibly other kinds of processes. For example, Gardner includes in his theory bodily–kinesthetic and musical intelligences, which are not included in other theories. Sternberg includes creative (Niu & Sternberg, 2003) and practical skills (Sternberg, 1997; Sternberg & Hedlund, 2002; Sternberg & Smith, 1985) that also are typically missing from other theories. Sternberg's theory posits a set of processes that act upon experience in order to adapt to, shape, and select environments.

The approaches, as mentioned above, are not necessarily mutually exclusive. Rather, they provide different lenses for understanding intelligence in different ways. A comprehensive approach ultimately would integrate these different single approaches.

KEY TERMS

accommodation • assimilation • chronological age • dynamic testing • factor analysis • general intelligence (*g*) • heritability • intelligence quotient (IQ) • mental age • percentile • reasoning ability • static testing • verbal ability • zone of proximal development

COMPREHENSION AND REFLECTION QUESTIONS

1. Describe the psychometric approach to understanding intelligence.
2. What do you see as some of the strengths and weaknesses of the cognitive approach to intelligence?
3. Can the biological approach to intelligence give us final answers as to what intelligence is? Why or why not?
4. Do you believe intelligence is, at least in part, a cultural invention? Why or why not?
5. What advantages might systems approaches to intelligence have in terms of understanding people from a holistic or integrative perspective?

References

Anderson, J. R. (2015). *The adaptive character of thought*. New York: Psychology Press.

Berry, J. W. (1974). Radical cultural relativism and the concept of intelligence. In J. W. Berry, & P. R. Dasen (eds.), *Culture and cognition: Readings in cross-cultural psychology* (pp. 225-229). London: Methuen.

Berry, J. W., & Irvine, S. H. (1986). Bricolage: Savages do it daily. In R. J. Sternberg & R. K. Wagner (eds.), *Practical intelligence: Nature and origins of competence in the everyday world* (pp. 271-306). New York: Cambridge University Press.

Binet. A., & Simon, T. (1916). *The development of intelligence in children*. Baltimore, Williams & Wilkins. (Reprinted 1973, New York: Arno Press; 1983, Salem, NH: Ayer Company).

Carroll, J. B. (1993). *Human cognitive abilities: A survey of factor-analytic studies*. New York: Cambridge University Press.

Chi, M. T. H., Glaser, R., & Farr, M. J. (eds.) (1988). *The nature of expertise*. New York: Psychology Press.

Cronbach, L. J. (1957). The two disciplines of scientific psychology. *American Psychologist, 12*, 671-684.

Deary, I. J. (2000). *Looking down on human intelligence: From psychometrics to the brain*. Oxford: Oxford University Press.

Eysenck, H. J., & Kamin, L. (1981). *Intelligence: The battle for the mind*. New York: Macmillan.

Feuerstein, R. (1979). *The dynamic assessment of retarded performers: The learning potential assessment device, theory, instruments, and techniques*. Baltimore, MD: University Park Press.

Flynn, J. R. (2016). *Does your family make you smart? Nature, nurture, and human autonomy*. New York: Cambridge University Press.

Gardner, H. (1983). *Frames of mind: The theory of multiple intelligences*. New York: Basic Books.

Gardner, H. (2011). *Frames of mind: The theory of multiple intelligences*. New York: Basic Books.

Gazzaniga, M. S. (1970). *The bisected brain*. East Norwalk, CT: Appleton-Century-Crofts.

Goswami, U. (ed.) (2013). *The Wiley-Blackwell handbook of child cognitive development* (2nd ed.). New York: Wiley-Blackwell.

Grigorenko, E. L., & Sternberg, R. J. (1998). Dynamic testing. *Psychological Bulletin, 124*, 75–111.

Guilford, J. P. (1967). *The nature of human intelligence*. New York: McGraw-Hill.

Guilford, J. P. (1988). Some changes in the structure-of-intellect model. *Educational and Psychological Measurement, 48*, 1-4.

Gur, R. C., Turetsky, B. I., Matsui, M., Yan, M., Bilker, W., Hughett, P., & Gur, R. E. (1999). Sex differences in brain gray and white matter in healthy young adults: correlations with cognitive performance. *Journal of Neuroscience, 19*(10), 4065–4072.

Haier, R. J. (2017). *The neuroscience of intelligence.* New York: Cambridge University Press.

Haier, R. J., Siegel, B., Tang, C., Abel, L., & Buchsbaum, M. S. (1992a). Intelligence and changes in regional cerebral glucose metabolic-rate following learning. *Intelligence, 16*, 415-426.

Haier, R. J., Siegel, B. V., Jr., MacLachlan, A., Soderling, E., Lottenberg, S., & Buchsbaum, M. S. (1992b). Regional glucose metabolic changes after learning a complex visuospatial/ motor task: A positron emission tomographic study. *Brain Research, 570*, 134-143.

Herrnstein, R. (1973). *IQ in the meritocracy.* New York: Little-Brown.

Hickendorff, M., van Putten, C. M., Verhelst, N. D., & Heiser, W. J. (2010). Individual differences in strategy use on division problems: Mental versus written computation. *Journal of Educational Psychology, 102*, 438-452.

Hunt, E. (1980). Intelligence as an information processing concept. *British Journal of Psychology, 71*, 449-474.

Hunt, E. (2010). *Human intelligence.* New York: Cambridge University Press.

Hunt, E. B., Frost, N., & Lunneborg, C. (1973). Individual differences in cognition: A new approach to intelligence. In G. H. Bower (ed.), *The psychology of learning and motivation* (vol. 7, pp. 87-122). New York: Academic Press.

Hunt, E. B., Lunneborg, C., & Lewis, J. (1975). What does it mean to be high verbal? *Cognitive Psychology, 7*, 194–227.

Jensen, A. R. (1998). *The g factor.* Westport, CT: Praeger.

Kamin, L. (1974). *The science and politics of IQ.* Hillsdale, NJ: Lawrence Erlbaum Associates.

Levy, J., Trevarthen, C., & Sperry, R. W. (1972). Perception of bilateral chimeric figures following hemispheric disconnection. *Brain, 95*, 61-78.

Levy, J., Trevarthen, C., & Sperry, R. W. "Mainstream Science on Intelligence" (December 13, 1994). *Wall Street Journal,* p. A18.

Mandelman, S. D., & Grigorenko, E. L. (2011). Genes, environments, and their interactions. In R. J. Sternberg & S. B. Kaufman (eds.), *Cambridge handbook of intelligence* (pp. 85-106). New York: Cambridge University Press.

Miller, G. A., Galanter, E. H., & Pribram, K. H. (1960). *Plans and the structure of behavior.* New York: Holt, Rinehart and Winston.

Neisser, U., Boodoo, G., Bouchard, T. J., Boykin, W. A., Brody, N., Ceci, S. J., Halpern, D. F., Loehlin, J. C., Perloff, R., Sternberg, R. J., & Urbina, S. (1996). Intelligence: Knowns and unknowns. *American Psychologist, 51*(2), 77–101.

Neubauer, A., Freudenthaler, H. H., & Pfurtscheller, G. (1995). Intelligence and spatiotemporal patterns of event-related desynchronization (ERD). *Intelligence, 20*, 249-266.

Newell, A., Shaw, J. C., & Simon, H. A. (1957). Problem solving in humans and computers. *Carnegie Technical, 21*(4), 34-38.

Newell, A., Shaw, J. C., & Simon, H. A. (1958). Elements of a theory of human problem solving. *Psychological Review, 65*(3), 151-166.

Newell, A., & Simon, H. A. (1972). *Human problem solving.* Englewood Cliffs, NJ: Prentice Hall.

Niu, W., & Sternberg, R. J. (2003). Societal and school influences on student creativity: The case of China. *Psychology in the Schools, (40)*1, 103–114.

Piaget, J. (1972). *The psychology of intelligence.* Totowa, NJ: Littlefield Adams.

Pietschnig, J., Penke, L., Wicherts, J. M., Zeiler, M., & Voracek, M. (2015). Meta-analysis of associations between human brain volume and intelligence differences: How strong are they and what do they mean? *Neuroscience & Biobehavioral Reviews, 57,* 411–32.

Plomin, R., DeFries, J. C., Knopik, V. S., & Neiderhiser, J. (2012). *Behavioral genetics* (6th edn.). New York: Worth.

Roid, G. H. (2003). *Stanford-Binet Intelligence Scales* (5th ed.). Itasca, IL: Riverside Publishing Company.

Schank, R. C. (1972). Conceptual dependency: A theory of natural language understanding. *Cognitive Psychology, 3,* 552-631.

Shipstead, Z., Harrison, T. L., & Engle, R. W. (2016). Working memory capacity and fluid intelligence: Maintenance and disengagement. *Perspectives on Psychological Science, 11,* 771-799.

Spearman, C. (1923). *The nature of "intelligence" and the principles of cognition.* London: Macmillan.

Spearman, C. (1927). *The abilities of man: Their nature and assessment.* New York: Macmillan.

Sternberg, R. J. (1977). *Intelligence, information processing, and analogical reasoning: The componential analysis of human abilities.* Hillsdale, NJ: Lawrence Erlbaum Associates.

Sternberg, R. J. (1981a). A componential theory of intellectual giftedness. *Gifted Child Quarterly, 25,* 86–93.

Sternberg, R. J. (1981b). Testing and cognitive psychology. *American Psychologist, 36,* 1181–1189.

Sternberg, R. J. (1983). Components of human intelligence. *Cognition, 15,* 1–48.

Sternberg, R. J. (ed.). (1984). *Mechanisms of cognitive development.* San Francisco: Freeman.

Sternberg, R. J. (1985a). *Beyond IQ: A triarchic theory of human intelligence.* New York: Cambridge University Press.

Sternberg, R. J. (ed.). (1985b). *Human abilities: An information-processing approach.* San Francisco: Freeman.

Sternberg, R. J. (1985c). Human intelligence: The model is the message. *Science, 230,* 1111–1118.

Sternberg, R. J. (1986). Inside intelligence. *American Scientist, 74,* 137–143.

Sternberg, R. J. (1990). *Metaphors of mind: Conceptions of the nature of intelligence.* New York: Cambridge University Press.

Sternberg, R. J. (1997). What does it mean to be smart? *Educational Leadership, 54*(6), 20–24.

Sternberg, R. J. (2003). *Wisdom, intelligence, and creativity synthesized.* New York: Cambridge University Press.

Sternberg, R. J. (2004). Culture and intelligence. *American Psychologist, 59*(5), 325–338.

Sternberg, R. J. (ed.) (in press). *Cambridge handbook of human intelligence* (2nd ed.). New York: Cambridge University Press.

Sternberg, R. J., & Grigorenko, E. L. (1999). Genetics and intelligence. *Journal of American Academy of Child and Adolescent Psychiatry, 38,* 486–488.

Sternberg, R. J., & Grigorenko, E. L. (2002a). *Dynamic testing.* New York: Cambridge University Press.

Sternberg, R. J., & Grigorenko, E. L. (eds.). (2002b). *The general factor of intelligence: How general is it?* Mahwah, NJ: Lawrence Erlbaum Associates.

Sternberg, R. J., Grigorenko, E. L., Ngorosho, D., Tantufuye, E., Mbise, A., Nokes, C., Jukes, M., & Bundy, D. A. (2002). Assessing intellectual potential in rural Tanzanian school children. *Intelligence, 30,* 141–162.

Sternberg, R. J., Nokes, K., Geissler, P. W., Prince, R., Okatcha, F., Bundy, D. A., & Grigorenko, E. L. (2001). The relationship between academic and practical intelligence: A case study in Kenya. *Intelligence, 29,* 401–418.

Sternberg, R. J., & Hedlund, J. (2002). Practical intelligence, *g*, and work psychology. *Human Performance 15*(1/2), 143–160.

Sternberg, R. J., & Kaufman, S. B. (eds.) (2011). *Cambridge handbook of intelligence.* New York: Cambridge University Press.

Sternberg, R. J., & Smith, C. (1985). Social intelligence and decoding skills in nonverbal communication. *Social Cognition,* 2, 168–192.

Sternberg, R. J., & Weil, E. M. (1980). An aptitude–strategy interaction in linear syllogistic reasoning. *Journal of Educational Psychology, 72,* 226–234.

Thurstone, L. L. (1938). *Primary mental abilities.* Chicago, IL: University of Chicago.

Turkheimer, E., Haley, A., Waldron, M., D'Onofrio, B., & Gottesman, I. I. (2003). Socioeconomic status modifies heritability of IQ in young children. *Psychological Science,* 6, 623–628.

Visser, B. A., Ashton, M. C., & Vernon, P. A. (2006). Beyond *g*: Putting multiple intelligences theory to the test. *Intelligence, 34*(5), 487–502.

Vygotsky, L. (1978). *Mind in society.* Cambridge, MA: Harvard University Press.

Wechsler, D. (1940). Non-intellective factors in general intelligence. *Psychological Bulletin, 37,* 444–445.

Wechsler, D. (2008). *Wechsler Adult Intelligence Scale – Fourth Edition.* San Antonio, TX: Psychological Corporation.

Witelson, S. F., Beresh, H., & Kigar, D. L. (2006). Intelligence and brain size in 100 postmortem brains: Sex, lateralization and age factors. *Brain, 129,* 386–398.

3 Early History of Theory and Research on Intelligence

ROBERT J. STERNBERG

The early roots of modern thinking about intelligence perhaps extend back as far as the publication of Charles Darwin's (1859) *Origin of Species*. This volume had a profound impact on many fields of scientific endeavor. One of the lines of inquiry was the investigation of human intelligence. The book argued that the capabilities of humans are in some ways continuous with, rather than totally distinct from, those of lower animals. Hence, they could be understood through scientific investigations much like those directed at lower animals. Investigators of intelligence picked up on some of Darwin's ideas. As you read this chapter, consider how Darwin's ideas have permeated thinking throughout the history of attempts to understand intelligence (Sternberg, 1985b, 1986, 1990). What are some of these attempts?

Early Contributors to the Testing Movement in Intelligence

The testing movement in intelligence can be traced to the work of several scientists of the late nineteenth and early twentieth century. First, the British inventor, explorer, and researcher, Francis Galton, applied Darwin's theory to human behavior. He was one of the first scientists to carry out studies on human intelligence. Slightly thereafter, James McKeen Cattell followed up on Galton's work to create some of the first actual tests of intelligence. In France in the early 1900s, Alfred Binet turned this research toward a more practical goal – to develop some tests that would help place children in the most appropriate classes in school.

Francis Galton

Darwin's cousin, **Francis Galton** (1883), proposed a theory of the "human faculty and its development." Galton believed that Darwin's theory could be applied directly to human behavior. The combination of theory and measurement techniques Galton proposed opened a door to the understanding of human intelligence.

Galton proposed two general qualities that distinguish the more from the less intellectually able. The first is energy, which Galton, perhaps reflecting his times, viewed as the capacity for labor. Galton believed that individuals who are intellectually gifted in a variety of fields have in common that they show remarkable levels of energy. The second general quality that Galton observed is sensitivity to the environment. Galton observed that information can reach us concerning external events only if it first is transmitted through the senses. The more perceptive the senses are to differences in various properties of stimuli, for example, luminescence, pitch, odor, or other sensory qualities, the larger would be the range of information on which intelligence ultimately can act. Galton had a very negative perception of people in the lower ranges of the intellectual spectrum. Galton (1883) wrote:

> The discriminative facility of idiots is curiously low; they hardly distinguish between heat and cold, and their sense of pain is so obtuse that some of the more idiotic seem hardly to know what it is. In their dull lives, such pain as can be excited in them may literally be accepted with welcome surprise. (p. 28)

The quotation probably tells us much more about Galton and his times than it does about people with low intelligence. His statement shows his clear disdain for and condescension toward such people. Unfortunately, this problem of condescension and disparagement persisted among many other scholars who later studied intelligence in the twentieth century. Certainly, there is no compassion or even pity in his statements. Were it only Galton, perhaps one could write off the man as idiosyncratic. But too much of the history of intelligence work reveals similar attitudes toward people of low intelligence (e.g., Goddard, 1912, 1914; Terman, 1916).

For seven years (during the period of 1884-1890), Galton ran what he viewed as an anthropometric laboratory – a laboratory quantitatively studying the intelligence of people – at the South Kensington Museum (renamed the Victoria and Albert Museum) in London. At this museum, for a small amount of money, visitors could have themselves measured on a wide variety of psychophysical tests of Galton's invention. In this sense, Galton was the forerunner of another later trend – finding ways to make people pay to have their mental skills tested.

One of Galton's tests was weight discrimination – telling the difference between objects weighing different amounts. The apparatus Galton used to measure weight discrimination consisted of a number of cases of gun cartridges. Each case was filled with alternating layers of shot, wool, and wadding. The cases all appeared to be identical. They differed only in their respective weights. The weights of the cases formed a geometric series of heaviness, so that they were multiplicatively related. The examiner recorded the finest (smallest geometric) interval that a given participant could discriminate. Galton suggested that similar geometric sequences also could be used for assessing other human senses, such as taste and touch. For touch, Galton suggested using wirework of various degrees of fineness to assess discrimination. For taste, Galton suggested using stock bottles of salt solutions of various strengths to assess discrimination. For olfaction (sense of smell), Galton suggested the use of bottles of attar of rose at various levels of dilution.

Galton also designed a whistle to enable him to determine the highest pitch that different individuals could perceive. Tests on human participants with the whistle enabled Galton to discover that the ability of people to hear notes high in pitch tends to decline precipitously as they advance in age. Galton also discovered that people are less able than cats to perceive tones of high pitch. This test, and the others as well, certainly were sophisticated for the time. But this finding presents a problem for any psychophysically based theory of intelligence that subscribes to a notion of evolutionary continuity. It suggests that, in at least this one respect, cats are superior in intelligence to humans. Although one may grant this superiority to cats, one then will be obliged to grant superiority to various animals in many other psychophysical characteristics, leaving humans in a mediocre position to which they are not accustomed (but which perhaps they deserve)!

The critical thing to note about Galton is that he was the first to study intelligence in anything that reasonably could be labeled a scientific way. Even if his theory seems a bit quaint today – does a person who is nearsighted deserve to be labeled as less intelligent than a person with 20/20 vision? – Galton recognized the need to formulate a theory and to test it with empirical data. That was a first in the field of intelligence research.

James McKeen Cattell

James McKeen Cattell brought many of Galton's ideas across continents from the United Kingdom to the United States. Cattell was head of the psychological laboratory at Columbia University. As a result, he was in a favorable position to publicize Galton's psychophysical approach to both the theory and the measurement of intelligence. Cattell (1890) devised his own mental tests based on Galton's notions.

Cattell (1890) proposed a series of 50 distinct psychophysical tests. He described 10 of them in detail, for example:

1. *Dynamometer pressure.* This is the pressure resulting from the greatest possible squeeze of one's hand on an instrument called a dynamometer.
2. *Rate of movement.* This is the quickest possible movement of the right hand and arm, starting at rest and then proceeding through a distance of 50 cm.
3. *Sensation areas.* This is the distance on the skin by which two points of pressure, such as a pin prick, need to be separated in order for the two points actually to be felt as separate points.
4. *Pressure causing pain.* This is the point at which pressure on a part of the body, such as the center of the forehead, first causes pain.
5. *Least noticeable difference in weight.* This is the smallest possible difference in the weights of two objects, such as boxes, that one can detect as representing different weights.

Cattell thus took Galton's ideas, refined them, and made them into what arguably was the first truly structured and carefully constructed test of intelligence. Again, the theory may have left something to be desired, but Cattell set, at least in the United States, a standard for scientific research on intelligence. He moved much of intelligence research from the realm of philosophy to the realm of the budding discipline of psychology.

Psychophysical tasks, though, find little or no place in modern-day tests of intelligence as administered in schools and in industry. Indeed, such tests ceased to play an important role in practical mental measurement by the turn of the twentieth century, although, as will be discussed later in this volume, they are coming back into vogue among certain theoreticians. Cattell's tests eventually were abandoned because they were found to show nothing more than a chance pattern of correlations, both with each other and with external measures used to validate the tests. In other words, the tests were invalid.

Cattell's approach was dealt a more or less fatal blow by one of his own students. Wissler (1901) suggested that Cattell's tests should correlate with each other and with external criteria of academic success, such as grades in the undergraduate program at Columbia University. In fact, Wissler found Cattell's tests correlated with neither. His findings seemed conclusively to invalidate the Galton-Cattell theory. It was time for a new view on intelligence to come to the attention of scientists. That view proved to be the view of Alfred Binet and his collaborator, Theodore Simon.

Alfred Binet

In 1904, the minister of public instruction in Paris named a commission with an important task. The commission was charged with studying or creating tests that would ensure that children with intellectual deficits received an adequate education. The commission decided that no child suspected of mental challenges should be placed in a special class for such children unless it could be certified that the child truly was mentally challenged. Binet and Simon (1916a) devised tests (known as **the Binet–Simon Scale**) to meet this placement need.

Thus, whereas theory and research in the tradition of Galton grew out of purely scientific concerns, research in the tradition of Binet grew out of practical educational concerns. There was one other key difference between Binet and Galton. Whereas Galton showed obvious disdain for intellectually challenged children, Binet was intent on helping them. As we shall see, however, the tests he helped create could be used by people with a view toward challenged children similar to his own, or by people with a view toward such children similar to Galton's.

At the time, definitions of various degrees of subnormal intelligence lacked both precision and standardization. Personality deficits and intellectual deficits were both seen as being of the same ilk. So a child with a perceived personality issue might be placed in a class for intellectually subnormal children. The risk, of course, was that schools would dump children whom they perceived to be problematical in those classes simply to reduce their own workload. Binet and Simon presented a different point of view. They believed that the core of intelligence is judgment, otherwise called good sense, practical sense, initiative, the faculty of adapting one's self to circumstances. To judge well, to comprehend well, to reason well, these are the essential activities of intelligence. A person may be a moron or an imbecile if he is lacking in judgment; but with good judgment he can never be either. Indeed, the rest of the intellectual faculties seem of little importance in comparison with judgment (Binet & Simon, 1916a, pp. 42-43).

Binet cited the example of Helen Keller as someone of known extraordinary intelligence whose scores on psychophysical tests would be notably inferior. Yet Keller, given her accomplishments, could be expected to perform at a very high level on tests of judgment.

Binet is sometimes thought of as test-driven or as atheoretical (Hunt, Frost, & Lunneborg, 1973), but he was neither. Binet and Simon's (1916a) theory of intelligent thinking in many ways foreshadowed the research being done many years later on the development of metacognition (e.g., Brown & DeLoache, 1978; Flavell, 1981; Flavell & Wellman, 1977; Sternberg, 1984a). Binet and Simon (1916b) proposed that intelligent thought comprises three distinct elements: direction, adaptation, and control.

Direction involves knowing what one needs to do and how to do it. When we need to multiply two numbers of two digits each, for example, we give ourselves a series of instructions on how to do the multiplication. These instructions constitute the direction of thought. The instructions do not need always to be consciously executed.

In many respects, these ideas about the development of direction over time foreshadow much later theorizing regarding automaticity of information processing (see, e.g., Schneider & Shiffrin, 1977; Shiffrin & Schneider, 1977). According to Binet and Simon (1916b), mentally challenged individuals show an absence or weakness of direction that manifests itself in two different forms: "Either the direction, once commenced, does not continue, or it has not even been commenced because it has not been understood" (p. 138).

Adaptation refers to how an individual selects and monitors his or her strategy during the course of performing a task. Thoughts consist of a series of selections. One can think this way, or one can think that way. Brighter children are more likely to select and monitor their strategies in an efficient way. This idea is directly relevant to metacognitive ideas, such as Sternberg's theory of metacomponents in learning and problem solving (Sternberg, 2001).

Finally, control is the ability to criticize one's own thoughts and actions. Binet and Simon (1916b) believed that much of this ability is exercised below the conscious level. Less intelligent individuals show a lack of control. Their actions frequently are inappropriate to and not useful for performing the task at hand. For example, a mentally challenged child "told to copy an 'a' scribbles a formless mass at which he smiles in a satisfied manner" (p. 149).

Binet and Simon further distinguished between two types of intelligence, ideational and instinctive intelligence. Ideational intelligence operates by means of words and ideas. It uses logical analysis and verbal reasoning. Instinctive intelligence operates by means of feeling. It refers not to the instinct attributed to other animals and to simple forms of human behavior, but rather to the "lack of a logical perception, of a verbal reasoning, which would permit of explaining and of demonstrating a succession of truths" (Binet & Simon, 1916b, p. 316). It seems to be similar to an intuitive sense. Thus, Binet and Simon, like some of the philosophers who preceded them, had a sense of the kinds of fast and slow processing that would be important to cognitive theory many years later (Kahneman, 2013).

Binet and Simon's tests and the **Binet–Simon Scale** were early attempts to operationalize Binet's conception of intelligence. Binet came up with the concept of mental age, or the comparable age level at which a child performs on a test, regardless of his or her chronological age. Binet, unlike Galton, believed that intelligence is modifiable, and even designed what he called "mental orthopedics" to help children improve their cognitive skills. But it remained for Lewis Terman, his successor in the United States, to operationalize the tests in a standardized way. Terman never operationalized the mental orthopedics, nor is it likely he would have been interested, as he was strongly hereditarian.

Lewis Terman

Lewis M. Terman, a professor of psychology at Stanford University, was a follower of Binet. In collaboration with Maud Merrill, he constructed the earliest versions of what are now known as the **Stanford–Binet Intelligence Scales** (Terman & Merrill, 1937, 1973). Terman's historical versions of the test are described here. More recent versions are described in later chapters.

In the 1973 version of the tests, testing starts at age 2. Examples of tests at this level are a three-holed form board, which requires children to put circular, square, and triangular pieces into holes on a board of appropriate shape; identification of parts of the body, which requires children to identify body parts on a paper doll; block building, which requires children to build a four-block tower; and picture vocabulary, which requires children to identify pictures of common objects.

Six years later, by age 8, the character of the tests changes considerably, although the tests are still measuring the kinds of higher cognitive processes that the tests for age 2 attempt to tap. For age 8, the tests include vocabulary, requiring children to define words; verbal absurdities, requiring children to recognize why particular statements are foolish; similarities and differences, requiring children to say in what ways each of two objects is the same as and at the same time different from the other; comprehension, requiring children to solve practical problems of the kinds that they face in everyday life; and naming of the seven days of the week.

At age 14, there is some overlap in tests, although the tests are now more difficult. The tests include vocabulary; induction, in which the examiner makes a notch in an edge of a piece of folded paper and asks children how many holes the piece of paper will have when it is unfolded (as a note, the test seems to be more spatial than inductive in what it measures); reasoning, requiring solution of arithmetic word problems; ingenuity, requiring children to indicate the series of steps that could be taken to pour out a particular amount of liquid; spatial directions; and reconciliation of opposites, requiring children to say in what ways two words with opposite meanings are alike. The most difficult level is "Superior Adult III." It includes measures of vocabulary, interpretation of proverbs, spatial orientation, inductive reasoning, repetition of the main ideas of a story, and solution of analogies.

IQ on the Stanford-Binet scale was initially computed on the basis of the ratio of mental age to chronological age × 100. So if a child had a mental age of 10 (i.e., was capable of doing the mental work of a 10-year-old) and a chronological age of 8 (was 8 years old physically), the child's IQ would be (10/8) × 100 = 125. Today mental ages are not used because they never really worked past the age of about 16. After that age, one additional year of physical (chronological) age no longer seems to correspond to a year of mental growth.

Terman is best known for his applied work rather than for his theoretical work. Beyond his work on the intelligence test, he (with collaborators) is most well-known for a longitudinal study of the gifted (e.g., Terman, 1925; Terman & Oden, 1959). In his sample of gifted children, Terman included children from California under age 11 with IQs over 140 as well as children in the 11–14 age bracket with somewhat lower IQs (to allow for the lower ceiling at this age in test scores). The mean IQ of the 643 participants selected was 151; only 22 of the participants had IQs of under 140. The accomplishments in later life of the selected group were quite notable. By 1959, there were 70 listings among the group in *American Men of Science* and 3 memberships in the National Academy of Science. Further, 31 men were listed in *Who's Who in America* and 10 were listed in the *Directory of American Scholars*. There were numerous highly successful businessmen as well as individuals who were succeeding well in all of the professions. The sex bias in these references is readily apparent. In those days, the social convention was for most women to become housewives. It therefore is impossible to make any meaningful comparison between the men and the women in the study.

The Terman study was a landmark study in that it showed a clear association between IQ and various real-world measures of life success. Moreover, it helped dispel the notion that people with high IQs are oddballs, or physically infirm, or even tending toward the mentally ill. All of these were fairly common stereotypes at the time the study was commenced. At the same time, it was a correlational study, so it could not show causal effects. How much of any effect was due to confounding factors – such as socioeconomic status or parental investment – just is not clear. Moreover, although there were many successes, one might argue there were limitations in the findings: Few of the individuals seem to have reached levels (percentiles) of success comparable to the levels (percentiles) of their IQs. Indeed, the study generally has been touted as having large percentages of success, but would not the same be true of children who simply had high school marks at an early age? All that said, the study was tremendously important in suggesting that investment in the gifted could pay serious dividends. It was also important in a way that some, including myself, would argue was not so positive (Sternberg, 1984b, 1985a, 1985b, 2003; Sternberg & Davidson, 1982, 1983): It led to many gifted programs emphasizing IQ as a, or even the sole, basis for identification of the gifted at the expense of serious consideration of other measures as well.

David Wechsler

David Wechsler, a twentieth-century American psychologist, followed in the tradition of Alfred Binet in emphasizing higher cognitive processes in his test of intelligence (e.g., Wechsler, 1939, 1958, 1974). But his notion of intelligence, although related to Binet's, was somewhat different:

> Ultimately, intelligence is not a kind of ability at all, certainly not in the same sense that reasoning, memory, verbal fluency, etc., are so regarded. Rather it's something that is inferred from the way these abilities are manifested under different conditions and circumstances. (Wechsler, 1974, pp. 5-6)

> Intelligence is the aggregate or global capacity of the individual to act purposefully, to think rationally and to deal effectively with his environment. (Wechsler, 1944, p. 3)

The Wechsler scales, like the Stanford-Binet scales, are wide ranging in their content. The **Wechsler Adult Intelligence Scale (WAIS)** was designed for adults (ages 16 and up) and the **Wechsler Intelligence Scale for Children (WISC)** is appropriate for children aged 6 to under 16. However, these scales do not do full justice to the breadth of Wechsler's original conception of the nature of intelligence. Indeed, it is unlikely, even today, that any scale could be constructed that would do full justice to the broad conceptions of intelligence of Binet and Wechsler.

There are 12 subtests in the 1974 revision of the Wechsler Intelligence Scale for Children (WISC-R). Ten of these subtests are considered mandatory and two are optional. (Chapter 4 describes the twenty-first-century versions of the test, as they have changed quite a bit.) The content of the WISC-R test is almost identical to the content of the adult-level scale, except that the items are easier, as would be expected. The tests are divided into two equal parts, verbal tests and performance tests. Each part yields a separate deviation IQ, meaning that IQ is determined by converting percentile scores into an IQ using normal-distribution IQ equivalents of percentile scores. Like the Stanford–Binet, the test must be administered to individuals one at a time. In both tests, an examiner administers only items that are appropriate to the age and ability level of the test-taker. Test-takers begin with easier items appropriate for their age and work their way up. They end with items that are difficult enough to result in repeated failure to get the items correct.

The verbal part of the test includes as subtests the following: information, which requires demonstration of knowledge about the world; similarities, which requires an indication of a way in which two different objects are alike; arithmetic, which requires the solution of arithmetic word problems; vocabulary, which requires definition of common English words; comprehension, which requires understanding of societal customs; and optionally, digit span, which requires recall of strings of digits forward in one section and of digits backward in another section. The performance part of the tests includes as subtests the following: picture completion, which requires recognition of a missing part of a picture of an object; picture arrangement, which requires rearrangement of a scrambled set of pictures into an order that tells a coherent story from beginning to end; block design, which requires children to reproduce a picture of a design, constructed from a set of red, white, and half-red/half-white blocks, by actually building the design with physical blocks; object assembly, which requires children to manipulate jigsaw puzzle pieces to form a picture of a common object in the real world; coding (the analogue of digit-symbol at the adult level), which requires rapid copying of symbols that are paired with pictures of objects according to a prespecified key that links the pictures with the objects; and mazes, which requires tracing of a route through each of a set of mazes from beginning to end. See Focus on Contemporary Research for an examination of one researcher's ideas about intelligence.

FOCUS ON CONTEMPORARY RESEARCH: ROBERT J. STERNBERG'S EVOLUTION OF IDEAS ABOUT INTELLIGENCE

Is intelligence just what intelligence tests measure? Some of my research focuses on the question of just what intelligence is. In this sense, it continues with the tradition of Galton, Binet, Spearman, and others who have been trying to figure out what *intelligence* is.

Just as the field of intelligence has a history, so does the research trajectory of any intelligence researcher. In my early work (e.g., Sternberg, 1980, 1983), I believed that intelligence is best understood as a set of information-processing components. In other words, it comprises the mental processes a person uses from the time a person first sees an intelligence-test item to the time the person responds to the item. For example, in solving an analogy such as *black : white :: top : ?*, a person first needs to encode the terms of the analogy, then infer the relationship between the first two terms, then map that relationship to the second half of the analogy, then apply the relationship to generate an answer (in this case, *bottom*), and finally, respond.

I believed in this kind of componential theory for quite some time, but then decided it is an oversimplification of the nature of intelligence. The reason is that this view assumed that intelligence is fully captured by the kinds of items found on intelligence tests. But my experiences teaching students convinced me that this is not the case. In particular, I came across students who were very strong in creative or practical (common-sense) skills but not necessarily excellent in IQ-testing-based skills. Rather, there are important kinds of intellectual skills barely measured or not measured at all by conventional intelligence tests, namely, creative and practical skills. So I proposed a "triarchic theory" of intelligence that recognized the importance of these additional skills (Sternberg, 1984a, 1984b, 1993, 1997a; Sternberg & Smith, 1985).

After a while, I realized that the issue is more complex (Sternberg, 1985a, 1997a, 1997b). People who are adaptive to their environments are not merely strong in analytical, creative, and/or practical skills. More importantly, they figure out what their strengths and weaknesses are, and then find ways of capitalizing on their strengths and correcting or compensating for their weaknesses. At a more general level, what I came to call "successfully intelligent" people figure out what they want to do with their lives and what they realistically can do with them, and then find strategies to achieve their goals to the extent they can.

I continue to believe in the theory of successful intelligence, but today it is broader than in the past, including wisdom-based skills as well as analytical, creative, and practical ones (Sternberg, 2003). Successfully intelligent people are people who are not only adept at using their cognitive skills to advance themselves and those they care directly about, but they are also adept at using their cognitive skills to help attain a common good – that is, they are people who contribute toward making the world a better place.

Societal Uses of Intelligence Testing

Theories of intelligence never developed in close connection with the uses of intelligence tests in society. Indeed, Alfred Binet might have turned over in his grave were he aware of some of the uses to which his test was being put.

The Early Eugenics Movement

Henry Goddard was one of the earliest researchers to find what he thought was a societal use for intelligence tests. Goddard came to believe, like Galton, that intelligence is largely if not wholly inherited. But Goddard followed Binet's, not Galton's approach to assessment. As early as 1916, he already took charge of the translation of the Binet–Simon scales into English. He and his colleagues distributed thousands of copies of the translated test. In effect, he became the leading proponent of the test, which is ironic because his view on intelligence as fixed at birth was pretty much the opposite of Binet's view. Goddard was Director of Research at the Vineland Training School for Feeble-Minded Boys and Girls in Vineland, New Jersey, and in his role, was able to put his ideas into practice. Goddard (1912) wrote of what he had learned from his research in a popular (i.e., not essentially scholarly) book, *The Kallikak Family: A Study in the Heredity of Feeble-Mindedness*.

The story of the Kallikaks, at least as Goddard told it, was intended to convince Goddard's audience of the primacy of heredity in the development of intelligence. As Goddard told the story (and there is reason to question at least some of the details), a young man of a family of supposedly good genetic stock, Martin Kallikak, Sr., engaged in a fling with a bar woman, out of which emerged a son, Martin, Jr. The son then went on to produce a family tree of allegedly feeble-minded progeny, including Deborah, a resident at the school. Deborah's immediate relatives, according to Goddard, included 36 children born outside wedlock (at the time, labeled "illegitimate"), 24 alcoholics, and many other individuals with lives that people of the time considered immoral or disgraceful. But Martin, Sr., sowed his wild oats and then went on to marry a woman of excellent repute. As one might expect, the children of the marriage went on to become doctors, lawyers, judges, educators, and other distinguished individuals. In sum, Goddard believed, the father was bright – whether the children turned out to be society's winners or losers depended in this case on the genetics of the mother. So for Goddard and many of his contemporaries, including Lewis Terman, the case was open and shut: Heredity is the determining factor behind individual differences in intelligence.

The details of the story of the Kallikaks do not provide real support for Goddard's hereditarian position. Consider why.

First, the environment in which the within-wedlock family grew up was undoubtedly much superior to the environment in which the out-of-wedlock family grew up. Goddard, like Galton with his beliefs in hereditary genius, failed to appreciate that environment and heredity were totally confounded by the research designs they used.

Second, Goddard clearly had an ideology that he wanted to sell. He was a staunch believer in **eugenics** – the idea that people could be bred (much as other animals can be) to encourage the development of desirable traits or the suppression of undesirable ones. Goddard's book was a way of promoting that ideology. One might wonder on what basis anyone would conclude that the ideology came first. Goddard's activity in the eugenics movement is one indicator – he was hoping that mentally challenged people would be sterilized, or at least that they would be separated from the rest of society through institutions such as the Vineland one. Further evidence for his motivations is shown by the fact that he published doctored photographs to make the "bad" side of the family look even worse. In other words, he "faked" his photographic data. (Doctoring photographs is enough by contemporary standards to lead to a compulsory retraction of a scientific article or book.)

Third, Goddard went way beyond his data not in a scholarly article, where scholars could have the opportunity to ponder and debate the meaning of his findings, but rather in a popular book read by people who would lack the scientific training that could lead them to be skeptical of Goddard's claims.

Fourth, Goddard went well beyond IQ or intelligence or any intellectual measurement in his discussion of people with intellectual challenges. Many of his judgments appear not to have been made on the basis of the Stanford-Binet or any other intelligence test. Rather, they were more along the lines of moral judgments or even judgments of people's supposed worth. A problem in the history of intelligence testing has been scholars who go beyond their data to make judgments about people's value to society, and Goddard was one of the early proponents of such judgments, as with his avid support of eugenics. In this respect, he had a lot of company with similar biases. Goddard tapped into a societal fear that the United States was being somehow contaminated – whether by foreigners or by people who otherwise did not fit in – and he successfully persuaded others that his broader judgments were sound. In the second decade of the twenty-first century, Americans are witnessing similar concerns, with similar unfortunate results. In the end, people often are suspicious of people who are "not like them," and they find all kinds of spurious reasons to denigrate those who do not live up to whatever standards they set for humanity.

Henry Goddard went well beyond his data, but he was not the only scholar who did. Some years later, Sir Cyril Burt, who was greatly admired during his lifetime and even was knighted, wrote scholarly papers describing his studies of twins (e.g., Burt, 1966), especially monozygotic (identical) twins reared apart. Such twins are valuable for the study of genetic determination, in theory, because they have identical heredity but wholly different environments. But it is not clear how many twins Burt really studied, if any. As the years went by, Burt supposedly added to his number of cases, but some of his statistics (correlations) remained identical. This outcome is pretty much a statistical impossibility. Moreover, anyone attempting to gain Burt's data had great difficulty doing so. When data were finally provided, they appeared to have been faked, at least in part, to provide the statistics Burt claimed for them (Fancher, 1985). Today, Burt, another strong believer in eugenics, is viewed as having left a very questionable legacy (Hearnshaw, 1981; Kamin, 1977; Mackintosh, 1995).

It might sound as though only those who are strong hereditarians are prepared to stretch the data. This is by no means the case. Strong ideologies can affect arguments on any side of a scientific issue. Kamin (1974) probably stretched things a bit far when he said that there was no evidence to suggest anything to a reasonable person but environmental origins of intelligence. And Gould (1981) sometimes misrepresented the work of others in his attempt to demonstrate that much work on intelligence was bogus. The truth is: All scientists need to take care that their ideology does not affect the conclusions they draw from their data.

IQ Testing in the Military

Probably the greatest societal impact of work on intelligence came neither from studies of heritability, such as those of Goddard and Burt, but rather directly from the IQ testing movement. During World War I, there was a sudden need to screen soldiers in terms of what they were capable of doing that had not existed before at any time in the history of the United States. The US was entering not just a war, but a world war. Led by Robert Yerkes, at one time the President of the American Psychological Association (and also, at one point in his life, a eugenicist), a team of early twentieth-century Army psychologists developed two tests, the Army Alpha and the Army Beta. The former was a verbal test of intelligence, the latter, a nonverbal (performance-based) test that required no language. The tests were used to screen recruits, close to two million by the end of the war. More recent intelligence tests are still used today in the military as well as in industry. Because intelligence test scores correlate with much real-world performance (Deary, Whalley, & Starr, 2009), such a procedure could be viewed as reasonable. What was not so reasonable were the conclusions drawn from the tests regarding differences in the intelligence of different groups of recruits, for example, recruits of different races or national origins. Again, differences in environment were confounded with differences in gene pools, but people's desires to draw the conclusions they want to draw sometimes leave even well-meaning scholars concluding what they want to conclude rather than what their data show.

CONCLUSION

We have seen in this chapter how thinking about intelligence evolved from the later nineteenth-century views of Sir Francis Galton to early and even mid-twentieth-century views, such as those of Alfred Binet, Lewis Terman, and Charles Spearman. Although these men lived long ago, many of their beliefs persist today, at least among some psychologists. Galton believed that intelligence could best be understood in terms of simple sensorimotor processing. Binet, in contrast, emphasized judgment and self-direction. Binet's views about the nature of intelligence prevailed in much of the twentieth century and even into present times; but Galton's views suggesting high heritability of intelligence were prominent in the early twentieth century.

Psychological scientists always have to be careful not to let their prior ideologies influence their work. Not all of the scientists have succeeded. For example, Goddard touched up photographs to strengthen the points he was trying to make, and Cyril Burt appears to have falsified at least some of his data. Although many intelligence theorists early in the twentieth century were strong believers in the heritability of intelligence, today people have more sophisticated views, realizing that genes and environment often work together to produce the cognitive outcomes we observe in everyday life.

CHAPTER SUMMARY

Early work on intelligence in the late nineteenth and early twentieth centuries developed in large part out of efforts to construct tests of intelligence. The tradition of Francis Galton emphasized psychophysical skills whereas the tradition of Alfred Binet emphasized judgmental skills. Binet's tradition won out. David Wechsler constructed a test that measured skills somewhat similar to those measured by Binet; however, there was more emphasis on performance-based tests. Modern versions of these two tests are still used today.

Mental testing has, in some respects, come far and in other ways hardly at all. The tests used today are very different from Galton's original tests, but little different from Binet's. Certainly the cosmetic appearance has changed, but the fundamental items types have changed little. Perhaps Binet just hit on the best way to measure intelligence. Or perhaps test-constructors became entrenched, and simply failed to move beyond where Binet brought them so long ago. Only time will tell.

Early theorists of intelligence were, in many cases, strongly hereditarian in their beliefs. (Alfred Binet was a notable exception.) In some cases, these strong beliefs appear to have had an effect on the way the scholars reported their data. In some rare cases, there may have been outright faking. Social policies were implemented on the basis of ideology but that were credited with much more of a scientific basis than they truly had. Today, most scientists try to be careful in their scientific claims so that policy-makers do not claim scientific bases for policies that are fundamentally ideological. We look at the ideas of many early researchers in the field of intelligence as erroneous. But future researchers well may look back on our times and wonder how we could have had beliefs as erroneous as those we have.

Current theories of intelligence take many different forms. Many theorists, at least those who view intelligence as well measured by conventional intelligence tests, believe that mental abilities are hierarchically structured, with general ability at the top and successively narrower abilities as one goes down the hierarchy (see Sternberg & Grigorenko, 2002). Tests of intelligence today, which are largely based on hierarchical theories, are in many ways similar to those of Binet and his early successors. But in other ways, they have been updated to reflect current times, as discussed in the next chapter.

KEY TERMS

Alfred Binet • Binet–Simon Scale • eugenics • Francis Galton • Stanford–Binet Intelligence Scales • Wechsler Adult Intelligence Scale (WAIS) • Wechsler Intelligence Scale for Children (WISC)

COMPREHENSION AND REFLECTION QUESTIONS

1. How did the views of Galton and Binet differ regarding the nature of intelligence?
2. Why are Galtonian types of tests almost never used today to measure intelligence?
3. What evidence did Goddard use to argue for the importance of heredity in the development of intelligence? How good was the evidence?
4. Why do scientists sometimes (although rarely!) distort or even outright fake their data?
5. Why did mental testing blossom during the period of World War I?

References

Binet, A., & Simon, T. (1916a). *The development of intelligence in children* (E. S. Kite, trans.). Baltimore: MD: Williams & Wilkins.

Binet, A., & Simon, T. (1916b). *The intelligence of the feeble-minded* (E. S. Kite, trans.). Baltimore: Williams & Wilkins.

Brown, A. L., & DeLoache, J. S. (1978). Skills, plans, and self-regulation. In R. Siegler (ed.), *Children's thinking: What develops?* (pp. 3-35). Hillsdale, NJ: Lawrence Erlbaum Associates.

Burt, C. (1966). The genetic determination of differences in intelligence: A study of monozygotic twins reared together and apart. *British Journal of Psychology, 57,* 137-153.

Cattell, J. McK. (1890). Mental tests and measurements. *Mind, 15,* 373-380.

Darwin, C. (1859). *Origin of species.* London: John Murray.

Deary, I. J., Whalley, L. J., & Starr, J. M. (2009). *A lifetime of intelligence: Follow-up studies of the Scottish mental surveys of 1932 and 1947.* Washington, DC: American Psychological Association.

Fancher, R. E. (1985). *The intelligence men.* New York: W. W. Norton.

Flavell, J. H. (1981). Cognitive monitoring. In W. P. Dickson (ed.), *Children's oral communication skills* (pp. 35-60). New York: Academic Press.

Flavell, J. H., & Wellman, H. M. (1977). Metamemory. In R. V. Kail & J. W. Hagen (eds.), *Perspectives on the development of memory and cognition* (pp. 3-33). Hillsdale, NJ: Lawrence Erlbaum Associates.

Galton, F. (1869). *Hereditary genius: An inquiry into its laws and consequences.* London: Macmillan.

Galton, F. (1883). *Inquiry into human faculty and its development.* London: Macmillan.

Goddard, H. H. (1912). *The Kallikak family: A study in the heredity of feeble-mindedness.* New York: Macmillan.

Goddard, H. H. (1914). *Feeble-mindedness: Its causes and consequences.* New York: Macmillan.

Gould, S. J. (1981). *The mismeasure of man.* New York: W. W. Norton.

Hearnshaw, L. (1981). *Cyril Burt, psychologist.* New York: Vintage.

Hunt, E. B., Frost, N., & Lunneborg, C. (1973). Individual differences in cognition: A new approach to intelligence. In G. Bower (ed.), *The psychology of learning and motivation* (vol. 7, pp. 87-122). New York: Academic Press.

Kahneman, D. (2013). *Thinking, fast and slow.* New York: Farrar, Straus, & Giroux.

Kamin, L. (1974). *The science and politics of IQ.* Hillsdale, NJ: Lawrence Erlbaum Associates.

Kamin, L. (1977). *The science and politics of IQ.* Hillsdale, NJ: Lawrence Erlbaum Associates.

Mackintosh, N. J. (1995). *Cyril Burt: Fraud or framed?* Oxford: Oxford University Press.

Schneider, W., & Shiffrin, R. W. (1977). Controlled and automatic human information processing: I. Detection, search, and attention. *Psychological Review, 84,* 1-66.

Shiffrin, R. M., & Schneider, W. (1977). Controlled and automatic human information processing: 2. Perceptual learning, automatic attending, and a general theory. *Psychological Review, 84,* 127-190.

Spearman, C. (1927). *The abilities of man.* New York: Macmillan.

Sternberg, R. J. (1977). *Intelligence, information processing, and analogical reasoning: The componential analysis of human abilities.* Hillsdale, NJ: Lawrence Erlbaum Associates.

Sternberg, R. J. (1980). Sketch of a componential subtheory of human intelligence. *Behavioral and Brain Sciences, 3,* 573–584.

Sternberg, R. J. (1983). Components of human intelligence. *Cognition, 15,* 1–48.

Sternberg, R. J. (1984a). Toward a triarchic theory of human intelligence. *Behavioral and Brain Sciences, 7,* 269–287.

Sternberg, R. J. (1984b). What should intelligence tests test? Implications of a triarchic theory of intelligence for intelligence testing. *Educational Researcher, 13,* 5–15.

Sternberg, R. J. (ed.). (1985a). *Human abilities: An information-processing approach.* San Francisco: Freeman.

Sternberg, R. J. (1985b). Human intelligence: The model is the message. *Science, 230,* 1111–1118.

Sternberg, R. J. (1985c). Teaching critical thinking, Part 1: Are we making critical mistakes? *Phi Delta Kappan, 67,* 194–198.

Sternberg, R. J. (1986). Inside intelligence. *American Scientist, 74,* 137–143.

Sternberg, R. J. (1990). *Metaphors of mind.* New York: Cambridge University Press.

Sternberg, R. J. (1993). *Sternberg Triarchic Abilities Test.* Unpublished test.

Sternberg, R. J. (1997a). The triarchic theory of intelligence. In D. P. Flanagan, J. L. Genshaft, & P. L. Harrison (eds.), *Contemporary intellectual assessment: Theories, tests, and issues* (pp. 92–104). New York: Guilford Press.

Sternberg, R. J. (1997b). What does it mean to be smart? *Educational Leadership, 54*(6), 20–24.

Sternberg, R. J. (2001). Metacognition, abilities, and developing expertise: What makes an expert student? In H. J. Hartman (ed.), *Metacognition in learning and instruction: Theory, research and practice* (pp. 247–260). Boston, MA: Kluwer Academic Publishers.

Sternberg, R. J. (2003). WICS: A model for leadership in organizations. *Academy of Management Learning & Education, 2,* 386–401.

Sternberg, R. J., & Davidson, J. E. (1982). The mind of the puzzler. *Psychology Today, 16,* 37–44.

Sternberg, R. J., & Davidson, J. E. (1983). Insight in the gifted. *Educational Psychologist, 18,* 51–57.

Sternberg, R. J., & Grigorenko, E. L. (eds.). (2002). *The general factor of intelligence: How general is it?* Mahwah, NJ: Lawrence Erlbaum Associates.

Sternberg, R. J., & Smith, C. (1985). Social intelligence and decoding skills in nonverbal communication. *Social Cognition, 2,* 168–192.

Terman, L. M. (1916). *The measurement of intelligence.* Boston, MA: Houghton-Mifflin.

Terman, L. M. (1925). *Genetic studies of genius: Mental and physical traits of a thousand gifted children* (vol. 1). Stanford, CA: Stanford University Press.

Terman, L. M., & Merrill, M. A. (1937). *Measuring intelligence.* Boston, MA: Houghton-Mifflin.

Terman, L. M., & Merrill, M. A. (1973). *Stanford–Binet intelligence scale: Manual for the third revision.* Boston, MA: Houghton-Mifflin.

Terman, L. M., & Oden, M. H. (1959). *Genetic studies of genius,* vol. 4: *The gifted group at midlife.* Stanford, CA: Stanford University Press.

Wechsler, D. (1939). *The measurement of adult intelligence.* Baltimore, MD: Williams & Wilkins.

Wechsler, D. (1944). *The measurement of adult intelligence* (3rd ed.). Baltimore: Williams & Wilkins.

Wechsler, D. (1958). *The measurement and appraisal of adult intelligence* (5th ed.). Baltimore, MD: Williams & Wilkins.

Wechsler, D. (1974). *Manual for the Wechsler Intelligence Scale for Children* (rev.). New York: The Psychological Corporation.

Wissler, C. (1901). The correlation of mental and physical tests. *Psychological Review, Monograph Supplement, 3*, no. 6.

PART II
Approaches to Studying Intelligence

4 Psychometric Approaches to Intelligence

ALAN S. KAUFMAN, W. JOEL SCHNEIDER, AND JAMES C. KAUFMAN

People have been appraising each other's capacities for a long time, at least informally. In any society, knowing who is clever, quick-witted, and knowledgeable – and who is not – confers significant advantages as we cultivate friendships, build alliances, compete with rivals, and contend with enemies. In everyday interactions, our appraisals need only be approximately correct rather than rigorously precise. For the same reasons we do not need formal measurements to decide who is trustworthy, loyal, helpful, friendly, courteous, or kind, we do not need intelligence tests – tests of people's cognitive abilities – to know which of our acquaintances are bright. We can see their intelligence easily enough in their vocabulary, in their humor, in their creativity, and in their achievements (Borkenau & Liebler, 1995; Borkenau, Mauer, Riemann, Spinath, & Angleitner, 2004; J. Kaufman, 2016; Murphy, Hall, & Colvin, 2003). Such outward signs of intellect allow us to judge quickly and with reasonable accuracy if someone is about average in intellect, well above average, or well below. If our appraisals prove to be grossly inaccurate, we can update them as needed.

The First Intelligence Tests

If we can manage our daily concerns without knowing official IQ scores of friends, family, and co-workers, what purpose do the tests serve? The first verbal and nonverbal intelligence tests were developed in an era in which corporations were merging, government bureaucracies were expanding, public education became universal, and world wars pitted whole populations against each other. Increasingly, large organizations faced a high volume of time-consuming, complex, high-stakes decisions about individuals. These organizations needed such decisions to be quick, inexpensive, transparent, and plausibly based in science. Intelligence tests were one of many tools that met these needs – though not without controversy. Many organizations continue to use intelligence tests because they streamline personnel selection procedures, cut training costs, and increase worker productivity (Schmidt & Hunter, 1998).

As described in Chapter 3, the first modern intelligence tests were developed in France at the beginning of the twentieth century to identify children who needed special education services (Binet & Simon, 1905). Although all children can learn, children with severe intellectual disabilities require far more hands-on training than regular education can provide. Regular education is simply too fast and insufficiently structured for such children.

With his collaborator Théodore Simon, Binet devised a series of diagnostic tests that were easy to administer, score, and interpret. Their tests sidestepped the impossible task of measuring a person's "true" intelligence, whatever that might mean. Their purpose was simply to find test items that would distinguish between children who would likely have difficulty in regular education and those who would not. Example items include naming body parts, repeating short sentences, defining words, and recreating simple drawings from memory (Binet & Simon, 1905, 1916). Children who could not do such tasks were likely to need more attention than regular education could provide.

Tests are as old as education, but not until the modern era were formal methods developed to evaluate empirically whether a test validly measured what it was intended to measure. One can easily claim to measure a mental process, but proving the validity of the measure requires a surprising amount of time and effort. In the late nineteenth century, statisticians invented the discipline of psychometrics (Galton, 1879), a set of conceptual tools and mathematical methods for measuring mental processes, personality traits, interests, attitudes, and abilities. More broadly, **psychometrics** is the scientific study of psychological measurement and the methods by which we verify that our measures are trustworthy and psychologically meaningful (Furr & Bacharach, 2013, p. 2). Psychometrics has matured into a broad and sophisticated discipline that takes years of intensive study to master.

Chapter 2 briefly described the uses of mental age in IQ testing. Binet and Simon were psychometric pioneers who invented the concept of the **mental age**, a person's level of performance which could be compared to the performance typical of a given child's true chronological age. If an 8-year-old's score on an intelligence test was equal to the score obtained by the average 10-year-old, then the child was considered to have a mental age of 10, which is two years ahead of the child's chronological age. If an 8-year-old scored as well as the average 6-year-old, the child's mental age was two years behind the child's chronological age. By definition, children scoring at the average for their age have matching mental and chronological ages. The concept of the mental age made it possible to use **population norms** – typical performance of children of various ages – to compare children across ages and across tests. Later innovations allowed psychologists to interpret test scores in terms of the intelligence quotient (IQ), which is used to evaluate and compare the overall mental capacity of same-age peers on a single scale. At every age, the average IQ is set at 100. As seen in Figure 4.1, there is no upper or lower bound to IQ, but scores lower than 40 or higher

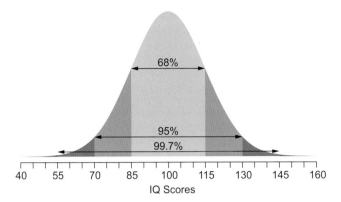

Figure 4.1 Distribution of IQ scores

than 160 are quite rare. About 68 percent of all scores fall between 85 and 115, and 95 percent of scores are between 70 and 130.

Interestingly, the inventor of the IQ concept, William Stern, was appalled at how his idea morphed into an oversimplified synonym for intelligence (Lamiell, 2003). Although he believed that intelligence tests were useful for understanding an individual, he condemned his contemporaries for investing the scores with too much meaning, conflating a person's score with the person's worth. He especially disapproved when intelligence tests were used to benefit institutions at the expense of individuals.

How Are Intelligence Tests Used Today?

The most popular intelligence tests, for at least the past half century, were developed by David Wechsler (1939), who emphasized the measurement of verbal and perform-ance (nonverbal) abilities, and the importance of thinking of IQ tests as clinical instruments, not merely as psychometric tools (A. Kaufman, 2009; A. Kaufman, Raiford, & Coalson, 2016). Chapter 3 described the development of the early Wechs-ler scales. Today, current versions of his tests are popular worldwide (Wechsler, 2008, 2014). These IQ tests, as well as other popular individually administered instruments (A. Kaufman & Kaufman, 2004; McGrew, 2009; Naglieri, Das, & Goldstein, 2014; Reynolds & Kamphaus, 2015; Woodcock, 1993), are used for educational, medical (neuropsychological), and legal purposes. Other IQ tests, often administered to large groups of people simultaneously, are used for personnel selection.

Educational Uses of Intelligence Tests
The first use of intelligence tests – identifying intellectual disabilities so that children could receive intensive services as soon as possible – remains its least controversial. Intelligence tests are used for a variety of other purposes in education

as well. Not all intelligence deficits are extreme, and some are subtle enough to escape notice for years. Sometimes otherwise bright children have specific deficits that interfere with learning. Identifying such deficits requires an understanding not only of overall intelligence as measured by IQ, but of the various components of intelligence. For example, children with dyslexia often fall behind their peers in learning to read, not because they are generally unintelligent, but because they have difficulty hearing how the individual sounds in spoken words correspond to individual letters in written words (e.g., /k/-/a/-/t/ = cat). Intelligence tests combined with reading tests can help school personnel identify and help such children early – before they fall behind their peers and frustration undermines their motivation to learn.

The use of intelligence tests to identify children who need extra help is relatively uncontroversial provided the process is conducted with integrity, compassion, and professionalism. Somewhat more controversial is the use of intelligence tests to select children for inclusion in gifted education programs. If the pace of gifted education is too fast for most children, and the pace of regular education is too slow for children with high scores on intelligence tests, then using intelligence tests for this purpose can be justified, particularly since children in gifted programs tend to become productive adults whose innovations benefit society as a whole (Lubinski, 2016).

Nevertheless, many scholars concerned about fairness and inclusion of under-represented groups have advocated alternative methods of assessing giftedness and for reforms in gifted education as a whole (Gardner, 2011; J. Kaufman, 2017; S. Luria, O'Brien, & Kaufman, 2016; Renzulli, & Reis, 2014; Subotnik, Olszewski-Kubilius, & Worrell, 2011). Even so, cognitive ability tests in one form or another are likely to play a role in gifted education selection for a long time.

There is some debate in the field about whether intelligence tests should be used to identify specific learning disabilities. See the Focus on Contemporary Research box for a look at some research that asks whether it is possible to correlate different patterns of cognitive strengths and weaknesses with specific patterns of academic strengths and weaknesses.

FOCUS ON CONTEMPORARY RESEARCH: ALAN S. KAUFMAN'S WORK ON THE MEASUREMENT OF COGNITIVE STRENGTHS AND WEAKNESSES

One of the current controversies about intelligence tests is whether they should be used in the identification of specific learning disabilities, with some scholars arguing that much of the useful information cognitive ability tests provide is redundant with measures of academic functioning that are routinely administered (c.f. Schneider & Kaufman, 2017 and Miciak & Fletcher, 2017). Other scholars have argued that the particular mix of cognitive abilities people have is relatively unimportant and that the main focus of interpretation should be on the general factor of intelligence (Canivez, 2013; McGill, 2015).

One of several steps toward resolving these controversies is to show that different patterns of cognitive strengths and weaknesses are associated with distinct kinds of academic difficulties. For example, do people with strong verbal skills but poor working memory abilities have reading problems that are distinct from people with weak verbal skills but strong working memory abilities? There is evidence that people with strong verbal skills are better able to infer the meaning of unfamiliar vocabulary in text. However, because of difficulty holding information in short-term memory they might have difficulty understanding multi-part sentences in which the meaning of the first part of the sentence is unclear until the end of the sentence has been read (Calvo, 2005). People with the reverse cognitive profile might have the opposite pattern of reading difficulties.

A recent paper authored by Liu, Marchis, DeBiase, Breaux, Courville, Pan, & Kaufman (2017) asked a simple but important question: Are different patterns of cognitive strengths and weaknesses associated with specific patterns of academic strengths and weaknesses?

From the KTEA-3 standardization sample, 304 individuals were identified who had higher knowledge (Gc) than memory retrieval fluency (Gr); 288 individuals had the reverse pattern; and 198 individuals had relatively high knowledge (Gc) but low auditory processing (Ga). That is, each group had one relative cognitive strength and one relative cognitive weakness.

Literacy skills can be categorized and measured in many ways. To understand the results of this study, we can make two distinctions in reading abilities: Decoding vs. Comprehension and Level vs. Fluency. That is, some reading abilities refer to technical skills like decoding single words. For example, if shown a single unfamiliar word, can you sound it out according to the typical rules of your native language? Other literacy skills have to do more with higher-level skills like reading comprehension and written communication. For example, can you read a story, follow the plot, and appreciate the author's sense of humor?

Some literacy skills are measured in terms of the level of performance, with questions that vary from easy to difficult. Other skills are measured in terms of speed or fluency. The speed/fluency tests require you to complete a series of simple tasks quickly (e.g., read a series of simple words or write several simple sentences). Thus, there are decoding tests that measure the level of one's ability to read words, decoding tests that measure one's fluency of reading words, tests that measure the level of one's ability to comprehend and communicate with text,

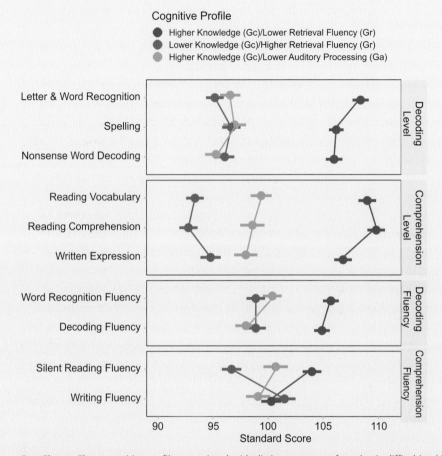

Box Figure. Three cognitive profiles associated with distinct patterns of academic difficulties (data from Table 2 in Liu et al., 2017)

and tests that measure the fluency and speed at which one can read with comprehension and write meaningful sentences.

In the figure, the average performance of the three cognitive profile groups is plotted on different kinds of literacy tests (i.e., Decoding vs. Comprehension, Performance Level vs. Fluency). The sample means in the figure below are circles, and the horizontal lines through the circles indicate the confidence intervals of the sample means (i.e., the range where the true population means are likely to be).

Shown in blue, the group with higher knowledge (Gc) and lower retrieval fluency (Gr) has strong language skills, but they sometimes have difficulty recalling quickly what they know. This group performed relatively well across tasks, but less well on the academic fluency tests (i.e., tests that measure how quickly and easily one can read and write words and sentences). This finding makes sense. They performed well because strong knowledge and language skills are the most important predictors of literacy. Nevertheless, their weaker memory retrieval fluency seems to have slowed their ability to read and write fluently.

The second group (shown in red) had the opposite cognitive profile compared to the first group shown in blue: lower verbal knowledge (Gc) and higher retrieval fluency (Gr). As expected, their academic profile is the mirror image of the red group – lower scores overall, but relatively better scores on academic fluency tasks.

The third group (shown in violet) had higher verbal knowledge (Gc) but lower auditory processing ability (Ga). Poor auditory processing interferes with learning to decode words because having difficulty hearing the parts of words distinctly is associated with difficulty sounding out written words (Wagner & Torgesen, 1987). With lower reading decoding skills, development of other aspects of literacy (i.e., comprehension and fluency in reading and writing) is difficult. Nevertheless, many children with poor auditory processing but good verbal ability are able to work around this difficulty, often learning unfamiliar words by brute-force memorization so that they can still comprehend text reasonably well. Thus, the main way in which the third group differed from the children with poor verbal skills in the second group is that they were better able to demonstrate their understanding of text, even though they had similar difficulties with single-word decoding and reading fluency tasks.

In summary, all three groups of children had cognitive weaknesses, but different profiles of cognitive strengths and weaknesses are associated with distinct kinds of academic difficulty. If referred for help, the children from the first group would be likely to need interventions emphasizing reading and writing fluency. The second group is likely to need interventions emphasizing background knowledge and vocabulary building. The third group is likely to need interventions emphasizing reading decoding skills. This study by Liu and colleagues does not answer every controversial question in the field, but it gives reassurance that careful assessment of cognitive abilities can yield valuable information that may prove useful in understanding how to help a child struggling to read and write.

Medical (Neuropsychological) Uses of Intelligence Tests

Intelligence tests are an integral part of neuropsychological assessments – evaluating the effects of disease, injuries, and strokes on the brain (Lezak, 2004). Evaluations of which cognitive functions – perception, attention, memory, reasoning, language, and knowledge – are intact and which have been compromised is essential for treatment planning. Thus, neuropsychologists de-emphasize overall intelligence and instead use portions of intelligence tests to measure narrower cognitive abilities (Lezak, 1988). For example, focal injuries to the visual cortex in the occipital lobes and adjacent areas typically result in specific visual-spatial deficits and focal injuries to other regions generally leave visual-spatial abilities intact (Landau, 2017).

Uses of Intelligence Tests within the Legal System

Intelligence tests are used in a variety of contexts within the legal system and are sometimes decisive in determining the outcome of court cases. They are used to assess damages if a plaintiff has had a brain injury, to evaluate whether a person is fit to stand trial, and to evaluate disability status. Because it is unconstitutional in the United States to execute criminals with intellectual disabilities (historically known as mental retardation) (Atkins v. Virginia, 2002), IQ tests are also used to evaluate whether a convict can be subject to the death penalty. That determination requires the testimony of expert witnesses who specialize in psychometrics because the diagnosis of intellectual disabilities is subtle. The person with that diagnosis must demonstrate low IQ (the cutoff is usually 70) as well as a similarly low level of adaptive behavior (the person's ability to function in society and to perform everyday tasks such as making change when shopping and interacting appropriately with other people). Further, criminals have often been administered IQ tests as many as five or six times since adolescence as they have moved through the criminal justice system. Are they intellectually disabled if some of their IQs are below 70, while others are in the low 80s? The answer depends on a variety of concepts that include the "practice effect" (scoring better the second or third time tested because of the experience with the same kinds of tasks), errors of measurement, and the general increase in average IQ scores over time, a phenomenon that has come to be called the **Flynn effect**.

James Flynn (1987) noted that **test norms** – the reference groups for determining how well children and adults score, on average, on an IQ test – get out of date at the rate of about 3 points per decade in the United States. Norms become steeper as time goes by. The bar continues to rise from generation to generation because children score higher on mental tasks than did their parents who, in turn, outstrip the previous generation. Thus, if a person recently earned an IQ of 74 on an intelligence test with 20-year-old norms (standards), many psychologists would argue that the IQ of 74 should be adjusted to 68, three points for each decade that the norms are out of date. There is healthy debate on this topic of adjusting IQs of criminals (A. Kaufman & Weiss, 2010), and judges differ in how they interpret expert testimony (Fletcher, Stuebing, & Hughes, 2010). Regardless of one's position on how to best integrate measures of adaptive behavior with IQ tests, how to best account for known errors of measurement, and whether to adjust a person's IQs for the Flynn effect and practice effect, it is clear that IQ tests can determine whether a criminal who has committed a capital offense will live or die.

Uses of Intelligence Tests in Personnel Selection

The United States Armed Forces use tests similar to intelligence tests to screen out applicants who would otherwise be a danger to themselves and to their fellow soldiers if permitted to serve on the battlefield. From time to time, military commanders experiment with lowering the standards to meet recruiting goals, often with disastrous results. For example, when the US Army was facing pressure to meet recruiting goals during the increasingly unpopular Vietnam War, standards were lowered to allow over 300,000 men to serve in the military. The soldiers who scored too low on an aptitude test to be admitted under previous standards, often failed to complete training in a timely manner, and when they served in combat roles were several times more likely to be killed in action or to inadvertently hurt their comrades (Gregory, 2015). The US military also uses aptitude tests to make decisions about the kinds of training a soldier will receive, with high-scoring recruits given greater responsibility.

Businesses that hire thousands of people a year can use intelligence test scores to guide hiring decisions, resulting in greater productivity and higher profits (Schmidt & Hunter, 1998). The first advocates of using intelligence tests for personnel selection argued that selecting employees based on test scores instead of family connections and degrees from expensive schools would reduce the injustice faced by bright applicants who do not come from privileged backgrounds. Although the use of intelligence tests has indeed given many people from poor families and from disadvantaged groups opportunities they otherwise would not have enjoyed, the improper use of IQ tests can create a different set of injustices, hurting the populations they were intended to help.

People of lower socioeconomic status or members of underrepresented groups can score lower on average on cognitive ability tests for reasons that have little to do with intelligence. For example, language barriers can result in underestimating linguistic minorities' intelligence unless the examiner follows sound cross-cultural assessment practices (Bainter & Tollefson, 2003). Because cultural groups emphasize different sets of cognitive skills, the same test scores do not always have the same meaning across populations (Wicherts & Dolan, 2010). Supplementing traditional cognitive ability assessments with alternative measures of talent (e.g., creativity and practical intelligence) can help organizations increase diversity and excellence simultaneously in their workforce (J. Kaufman, 2010, 2015; Outtz & Newman, 2010; Schneider & Newman, 2015; Sternberg, 2008; Wee, Newman, & Joseph, 2014).

People growing up in poverty and/or in disadvantaged minority groups are more likely to have experiences that interfere with brain functioning such as chronic, continuous stress, exposure to environmental toxins (e.g., lead, mercury, and mold), and less cognitively stimulating environments at home and at school (Armor, 2003; Nisbett, Aronson, Blair, Dickens, Flynn, Halpern, & Turkheimer, 2012). Thus, not only do differences in intelligence cause inequality, but inequality causes differences in intelligence. If we use intelligence tests to deny societal benefits to low-scoring individuals, and denying those benefits reduces cognitive abilities in the next generation, then the tests are being used to perpetuate injustice. For this

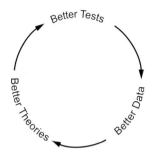

Figure 4.2 The importance of measurement in theory development

reason, many intelligence researchers and concerned citizens have worked hard to prevent intelligence tests from being misused in this manner, focusing instead on the use of intelligence tests to expand opportunities for those who otherwise might have been overlooked and to guide treatment of those in need.

Psychometric Models of Intelligence

Ironically, one of the reasons we need intelligence tests is so that we can study the construct of intelligence itself. IQ tests are used to examine the structure and development of intelligence, or as a way of including (or controlling for) intelligence in studies on different topics. Psychometrics can be used to identify flaws in existing measures and suggest how to improve them. That is, before we have a good theory to guide test construction, our measures are based on crude guesses about what should be measured. If we refine our measures, previously hidden relationships between intelligence and other variables emerge, helping us refine our theories, which, in turn, prompts us to further refine our measurements. As illustrated in Figure 4.2, measurement and theory reinforce each other in a cycle: With better tests, we obtain better data, and with better data, we can refine our theories, and with better theories, we can create better tests.

Structural Models of Intelligence

Working within the psychometric tradition, researchers can develop useful theories of intelligence with persuasive empirical evidence. Of course, scholars who use psychometrics also pay attention to, and borrow from scholars who study intelligence using different methods. A strong theory of intelligence is consistent with evidence from many disciplines, including developmental psychology, evolutionary psychology, cognitive neuroscience, and artificial intelligence.

How Do Psychometric Researchers Study the Structure of Intelligence?

You cannot see the rocks below the surface of whitewater rapids, but an experienced rafting guide can read the water to deduce what lurks beneath. In a similar manner, we cannot observe cognitive abilities directly, but we can read the patterns in observable behavior to deduce what lurks beneath the surface, producing those patterns.

Psychometric researchers hope to understand the structure of individual differences in intelligence. In this context, studying the *structure* of intelligence refers to two kinds of questions:

1. *What is the composition of intelligence?* That is, what are its parts? How many parts are there? What shall we call them? What do they do? What are they for?
2. *How do the components of intelligence interact?* That is, how do the parts influence each other to produce adaptive behavior? For example, how does speed of perception influence reasoning? How does reasoning produce useful knowledge? How does prior knowledge affect reading comprehension?

To understand the composition of intelligence, researchers use a wide variety of tools, but foremost of these is a family of statistical procedures called **factor analysis**. These procedures allow researchers to study many variables at a time and understand how overwhelmingly complex data patterns among those variables can arise from a smaller and simpler set of processes. In the next section we will present the underlying logic of factor analysis, largely omitting its mathematical foundations and glossing over unnecessary technical details.

Factor Analysis: A Gentle, Non-Technical Introduction

How many cognitive abilities are there? It seems like a simple question at first, until you try to answer it to everyone's satisfaction. Individual-difference domains like intelligence are open-ended and endlessly divisible. To ask how many abilities exist is like asking, "How many kinds of food are there?" and then expecting a specific number (8,675,309?). Obviously, there is no end to the variety of recipes we can create. Likewise, if we assume a separate ability for every conceivable task, we quickly find ourselves overwhelmed by the implications of an infinite number of task variations.

To bring order to the chaos of endless particulars, scholars try to find useful criteria by which to divide open-ended domains. For example, biologists group organisms by similarities in outward appearance, and in recent decades, by genetic similarity. Linguists have followed a similar approach in constructing language family trees. Psychologists have classified many domains of functioning, such as personality, emotions, psychopathology, and abilities, using a powerful tool for quantifying similarity: the correlation coefficient.

Two tests can correlate for a variety of reasons, but the default assumption among factor-analytic researchers is that the tests correlate because they were both influenced by a common cause. This assumption may prove to be false later (e.g., one variable might cause the other or there is more than one common cause), but it is a useful starting place. The two tests are observed variables and the hypothesized common cause is the latent variable. **Latent variables** are not observed directly, but like the rocks beneath the rapids, we infer their presence from their effects.

Suppose that you decide to create an intelligence test with five diverse tests:

1. **Logical Reasoning**: Decide whether a conclusion is valid, given a set of premises.
2. General Knowledge: Answer questions about civics, culture, history, and science.
3. **Spatial Visualization**: Read instructions for folding paper shapes in particular ways, and imagine what the result would look like.
4. **Associative Learning**: Study pictures of unfamiliar people and remember their names.
5. **Perceptual Speed**: Decide as quickly as possible whether, for many pairs of objects, the objects in each pair are the same or different.

If you give these tests to hundreds of adults, you might find that the tests are correlated positively and moderately, as seen in Table 4.1.

What would account for this pattern of correlations? If a single explanation could be deduced from the correlation matrix, intelligence theorists would have little left to do. Amazingly, however, these correlations could have arisen from an infinite number of alternate models, all of which account for this pattern perfectly. Maybe there are 180 separate influences that combine in a fantastically complex way to produce precisely this pattern. Or there might just be 10 (or 2 or 45). We could postulate an infinite number of models, all of which are slightly different from each other.

If the number of options is infinite, by what criteria should we prefer one option over the other? As Aristotle wrote long ago in *Posterior Analytics* (Mure, 2007): "All else equal, we may assume the superiority of the demonstration which derives from fewer postulates." In general, we would like to propose the simplest explanation that can still account for all the facts. We allow more complex explanations into our theories only when simpler models fail to account for the facts.

Table 4.1 Correlations among hypothetical tests

	1	2	3	4	5
1. Logical Reasoning	1	.72	.63	.54	.45
2. General Knowledge	.72	1	.56	.48	.40
3. Spatial Visualization	.63	.56	1	.42	.35
4. Associative Learning	.54	.48	.42	1	.30
5. Perceptual Speed	.45	.40	.35	.30	1

The First Factor-Analytic Theory of Intelligence

Charles Spearman, the inventor of factor analysis, gave similar kinds of tests as in our example and observed a similar pattern in the correlation matrices. He proposed the simplest possible explanation: the *two-factor theory of intelligence* (Spearman, 1904, 1927). In this model, there are two kinds of influences on performance, one general, and one specific. Every test is influenced by a **general factor** of intelligence that is relevant to every test, and each test has its own **specific factor**. If Spearman's two-factor theory were applied to the moderate correlations among the five hypothetical tests mentioned above, the model of intelligence would look like the path diagram in Figure 4.3.

Path diagrams show a model's structure. By convention, latent variables like g and the specific abilities are depicted with circles, and observed variables (i.e., the tests) are depicted as rectangles. The path from g to the Logical Reasoning test has a coefficient of .90, meaning that g is a causal influence on Logical Reasoning and correlates with a strength of .90. Note that g is a causal influence on all the tests, but its influence differs from test to test. Tests that are less influenced by g are more influenced by their respective specific abilities. For the sake of simplicity, Figure 4.3 omits the psychometric concept of **measurement error**, which refers to influences that muddy psychological measurement, such as examiner error, examinee inattention, and other chance factors that influence performance but have nothing to with intelligence.

Simply drawing g on a path diagram does not explain what g is any more than drawing Paris on a map explains the city's cultural and historic significance. All that is asserted in Figure 4.3 is that a single common cause explains the correlations among the five tests. Spearman noticed that tests that were highly correlated with the g factor tended to be tests that required reasoning, particularly those that required examinees to figure out logical relationships and patterns. Spearman (1923) hypothesized that his general factor of intelligence was a general relationship-perceiving mechanism that was central to the process of acquiring new knowledge. Although his theory was called the two-factor theory, to others in the field it was consistently interpreted as a one-factor theory, namely *Spearman's g theory*.

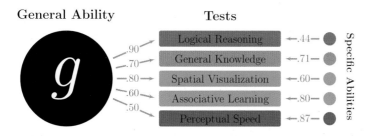

Figure 4.3 Path diagram illustrating Spearman's two-factor theory

The Glorious Death of Spearman's Two-Factor ("*g*") Theory

In healthy disciplines, unsuccessful theories die and become fertilizer for new theories. In unhealthy disciplines, old theories languish undead, neither proven nor disproven, each groaning to be heard above the others. Factor analysis not only helps researchers generate new theories, but kills off unsuccessful ones. Spearman's *g* theory of intelligence was both factor analysis's firstborn and later its first casualty.

Spearman hypothesized that the general factor of intelligence was a sufficient explanation of the correlation between any two tests, provided that the tests were not so similar that they measure the same specific ability (e.g., two tests of simple arithmetic). The strict version of the Two-Factor Theory holds that no additional abilities need be hypothesized to explain the correlations among ability tests.

Shortly after Spearman's theory was proposed, several scholars (e.g., Cattell, 1941; Thurstone, 1931) obtained data showing that there were many correlations that could not be fully explained by a general factor. Two decades after the strict version of Spearman's theory was proposed, he was still calling his theory the "Two-Factor Theory" and he focused on general ability as the essence of intelligence, but even his own data obliged him to acknowledge the existence of a third kind of factor, the **group factor**, by which similar tests could be grouped together (Spearman, 1927, p. 222).

The fact that Spearman initially was wrong about the existence of group factors does not undercut the brilliance of his theory. It was not just a triumph of mathematical ingenuity, it set the standard of scientific excellence in the psychometric tradition – not because it was correct, but because it was *falsifiable*. Good scientific theories set the conditions by which they could potentially be disproven (Popper, 1959).

Multiple Factor Analysis and Thurstone's Primary Mental Abilities

After it was conceded that group factors exist, researchers went to work finding and classifying them. Although Spearman's version of factor analysis was a brilliant advance, it was too computationally intensive in the pre-computer age to explore complex models of intelligence. Louis Thurstone wanted to find the fundamental elements of intelligence in the same way physicists were identifying the fundamental elements of matter. He invented a newer, more flexible kind of factor analysis that allowed him to do just that. He gave participants a much larger set of diverse tests than most researchers gave, and used his new *multiple factor analysis* to isolate several factors that he called *primary mental abilities* (Thurstone, 1931, 1938). His answers varied slightly from study to study, but seven factors emerged consistently: verbal comprehension ability, inductive reasoning, perceptual speed, word fluency, memory, spatial reasoning, and numerical ability (See Figure 4.4).

Given how closely results from later studies resemble Thurstone's Primary Mental Abilities (Schneider & Flanagan, 2015), Thurstone's model has held up remarkably

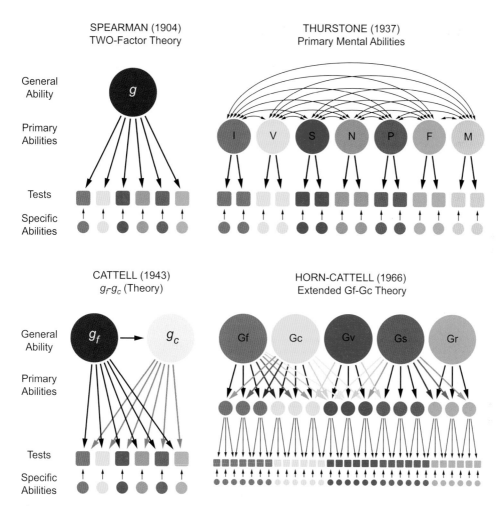

Figure 4.4 Early psychometric models of intelligence. *g* = general intelligence, I = Induction, V = Verbal, S = Space, N = Number, P = Perceptual Speed, F = Fluency, M = Memory, Gf = Fluid Reasoning, Gc = Crystallized Intelligence, Gv = Visual-Spatial, Gs = Processing Speed, Gr = Retrieval

well: His seven factors of ability would fit nicely in any contemporary factor-analytic model. However, later evidence proved that his primary mental abilities were not primary in the way that primary colors are primary. That is, his list omitted several important abilities, and each of his "primary" abilities could be subdivided into ever narrower abilities (Carroll, 1993; Cattell, 1987; Horn & Blankson, 2005). For example, Thurstone's spatial ability factor has several distinguishable components, such as the ability to generate mental images, rotate mental images, visualize a scene from another person's perspective, navigate in three-dimensional space, perceive patterns, estimate length of objects, and visualize what is missing in partially obscured objects (Carroll, 1993; Hegarty, 2010; Hegarty & Waller, 2004;

Wolbers & Hegarty, 2010). All of Thurstone's primary mental abilities likewise have multiple components.

As evidence accumulated that Thurstone's primary mental abilities had distinguishable components, scholars began to distinguish between broad and narrow group factors. **Narrow abilities** (such as visual short-term memory span, emotion recognition accuracy, or the speed at which you can recall names of people and things) influence performance on a small number of tests specifically designed to measure the same cognitive ability. **Broad abilities** influence performance on a wider variety of tests, spanning at least two narrow abilities. For example, the broad ability of auditory processing encompasses many narrower abilities such as the ability to distinguish musical pitch, judge where sounds are coming from, and understand speech when the level of ambient noise is high (e.g., understanding a person talking in a crowded room or over a weak telephone signal).

Later, more systematic attempts to measure the spectrum of mental abilities led to a consistent pattern of results. First, all cognitive abilities are positively correlated, but with a hierarchical structure of general, broad, and narrow abilities (Carroll, 1993; see Figure 4.4). Second, the number of broad abilities is not large, on the order of eight to ten, with the possibility of several more (McGrew, 2009). Third, each broad ability can be divided into smaller factors with an ever-narrower scope, with about 80 to 100 identified so far, and with many more likely to be discovered (Schneider & McGrew, 2012).

Splitting *g* in Two: Cattell's Theory of Fluid and Crystallized Intelligence

Even in his first paper on general intelligence, Spearman (1904) conceded that what he called general intelligence might consist of more than one general ability factor. Though Spearman never developed this idea further, his former student Raymond Cattell did. Cattell (1941, 1943) used factor analysis to isolate two general factors of intelligence: fluid intelligence and crystallized intelligence. Cattell used the neuropsychological studies by Hebb (1942) and others to understand their meaning.

Hebb's work, along with factor-analytic results suggesting the separation of verbal knowledge from reasoning ability, implied to Cattell that the processes that govern knowledge acquisition via reasoning were not the same as those that govern knowledge retention. He hypothesized the existence of two general ability factors that influence performance in a wide variety of contexts. The first factor, general fluid intelligence (g_f), is essentially identical to Spearman's general factor in that it consists of the ability to perceive complex patterns and relationships in unfamiliar situations. The factor is "fluid" in the sense that it can be applied to any kind of intellectual performance. It increases from infancy to early adulthood and then decreases steadily thereafter (A. Kaufman, Salthouse, Scheiber, & Chen, 2016). Notably, fluid intelligence increases and decreases across the lifespan at different rates for different people; nonetheless, its substantial decline in middle age and old age seems to show little or no relationship to real-world performance in the workplace or in everyday life (Salthouse, 2012).

The second factor, general crystallized intelligence (g_c), consists of acquired knowledge. It is "crystallized" in the sense that it consists of specific bits of knowledge that are either present or not. In Cattell's (1963) Investment Theory, crystallized intelligence builds on prior knowledge and is expanded via the "investment" of fluid intelligence. Crystallized intelligence depends on the action of fluid intelligence to grow. It is more robust to the effects of injury and disease than fluid intelligence, but its growth can slow dramatically if fluid intelligence is compromised.

Crystallized intelligence rapidly increases with age until early adulthood and then gradually increases throughout middle and late adulthood – so long as the learning rate exceeds the forgetting rate – before declining at some point in old age (A. Kaufman, Salthouse et al., 2016). Thus, crystallized intelligence remains high over most of the lifespan unless the effects of dementia or severe injury to the brain decrease it. If fluid intelligence is compromised in childhood, crystallized intelligence never has the chance to develop to its full potential.

Despite its name, crystallized intelligence is not inert, but an active aid in further knowledge acquisition (Cattell, 1963). Certain kinds of knowledge act as conceptual tools that aid further knowledge acquisition. For example, once a person understands that letters can substitute for numbers in algebraic equations, the person can apply this conceptual tool in a wide range of mathematical applications. In most domains of achievement, knowledge truly is power.

The primary effect of fluid intelligence is that it facilitates the acquisition of knowledge (Hunter, 1986). If the task is simple (e.g., sweeping floors, unloading trucks, data entry), one may train for as many hours as it takes to master the necessary skills. People with high fluid intelligence might require less training time to master simple skills, but they do not necessarily perform better after training is complete. However, many tasks are too complex to be routinized. No simple recipe can be followed to perform well in complex domains. These tasks require judgment in deciding what to do in situations one has not trained for, such as deciding how to present an argument to a jury in an unusual lawsuit, anticipating how a new weapons system will alter battlefield strategy, or adapting a scientific theory in the face of unanticipated experimental results. In such tasks, fluid intelligence has direct effects on performance beyond the effects of knowledge and training (Hunter, 1986).

Although Cattell's two general factors do not explain all of intelligence (nor were they meant to), his theory remains viable as a partial explanation of some of the most important phenomena in cognitive ability research. When researchers want a short measure of overall intelligence, they often select one measure of fluid intelligence and another measure of crystallized intelligence, as these have the strongest correlates with a wide variety of life outcomes (e.g., grades, degrees, wealth, and health). A number of scholars have challenged some of the finer points of Cattell's theory – pointing out that crystallized intelligence is not just an accumulation of knowledge but reflects a distinct language component that is likely to be hardwired into development (Johnson & Bouchard, 2005; Kan, Kievit, Dolan, & Maas, 2011) – but there are no radical departures from Cattell that give a satisfying explanation of the differing developmental growth patterns in reasoning and knowledge and their differing vulnerability to injury and disease.

The Theory of Fluid and Crystallized Intelligence Expands

Cattell's (1943) original theory of fluid and crystallized intelligence had a large body of indirect evidence, but 20 years passed before he and his student John Horn tested it directly. Their data led them to recognize additional broad and general abilities beyond fluid and crystallized intelligence (Cattell, 1963; Horn & Cattell, 1966). John Horn later became a major theorist in his own right, sometimes refining his mentor's ideas, sometimes departing from them. Horn's (1985) expansion of the theory of fluid and crystallized intelligence recognized several general factors of ability (fluid intelligence, short-term memory, and processing speed), at least two perceptual abilities (auditory, visual-spatial), and abilities related to expertise (crystallized intelligence, quantitative knowledge, and the fluent retrieval of knowledge). Horn elaborated the theoretical basis of these abilities, showing how each consisted of multiple empirically distinguishable narrow abilities.

Carroll's (1993) Reanalysis Largely Confirms the Horn–Cattell Model

As Cattell and Horn were developing their theory, it was not the dominant psychometric model among intelligence researchers, but one of several competing models vying for attention. The Horn–Cattell model received a major boost in credibility when its major findings were confirmed in an empirical research *tour de force*. John Carroll, known for decades primarily for his psychometric models of language abilities, spent his retirement years hunting down and reanalyzing all 461 studies of the structure of intelligence available at the time. He applied identical factor-analytic methods to each dataset and systematically compiled his results. After years of solitary labor, he published his masterpiece, *Human Cognitive Abilities: A Survey of Factor-Analytic Studies* (Carroll, 1993).

As seen in Figure 4.5, Carroll hypothesized that general intelligence was the largest factor of ability. He hypothesized that there are about eight broad abilities, each of which consist of numerous narrow abilities. Fluid intelligence is closely aligned with general intelligence and, moving counterclockwise toward the ability called *decision speed*, the broad abilities are increasingly independent of general intelligence. Each broad ability consists of several narrow abilities, represented by the smaller circles on each broad ability. For example, the broad ability of visual

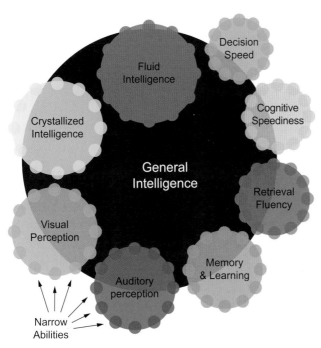

Figure 4.5 General, broad, and narrow abilities in Carroll's (1993) Three-stratum theory of cognitive abilities

perception (often called visual-spatial processing) consists of narrow abilities such as remembering complex, detailed images; imagining what an object might look like from a different angle; and recognizing a whole object when shown only parts of it.

Carroll's work did not answer every question, nor did it settle all disputes, but to overturn Carroll's findings would require extremely high-quality evidence. Carroll's *Three-Stratum Theory of Cognitive Abilities* and *the Horn–Cattell expanded theory of fluid and crystallized intelligence* have been the dominant psychometric models for a generation now. The Carroll and Horn–Cattell models did not displace all competing models, but they gave the field a common framework and nomenclature with which they could compare their findings. Test developers increasingly drew on these models to guide their work, to the point that nearly all commercially available intelligence tests are either explicitly derived from their models, indirectly inspired by them, or can be easily reconfigured to align with them (Alfonso, Flanagan, & Radwan, 2005; Flanagan, Ortiz, & Alfonso, 2013).

The Cattell–Horn–Carroll (CHC) Theory of Cognitive Abilities

Carroll's model largely confirmed the Horn–Cattell model, but it differed in what at first glance seems to be a major way. Carroll's model puts Spearman's *g* back at the apex of the hierarchy. Horn and Carroll agreed about many topics but could not reconcile their differences about g (McGrew, 2005). Horn had spent his entire career explaining why the general factor was a statistical illusion and a theoretical misstep, and thus Carroll's 461 factor analyses were simply not convincing to him (Horn & Blankson, 2005; Horn & McArdle, 2007). Fortunately, through the diplomatic efforts of test developers and psychometric theorists Richard Woodcock and Kevin McGrew, Horn and Carroll were able to move past their differences and agreed to have their models yoked in a common framework called the **Cattell-Horn-Carroll Theory of Cognitive Abilities** (**CHC** Theory; McGrew, 1997, 2005). CHC theory does not settle the primary dispute between Horn and Carroll. Rather, it is a neutral space in which scholars of different orientations can politely ignore each other's differences on the interpretation of the g factor so that they can work together to advance their common goals. Ultimately, CHC theory focuses on the group factors, especially the broad abilities (see Figure 4.6).

In CHC theory, the general factor sits atop the hierarchy, and any scholar who wishes to make use of it can do so. Scholars convinced by Horn's arguments that the general factor does not really exist can ignore it as needed. Clinicians, by contrast, cannot ignore g completely because all major intelligence tests interpret global scores – scores that give an overall summary of many cognitive abilities such as the **Full-Scale IQ (FSIQ)** on Wechsler's (2008, 2014) tests – and placement decisions in educational settings and life-and-death decisions in legal settings often depend on global scores measuring g. In truth, the difference between Horn and Carroll is smaller than it appears at first glance. Both Carroll (1993) and Horn (Horn & Blankson, 2005; Horn & McArdle, 2007) agreed that the general factor of intelligence and fluid reasoning are nearly identical, both empirically and theoretically (Undheim & Gustafsson, 1987). For now, it is largely a distinction without a difference.

Now that CHC theory's source theorists – Cattell, Horn, and Carroll – have passed away, Kevin McGrew (1997, 2005, 2009), Dawn Flanagan, and Joel Schneider (Schneider & Flanagan, 2015) have been its primary caretakers, but all scholars are invited to participate in the theory's evolution (Schneider & McGrew, 2012). Recent developments in the theory have focused on integrating the model with information processing models from cognitive psychology, reconciling CHC theory with other psychometric models of intelligence, and emphasizing the causal relationships among cognitive abilities rather than just listing them (Schneider, Mayer, & Newman, 2016; Schneider & McGrew, 2013; Schneider & Newman, 2015).

Fluid Reasoning (Gf)

Fluid reasoning (Gf) is a domain-general pattern recognition system that allows for logical reasoning. Fluid reasoning is domain-general in the sense that it can be applied to any kind of stimulus – visual, auditory, tactile, verbal, quantitative,

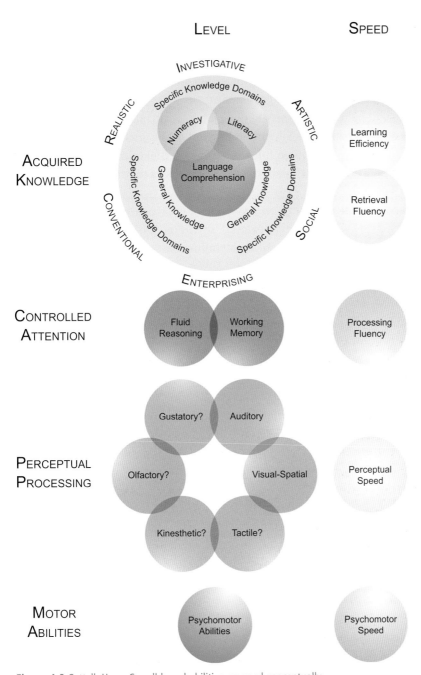

Figure 4.6 Cattell–Horn–Carroll broad abilities grouped conceptually

musical, mechanical, etc. Most importantly, fluid reasoning allows for **inductive reasoning** – discovering the pattern or rule that governs a phenomenon. Once a pattern has been learned – whether by inductive reasoning or by direct instruction – we can make use of the information via **deductive reasoning** (i.e., using a rule to generate specific new knowledge). For example, if you are looking for a house at 225 Sycamore Drive, and the houses on the right side of the street are numbered 195, 200, 205, 210, and 215, you can induce that, unlike most streets, the numbers are increasing by fives, and you can deduce that the next house is 220 and the one after that is likely to be your destination. Of course, there is no guarantee that the pattern will hold – our brains did not evolve specifically to discover ironclad rules that stand for all time. Instead, our brains evolved to forecast constantly what is likely to happen in the immediate future (Hawkins & Blakeslee, 2004); being able to infer simple rules and abstract patterns gave humans extraordinary control over their environments.

The influence of fluid reasoning on academic and occupational achievement is primarily indirect. That is, fluid reasoning drives acquisition of general and **domain-specific knowledge**, which then influences performance in specific domains (Hunter, 1986; Schmidt & Hunter, 1998). However, fluid reasoning has an intimate and direct relationship with achievement in mathematics (Floyd, Evans, & McGrew, 2003; Primi, Ferrão, & Almeida, 2010; Taub, Keith, Floyd, & McGrew, 2008). Mathematics seems to require direct application of fluid reasoning because it is much more abstract than most other academic disciplines.

Acquired Knowledge (Gc)

At the core of the acquired knowledge cluster of abilities (Gc) are language skills, including oral language comprehension and oral language communication skills. There are many ways to communicate knowledge, but language is the clearest and most efficient vehicle for knowledge transmission. Language comprehension has many subcomponents, including knowledge of vocabulary and grammar.

In CHC theory, individual differences in knowledge are manifested both as general and domain-specific. Every culture emphasizes certain kinds of knowledge over others. For example, because of their specific role in shaping US society, American schoolchildren spend far more time learning about Greece, Rome, and Great Britain than about most other countries. **General knowledge** refers to knowledge all members of a society are likely to be taught or is given special priority among influential members of the society. In contrast, domain-specific knowledge refers to facts and skills that only members of specific professions are expected to know. Although adults in the United States are expected to know a little about Africa (e.g., where it is or which animals live there), only specialists in African history would be expected to know, for example, about the role of the University of Sankore in the Sahelian kingdoms or the tactics by which Ethiopians resisted European colonization.

Ackerman (2000) refers to domain-specific knowledge as the "dark matter" of adult intelligence because it constitutes most of human knowledge, yet it is extremely difficult to measure with psychometric tests because it is so sensitive to individual context and history. He notes that older workers have significantly greater stores of domain-specific knowledge compared to their younger, less-experienced colleagues, which is why older employees are particularly valuable in managerial and specialist positions in which large knowledge repertoires are needed.

Individual differences in general knowledge are driven largely by individual differences in fluid intelligence and general interest in learning (Schmidt, 2011, 2014). In contrast, individual differences in domain-specific knowledge are more driven by domain-specific interests and also by the "tilt" of one's specific abilities (Coyle, Purcell, Snyder, & Richmond, 2014; Pässler, Beinicke, & Hell, 2015). For example, children with excellent auditory processing ability are more likely to become interested in music – and musical training, in turn, further enhances auditory processing (Strait, Hornickel, & Kraus, 2011; Strait, O'Connell, Parbery-Clark, & Kraus, 2013).

Perceptual Processing (Gv, Ga)

Differences in sensory acuity arising from physical impairments (such as near-sightedness) are not thought to be part of intelligence. What the brain does with information from the sense organs, however, is clearly within the intellectual domain. **Visual–spatial processing (Gv)** refers to the ability to detect visual patterns, remember visual images, and mentally rotate internal representations of objects (e.g., imagining how a large sofa might fit through a narrow doorway). **Auditory processing (Ga)** refers to comparable abilities related to sound, such as detecting sound patterns, remembering pitch sequences, and manipulating sounds in one's head (e.g., imagining how two singers' voices might harmonize). The evidence for distinct cognitive abilities related to other sensory modalities is promising but not yet compelling (Schneider & McGrew, 2012).

Visual-spatial abilities have subtle effects on academic and occupational achievement. People with greater spatial ability than verbal ability are more likely to choose careers in the STEM (Science, Technology, Engineering, and Mathematics) fields and people with greater verbal than spatial ability are more likely to enter fields related to education, social sciences, arts, and humanities (Lubinski, 2010; Wai, Lubinski, & Benbow, 2009).

Auditory processing deficits are one of several causes of reading disorders. When children learn phonics skills, they learn that specific letters indicate specific sounds. When confronted with an unfamiliar word, children with phonics skills can "sound it out." Children with auditory processing deficits have trouble hearing the distinct letter-sounds in words and thus take much longer to read fluently (Torgesen, Wagner, Rashotte, Burgess, & Hecht, 1997; Wagner & Torgesen, 1987).

Attention and Memory (Gl, Gr, Gwm)

Some people learn new information more quickly than others, although the rate of learning depends on the type of information learned, the complexity of the material, and previous experience with the subject matter. In CHC theory, the overall speed at which new information is learned is called **learning efficiency (Gl)**, which encompasses diverse abilities such as remembering stories, remembering lists, and remembering associated pairs (e.g., remembering which name goes with which face).

An important aspect of memory functioning is **retrieval fluency (Gr)**, the speed and ease with which previously learned information is retrieved from memory. Everyone has had the tip-of-the-tongue experience in which you know that you know something but cannot find it in memory. As we age, retrieval fluency tends to slow considerably, which is why older adults often speak more slowly than they did in their youth and with more hesitations, *ah*s, and *um*s. Children with memory retrieval fluency problems often fail to read smoothly and cannot recall math facts without effort (Norton & Wolf, 2012; Reber & Greifeneder, 2017).

A particularly important kind of retrieval fluency is **divergent production**, the ability to draw on memory to generate many answers to an open-ended prompt quickly (e.g., describe different ways to get a kite out of a tree, list different ways of saying that a person is drunk, make four-word sentences with words starting with the letter "B"). This is the ability that quick-witted talk-show hosts and improvisational rap artists have in abundance. Creativity is included under the auspices of retrieval fluency, and there is some theoretical (J. Kaufman, Kaufman, & Lichtenberger, 2011) and empirical (Avitia & Kaufman, 2014; Beaty, Silvia, Nusbaum, Jauk, & Benedek, 2014) support for this placement. However, others have challenged the idea that creativity is a component of retrieval fluency in the current CHC model, arguing that creativity is a diverse construct that is related to additional factors in the CHC model (J. Kaufman, 2016; J. Kaufman & Plucker, 2011).

Learning efficiency and retrieval fluency are related to long-term memory functioning. **Working memory capacity (Gwm)** refers to the ability to store and process information in short-term memory. The term "working memory" emphasizes the fact that memory is not just a passive storage tank but is intimately related to the effortful control of attention (Baddeley, 2012). When we engage in a routine task (e.g., brushing our teeth or driving to work), we only barely need to pay attention. If something unusual disrupts our routine, we must direct the focus of attention to the task. Often when we are engaging in a sequence of tasks, we need to temporarily store information in memory to be used in a later step. For example, cooking multiple dishes requires dividing one's attention among several processes and remembering where in the sequence one left off on each task.

Working memory capacity is measured with tasks that require people both to store and to process information in memory. For example, the examiner might say a list of numbers and animals and the examinee would have to repeat them back but rearranged separately by size. Thus, *Elephant-6-Cat-9-Horse-2* becomes *Cat, Horse, Elephant; 2, 6, 9.* Working memory is fragile and easily disrupted. Extreme levels of emotion, hunger, fatigue, or pain can lead to being temporarily more impulsive, distractible, and thinking in the short term. These symptoms, referred to as *dysexecutive syndrome* (Baddeley & Wilson, 1988), are more chronic and severe in people with brain injuries, brain diseases, and developmental disruptions (e.g., attention-deficit/hyperactivity disorder).

Processing Speed (Gs)

Processing Speed (Gs) refers to the fluency and ease with which a person can direct the focus of attention to accomplish a series of tasks. For example, quickly alphabetizing files requires concentration as one quickly performs a series of simple steps. Because processing speed is the most fragile of abilities, tests of processing speed are often used to evaluate the severity of brain injuries (Mathias & Wheaton, 2007). Injuries and diseases of the brain have diverse manifestations, but in almost every case of brain disfunction the ability to concentrate and deliberately control one's attention is markedly disrupted. The cognitive abilities that are particularly sensitive to disturbances of attention are processing speed, working memory, and fluid intelligence (Jurado & Rosselli, 2007; McCabe, Roediger, McDaniel, Balota, & Hambrick, 2010), which is why they constitute the Controlled Attention cluster in Figure 4.6.

Motor Abilities (Gp, Gps)

Gp refers to psychomotor ability in general, and Gps refers to psychomotor speed. Carroll (1993) did not set out to map the motor ability domain because it is not strictly cognitive, but many of the studies he used included motor abilities measures, and thus he presented an abbreviated list of motor abilities that could be distinguished in factor-analytic studies: manual dexterity, aiming, arm–hand steadiness, balance, and multi-limb coordination. Gardner (1983, 1999) argues that some aspects of movement abilities constitute a full-fledged component of intelligence (bodily–kinesthetic). This intriguing idea has only preliminary (and inconsistent) support in psychometric studies (Roberts, Stankov, Pallier, & Dolph, 1997; Stankov, Seizova-Cajić, & Roberts, 2001).

What Do Psychometric Models Miss?

Factor analysis is but one tool that can guide theory development. One of its primary weaknesses is that it summarizes data from large samples of people, most of whom are neurologically intact. The unusual effects of specific brain injuries do not emerge unless the sample includes large homogeneous subgroups of people with similar brain injuries, which are hard to find. Thus, psychometric models of intelligence are generally too coarse to help us understand individuals with highly specific brain injuries.

The *PASS Theory of Intelligence* (Das, Naglieri, & Kirby, 1994) emphasizes the distinct roles of Planning, Attention, Simultaneous Processing, and Successive Processing in intelligent behavior and, though interdependent, correspond to separate functional systems of the brain. The theory was derived from the pioneering research of Soviet neuropsychologist Alexander Luria, who was able to observe a wide variety of special populations, including many brain-injured soldiers returning from World War II. By noting the common deficits of soldiers with similar injuries, A. Luria (1963, 1966) proposed a complex set of influential theories that remain relevant. The primary constructs of PASS theory (Planning, Attention, Simultaneous Processing, and Successive Processing) do not always emerge in factor analyses (Keith, Kranzler, & Flanagan, 2001; Kranzler & Keith, 1999), in part because they are extremely broad constructs with many components. However, guided by PASS theory, researchers have constructed tests that perform as well as or better than tests derived from factor-analytic methods (A. Kaufman & Kaufman, 2004; Naglieri et al., 2014), and interventions guided by PASS theory are among the few empirically supported uses of the assessment of specific abilities to select specific academic interventions (Haddad et al., 2003; Iseman & Naglieri, 2011; Naglieri & Johnson, 2000). It is likely that PASS theory and CHC theory can coexist peacefully, and efforts are underway to integrate them. For example, the Kaufman Assessment Battery for Children, 2nd edition (KABC-II; A. Kaufman & Kaufman, 2004, 2018) is founded on a dual theoretical model that merges CHC and Luria-based models. This integration is based on the conceptual similarity of constructs that underlie the separate models, e.g., Luria's notion of planning ability closely resembles fluid reasoning ability from the CHC model, and the Simultaneous processing construct from PASS theory may provide a good account of the underlying processes in visual–spatial ability from CHC theory (Flanagan, Alfonso, & Dixon, 2014; A. Kaufman, Lichtenberger, Fletcher-Janzen, & Kaufman, 2005).

CONCLUSION

Factor-analytic methods are well suited for ability measures. Any construct that also incorporates traits, mood, or context lends itself less to this methodology. Although factor analysis is commonly used in personality research (DeYoung, 2015) and occasionally in creativity research (J. Kaufman, 2012), it is not necessarily the ideal approach. Many intelligence theorists, most notably Robert Sternberg (1997;

Sternberg, Kaufman, & Grigorenko, 2008) and Howard Gardner (1983, 1999), do not deny psychometric findings of intelligence but rather take a broader scope. The main argument is that psychometric findings are but a small part of the larger picture, with related constructs such as creativity, wisdom, tacit knowledge, and interpersonal skills being mostly absent.

We do not foresee any conceptual barriers to a successful integration of psychometric theories with Sternberg's and Gardner's approaches. Listening to outsider perspectives is an important pathway to creative theoretical breakthroughs. Many attempts have been made to bridge the gap between theories of intelligence derived from studies of individual differences and theories of cognition derived from experimental work, but none has achieved consensus (Floyd & Kranzler, 2012; Hunt, 1980; Schneider & McGrew, 2013; Woodcock, 1993). We predict that the two disciplines will eventually be reconciled, making intelligence tests more accurate, useful, and helpful for individuals who need assessments.

CHAPTER SUMMARY

In the early 1900s, researchers began to use psychometrics (a scientific approach for measuring psychological traits such as intelligence) to help meet practical demands of society such as identifying children who are likely to fail in school, assisting large organizations to make better personnel decisions in industry, and helping to choose soldiers and officers in wartime. Alfred Binet and Théodore Simon developed the first modern intelligence test in Paris in 1905. Their goal was practical – identifying students with intellectual deficits who require more specialized training than regular education can provide – by measuring the students' overall capacity to understand complex ideas, learn from experience, and apply reasoning ability. Theories of intelligence also emerged just after the turn of the century when Charles Spearman proposed his Two-Factor Theory, composed of a general factor (g) and the specific abilities measured by each test. That theory became known as g theory because of its emphasis on a person's general intelligence, a global ability that is roughly summarized by a single number ("IQ"). Subsequent theories, developed in the 1930s and 1940s by Louis Thurstone (Primary Mental Abilities) and Raymond Cattell (Fluid and Crystallized Intelligence), stressed the importance of separate abilities such as perceptual speed and visual–spatial ability rather than g. These theories were taken to the next level by the exceptional psychometric research conducted independently by John Carroll and Cattell's student John Horn starting in the 1960s. Carroll and Horn refined and expanded the pioneering work of Thurstone and Cattell, and their multiple ability theories were merged in the late 1990s to form the Cattell–Horn–Carroll (CHC) theory. IQ tests, starting with the Binet–Simon and continuing in 1939 with the first of David Wechsler's popular series of tests, coexisted with theories of intelligence but did not embrace them until the 1980s. CHC theory has been the predominant foundation of contemporary IQ tests, but Alexander Luria's neuropsychological model has also been influential. The comprehensive, popular theories of intelligence developed by Robert Sternberg and Howard Gardner have not yet entered the realm of IQ testing. Thus, current intelligence tests seem to serve useful functions in the present but may, in the future, be supplemented by tests that provide an even more extensive profile of people's intellectual abilities.

KEY TERMS

auditory processing (Ga) • broad abilities • Cattell–Horn–Carroll Theory of Cognitive Abilities (CHC) • deductive reasoning • divergent production • domain-specific knowledge • factor analysis • Flynn effect • Full-Scale IQ (FSIQ) • general factor • general knowledge • group factor • inductive reasoning • latent variable • learning efficiency (gl) • measurement error • narrow abilities • path diagram • population norms • processing speed (gs) • psychometrics • retrieval fluency (gr) • specific factor • test norms • visual–spatial processing (gv) • working memory capacity (gwm)

COMPREHENSION AND REFLECTION QUESTIONS

1. Charles Spearman emphasized general ability (*g*) and ignored "group" abilities such as fluid (reasoning) ability and crystallized (acquired) knowledge. Which notion of intelligence – *g* or separate "group" abilities – accords best with your own experiences and worldview?
2. The Flynn effect demonstrates that IQ test norms in the 20th century got out-of-date in the US at the rate of 3 IQ points per decade. Should criminals' IQs be adjusted (e.g., an IQ of 72 adjusted to 69) if they were administered tests with old norms, or should the actual IQs they obtained be used to determine their fate in capital punishment cases? Why or why not?
3. Fluid intelligence refers to a person's ability to use reasoning to solve novel problems whereas crystallized intelligence pertains to a person's store of acquired knowledge. Can you think of the kinds of jobs that are particularly suited to people who are especially high in one kind of intelligence or the other? Can you think of friends or acquaintances who seem to be high in fluid reasoning and low in crystallized knowledge, or vice versa?

4. Intelligence tests are used in educational, industrial, medical, and legal settings. The use of IQ tests remains controversial. Do you believe that IQ tests should be commonly used for various societal purposes? Has reading this chapter on Psychometric Approaches changed your mind in any way?

5. Intelligence tests built from CHC theory or Luria's neuropsychological theory provide scores on a profile of mental abilities such as fluid reasoning, crystallized knowledge, visual–spatial ability, short-term memory, long-term memory, and processing speed. Do you think that these areas of intelligence are equally important, or do you believe that some of these abilities are more important than others for describing a person's intelligence? Explain your thinking.

References

Ackerman, P. L. (2000). Domain-specific knowledge as the "dark matter" of adult intelligence: Gf/Gc, personality and interest correlates. *The Journals of Gerontology Series B: Psychological Sciences and Social Sciences, 55*(2), 69–84.

Alfonso, V. C., Flanagan, D. P., & Radwan, S. (2005). The impact of the Cattell–Horn–Carroll Theory on test development and interpretation of cognitive and academic abilities. In D. P. Flanagan & P. L. Harrison (eds.), *Contemporary intellectual assessment: Theories, tests, and issues* (2nd ed., pp. 185–202). New York: Guilford Press.

Armor, D. J. (2003). *Maximizing intelligence.* New Brunswick, NJ: Transaction Publishers.

Atkins v. Virginia (2002), 536 U.S. 304, 122 S. CT 2242.

Avitia, M. J., & Kaufman, J. C. (2014). Beyond *g* and *c*: The relationship of rated creativity to long-term storage and retrieval (*glr*). *Psychology of Aesthetics, Creativity, and the Arts, 8,* 293–302.

Baddeley, A. D. (2012). Working memory: Theories, models, and controversies. *Annual Review of Psychology, 63,* 1–29.

Baddeley, A. D., & Wilson, B. (1988). Frontal amnesia and the dysexecutive syndrome. *Brain and Cognition, 7*(2), 212–230.

Bainter, T. R., & Tollefson, N. (2003). Intellectual assessment of language minority students: What do school psychologists believe are acceptable practices? *Psychology in the Schools, 40*(6), 599–603.

Beaty, R. E., Silvia, P. J., Nusbaum, E. C., Jauk, E., & Benedek, M. (2014). The roles of associative and executive processes in creative cognition. *Memory & Cognition, 42*(7), 1186–1197.

Binet, A., & Simon, T. (1905). New methods for the diagnosis of the intellectual level of subnormals. *L'Année Psychologique, 12,* 191–244.

Binet, A., & Simon, T. (1916). *The development of intelligence in children: The Binet–Simon Scale.* Vineland, NJ: Williams & Wilkins Company.

Borkenau, P., & Liebler, A. (1995). Observable attributes as manifestations and cues of personality and intelligence. *Journal of Personality, 63*(1), 1–25.

Borkenau, P., Mauer, N., Riemann, R., Spinath, F. M., & Angleitner, A. (2004). Thin slices of behavior as cues of personality and intelligence. *Journal of Personality and Social Psychology, 86*(4), 599–614.

Breaux, K. C., Bray, M. A., Root, M. M., & Kaufman, A. S. (2017). Introduction to special issue and to KTEA-3 error analysis. *Journal of Psychoeducational Assessment, 35*(1–2), 4–6.

Calvo, M. G. (2005). Relative contribution of vocabulary knowledge and working memory span to elaborative inferences in reading. *Learning and Individual Differences, 15,* 53–65.

Canivez, G. L. (2013). Psychometric versus actuarial interpretation of intelligence and related aptitude batteries. In D. Saklofske, C. Reynolds, & V. Schwean (eds.), *Oxford handbook of psychological assessment of children and adolescents* (pp. 84–112). New York: Oxford University Press.

Carroll, J. B. (1993). *Human cognitive abilities: A survey of factor-analytic studies.* New York: Cambridge University Press.

Cattell, R. B. (1941). Some theoretical issues in adult intelligence testing. *Psychological Bulletin, 38*(592), 10.

Cattell, R. B. (1943). The measurement of adult intelligence. *Psychological Bulletin, 40*(3), 153–193.

Cattell, R. B. (1963). Theory of fluid and crystallized intelligence: A critical experiment. *Journal of Educational Psychology, 54,* 1–22.

Cattell, R. B. (1987). *Intelligence: Its structure, growth and action.* New York: Elsevier.

Coyle, T. R., Purcell, J. M., Snyder, A. C., & Richmond, M. C. (2014). Ability tilt on the SAT and ACT predicts specific abilities and college majors. *Intelligence, 46,* 18–24.

Das, J. P., Naglieri, J. A., & Kirby, J. R. (1994). *Assessment of cognitive processes: The PASS theory of intelligence.* Boston, MA: Allyn & Bacon.

DeYoung, C. G. (2015). Cybernetic Big Five Theory. *Journal of Research in Personality, 56,* 33–58.

Flanagan, D. P., Alfonso, V. C., & Dixon, S. G. (2014). Cross-battery approach to the assessment of executive functions. In S. Goldstein & J. A. Naglieri (eds.), *Handbook of executive functioning* (pp. 379–409). New York: Springer.

Flanagan, D. P., Ortiz, S. O., & Alfonso, V. C. (2013). *Essentials of cross-battery assessment* (vol. 84). Hoboken, NJ: John Wiley & Sons.

Fletcher, J. M., & Miciak, J. (2017). Comprehensive cognitive assessments are not necessary for the identification and treatment of learning disabilities. *Archives of Clinical Neuropsychology, 32*(1), 2–7.

Fletcher, J. M., Stuebing, K. K., & Hughes, L. C. (2010). IQ scores should be corrected for the Flynn effect in high-stakes decisions. *Journal of Psychoeducational Assessment, 28,* 469–473.

Floyd, R. G., Evans, J. J., & McGrew, K. S. (2003). Relations between measures of Cattell–Horn–Carroll (CHC) cognitive abilities and mathematics achievement across the school-age years. *Psychology in the Schools, 40*(2), 155–171.

Floyd, R. G., & Kranzler, J. (2012). Processing approaches to interpretation of information from cognitive ability tests: A critical review. In D. P. Flanagan & P. L. Harrison (eds.), *Contemporary intellectual assessment: Theories, tests, and issues* (3rd ed., pp. 526–552). New York: Guilford Press.

Flynn, J. R. (1987). Massive IQ gains in 14 nations: What IQ tests really measure. *Psychological Bulletin, 101*, 171–191.

Furr, R. M., & Bacharach, V. R. (2013). *Psychometrics: an introduction.* Thousand Oaks, CA: Sage.

Galton, F. (1879). Psychometric experiments. *Brain, 2*(2), 149–162.

Gardner, H. (1983). *Frames of mind.* New York: Basic Books.

Gardner, H. (1999). *Intelligence reframed: Multiple intelligences for the 21st century.* New York: Basic Books.

Gardner, H. (2011). Intelligence, creativity, ethics: Reflections on my evolving research interests. *Gifted Child Quarterly, 55*, 302–304.

Gregory, H. (2015). *McNamara's folly: The use of low-IQ troops in the Vietnam War.* West Conshohocken, PA: Infinity Publishing.

Haddad, F. A., Garcia, Y. E., Naglieri, J. A., Grimditch, M., McAndrews, A., & Eubanks, J. (2003). Planning facilitation and reading comprehension: Instructional relevance of the PASS theory. *Journal of Psychoeducational Assessment, 21*(3), 282–289.

Hawkins, J., & Blakeslee, S. (2004). *On intelligence.* New York: Times Books.

Hebb, D. O. (1942). The effect of early and late brain injury upon test scores, and the nature of normal adult intelligence. *Proceedings of the American Philosophical Society, 85*(3), 275–292.

Hegarty, M. (2010). Components of Spatial Intelligence. In B. H. Ross (ed.), *The Psychology of Learning and Motivation* (vol. 52, pp. 265–297). San Diego, CA: Academic Press.

Hegarty, M., & Waller, D. (2004). A dissociation between mental rotation and perspective-taking spatial abilities. *Intelligence, 32*(2), 175–191.

Horn, J. L. (1968). Organization of abilities and the development of intelligence. *Psychological Review, 75*(3), 242–259.

Horn, J. L. (1985). Remodeling old models of intelligence. In B. B. Wolman (ed.), *Handbook of intelligence* (pp. 267–300). New York: Wiley.

Horn, J. L., & Blankson, N. (2005). Foundations for better understanding of cognitive abilities. In D. P. Flanagan & P. L. Harrison (eds.), *Contemporary intellectual assessment: Theories, tests, and issues* (2nd ed., pp. 41–68). New York: Guilford Press.

Horn, J. L., & Cattell, R. B. (1966). Refinement and test of the theory of fluid and crystallized general intelligences. *Journal of Educational Psychology, 57*(5), 253–270.

Horn, J. L., & McArdle, J. J. (2007). Understanding human intelligence since Spearman. In R. Cudeck & R. C. MacCallum (eds.), *Factor analysis at 100: Historical developments and future directions* (pp. 767–782). Mahwah, NJ: Lawrence Erlbaum Associates.

Hunt, E. (1980). Intelligence as an information-processing concept. *British Journal of Psychology, 71*(4), 449–474.

Hunter, J. E. (1986). Cognitive ability, cognitive aptitudes, job knowledge, and job performance. *Journal of Vocational Behavior, 29*(3), 340–362.

Iseman, J. S., & Naglieri, J. A. (2011). A cognitive strategy instruction to improve math calculation for children with ADHD and LD: A randomized controlled study. *Journal of Learning Disabilities, 44*(2), 184–195.

Johnson, W., & Bouchard, T. J. (2005). The structure of human intelligence: It is verbal, perceptual, and image rotation (VPR), not fluid and crystallized. *Intelligence, 33*(4), 393–416.

Jurado, M. B., & Rosselli, M. (2007). The elusive nature of executive functions: a review of our current understanding. *Neuropsychology review, 17*(3), 213–233.

Kan, K.-J., Kievit, R. A., Dolan, C., & Maas, H. van der. (2011). On the interpretation of the CHC factor Gc. *Intelligence, 39*(5), 292–302.

Kaufman, A. S. (2009). *IQ testing 101.* New York: Springer.

Kaufman, A. S., & Kaufman, N. L. (2004). *Kaufman Assessment Battery for Children – Second Edition (KABC-II).* Circle Pines, MN: American Guidance Service.

Kaufman, A. S., & Kaufman, N. L. (2014). *Kaufman Test of Educational Achievement – Third Edition (KTEA-3).* Bloomington, MN: Pearson.

Kaufman, A. S., & Kaufman, N. L. (2018). *Kaufman Assessment Battery for Children – Second Edition – Normative Update (KABC-II NU).* Bloomington, MN: Pearson.

Kaufman, A. S., Lichtenberger, E. O., Fletcher-Janzen, E., & Kaufman, N. L. (2005). *Essentials of KABC-II assessment.* New York: Wiley.

Kaufman, A. S., Raiford, S. E., & Coalson, D. L. (2016). *Intelligent testing with the WISC-V.* Hoboken, NJ: Wiley.

Kaufman, A. S., Salthouse, T. A., Scheiber, C., & Chen, H. (2016). Age differences and educational attainment across the lifespan on three generations of Wechsler adult scales. *Journal of Psychoeducational Assessment, 34*, 421–441.

Kaufman, A. S., & Weiss, L. G. (eds.) (2010). Special issue on the Flynn Effect. *Journal of Psychoeducational Assessment, 28*(5). Thousand Oaks, CA: Sage.

Kaufman, J. C. (2010). Using creativity to reduce ethnic bias in college admissions. *Review of General Psychology, 14*, 189–203.

Kaufman, J. C. (2012). Counting the muses: Development of the Kaufman-Domains of Creativity Scale (K-DOCS). *Psychology of Aesthetics, Creativity, and the Arts, 6*, 298–308.

Kaufman, J. C. (2015). Why creativity isn't in IQ tests, why it matters, and why it won't change anytime soon ... Probably. *Journal of Intelligence, 3*, 59–72.

Kaufman, J. C. (2016). *Creativity 101* (2nd ed.). New York: Springer.

Kaufman, J. C. (2017). Looking forward: The potential of creativity for social justice and equity (and other exciting outcomes). *Journal of Creative Behavior, 4*, 305–307.

Kaufman, J. C., Kaufman, S. B., & Lichtenberger, E. O. (2011). Finding creativity on intelligence tests via divergent production. *Canadian Journal of School Psychology, 26*, 83–106.

Kaufman, J. C., & Plucker, J. A. (2011). Intelligence and creativity. In R. J. Sternberg & S. B. Kaufman (eds.), *Cambridge handbook of intelligence* (pp. 771–783). New York: Cambridge University Press.

Keith, T. Z., Kranzler, J. H., & Flanagan, D. P. (2001). What does the Cognitive Assessment System (CAS) measure? Joint confirmatory factor analysis of the CAS and the Woodcock-Johnson Tests of Cognitive Ability. *School Psychology Review, 30*(1), 89–119.

Keyes, K. M., Platt, J., Kaufman, A. S., & McLaughlin, K. A. (2017). Fluid intelligence and psychiatric disorders in a population representative sample of US adolescents. *JAMA Psychiatry, 74* (2), 179–188.

Kranzler, J. H., & Keith, T. Z. (1999). Independent confirmatory factor analysis of the Cognitive Assessment System (CAS): What does the CAS measure? *School Psychology Review, 28*(1), 117–144.

Lamiell, J. T. (2003). *Beyond individual and group differences: Human individuality, scientific psychology, and William Stern's critical personalism.* Thousand Oaks, CA: Sage.

Landau, B. (2017). Update on "What" and "Where" in spatial language: A new division of labor for spatial terms. *Cognitive Science, 41*(S2), 321–350.

Lezak, M. D. (1988). IQ: RIP. *Journal of Clinical and Experimental Neuropsychology, 10*(3), 351–361.

Lezak, M. D. (2004). *Neuropsychological assessment* (4th ed.). New York: Oxford University Press.

Liu, X., Marchis, L., DeBiase, E., Breaux, K. C., Courville, T., Pan, X., . . . & Kaufman, A. S. (2017). Do cognitive patterns of strengths and weaknesses differentially predict errors on reading, writing, and spelling? *Journal of Psychoeducational Assessment, 35*(1–2), 186–205.

Lubinski, D. (2010). Spatial ability and STEM: A sleeping giant for talent identification and development. *Personality and Individual Differences, 49*(4), 344–351.

Lubinski, D. (2016). From Terman to today: A century of findings on intellectual precocity. *Review of Educational Research, 86*(4), 900–944.

Luria, A. R. (1963). *Restoration of function after brain injury.* New York: Macmillan.

Luria, A. R. (1966). *Higher cortical functions in man.* New York: Basic Books.

Luria, S. R., O'Brien, R. L., & Kaufman, J. C. (2016). Creativity in gifted identification: Increasing accuracy and diversity. *Annals of the New York Academy of Sciences, 1377*, 44–52.

Mathias, J. L., & Wheaton, P. (2007). Changes in attention and information-processing speed following severe traumatic brain injury: A meta-analytic review. *Neuropsychology, 21*(2), 212–223.

McCabe, D. P., Roediger, H. L., McDaniel, M. A., Balota, D. A., & Hambrick, D. Z. (2010). The relationship between working memory capacity and executive functioning. *Neuropsychology, 24*(2), 222–243.

McGill, R. J. (2015). Interpretation of KABC-II scores: An evaluation of the incremental validity of Cattell–Horn–Carroll (CHC) factor scores in predicting achievement. *Psychological Assessment, 27*(4), 1417–1426.

McGrew, K. S. (1997). Analysis of the major intelligence batteries according to a proposed comprehensive Gf-Gc framework. In D. P. Flanagan, J. L. Genshaft, & P. L. Harrison (eds.), *Contemporary intellectual assessment: Theories, tests, and issues* (pp. 151–179). New York: Guilford Press.

McGrew, K. S. (2005). The Cattell–Horn–Carroll Theory of Cognitive Abilities: past, present, and future. In D. P. Flanagan & P. L. Harrison (eds.), *Contemporary intellectual assessment: Theories, tests, and issues* (2nd ed., pp. 136–181). New York: Guilford Press.

McGrew, K. S. (2009). CHC theory and the human cognitive abilities project: Standing on the shoulders of the giants of psychometric intelligence research. *Intelligence, 37*(1), 1–10.

Mure, G. R. G. (trans.) (2007), *Posterior Analytics*. The University of Adelaide: eBooks @ Adelaide.

Murphy, N. A., Hall, J. A., & Colvin, C. R. (2003). Accurate intelligence assessments in social interactions: Mediators and gender effects. *Journal of Personality, 71*(3), 465–493.

Naglieri, J. A., Das, J. P., & Goldstein, S. (2014). *Cognitive Assessment System, Second Edition*. Austin, TX: PRO-ED.

Naglieri, J. A., & Johnson, D. (2000). Effectiveness of a cognitive strategy intervention in improving arithmetic computation based on the PASS theory. *Journal of Learning Disabilities, 33*(6), 591–597.

Neisser, U., Boodoo, G., Bouchard Jr, T. J., Boykin, A. W., Brody, N., Ceci, S. J., . . . & Urbina, S. (1996). Intelligence: Knowns and unknowns. *American Psychologist, 51*(2), 77–101.

Niileksela, C. R., Reynolds, M. R., & Kaufman, A. S. (2013). An alternative Cattell-Horn-Carroll (CHC) factor structure of the WAIS-IV: Age invariance of an alternative model for ages 70-90. *Psychological Assessment, 25*, 391–404.

Nisbett, R. E., Aronson, J., Blair, C., Dickens, W., Flynn, J., Halpern, D. F., & Turkheimer, E. (2012). Intelligence: New findings and theoretical developments. *American Psychologist, 67*(2), 130–159.

Norton, E. S., & Wolf, M. (2012). Rapid automatized naming (RAN) and reading fluency: Implications for understanding and treatment of reading disabilities. *Annual Review of Psychology, 63*, 427–452.

Outtz, J. L., & Newman, D. A. (2010). A theory of adverse impact. In J. L. Outtz (ed.), *Adverse impact: Implications for organizational staffing and high stakes selection* (pp. 53–94). New York: Routledge.

Pässler, K., Beinicke, A., & Hell, B. (2015). Interests and intelligence: A meta-analysis. *Intelligence, 50*, 30–51.

Popper, K. (1959). *The logic of scientific discovery.* New York: Basic Books.

Primi, R., Ferrão, M. E., & Almeida, L. S. (2010). Fluid intelligence as a predictor of learning: A longitudinal multilevel approach applied to math. *Learning and Individual Differences, 20*(5), 446–451.

Reber, R., & Greifeneder, R. (2017). Processing fluency in education: How metacognitive feelings shape learning, belief formation, and affect. *Educational Psychologist, 52*(2), 84–103.

Renzulli, J. S., & Reis, S. M. (2014). *The Schoolwide Enrichment Model: A how-to guide for talent development* (3rd ed.). Waco, TX: Prufrock Press.

Reynolds, C. R., & Kamphaus, R. W. (2015). *Reynolds Intellectual Assessment Scales* (2nd ed.). Lutz, FL: Psychological Assessment Resources.

Roberts, R. D., Stankov, L., Pallier, G., & Dolph, B. (1997). Charting the cognitive sphere: Tactile-kinesthetic performance within the structure of intelligence. *Intelligence, 25*(2), 111–148.

Salthouse, T. (2012). Consequences of age-related cognitive declines. *Annual Review of Psychology, 63*, 201–226.

Scheiber, C. & Kaufman, A. S. (2015). Which of the three KABC-II global scores is the least biased? *Journal of Pediatric Neuropsychology, 1* (4), 21–35.

Schmidt, F. L. (2011). A theory of sex differences in technical aptitude and some supporting evidence. *Perspectives on Psychological Science, 6*(6), 560–573.

Schmidt, F. L. (2014). A general theoretical integrative model of individual differences in interests, abilities, personality traits, and academic and occupational achievement: A commentary on four recent articles. *Perspectives on Psychological Science, 9*(2), 211–218.

Schmidt, F. L., & Hunter, J. E. (1998). The validity and utility of selection methods in personnel psychology: Practical and theoretical implications of 85 years of research findings. *Psychological Bulletin, 124*(2), 262–274.

Schneider, W. J., & Flanagan, D. P. (2015). The relationship between theories of intelligence and intelligence tests. In S. Goldstein, D. Princiotta, & J. A. Naglieri (eds.), *Handbook of intelligence: Evolutionary theory, historical perspective, and current concepts* (pp. 317–340). New York: Springer.

Schneider, W. J., & Kaufman, A. S. (2017). Let's not do away with comprehensive cognitive assessments just yet. *Archives of Clinical Neuropsychology, 32*(1), 8–20.

Schneider, W. J., Mayer, J. D., & Newman, D. A. (2016). Integrating hot and cool intelligences: Thinking broadly about broad abilities. *Journal of Intelligence, 4*(1), 1–25.

Schneider, W. J., & McGrew, K. S. (2012). The Cattell–Horn–Carroll model of intelligence. In D. P. Flanagan & P. L. Harrison (eds.), *Contemporary intellectual assessment: Theories, tests and issues* (3rd ed., pp. 99–144). New York: Guilford Press.

Schneider, W. J., & McGrew, K. S. (2013). Cognitive performance models: Individual differences in the ability to process information. In B. Irby, G. Brown, R. Laro-Alecio, & S. Jackson (eds.), *Handbook of educational theories* (pp. 767–782). Charlotte, NC: Information Age Publishing.

Schneider, W. J., & Newman, D. A. (2015). Intelligence is multidimensional: Theoretical review and implications of specific cognitive abilities. *Human Resource Management Review, 25*(1), 12–27.

Spearman, C. E. (1904). "General intelligence," objectively determined and measured. *American Journal of Psychology, 15*(2), 201–292.

Spearman, C. E. (1923). *The nature of "intelligence" and the principles of cognition.* London: Macmillan.

Spearman, C. E. (1927). *The abilities of man: Their nature and measurement.* London: Macmillan.

Stankov, L., Seizova-Cajić, T., & Roberts, R. D. (2001). Tactile and kinesthetic perceptual processes within the taxonomy of human cognitive abilities. *Intelligence, 29*(1), 1–29.

Stern, W. (1914). *The psychological methods of testing intelligence.* Baltimore, MD: Warwick & York.

Sternberg, R. J. (1997). *Successful intelligence.* New York: Plume.

Sternberg, R. J. (2008). Increasing academic excellence and enhancing diversity are compatible goals. *Educational Policy, 22*(4), 487–514.

Sternberg, R. J., Kaufman, J. C., & Grigorenko, E. L. (2008). *Applied intelligence.* New York: Cambridge University Press.

Strait, D. L., Hornickel, J., & Kraus, N. (2011). Subcortical processing of speech regularities underlies reading and music aptitude in children. *Behavioral and Brain Functions, 7*(1), 44:1–11.

Strait, D. L., O'Connell, S., Parbery-Clark, A., & Kraus, N. (2013). Musicians' enhanced neural differentiation of speech sounds arises early in life: developmental evidence from ages 3 to 30. *Cerebral Cortex, 24*(9), 2512–2521.

Subotnik, R. F., Olszewski-Kubilius, P., & Worrell, F. C. (2011). Rethinking giftedness and gifted education: A proposed direction forward based on psychological science. *Psychological Science in the Public Interest, 12*(1), 3–54.

Taub, G. E., Keith, T. Z., Floyd, R. G., & McGrew, K. S. (2008). Effects of general and broad cognitive abilities on mathematics achievement. *School Psychology Quarterly, 23*(2), 187–198.

Thurstone, L. L. (1931). Multiple factor analysis. *Psychological Review, 38*(5), 406–427.

Thurstone, L. L. (1938). *Primary mental abilities.* Chicago: University of Chicago Press.

Torgesen, J. K., Wagner, R. K., Rashotte, C. A., Burgess, S., & Hecht, S. (1997). Contributions of phonological awareness and rapid automatic naming ability to the growth of word-reading skills in second- to fifth-grade children. *Scientific Studies of Reading, 1*(2), 161–185.

Undheim, J. O. & Gustafsson, J.-E. (1987). The hierarchical organization of cognitive abilities: Restoring general intelligence through the use of linear structural relations (LISREL). *Multivariate Behavioral Research, 22,* 149–171.

Wagner, R. K., & Torgesen, J. K. (1987). The nature of phonological processing and its causal role in the acquisition of reading skills. *Psychological Bulletin, 101*(2), 192–212.

Wai, J., Lubinski, D., & Benbow, C. P. (2009). Spatial ability for STEM domains: Aligning over 50 years of cumulative psychological knowledge solidifies its importance. *Journal of Educational Psychology, 101*(4), 817–835.

Wechsler, D. (1939). *The measurement of adult intelligence.* Baltimore, MD: Williams & Wilkins Co.

Wechsler, D. (2008). *Wechsler Adult Intelligence Scale* (4th ed.). San Antonio, TX: Pearson.

Wechsler, D. (2014). *Wechsler Intelligence Scale for Children* (5th ed.). Bloomington, MN: Pearson.

Wee, S., Newman, D. A., & Joseph, D. L. (2014). More than *g*: Selection quality and adverse impact implications of considering second-stratum cognitive abilities. *Journal of Applied Psychology, 99*(4), 547–563.

Wicherts, J. M., & Dolan, C. V. (2010). Measurement invariance in confirmatory factor analysis: An illustration using IQ test performance of minorities. *Educational Measurement: Issues and Practice, 29*(3), 39-47.

Wolbers, T., & Hegarty, M. (2010). What determines our navigational abilities? *Trends in Cognitive Sciences, 14*(3), 138–146.

Woodcock, R. W. (1993). An information processing view of the Gf-Gc theory. *Journal of Psychoeducational Assessment,* Monograph Series: Woodcock-Johnson Psycho-Educational Assessment Battery–Revised (pp. 80–102). Cordova, TN: Psychoeducational Corporation.

5 Cognitive Approaches to Intelligence

VICTOR J. ELLINGSEN AND RANDALL W. ENGLE

You learned in Chapter 4 that the psychometric approach to studying intelligence involves identifying cognitive abilities and the relationships between them. Psychometricians administer test batteries to participants, and infer an ability structure by factor analyzing the results. At its core, the psychometric approach is a descriptive one. It describes how people tend to differ in their performance on various mental tests, but it cannot explain *why* these differences occur.

Cognitive psychology tackles the question of intelligence from a different angle. The cognitive approach to psychology in general is focused on understanding the processes involved in cognition by reducing cognitive tasks to one or more measurable component processes. Cognitive psychologists who are interested in individual differences in intelligence ask whether the ability to perform these component processes varies between people, and if so, whether this variability can explain differences in intelligence (Hunt, Lunneborg, & Lewis, 1975). This is a fundamentally different question from the one that drives the psychometric approach: The psychometric approach is focused on *whether* people answer items correctly, while the cognitive approach is focused on *how* people answer the items, and *why* some people are better than others at answering items of various types (Anderson, 2015).

Precursors to the Cognitive Approach to Intelligence

Although cognitive psychology as a field came into being in the mid-1900s (Anderson, 2015), some of the earliest research on human intelligence had a distinctly cognitive flavor. While some early psychologists (e.g., Thorndike, 1898) took a strong "nurture" view of intelligence as the sum total of acquired knowledge,[1] others (e.g., Galton, 1883) sought to explain differences in intelligence by way of basic mental processes. Galton suggested that mental ability should be

---

[1] This idea is still common today, reflected in computer-inspired computational models of cognition such as Anderson's ACT-R model (Anderson, 1996).

related to measures that he believed reflected these basic processes, such as reaction time and sensory discrimination tasks. Establishing an empirical relationship between intelligence and basic processes proved difficult, however. In 1901, Clark Wissler, a student with James McKeen Cattell, reported a failed attempt to find a link between mental speed, as measured by five trials of a reaction time task, and academic achievement among students at Columbia University. Following Wissler's disappointing result, intelligence research in general shifted away from trying to identify such primitive causes of between-person differences in intelligence. Instead, psychologists focused on measuring these differences, whether in the context of education (as exemplified by Binet; Hunt, 2011) or in the interest of developing theories about the structure of cognitive abilities (as exemplified by the factor-analytic/differential methods of Spearman, 1927, and Thurstone, 1948). Meanwhile, in psychology more broadly, the rise of behaviorism in the 1920s led to a strong focus on observable behavior and experimental methods, especially in the United States. Mental processes, along with everything else taking place within the "black box" of the mind, were not considered appropriate objects of inquiry if psychology was to establish itself as a serious science (J. B. Watson, 1913). Over the next few decades, the two branches of intelligence research (educational and differential) proceeded separately from the behaviorist approach to psychology, and largely separately from each other.

In the 1960s, the field of psychology as a whole pivoted again, as theorists realized the limitations of behaviorism for explaining complex human behavior. As computers worked their way into the popular imagination, psychologists began to think of the mind as something like a computer, in that it took in information, processed the information, and generated output based on the information (Neisser, 1967). Psychologists began to develop cognitive models, which generated testable hypotheses about the cognitive architecture and the processes involved in various mental activities. Relying heavily on the experimental method that was refined during the heyday of behaviorism, researchers in the new subdiscipline of cognitive psychology devised tightly controlled laboratory studies in order to test predictions about how the human mind works. In just a few decades, cognitive psychologists made tremendous progress in understanding human attention (Broadbent, 1958; Treisman, 1964), memory (Atkinson & Shiffrin, 1968), knowledge representation (Collins & Quillian, 1969), problem-solving (Newell & Simon, 1972), and reasoning (Wason, 1968). All of these topics are relevant to intelligence, insofar as they play a role in intelligent behavior. According to colloquial definitions of intelligence, a person who has a better memory, who learns faster, and who solves problems and makes decisions more effectively, typically will be seen as more intelligent than another person who is not as able in these domains, all else being equal. But, if a student interested in intelligence reads a cognitive psychology textbook, he or she may be disappointed to find that it barely, if at all, covers research on intelligence. How can this be?

Two Branches of Psychology: Experimental and Differential

There are two general branches of psychology: experimental and differential (also called correlational; Cronbach, 1957). The cognitive research mentioned in the paragraph above was a product of the first branch of psychology, the *experimental tradition*, meaning that most of the research was designed to test mean differences between two or more *experimental groups* that receive different treatments in an experiment. (In cognitive psychology, "different treatments" often means different versions of one or more cognitive tasks used in an experiment.) Such differences in performance across treatments can allow psychologists to infer things such as the organization of concepts in the mind (Collins & Quillian, 1969) or the structure of memory (Atkinson & Shiffrin, 1968). The goal of **experimental research** is to identify processes that are common to all people – that is, to explain how human cognition operates in general.

The second branch of psychology, the *differential tradition*, is focused on describing differences between *individuals*, especially in the degree to which they can adapt to their environment (Cronbach, 1957). **Differential research** focuses on constructs such as intelligence and personality, which cannot readily be manipulated in a laboratory and which are inherently between-person constructs. It is difficult to talk about a given person's level of intelligence or extraversion, for example, without at least an implicit reference to where that person stands in relation to others. Intelligence is not a binary characteristic that a person either does or does not possess; it exists along a continuum. Differential researchers are concerned with the variance of these constructs and their covariance with other constructs.

The experimental and differential traditions of psychology evolved separately from each other. Cronbach (1957) called for a unification of the two branches of psychology, arguing that each approach could be strengthened by incorporating methods that were commonplace in one but not the other. By the 1970s, the advantages of a unified field were especially salient for intelligence research. Differential psychologists drew from nearly a century of research measuring how people differ in intelligence, while theories about how the mind works had been offered by cognitive psychologists engaging in experimental work. Seeking to bring these two traditions together, Hunt and colleagues (Hunt et al., 1975) asked whether individual differences in intelligence (as measured by scores on intelligence tests, developed from the differential tradition) could be explained by individual differences in the ability to carry out basic cognitive processes (as measured by laboratory tasks, developed from the experimental tradition). In the 40 years since then, a robust literature of cognitive-oriented research on intelligence has developed, and is still vibrantly active today.

Psychometric *g* versus Psychological *g*

More than a century of intelligence research in the differential tradition (dating to Spearman, 1904) has left no doubt that there is a positive correlation (also called "positive manifold") between scores on a wide variety of mental tests (i.e., **psycho-metric** *g*; Conway & Kovacs, 2015). However, the existence of a single *factor* does not necessarily imply the existence of a single *process* underlying it. This was first demonstrated mathematically by Thomson (1916), but the idea did not gain much traction at the time. Even decades later, when cognitively oriented psychologists redeveloped an interest in explaining psychometric *g*, they attempted to identify a single underlying explanatory mechanism (i.e., **psychological *g***; Conway & Kovacs, 2015), such as mental speed (Eysenck, 1982; Jensen, 1998), or attention control (Shipstead et al., 2016).

These attempts to identify a single mechanism have met with little success, despite decades of effort and hundreds of studies. The threshold for identifying such a mechanism is high: Detterman (2002) suggested that in order for something to qualify as *the* mechanism underlying *g*, tasks designed to assess that mechanism should correlate at least $r = .80$ with intelligence test performance. Although this threshold is somewhat arbitrary, Detterman argued that a correlation of this magnitude would indicate that the mechanism accounts for most of the reliable variance in intelligence tests. In other words, if a single cognitive process is in fact responsible for the positive manifold, then it should be possible to find a relatively simple test that measures this process, and this test should provide an accurate indication of intelligence as measured by traditional intelligence tests (Mackintosh, 2011). Although this may be an impossibly high threshold – intelligence tests only correlate about $r = .80$ with each other – no measures of mental processes (such as mental speed or attention control) yet reported have come anywhere close. This has led some observers (Conway & Kovacs, 2013; Detterman, 2000; Mackintosh, 2011) to conclude that psychology's failure to identify such a task, despite a century of work, suggests that such a process does not exist. That is, *g* does not seem to correspond to a single mental process or biological factor. Although psychometric *g* clearly exists, few modern cognitive psychologists believe that there is a unitary psychological *g* (Conway & Kovacs, 2015).

Understanding the Cognitive Approach

The psychometric approach to studying intelligence involves obtaining scores from many people on a variety of tests. The results are factor analyzed in order to describe the pattern of correlations between the tests, and the factors are named according to the tests that load on them. Theories regarding the structure of cognitive abilities have been developed based on the results of these studies, but the psychometric approach is primarily centered on observing relationships between test scores. In other words, the psychometric approach is data-driven.

Cognitive psychologists who study the processes underlying intelligence seek to understand why psychometric *g* exists, rather than describe the relationships between various mental tests. Believing that intelligence will be best understood and measured when it can be connected to models of how cognition operates (Hunt et al., 1975), cognitive psychologists work to identify individual differences on relatively well-understood cognitive processing tasks that may be related to (and may help to explain) individual differences on traditional psychometric tests of intelligence. The idea is that if one or more basic cognitive mechanisms are used to carry out many different types of intelligent behavior (such as the myriad tests used in the psychometric approach), then the positive correlations between these intelligent behaviors can be explained by the fact that they rely on the same basic mechanisms. The cognitive approach is theory-driven: It begins with a model of how cognition works, and seeks to explain individual differences in intelligence via individual differences in the ability to perform the processes specified in the model.

Defining Intelligence for Research

Any research program studying intelligence must decide on a way to operationally define intelligence. Although intelligence tests were designed to predict academic or job success, not serve as the operational definition of intelligence itself (i.e., they were meant to be *predictor variables*, not *criterion variables*), they have long been used as indicators of intelligence for research purposes (see Hunt et al., 1975, for the original justification for taking this approach). Real-world intelligent behavior is difficult to define and measure, so cognitive psychologists often use intelligence test performance as a quantifiable proxy. The assumption is that because intelligence test scores correlate with real-world intelligent behavior, uncovering the cognitive processes that are related to intelligence test performance is theoretically meaningful and interesting.[2]

Practical considerations, such as the need for tests that can be administered in a group setting and the need to reduce the time burden on participants and researchers alike, mean that the use of full-scale IQ tests is relatively uncommon in cognitive research. More frequently, researchers obtain an estimate of general intelligence using one or a few highly *g*-loaded tests (that is, tests with a strong correlation to psychometric *g*), such as Raven's Advanced Progressive Matrices[3] (Raven, 1965). You may recall from Chapter 4 that psychometric *g* is derived from fluid intelligence

---

[2] There are, of course, many accounts of intelligence that are not centered exclusively (or at all) on intelligence tests – for example, Gardner's (1983) theory of multiple intelligences, R. J. Sternberg's (1999) theory of successful intelligence, Stanovich's (2009) description of rational thought, and investment theories of intelligence (Ackerman, 1996; Chamorro-Premuzic & Furnham, 2005). However, intelligence as defined by these theories is often difficult to measure. Researchers need an operational definition of intelligence to serve as the criterion measure in their studies. Despite their limitations, intelligence tests fill this need.

[3] In the literature, tests like Raven's matrices are sometimes referred to as Gf measures and sometimes as *g* measures. In reality, Gf and *g* are strongly related to each other (after all, *g* is derived

(Gf; the ability to perceive complex patterns and relationships in unfamiliar situations) and crystallized intelligence (Gc; acquired knowledge), as well as other factors. Tests of Gf are more commonly used in cognitive research than tests of Gc. This is because cognitive processes are hypothesized to underlie information-processing, which corresponds to Gf. Cognitive processes would be expected to relate to Gc only indirectly, through the investment of Gf in acquiring knowledge over time (Cattell, 1943). For these reasons, when we refer to intelligence in this chapter, we mean Gf unless otherwise specified.

In the rest of this chapter, we will give a brief overview of some methods that are commonly employed by cognitive psychologists studying intelligence. Then, we will review research related to the relationship between measures of speed (such as reaction time) and intelligence. For many researchers, this work represents the earliest modern efforts that sought to explain individual differences in intelligence from a cognitive perspective, although, as we will see, it is debatable whether this research should be classified as part of the cognitive approach. From there, we will consider how variability in performance on simple tasks led researchers to propose explanations based on cognitive processes such as attention. We finish with a review of the current state of research on the relationship between intelligence and working memory capacity (which we abbreviate in this chapter as **WMC**). This is the area which much of the field is focused on today.

Methods in the Cognitive Approach to Intelligence

Cognitive psychologists have used several different methods in order to study the relationship between cognitive processing and intelligence (R. J. Sternberg, 1985). Some of the more common methods are described in this section.

Cognitive Correlates Method

Cognitive psychologists have developed many laboratory tasks in order to study how humans process information. As mentioned above, in the 1970s, Hunt and colleagues (e.g., Hunt et al., 1975) had the insight that tasks that had been used to study cognition in general, could also be used to study individual differences in cognition. They reasoned that performance differences on complex tasks, such as a verbal ability test, might be explained by primitive cognitive elements reflected by performance on basic tasks, such as a short-term memory scanning task (S. Sternberg, 1966). Identifying one or a few cognitive processes that correlate with intelligence test performance would clarify what intelligence tests measure from an

---

from Gf and other factors), making the distinction something of a moot point from the perspective of a cognitive researcher.

information-processing perspective, and explain why some people perform better than others (Hunt et al., 1975).

The cognitive correlates approach can be divided further into two general types of research designs: microanalytic and macroanalytic. In the **microanalytic approach**, researchers examine the effect of experimental manipulations on the correlation between an intelligence test and another test that measures a cognitive process of interest (Hambrick, Kane, & Engle, 2005). For example, researchers might examine changes in the relationship between response time and intelligence by comparing the correlations between intelligence and two conditions of a Stroop task: one in which a color word is written in the same color text as its name (e.g., the word "red" written in red) and another in which a color word is written in a different color text (e.g., "red" is written in blue). In both conditions, the participant must say the color of the text (not the word that is written). This is very easy when the word and the text are the same color, but difficult when they are different because reading is automatic in literate adults. If there is a correlation between response time and intelligence in one condition and not in the other, then the researcher concludes that the manipulation affects a process that contributes to variance on intelligence test performance. In this case, there is not a correlation between response time and intelligence when the word and text are the same color, but there is a correlation when they do not match. This suggests that the cognitive processes involved in suppressing the automatic response of reading the word itself, and instead saying the color of the text, is related to intelligence more generally.

Many research studies in the microanalytic approach have used an *extreme groups design*, in which the top and bottom quartiles of performers on a test of a cognitive trait of interest are compared on another trait. For example, working memory capacity (WMC) might be compared to intelligence. This design has several limitations, including overestimation of effect sizes, exclusion of the middle 50 percent of the population for the trait under investigation, and often relatively small sample sizes. The extreme-groups design has become somewhat less common in recent years as researchers have come to acknowledge these limitations, but many of these studies are still cited frequently, and their results should be interpreted with some caution, including those published by one of the authors of this chapter (RWE; e.g., Conway & Engle, 1994; Unsworth & Engle, 2005).

The **macroanalytic approach** (Hambrick et al., 2005) involves examining relationships between **latent factors**, which are representations of variables that cannot be directly measured. For example, intelligence cannot be measured directly; there are many tests that are designed to reflect intelligence, but no test measures it perfectly or captures the entire construct of intelligence. As a result, a score on a single intelligence test is only an estimate of a person's intelligence – the score is influenced both by the person's actual intelligence, and also by other factors, such as the exact content of the test. Individual tests of intelligence correlate with each other, but do not correlate perfectly because of these extraneous factors. Researchers can obtain a more stable estimate of intelligence by administering multiple intelligence tests, and then using advanced statistical techniques to create a latent factor from the variance that is common to all of the tests. Researchers can then examine relationships between this latent factor and others created in the same way for other constructs (for example, attention control). We discuss this approach, and how cognitive psychologists use it in order to test hypotheses, in more detail in the section "Working toward Reliable Estimates of WMC."

Componential Analysis Method

Another method used by cognitive psychologists is componential analysis. This method can be used to develop and validate information-processing models of the cognitive steps (components) involved in solving complex test items, such as analogies (R. J. Sternberg, 1977) or matrix reasoning tests (Carpenter, Just, & Shell, 1990). These models can then be used to identify the sources of individual differences in performance on the task overall.

The general process is as follows. The researcher identifies the steps that are presumed to be involved in solving a given type of item. Take verbal analogies as an example. The stems of these items take the form "Food : Eat :: Beverage : ???" with the answer choices "(A) drink; (B) inhale." R. J. Sternberg (1977) suggested that solving these problems requires (1) *encoding* the three given terms and two answer choices; (2) *inferring* the relationship between the first two terms; (3) *mapping* the relationship between the first and third terms (in this case, realizing that food and beverages are things that can be consumed); (4) *applying* the relationship identified in Step 2 to the third term and the two answer choices (here, recognizing that food is consumed by eating it, meaning that the answer choice should indicate the way that beverages are consumed); and (5) *responding* by indicating the correct answer choice. In order to test this five-step model, a precueing procedure is used to isolate the component processes (R. J. Sternberg, 1977). In precueing, part of the analogy is presented. For example, only the first two terms might be presented, allowing the participant to complete the first two steps (encoding the first two terms, and inferring the relationship between them). The participant presses a button to indicate that he or she is ready to see the rest of the terms, and then solves the analogy. The time elapsed for each of these two parts is recorded. Other trials present only the first term or the first three terms before presenting the full analogy, corresponding to one or three of the steps involved in solving the item. The amount of time to complete each individual processing step is then estimated using the *subtraction method* (Donders, 1868/1969). For example, to obtain the amount of time required for applying the relationship from the first two terms of the analogy to the last two terms (Step 4), the researcher subtracts the response time for items that only required Steps 1 through 3, from the response time for items that required Steps 1 through 4.

In other words, the time taken to process Steps 1 through 3 is removed, leaving only the time required to complete Step 4. A variant on this approach, often used with spatial stimuli, allows researchers to examine accuracy at each step in addition to response time (Mumaw & Pellegrino, 1984).

Using this method, researchers can test models of the component processes involved in solving items of a particular type. An overarching goal of this method is to identify the components that give rise to individual differences in task performance and, by extension, differences in general intelligence (R. J. Sternberg, 1983). Components that correlate substantially with overall intelligence test performance may be relevant to cognition in general, especially if they are part of the model for many different cognitive tasks. R. J. Sternberg (1977) found that the time that elapsed during all steps after Step 1 (encoding) was negatively related to general intelligence, indicating that more intelligent people complete the steps after encoding more quickly than less intelligent people. To the extent that the components that are involved in analogical reasoning are also involved in other types of mental tasks, this suggests that more intelligent people execute these components more efficiently than people who are less intelligent.

Speed of Mental Processing

Although mental speed is not a *process*, it has been invoked as an explanatory mechanism for individual differences in intelligence (Deary & Stough, 1996; Eysenck, 1982; Jensen, 1998), and speed-related research is often included in cognitive-oriented reviews of intelligence research (e.g., Hunt, 2011; Mackintosh, 2011). Therefore, we include a review of speed-related theories and evidence here. We will also point out the limitations of these theories.

Like all cognitive approaches to the study of intelligence, the explanation for the relationship between mental speed and intelligence is a reductionist one. That is, it represents an attempt to explain intelligence in terms of a much simpler process – in this case, mental speed. Speed theories of intelligence are based on the long-standing observation that the capacity of the cognitive system is limited (Moray, 1967), in terms of both the amount of information that it can handle at any one time, and the length of time that information remains activated before it begins to decay. Proponents of speed theories claim that faster information processing effectively increases the capacity of the system, allowing more information to be processed before it decays (Jensen, 1998). This increased capacity means that a person with a faster "operating system" is able to incorporate more information per unit of time when solving a problem, making that person better able to answer complex items and attain better scores on ability tests. Meanwhile, people with slower systems become overwhelmed by the information processing demands of complex items, and are unable to solve them correctly.

Measuring Speed: Inspection Time and Reaction Time

Most research on the speed-intelligence relationship has centered on two constructs purported to reflect mental speed: reaction time and inspection time.

Reaction Time

Reaction time (RT) is defined as the amount of time it takes a person to complete some simple action in response to the appearance of a target stimulus. The basic RT tasks that were used by Galton and Wissler over a century ago are still in use today, albeit with more precise measuring equipment. Different varieties of RT tasks exist, but they all require the examinee to respond as quickly as possible (usually by pressing a button) to a stimulus (usually a light that appears on a screen). This is obviously a very simple task, so the main variable of interest is how long it takes the examinee to respond, rather than whether or not he or she responds correctly.

Although reaction time tasks are very simple, they are not direct measures of mental speed. A pure mental-speed measure would isolate the amount of time it takes the examinee to decide that the stimulus is present. RT includes this *decision time*, but also time for other response components, such as the time that the nerve impulse takes to travel from the brain to the finger, and the time that the muscles take to contract in order to press the button. These components may be slower in some populations, especially older adults (Salthouse, 1996). RT measures cannot separate out these components from mental-processing speed.

Inspection Time

In order to address this limitation of RT tasks, researchers devised the even simpler **inspection time** (IT) task. IT is intended to reflect the amount of time it takes a person to merely process a stimulus; it does not include the time required to initiate and complete the response. In a typical IT task, a simple stimulus is flashed on the screen, followed by a visual mask. The stimulus is similar to the shape of a capital Greek letter *pi* (Π) except that the two vertical "legs" are not the same length. The participant must indicate which "leg" is longer. The lengths of the legs are quite different, and identifying the longer one would be a trivially easy task for any participant with normal visual acuity if the stimulus were left on the screen. The task is made difficult by the visual mask, which replaces the stimulus after a variable amount of time has passed (usually less than 100 milliseconds). Across trials, the amount of time before the onset of the mask is varied, in order to establish the length of stimulus exposure a person requires to consistently respond correctly (usually defined as a threshold of, say, 85 percent accuracy). Researchers who use this task claim that it is a nearly pure measure of processing speed because it only requires the participant to view and process the stimulus. The speed of the response itself does not matter, because a person's processing speed is estimated from the exposure time, which is manipulated by the experimenter (Deary & Stough, 1996). Therefore, some researchers have argued that inspection time measures a process that is sufficiently basic to serve as a limiting factor of cognition in general (Vickers & Smith, 1986). However, others (e.g., White, 1993) have argued that the task is so basic that it does not meaningfully involve cognitive processing at all, and that it only reflects sensory processes. Based on the observed relationship between IT and intelligence, the reality seems to be somewhere in the middle, as we will see in the next section.

The Speed–Intelligence Relationship

A large body of research has examined the relationship between speed tasks (RT and IT) and intelligence. Early inspection time studies found very large correlations with intelligence (Nettelbeck & Lally, 1976). However, these early studies used very small sample sizes (e.g., $n = 10$; Nettelbeck & Lally, 1976), and included people with a very wide range of cognitive abilities, including people with intellectual disabilities. More recent reviews (Deary & Stough, 1996; Nettelbeck, 1987) and meta-analyses (Grudnik & Kranzler, 2001; Kranzler & Jensen, 1989; Sheppard & Vernon, 2008) have consistently reported uncorrected correlations between inspection time and general intelligence in the $r = -.30$ range in samples that do not include people with intellectual disabilities.[4] However, most samples consist mainly or exclusively of college students, which restricts the range of scores on both IT (because they are young adults) and intelligence tests (because they are college students). This range restriction depresses the correlation between IT and intelligence. After correcting for restriction of range, estimated IT–intelligence correlations increase to the $r = -.50$ range (Kranzler & Jensen, 1989). Similar results have been obtained for RT. A meta-analysis by Sheppard and Vernon (2008) reported uncorrected correlations between mean RT task performance and intelligence test scores ranging from $r = -.22$ for simple RT tasks to $r = -.40$ for more complex, 8-choice RT tasks.

Clearly, IT and RT tasks do not come close to reaching Detterman's (2002) $r = .80$ threshold correlation with intelligence (remember that this threshold is somewhat arbitrary, however). But do the relatively modest but consistent correlations suggest that mental speed, in itself, is at least somewhat important to intelligence? In the next section, we argue that they do not.

---

[4] Note that intelligence–speed correlations are negative because higher intelligence is associated with greater speed (lower response time).

Challenges for Intelligence-as-Speed Theories

Despite the existence of well-cited theories that have offered explanations of intelligence in terms of speed (Eysenck, 1982; Jensen, 1998), this stance faces many challenges. From the perspective of cognitive psychology, speed theories do not answer the question, "Speed of *what*?" Both Eysenck (1982) and Jensen (1998) have argued that mental speed reflects neural transmission speed, although there is no evidence that speed of nerve conduction is related to intelligence among individuals in the normal range of intelligence. Furthermore, it is not clear that RT or IT actually reflects the speed of neural conduction. By skipping directly to the cellular level, this extremely reductionist view of intelligence does not offer any insight into the cognitive processes involved in intelligent behavior. For this reason alone, speed-based theories of intelligence are unsatisfying to many cognitive psychologists (Conway, Kane, & Engle, 1999).

Despite the limitations and ambiguities of speed-based theories of intelligence, the fact remains that IT and RT tasks do correlate reliably with intelligence (Deary & Stough, 1996; Jensen, 1998). Why performance on a full-scale intelligence test would be related to performance on the simplest of laboratory tasks, which some (e.g., White, 1993) have argued do not even involve cognitive processing, is a question worth examining. The correlation between speed and intelligence does not mean that speed *causes* intelligence. But correlations *do* have causes. So what causes the speed–intelligence correlation?

Modern psychologists measure RT using many trials, which yields a distribution of response times for each participant.[5] Speed theorists (Eysenck, 1982; Jensen, 1998) often have focused on measures of *central tendency* (usually, mean RT) as the primary speed indicator of interest. However, central tendency is not the only way to quantify a distribution. RT distributions are highly positively skewed, with most RTs clustering near a person's fastest time, and progressively fewer trials having longer RTs. Is it possible that some subset of RTs drive the relationship between mean RT and intelligence? In other words, is the RT–intelligence correlation consistent across the distribution of observed RTs, or does the relationship change at different points on the RT distribution?

There is good evidence for the latter. Researchers have consistently found that the longest RTs in the distribution are more strongly correlated with intelligence than the shortest RTs (see Coyle, 2003, for a review). A common strategy for examining this phenomenon is to divide RTs into "bins." A researcher might create five bins, so that the first bin has the fastest 20 percent of RTs, the second bin has the next fastest 20 percent of RTs, and so on, with the last bin having the slowest 20 percent of RTs.

---

[5] Performance varies from trial to trial in IT tasks also, but this variability is somewhat more difficult to describe because of the dichotomous (correct/incorrect) nature of the responses. For simplicity, we will focus on RT tasks for the remainder of the section.

The mean RT for each bin is then computed, and the correlation between intelligence and the mean of each bin is examined separately. Correlations with intelligence increase from the fastest bin to the slowest (Larson & Alderton, 1990), meaning that an individual's slowest RTs are the most predictive of intelligence. This effect is known as the **worst performance rule**, and it cannot be fully explained by statistical artifacts such as outliers or variance compression (Coyle, 2003).

There are limitations to the binning method, such as a relatively small number of observations in each bin and the arbitrary division of the distribution (Unsworth, Redick, Lakey, & Young, 2010). Recently, researchers have employed more advanced statistical methods to describe the RT distribution (Schmiedek, Oberauer, Wilhelm, Süß, & Wittmann, 2007; Unsworth et al., 2010; van Ravenzwaaij, Brown, & Wagenmakers, 2011). The positively skewed RT distribution approximates an ex-Gaussian distribution, which is a combination of a Gaussian (normal) distribution and an exponential distribution. The exponential component of the distribution reflects the slower RTs. Researchers can extract separate parameters describing the normal and exponential components of the distribution, and examine how they relate to intelligence. Importantly, these parameters do not reflect cognitive processes directly (Unsworth et al., 2010). However, experimental manipulations known to affect certain cognitive processes have been shown to affect some parameters in predictable ways.

Using various experimental methods, multiple research groups have converged on the interpretation that the normal part of the distribution reflects automatic and sensori-motor processes, while the exponential part of the distribution is associated with controlled attentional processes, including the ability to maintain attentional focus on the task (Schmiedek et al., 2007; Unsworth et al., 2010). We will have much more to say about attentional processes later in this chapter, but for the purpose of the present discussion, the main idea is that people who are better able to keep their attention focused on a simple RT task are able to respond more quickly when the stimulus appears. People whose minds wander away from the task – even if their eyes do not – must bring their attention back to the task when the stimulus appears in order to respond to it. This takes time, and results in a long RT for the affected trial. Frequent attentional lapses lead to a greater proportion of long RTs, which increases the exponential component of the distribution.

The exponential component of the RT distribution is negatively correlated with intelligence ($r = -.71$; Schmiedek et al., 2007). That is, people with a higher proportion of slower responses on RT tasks also perform worse on intelligence tests, compared to people with fewer slow responses. (Note that this is consistent with findings that mean RT is negatively related to intelligence, because a greater proportion of slow responses would increase the overall mean of the distribution.) A speed-based explanation for this relationship may seem tempting on the surface, but does not in fact make much sense. A relationship between the exponential part of the distribution (i.e., the slowest RTs) and intelligence does not provide much support for the idea that faster speeds make a person smarter. The finding that "occasionally much slower equals less intelligent" does not support the idea that "faster equals smarter," because the results and the theory pertain to opposite ends of the RT spectrum (Mackintosh, 2011).

If attentional lapses can disrupt performance on something as simple as an RT task, while the participant (presumably) is trying to concentrate, then such lapses may be regular occurrences that negatively affect cognition. People who experience more attentional lapses during RT tasks may also experience them more often during other laboratory tasks and in real life. Thus, attentional lapses may drive the correlation between longer RTs and other cognitive tasks, including intelligence tests (Schmiedek et al., 2007; Unsworth et al., 2010, but see Kane, Gross, Chun, & Smeekens, 2017, for evidence that the relationship between mind-wandering in the lab and in real life is not as strong as one might assume). With the suggestion that attention lapses might *cause* the relationship between RT task performance and intelligence, we have moved squarely into the realm of cognitive psychology. We have identified a process which is part of a theory of how the mind works, and we have specified a way in which it might be related to intelligence. For the rest of the chapter, we will concentrate on the process that has become the focus of most cognitive intelligence research: executive attention.

Working Memory and Executive Attention

As noted in the introduction to this chapter, the cognitive approach to psychology focuses on models that describe how the cognitive system processes information. Most cognitive psychologists work to develop models of the processes involved in human cognition in general (for example, a model of the memory system), and are not interested in individual differences in the ability to carry out those processes. However, some cognitively oriented psychologists do use laboratory tests measuring cognitive processes to study differences between people. They then attempt to link differences between people in performance on these tasks to differences in intelligence. Much of this research has focused on working memory capacity and executive attention.

Measuring Working Memory Capacity (WMC)

Daneman and Carpenter (1980) were the first to use what would now be called a complex span task for measuring **working memory capacity (WMC)**. Earlier researchers had not found a relationship between simple short-term memory span tasks and complex cognitive indicators such as reading comprehension, leading to speculation that short-term memory was not important to complex cognition. (An article by Crowder in 1982, ominously titled "The Demise of Short-term Memory," argued exactly this point; see also Estes, 1982.) Daneman and Carpenter were skeptical of this conclusion, given that a relationship was predicted by theoretical models of both reading comprehension and WMC. At the time, WMC had been defined as involving both processing and storage of information, but it was typically measured using tasks that only required storage. So Daneman and Carpenter designed a task that would tax both the processing and storage components of working memory. In their reading span task, participants were asked to read or listen to a sentence and remember the last word of the sentence. After a set of sentences had been presented (set sizes ranged from 2 to 6), participants recalled the last word of each sentence. The number of correctly recalled words was the person's reading span, which operationally defined WMC. Daneman and Carpenter (1980) found strong correlations (ranging from $r = .42$ to $r = .86$) between reading span and various measures of reading comprehension, as well as SAT-Verbal scores. However, a simple word-span task that required participants to recall lists of words (i.e., a task that involved storage but not processing) did not significantly correlate with reading comprehension or SAT-Verbal scores. Although their sample sizes were very small for correlational research ($n = 20$ for Experiment 1, $n = 21$ for Experiment 2), Daneman and Carpenter's work provided important early evidence that WMC is critical to complex cognition.

Today, many different tasks are used to measure WMC, including a wide variety of **complex span tasks**. Like the reading span task, the complex span tasks all involve a processing task and a memory task, and participants must shift their attention between the memory task and the processing task before finally recalling all the memory items for the current trial. Figure 5.1 shows example stimuli from three common complex span tasks and explains how they work.

Span tasks are not the only method of measuring WMC. Two other frequently used tasks are the *n*-back task and the change-detection task. In the **n-back task**, a string of items (for example, digits) is presented and the person being tested must press a button whenever an item is identical to the item presented *n* items ago. For instance, in the 3-back version of the task, the examinee must press a button when the digit on the screen was also presented three items ago. In the **change-detection task**, a display showing some number of objects is presented briefly, followed by another similar display. Figure 5.2 shows an example of this task. The left box of the figure shows the initial display, and the right box of the figure shows the second display. The person being tested must indicate whether one of the objects, called the target object, was the same or different in the first and second displays. The probe indicating the target object does not appear until after the screen has changed. This means that, to respond correctly, participants must keep the original array in

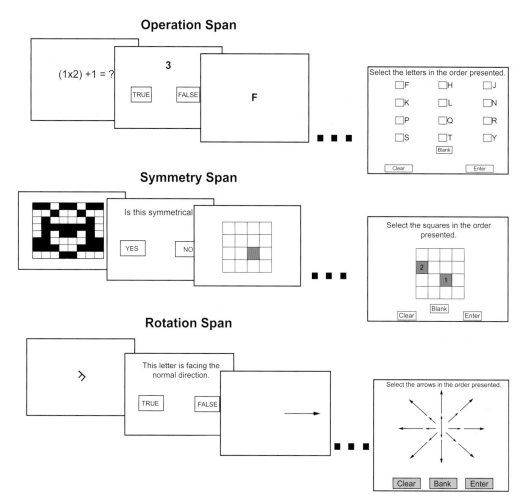

Figure 5.1 Example stimuli for three commonly used span tasks. For each task, the boxes represent what the participant sees during a trial, proceeding from left to right. First, the participant is shown a stimulus (arithmetic problem for the operation span task, array of squares for the symmetry span task, and a rotated letter for the rotation span task). Next, the participant must make a judgment about the stimulus (e.g., whether the number shown is the correct solution to the arithmetic problem, or whether the array is symmetrical). These two steps constitute the processing task. The participant is then shown another stimulus, represented in the third box, which is to be held in memory. This is the memory part of the task. This sequence of processing and memory tasks is repeated between two and seven times. Finally, the participant is prompted to recall all of the stimuli presented in the memory component, in the order in which they were presented. This is shown in the boxes on the right side of the figure.

memory until the probe appears. In this task, a person's WMC is the greatest number of objects in the display for which the person consistently responds correctly. There is growing evidence that although complex span tasks, *n*-back tasks, and change-detection tasks are highly correlated with each other, they emphasize different functions of working memory itself.

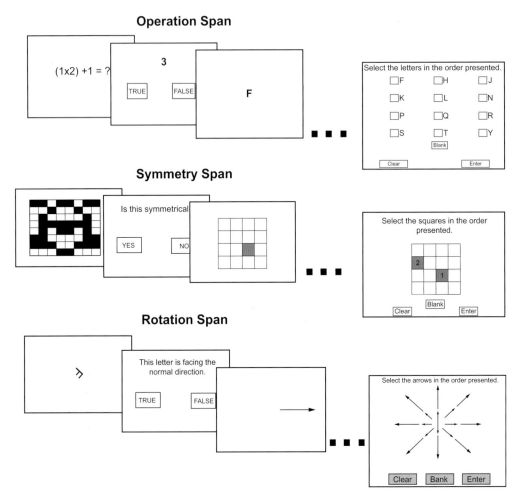

Figure 5.2 Example stimuli for the change detection task. The participant first sees an array like the one on the left. After a brief visual mask, a second array appears, such as the one on the right. After a brief delay, one shape in the array is identified as the target stimulus, and the participant indicates whether the shape changed color in the new array. The number of shapes in the array varies from trial to trial. A person's working memory capacity is the number of shapes in the largest array for which the person can consistently identify changes correctly.

Working toward Reliable Estimates of WMC

Before continuing with our discussion of working memory, we must offer a caveat about cognitive tasks: There is no such thing as a process-pure measure of cognition in humans. In even the simplest of tasks, different people will use different strategies, different coding schemes, different rehearsal techniques, and therefore probably different functions in their brains. Further, despite researchers' best efforts, no task is content-free. All memory or processing tasks require a person to remember or process *something*. Factors not related to WMC may make some content easier to manipulate for some people than for others, meaning that content plays a role in a person's performance on a WMC task. For example, people differ in their ability to manipulate visuospatial information: People who have lower spatial abilities do not perform as well on WMC tasks with spatial content as on WMC tasks with other types of content (Shah & Miyake, 1996). For these people, domain-general WMC would be underestimated if only WMC tasks with spatial content were used. The same is true for any other type of content. This presents a problem for cognitive researchers: They want to measure general cognitive processes, not the ability to work with specific types of content, but it is impossible to measure a process without using some kind of content. How can they do this?

One solution is to use the macroanalytic approach described earlier. Recall that in this approach, latent factors are created by administering multiple indicators of a construct that cannot be measured directly. If a cognitive researcher wants to measure WMC, for example, he or she may use three WM tasks that use different types of content in order to obtain an estimate of WMC that is not strongly influenced by any particular type of content. Latent factors for other constructs of interest, such as attention control, would be created in the same way. Then, the researcher would use methods such as structural equation modeling to explore relationships between the factors. **Structural equation modeling** is an advanced statistical technique that allows researchers to examine correlations between latent factors. These correlations are often more stable and meaningful than correlations between individual tests, and they offer a clearer picture of the relationship between factors than can be obtained from individual test scores. Structural equation modeling can also provide limited evidence supporting hypothesized causal relationships between variables.

The macroanalytic design is common in cognitive intelligence research (e.g., Kane et al., 2004; Süß, Oberauer, Wittmann, Wilhelm, & Schulze, 2002), and studies using it typically report stronger correlations between WMC and intelligence at the latent factor level than studies that examine pairwise correlations between individual WMC and intelligence tests (Oberauer, Schulze, Wilhelm, & Süß, 2005). This would be expected, because latent factors include only the variance that is common to all of the tests measuring that factor, and therefore are considered to reflect the influence of processes that are common to all of the tests measuring the construct. The latent factors do not include variance that arises from idiosyncrasies of particular tests. Thus, latent factors are presumed to represent something approaching the elusive process-pure measure of cognitive processes. Much of the literature that we will review in this section uses latent factors and structural equation modeling to make inferences about WMC and fluid intelligence.

Despite the significant advantages just described, the macroanalytic approach also has some limitations that must be kept in mind when interpreting the results of studies that have used this method. Two limitations are particularly relevant to the current discussion. The first limitation relates to claims of causality (e.g., "Working memory gives rise to Gf"). Researchers can examine whether the data are consistent with their proposed model, but the proposed model is never the only model that could fit the data. Testing a model with structural equation modeling requires a combination of statistics and theory: The statistics indicate the strength of the proposed relationships, but theory has to define the existence and direction of the relationships. Other theories could propose different relationships, and structural equation modeling alone usually cannot definitively support one theory over another. The second limitation relates to the ability to define two factors as the same or different. Statistical tests to determine whether the correlation between two factors, such as WMC and Gf, is $r = 1.0$ (meaning that they are the same) or significantly less than $r = 1.0$ (meaning that they are different) requires a large sample (over 200, but sample sizes closer to 100 are not uncommon in this area of research; Gignac, 2014; Matzke, Dolan, & Molenaar, 2010). It is important to keep this limitation in mind when reviewing evidence of the relationship (or unity) between WMC and Gf, which we will review in a later section.

Theories of Working Memory (WM)

Although there is general agreement about how WMC should be measured, there are different theories about its structure and the processes involved. Early researchers (and some more modern researchers, such as Cowan, 1988) conceptualized WMC as the number of chunks of information that a person's working memory can "hold" at a given time, a position that is very similar to the classical view of short-term memory (Atkinson & Shiffrin, 1968). However, many current researchers (e.g., Engle & Kane, 2004; Engle, Tuholski, Laughlin, & Conway, 1999; Oberauer, 2002) view WMC as reflecting not the "size" of the storage unit, but rather a person's ability to deploy attention in order to control and regulate the flow of information into and through the system. Between-person differences in attention control lead to differences in the ability to maintain multiple pieces of relevant information in a sufficiently activated state (in consciousness, if you will), which is reflected in performance on WMC tasks. Theories differ in terms of how this is accomplished. Two prominent theories are Engle's theory of attention control, and Oberauer's binding theory.

Engle and colleagues (Engle & Kane, 2004; Engle et al., 1999) argue that the main driver of individual differences in WMC is **executive attention** – the ability to control one's attention and prevent having attention captured by distractions, whether internal (such as thoughts and emotions) or external (events in the environment such as people talking or loud noises). In everyday experience, this is reflected in differences in mind wandering and tendency to be distracted. People with good attention control are able to manage their attention in such a way that allows them to complete tasks effectively with minimal disruption. What constitutes effective attention management depends on the task. For some tasks, it means maintaining task-relevant information above a minimal level of activation so that it can be accessed when needed. Maintaining increasing amounts of information requires increasingly tight control over attention, because there are fewer attentional resources that can be spared on task-irrelevant thoughts. For other tasks, effective attention management means actively disengaging from information that is no longer relevant to the task, thereby reducing the risk of interference from outdated information (Shipstead, Harrison, & Engle, 2016). Individual differences in capacity limitations, as measured by WMC tasks, reflect differences in the ability to manage attention during these tasks.

Oberauer and his colleagues (e.g., Oberauer, 2002; Oberauer, Süß, Wilhelm, & Sander, 2007) have taken a somewhat different view of WMC. Oberauer's model conceptualizes WM as an attentional system that is aimed at memory, rather than a memory system in its own right (Oberauer et al., 2007). In this model, WM comprises three regions, which represent different levels of activation. The highest level of activation is at the **focus of attention** (akin to what most people would think of as the contents of consciousness), which can accommodate the one chunk of information that the person is engaging with at a given moment. The **region of direct access** consists of a few chunks of information that are not actively being manipulated, but that are immediately available for processing. The lowest level of activation is the activated region of long-term memory, which can briefly store information in a less-activated state before it fades out of the activated region entirely. (There is also a vast region of long-term memory that is not meaningfully activated at a given time. This region does not play an important role in Oberauer's WM model, because information in this region is, by definition, not in WM.)

For Oberauer (2002; Oberauer et al., 2007), WM keeps chunks of information available by temporarily binding them to positions in a cognitive coordinate system that provides an "address" for the information. Temporary bindings can also be made between activated chunks. These bindings allow people to carry out tasks and solve problems by linking different problem components together. Capacity limitations arise when it becomes difficult to keep the bindings intact, which leads to features of different chunks of information being mixed up (which Oberauer calls *overwriting*) or to different chunks of information competing for the same location in the cognitive coordinate system (which Oberauer calls *crosstalk*). Overwriting and crosstalk both contribute to processing errors by making it difficult or impossible to access the correct information when it is needed.

We have spent a great deal of time describing the processes involved in these theories, because these processes are essential to a cognitive explanation for the relationship between WMC and intelligence. These two theories illustrate both the greatest challenge and the solidly scientific approach of cognitive psychology. The challenge is that there is no way to peer inside the brain and directly observe the processes that are involved in cognition. Both of these models are consistent with data from WMC and many other related tasks. This ambiguity is a major challenge for cognitive psychology. However, these two theories also show the strength of the cognitive approach, which is that well-constructed models of cognitive processes lead to testable hypotheses that can be examined empirically. A great deal of research has been conducted to test the predictions of both theories. A review of this research is beyond the scope of this chapter; for our purposes, the important thing to know is that, regardless of the theoretical orientation of the researchers, WMC tasks consistently are found to correlate with measures of intelligence, particularly Gf. The relevant question here is not which WM model is "correct," but rather why there should be such a consistent relationship between relatively simple cognitive tasks (WMC tasks) and much more complex cognitive tasks (intelligence test items).

The Relationship between WMC and Gf

Much working memory research has directly or indirectly addressed the question of how WMC is related to intelligence. While some researchers (Colom, Rebollo, Palacios, Juan-Espinosa, & Kyllonen, 2004; Kyllonen & Christal, 1990) have found such strong relationships between WMC and Gf that they have concluded that the two are the same construct, this is not the prevailing view. A more common position is that the two are strongly related, but meaningfully different. For example, Kane and colleagues (2004) reported a correlation of $r = .64$ between a latent WMC factor and Gf, as measured by conventional intelligence tests. In general, the relationship between WMC and Gf at the latent factor level is in the range of $r = .60$ to $r = .80$, with the variability in the correlations most likely arising from differences across studies in the range of abilities in the people tested and the exact nature of the tests used. While the strength of the relationship is still subject to some debate, it is clear that a strong relationship exists. The question then becomes *why* WMC and Gf are so strongly related.

As with all correlational research, there are at least three possibilities for the relationship between WMC and Gf. Differences in Gf may cause differences in WMC; differences in WMC may cause differences in Gf; or differences in both Gf and WMC may be caused by a third variable.

Differences in Gf May Cause Differences in WMC

This first option is hypothetically possible – for example, perhaps people with higher Gf are able to devise strategies that help them perform better on WMC tasks – but there is little empirical support for this position (Kane et al., 2004). Moreover, a theoretical justification for a causal path from Gf to WMC must grapple with a key definitional issue. WMC is based on theoretical accounts of mental processes that are grounded in cognitive, clinical, and neuroscientific evidence. Multiple lines of research have converged on similar conclusions about the general nature of the cognitive architecture and functions, and WMC task performance has been linked both to simpler cognitive tasks and to biology (Kane et al., 2004). In contrast, Gf is the common factor derived from exploratory factor analyses of tests that have traditionally been used to measure fluid intelligence. It is a description of relationships between tests, not an explanation for them. From a theoretical perspective, therefore, it is difficult to justify the position that Gf causes WMC. It seems that Gf is not a cause of the correlation between scores on various ability tests, but rather the effect of some underlying process(es) that impact performance on all of the tests. In other words, it is a psychometric phenomenon, not a psychological one (Conway & Kovacs, 2015).

Differences in WMC Cause Differences in Gf

The second possibility, that differences in WMC cause differences in Gf, is more plausible (Kane et al., 2004; Kyllonen & Christal, 1990). A naive position in line with this view is that WM, in itself, is the cognitive process underlying Gf. That is, people differ on Gf because they differ on WMC, and that is the end of the story; the correlation between them is less than $r = 1.0$ only because of error variance. A possible explanation for the relationship between WMC and performance on an inductive reasoning task, for example, is that WMC is used to keep track of relevant information such as patterns that have been identified and hypotheses that have been tested while attempting to solve the problem. People perform better on Gf tests when they are better able to keep track of these things. This position is likely to be overly simplistic, however. Suggesting a direct one-to-one relationship between WMC and Gf confuses cognitive tasks with the cognitive processes assumed to underlie them (Shipstead et al., 2016). That is, it assumes that WMC tests are pure measures of a single process – that a person's score on a symmetry span task, for example, accurately reflects his or her WMC, and is not influenced by any other factors. We have already asserted that this is unlikely.

Differences in both Gf and WMC May Be Caused by a Third Variable

Recent work indicates that performance on WMC tasks can be decomposed into more basic processes (Shipstead et al., 2016; see also Conway & Kovacs, 2015). This observation leads to the third possibility for interpreting the WMC–Gf correlation: It arises from processes that contribute to both. For example, Shipstead et al. (2016) suggested a model of the WMC–Gf relationship based on two more basic functions: **maintenance** of information in the face of distraction or decay, and **disengagement** from old, potentially interfering information to allow attention to new, potentially

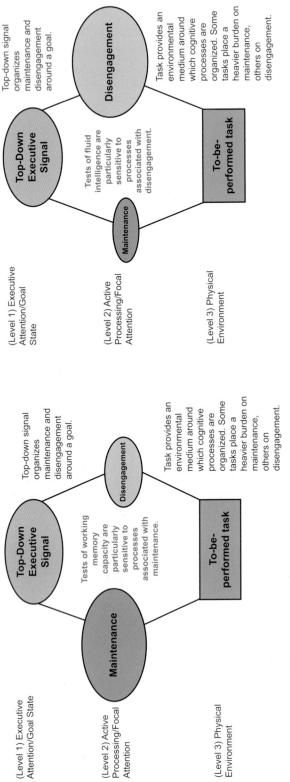

(Level 1) Executive Attention/Goal State

(Level 2) Active Processing/Focal Attention

(Level 3) Physical Environment

Top-down signal organizes maintenance and disengagement around a goal.

Tests of working memory capacity are particularly sensitive to processes associated with maintenance.

Task provides an environmental medium around which cognitive processes are organized. Some tasks place a heavier burden on maintenance, others on disengagement.

Top-Down Executive Signal

Maintenance

Disengagement

To-be-performed task

(Level 1) Executive Attention/Goal State

(Level 2) Active Processing/Focal Attention

(Level 3) Physical Environment

Top-down signal organizes maintenance and disengagement around a goal.

Tests of fluid intelligence are particularly sensitive to processes associated with disengagement.

Task provides an environmental medium around which cognitive processes are organized. Some tasks place a heavier burden on maintenance, others on disengagement.

Top-Down Executive Signal

Maintenance

Disengagement

To-be-performed task

Figure 5.3 Schematic representation of the roles of maintenance and disengagement in WMC and Gf tasks

relevant and useful information. Both of these processes are important for perform-ance both on WMC tasks and Gf tasks, but to different degrees (see Figure 5.3).

Shipstead and colleagues note that WMC tasks appear to mainly tax the ability to maintain information, whereas Gf tests rely more heavily on disengaging from information (for example, in hypothesis testing, during which an examinee must discard previously tested hypotheses in order to move on to new ones). However, both processes are used to some degree in both types of tasks, and both functions are effortful and demanding of limited-capacity attention. The common underlying processes and their reliance on limited-capacity attention cause the correlation between two quite different types of tasks; the difference in the importance of those underlying processes to the two tasks is the reason that they are not correlated more strongly. For a specific example of a recent study from the Randall W. Engle's lab investigating the role of maintenance and disengagement in a complex cognitive task (reading comprehension), see the Focus on Contemporary Research box.

FOCUS ON CONTEMPORARY RESEARCH: RANDALL W. ENGLE'S WORK ON WORKING MEMORY CAPACITY AND READING COMPREHENSION

Individual differences in working memory capacity (WMC) have been shown to be strongly associated with differences in reading comprehension (Daneman & Carpenter, 1980; Turner & Engle, 1989). The mechanism underlying this relationship is not yet known. One possibility is that the relationship is primarily due to individual differences in the ability to maintain information: High WMC individuals can maintain more idea units and more complex language structures in an active state, which results in better comprehension. Another possibility is that the WMC– reading comprehension relationship is primarily due to the ability to disengage from previously attended information (Hasher & Zacks, 1988; Gernsbacher, 1991). Although it may seem counterintuitive that disengaging from information aids comprehension, consider the many ambiguous words that are encountered when reading a passage in English. For example, if you read, "The violinist picked up the bow," you are likely to think of a bow that is used to play the violin. However, if the next sentence is, "She placed the bow in her daughter's hair to keep it in place," you must change the meaning of "bow" to a ribbon. High-ability individuals are better able to block, inhibit, or disengage from the first meaning after reading the second sentence, and to replace it with the new meaning. Low-ability individuals are more likely to keep both meanings active in working memory. Failing to suppress the now-irrelevant meaning of "bow" consumes WM resources that could otherwise be allocated toward understanding the passage.

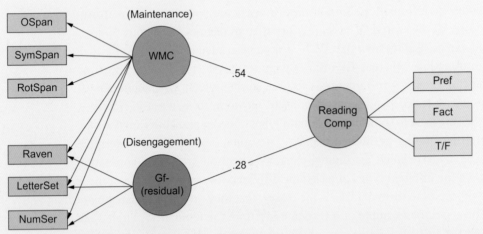

Box Figure. Structural equation modeling EM analysis from Martin et al. (unpublished), showing the contributions of maintenance and disengagement to reading comprehension. The arrows from WMC to all of the tasks, including the Gf tasks, reflect an attempt to attribute all of the variance due to maintenance to the WMC construct. Putatively, that means the Gf construct reflects largely disengagement. The result is that both WMC or maintenance and Gf or disengagement are shown to be important to reading comprehension. Martin et al. also found a similar result for learning second language vocabulary. The conclusion is that both maintenance and disengagement are important in reading and second language learning but it is likely that different real-world tasks will show differential reliance on these two important functions of intelligence.

A recent study by Martin, Shipstead, Harrison, and colleagues (unpublished) examined the relative importance of maintenance and disengagement in reading comprehension. Although earlier studies found a relationship between WMC and reading comprehension, these studies did not include measures of Gf. (Recall from the chapter that WMC tasks are thought to rely more heavily on maintenance, whereas Gf tasks are thought to rely more heavily on disengagement; this means that previous studies that did not measure Gf may not have adequately measured disengagement.) Using the macroanalytic approach described in the chapter, Martin et al. examined the relationship between maintenance, disengagement, and reading comprehension. They created a latent reading comprehension factor using three measures of reading comprehension for a series of paragraphs. One measure was a set of fact questions based on events described in the paragraph, the second was a set of true/false questions regarding events in the paragraph, and the third was a pronominal reference question in which participants were asked to identify the noun that a pronoun referred to (this was made somewhat difficult by the fact that the noun appeared four to seven sentences before the pronoun). A latent maintenance factor was created using three WM tasks plus the variance in three Gf tasks that was due to maintenance. (Remember that Gf tasks are thought to require *some* maintenance, even though they *primarily* require disengagement.) The latent disengagement factor was created from the remaining variance in the Gf tasks.

The results of the study are summarized graphically in the figure in this box. The lines connecting the maintenance and disengagement factors with the reading comprehension factor indicate that both maintenance and disengagement are important to reading comprehension. Put differently, both WMC and Gf reflect processes that are important to complex cognitive tasks, and measuring both of these factors explains more of the complex task performance than measuring only one of them. It is likely that different real-world tasks will show differential reliance on these two functions of intelligence, making it even more important to measure both processes when studying complex cognition.

This "third variable" view of the WMC–Gf relationship is arguably both the most plausible, and the most consistent with the cognitive approach to intelligence research. It explains Gf in terms of the basic processes that allow humans to process information, even if the individual processes have not yet been completely identified. One advantage of the theory that the ability to control attention is at least partly responsible for differences in Gf is that a single construct, attention control, can be used to understand a wide variety of phenomena in human psychology, from the ability to inhibit inappropriate behavior in young children (Skogan, Zeiler, Egeland, Rohrer-Baumgartner, & Urnes, 2014), to why depression and schizophrenia cause cognitive deficits (Forbes, Carrick, McIntosh, & Lawrie, 2009; Joormann & Gotlib, 2008; Lee & Park, 2005), to why sleep deprivation hurts performance in skilled pilots (Lopez, Previc, Fischer, Heitz, & Engle, 2012), to why stereotype threat leads some women to do poorly on math tests (Schmader, 2010), to why some point guards in basketball are more strategic in making passes than others (Furley & Wood, 2016), to why some police officers are more likely to shoot in a stressful situation (Kleider-Offutt, Clevinger, & Bond, 2016), to why some people are more likely to be distracted while driving (J. M. Watson et al., 2016), and to why some people are better at multi-tasking than others (Redick, 2016). The evidence suggests that people differ in their ability to control the deployment of attention in all situations where the control of thought, emotion, and behavior is important. In other words, attention control is critical to most of human psychology.

Before closing this chapter, we should address some criticisms that have been leveled against cognitive theories of intelligence, which mirror criticisms of cognitive psychology more broadly. Specifically, critics have argued that (a) real-world intelligent behavior (often, but not always, defined as academic or job success) does not correlate as strongly with tests of narrow cognitive processes as with full-scale IQ tests; and (b) cognitive researchers improperly focus on explaining performance on tests of Gf, which were designed to *predict* intelligent behavior, not to *define* it (Ackerman, 2017; Hunt, 2005). Both of these criticisms somewhat miss the point of the cognitive approach. Although it is true that cognitive researchers have not identified a single test, measuring a single process, that can replace comprehensive intelligence tests, that has not been the aim of most cognitive researchers in the last few decades. Instead, as we hope we have made clear in this chapter, cognitive psychologists strive to develop an understanding of intelligence grounded in models of how the mind works (Hunt, 2005). In other words, they are interested in identifying the *causes* of intelligence, which is different from identifying a set of basic cognitive tests that rival traditional measures of intelligence in their ability to predict intelligent behavior in situations encountered in the real world.

As you will learn in this book, intelligence is a complex concept that is difficult to operationally define. One option is to use intelligence tests as proxies, as cognitive psychologists have done since the early days of the cognitive approach (Hunt et al., 1975), even though the tests were not intended to define intelligence (Ackerman, 2017). Another option is to use specific performance indicators such as the ones mentioned in the previous paragraph. Neither option fully captures the breadth of human intelligence and the many ways it can manifest itself in the world outside the laboratory. However, both options do provide researchers with standardized indicators of intelligence (or intelligent behavior) that can be correlated with basic cognitive characteristics such as ability to control attention. While correlations cannot prove causation, the existence of the relationship indicates that something that affects performance on attention control tasks also affects performance on much more complex tasks. And while psychologists (and psychology students) should always keep in mind that Gf tests provide only a shadow of the complex reality of human intelligence, they nevertheless offer a starting point for understanding the processes that enable and support the many ways that intelligence is manifested.

CONCLUSION

The cognitive approach to studying intelligence is centered on identifying cognitive processes that explain individual differences in intelligence. Hints of the cognitive approach were present in the earliest days of intelligence research, long before the advent of cognitive psychology as a subfield. Although those early efforts (Galton, 1883; Wissler, 1901) were not particularly successful, they laid the groundwork for research programs that emerged many decades later, beginning in the 1970s and continuing today. The unifying theme of all of this work has been a quest to understand *why* some people are more intelligent than others.

We do not yet know the answer to this question. We can be fairly confident that there is not one single process, such as working memory, or characteristic of the cognitive system, such as speed, that fully accounts for between-person differences in intelligence (Detterman, 2002; Mackintosh, 2011). Modern models of intelligence in the cognitive tradition feature multiple processes that are tapped to different degrees by different types of cognitive tests. In these models, Gf is not understood as a psychological entity in itself. Instead, it is a psychometric property that emerges as a result of these various processes, each of which contributes to, but does not completely determine, performance on a subset of cognitive tests (Conway & Kovacs, 2015).

Because cognitive processes cannot be observed directly, there are always likely to be competing theories and room for multiple interpretations. One strength of the cognitive approach is that it is rooted in the experimental tradition, which pits the prediction of one theory against that of another. Experimental methods and tasks will evolve as theories do, leading researchers ever closer to an understanding of intelligence that is based on what is known about how the human cognitive system works.

CHAPTER SUMMARY

Cognitive psychology is the study of the mental processes involved in cognition. In the context of intelligence research, the cognitive approach is focused on identifying the mental processes involved in intelligent behavior and, further, exploring whether between-person differences in intelligence can be explained by differences in the ability to carry out those processes. While early research efforts were aimed at isolating a single process that could explain individual differences in intelligence, most modern cognitive researchers do not seek a single process. Instead, they work to identify a set of processes that together give rise to intelligence.

Cognitive researchers use a combination of experimental and correlational methods in their intelligence research, and we reviewed some of these methods. We reviewed research on the relationship between intelligence and mental processing speed, which is often considered to be an early example of cognitive research, and considered its explanatory power from a cognitive perspective. We then moved to more modern efforts to construct a cognitive account of intelligence, which are centered on attention control and working memory. These cognitive functions have been shown to be related to a wide variety of indicators of intelligence and intelligent behavior, both inside and outside the laboratory.

We closed by addressing some of the criticisms of the cognitive approach in the context of its particular strengths.

KEY TERMS

change-detection task • cognitive psychology • complex span tasks • differential research • disengagement • executive attention • experimental research • focus of attention • inspection time (IT) • latent factor • macroanalytic approach • maintenance • microanalytic approach • *n*-back task • psychological *g* • psychometric *g* • reaction time (RT) • region of direct access • structural equation modeling • working memory capacity (WMC) • worst performance rule

COMPREHENSION AND REFLECTION QUESTIONS

1. How does the cognitive approach to the study of intelligence differ from the psychometric approach?
2. Explain the two major theories of working memory. How does each one explain the relationship between working memory tasks and intelligence?
3. Why did some theorists believe that speed was related to intelligence? Do you think that speed theories of intelligence are satisfying from a cognitive perspective? Why or why not?
4. Describe the macroanalytic and microanalytic approaches to studying the relationship between intelligence and cognitive processes. What are the advantages and limitations of each?
5. If you were designing an experiment in the cognitive tradition, how would you measure intelligence? How would you defend your choice?

References

Ackerman, P. L. (1996). A theory of adult intellectual development: Process, personality, interests, and knowledge. *Intelligence, 22*(2), 227-257.

Ackerman, P. L. (2017). Adult intelligence: The construct and the criterion problem. *Perspectives on Psychological Science, 12*(6), 987-998. https://doi.org/10.1177/1745691617703437

Anderson, J. R. (1996). *The architecture of cognition.* New York: Psychology Press.

Anderson, J. R. (2015). *Cognitive psychology and its implications.* New York: Worth.

Atkinson, R. C., & Shiffrin, R. M. (1968). Human memory: A proposed system and its control processes. In K. W. Spence & J. T. Spence (eds.), *Psychology of Learning and Motivation* (vol. 2, pp. 89–195). New York: Academic Press.

Broadbent, D. E. (1958). *Perception and communication*. New York: Pergamon.

Carpenter, P. A., Just, M. A., & Shell, P. (1990). What one intelligence test measures: A theoretical account of the processing in the Raven Progressive Matrices Test. *Psychological Review, 97*(3), 404–31. Retrieved from www.ncbi.nlm.nih.gov/pubmed/2381998

Cattell, R. B. (1943). The measurement of adult intelligence. *Psychological Bulletin, 40*(3), 153–193. https://doi.org/10.1037/h0059973

Chamorro-Premuzic, T., & Furnham, A. (2005). *Personality and intellectual competence*. New York: Lawrence Erlbaum Associates.

Collins, A. M., & Quillian, M. R. (1969). Retrieval time from semantic memory. *Journal of Verbal Learning and Verbal Behavior, 8*, 240–247.

Colom, R., Rebollo, I., Palacios, A., Juan-Espinosa, M., & Kyllonen, P. C. (2004). Working memory is (almost) perfectly predicted by *g. Intelligence, 32*(3), 277–296. https://doi.org/10.1016/j.intell.2003.12.002

Conway, A. R. A., & Engle, R. W. (1994). Working memory and retrieval: A resource-dependent inhibition model. *Journal of Experimental Psychology: General, 123*(4), 354–373.

Conway, A. R. A., Kane, M. J., & Engle, R. W. (1999). Is Spearman's *g* determined by speed or working memory capacity? *Psycoloquy, 10*(74). Retrieved from www.cogsci.ecs.soton.ac.uk/cgi/psych/newpsy?10.074

Conway, A. R. A., & Kovacs, K. (2013). Individual differences in intelligence and working memory: A review of latent variable models. In B. H. Ross (ed.), *Psychology of Learning and Motivation* (vol. 58, pp. 233–270). Waltham, MA: Academic Press.

Conway, A. R. A., & Kovacs, K. (2015). New and emerging models of human intelligence. *Wiley Interdisciplinary Reviews: Cognitive Science, 6*(5), 419–426. https://doi.org/10.1002/wcs.1356

Cowan, N. (1988). Evolving conceptions of memory storage, selective attention, and their mutual constraints within the human information-processing system. *Psychological Bulletin, 104*(2), 163–191.

Coyle, T. R. (2003). A review of the worst performance rule: Evidence, theory, and alternative hypotheses. *Intelligence, 31*(6), 567–587. https://doi.org/10.1016/S0160-2896(03)00054-0

Cronbach, L. J. (1957). The two disciplines of scientific psychology. *American Psychologist, 12*, (671–684).

Crowder, R. G. (1982). The demise of short-term memory. *Acta Psychologica, 50*(3), 291–323.

Daneman, M., & Carpenter, P. A. (1980). Individual differences in working memory and reading. *Journal of Verbal Learning and Verbal Behavior, 19*, 450–466.

Deary, I. J., & Stough, C. (1996). Intelligence and inspection time. *American Psychologist, 5*(6), 599–608.

Detterman, D. K. (2000). General intelligence and the definition of phenotypes. In G. R. Bock, J. A. Goode, & K. Webb (eds.), *The nature of intelligence* (pp. 136–148). Chichester: John Wiley & Sons.

Detterman, D. K. (2002). General intelligence: Cognitive and biological explanations. In R. J. Sternberg & E. L. Grigorenko (eds.), *The general factor of intelligence: How general is it?* Mahwah, NJ: Lawrence Erlbaum Associates.

Donders, F. C. (1969). On the speed of mental processes (W. G. Koster, trans.). *Acta Psychologica, 30*, 412-431. (First published 1868.)

Engle, R. W., & Kane, M. J. (2004). Executive attention, working memory capacity, and a two-factor theory of cognitive control. In *Psychology of Learning and Motivation* (vol. 44, pp. 145–199). https://doi.org/10.1016/S0079-7421(03)44005-X

Engle, R. W., Tuholski, S. W., Laughlin, J. E., & Conway, A. R. A. (1999). Working memory, short-term memory, and general fluid intelligence: A latent-variable approach. *Journal of Experimental Psychology: General, 128*(3), 309–331. https://doi.org/10.1037/0096-3445.128.3.309

Estes, W. K. (1982). Learning, memory, and intelligence. In R. J. Sternberg (ed.), *Handbook of human intelligence* (pp. 170-224). Cambridge: Cambridge University Press.

Eysenck, H. J. (ed.). (1982). *A model for intelligence.* New York: Springer-Verlag.

Forbes, N. F., Carrick, L. A., McIntosh, A. M., & Lawrie, S. M. (2009). Working memory in schizophrenia: A meta-analysis. *Psychological Medicine, 39*, 889–905.

Furley, P., & Wood, G. (2016). Working memory, attentional control, and expertise in sports: A review of current literature and directions for future research. *Journal of Applied Research in Memory and Cognition, 5*(4), 415–425.

Galton, F. (1883). *An inquiry into human faculty.* London: Macmillan.

Gardner, H. (1983). *Frames of mind: The theory of multiple intelligences.* New York: Basic Books.

Gernsbacher, M. A. (1991). Cognitive processes and mechanisms in language comprehension: The structure building framework. In G. H. Bower (ed.), *The psychology of learning and motivation* (vol. 27, pp. 217-263). New York: Academic Press.

Gignac, G. E. (2014). Fluid intelligence shares closer to 60% of its variance with working memory capacity and is a better indicator of general intelligence. *Intelligence, 47*, 122–133. https://doi.org/10.1016/j.intell.2014.09.004

Grudnik, J. L., & Kranzler, J. H. (2001). Meta-analysis of the relationship between intelligence and inspection time. *Intelligence, 29*(6), 523–535. https://doi.org/10.1016/S0160-2896(01)00078-2

Hambrick, D. Z., Kane, M. J., & Engle, R. W. (2005). The role of working memory in higher-level cognition: Domain-specific versus domain-general perspectives. In R. J. Sternberg & J. E. Pretz (eds.), *Cognition and intelligence* (pp. 104–121). New York: Cambridge University Press.

Hasher, L., & Zacks, R. T. (1988). Working memory, comprehension, and aging: A review and a new view. In G. H. Bower (ed.), *The psychology of learning and motivation* (vol. 22, pp. 193-225). New York: Academic Press.

Hunt, E. (2005). Information processing and intelligence: Where we are and where we are going. In R. J. Sternberg & J. E. Pretz (eds.), *Cognition and intelligence* (pp. 1-25). New York: Cambridge University Press.

Hunt, E. (2011). *Human intelligence.* Cambridge: Cambridge University Press.

Hunt, E., Lunneborg, C., & Lewis, J. (1975). What does it mean to be high verbal? *Cognitive Psychology, 7*, 194–227.

Jensen, A. R. (1998). The *g* factor. Westport, CT: Praeger.

Joormann, J., & Gotlib, I. H. (2008). Updating the contents of working memory in depression: Interference from irrelevant negative material. *Journal of Abnormal Psychology, 117*(1), 182–192.

Kane, M. J., Gross, G. M., Chun, C. A., & Smeekens, B. A. (2017). For whom the mind wanders, and when, varies across laboratory and daily-life settings. *Psychological Science.* https://doi.org/10.1111/j.1467-9280.2007.01948.x

Kane, M. J., Hambrick, D. Z., Tuholski, S. W., Wilhelm, O., Payne, T. W., & Engle, R. W. (2004). The generality of working memory capacity: A latent-variable approach to verbal and visuospatial memory span and reasoning. *Journal of Experimental Psychology: General, 133*(2), 189–217. https://doi.org/10.1037/0096-3445.133.2.189

Kleider-Offutt, H. M., Clevinger, A. M., & Bond, A. D. (2016). Working memory and cognitive load in the legal system: Influences on police shooting decisions, interrogation, and jury decisions. *Journal of Applied Research in Memory and Cognition, 5*(4), 426–433.

Kranzler, J. H., & Jensen, A. R. (1989). Inspection time and intelligence: A meta-analysis. *Intelligence, 13*, 329–347.

Kyllonen, P. C., & Christal, R. E. (1990). Reasoning ability is (little more than) working-memory capacity?! *Intelligence, 14*(4), 389–433. https://doi.org/10.1016/S0160-2896(05)80012-1

Larson, G. E., & Alderton, D. L. (1990). Reaction time variability and intelligence: A "worst performance" analysis of individual differences. *Intelligence, 14*, 309–325.

Lee, J., & Park, S. (2005). Working memory impairments in schizophrenia: A meta-analysis. *Journal of Abnormal Psychology, 114*(599–611).

Lopez, N., Previc, F. H., Fischer, J., Heitz, R. P., & Engle, R. W. (2012). Effects of sleep deprivation on cognitive performance by United States Air Force pilots. *Journal of Applied Research in Memory and Cognition, 1*(1), 27–33.

Mackintosh, N. J. (2011). *IQ and human intelligence* (2nd ed.). Oxford: Oxford University Press.

Martin, J. D., Shipstead, Z., Harrison, T.L., Reddick, T.S., Bunting, M., & Engle, R.W. (Unpublished). The role of maintenance and disengagement in predicting reading comprehension and vocabulary learning. MS.

Matzke, D., Dolan, C. V., & Molenaar, D. (2010). The issue of power in the identification of "g" with lower-order factors. *Intelligence, 38*(3), 336–344. https://doi.org/10.1016/j .intell.2010.02.001

Moray, N. (1967). Where is capacity limited? A survey and a model. *Acta Psychologica, 27*, 84–92.

Mumaw, R. J., & Pellegrino, J. W. (1984). Individual differences in complex spatial processing. *Journal of Educational Psychology, 75*(5), 920–939.

Neisser, U. (1967). *Cognitive psychology*. New York: Appleton-Century-Crofts.

Nettelbeck, T. (1987). Inspection time and intelligence. In P. A. Vernon (ed.), *Speed of information-processing and intelligence* (pp. 295–346). Norwood, NJ: Ablex.

Nettelbeck, T., & Lally, M. (1976). Inspection time and measured intelligence. *British Journal of Psychology, 67*(1), 17–22. https://doi.org/10.1111/j.2044-8295.1976 .tb01493.x

Newell, A. & Simon, H. (1972). *Human problem solving*. Englewood Cliffs, NJ: Prentice Hall.

Oberauer, K. (2002). Access to information in working memory: Exploring the focus of attention. *Journal of Experimental Psychology: Learning, Memory, and Cognition, 28*(3), 411–421. https://doi.org/10.1037//0278-7393.28.3.411

Oberauer, K., Schulze, R., Wilhelm, O., & Süß, H.-M. (2005). Working memory and intelligence – Their correlation and their relation: Comment on Ackerman, Beier, and Boyle (2005). *Psychological Bulletin, 131*(1), 61–65. https://doi.org/10.1037/ 0033-2909.131.1.61

Oberauer, K., Süß, H.-M., Wilhelm, O., & Sander, N. (2007). Individual differences in working memory capacity and reasoning ability. In A. R. A. Conway, C. Jarrold, M. J. Kane, A. Miyake, & J. N. Towse (eds.), *Variation in working memory* (pp. 49–75). New York: Oxford University Press.

Raven, J. C. (1965). *Advanced Progressive Matrices Sets I and II*. London: Lewis.

Redick, T. S. (2016). On the relation of working memory and multitasking: Memory span and synthetic work performance. *Journal of Applied Research in Memory and Cognition, 5*(4), 401–409.

Salthouse, T. A. (1996). The processing speed theory of adult age differences in cognition. *Psychological Review, 103*(3), 403–428.

Schmader, T. (2010). Stereotype threat deconstructed. *Current Directions in Psychological Science, 19*(1), 14–18.

Schmiedek, F., Oberauer, K., Wilhelm, O., Süß, H.-M., & Wittmann, W. W. (2007). Individual differences in components of reaction time distributions and their relations to working memory and intelligence. *Journal of Experimental Psychology: General, 136*(3), 414–429. https://doi.org/10.1037/0096-3445.136.3.414

Shah, P., & Miyake, A. (1996). The separability of working memory resources for spatial thinking and language processing: An individual differences approach. *Journal of Experimental Psychology: General, 125*(1), 4–27. https://doi.org/10.1037/0096-3445 .125.1.4

Sheppard, L. D., & Vernon, P. A. (2008). Intelligence and speed of information-processing: A review of 50 years of research. *Personality and Individual Differences, 44*(3), 535–551. https://doi.org/10.1016/j.paid.2007.09.015

Shipstead, Z., Harrison, T. L., & Engle, R. W. (2016). Working memory capacity and fluid intelligence: Maintenance and disengagement. *Perspectives on Psychological Science, 11*(6), 771–799. https://doi.org/10.1177/1745691616650647

Skogan, A. H., Zeiler, P., Egeland, J., Rohrer-Baumgartner, N., & Urnes, A.-G. (2014). Inhibition and working memory in young preschool children with symptoms of ADHD and/or oppositional-defiant disorder. *Child Neuropsychology, 20*(5), 607–624.

Spearman, C. (1904). "General intelligence," objectively determined and measured. *American Journal of Psychology, 15*(2), 201–292.

Spearman, C. (1927). *The abilities of man.* London: Macmillan.

Stanovich, K. E. (2009). *What intelligence tests miss: The psychology of rational thought.* New Haven, CT: Yale University Press.

Sternberg, R. J. (1977). Component processes in analogical reasoning. *Psychological Review, 84*(4), 353–378. https://doi.org/10.1037/0033-295X.84.4.353

Sternberg, R. J. (1983). Components of human intelligence. *Cognition, 5*, 1-48.

Sternberg, R. J. (1985). Introduction: What is an information-processing approach to human abilities? In R. J. Sternberg (ed.), *Human abilities: An information processing approach* (pp. 1–4). New York: W. H. Freeman.

Sternberg, R. J. (1999). The theory of successful intelligence. *Review of General Psychology, 3*, 292-316.

Sternberg, S. (1966). High-speed scanning in human memory. *Science, 153*, 652-654.

Süß, H.-M., Oberauer, K., Wittmann, W. W., Wilhelm, O., & Schulze, R. (2002). Working-memory capacity explains reasoning ability – and a little bit more. *Intelligence, 30*, 261–288.

Thomson, G. H. (1916). A hierarchy without a general factor. *British Journal of Psychology, 8*, 271–281.

Thorndike, E. L. (1898). Animal intelligence: An experimental study of the associate processes in animals. *Psychological Review Monograph Supplement, 2*(4), 1–8.

Thurstone, L. L. (1948). *Primary mental abilities.* Chicago: University of Chicago Press.

Triesman, A. M. (1964). Monitoring and storage of irrelevant messages and selective attention. *Quarterly Journal of Experimental Psychology, 12*, 242-248.

Turner, M. L., & Engle, R. W. (1989). Is working memory capacity task dependent? *Journal of Memory and Language, 28*, 127-154. doi:10.1016/0749-596X(89)90040- 5

Unsworth, N., & Engle, R. W. (2005). Individual differences in working memory capacity and learning: Evidence from the serial reaction time task. *Memory & Cognition, 33*(2), 213-220.

Unsworth, N., Redick, T. S., Lakey, C. E., & Young, D. L. (2010). Lapses in sustained attention and their relation to executive control and fluid abilities: An individual differences investigation. *Intelligence, 38*(1), 111–122. https://doi.org/10.1016/j.intell.2009.08.002

van Ravenzwaaij, D., Brown, S., & Wagenmakers, E. J. (2011). An integrated perspective on the relation between response speed and intelligence. *Cognition, 119*(3), 381–393. https://doi.org/10.1016/j.cognition.2011.02.002

Vickers, D., & Smith, P. L. (1986). The rationale for the inspection time index. *Personality and Individual Differences, 7,* 609–624.

Wason, P. C. (1968). Reasoning about a rule. *Quarterly Journal of Experimental Psychology, 20*(3), 273-281.

Watson, J. B. (1913). Psychology as the behaviorist views it. *Psychological Review, 20,* 158–177. https://doi.org/10.1037/h0074428

Watson, J. M., Memmott, M. G., Moffitt, C. C., Coleman, J., Turrill, J., Fernandez, A., & Strayer, D. L. (2016). On working memory and a productivity illusion in distracted driving. *Journal of Applied Research in Memory and Cognition, 5*(4), 445–453.

White, M. (1993). The inspection time rationale fails to demonstrate that inspection time is a measure of the speed of post-sensory processing. *Personality and Individual Differences, 15*(2), 185–198. https://doi.org/10.1016/0191-8869(93)90025-X

Wissler, C. (1901). The correlation of mental and physical tests. *Psychological Review [Monograph], 16*(suppl. 3), 1–62.

6 Biological Approaches to Intelligence

RICHARD J. HAIER

In the last decade, biological approaches have dramatically advanced our understanding of human intelligence. The weight of evidence is overwhelming from large-sample neuroimaging and DNA studies in showing that genetic factors and brain characteristics are major influences on why some people are smarter than others. This progress energizes the hunt for specific genes that influence intelligence, perhaps many hundreds of them, and sets the stage for identifying how these genes work to effect brain structure and function and their development. This chapter reviews key studies that support this conclusion. For a more in-depth examination of these research advances, see Haier (2017).

Genes influence virtually all complex human behaviors to some extent (Polderman et al., 2015; Turkheimer, 2000). We know that genetic influences on intelligence are strong from an abundance of modern studies of many identical twins reared together and many others separated at an early age and reared apart by different families (Bouchard, 2009; Deary, Johnson, & Houlihan, 2009), as well as from DNA studies with large samples (Davies et al., 2015; Davies et al., 2017; Rietveld et al., 2013). Since genes work through biology, there must be a biological basis to intelligence. A major challenge for neuroscience is to identify specific properties of the brain that are responsible for intelligence. Modern neuroimaging research techniques are providing important data and insights.

Before describing the newest findings, this chapter will review some earlier, pre-imaging attempts to study the relationship between brain properties and intelligence. These early studies are important historically because they introduce concepts of current interest such as whether or not intelligence is localized in the brain and whether efficient communication among brain areas helps explain intelligence. Then we will describe the first phase of neuroimaging/intelligence studies, beginning in 1988 and ending with a comprehensive review in 2007 that proposed a specific model of the neuro-anatomy of intelligence. By today's standards, these early imaging studies had tiny samples and the analyses were unsophisticated. Nonetheless, they demonstrate the power of neuroimaging. Many of the early findings have proved reliable, based on subsequent better studies. The most recent studies combine DNA, neuroimaging, and intelligence assessments in large samples of people collected by multinational consortia. These findings are considered a second phase of modern intelligence research and the results are compelling because they include large, diverse samples, sophisticated quantitative analyses, and independent replications. The new DNA studies are the basis for advances in molecular genetics and the hunt for genes that contribute to the relevant brain characteristics identified by neuroimaging. These developments have moved intelligence research beyond the limits of psychometric analyses of intelligence tests to modern neuroscience and into the brain itself. It is a historic shift.

Before we begin, two more brief introductory comments are necessary. First, the definition of intelligence and how it is measured develop hand in hand. Consensus agreement is not necessary for progress. After all, there is still controversy about the definition of a "gene" (Silverman, 2004). Neuroimaging offers the possibility for new, objective assessment of intelligence using brain parameters (Haier, 2009a, 2009b). Already, psychometric measures of intelligence, once alleged to be "meaningless" by some critics, have demonstrated powerful new validity based on their relationship to brain structure and function. Understanding these relationships and their genetic basis is now the focus of many research groups around the world.

Second, once any brain property is found to be associated with intelligence, a separate issue is how that property develops and how it may be influenced by other biological and nonbiological factors to create individual differences. Genes turn on and off throughout a lifetime. The triggers for these on/off switches may depend on interaction with environmental factors like stress or other biological factors like hormone fluctuations associated with aging. The emerging field of **epigenetic research** focuses on how such factors interact with each other. The importance of identifying these factors and interactions is that there may be ways to influence them to maximize intelligence, especially during brain development in early life. In some cases, treatments might be possible for the low IQ that defines intellectual disability. It may even be possible to develop drugs to increase IQ across the normal range so that everyone is smarter, just as personalized genetic medicine hopes to improve health. As we learn more and more about brain properties and neural mechanisms associated with intelligence, the possibilities for increasing intelligence become less and less far-fetched.

Understanding the biological basis of intelligence can be a complicated enterprise. As you read this chapter, keep in mind the following: (1) No story about the brain is simple. (2) No one study is definitive. (3) It takes many studies and many years to sort out inconsistent results and establish a weight of evidence (Haier, 2017).

Pre-Imaging Studies

The brain is constantly active as billions of neurons react to chemical and electrical interactions. The main measure of the electrical activity produced as neurons fire on and off is the **electroencephalogram** (EEG). EEG is measured millisecond by milli-second in real time from multiple electrodes on the scalp and each electrode produces scribbly waves with peaks and valleys that reflect fluctuations in electrical activity. Since the 1960s, many studies have correlated EEG wave forms assessed under a wide variety of experimental conditions and stimulus types, with measures of intelligence. In general, modest correlations have been reported between .3 and .6 (Jensen, 1998).

Brain Waves and Efficient Information Processing

One explanation for the existence of the correlations in brain wave activity and intelligence is that higher-IQ subjects process information *more efficiently* than lower-IQ subjects. Some studies used a variation of real-time EEG that is called the **average evoked response (AER)**. This method collects EEG for a short time; say 500 milliseconds after a single stimulus like a light flash. The flash is repeated many times and the 500 millisecond EEG after each flash is averaged together to create the average evoked response to the flash. Schafer reported different AERs to unexpected stimuli (e.g., occasional flashes brighter than most other flashes) were found in higher-IQ subjects that reflected a weaker neural response (Schafer, 1982). In other words, he suggested, "A brain that uses fewer neurons to process a foreknown sensory input saves its limited neural energy and functions in an inherently efficient manner" (p. 184). Other studies also reported AER differences in higher-IQ subjects that suggested they had faster minds (Chalke & Ertl, 1965; Ertl & Schafer, 1969). Another early study reported that the complexity of AER wave-forms was greater in higher-IQ subjects than in lower-IQ subjects, suggesting less neural transmission error and more efficiency in the high-IQ subjects (Hendrickson & Hendrickson, 1980). Because EEG measured brain activity, these early studies raised exciting possibilities for understanding the neural basis of intelligence. Unfortunately, most of these early findings were based on idiosyncratic EEG methods so not surprisingly they did not replicate reliably (Barrett & Eysenck, 1994).

A more recent series of AER studies focused on how high- and low-IQ individuals differ with respect to the temporal sequence of activation of different brain areas as various cognitive stimuli are processed. Using multiple electrodes across the entire scalp and mathematical interpolations of the waveforms among the electrodes, researchers can now create maps of brain activity as information flows among cortical areas millisecond by millisecond. These studies suggest that high- and low-IQ subjects show differences in the sequence of brain activity across multiple areas during performance on cognitive tasks related to intelligence. The differences have been interpreted as consistent with the view that higher IQ is associated with more efficient brain processing (Neubauer & Fink, 2008, 2009).

EEG methods were never sufficiently standardized among researchers and gener-ally EEG research has been replaced by more advanced neuroimaging as discussed later in this chapter. The primary historical relevance of these EEG/AER studies is with respect to introducing the concept of *brain efficiency*, which is now investigated with modern imaging studies. We will cover these studies later in the chapter.

Lesion Studies

Figure 6.1 illustrates the four lobes of the brain (frontal, temporal, parietal, and occipital) and their primary functions. Where in the brain is intelligence located? It has long been observed that significant brain damage often does not result in a dramatic lowering of IQ. Even "psychosurgery" to sever the connections between the frontal lobes and the rest of the brain, practiced in earlier decades (but rarely used today) to treat schizophrenia and other mental conditions, produced little apparent impairment in tests of general intelligence (O'Callaghan & Carroll, 1982). Similarly, early animal lesion experiments found that the severity of impaired performance during learning experiments was related to the size rather than to the location of a

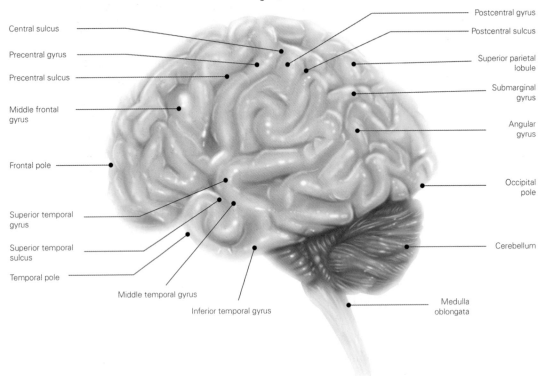

Brain Anatomy (Lateral View)

Central sulcus

Precentral gyrus

Precentral sulcus

Middle frontal gyrus

Frontal pole

Superior temporal gyrus

Superior temporal sulcus

Temporal pole

Middle temporal gyrus

Inferior temporal gyrus

Postcentral gyrus

Postcentral sulcus

Superior parietal lobule

Submarginal gyrus

Angular gyrus

Occipital pole

Cerebellum

Medulla oblongata

Figure 6.1 Anatomy of the brain. Although human brain tissue may look the same everywhere to the naked eye, there are areas with different functions and tissue makeups. Some of the major anatomical areas of the cerebral hemispheres are labeled here. Most brain imaging studies of intelligence have findings in the outer cortex.

brain injury (Lashley, 1964). This indicated that general intelligence might be diffusely represented throughout the brain rather than residing in specific "centers." It may also be the case that non-damaged areas take over the functions of damaged areas after some period of time. Retrospective clinical studies of humans after brain injury do not provide definitive maps of "intelligence areas" and the brain injury data related to intelligence are inconsistent (Duncan, Emslie, Williams, Johnson, & Freer, 1996). As discussed later, however, new neuroimaging data of lesion patients shows considerable progress (Glascher et al., 2010; Glascher et al., 2009).

Experimental animal lesion studies suggest one set of brain areas may be related to performance on specific problem-solving tasks and another set of areas may be related to a general problem-solving ability (R. Thompson, Crinella, & Yu, 1990). In these studies, researchers created lesions in more than 1,000 rats to determine "the functional organization of the brain in relation to problem solving ability and intelligence" (p. 7). They systematically created surgical lesions in 50 brain areas; each rat received a lesion to only one area (and there were at least seven rats with each lesion). Following recovery from the surgery, each rat was trained to perform a battery of problem-solving tasks. A control group of rats with sham surgery was also trained on the same battery of tasks. The tasks included a variety of climbing detour problems, puzzle box problems, and maze learning problems.

The results identified eight brain areas where lesions caused significant impairment in the performance of all tasks in the battery. These areas were thought to represent a nonspecific mechanism that influenced general problem-solving ability, termed "biological g." Lesions in any of these eight areas resulted in poor performance on all tasks. In the next step, the statistical technique of factor analysis (described in Chapter 4) was used to determine how performance on each problem-solving task in the sham group was related to performance on the other tasks. One factor accounted for most task variance, just as one factor accounts for most variance among humans on psychometric measures of intelligence. This main factor is usually referred to as "g," following Spearman (1904) who first described a general (g) factor of intelligence common to all tests of mental abilities. In the rat data, the g factor was most related to the complex tasks, just as it is in humans. Each of the 50 lesion locations was ranked for its statistical relationship to this g factor. Six regions were most related and these may represent those brain areas required for good performance on complex tasks, similar to Spearman's "psychometric g" in humans.

The importance of this elaborate rat lesion study is that it indicates specific brain areas that underlie individual differences in performance of general problem-solving ability. To the extent that the tasks used in the rats are similar to measures of human intelligence (and this seems also to be the case in mice; Matzel et al., 2003), the search for analogous areas in humans could be successful. Of course, the rat and human brains are quite different and experimental lesion studies cannot be done in humans. But if human "intelligence areas" exist, modern noninvasive neuroimaging techniques should be able to identify them. We will review studies that have imaged patients with brain lesions as the second part of the next section.

The First Phase of Neuroimaging Studies (1988–2007)

After a hundred years of research based on statistical analyses of paper and pencil tests and fifty years of EEG studies with low spatial resolution recordings from scalp electrodes, new brain imaging technologies changed the course of intelligence research in the 1980s. For the first time, researchers could make reliable measurements of brain function and structure in live human beings and relate them to mental ability test scores. It was the beginning of modern cognitive neuroscience approaches to understanding intelligence. Every image was exciting and the earliest findings clearly showed that intelligence test scores were related to quantifiable brain characteristics, findings that would be impossible if, as many critics charged, these test scores were meaningless.

Positron Emission Tomography (PET)

Positron emission tomography (PET) scanning was the first modern imaging technique applied to the study of intelligence. It provides unique information about brain function. The technique is based on injecting a low-level radioactive tracer into a subject. The tracer is chemically designed to carry a positron-emitting chemical isotope like fluorine18 (F^{18}) into neurons by attaching the F^{18} to a special glucose. The result is fluorodeoxyglucose (FDG). Glucose is sugar, and every time a neuron fires, glucose is consumed. The harder a brain area is working, the more glucose it uses and the more FDG is deposited in that area. PET scanning reveals the amount of radiation coming from the FDG in all parts of the brain and computes an image showing where the most activity occurred. This is a measure of **glucose metabolic rate (GMR)**. The pattern of GMR in the brain changes depending on what the brain is doing following the injection of the FDG. For example, the pattern will differ if the person is awake or asleep, dreaming or not dreaming, doing mental arithmetic or silent reading. This is a powerful technique for psychology because it ties regional brain function to psychological processes.

One of the earliest uses of PET was in a series of studies to determine whether there are "intelligence centers" in the brain. In the first study (Haier et al., 1988), eight males were injected with FDG and then solved problems on the Raven's Advanced Progressive Matrices (RAPM). The study was limited to eight participants because each scan cost $2,500 and no grant funds were available at this early stage of PET research. The RAPM is a standard test of nonverbal abstract reasoning problems with a high loading on the g factor. Each test item is a matrix of symbols arranged according to a pattern or rule, but one symbol is missing from the matrix. Once the pattern or rule is discerned, the missing symbol can be identified from eight choices. The test has 36 items that get progressively more difficult. The harder any brain area worked while solving these problems, the more FDG would accumulate.

Control subjects performed a simple test of attention that required no problem solving. Results revealed that several cortical regions distributed throughout the brain were uniquely activated during the RAPM (i.e., higher GMR) compared to the control conditions. Taking an approach that was novel at the time for imaging studies, each person's RAPM score was correlated with his GMR in each cortical region that was significantly different from the comparison tasks. The expectation was that the higher the score, the higher the GMR would be in these brain areas because better test performance would be associated with more brain activity. Several correlations were statistically significant but, surprisingly, they were all negative (–.72 to –.84). That is, high RAPM scores were correlated with *low* GMR. The researchers interpreted this as evidence consistent with a brain efficiency hypothesis for complex problem solving and intelligence. The **brain efficiency hypothesis** predicts that higher intelligence test scores will be associated with less brain activity because more efficient use of brain resources is what makes a smart brain. Brain resources could include, for example, more gray matter with more neurons and synapses and/or more white matter connections among brain areas (see Figure 6.2).

At the time, inverse correlations between brain activation and test performance were novel and researchers wondered what might make a brain efficient. In a second study, Haier et al. tested whether there were brain activity decreases after learning, using the computer game *Tetris* (Haier, Siegel, MacLachlan, et al., 1992). Eight subjects completed PET before and after 50 days of practice. At the time, *Tetris* had just been introduced in the United States and none of the subjects had ever seen or played it. As predicted by an efficiency hypothesis, activity decreased in some brain areas after practice even though game performance was better and required faster processing and decision making for more stimuli than at the baseline. Moreover, each subject in the *Tetris* experiment completed the RAPM on a separate occasion. Those subjects with the highest scores on the RAPM showed the largest GMR decreases with practice, especially in frontal cortical and in cingulate areas (Haier, Siegel, Tang, Abel, & Buchsbaum, 1992). Thus, the most intelligent subjects showed the greatest brain efficiency with learning.

After the *Tetris* study, Haier et al. also tested whether people with mild to moderate intellectual disability (IQ between 50 and 75; n = 10) of unknown cause had *higher* cerebral GMR than 10 normal controls (Haier, Chueh, Touchette, Lott, et al., 1995). A group with Down syndrome (n = 7) was included for comparison. At the time, no other PET studies of low-IQ individuals had been done, and the expectation of most researchers was that they would find lower GMR reflecting brain damage. That low-IQ people would show high GMR because they had

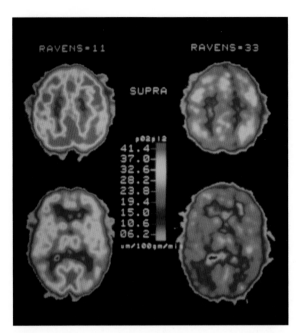

Figure 6.2 PET scans of the brain. An upper and a lower slice of brain are shown for two individuals. These scans were made with PET while each person solved reasoning problems. The person on the left had a low score; the person on the right had a high score. Red and yellow colors show where the brain was more active during the problem solving. Note the high scoring person on the right used less energy than the low scoring person on the left. This was opposite of what was expected and was interpreted as evidence that higher intelligence was associated with an efficient brain. (Photo courtesy of R. Haier)

over-active brains (i.e., the inefficiency hypothesis) was counterintuitive, but this is exactly what was found. GMR for the normal controls was lower than for either of the low-IQ groups. These results were consistent with the brain inefficiency prediction, although in Down syndrome the explanation for increased GMR may be related to a compensatory brain reaction in response to a very early stage of dementia (Haier, Alkire, et al., 2003; Haier, Head, Head, & Lott, 2008; Head, Lott, Patterson, Doran, & Haier, 2007).

Using PET to Investigate Sex Differences in Cognitive Ability

In addition to general intelligence, PET has been used to investigate a specific cognitive ability, including one of the first studies to examine sex differences with neuroimaging (Haier & Benbow, 1995). Male and female college students were selected for high or average mathematical reasoning ability using the SAT. Each person then solved mathematical reasoning problems during FDG uptake. Based on the brain efficiency hypothesis, researchers expected students selected for high math ability would have lower cerebral GMR than the subjects selected for average ability.

A total of 44 right-handed students participated. Eleven males and 11 females had SAT-Math scores (for college entrance) of 700 or higher (95th percentile of college-bound high school seniors). Another 11 males and 11 females had SAT-Math scores between 410 and 540 (30th to 68th percentile). Contrary to the prediction of brain efficiency, the subjects selected for high math ability did not show lower cerebral GMR. In the 22 males, there were, however, positive correlations between GMR in temporal lobe areas (bilaterally) and math score attained on the test given during the FDG uptake period. These correlations ranged between .42 and .55 for the areas of middle, inferior, and posterior temporal cortex in left and in right hemispheres. These differences in magnitude of correlations may reflect random noise with only 22 participants; they may also reflect different roles in mathematical reasoning for these brain areas. There were no significant correlations between GMR and math score for the 22 females. Thus, although it failed to substantiate brain efficiency in the high-ability group, this study suggested a clear sex difference. Recent imaging research has clarified sex differences in math performance (Keller & Menon, 2009), and new structural imaging studies of intelligence described later in the chapter also reveal sex differences. Sex differences mean that not all brains work the same way and this is the fundamental basis for approaching neuroimaging studies with an individual differences perspective.

One inherent challenge with functional imaging is that results depend on the problem-solving task used, so any correlations between brain activity and intelligence test scores can be confounded with specific task demands. In another study, PET was used in students while they watched videos with no problem-solving task. Based on 44 scans, activation during this "passive" task was compared with RAPM scores. Activation in posterior areas was positively correlated with scores on the RAPM (Haier, White, & Alkire, 2003). Since watching videos had no problem-solving component, it appears that more intelligent people activate sensory processing and integration brain areas more than less intelligent ones. The results of this study are consistent with the view that brain areas related to intelligence are distributed throughout the brain and that intelligence depends on the integration of activity among these areas.

It should be noted that one PET study of 13 subjects reported that only frontal lobe areas were activated when tasks related to different levels of "g" were performed (Duncan et al., 2000). However, the subjects did not complete any IQ testing so we don't know their level of intelligence (this is relevant because high-IQ subjects might need to expend less effort). Moreover, the tasks used did not represent a sufficient range of g-loadings, only a single trial of each task was used (dramatically reducing reliability), and the small sample size of this study limited the statistical power to determine whether other areas might also be activated. In fact, the idea that intelligence is related to activation of only frontal lobe areas is not consistent with either previous or subsequent imaging studies and is considered unlikely by most researchers, especially in view of the newer research described in phase 2 of imaging studies found later in this chapter.

Magnetic Resonance Imaging

Magnetic resonance imaging (MRI) is based on strong magnetic fields that create a north/south alignment of protons in hydrogen atoms found in water throughout the body. This alignment by itself does not produce an image. However, when radio frequencies are rapidly pulsed into the magnetic field, each pulse briefly throws the protons out of the north/south alignment. Since the body is still in the magnetic field, the protons snap back into alignment between pulses. As this sequence is repeated rapidly, different radio frequencies are produced from the changing energy emanating from the spinning protons. Antenna-like coils inside the scanner detect these frequencies. By using a gradient magnetic field, the radio frequencies produced also contain spatial information that is mathematically converted to an image. Since the brain has high water content, it shows considerable structural detail with this technique. MRI can also be used to produce functional images (fMRI) by rapidly scanning changes in oxygen content in blood to infer blood flow to different brain areas. Prabhakaran and colleagues first used fMRI to study intelligence using RAPM items (Prabhakaran, Smith, Desmond, Glover, & Gabrieli, 1997). A number of fMRI studies of intelligence subsequently appeared; most findings supported earlier PET results (Jung & Haier, 2007).

Functional MRI is easier and cheaper to use than PET because no radioactive isotopes are required, and the shorter time resolution allows for better experimental control. Nonetheless, interpretation of fMRI results, like those in PET studies, is dependent on the cognitive tasks used during the scanning. Structural MRI results are the same no matter what the cognitive or mental state of the subject, so interpretation of structural imaging results is more straightforward.

MRI Studies Examining Gray Matter Concentrations and Intelligence

Structural MRI studies confirmed earlier research using head measurements that showed higher intelligence was associated with bigger brains (Willerman, Schultz, Rutledge, & Bigler, 1991). It is now generally accepted that the correlation between brain size, as measured by MRI scans, and most intelligence measures is about $r = .40$ (Gignac, Vernon, & Wickett, 2003; McDaniel, 2005). But is whole brain size the most important variable or is the size of specific areas more important? This was difficult to determine with methods based on defining a region-of-interest (ROI) and then outlining this region on individual brain images, where there often is no clear visual boundary between one area and another, especially in cortex. Newer techniques to assess gray and white matter concentrations in the brain addressed this problem. **Voxel-Based Morphometry (VBM)** uses algorithms to differentiate and quantify gray and white matter for each voxel of the image throughout the entire brain. A voxel is a three-dimensional pixel that has depth as well as height

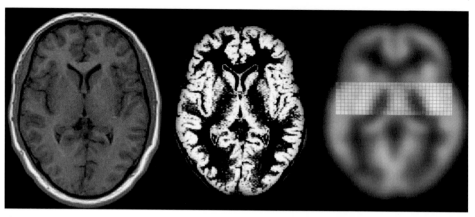

Figure 6.3 MRI scans of the brain. Left image is an MRI scan before VBM processing; middle scan shows first step of VBM processing to segment gray and white matter by algorithm; right scan illustrates how each square voxel is superimposed on entire image. Gray and white matter densities are computed within each voxel and this quantified value can be compared to other variables like age or IQ score. (Photo courtesy of R. Haier)

and width. This means volume can be calculated in addition to area. No predefined ROIs are required for this technique. Even newer, the geometric assessment of cortical thickness has advantages over VBM and may be more accurate. **Diffusion Tensor Imaging (DTI)** shows white matter tracts in great detail. These methods have been applied to intelligence studies (see Figure 6.3).

Using data collected from two research centers, gray and white matter assessed with VBM was compared to Full-Scale IQ (FSIQ) scores in 47 normal volunteers (Haier, Jung, Yeo, Head, & Alkire, 2004). The amount of gray matter was strongly correlated with FSIQ in six areas of the frontal lobes as well as in five areas of the temporal lobes. White matter showed the strongest relationship to intelligence near the one area where Albert Einstein's brain differed from controls (Diamond, Scheibel, Murphy, & Harvey, 1985) (see Figure 6.4).

However, when these data were analyzed separately for males and females (Haier, Jung, Yeo, Head, & Alkire, 2005), a completely different picture emerged. The areas where brain tissue was correlated with IQ in the males were different from those in the females. Frontal areas were more prominent in the females; posterior areas were more prominent in the males. Since the men and women were matched on IQ scores, this was a surprising result. Could it be that evolution has created at least two different brain architectures equally related to intelligence? If so, there is likely to be considerable overlap between the sexes. But, as noted earlier, this possibility implies that not all brains work in the same way and that there may be alternative combinations of brain parameters that lead to equal cognitive abilities. This view reinforces the importance of individual differences for interpreting imaging results and the need to analyze data separately for males and females. Schmithorst and Holland (2007) demonstrated this convincingly using fMRI during a verb generation

Figure 6.4 The brain of Albert Einstein. Albert Einstein's brain was studied after he died. Areas in the frontal and parietal lobes showed more of one type of brain cell called glia.

task. They studied over 300 children and adolescents aged 5–18 years old, and showed brain development pattern differences between males and females for the areas related to intelligence scores; they also showed sex differences in the connectivity among the areas related to intelligence, with girls showing greater inter-hemispheric connectivity with age (Schmithorst & Holland, 2007).

One major issue not addressed in most of the early imaging studies concerned the intelligence measures used. Most used only one measure either as a summary of several intelligence factors (like IQ scores) or as an estimate of the g factor (the general factor underlying all mental tests, as first identified by Spearman [1904]). Colom and colleagues addressed this issue in two complementary studies using voxel-based morphometry (VBM) to assess gray matter. First, they correlated gray matter volumes with three subtest scores of the Wechsler Adult Intelligence Scale (WAIS) IQ test. Each subtest has a different g-loading: low, medium, and high. The higher the g-loading, the more gray matter clusters were correlated to the subtest score (Colom, Jung, & Haier, 2006a). In the second study, they used Jensen's Method of Correlated Vectors (Jensen, 1998) and showed a near-perfect correlation between the g-loading of the subtest and the number of brain areas where gray matter correlated with the subtest score (Colom, Jung, & Haier, 2006b). A more recent study expands these findings (Roman et al., 2014).

Efficiency Follow-up Studies (MRI)
One hypothesis to explain increased brain efficiency is that decreased activity results from an increase in gray matter. More gray matter might mean that having

more brain resources would result in less work required for solving a problem. To examine this hypothesis, Haier et al. conducted a new study using Magnetic Resonance Imaging (MRI), a technique that uses magnetic fields to generate images of structural and functional details of the brain (Haier, Karama, Leyba, & Jung, 2009) to assess structural and functional brain changes after learning. (Magnetic Resonance Imaging was explained in much greater detail earlier in this chapter.) The subjects were adolescent girls; 15 played *Tetris* for three months and 11 controls did not. The functional (fMRI) results showed activity decreases after three months of practice, especially in frontal areas (whereas the 1992 study in young men found decreases mostly in parietal areas). The structural MRI results showed thicker cortex, relative to controls, in the girls who practiced *Tetris*; these changes were most significant in the frontal and temporal lobe regions. Contrary to the researchers' prediction, there was no overlap between the structural and functional changes, suggesting that efficiency is not a function of increased gray matter. Moreover, this study, unlike the 1992 study, found no relationship between brain changes and intelligence scores.

Both this study and the one from 1992 had small samples with limited statistical power to identify robust, consistent results. False positive results were common among the early studies but there was so much excitement about the imaging methods that many underpowered studies were published. This was a central problem in most of the studies in phase 1, which can be called exploratory. As we shall see, phase 2 studies were better funded and had larger sample sizes. Nonetheless, there are some additional phase 1 studies to summarize before moving to phase 2 because they illustrate a sequence of thinking about intelligence and brain efficiency.

The P-FIT Model of Intelligence

In December 2003, the International Society of Intelligence Researchers (ISIR) hosted a symposium at their annual meeting on brain-imaging studies of intelligence, the first symposium of its kind. One outcome of that symposium was an appreciation of an emerging field of "neuro-intelligence" research. At that meeting, two researchers – Rex Jung and I – independently concluded that the brain areas most likely involved with intelligence were distributed throughout the brain rather than only in the frontal lobes. Subsequently, Jung and Haier worked together and reviewed the 37 neuroimaging studies of intelligence that existed at the time. These included functional imaging (PET, fMRI, MRI spectroscopy) and structural MRI imaging; a wide variety of intelligence measures were represented. Brain areas related to intelligence were identified with some consistency across these methodologically disparate studies (Jung & Haier, 2007). These areas were distributed throughout the brain but were most prominent in the parietal and frontal areas. Out of this work grew a model called the **parieto-frontal integration theory (P-FIT) of intelligence**, which emphasizes the importance of information flow among these areas.

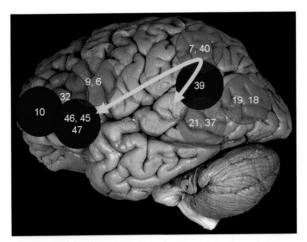

Figure 6.5 The P-FIT model brain regions associated with performance on measures of intelligence. Numbers refer to Brodmann areas (BAs); blue circles denote predominant left hemisphere associations; red circles denote predominant bilateral associations; yellow arrow denotes a critical tract of white matter, the arcuate fasciculus. (Courtesy of Rex Jung)

The P-FIT areas are shown in Figure 6.5. These areas may not be engaged during problem solving/reasoning all at once. They can be characterized as stages of information processing generally moving from the back of the brain toward the front. In the first stage, temporal and occipital areas process sensory information: the extrastriate cortex (BAs 18 and 19) and the fusiform gyrus (BA 37), involved with recognition, imagery, and elaboration of visual inputs, as well as Wernicke's area (BA 22) for analysis and elaboration of syntax of auditory information. The second stage implicates integration and abstraction of this information by parietal BAs 39 (angular gyrus), 40 (supra-marginal gyrus), and 7 (superior parietal lobule). In the third stage, these parietal areas interact with the frontal lobes, which serve to problem solve, evaluate, and hypothesis test. Frontal BAs 6, 9, 10, 45, 46, and 47 are prominent. In the final stage, the anterior cingulate (BA 32) is implicated for response selection and inhibition of alternative responses, once the best solution is determined in the previous stage. White matter, especially the arcuate fasciculus, plays a critical role for reliable communication of information among these processing units.

The P-FIT framework recognizes that there may be different combinations of areas that lead to the same cognitive performance. Individual differences in the pattern of P-FIT areas, and the white matter tracts that connect them, may account for individual differences in cognitive strengths and weakness assessed by scores on factors of intelligence denoting specific abilities as well as on the *g* factor. The 2007 P-FIT review included commentaries by 19 other researchers and responses (Haier & Jung, 2007; Jung & Haier, 2007). The comments mostly supported the fundamental idea of a distributed network and enumerated many testable hypotheses and issues for future research, including the need for larger samples and multiple measures of intelligence. Most of these recommendations have been met in phase 2 studies, as detailed in the next section.

Phase 2 of Imaging Studies – Post-2007 to the Present

The first 37 neuroimaging studies of intelligence appeared over a 20-year period. Now, a decade later, there are over a hundred imaging studies of intelligence and there are important new findings to review here. This rapid increase in imaging studies of intelligence marks phase 2 and is characterized by much larger samples, more sophisticated image analyses, the use of multiple measures of intelligence, and the combination of imaging and genetic assessments in the same individuals. Some of these studies have replicated major aspects of the P-FIT. For example, a German group computed a detailed meta-analysis that included imaging/intelligence studies through 2015 with a combined sample of over a thousand individuals (Basten, Hilger, & Fiebach, 2015). Whereas the Jung and Haier review was qualitative, this meta-analysis was a quantitative analysis of commonality among imaging studies on a voxel-by-voxel basis. This analysis supported the P-FIT and added three additional areas for consideration in future studies. At this point, the weight of evidence supports the idea that intelligence is related to multiple networks distributed across the brain, especially parietal/frontal ones. As described below, new methods of assessing connectivity among brain areas are helping advance our understanding of what makes a smart brain.

Intelligence Components and Brain Chemistry – Functional Studies

A number of new functional imaging studies use sophisticated experimental designs to examine cognitive and psychometric components of intelligence, although sample sizes still tend to be relatively small and sex differences are not routinely examined. Nonetheless, these studies are of interest. Rypma and Prabhakaran studied young adults with fMRI in two separate experiments (n = 12 each) focused on separating effects of processing capacity and processing speed as determinants of brain efficiency (Rypma & Prabhakaran, 2009). Their results "support a model of neural efficiency in which individuals differ in the extent of direct processing links between neural nodes. One benefit of direct processing links may be a surplus of resources that maximize available capacity permitting fast and accurate performance" (p. 207). With respect to the P-FIT, they note, "Our results extend [the P-FIT model] by suggesting that optimal performance occurs when posterior brain regions (parietal cortex and ventrolateral pre-frontal cortex…) can operate with minimal executive dorsolateral pre-frontal cortex control. Slower performance occurs when greater dorsolateral pre-frontal cortex involvement is required to provide top-down control of task-relevant brain regions" (p. 218).

As we saw in Chapter 4, *fluid intelligence* is another term for reasoning and problem-solving ability; it is so highly correlated with the *g* factor that the two terms are often used synonymously. Analogical reasoning is a key component of fluid intelligence (Geake & Hansen, 2005; Spearman, 1923; Sternberg, 1977). Geake and Hansen (2010) used fMRI and tests of analogical reasoning in 16 subjects (Geake & Hansen, 2010). Activations during an analogy test that required fluid reasoning were compared to activations during an analogy test that required crystallized intelligence (another intelligence factor based on the factual knowledge one has acquired). Areas where activations differed between tasks included bilateral frontal and parietal areas associated with working memory load and fronto-parietal models of general intelligence. Wartenburger and colleagues studied 15 males with fMRI during a geometric analogy task with easy and hard conditions before and after training (Wartenburger, Heekeren, Preusse, Kramer, & van der Meer, 2009). They found both increased activity in a fronto-parietal network as the task got harder and increased brain efficiency in this network after training. Masunaga and colleagues used another nonverbal measure of fluid intelligence, the Topology Test; it assesses the ability to locate objects in space (Masunaga, Kawashima, Horn, Sassa, & Sekiguchi, 2008). They found activations in parietal and frontal areas during fMRI (N = 18 graduate students). All these results come from small samples so they can only be interpreted tentatively until a weight of evidence emerges from multiple studies. Nonetheless, they illustrate the importance of using different tests and item difficulties to accentuate individual differences in brain function (see Figure 6.6).

Finally, Jung and colleagues used a newer MRI method called proton magnetic resonance spectroscopy to investigate a neurochemical correlate of IQ scores in 63 young adults (Jung et al., 2009). This technique assays specific brain neurochemistry in vivo – in this case, N-acetylaspartate (NAA), a marker of neuronal density. They found that lower NAA within right anterior gray matter predicted better scores on verbal IQ, possibly consistent with efficient function; higher NAA within the right posterior gray matter region predicted better-performance IQ scores. The findings tended to be stronger in the males. One limitation of this method is that

+

Figure 6.6 Sample topology test item based on Cattell's Culture-Fair Intelligence Test. The target is the upper center figure. The participant must choose the one figure from the bottom row that shows where a dot could be placed in the same way as in the target. The correct answer here is the figure on the bottom left (a dot could be placed both below the line and in the oval like in the target). The topology test is a good estimate of fluid intelligence and the *g* factor.

it cannot assess the entire brain at once. Regions of interest must be selected in advance and the regions are relatively large blocks of tissue. The observation of different patterns of correlations for verbal IQ (VIQ) and performance (PIQ) requires replication in even larger samples. At this point, these findings show that brain chemistry assessments also are related to psychometric scores even though the weight of evidence for a role of efficiency is still evolving. MRI spectroscopy has considerable potential for identifying details of the neurochemistry underlying other functional and structural correlates of intelligence test scores.

Anatomical Correlates – Structural Studies of Brain Areas

Structural imaging with MRI shows anatomical detail but contains no functional information (e.g., a structural scan can show the location of a tumor, but a functional scan can show how active the tumor is). Structural MRI continues to be used in studies of intelligence with more sophisticated designs, image analyses, and larger samples. Luders and colleagues have reviewed neuro-anatomical correlates of intelligence (Luders, Narr, Thompson, & Toga, 2009), including studies of regional and global volume, gray and white matter assessments, cortical thickness (Narr et al., 2007), cortical convolution (Luders et al., 2008), and assessment of the corpus callosum (Luders et al., 2007). Their review supports the distributed nature of intelligence-related areas throughout the brain and reinforces the P-FIT.

An interesting paper by Amat et al. compared IQ scores with the size of the hippocampus and amygdala (two deep brain structures), as determined by region-of-interest analysis of high-resolution MRIs, in 34 adults (Amat et al., 2008). There were no findings for the amygdala, but hippocampus volumes correlated significantly and inversely with FSIQ. The findings suggested to the authors that a smaller anterior hippocampus "contributes to an increased efficiency of neural processing that subserves overall intelligence." They did not explain this interpretation of the findings; generally, however, larger structures are thought to have more neurons and more synapses and these features could lead to more efficient processing. Another view is that smaller structures have more/better white matter connections that result in more efficient/faster processing. Both might be true to some extent in different brain areas. Variations of these possibilities among people might underlie individual differences in intelligence test scores. This is another example of why individual difference analyses may be key in understanding neuroimaging results that are based on group averages. New connectivity studies, detailed in the next section, provide such analyses regarding efficiency.

Two of the most compelling studies used MRI and voxel-based lesion-symptom mapping in 241 patients with focal brain damage. In the first study (Glascher et al., 2009), four cognitive indices of intelligence (perceptual organization, working memory, verbal comprehension, and processing speed) were determined from the WAIS subtests and correlated to lesion location. Each index showed correlates distributed throughout the brain, with considerable anatomical overlap for verbal comprehension and working memory; perceptual organization and processing speed had more distinct anatomical correlates most similar to the P-FIT with the pattern for processing speed. Interestingly, separate analyses by age and sex revealed no inter-actions, suggesting that any influence of these variables was overwhelmed by lesion location. In their second study, Glascher et al. (2010) extracted a *g* factor from the cognitive tests. They found that lesions in frontal/parietal areas had the most impact on *g* scores. Two other papers, by Barbey and colleagues, also studied intelligence in lesion patients. In one study of 182 patients (Barbey et al., 2012), results indicated that *g* scores were related to frontal, parietal networks. Another study (Barbey, Colom, & Grafman, 2013) compared patients with frontal lobe lesions to others with different lesions and to patients without lesions. The results supported an integrative role for parts of the frontal with connections to parietal areas. Following the seminal experimental lesion studies in rats (Lashley, 1964; R. Thompson et al., 1990), these newer studies clearly illustrate that neuroimaging techniques in humans with lesions can provide important insights about intelligence and cognition.

One feature shared by these studies is the use of *g* scores derived from combining multiple tests of intelligence. As you've read in previous chapters, over 100 years of psychometric research have led most researchers to assume that mental abilities are organized in a hierarchy with a general factor (*g*) underlying all tests and that a small number of primary factors account for specific abilities (Jensen, 1998). The first phase of imaging studies mostly focused on single measures of the general factor. Many newer studies use a battery of tests from which a general factor can be extracted along with specific factors. Colom and colleagues used this approach in 100 college students and correlated intelligence factors with gray matter using VBM (Colom et al., 2009). The results showed some overlap for certain factors and some unique neuro-anatomy for others. Many P-FIT areas were found where more gray matter was associated with higher factor scores. Haier and colleagues used a different battery of tests in 40 young adults and extracted a general factor and specific factors (Haier, Colom, et al., 2009). Correlations with amount of gray matter determined by VBM for the general factor did not match the areas found in the Colom analysis very well, although there was a good match for the spatial factor. The inconsistencies for the general factor may be due to the small sample size studied by Haier et al, although *g* factors extracted from different test batteries should be nearly equivalent (Johnson, te Nijenhuis, & Bouchard, 2008). It is not yet determined whether there is an anatomic network specific for the *g* factor ("neuro-*g*") that is unique from networks associated with specific factors (derived with *g* variance removed). Colom and colleagues, for example, found considerable overlap in the brain areas where gray matter correlated with scores on general intelligence and working memory (Colom, Jung, & Haier, 2007). Johnson and colleagues investigated gray and white matter correlates of other cognitive factors that were derived independently of IQ (Johnson, Jung, Colom, & Haier, 2008). Two dimensions, rotation/verbal and focus/diffusion, were studied in adults (N = 45).

There were correlations in brain areas that did not correspond to those reported for IQ. These data demonstrate that there is more to learn about the neural basis of cognitive abilities after removing variance contributed by general intelligence.

Network and Efficiency Connectivity Studies

An important development that is driving many phase 2 neuroimaging studies is based on new methods of assessing connectivity among brain areas. As noted, every brain image is made of many thousands voxels and each voxel has a quantitative value. It can be a functional value in PET (e.g., glucose metabolic rate) or fMRI (e.g., blood flow) scans or a structural value (e.g., gray or white matter volume) in MRI scans. The value of every voxel can be correlated to the values of all other voxels, and algorithms can assess patterns of connectivity (termed **brain connectivity patterns**) among clusters of voxels that define specific brain areas. Generally these methods are called **graph analysis** (Reijneveld, Ponten, Berendse, & Stam, 2007). An example is illustrated in Figure 6.7 (van den Heuvel & Sporns, 2011).

In an early study Li and colleagues assessed connectivity using Diffusion Tensor Tractography (DTT – an MRI-based method) in 79 young adults and found higher intelligence scores corresponded to a shorter path length and a higher efficiency of the networks, suggesting more efficient parallel information transfer in the brain (Li et al., 2009). They concluded that their findings supported the P-FIT framework and added direct evidence that, as predicted by the P-FIT, efficient information flow

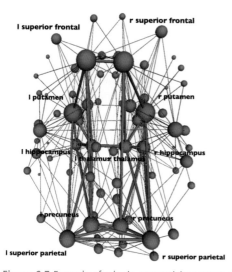

Figure 6.7 Example of a brain connectivity pattern determined by graph analysis. Circles show nodes where connections meet. Nodes with many connections are called hubs (larger circles have more connections) and the lines (called edges) show the strength of connection between two nodes or hubs (thicker line is a stronger connection). These connectivity patterns vary from person to person for structural and functional imaging data. (Adapted with permission from van den Heuvel & Sporns, 2011)

in this network was positively related to IQ scores. Song and colleagues (2008) used resting-state fMRI (i.e., lying quietly with eyes closed and no task to perform during the scan) and examined functional connectivity based on correlations among all voxels of BOLD signal (the basis for inferring blood flow). Even though no task was involved during the imaging, they found correlations between IQ scores and connectivity measures, especially frontal/posterior areas. Another group of researchers assessed white matter fibers in 420 older adults and found that 10 percent of the differences in intelligence test scores could be accounted for by a general factor of global white matter integrity computed by combining all tracts (Booth et al., 2013). Ten percent may not sound like much, but individual differences are likely to be due to many factors, so finding one brain characteristic that can be measured from a brain image that accounts for 10 percent is actually quite important. Another early intelligence study that used graph analysis was based on fMRI during rest in 19 adults (van den Heuvel, Stam, Kahn, & Pol, 2009). Van den Heuvel and colleagues calculated a measure of brain efficiency based on the length of functional connections among brain areas. They found that shorter pathways were associated with higher IQ scores, especially frontal/parietal pathways. This, too, was consistent with the brain efficiency hypothesis.

Brain connectivity patterns have now been associated with intelligence in a number of studies. One group used resting-state fMRI data from 207 individuals and reported IQ scores were related to connections among areas across the brain including P-FIT areas (Santarnecchi, Galli, Polizzotto, Rossi, & Rossi, 2014). Surprisingly, they found that IQ was most related to the weaker long-distance connections rather than to the shorter ones connecting local areas. They also introduced artificial brain "damage" mathematically into the connectivity analyses to see the effect on specific connections (Santarnecchi, Rossi, & Rossi, 2015). Interestingly, individuals with higher IQ scores tended to show less impact of the mathematical "damage" on connectivity patterns. Also, the ongoing longitudinal study of children identified in the 1930s throughout Scotland has reported MRI correlates of intelligence in 672 adults (average age 73) still living (Ritchie et al., 2015). Using multivariate statistics, they reported that a combination of structural brain features predicted about 20 percent of the variance in g scores. Most of the predictive power was due to total brain volume.

The most recent and exciting intelligence/connectivity studies are based on large samples from multicenter consortia. One study that is especially noteworthy and controversial is Finn et al. (2015). This study reports that IQ can be predicted from brain images. It is not the first study to make this claim, but it is the most impressive one to do so to date. The data come from one of the largest consortia of imaging studies called the Human Connectome Project. Their goal is to map all connectivity in the human brain, and their rich database is available freely to researchers. Using a version of graph analysis, Finn et al. computed individual connectivity patterns for 126 people from fMRI scans. Each person was scanned six times: four times while performing different cognitive tasks and twice during resting state. They found that each person's pattern of connectivity was unique and stable across conditions. In fact, each person's pattern was so stable and unique that they were termed "brain fingerprints." These patterns are like the ones shown in Figure 6.7. Finn et al. also reported that the patterns were correlated to intelligence test scores, especially the parts of the patterns connecting frontal-parietal regions. A cross-validation replication was included. If these findings hold up after independent replication by other researchers, we will have reached a major goal in this field – predicting individual differences in intelligence from brain images. As the authors note, this "may eventually be used to personalize educational and clinical practice and improve outcomes" (Finn et al., 2015, p. 1669).

As with all methods of predicting behavior (including parent/teacher ratings, intelligence and other standardized test scores, and previous behavior) the best predictions are often based on multiple methods and evaluations. Brain image data are not any more or less inherently problematic than other measures for making predictions about educational, vocational, or life success. Think about whether students and parents might prefer a 10-minute MRI costing a few hundred dollars and requiring no preparation, or the hours-long SAT test and an expensive pre-test preparation course lasting weeks. Whether brain image data predicts as well or better than the SAT is an empirical question. Which would you prefer?

Developmental Studies

Structural neuroimaging studies with large samples continue to relate intelligence to brain development. Karama and colleagues studied 216 children and adolescents aged 6 to 18 years old from an NIH-sponsored multicenter sample (Karama et al., 2009). They correlated g scores derived from WAIS subtests with cortical thickness. Results confirmed a distributed network including P-FIT areas, especially multimodal association areas. These areas were the same for the full range of ages studied and largely replicated the findings of Shaw and colleagues (2006). Further analyses found that cortical thickness associations in different brain areas with performance on specific individual tests were reduced to nearly nil when the g factor was removed (Karama et al., 2011). This indicated that some assessment of g is necessary for neuroimaging studies of cognitive tasks in children and adolescents. These researchers further studied cortical thickness and g in a sample of 588 older people (mean age 73 years). These individuals were part of the longitudinal study in Scotland that began in the 1930s. Each person had completed intelligence testing at age 11 and again at age 70. There were strong correlations between cortical thickness in different P-FIT areas and IQ scores in old age, but most of these associations were related to childhood IQ (Karama et al., 2014). In other words, having higher IQ in childhood helped explain why higher IQ in old age was related to cortical thickness. People who start out with high scores continue to have high scores as they age. Without the childhood IQ scores, the old-age correlation between cortical thickness and IQ might be erroneously interpreted as a result of the aging process alone.

There are also noteworthy genetic/imaging findings related to intelligence in children. Van Leeuwen and colleagues studied 112 twin pairs (48 identical pairs and 64 fraternal pairs) at age 9 years (van Leeuwen, van den Berg, Hoekstra, & Boomsma, 2009). Phenotypic correlations between whole brain volumes and different intelligence tests were modest, but the correlation between brain volume and intelligence was entirely explained by a common set of genes influencing both sets of phenotypes. Schmithorst and colleagues continued their impressive series of developmental studies with new findings in more than 100 children and adolescents aged 5–18 years old studied with Diffusion Tensor Imaging (DTI), an MRI technique that images the integrity of white matter tracts. The focus was specifically on sex differences (Schmithorst, 2009; Schmithorst & Holland, 2007). The findings showed significant sex-by-IQ interactions, especially in left frontal lobe, in fronto-parietal areas bilaterally, and in the arcuate fasciculus bilaterally, consistent with the P-FIT. Girls showed positive correlations of white matter integrity with IQ, and boys showed a negative correlation. That is, *less* white matter in a specific tract may be related to higher IQs in older boys. These opposite findings demonstrate the necessity of analyzing imaging data separately for males and females and emphasize the growing recognition that not all brains work or necessarily develop the same way. Similar results were reported more recently in a study of 1,070 children (Muetzel et al., 2015) and in a study of adolescent twins (Koenis et al., 2015). There is more on combining genetic and neuroimaging methods in adult samples in the next section.

Genetic/Imaging Studies

The combination of neuroimaging and genetic methods in the same sample is one of the most powerful new approaches to understanding the neural basis of intelligence. Earlier studies showed that regional gray matter and white matter are largely under genetic control and share common genes with intelligence (Hulshoff Pol et al., 2006; Peper, Brouwer, Boomsma, Kahn, & Poll, 2007; Posthuma et al., 2002; P. M. Thompson et al., 2001; Toga & Thompson, 2005). Particularly noteworthy, for example, Chiang and colleagues (Chiang et al., 2009) studied identical (N = 22 pairs) and fraternal twins (N = 23 pairs) who had completed MRI-based DTI and IQ testing in young adulthood. White-matter integrity was highly heritable (75%–90% variance accounted for by genes; contributions from shared environmental factors were not detectable) and most significant in parietal, frontal, and occipital tracts. White-matter integrity in several regions was also correlated with IQ scores. The authors concluded "common genetic factors mediated the correlation between IQ and white matter integrity, suggesting a common physiological mechanism for both, and common genetic determination" (p. 2212). Expanding this research with more twins (*n* = 472) and their non-twin siblings, this group added DNA testing and found a network of candidate genes related to the white-matter tracts most related to IQ (Chiang et al., 2012). As with similar studies, each candidate gene contributed to only a tiny portion of the IQ variance. Even though this sample is large compared to earlier studies, it still was insufficient to reliably detect small effects. In fact, most of the candidate genes identified in early studies have not replicated in new samples. The newest gene-hunting studies, however, have very large discovery samples and include independent replication samples. We cover these studies in the next section.

The problem of sample size is being addressed with multinational consortia that combine data from several sites. Getting different research groups and individual investigators collaborating in these efforts is not easy, and the success of these collaborations is a major advance in science. For example, one large consortium is ENIGMA (Enhancing Neuro-Imaging Genetics through Meta Analysis). This group has published data relating individual differences in intelligence to a gene (HMGA2) related to brain size (Stein et al., 2012). This report included a replication sample and was based on thousands of participants who had completed DNA testing, neuroimaging, and cognitive testing.

Other large multinational consortia also are providing important data sets and exciting findings. For example, the Social Science Genetic Association Consortium (SSGAC) found genetic variants that were associated with cognitive function and educational attainment, a variable highly correlated with IQ. This was in a sample of over 101,000 participants with an independent replication sample of nearly 25,000 people (Rietveld et al., 2013). Again the associations were small, and combined genetic variants predicted about 2 percent of variance in educational attainment. But this study demonstrated the importance of even larger samples. As predicted, a follow-up study with a larger sample of over 329,000 people increased the score of variance to 4 percent (Okbay et al., 2016). Another group carried out similar analyses on education achievement scores in schoolchildren of different ages (7, 11, 16 years old); these researchers found that the genetic variables predicted best in the 16-year-olds, accounting for about 9 percent of the variance (Selzam et al., 2016). Another group reported the identification of 40 specific genes, mostly involved with cell development, which predicted intelligence scores (Sniekers et al., 2017). This study was featured in an editorial in the scientific journal *Nature* for its positive impact on developing a molecular biology of intelligence, a major advance for bringing intelligence research into the realm of neuroscience (*Nature*, *545*, 385-386). Note the increases in intelligence score variance accounted for by genes have gone from 2 percent in 2013 to 9 percent in just three years. This is rapid progress and the *Nature* editorial is a major acknowledgment that intelligence research is moving into mainstream science after decades of controversy about whether genes had any influence at all (Haier, 2017).

What's Next?

The exciting examples described above demonstrate the rapid progress of neuroimaging and genetic studies of intelligence. So what is next? There is another wave of neuroimaging studies, independent of genetics, taking shape now that may become phase 3 in the history of neuroimaging studies of intelligence. These studies use imaging in conjunction with experiments aimed at manipulating brain systems to improve performance on cognitive tests, including ones that assess intelligence. Some of these studies use electrical stimulation of the brain to enhance cognitive performance (Santarnecchi et al., 2013; Santarnecchi & Rossi, 2016), and imaging can determine if there are any effects related to brain changes. So far, it's too early to know if these studies will be successful, but they also demonstrate how far we have come since our first PET study back in 1988 asked the question, where in the brain is intelligence?

In the long run, the genetic findings are setting the stage for molecular biology studies that will target neurotransmitter systems and actions in the synapse for their associations with individual differences in intelligence. One key consequence of understanding details about the biological basis of intelligence is that neural mechanisms can be adjusted. This is the goal of research into the biology of all health-related issues, especially those that are brain-based like Alzheimer's disease or schizophrenia. Certainly, a laudable goal of intelligence research is to find a way to increase intelligence in those with low IQ. What about increasing intelligence in everyone else?

Consider if there were a safe drug that influenced gray-matter volume development, white-matter integrity, or relevant neurotransmitter activity that regulated communication among neurons and across brain areas and, consequently increased IQ by 15 points (one standard deviation). This is a substantial increase that would most likely result in much improved school and work performance and new possibilities for personal and professional development. Would you take the drug? Should the drug be mandated for everyone, like fluoride in the municipal water supply? Is there a moral prescription that more intelligence is always better than less? Imagine that this drug was expensive so that only wealthy people could afford it. Should insurance companies pay for the drug just for low-IQ people or for anyone who wished to be smarter? Suppose it only worked in children as the brain developed; should parents be allowed to give a child the drug? Would it be regarded as cheating if college students took the drug? Learning and memory are key components of intelligence and they are the mental abilities that deteriorate in Alzheimer's disease (AD). Given the intense worldwide efforts to find drugs to slow, stop, or reverse these declines in AD, drugs to increase intelligence are on the way. It is only a matter of time before difficult and complex questions about their use in nonpatients will need answers.

CONCLUSION

As the twenty-first century is now in its second decade, neuroimaging research into the biological basis of intelligence is progressing rapidly: 37 studies were published between 1988 and 2007, and there are about 100 new studies since 2007. (See the

Focus on Contemporary Research box below for a description of one person's path in this field.) So far, the data show that brain areas related to intelligence are distributed throughout the brain. Brain efficiency continues to develop as a concept that shows promise as a measurable feature of connectivity and information flow around brain networks that may help define intelligence in a new way. The relevant networks may depend on whether intelligence is assessed as g or as specific factors. Apparently, not all brains work the same way, as evidenced by the imaging data that show different brain areas related to intelligence according to age and sex. Therefore, influences of age, sex, and intelligence need to be addressed systematically in future studies of cognition. The evolution of imaging studies of intelligence already includes greatly increased sample sizes, more sophisticated image analyses, and more complex, hypothesis-driven research designs. We have data on brain development trajectories related to intelligence and we have genetic analyses that indicate common genes for brain structures and intelligence. We may be on the verge of using neuroimaging data to assess individual differences in intelligence using measures of gray-matter volume, white-matter integrity, structural and functional connectivity among brain areas, and the efficiency of information flow through specific networks. Genetic studies are pointing to specific genes and understanding how they function may afford opportunities to manipulate brain systems with the goal of increasing intelligence. Certainly, such advances will have major implications for education, aging, and the treatment of brain deficits, damage, and disorders. It is not too early to have public discussions about how these advances can be used for maximum benefits or, perhaps, regulated to avoid potential misuses. Intelligence research is no longer bound by psychometric controversies, as it becomes a focus of neuroscience (Haier, 2017). Neuroimaging tools along with genetic methods continue to advance our understanding of what intelligence is and how the brain makes it so. It is an exciting time to be an intelligence researcher.

FOCUS ON CONTEMPORARY RESEARCH: RICHARD HAIER'S PATH TO NEUROIMAGING RESEARCH

When I started doing imaging research, I had to fund the acquisition of expensive PET and MRI data with grants (and a portion of the multimillion-dollar imaging equipment), so my sample sizes were necessarily small. Now it is possible without charge to access large imaging data sets collected by well-funded multinational consortia. This is a major advance in science and I encourage budding researchers to learn about image analysis methods in order to take advantage of these data sets. There really are no insurmountable barriers if you are interested in this kind of research. Accessing these databases will open opportunities to use cutting-edge structural and functional brain connectivity information to understand more about how intelligence factors work. Many of these databases include DNA assessments, so researchers can identify genetic influences on the brain structures and functions that are relevant for individual differences in intelligence. The newest findings are exciting and the pace of progress is accelerating. That's why I am optimistic that the complex puzzles about intelligence are finite and will be solved. When they are solved and we understand the neuroscience of intelligence, we may have the ability to increase intelligence for everyone, perhaps dramatically. Imagine that.

CHAPTER SUMMARY

No matter how you define intelligence, the brain is the source of all mental abilities. Based on decades of behavioral genetics, we know genes influence brain development and intelligence. Genes always work through biology, so there must be a biological basis to intelligence. In this chapter, we review neuroimaging studies that show intelligence test scores are related to specific brain structures and function assessed by a variety of modern neuroimaging methods. One surprising early finding was that the brain seems to work less hard as more intelligent people solved abstract problems, a finding that suggested a brain efficiency hypothesis about intelligence. Other early studies supported a model of brain/intelligence relationships called the Parieto-Frontal Integration Theory (P-FIT). This model indicates that intelligence is a function of a network of brain areas distributed throughout the brain and not limited only to the frontal lobes. Subsequent studies provide independent evidence for this model and other studies continue to explore the brain efficiency hypothesis. Some studies combine behavioral genetics and neuroimaging in twins to demonstrate that brain structure and intelligence have genes in common.

Even beyond such studies, the field of biological studies of intelligence has advanced dramatically in the last decade. New DNA methods and new neuroimaging methods have been applied to intelligence research and many of these studies are coming from multinational consortia that pool resources and assess thousands of individuals with standard DNA, neuroimaging, and mental ability assessments. One of the most exciting advances is the use of mathematical methods to identify patterns of connectivity among brain areas. These patterns appear to be stable within individuals and have been likened to fingerprints. Brain connectivity patterns might predict IQ scores. The establishment of multinational consortia that combine samples is also a major advance, especially for identifying specific genes related to intelligence differences among people. This is necessary because it appears that many genes, perhaps hundreds, influence intelligence and each gene accounts for a tiny portion of intelligence differences among individuals. The hunt for these genes is underway and once they are identified, molecular genetic studies will try to understand how they work on brain development and neuron activity.

All together, applying biological approaches to the study of intelligence has generated excitement among intelligence researchers and neuroscientists with the prospect of finding ways to manipulate brain systems to increase intelligence, a science fiction topic that seems less farfetched everyday. If you are just starting out or considering a research career, think about these developments and the questions they raise as challenges waiting for you to tackle.

KEY TERMS

average evoked response (AER) • **brain connectivity patterns** • **brain efficiency hypothesis** • **diffusion tensor imaging (DTI)** • **electroencephalogram (EEG)** • **epigenetic research** • **glucose metabolic rate (GMR)** • **magnetic resonance imaging (MRI)** • **parieto-frontal integration theory (P-FIT) of intelligence** • **positron emission tomography (PET)** • **voxel-based morphometry (VBM)**

COMPREHENSION AND REFLECTION QUESTIONS

1. What definition of intelligence is the basis for most research?
2. Why is it important to establish the genetics of intelligence?
3. Why are individual differences in intelligence an important area for research?
4. What is the relationship between environment and genetic factors when it comes to explaining individual differences in intelligence?
5. If there were a safe "IQ Pill" to boost your intelligence by a standard deviation, would you want to take it or give it to your children?

References

Amat, J. A., Bansal, R., Whiteman, R., Haggerty, R., Royal, J., & Peterson, B. S. (2008). Correlates of intellectual ability with morphology of the hippocampus and amygdala in healthy adults. *Brain and Cognition, 66*(2), 105-114.

Barbey, A. K., Colom, R., & Grafman, J. (2013). Dorsolateral prefrontal contributions to human intelligence. *Neuropsychologia, 51*(7), 1361-1369. doi:10.1016/j. neuropsychologia.2012.05.017

Barbey, A. K., Colom, R., Solomon, J., Krueger, F., Forbes, C., & Grafman, J. (2012). An integrative architecture for general intelligence and executive function revealed by lesion mapping. *Brain, 135*(4), 1154-1164. doi: 10.1093/brain/aws021

Barrett, P. T., & Eysenck, H. J. (1994). The relationship between evoked-potential component amplitude, latency, contour length, variability, zero-crossings, and psychometric intelligence. *Personality and Individual Differences, 16*(1), 3-32.

Basten, U., Hilger, K., & Fiebach, C. J. (2015). Where smart brains are different: A quantitative meta-analysis of functional and structural brain imaging studies on intelligence. *Intelligence, 51*, 10-27. doi: http://dx.doi.org/10.1016/j.intell.2015.04.009

Booth, T., Bastin, M. E., Penke, L., Maniega, S. M., Murray, C., Royle, N. A., . . . & Deary, I. J. (2013). Brain white matter tract integrity and cognitive abilities in community-dwelling older people: The Lothian birth cohort, 1936. *Neuropsychology, 27*(5), 595-607. doi: 10.1037/A0033354

Bouchard, T. J. (2009). Genetic influence on human intelligence (Spearman's *g*): How much? *Annals of Human Biology, 36*(5), 527-544.

Chalke, F. C., & Ertl, J. (1965). Evoked potentials and intelligence. *Life Sciences, 4*(13), 1319-1322.

Chiang, M. C., Barysheva, M., McMahon, K. L., de Zubicaray, G. I., Johnson, K., Montgomery, G. W., . . . & Thompson, P. M. (2012). Gene network effects on brain microstructure and intellectual performance identified in 472 twins. *Journal of Neuroscience, 32*(25), 8732-8745. doi: 10.1523/JNEUROSCI.5993-11.2012

Chiang, M. C., Barysheva, M., Shattuck, D. W., Lee, A. D., Madsen, S. K., Avedissian, C., . . . & Thompson, P. M. (2009). Genetics of Brain Fiber Architecture and Intellectual Performance. *Journal of Neuroscience, 29*(7), 2212-2224. doi: 10.1523/Jneurosci.4184-08.2009

Colom, R., Haier, R. J., Head, K., Alvarez-Linera, J., Quiroga, M. A., Shih, P. C., & Jung, R. E. (2009). Gray matter correlates of fluid, crystallized, and spatial intelligence: Testing the P-FIT model. *Intelligence, 37*(2), 124-135.

Colom, R., Jung, R. E., & Haier, R. J. (2006a). Distributed brain sites for the g-factor of intelligence. *Neuroimage, 31*(3), 1359-1365.

Colom, R., Jung, R. E., & Haier, R. J. (2006b). Finding the *g*-factor in brain structure using the method of correlated vectors. *Intelligence, 34*(6), 561-570.

Colom, R., Jung, R. E., & Haier, R. J. (2007). General intelligence and memory span: Evidence for a common neuroanatomic framework. *Cognitive Neuropsychology, 24*(8), 867-878.

Davies, G., Armstrong, N., Bis, J. C., Bressler, J., Chouraki, V., Giddaluru, S., . . . & Deary, I. J. (2015). Genetic contributions to variation in general cognitive function: a meta-analysis of genome-wide association studies in the CHARGE consortium (N=53949). *Molecular Psychiatry, 20*(2), 183-192. doi: 10.1038/mp.2014.188

Davies, G., Lam, M., Harris, S. E., Trampush, J., Luciano, M., Hill, W. D., . . . & Deary, I. J. (2017). Ninety-nine independent genetic loci influencing general cognitive function include genes associated with brain health and structure (N = 280,360). *bioRxiv*. doi:10.1101/176511

Deary, I. J., Johnson, W., & Houlihan, L. M. (2009). Genetic foundations of human intelligence. *Human Genetics, 126*(1), 215-232. doi: 10.1007/s00439-009-0655-4

Diamond, M. C., Scheibel, A. B., Murphy, G. M., Jr., & Harvey, T. (1985). On the brain of a scientist: Albert Einstein. *Experimental Neurology*, *88*(1), 198-204.

Duncan, J., Emslie, H., Williams, P., Johnson, R., & Freer, C. (1996). Intelligence and the frontal lobe: the organization of goal-directed behavior. *Cognitive Psychology*, *30*(3), 257-303.

Duncan, J., Seitz, R. J., Kolodny, J., Bor, D., Herzog, H., Ahmed, A., . . . Emslie, H. (2000). A neural basis for general intelligence. *Science*, *289*(5478), 457-460.

Ertl, J. P., & Schafer, E. W. (1969). Brain response correlates of psychometric intelligence. *Nature*, *223*(204), 421-422.

Finn, E. S., Shen, X., Scheinost, D., Rosenberg, M. D., Huang, J., Chun, M. M., . . . & Constable, R. T. (2015). Functional connectome fingerprinting: identifying individuals using patterns of brain connectivity. *Nature Neuroscience*, *18*(11), 1664-1671. doi: 10.1038/nn.4135

Geake, J. G., & Hansen, P. C. (2005). Neural correlates of intelligence as revealed by fMRI of fluid analogies. *Neuroimage*, *26*(2), 555-564.

Geake, J. G., & Hansen, P. C. (2010). Functional neural correlates of fluid and crystallized analogizing. *Neuroimage*, *49*(4), 3489-3497. doi: 10.1016/j.neuroimage.2009.09.008

Gignac, G., Vernon, P. A., & Wickett, J. C. (2003). Factors influencing the relationship between brain size and intelligence. In H. Nyborg (ed.), *The Scientific Study of general Intelligence* (pp. 93-106). Amsterdam: Pergamon.

Glascher, J., Rudrauf, D., Colom, R., Paul, L. K., Tranel, D., Damasio, H., & Adolphs, R. (2010). Distributed neural system for general intelligence revealed by lesion mapping. *Proceedings of the National Academy of Sciences of the United States of America*, *107*(10), 4705-4709. doi: 10.1073/Pnas.0910397107

Glascher, J., Tranel, D., Paul, L. K., Rudrauf, D., Rorden, C., Hornaday, A., . . . & Adolphs, R. (2009). Lesion mapping of cognitive abilities linked to intelligence. *Neuron*, *61*(5), 681-691. doi: 10.1016/j.neuron.2009.01.026

Haier, R. J. (2009a). Neuro-intelligence, neuro-metrics and the next phase of brain imaging studies. *Intelligence*, *37*(2), 121-123.

Haier, R. J. (2009b). What does a smart brain look like? *Scientific American Mind,* November/December, 26-33.

Haier, R. J. (2017). *The neuroscience of intelligence*. Cambridge: Cambridge University Press.

Haier, R. J., Alkire, M. T., White, N. S., Uncapher, M. R., Head, E., Lott, I. T., & Cotman, C. W. (2003). Temporal cortex hypermetabolism in Down syndrome prior to the onset of dementia. *Neurology*, *61*(12), 1673-1679.

Haier, R. J., & Benbow, C. P. (1995). Sex differences and lateralization in temporal lobe glucose metabolism during mathematical reasoning. *Developmental Neuropsychology*, *11*(4), 405-414.

Haier, R. J., Chueh, D., Touchette, P., Lott, I., et al. (1995). Brain size and cerebral glucose metabolic rate in nonspecific mental retardation and Down syndrome. *Intelligence*, *20*(2), 191-210.

Haier, R. J., Colom, R., Schroeder, D. H., Condon, C. A., Tang, C., Eaves, E., & Head, K. (2009). Gray matter and intelligence factors: Is there a neuro-g? *Intelligence*, *37*(2), 136-144. doi: 10.1016/j.intell.2008.10.011

Haier, R. J., Head, K., Head, E., & Lott, I. T. (2008). Neuroimaging of individuals with Down's syndrome at-risk for dementia: Evidence for possible compensatory events. *Neuroimage*, *39*(3), 1324-1332.

Haier, R. J., & Jung, R. E. (2007). Beautiful minds (i.e., brains) and the neural basis of intelligence. *Behavioral and Brain Sciences*, *30*(02), 174-178.

Haier, R. J., Jung, R. E., Yeo, R. A., Head, K., & Alkire, M. T. (2004). Structural brain variation and general intelligence. *Neuroimage*, *23*(1), 425-433.

Haier, R. J., Jung, R. E., Yeo, R. A., Head, K., & Alkire, M. T. (2005). The neuroanatomy of general intelligence: sex matters. *Neuroimage*, *25*(1), 320-327.

Haier, R. J., Karama, S., Leyba, L., & Jung, R. E. (2009). MRI assessment of cortical thickness and functional activity changes in adolescent girls following three months of practice on a visual–spatial task. *BMC Research Notes*, *2*, 174. doi: 1756-0500-2-174 [pii] 10.1186/1756-0500-2-174

Haier, R. J., Siegel, B., Tang, C., Abel, L., & Buchsbaum, M. S. (1992). Intelligence and changes in regional cerebral glucose metabolic-rate following learning. *Intelligence*, *16*(3-4), 415-426.

Haier, R. J., Siegel, B. V., Jr., MacLachlan, A., Soderling, E., Lottenberg, S., & Buchsbaum, M. S. (1992). Regional glucose metabolic changes after learning a complex visuospatial/ motor task: A positron emission tomographic study. *Brain Research*, *570*(1-2), 134-143.

Haier, R. J., Siegel, B. V., Nuechterlein, K. H., Hazlett, E., Wu, J. C., Paek, J., . . . & Buchsbaum, M. S. (1988). Cortical glucose metabolic-rate correlates of abstract reasoning and attention studied with positron emission tomography. *Intelligence*, *12*(2), 199-217.

Haier, R. J., White, N. S., & Alkire, M. T. (2003). Individual differences in general intelligence correlate with brain function during nonreasoning tasks. *Intelligence*, *31*(5), 429-441.

Head, E., Lott, I. T., Patterson, D., Doran, E., & Haier, R. J. (2007). Possible compensatory events in adult Down syndrome brain prior to the development of Alzheimer disease neuropathology: Targets for non-pharmacological intervention. *Journal of Alzheimer's Disease*, *11*(1), 61-76.

Hendrickson, D. E., & Hendrickson, A. E. (1980). The biological basis of individual-differences in intelligence. *Personality and Individual Differences*, *1*(1), 3-33.

Hulshoff Pol, H. E., Schnack, H. G., Posthuma, D., Mandl, R. C., Baare, W. F., van Oel, C., . . . & Kahn, R. S. (2006). Genetic contributions to human brain morphology and intelligence. *Journal of Neuroscience*, *26*(40), 10235-10242. doi: 10.1523/ JNEUROSCI.1312-06.2006

Jensen, A. R. (1998). *The g factor: The Science of Mental Ability*. Westport, CT: Praeger.

Johnson, W., Jung, R. E., Colom, R., & Haier, R. J. (2008). Cognitive abilities independent of IQ correlate with regional brain structure. *Intelligence, 36*(1), 18-28.

Johnson, W., te Nijenhuis, J., & Bouchard, T. J. (2008). Still just 1 *g*: Consistent results from five test batteries. *Intelligence, 36*(1), 81-95.

Jung, R. E., Gasparovic, C., Chavez, R. S., Flores, R. A., Smith, S. M., Caprihan, A., & Yeo, R. A. (2009). Biochemical support for the "threshold" theory of creativity: A magnetic resonance spectroscopy study. *Journal of Neuroscience, 29*(16), 5319-5325. doi: 10.1523/jneurosci.0588-09.2009

Jung, R. E., & Haier, R. J. (2007). The parieto-frontal integration theory (P-FIT) of intelligence: Converging neuroimaging evidence. *Behavioral and Brain Sciences, 30*(2), 135-154; discussion 154-187. doi: 10.1017/S0140525X07001185

Karama, S., Ad-Dab'bagh, Y., Haier, R. J., Deary, I. J., Lyttelton, O. C., Lepage, C., ... & Grp, B. D. C. (2009). Positive association between cognitive ability and cortical thickness in a representative US sample of healthy 6 to 18 year-olds. *Intelligence, 37*(2), 145-155.

Karama, S., Bastin, M. E., Murray, C., Royle, N. A., Penke, L., Munoz Maniega, S., ... & Deary, I. J. (2014). Childhood cognitive ability accounts for associations between cognitive ability and brain cortical thickness in old age. *Molecular Psychiatry, 19*(5), 555-559. doi: 10.1038/mp.2013.64

Karama, S., Colom, R., Johnson, W., Deary, I. J., Haier, R., Waber, D. P., ... & Brain Dev Cooperative G. (2011). Cortical thickness correlates of specific cognitive performance accounted for by the general factor of intelligence in healthy children aged 6 to 18. *Neuroimage, 55*(4), 1443-1453. doi: 10.1016/j.neuroimage.2011.01.016

Keller, K., & Menon, V. (2009). Gender differences in the functional and structural neuroanatomy of mathematical cognition. *Neuroimage, 47*(1), 342-352. doi: 10.1016/j.neuroimage.2009.04.042

Koenis, M. M., Brouwer, R. M., van den Heuvel, M. P., Mandl, R. C., van Soelen, I. L., Kahn, R. S., ... & Hulshoff Pol, H. E. (2015). Development of the brain's structural network efficiency in early adolescence: A longitudinal DTI twin study. *Human Brain Mapping.* doi: 10.1002/hbm.22988

Lashley, K. S. (1964). *Brain mechanisms and intelligence.* New York: Hafner.

Li, Y., Liu, Y., Li, J., Qin, W., Li, K. C., Yu, C. S., & Jiang, T. Z. (2009). Brain anatomical network and intelligence. *PLoS Computational Biology, 5*(5). doi: 10.1371/journal.pcbi.1000395

Luders, E., Narr, K. L., Bilder, R. M., Thompson, P. M., Szeszko, P. R., Hamilton, L., & Toga, A. W. (2007). Positive correlations between corpus callosum thickness and intelligence. *Neuroimage, 37*(4), 1457-1464. doi: 10.1016/j.neuroimage.2007.06.028

Luders, E., Narr, K. L., Bilder, R. M., Szeszko, P. R., Gurbani, M. N., Hamilton, L., ... & Gaser, C. (2008). Mapping the relationship between cortical convolution and intelligence: effects of gender. *Cerebral Cortex, 18*(9), 2019-2026. doi: 10.1093/cercor/bhm227

Luders, E., Narr, K. L., Thompson, P. M., & Toga, A. W. (2009). Neuroanatomical correlates of intelligence. *Intelligence*, *37*(2), 156-163. doi: 1 0.1016/j.intell.2008.07.002

Masunaga, H., Kawashima, R., Horn, J. L., Sassa, Y., & Sekiguchi, A. (2008). Neural substrates of the Topology Test to measure fluid reasoning: An fMRI study. *Intelligence*, *36*(6), 607-615. doi: 10.1016/j.intell.2008.01.006

Matzel, L. D., Han, Y. R., Grossman, H., Karnik, M. S., Patel, D., Scott, N., . . . Gandhi, C. C. (2003). Individual differences in the expression of a "general" learning ability in mice. *Journal of Neuroscience*, *23*(16), 6423-6433.

McDaniel, M. A. (2005). Big-brained people are smarter: A meta-analysis of the relationship between in vivo brain volume and intelligence. *Intelligence*, *33*(4), 337-346.

Muetzel, R. L., Mous, S. E., van der Ende, J., Blanken, L. M. E., van der Lugt, A., Jaddoe, V. W. V., . . . White, T. (2015). White matter integrity and cognitive performance in school-age children: A population-based neuroimaging study. *Neuroimage*, *119*, 119-128. doi: 10.1016/j.neuroimage.2015.06.014

Narr, K. L., Woods, R. P., Thompson, P. M., Szeszko, P., Robinson, D., Dimtcheva, T., . . . & Bilder, R. M. (2007). Relationships between IQ and regional cortical gray matter thickness in healthy adults. *Cerebral Cortex*, *17*(9), 2163-2171. doi: 10.1093/cercor/bhl125

Neubauer, A. C., & Fink, A. (2008). Intelligence and neural efficiency: A review and new data. *International Journal of Psychophysiology*, *69*(3), 168-169.

Neubauer, A. C., & Fink, A. (2009). Intelligence and neural efficiency: Measures of brain activation versus measures of functional connectivity in the brain. *Intelligence*, *37*(2), 223-229.

O'Callaghan, M. A., & Carroll, D. (1982). *Psychosurgery: A scientific analysis*. Ridgewood, NJ: George A. Bogden & Son.

Okbay, A., Beauchamp, J. P., Fontana, M. A., Lee, J. J., Pers, T. H., Rietveld, C. A., . . . & Benjamin, D. J. (2016). Genome-wide association study identifies 74 loci associated with educational attainment. *Nature*, *533*(7604), 539-542. doi: 10.1038/nature17671

Peper, J. S., Brouwer, R. M., Boomsma, D. I., Kahn, R. S., & Poll, H. E. H. (2007). Genetic influences on human brain structure: A review of brain imaging studies in twins. *Human Brain Mapping*, *28*(6), 464-473.

Polderman, T. J., Benyamin, B., de Leeuw, C. A., Sullivan, P. F., van Bochoven, A., Visscher, P. M., & Posthuma, D. (2015). Meta-analysis of the heritability of human traits based on fifty years of twin studies. *Nature Genetics*, *47*(7), 702-709. doi: 10.1038/ng.3285

Posthuma, D., De Geus, E. J., Baare, W. F., Hulshoff Pol, H. E., Kahn, R. S., & Boomsma, D. I. (2002). The association between brain volume and intelligence is of genetic origin. *Nature Neuroscience*, *5*(2), 83-84.

Prabhakaran, V., Smith, J. A., Desmond, J. E., Glover, G. H., & Gabrieli, J. D. (1997). Neural substrates of fluid reasoning: An fMRI study of neocortical activation during performance of the Raven's Progressive Matrices Test. *Cognitive Psychology*, *33*(1), 43-63.

Reijneveld, J. C., Ponten, S. C., Berendse, H. W., & Stam, C. J. (2007). The application of graph theoretical analysis to complex networks in the brain. *Clinical Neurophysiology, 118*(11), 2317-2331. doi: 10.1016/j.clinph.2007.08.010

Rietveld, C. A., Medland, S. E., Derringer, J., Yang, J., Esko, T., Martin, N. W., ... & Koellinger, P. D. (2013). GWAS of 126,559 individuals identifies genetic variants associated with educational attainment. *Science, 340*(6139), 1467-1471. doi: 10.1126/science.1235488

Ritchie, S. J., Booth, T., Hernandez, M., Corley, J., Maniega, S. M., Gow, A. J., ... & Deary, I. J. (2015). Beyond a bigger brain: Multivariable structural brain imaging and intelligence. *Intelligence, 51*, 47-56. doi: 10.1016/j.intell.2015.05.001

Roman, F. J., Abad, F. J., Escorial, S., Burgaleta, M., Martinez, K., Alvarez-Linera, J., ... & Colom, R. (2014). Reversed hierarchy in the brain for general and specific cognitive abilities: A morphometric analysis. *Human Brain Mapping, 35*(8), 3805-3818. doi: 10.1002/hbm.22438

Rypma, B., & Prabhakaran, V. (2009). When less is more and when more is more: The mediating roles of capacity and speed in brain-behavior efficiency. *Intelligence, 37* (2), 207-222. doi: 10.1016/j.intell.2008.12.004

Santarnecchi, E., Galli, G., Polizzotto, N. R., Rossi, A., & Rossi, S. (2014). Efficiency of weak brain connections support general cognitive functioning. *Human Brain Mapping, 35*(9), 4566-4582. doi: 10.1002/hbm.22495

Santarnecchi, E., Polizzotto, N. R., Godone, M., Giovannelli, F., Feurra, M., Matzen, L., ... & Rossi, S. (2013). Frequency-dependent enhancement of fluid intelligence induced by transcranial oscillatory potentials. *Current Biology, 23*(15), 1449-1453. doi: 10.1016/j.cub.2013.06.022

Santarnecchi, E., & Rossi, S. (2016). Advances in the neuroscience of intelligence: From brain connectivity to brain perturbation. *Spanish Journal of Psychology, 19*. doi: 10.1017/sjp.2016.89

Santarnecchi, E., Rossi, S., & Rossi, A. (2015). The smarter, the stronger: Intelligence level correlates with brain resilience to systematic insults. *Cortex, 64*, 293-309. doi: 10.1016/j.cortex.2014.11.005

Schafer, E. W. (1982). Neural adaptability: A biological determinant of behavioral intelligence. *International Journal of Neuroscience, 17*(3), 183-191.

Schmithorst, V. J. (2009). Developmental sex differences in the relation of neuroanatomical connectivity to intelligence. *Intelligence, 37*(2), 164-173. doi: 10.1016/j.intell.2008.07.001

Schmithorst, V. J., & Holland, S. K. (2007). Sex differences in the development of neuroanatomical functional connectivity underlying intelligence found using Bayesian connectivity analysis. *Neuroimage, 35*(1), 406.

Selzam, S., Krapohl, E., von Stumm, S., O'Reilly, P. F., Rimfeld, K., Kovas, Y., ... & Plomin, R. (2016). Predicting educational achievement from DNA. *Molecular Psychiatry*. doi: 10.1038/mp.2016.107

Shaw, P., Greenstein, D., Lerch, J., Clasen, L., Lenroot, R., Gogtay, N., ... & Giedd, J. (2006). Intellectual ability and cortical development in children and adolescents. *Nature*, *440*(7084), 676-679.

Silverman, P. H. (2004). Rethinking genetic determinism. *The Scientist*, *18*(10), 32-33.

Sniekers, S., Stringer, S., Watanabe, K., Jansen, P. R., Coleman, J. R. I., Krapohl, E., ... & Posthuma, D. (2017). Genome-wide association meta-analysis of 78,308 individuals identifies new loci and genes influencing human intelligence. *Nature Genetics*, *49*(7), 1107-1112. doi: 10.1038/ng.3869

Song, M., Zhou, Y., Li, J., Liu, Y., Tian, L., Yu, C., & Jiang, T. (2008). Brain spontaneous functional connectivity and intelligence. *Neuroimage*, *41*(3), 1168-1176. doi: 10.1016/j.neuroimage.2008.02.036

Spearman, C. (1904). General intelligence objectively determined and measured. *American Journal of Psychology*, *15*, 201-293.

Spearman, C. (1923). *The nature of "intelligence" and the principles of cognition*. London: Macmillan.

Stein, J. L., Medland, S. E., Vasquez, A. A., Hibar, D. P., Senstad, R. E., Winkler, A. M., et al. (2012). Identification of common variants associated with human hippocampal and intracranial volumes. *Nature Genetics*, *44*(5), 552-561. doi: 10.1038/ng.2250

Sternberg, R. J. (1977). *Intelligence, information processing, and analogical reasoning: The componential analysis of human abilities*. Hillsdale, N.J.: Lawrence Erlbaum Associates.

Thompson, P. M., Cannon, T. D., Narr, K. L., van Erp, T., Poutanen, V. P., Huttunen, M., ... & Toga, A. W. (2001). Genetic influences on brain structure. *Natural Neuroscience*, *4*(12), 1253-1258.

Thompson, R., Crinella, F. M., & Yu, J. (1990). *Brain mechanisms in problem solving and intelligence: A survey of the rat brain*. New York: Plenum Press.

Toga, A. W., & Thompson, P. M. (2005). Genetics of brain structure and intelligence. *Annual Review of Neuroscience*, *28*, 1-23.

Turkheimer, E. (2000). Three laws of behavior genetics and what they mean. *Current Directions in Psychological Science*, *9*(5), 160-164.

van den Heuvel, M. P., & Sporns, O. (2011). Rich-club organization of the human connectome. *Journal of Neuroscience*, *31*(44), 15775-15786. doi: 10.1523/JNEUROSCI.3539-11.2011

van den Heuvel, M. P., Stam, C. J., Kahn, R. S., & Pol, H. E. H. (2009). Efficiency of functional brain networks and intellectual performance. *Journal of Neuroscience*, *29*(23), 7619-7624. doi: 10.1523/jneurosci.1443-09.2009

van Leeuwen, M., van den Berg, S. M., Hoekstra, R. A., & Boomsma, D. I. (2009). The genetic and environmental structure of verbal and visuospatial memory in young adults and children. *Neuropsychology*, *23*(6), 792-802.

Wartenburger, I., Heekeren, H. R., Preusse, F., Kramer, J., & van der Meer, E. (2009). Cerebral correlates of analogical processing and their modulation by training. *Neuroimage, 48*(1), 291-302. doi: 10.1016/j.neuroimage.2009.06.025

Willerman, L., Schultz, R., Rutledge, J. N., & Bigler, E. D. (1991). In vivo brain size and intelligence. *Intelligence, 15*(2), 223-228.

7 Cultural Approaches to Intelligence

ROBERT J. STERNBERG

The study of the relation between culture and intelligence starts with the idea that behavior that in one particular cultural context is considered intelligent or somehow adaptive may, in another and different cultural context, be considered unintelligent and quite possibly maladaptive (Cole, Gay, Glick, & Sharp, 1971; Sternberg, 2004a, 2007, 2012, 2014). In one country, stating one's political views honestly and openly may win an individual the top political job, such as the presidency; in another country with another culture, stating one's political views honestly and openly may lead to a death sentence.

Culture and intelligence are inextricably interlinked. On a related note, Tomasello (2001) has suggested that culture, in large part, is what distinguishes human intelligence from animal intelligence. Tomasello believes that humans have evolved as they have, at least in part, because of their cultural adaptations. These adaptations in turn develop from their ability, starting in infancy, to understand others as intentional agents. At the same time that humans evolve, so do cultures (Greenfield, 1998, 2017): That is, what is true of a culture at one time may not be true of the same culture at another (Cole, 2017).

The conceptualization, assessment, and development of intelligence can only be fully or even meaningfully understood within their cultural context. Work that seeks to study intelligence outside any cultural context may overlay a modern Western view of how the world is on other parts of the world.

The upshot of such an effort typically is to show that individuals who are more similar to the prototypical Westerner are more intelligent than are individuals who are less similar. For example, an intelligence test that is developed and then validated in one cultural context may be less valid, or even not valid at all, in a different cultural context (Sternberg & Grigorenko, 2008). Not only intelligence, but also the heritability of intelligence – the extent of its transmission through genetic means – varies from one culture to another (Henrich, Heien, & Norenzayan, 2010a, 2010b).

Moreover, everyday behavior we see as intelligent does not occur in a vacuum – it is culturally defined. Laws come to embody cultural conventions. Driving on the right side of the street is lawful and intelligent in the United States; in the United Kingdom, it is unlawful and can get you killed. Moreover, jaywalking is viewed as acceptable and is common in some places (e.g., New York City) but is uncommon and viewed as unacceptable in others places (e.g., Tokyo). What constitutes legal and reasonable use of certain psychoactive drugs varies even between states; in the United States, for example, there are differences between Colorado and Mississippi. Gelfand and her colleagues have referred to the relevance of tight versus loose cultures (Gelfand et al., 2006, 2011, 2017). Tight cultures have strong social norms and severe punishments for transgressions. Loose cultures have weaker social norms and punishments for transgressions. It may not ever be intelligent to smoke marijuana (except for the alleviation of severe pain), but it definitely is unintelligent in societies where the death penalty might apply.

Just as culture evolves, so does intelligence. As the results of large-scale globalization have become more embedded in diverse cultures around the world, the standards for intelligent behavior probably have risen, and IQs with them (Flynn, 2016). People now have to compete intellectually on an international stage on tasks that formally entailed merely local competition (Hong & Cheon, 2017). The same behavior that might have brought one success in a small-scale local environment may no longer be viewed as favorably in the competition of a global environment.

What Is Culture and What Is Intelligence?

So far in this book we have used the term "culture" without strictly defining it. But what, exactly, is culture?

There have been many different and quite diverse definitions of the concept of culture (e.g., Brislin, Lonner, & Thorndike, 1973; Kroeber & Kluckhohn, 1952). **Culture** is defined here as "the set of attitudes, values, beliefs and behaviors shared by a group of people, communicated from one generation to the next via language or some other means of communication (Barnouw, 1985)" (Matsumoto, 1994, p. 4). The term "culture" is used by people in various ways. These uses have a long and distinguished history (Benedict, 1946; Boas, 1911; Mead, 1928; see Matsumoto, 1996). For example, Berry, Poortinga, Segall, and Dasen (1992) described six different uses of the term "culture." First, it can be used descriptively to characterize a culture. Second, it can be used historically to describe the traditions of a group. Third, it can be used normatively to express rules and norms of a group. Fourth, it can be used psychologically to emphasize how a group learns and solves problems. Fifth, it can be used structurally to emphasize the organizational elements of a culture. Finally, it can be used genetically to describe cultural origins. Indeed, whereas we in the United States often view intelligence primarily as an individual phenomenon, people in other cultures, such as the Maya, view it more as a collective phenomenon (Rogoff et al., 2017).

In cultural research, it is challenging to separate linguistic differences from conceptual differences with regard to the meaning of "intelligence." **Converging operations** – a variety of methods that are used in the hope of their leading to the same scientific conclusion – can be used in order to achieve some separation. That is, different and diverse empirical operations can be employed in order to ascertain notions of intelligence. So one may ask in one study that people identify aspects of competence; in another study, that they identify competent people; in a third study, that they characterize the meaning of "intelligence," and so forth.

Implicit Theories of Intelligence

Intelligence can be conceptualized differently in different cultures (see reviews in Ang, Van Dyne, & Tan, 2011; Niu & Brass, 2011; Serpell, 2000; and Sternberg & Kaufman, 1998). Such conceptions are called implicit theories of intelligence. An **implicit theory** is a folk conception of a construct, such as intelligence, that is, what people believe the construct to be, in contrast to what it actually is. These differences in implicit theories are important. The reason is that cultures judge their members and also members of other cultures according to the norms of their own views about intelligence. As an example, in parts of Latin America, teachers' implicit theories of intelligence often stress academic knowledge and skills as the primary basis of intelligence (Kaplan, 1997). In Argentina, teachers were found to emphasize good discipline as important to intelligence. They also emphasized excitement about learning, ability to learn and think, and also growing up in a stable home (Kaplan, 1997). Many of the teachers queried in this particular research believed as well in the notion of a "bad head," that is, a mind not well suited to studying.

Western and Eastern Conceptions of Intelligence

Western notions regarding intelligence are not the same as those to be found in many other cultures. For example, the Western emphasis on the importance for intelligence of speed of mental processing (Sternberg, Conway, Ketron, & Bernstein, 1981) is quite different from that of many other cultures. People in non-Western cultures may be suspicious of the quality of work that is done very quickly. Even people in the West may share this suspicion. Indeed, many other cultures emphasize how deeply information is processed rather than merely how quickly it is processed. They are not alone in this regard: Some prominent Western researchers have argued for the importance of deep processing for true command of academic and other knowledge (e.g., Craik & Lockhart, 1972).

How important is memory for knowledge, anyway? Chen (1994) showed that Chinese students considered factual memory as particularly important for intelligence; in contrast, Australian students considered these skills to be only trivially important. Furthermore, Das (1994), analyzing Eastern notions of intelligence, argued that in Buddhist and Hindu philosophies, intelligence requires waking up, noticing, and recognizing things, and understanding and comprehending concepts and things in the environment. But, on this view, intelligence also involves such attributes as determination and mental effort.

Researchers for many years have recognized differences between cultures in conceptions of intelligence. Gill and Keats (1980) observed that Australian University students value academic skills and the ability to adapt to new events as essential to high intelligence. By contrast, Malay students more value practical skills, in addition to speed and creativity. Dasen (1984) found Malay students tend to emphasize both social and cognitive attributes in their conceptions of the nature of intelligence. Motivation also can be an important element (Dai & Sternberg, 2004). See the Focus on Contemporary Research Box below for a discussion of research that looks at the correlation of practical skills and health.

FOCUS ON CONTEMPORARY RESEARCH: ROBERT STERNBERG'S WORK ON WHETHER PRACTICAL SKILLS CAN PREDICT HEALTH

Practical intellectual skills may, in some instances, be better predictors of health than are academic ones. In a study we carried out in Russia (Grigorenko & Sternberg, 2001), we developed separate measures of analytical, creative, and practical intelligence with at least two summative indicators for each construct. Principal-component analysis yielded clear-cut analytical, creative, and practical factors for the tests (for details, see Grigorenko & Sternberg, 2001).

The main goal of this study was to use analytical, creative, and practical tests to predict mental and physical health among Russian adults. Mental health was assessed by standard paper-and-pencil tests of depression and anxiety. Physical health was assessed by self-reports of the participants. The best predictor of both mental and physical health were the practical-intelligence measures for mental and physical health, respectively. Analytical intelligence was the second-best predictor and creative intelligence was the third-best predictor. All three measures contributed to prediction, however. Analytical thinking of the kind emphasized in school is important (Sternberg, 1985b, 1985c, 1986, 1997c), but it is not enough to get people through life.

The results in Russia suggested the importance of studying health-related outcomes as one way of measuring successful adaptation to the environment. Health-related variables can affect one's ability to perform well on tests or even to achieve one's goals in life.

The differences between Eastern and Western ideas about human intelligence may be partly a function of differences between the types of knowledge and skills that are valued by Eastern and Western cultures (Srivastava & Misra, 1996). Western cultures and the schools they create stress what one might call "technological intelligence" (Mundy-Castle, 1974). African cultures tend more to emphasize what one might call "social intelligence" (Mundy-Castle, 1974).

Western schooling also emphasizes other skills (Srivastava & Misra, 1996). These other skills include generalization, or going beyond the given information (Connolly & Bruner, 1974; Goodnow, 1986), speed of mental processing (Sternberg, 1985a), making minimal moves to reach a solution (Newell & Simon, 1972), and thinking creatively (Goodnow, 1986; Sternberg & Davidson, 1982). Moreover, silence often is construed as a lack of knowledge (Irvine, 1988).

In contrast, many Asian cultures place more emphasis on the social aspect of intelligence than on the conventional Western notion, which is largely IQ-based notion (Azuma & Kashiwagi, 1987; Lutz, 1985; Poole, 1985; White, 1985). The Confucian perspective in China emphasizes the characteristic of benevolence and of doing what is morally correct (Shi, 2004; Yang, 2001; Yang & Sternberg, 1997a). In agreement with the Western notion of intelligence, the intelligent individual expends a lot of effort in learning, enjoys learning, and persists, with a great deal of enthusiasm, in life-long learning. The Taoist tradition instead emphasizes the importance of possessing humility, freedom from embracing conventional standards of judgment, and having full knowledge of oneself as well as of external conditions.

China is widely considered to be the first country seriously to have employed intelligence tests (Shi, 2004). Tests were utilized in ancient China for the purpose of hiring people. The tangram, requiring a person to construct shapes in various forms, was first developed in the Song dynasty, which lasted from 1127 to 1279 (Lin, 1980). Even young children were assessed for their intellectual development, for example by having them place objects where they were supposed to be (Yan, 2001).

The difference between conceptions of intelligence in the East and in the West appears to persist even in modern times. Yang and Sternberg (1997b) studied modern Taiwanese Chinese conceptions of the nature of intelligence. They found five factors underlying these conceptions of intelligence: (a) a general cognitive factor (closely resembling the g factor in Western intelligence tests); (b) interpersonal intelligence (which is, more or less, social competence); (c) intrapersonal intelligence (which is, more or less, self-understanding); (d) intellectual self-assertion (which is knowing when to show you are smart); and (e) intellectual self-effacement (which is knowing when not to show you are smart).

The factors revealed for individuals living in Taiwan differ rather substantially from the factors identified by Sternberg, et al. (1981) in people's conceptions of intelligence in the United States: (a) everyday problem solving, (b) verbal skills, and (c) social competence. However, in both cases, people's implicit theories of intelligence seem to extend quite far beyond what conventional intelligence tests measure.

Conceptions of Intelligence among African Cultures

Studies in Africa provide a further window on the substantial and meaningful differences in conceptions of intelligence across various cultures. Ruzgis and Grigorenko (1994) found that, in parts of Africa, conceptions of intelligence emphasize the importance of people helping to facilitate and maintain harmonious and stable intergroup relations. Intragroup relations (i.e., relations of people within a particular group) are just as important and at times can be more important. For example, Serpell (1974, 1996) discovered that Chewa adults in Zambia emphasize in their conception of intelligence the importance of social responsibilities, cooperation, and obedience. Intelligent children are supposed to show respect toward, and be obedient to adults. Kenyan parents also emphasize the importance of active and responsible participation in family and social life as key aspects of intelligence (Super & Harkness, 1982, 1986, 1993).

In Zimbabwe, one of the words for intelligence, *ngware*, means to be prudent and cautious, particularly in the context of social relationships. Among the Baoule people, keys to intelligence include service to the family and community and politeness toward, and respect for, elders (Dasen, 1984). In Zimbabwe, conceptions of intelligence are further represented by the words *njere* (in the Shona language) and *ukaliphile* (in the Ndebele language) (Mpofu, 2004). These terms signify behavior that is deliberate, socially responsible, altruistic, and public-spirited (Chimhundu, 2001; Hadebe, 2001; Irvine, 1988; Mpofu, 1993, 2004). These words also can mean "wise," suggesting that, as in Taiwanese Chinese culture (Yang & Sternberg, 1997a, 1997b), wisdom and intelligence are seen as being very closely related. Behavior is considered intelligent to the extent that it benefits not just the individual, but also the community as a whole (Mpofu, 2004). Figure 7.1 shows a photo of a boy who has caught two catfish. In many African as well as other cultures, practical skills such as fishing are more important than in some European and North American cultural settings.

Neither African nor Asian conceptions of intelligence emphasize *exclusively* social notions. While they place more emphasis on social skills than do conventional US conceptions of intelligence, they also recognize the importance of cognitive aspects of intelligence. In a study of rural Kenyan conceptions of the nature of intelligence, Grigorenko and colleagues (2001) showed that four different terms constitute conceptions of intelligence among rural Kenyans – *rieko* (referring to academic but also other knowledge and skills), *luoro* (respect and obedience), *winjo* (common sense or practical intelligence), and *paro* (initiative and motivation). Only the first of these terms directly refers to knowledge-based skills (including but not

Figure 7.1 A young boy from Africa showing his catch. Practical skills can be more important
in African cultures than in many cultural settings in the West.

limited to the academic). More generally, Keller (2007, 2017) has pointed out that
Western urbanized cultures and farm cultures raise children in very different ways
with goals of developing different sets of skills. As a result, farm children become
adept at the tasks needed to be a successful farmer, including aspects of what
Gardner (2011) refers to as "naturalist intelligence." Urbanized Western children
develop different sets of more abstracted skills, which will serve them well on
standardized tests of intelligence, but which will be of little use to them on a farm.
A high IQ does not translate into knowledge of how to combat the effects on crops
of droughts, or even of how to milk a cow.

Differences in the Conception of Intelligence among US Ethnic Groups

While it is possible to compare general notions of the conception of intelligence
among Western and Eastern cultures, that doesn't mean that Western cultures or
even the United States share one overall conception of intelligence. Indeed, as

described in the Focus on Contemporary Research box in Chapter 1, Okagaki and Sternberg (1993) discovered that members of different ethnic groups in San Jose, California, had quite different ideas about what it means to be intelligent. For example, Latino-American parents of schoolchildren tended to emphasize the importance of social-competence skills in their conceptions of intelligence, whereas Asian American parents tended to emphasize the importance of cognitive skills rather heavily. Anglo-American parents also emphasized cognitive skills more. Teachers, representing the dominant culture of the school and of society, emphasized cognitive skills more heavily than skills of social competence. Children were viewed as more intelligent by teachers as a function of the extent to which their parents agreed with the teachers in their conception of the nature of intelligence. Put another way, teachers generally rewarded children who grew up with a view of intelligence that was similar to the teachers' own view of intelligence. The Asian American and Latino-American children, however, share an attribute not shared with the Anglo-Americans: The former tend to be more interdependent on each other in their thinking and in their lives (Kitayama & Salvador, 2017; Sanchez-Burks, Nisbett, & Ybarra, 2000). In other words, they recognize that intelligence often occurs in group efforts, not just in individual ones.

The Importance of Intelligence to Western Culture

Beyond the notions of what constitutes intelligence, people in the West and in other cultures as well consider intelligence to be of great importance. This emphasis is not common throughout the world, however. In Japan, for instance, people rarely talk about an individual's level of intelligence (Sato, Namiki, Ando, & Hatano, 2004). Instead, they place much more emphasis on a person's motivation and on the person's diligence. They view success as much more dependent on motivation and determination than on intelligence (Sato et al., 2004; see also Dai & Sternberg, 2004). When participants are given a task and then are given feedback denoting either success or failure, Japanese students are more likely than American students to view their success as resulting from effort, good luck, or various other situational factors. In contrast, American students are more likely to attribute their success to ability. Relatedly, Japanese students are likely to attribute their failure to a lack of effort. Americans are more likely to attribute failure to lack of ability (Miyamoto, 1985).

Expert Versus Lay Theories of Intelligence

Although researchers tend to emphasize lay implicit theories of intelligence in cultural studies, it is important to realize that it is not only cultural conceptions of intelligence that differ: Implicit theories of experts also are different. As an example, thinking about intelligence of Continental European researchers, especially in French-speaking countries, was swayed by Jean Piaget in the latter half of the twentieth century. This influence continues to be felt in the twenty-first century (Lautrey & de Ribaupierre, 2004). Vygotsky and Luria heavily influenced Russian thinking about intelligence (Grigorenko, 2004). Spearman heavily influenced English thinking (Deary & Smith, 2004). And Thurstone and Spearman both heavily influenced North American thinking (Sternberg, 2004c). Eastern philosophy heavily influenced Indian thinking (Baral & Das, 2004).

Models of the Relationship of Culture to Intelligence

Traditionally, research used more or less the same measures in various cultures, sometimes doing minor adaptations in order to fit the measures to the culture (Carlstedt, Gustafsson, & Hautamäki, 2004; Deary & Smith, 2004; Demetriou & Papadopoulos, 2004; Fernández-Ballesteros & Colom, 2004; Gulgoz & Kagitcibasi, 2004; Rosas, 2004; Stankov, 2004; see, in general, essays in Sternberg, 2004b). Today, however, research suggests that although the tests given to people in different cultures may have more or less the same items, people in different cultures may think about the problems in different ways (Nisbett, 2003; de Oliveira & Nisbett, 2017; Sternberg, 1997b, 2008, 2015). Some researchers even believe that both the instruments that should be used to measure intelligence and the alleged dimensions of intelligence differ as a function of the culture (Berry, 1974; Sarason & Doris, 1979). This position, as advocated by John Berry and others, is sometimes called radical cultural relativism.

Studies of Intelligence in Its Cultural Contexts

There are some aspects of intelligence that seem to transcend cultures. For example, the mental processes underlying intelligence and the mental representations upon which these processes act, appear to be largely uniform across cultures. But as the discussion above implies, any conception of intelligence that is understood without regard to its cultural context is likely to be incomplete and possibly misleading.

The Dangers of Single-Culture Research

Most psychological research is conducted within the context of a single culture. Single-culture studies whose results are generalized across cultures potentially mislead the field in a number of ways. First, they may limit the ways in which psychological phenomena and problems are defined. Second, they may give rise to unjustified assumptions about the phenomena being studied. Third, they may leave unanswered questions about the cultural generalizability of findings. Fourth, they may engender cultural imperialism, whereby members of one culture view their culture as better than others. And finally, they may represent lost opportunities for psychologists to collaborate and to develop psychological research around the world. Single-culture research programs show the potential hazards of research that is conducted within just a single culture. Greenfield (1997), for example, argued that it means a different thing for Mayan children to take a test than it does for many children in the United States to do so. The Mayan expectation is that collaboration is both permissible and proper. In the Mayan culture, it is quite unnatural for children to be forced to work individually rather than to collaborate.

Markus and Kitayama (1991) have found that there are different cultural constructions of the self in individualistic cultures, in contrast with collectivistic cultures. Indeed, Nisbett (2003; de Oliveira & Nisbett, 2017) has suggested that some cultures, especially Asian cultures, are more dialectical, or nonlinear, in their thinking, whereas other cultures, especially European and North American ones, are generally more linear. The difference is an important and meaningful one. For Westerners, an "intelligent" person is someone who can figure out as close to a linear progression as possible to reach a solution to a complex problem (Newell & Simon, 1972). The smart person reduces the difference between where he or she is in problem solving and where he or she needs to go until a solution is reached. In the Eastern mode, the smart person recognizes that real-life problems are more complex than that. They often have mutually incompatible or contradictory elements that may or may not be resolvable, resulting in solutions that may maximize on some dimensions while leaving other dimensions to be dealt with at some future time. The solution of problems is nonlinear.

Individuals living in different cultures may build concepts in quite different ways, rendering suspect data from concept-formation or concept-identification research studies in a single culture (Atran, 1999; Cole, Medin, Proffitt, Lynch, & Atran, 1999; Medin & Atran, 1999). Different groups may think differently about what appears to be the same phenomenon – whether a concept, an object, or an action such as the taking of a test. What appear as differences in intelligence across different groups may actually reflect little more than differences in cultural attributions (Helms-Lorenz, Van de Vijver, & Poortinga, 2003; Sternberg & Grigorenko, 2002). Helms-Lorenz et al. (2003) have suggested that measured differences in intellectual performance may be a result of differences in cultural complexity. That said, the complexity of a culture is extremely hard to define, and what appears to be simple or complex from the viewpoint of one culture may appear differently from the viewpoint of another.

Recognizing the Importance of Cultural Context for Research

Many psychologists have recognized the importance of cultural context for understanding intelligence and other related constructs. For example, Berry (1974) analyzed concepts regarding the nature of intelligence across many different cultural contexts. He found that there are substantial differences across these cultural contexts (see also Berry & Irvine, 1986). Cole (1998) and Shweder (1991, 2002) were instrumental in defining "cultural psychology" as a distinct field. They differentiated it from "cross-cultural psychology" (e.g., Irvine, 1979; Irvine & Berry, 1983; Marsella, Tharp, & Cibrorowski, 1979), which, they argued, is generally less sensitive to differences in thought and behavior among members of various cultures.

The various theories and empirical studies described in this chapter are drawn from both approaches, although our own research is in the "cultural" rather than the "cross-cultural" tradition. Cole's analysis of the field builds on his earlier work (Cole, Gay, Glick, & Sharp, 1971; Cole & Means, 1981; see also Cole & Scribner, 1974; Laboratory of Comparative Human Cognition, 1982), which demonstrated how cognitive performance among indigenous populations, such as the Kpelle in parts of Africa, can be different from that of North Americans. North Americans typically are tested in the context of lab studies of thinking and reasoning. What North Americans might view as sophisticated thinking – for example, sorting objects taxonomically (as in a bluebird being a kind of bird) – might be viewed as relatively unsophisticated thinking by members of the Kpelle tribe. Their sorting things functionally on sorting tasks reflected the demands of their everyday environment and life (as in a robin flying). In related work, Bruner, Olver, and Greenfield (1966) found that for members of the Wolof tribe of Senegal, increasingly greater Western-style schooling appeared to lead to increased use of taxonomic kinds of classification.

Some Examples Where Context Matters

Cole's work built upon earlier work, especially that of Luria. Luria (1931, 1976) demonstrated that Asian peasants in the former Soviet Union might fail to perform well on cognitive tasks as a result of their refusal to accept the tasks as they were presented. Gladwin (1970), studying the Puluwat people who inhabit the Caroline Islands in the South Pacific, discovered that the Puluwat were able to master diverse important knowledge domains, including ocean currents, wind and weather, and movements of the stars. The Puluwat integrate this knowledge with their mental maps of the islands to become navigators who respect and are highly respected in the environmental milieu in which they live.

In related work, Serpell (1974; see also Serpell, 2017) conducted research to discriminate between a general perceptual-deficit hypothesis and an opposing context-specific hypothesis regarding why children in certain cultures may sometimes show inferior perceptual abilities. Serpell found that English children did better than the rural Zambian children on a drawing task, but that the rural Zambian children did better than the English children on a task requiring wire-shaping. Thus, children performed better on those stimulus materials that were more relevant in their lives and that were more familiar to them in their own environments.

Wagner (1978) asked Moroccan and North American individuals to remember patterns of Oriental rugs as well as pictures of common everyday objects, for example, a rooster and a fish. He found no evidence of a difference in the structure of memory between the Moroccans and the North Americans. But the Moroccans were better with their memory for Oriental rugs. Kearins (1981), in a related study, found that when they were asked to remember visual displays, Anglo-Australians used verbally based school-appropriate strategies, whereas aboriginals used visual strategies appropriate for desert nomads.

Children from non-European and non-North American cultures do not always perform worse than children from modern Western cultures on tests of cognitive skills. Super (1976), for example, found that many African infants sit and walk earlier in life than do their counterparts in Europe and in the United States. Super further found that mothers in the African cultures he investigated made a serious effort to teach their babies at the earliest possible time how to sit and also to walk. At more mature levels of development, Stigler, Lee, Lucker, and Stevenson (1982; see also Stevenson & Stigler, 1994) found that both Chinese and Japanese children typically excel in developed mathematical skills relative to North American children.

Intelligence as Adaptation to the Environment

One study of a group of children carried out by Carraher, Carraher, and Schliemann (1985) is especially useful for evaluating intelligence as adaptation to the environment. The group comprised Brazilian street children. Brazilian street children are under serious environmental pressure to create and maintain a successful street business. The alternative for them may be death. In particular, if they do not form a successful street business, they risk death at the hands of so-called "death squads." These death squads may murder children who, unable to earn money, resort to robbing stores (or who are suspected of robbing stores). Thus, if the children are not intelligent in the basic sense of adapting to the environment, they risk death at the hands of death squads. The researchers discovered that the very same children who were perfectly able to do the mathematics they needed to run their street businesses were often unable to do the mathematics required in school successfully. The more abstracted and distant from real-world contexts the problems are as presented, the worse the children typically do on the problems. For middle-class children in regular school, the street context would be more distant from their lives. These results suggest that differences in environmental contexts can and do have a strong effect on performance. (See also Ceci & Roazzi, 1994; Nuñes, 1994; Saxe, 1990, for related work.) Figure 7.2 shows a photo of Brazilian street children. Their skills in forming a street business can be crucial to their survival.

Such differences in mathematical performance are not limited just to street children in Brazil. Lave (1988) demonstrated that housewives in Berkeley, California,

Figure 7.2 A group of young Brazilian drummers make their way around the historic tourist neighborhood of Pelourinho. (lazyllama / Shutterstock.com)

who could successfully do the mathematics needed to do comparison-shopping in the supermarket were often unable to do the same mathematics when they were placed in a classroom and given the same kinds of problems presented in an abstract, classroom-like form. In other words, the problem for the housewives was not at the level of mental processes, but rather at the level of applying the processes in specific environmental contexts that varied in their relevance to the housewives' lives.

To sum up, a number of researchers have conducted studies suggesting that how one assesses abilities, competences, and expertise can have a major effect on how "intelligent" students appear to be. Street children in Brazil, for instance, need the same mathematical skills to solve problems involving buying, selling, and giving discounts as do children living in the United States. But the environmental contexts in which they express these mathematical skills, and hence the cultural contexts in which they can best display their mathematical knowledge on tests, are different.

Viewing Intelligence on a Continuum
The measurement of human intelligence may be considered
to be taking place on a continuum

As an example, a test of vocabulary, as found in tests of intelligence, is clearly a test of achievement. But so, equally, is a test of abstract reasoning, such as figural matrices, as shown by the Flynn effect. In particular, Flynn showed that abstract-reasoning skills experienced substantial secular increases over the course of the twentieth century in diverse cultures around the world (Flynn, 1984, 1987). Thus, a psychologist can test knowledge as being part of intelligence, but all tests of intelligence require knowledge, even if the knowledge is merely with respect to test-taking skills – how to take the tests and maximize scores on them.

Children May Develop Skills that Are Contextually Important at the Expense of Skills that Are Academically Important

Investigations of intelligence that are conducted in settings outside the developed world can yield a picture of intelligence that is quite different from the picture one would obtain from investigations conducted only in the developed world. In a study in rural Kenya, my colleagues and I studied the ability of school-age children to adapt to their indigenous environment. My colleagues and I devised a test of practical intelligence that was relevant to the measurement of one aspect of adaptation to the environment (see Sternberg & Grigorenko, 1997; Sternberg et al., 2001; see also Sternberg, 1997a). The particular test of practical intelligence measured rural Kenyan children's informal tacit knowledge for the natural herbal medicines that the villagers used to combat various types of parasitic illnesses. Roughly speaking, tacit knowledge is what one needs to know to adapt to an environment, that is typically is not explicitly taught, and that often is not even verbalized – that is, people are not even sure of what it is (Sternberg et al., 2000; Sternberg & Hedlund, 2002; Sternberg & Smith, 1985).

Figure 7.3 shows a photograph of rural Kenyan schoolchildren. Schooling can be perceived as having a different value in a some rural Kenyan settings, where there

Figure 7.3 Rural Kenyan schoolchildren. In places where there are few jobs available that will require the use of information learned in school, school may be valued less than learning practical skills gained through an apprenticeship. (Photographed by Elena Grigorenko; photo courtesy of Robert Sternberg)

are very few jobs that students can ultimately pursue that will require them to use their schooling, as opposed to the practical skills they might gain through an early apprenticeship.

Middle-class Westerners of the modern era might find it a serious challenge to survive, much less to thrive, in some of the contexts described above. For example, in all likelihood, they would not know what any of the natural herbal medicines are, and certainly would not know how to use any of them. Yet, such knowledge is important for combating the diverse and abundant parasitic illnesses anyone might pick up in rural Kenya.

We measured the rural Kenyan children's skills in identifying the natural herbal medicines, where the herbs originate, what purposes they are used for, and how they are correctly dosed. We also administered to the children of the study the Raven Colored Progressive Matrices Test (Raven, Court, & Raven, 1992), which is a test of fluid (abstract-reasoning-based abilities), as well as the Mill Hill Vocabulary Scale (Raven et al., 1992 – which is a measure of crystallized or formal-knowledge-based abilities). In addition, we administered to the children a comparable test of vocabulary that was couched in their own language, Dholuo. The Dholuo language is usually spoken in the context of the home and community, whereas English is typically spoken in the context of the schools.

All the correlations we obtained between the test of practical intelligence, indigenous tacit knowledge, and scores on fluid ability and crystallized ability tests were *negative*. The correlations between the practical-intelligence tests and the tests of crystallized abilities were statistically significantly so. Put another way, higher scores by the children on the test of tacit knowledge were associated with lower scores on the tests of crystallized abilities (vocabulary). In this culture, staying in school may lead to increased performance on Western tests, but it is viewed as a failure: The successful children leave school to start work (see Prince & Geissler, 2001). As Rogoff (1990, 2003) and other investigators have noted, Western-type schooling is far from universal. It has not even been common through much of the history of humankind. Throughout history and still in many cultural settings, schooling, especially for boys, takes the form of apprenticeships in which the children learn a trade from an early age. They learn the knowledge and skills they will need so as to succeed in their chosen or assigned trade. They are not simultaneously involved in academic tasks that call upon the development of the particular blend of cognitive skills assessed by conventional intelligence tests.

Children May Have Substantial Practical Skills that Go Unrecognized in Academic Tests

Related data resulted from a study done among Yup'ik Eskimo children in south-western Alaska (Grigorenko, Meier, Lipka, Mohatt, Yanez, & Sternberg, 2004).

My colleagues and I assessed the importance of academic and practical intelligence for adaptation in rural as well as semi-urban Alaskan communities. We measured academic intelligence with standardized tests of fluid (the Cattell Culture Fair Test of *g*, Cattell & Cattell, 1973) and crystallized intelligence (the Mill Hill Vocabulary Scale, Raven et al., 1992). In contrast, we measured practical intelligence with a test of tacit knowledge of practical skills (hunting, fishing, using herbal medicines, coping with rapidly changing weather conditions, picking and preserving plant foods, and so on) as are relevant to, and acquired in rural Alaskan Yup'ik communities. The test was called the Yup'ik Scale of Practical Intelligence. As we expected, the semi-urban children outperformed the rural children on the measure of crystallized intelligence (vocabulary). But the rural children outperformed the semi-urban children on the practical-intelligence measure relevant to the Yup'ik. The test of tacit-knowledge skills was superior to the tests of academic intelligence in predicting practical adaptive skills as judged both by adults and by peers of the children from rural communities (for whom the test was created), but not of the children from semi-urban settings.

Dynamic Testing May Reveal Cognitive Skills Not Revealed by Static Testing

Do conventional tests of intelligence truly measure all of the skills that children in developing countries, or really, any countries, have to offer?

Dynamic testing, defined in Chapter 2, is like conventional static testing insofar as individuals are tested so that inferences can be drawn regarding their diverse abilities (Brown & Ferrara, 1985; Feuerstein, 1979; Grigorenko & Sternberg, 1998; Guthke, 1993; Haywood & Tzuriel, 1992; Lidz, 1991; Sternberg & Grigorenko, 2002; Tzuriel, 1995; Vygotsky, 1978). But in dynamic testing, individuals are given some kind of feedback in order to help them improve their performance – that is, they learn while being tested (Feuerstein, 1979; Grigorenko & Sternberg, 1998; Sternberg & Grigorenko, 2002; Tzuriel, 1995). Vygotsky (1978) noted that children's ability to profit from the guided, targeted instruction the children received during a testing session could serve as an assessment of children's zone of proximal development (ZPD), that is, the difference between their developed abilities, on the one hand, and their not yet developed, latent capacities, on the other. In dynamic testing, testing and instruction are treated as being of one integrated and holistic piece rather than as being distinct and easily separable processes. Such an integration fits into traditional definitions of intelligence. These definitions emphasize the nature of intelligence as the ability to learn and profit from experience ("Intelligence and its measurement," 1921; see also Sternberg & Detterman, 1986). Dynamic measurement is particularly critical when not all children being tested have had equal opportunities in the past to learn in school and in the home environment.

Culture-Fair and Culture-Relevant Testing

An **etic approach** to testing involves giving essentially the same tests or tasks to individuals across cultures. The etic approach is at least somewhat susceptible to criticism; because members of different cultures view intelligence differently, the same behaviors that may be considered intelligent in one cultural context may be viewed as unintelligent in another cultural context. Consider, for instance, the concept of mental quickness. In mainstream US culture, to say someone is "quick" is tantamount to saying that the person is intelligent. And as it happens, most group tests of intelligence are strictly timed.

Certainly, it is sometimes important to be fast in one's work. When a student has not yet started writing a term paper that is due the next day, it is definitely adaptive for the student to be quick in writing the paper. Similarly, an air-traffic controller has to be fast if he or she values the lives of the passengers on the airplanes he or she is monitoring. In many cultures, however, quickness is not generally viewed as a valuable disposition. People in some cultures may believe that more intelligent people do not rush into or through their work.

In theory, a **culture-fair test** is a test that is equally appropriate for members of all cultures. It comprises items that are equally fair to everyone. Performance on tests that have been designated "culture fair," however, seems to be influenced by cultural factors. Examples are years of schooling and levels of academic achievements (e.g., Ceci, 1996). In sum, researchers must be careful when drawing conclusions about levels or even the existence of between-group differences in measured intelligence (Greenfield, 1997; Loehlin, 2000).

We cannot now, given our present state of knowledge, create culture-free or culture-fair tests. But we can create culture-relevant tests, ones that will not make individuals from cultures other than the North American or European continents look intellectually challenged or learning disabled, and that should be our goal (Sternberg, 1981; Spear-Swerling & Sternberg, 1994). **Culture-relevant tests** require an array of skills and stored information that are relevant to the specific cultural and worldly experiences of the test-takers. Culture-relevant tests involve an **emic approach,** in which one takes into account the cultural context of the people being studied and adapts one's research or assessment to that context. The content of the tests and the procedures for administering them are appropriate to the cultural norms and expectations of the test takers. For instance, in one study, 14-year-old boys performed poorly on a task if it was presented in terms of baking cupcakes. But the boys performed well when the task instead was presented in terms of charging batteries (Ceci & Bronfenbrenner, 1985). Similarly, Brazilian maids had no trouble with proportional reasoning when they were hypothetically purchasing food. But they had great difficulty with the task when they were hypothetically purchasing medicinal herbs (Schliemann & Magalhües, 1990).

CONCLUSION

When people's cultural contexts are taken into account, (a) people are better recognized for and are better able to utilize their talents, (b) schools better can teach and assess children's performance, and (c) society is better able to utilize constructively rather than waste the talents of its members. Measuring intelligence across cultures simply by translating Western tests and giving the tests to individuals in a variety of cultures is nonideal. Rather, we need to understand the cultural context of the individuals we are testing.

CHAPTER SUMMARY

Intelligence needs to be understood in the cultural contexts in which it is displayed. For one thing, people in different cultures have different conceptions (implicit theories) of what intelligence is. Asian and African cultures tend to have broader and more encompassing views of intelligence than do Western cultures. Asians and Africans place less emphasis on mental speed and more emphasis on social and emotional aspects of behavior as well as wisdom. These implicit theories are important because in everyday life, people's behavior is guided not so much by scores on standardized or other tests but rather by people's implicit theories. For example, hiring and promotion decisions usually are based on such implicit theories, not on test scores.

Studies of performance by people and especially children in different cultures suggest that the strengths of individuals across cultures are not necessarily well represented by conventional intelligence tests. For example, in some cultures, knowledge of herbal medications to combat parasitic illnesses, or knowledge of hunting and gathering, or knowledge of how to do ice fishing effectively, can be more important to intelligence than scores on a standardized test. Eskimo children may know how to navigate across the frozen tundra in the winter without obvious landmarks, yet not be able to attain high scores on intelligence tests. Some of those who would score highly on such tests would be unable to do such navigation, to their peril.

There is no such thing as a culture-free test of intelligence and there probably is no test that genuinely is culture-fair either. At best, tests should be culture-relevant, measuring cognitive and other skills relevant to adaptation in particular cultures. These skills are likely to be partially but not fully overlapping across cultures. Thus, intelligence needs to be understood in its cultural contexts, not divorced from such contexts.

KEY TERMS

converging operations • **culture** • **culture-fair test** • **culture-relevant test** • **dynamic testing** • **emic approach** • **etic approach** • **implicit theory**

COMPREHENSION AND REFLECTION QUESTIONS

1. What is the difference between an etic and an emic approach to cultural research?
2. What did Sternberg and his colleagues find in their study of rural Kenyan children's knowledge of natural herbal medicines that can combat parasitic illnesses?
3. What are limitations of research that takes place in just one culture?
4. What are the advantages of assessing intelligence as it occurs in natural cultural contexts? What are the limitations?
5. What is dynamic testing?

References

Ang, S., Van Dyne, L., & Tan, M. L. (2011). Cultural intelligence. In R. J. Sternberg & S. B. Kaufman (eds.), *Cambridge handbook of intelligence* (pp. 582-602). New York: Cambridge University Press.

Atran, S. (1999). Itzaj Maya folkbiological taxonomy: Cognitive universals and cultural particulars. In D. L. Medin & S. Atran (eds.), *Folkbiology* (pp. 119–213). Cambridge, MA: MIT Press.

Azuma, H., & Kashiwagi, K. (1987). Descriptions for an intelligent person: A Japanese study. *Japanese Psychological Research, 29,* 17-26.

Baral, B. D., & Das, J. P. (2004). Intelligence: what is indigenous to India and what is shared? In R. J. Sternberg (ed.), *International handbook of intelligence* (pp. 270-301). New York: Cambridge University Press.

Barnouw, V. (1985). *Culture and personality.* Chicago: Dorsey Press.

Benedict, R. (1946). *The crysanthemum and the sword.* Boston, MA: Houghton Mifflin.

Berry, J. W. (1974). Radical cultural relativism and the concept of intelligence. In J. W. Berry, & P. R. Dasen (eds.), *Culture and cognition: Readings in cross-cultural psychology* (pp. 225-229). London: Methuen.

Berry, J. W., & Irvine, S. H. (1986). Bricolage: Savages do it daily. In R. J. Sternberg & R. K. Wagner (eds.), *Practical intelligence: Nature and origins of competence in the everyday world* (pp. 271-306). New York: Cambridge University Press.

Berry, J. W., Poortinga, Y. H., Segall, M. H., & Dasen, P. R. (1992). *Cross-cultural psychology: Research and applications.* New York: Cambridge University Press.

Binet, A., & Simon, T. (1916). *The development of intelligence in children* (E. S. Kite, trans.). Baltimore: Williams & Wilkins.

Boas, F. (1911). *The mind of primitive man*. New York: Macmillan.

Brislin, R. W., Lonner, W. J., & Thorndike, R. M. (eds.) (1973). *Cross-cultural research methods*. New York: Wiley.

Brown, A. L., & Ferrara, R. A. (1985). Diagnosing zones of proximal development. In J. V. Wertsch (ed.). *Culture, communication, and cognition: Vygotskian perspectives*, (pp. 273-305). New York: Cambridge University Press.

Bruner, J. S., Olver, R. R., & Greenfield, P. M. (1966). *Studies in cognitive growth*. New York: Wiley.

Carlstedt, B., Gustafsson, J.-E., & Hautamäki, J. (2004). Intelligence: Theory, research, and testing in the Nordic countries. In R. J. Sternberg (ed.), *International handbook of intelligence* (pp. 49-78). New York: Cambridge University Press.

Carraher, T. N., Carraher, D., & Schliemann, A. D. (1985). Mathematics in the streets and in schools. *British Journal of Developmental Psychology*, *3*, 21-29.

Cattell, R. B., & Cattell, A. K. S. (1973). *Measuring intelligence with the Culture Fair Tests*. Champaign, IL: Institute for Personality and Ability Testing.

Ceci, S. J. (1996). *On intelligence* (expanded ed.). Cambridge, MA: Harvard University Press.

Ceci, S. J., & Bronfenbrenner, U. (1985). Don't forget to take the cupcakes out of the oven: Strategic time-monitoring, prospective memory and context. *Child Development*, *56*, 175-190.

Ceci, S. J., & Roazzi, A. (1994). The effects of context on cognition: Postcards from Brazil. In R. J. Sternberg & R. K. Wagner (eds.), *Mind in context: Interactionist perspectives on human intelligence* (pp. 74-101). New York: Cambridge University Press.

Chen, M. J. (1994). Chinese and Australian concepts of intelligence. *Psychology and Developing Societies*, *6*, 101-117.

Chimhundu, H. (ed.) (2001). *Dura manzwi guru rechi Shona*. Harare, Zimbabwe: College Press.

Cole, M. (1998). *Cultural psychology: A once and future discipline*. Cambridge, MA: Belknap.

Cole, M. (2017). Idiocultural design as a tool of cultural psychology. *Perspectives on Psychological Science*, *12*, 772-781.

Cole, M., Gay, J., Glick, J., & Sharp, D. W. (1971). *The cultural context of learning and thinking*. New York: Basic Books.

Cole, M., & Means, B. (1981). *Comparative studies of how people think*. Cambridge, MA: Harvard University Press.

Cole, M., & Scribner, S. (1974). *Culture and thought*. New York: Wiley.

Coley, J. D., Medin, D. L., Proffitt, J. B., Lynch, E., & Atran, S. (1999). Inductive reasoning in folkbiological thought. In D. L. Medin & S. Atran (eds.), *Folkbiology* (pp. 205–232). Cambridge, MA: MIT Press.

Connolly, K., & Bruner, J. (eds.) (1974). *The growth of competence*. New York: Academic Press.

Craik, F. I. M., & Lockhart, R. S. (1972). Levels of processing: A framework for memory research. *Journal of Verbal Learning and Verbal Behavior, 11*, 671–684.

Dai, D. Y., & Sternberg, R. J. (eds.). (2004). *Motivation, emotion, and cognition: Integrative perspectives on intellectual functioning and development.* Mahwah, NJ: Lawrence Erlbaum Associates.

Das, J. P. (1994). Eastern views of intelligence. In R. J. Sternberg (ed.), *Encyclopedia of intelligence* (pp. 91-97). New York: Macmillan.

Dasen, P. (1984). The cross-cultural study of intelligence: Piaget and the Baoule. *International Journal of Psychology, 19*, 407-434.

Deary, I. J., & Smith, P. (2004). Intelligence research and assessment in the United Kingdom. In R. J. Sternberg (ed.), *International handbook of intelligence* (pp. 1-48). New York: Cambridge University Press.

Demetriou, A., & Papadopoulos, T. C. (2004). Human intelligence: From local models to universal theory. In R. J. Sternberg (ed.), *International handbook of intelligence* (pp. 445-474). New York: Cambridge University Press.

De Oliveira, S., & Nisbett, R. (2017). Culture changes how we think about thinking: From "human inference" to "geography of thought." *Perspectives on Psychological Science, 12*(5), 782-790.

Fernández-Ballesteros, R., & Colom, R. (2004). The psychology of human intelligence in Spain. In R. J. Sternberg (ed.), *International handbook of intelligence* (pp. 79-103). New York: Cambridge University Press.

Feuerstein, R. (1979). *The dynamic assessment of retarded performers: The Learning Potential Assessment Device theory, instruments, and techniques.* Baltimore, MD: University Park Press.

Flynn, J. R. (1984). The mean IQ of Americans: Massive gains 1932 to 1978. *Psychological Bulletin. 95*, 29-51.

Flynn, J. R. (1987). Massive IQ gains in 14 nations. *Psychological Bulletin, 101*, 171-191.

Flynn, J. R. (2016). *Does your family make you smarter? Nature, nurture, and human autonomy.* New York: Cambridge University Press.

Gardner, H. (2011). *Frames of mind: The theory of multiple intelligences.* New York: Basic Books.

Gelfand, M., Harrington, J., & Jackson, J. (2017). The strength of social norms across human groups: Insights from cultural psychology. *Perspectives on Psychological Science, 12*, 800-809.

Gelfand, M. J., Nishii, L. H., & Raver, J. L. (2006). On the nature and importance of cultural tightness-looseness. *Journal of Applied Psychology*, 91(6), 1225-1244.

Gelfand, M. J., Raver, J. L., Nishii, L., Leslie, L. M., Lun, J., Lim, B. C., ... & Aycan, Z. (2011). Differences between tight and loose cultures: A 33-nation study. *Science, 332*(6033), 1100-1104.

Gill, R., & Keats, D. M. (1980). Elements of intellectual competence judgments by Australian and Malay university students. *Journal of Cross-cultural Psychology, 11*(2), 233-243.

Gladwin, T. (1970). *East is a big bird*. Cambridge, MA: Harvard University Press.

Goodnow, J. J. (1986). Some lifelong everyday forms of intelligence behavior: Organizing and reorganizing. In R. J. Sternberg & R. K. Wagner (eds.), *Practical intelligence* (pp. 31-50). New York: Cambridge University Press.

Greenfield, P. M. (1997). You can't take it with you: Why abilities assessments don't cross cultures. *American Psychologist, 52*, 1115-1124.

Greenfield, P. M. (1998). The cultural evolution of IQ. In U. Neisser (ed.), *The rising curve: Long-term gains in IQ and related measures* (pp. 81-123). Washington, DC: American Psychological Association.

Greenfield, P. M. (2017). Cultural change over time: Why replicability should not be the gold standard in psychological science. *Perspectives on Psychological Science, 12*, 762-771.

Grigorenko, E. L. (2004). Is it possible to study intelligence without using the concept of intelligence? An example from Soviet/Russian psychology. In R. J. Sternberg (ed.), *International handbook of intelligence* (pp. 170-211). New York: Cambridge University Press.

Grigorenko, E. L., Geissler, P. W., Prince, R., Okatcha, F., Nokes, C., Kenny, D. A., Bundy, D.A., & Sternberg, R. J. (2001). The organization of Luo conceptions of intelligence: A study of implicit theories in a Kenyan village. *International Journal of Behavior Development, 25*, 367-378.

Grigorenko, E. L., Meier, E., Lipka, J., Mohatt, G., Yanez, E., & Sternberg, R. J. (2004). The relationship between academic and practical intelligence: A case study of the tacit knowledge of Native American Yup'ik people in Alaska. *Learning and Individual Differences, 14*, 183-207.

Grigorenko, E. L., & Sternberg, R. J. (1998). Dynamic testing. *Psychological Bulletin, 124*, 75-111.

Grigorenko, E. L., & Sternberg, R. J. (2001). Analytical, creative, and practical intelligence as predictors of self-reported adaptive functioning: A case study in Russia. *Intelligence, 29*, 57-73.

Gulgoz, S., & Kagitcibasi, C. (2004). Intelligence and intelligence testing in Turkey. In R. J. Sternberg (ed.), *International handbook of intelligence* (pp. 248-269). New York: Cambridge University Press.

Guthke, J. (1993). Current trends in theories and assessment of intelligence. In J. H. M. Hamers, K. Sijtsma, & A. J. J. M. Ruijssenaars (eds.), *Learning potential assessment* (pp. 13-20). Amsterdam: Swets & Zeitlinger.

Hadebe, S. (ed.) (2001). *Isichamazwi*. Harare, Zimbabwe: College Press.

Haywood, H. C. &. Tzuriel, D. (eds.). (1992). *Interactive assessment*. New York: Springer.

Helms-Lorenz, M., Van de Vijver, F. J. R., & Poortinga, Y. H. (2003). Cross-cultural differences in cognitive performance and Spearman's hypothesis: *g* or *c*? *Intelligence, 31*, 9-29.

Henrich, J., Heine, S. J., & Norenzayan, A. (2010a). Most people are not WEIRD. *Nature, 466*. www2.psych.ubc.ca/~anlab/Manuscripts/HHN_Nature_2010.pdf.

Henrich, J., Heine, S. J., & Norenzayan, A. (2010b). The weirdest people in the world? *Behavioral and Brain Sciences, 33*(2-3), 61-83.

Hong, Y.-Y., & Cheon, B. (2017). How does culture matter in the face of globalization? *Perspectives on Psychological Science, 12,* 810-823.

Hong, Y.-Y., & Cheon, B. "Intelligence and its measurement": A symposium (1921). *Journal of Educational Psychology, 12,* 123-147, 195-216, 271-275.

Irvine, S. H. (1979). The place of factor analysis in cross-cultural methodology and its contribution to cognitive theory. In L. Eckensberger, W. Lonner, & Y. Poortinga (eds.), *Cross-cultural contributions to psychology.* Amsterdam: Swets & Zeitlinger.

Irvine, S. H. (1988). Constructing the intellect of the Shona: A taxonomic approach. In J. W. Berry, S. H. Irvine, & E. B. Hunt (eds.), *Indigenous cognitive functioning in a cultural context* (pp. 3-59). New York: Cambridge University Press.

Irvine, S. H., & Berry, J. W. (eds.) (1983). *Human abilities in cultural context.* New York: Cambridge University Press.

Kaplan, K. (1997). Inteligencia, escuela y sociedad: Las categorias del judicio magisterial sobre la inteligencia. [Intelligence, school, and society: The categories of the teachers' judgment about intelligence.] *Propuesta Educativa, 16,* 24-32.

Kearins, J. M. (1981). Visual spatial memory in Australian Aboriginal children of desert regions. *Cognitive Psychology, 13,* 434-460.

Keller, H. (2007). *Cultures of infancy.* Mahwah, NJ: Lawrence Erlbaum Associates.

Keller, H. (2017). Culture and development: A systematic relationship. *Perspectives on Psychological Science, 12,* 833-840.

Kitayama, S., & Salvador, C. (2017). Culture embrained: Going beyond the nature-nurture dichotomy. *Perspectives on Psychological Science, 12,* 841-854.

Kroeber, A. L., & Kluckhohn, C. (1952). *Culture: A critical review of concepts and definitions.* Cambridge, MA: Peabody Museum.

Laboratory of Comparative Human Cognition (1982). Culture and intelligence. In R. J. Sternberg (ed.), *Handbook of human intelligence* (pp. 642-719). New York: Cambridge University Press.

Lautrey, J., & Ribaupierre, A. (2004). Psychology of human intelligence in France and French-speaking Switzerland. In R. J. Sternberg (ed.), *International handbook of intelligence* (pp. 104-134). New York: Cambridge University Press.

Lave, J. (1988). *Cognition in practice.* New York: Cambridge University Press.

Lidz, C. S. (1991). *Practitioner's guide to dynamic assessment.* New York: Guilford Press.

Lin, C. T. (1980). A sketch on the methods of mental testing in ancient China. *Acta Psychological Sinica, 1,* 75-80. (In Chinese.)

Loehlin, J. C. (2000). Group differences in intelligence. In R. J. Sternberg (ed.), *Handbook of intelligence* (pp. 176-194). New York: Cambridge University Press.

Luria, A. R. (1931). Psychological expedition to central Asia. *Science, 74,* 383-384.

Lutz, C. (1985). Ethnopsychology compared to what? Explaining behaviour and consciousness among the Ifaluk. In G. M. White & J. Kirkpatrick (eds.), *Person, self, and experience: Exploring Pacific ethnopsychologies* (pp. 35-79). Berkeley: University of California Press.

Markus, H. R., & Kitayama, S. (1991). Culture and the self: Implications for cognition, emotion, and motivation. *Psychological Review, 98*, 224-253.

Marsella, A. J., Tharp, R., & Ciborowski, T. (eds.) (1979). *Perspectives on cross-cultural psychology*. New York: Academic Press.

Matsumoto, D. (1994). *People: Psychology from a cultural perspective*. Pacific Grove, CA: Brooks-Cole.

Matsumoto, D. (1996). *Culture and psychology*. Pacific Grove, CA: Brooks-Cole.

Mead, M. (1928). *Coming of age in Samoa*. New York: Morrow.

Medin, D. L., & Atran, S. (eds.) (1999). *Folkbiology*. Cambridge, MA: MIT Press.

Miyamoto, M. (1985). Parents' and children's beliefs and children's achievement and development. In R. Diaz-Guerrero (ed.), *Cross-cultural and national studies in social psychology* (pp. 209-223). Amsterdam: Elsevier Science.

Mpofu, E. (1993). The context of mental testing and implications for psychoeducational practice in modern Zimbabwe. In W. Su (ed.), *Proceedings of the second Afro-Asian Psychological Conference* (pp. 17-25). Beijing: University of Peking Press.

Mpofu, E. (2004). Intelligence in Zimbabwe. In R. J. Sternberg (ed.), *International handbook of intelligence* (pp. 364-390). New York: Cambridge University Press.

Mundy-Castle, A. C. (1974). Social and technological intelligence in Western or nonwestern cultures. *Universitas, 4*, 46-52.

Newell, A., & Simon, H. A. (1972). *Human problem solving*. Englewood Cliffs, NJ: Prentice-Hall.

Nisbett, R. E. (2003). *The geography of thought: Why we think the way we do*. New York: The Free Press.

Niu, W. & Brass, J. (2011). Intelligence in worldwide perspective. In S. Kaufman & R. J. Sternberg (eds.), *Cambridge handbook of intelligence* (pp. 623-646). New York: Cambridge University Press.

Nuñes, T. (1994). Street intelligence. In R. J. Sternberg (ed.), *Encyclopedia of human intelligence* (vol. 2, pp. 1045-1049). New York: Macmillan.

Okagaki, L., & Sternberg, R. J. (1993). Parental beliefs and children's school performance. *Child Development, 64*, 36-56.

Poole, F. J. P. (1985). Coming into social being: Cultural images of infants in Bimin-Kuskusmin folk psychology. In G. M. White & J. Kirkpatrick (eds.). *Person, self, and experience: Exploring Pacific ethnopsychologies* (pp. 183-244). Berkeley: University of California Press.

Prince, R. J., & Geissler, P. W. (2001). Becoming "one who treats": A case study of a Luo healer and her grandson in western Kenya. *Educational Anthropology Quarterly, 32*, 447-471.

Raven, J. C., Court, J. H., & Raven, J. (1992). *Manual for Raven's Progressive Matrices and Mill Hill Vocabulary Scales*. Oxford: Oxford Psychologists Press.

Rogoff, B. (1990). *Apprenticeship in thinking: Cognitive development in social context.* New York: Oxford University Press.

Rogoff, B. (2003). *The cultural nature of human development.* London: Oxford University Press.

Rogoff, B., Coppens, A., Alcalá, L., Aceves-Azuara, I., López, A., Ruvalcaba, O., & Dayton, A. (2017). Noticing learners' strengths through cultural research. *Perspectives on Psychological Science, 12,* 876-888.

Rosas, R. (2004). Intelligence research in Latin America. In R. J. Sternberg (ed.), *International handbook of intelligence* (pp. 391-410). New York: Cambridge University Press.

Ruzgis, P. M., & Grigorenko, E. L. (1994). Cultural meaning systems, intelligence and personality. In R. J. Sternberg and P. Ruzgis (eds.). *Personality and intelligence* (pp. 248-270). New York: Cambridge University Press.

Sanchez-Burks, J., Nisbett, R. E., & Ybarra, O. (2000). Cultural styles, relationship schemas, and prejudice against out-groups. *Journal of Personality and Social Psychology, 79*(2), 174-189.

Sarason, S. B., & Doris, J. (1979). *Educational handicap, public policy, and social history.* New York: Free Press.

Sato, T., Namiki, H., Ando, J., & Hatano, G. (2004). Japanese conception of and research on intelligence. In R. J. Sternberg (ed.), *International handbook of intelligence* (pp. 302-324). New York: Cambridge University Press.

Saxe, G. B. (1990). *Culture and cognitive development: Studies in mathematical understanding.* Mahwah, NJ: Lawrence Erlbaum Associates.

Schliemann, A. D., & Magalhües, V. P. (1990). Proportional reasoning: From shops, to kitchens, laboratories, and, hopefully, schools. *Proceedings of the Fourteenth International Conference for the Psychology of Mathematics Education, Oaxtepec, Mexico.*

Scribner, S. (1984). Studying working intelligence. In B. Rogoff & J. Lave (eds.), *Everyday cognition: Its development in social context* (pp. 9-40). Cambridge, MA: Harvard University Press.

Scribner, S. (1986). Thinking in action: Some characteristics of practical thought. In R. J. Sternberg & R. K. Wagner (eds.), *Practical intelligence: Nature and origins of competence in the everyday world* (pp. 13-30). New York: Cambridge University Press.

Serpell, R. (1974). Aspects of intelligence in a developing country. *African Social Research, 17,* 576-596.

Serpell, R. (1996). Cultural models of childhood in indigenous socialization and formal schooling in Zambia. In C. P. Hwang & M. E. Lamb (eds.), *Images of childhood* (pp. 129-142). Mahwah, NJ: Lawrence Erlbaum Associates.

Serpell, R. (2000). Intelligence and culture. In R. J. Sternberg (ed.), *Handbook of intelligence* (pp. 549-580). New York: Cambridge University Press.

Serpell, R. (2002). The embeddedness of human development within sociocultural context: Pedagogical, and political implications. *Social Development, 11*(2) 290-295.

Serpell, R. (2017). How the study of cognitive growth can benefit from a cultural lens. *Perspectives on Psychological Science, 12*(5), 889-899.

Shi, J. (2004). Diligence makes people smart: Chinese perspectives on intelligence. In R. J. Sternberg (ed.), *International handbook of intelligence* (pp. 325-343). New York: Cambridge University Press.

Shweder, R. A. (1991). *Thinking through cultures: Multicultural expeditions in cultural psychology*. Cambridge, MA: Harvard University Press.

Shweder, R. A. (2002). *Engaging cultural differences: The multicultural challenge in liberal democracies*. New York: Russell Sage

Spear-Swerling, L., & Sternberg, R. J. (1994). The road not taken: An integrative theoretical model of reading disability. *Journal of Learning Disabilities, 27*(2), 91-103.

Srivistava, S., & Misra, G. (1996). Changing perspectives on understanding intelligence: An appraisal. *Indian Psychological Abstracts and Reviews, 3*. New Delhi: Sage.

Srivistava, S., & Misra, G. (2000). *Culture and conceptualization of intelligence*. New Delhi: National Council of Educational Research and Training.

Stankov, L. (2004). Similar thoughts under different stars: Conceptions of intelligence in Australia. In R. J. Sternberg (ed.), *International handbook of intelligence* (pp. 344-363). New York: Cambridge University Press.

Sternberg, R. J. (1985a). *Beyond IQ: A triarchic theory of human intelligence*. New York: Cambridge University Press.

Sternberg, R. J. (1985b). Human intelligence: The model is the message. *Science, 230*, 1111-1118.

Sternberg, R. J. (1985c). Teaching critical thinking, Part 1: Are we making critical mistakes? *Phi Delta Kappan, 67*, 194-198.

Sternberg, R. J. (1986). Inside intelligence. *American Scientist, 74*, 137-143.

Sternberg, R. J. (1990). *Metaphors of mind*. New York: Cambridge University Press.

Sternberg. R. J. (1997a). Managerial intelligence: Why IQ isn't enough. *Journal of Management, 23*(3), 475-463.

Sternberg, R. J. (1997b). *Successful intelligence*. New York: Plume.

Sternberg, R. J. (1997c). What does it mean to be smart? *Educational Leadership, 54*(6), 20-24.

Sternberg, R. J. (1999). The theory of successful intelligence. *Review of General Psychology, 3*, 292-316.

Sternberg, R. J. (2004a). Culture and intelligence. *American Psychologist, 59*, 325-338.

Sternberg, R. J. (ed.) (2004b). *International handbook of intelligence*. New York: Cambridge University Press.

Sternberg, R. J. (2004c). North American approaches to intelligence. In R. J. Sternberg (ed.), *International handbook of intelligence* (pp. 411-444). New York: Cambridge University Press.

Sternberg, R. J. (2005). There are no public-policy implications: A reply to Rushton and Jensen. *Psychology, Public Policy, and Law, 11*(2), 295-301.

Sternberg, R. J. (2007). Intelligence and culture. In S. Kitayama & D. Cohen (eds.), *Handbook of cultural psychology* (pp. 547-568). New York: Guilford Press.

Sternberg, R. J. (2008). Successful intelligence as a framework for understanding cultural adaptation. In S. Ang & L. Van Dyne (eds.), *Handbook on cultural intelligence* (pp. 306-317). New York: M. E. Sharpe.

Sternberg, R. J. (2012). Intelligence in its cultural context. In M. Gelfand, C. -Y. Chiu, & Y. -Y. Hong (eds.), *Advances in cultures and psychology* (vol. 2, pp. 205-248). New York: Oxford University Press.

Sternberg, R. J. (2014). The development of adaptive competence. *Developmental Review*, *34*, 208-224.

Sternberg, R. J. (2015). Successful intelligence: A new model for testing intelligence beyond IQ tests. *European Journal of Education and Psychology, 8*, 76-84.

Sternberg, R. J., Conway, B. E., Ketron, J. L., & Bernstein, M. (1981). People's conceptions of intelligence. *Journal of Personality and Social Psychology, 41*, 37-55.

Sternberg, R. J., & Davidson, J. E. (1982). The mind of the puzzler. *Psychology Today*, *16* (June), 37–44.

Sternberg, R. J., & Detterman, D. K. (1986). *What is intelligence?* Norwood, NJ: Ablex.

Sternberg, R. J., Forsythe, G. B., Hedlund, J., Horvath, J., Snook, S., Williams, W. M., Wagner, R. K., & Grigorenko, E. L. (2000). *Practical intelligence in everyday life.* New York: Cambridge University Press.

Sternberg, R. J., & Grigorenko, E. L. (eds.). (1997). *Intelligence, heredity, and environment.* New York: Cambridge University Press.

Sternberg, R. J., & Grigorenko, E. L. (1999). A smelly 113° in the shade, or, why we do field research. *APS Observer, 12*(1), 10–11, 20–21.

Sternberg, R. J., & Grigorenko E. L. (eds.). (2002). *The general factor of intelligence: How general is it?* Mahwah, NJ: Lawrence Erlbaum Associates.

Sternberg, R. J., & Grigorenko, E. L. (2008). Ability testing across cultures. In L. A. Suzuki & J. G. Ponterotto (eds.), *Handbook of multicultural assessment* (3rd ed., pp. 449-470). San Francisco: Jossey-Bass.

Sternberg, R. J., Grigorenko, E. L., Ngrosho, D., Tantufuye, E., Mbise, A., Nokes, C., Jukes, M., & Bundy, D. A. (2002). Assessing intellectual potential in rural Tanzanian school children. *Intelligence, 30*, 141-162.

Sternberg, R. J., & Hedlund, J. (2002). Practical intelligence, *g*, and work psychology. *Human Performance 15*(1/2), 143–160.

Sternberg, R. J., & Kaufman, J. C. (1998). Human abilities. *Annual Review of Psychology, 49*, 479–502.

Sternberg, R. J., Nokes, K., Geissler, P. W., Prince, R., Okatcha, F., Bundy, D. A., & Grigorenko, E. L. (2001). The relationship between academic and practical intelligence: A case study in Kenya. *Intelligence, 29*, 401-418.

Sternberg, R. J., & Smith, C. (1985). Social intelligence and decoding skills in nonverbal communication. *Social Cognition, 2*, 168–192.

Stevenson, H. W., & Stigler, J. W. (1994). *The learning gap: Why our schools are failing and what we can learn from Japanese and Chinese education.* New York: Simon & Schuster.

Stigler, J. W., Lee, S., Lucker, G. W., & Stevenson, H. W. (1982). Curriculum and achievement in mathematics: A study of elementary school children in Japan, Taiwan, and the United States. *Journal of Educational Psychology, 74*, 315-322.

Super, C. M. (1976). Environmental effects on motor development: The case of "African Infant Precocity." *Developmental Medicine & Child Neurology, 18*, 561-567.

Super, C. M., & Harkness, S. (1982). The development of affect in infancy and early childhood. In D. Wagner & H. Stevenson (eds.). *Cultural perspectives on child development* (pp. 1-19). San Francisco: W. H. Freeman.

Super, C. M., & Harkness, S. (1986). The developmental niche: A conceptualization at the interface of child and culture. *International Journal of Behavioral Development, 9*, 545-569.

Super, C. M., & Harkness, S. (1993). The developmental niche: A conceptualization at the interface of child and culture. In R. A. Pierce & M. A. Black (eds.), *Life-span development: A diversity reader* (pp. 61-77). Dubuque, IA: Kendall/Hunt Publishing Co.

Suzuki, L. A., Short, E. L., & Lee, C. S. (2011). Racial and ethnic group differences in intelligence in the United States. In R. J. Sternberg & S. B. Kaufman (eds.), *Cambridge handbook of intelligence* (pp. 273-292). New York: Cambridge University Press.

Tomasello, M. (2001). *The cultural origins of human cognition.* Cambridge, MA: Harvard University Press.

Tzuriel, D. (1995). Dynamic-interactive assessment: The legacy of L. S. Vygotsky and current developments. Unpublished manuscript.

Vygotsky, L. S. (1978). *Mind in society: The development of higher psychological processes.* Cambridge, MA: Harvard University Press.

Wagner, D. A. (1978). Memories of Morocco: The influence of age, schooling, and environment on memory. *Cognitive Psychology, 10*, 1-28.

White, G. M. (1985). Premises and purposes in a Solomon Islands ethnopsychology. In G. M. White & J. Kirkpatrick (eds.). *Person, self, and experience: Exploring Pacific ethnopsychologies* (pp. 328-366). Berkeley: University of California Press.

Wober, M. (1974). Towards an understanding of the Kiganda concept of intelligence. In J. W. Berry & P. R. Dasen (eds.), *Culture and cognition: Readings in cross-cultural psychology* (pp. 261-280). London: Methuen.

Yan, Z. (2001). *Yan's family rules: Piece of conduct.* In Chinese classic books series (multimedia version.). Beijing: Beijing Yinguan Electronic Publishing. (In Chinese.)

Yang, S.-Y. (2001). Conceptions of wisdom among Taiwanese Chinese. *Journal of Cross-cultural Psychology, 32*, 662-680.

Yang, S.-Y., & Sternberg, R. J. (1997a). Conceptions of intelligence in ancient Chinese philosophy. *Journal of Theoretical and Philosophical Psychology, 17*, 101-119.

Yang, S.-Y., & Sternberg, R. J. (1997b). Taiwanese Chinese people's conceptions of intelligence. *Intelligence, 25*, 21-36.

8 Systems Approaches to Intelligence

ROBERT J. STERNBERG

Rather than viewing intelligence as a "thing" (general intelligence, mental energy, or whatever), one can view intelligence as a system (Sternberg, 1985b, 1986). As you read in Chapter 2, systems approaches seek to understand intelligence in terms of multiple systems of intelligence. In this chapter, we describe two systems theories of intelligence: Howard Gardner's theory of multiple intelligences (Gardner, 1983, 2011) and Sternberg's theory of successful intelligence (Sternberg, 1997b, 2003, 2010, 2016).

The Theory of Multiple Intelligences

The theory of multiple intelligences (Gardner, 1983, 1995, 2011) holds that intelligence is not a single thing, but that intelligences are multiple and that people differ in how well-endowed they are in each of these areas.

Multiple Intelligences

Howard Gardner developed the theory of multiple intelligences in 1983 as a response to theories stressing IQ testing, which he felt presented a much too limited picture of human intelligence. In the current version of the theory (Gardner, 2011), there are eight distinct multiple intelligences: linguistic, logical-mathematical, visual–spatial, bodily–kinesthetic, interpersonal, intrapersonal, musical, and naturalist. Each of these intelligences is described below.

Linguistic Intelligence

Linguistic intelligence is involved in the use of words and language in general. Linguistic intelligence enables us to listen, read, speak, and write effectively. This intelligence is needed to understand poetry, novels, speeches, debates, and verbal media. Most tests of intelligence measure linguistic intelligence, as do many achievement-oriented tests, such as the SAT and the ACT. School achievement tests often draw heavily on linguistic intelligence.

Logical–mathematical intelligence

Logical–mathematical intelligence is used in solving logical and mathematical problems. It is heavily involved in school subjects such as arithmetic at the lower grade levels, and later, algebra, geometry, calculus, and trigonometry. It is also involved in causal reasoning. Logical–mathematical intelligence is measured by many intelligence tests as well as by achievement-oriented tests, again like the SAT and ACT. School achievement tests often draw heavily on logical–mathematical intelligence.

Visual–Spatial Intelligence

Visual–spatial intelligence is involved in mentally rotating objects in one's head, imagining how to fit suitcases into the trunk of a car, imagining what a building project will look like when it is done, solving jigsaw puzzles, making sense of maps and routes planned using maps, and finding one's way from one place to another without the use of a map. When we drive, we use visual–spatial intelligence to navigate from one place to another. And when we get lost, we use – or at least try to use – visual–spatial intelligence to find our way back to the correct route.

Bodily–Kinesthetic Intelligence

Bodily–kinesthetic intelligence involves the control and management of one's bodily movements and the positioning of them in space. It is used in dance, basketball, soccer, swimming, and tennis. But it is also used by hunters to position themselves for a shot, and by prey to position themselves to avoid harm by predators. Unlike the three intelligences discussed above, bodily–kinesthetic intelligence is not measured by conventional tests of intelligence.

Interpersonal Intelligence

Interpersonal intelligence is used to relate to other people. It is crucial to interpersonal relations. It involves recognizing other people's emotions, moods, and motives, and then responding appropriately. It overlaps with the construct of *emotional intelligence* (Mayer, Salovey, Caruso, & Sitarenios, 2003). Interpersonal intelligence would be especially important for people in jobs that heavily involve understanding and relating to other people, such as sales, marketing, and management (see Figure 8.1).

Intrapersonal Intelligence

Intrapersonal intelligence is involved in understanding oneself. People who are high in intrapersonal intelligence are self-reflective and understand their strengths as well as their weaknesses. They are introspective and continually question whether they are using their knowledge and skills to advantage.

Figure 8.1 Interpersonal intelligence. Interpersonal intelligence is especially important for people in jobs that require understanding and relating to other people, such as sales, marketing, and management.

Musical Intelligence

Musical intelligence involves the understanding and production of music. It is used in singing, playing musical instruments, reading music, and appreciating music. Cultures differ widely in the extent to which they promote musical intelligence, ranging from cultures that widely appreciate music to cultures in which music is largely banned.

Naturalist Intelligence

Naturalist intelligence is used to recognize patterns in nature. Examples would be recognizing kinds of rocks, classifying plants, distinguishing among the leaves of different kinds of trees, and distinguishing harmful from harmless animals. Such an intelligence would be important for hunters, but also for naturalists, botanists, ecologists, meteorologists, and the like (see Figure 8.2).

Criteria for Constructing the Theory of Multiple Intelligences

How did Gardner actually construct the theory of multiple intelligences? Gardner has suggested that eight criteria were relevant in his creation of the theory:

Figure 8.2 Naturalist intelligence. Naturalist intelligence is used to recognize patterns in nature, such as recognizing kinds of rocks. Here a jade digger carefully checks the stone dug from the riverbed of Yurungkash River, in Hotan, China.

- Presence of core operations. There are certain mental operations that are crucially associated with and largely unique to that particular intelligence.
- Symbol system. There is a symbol system associated with the intelligence, for example, musical notes for musical intelligence or letters and words for linguistic intelligence.
- Distinct developmental progression. It is possible to trace a distinctive developmental progression of the intelligence from childhood through adulthood, into old age. The developmental progression can differ from one intelligence to another.
- Potential for isolation through brain damage. Clinical studies of patient populations reveal areas in the brain that are distinctively associated with the intelligence.
- Evolutionary history. It is possible to trace an evolutionary trajectory for the intelligence.
- Existence of prodigies and/or savants. One can locate individuals who show exceptional skills in the areas defined by the intelligence.

- Support from experimental psychology. It is possible to isolate the intelligence experimentally (or clinically).
- Support from psychometric analysis. The intelligence can be assessed and there is support from psychometric assessments for the existence of that intelligence.

Evidence for the Theory

Gardner (1983, 2006, 2011) has offered a variety of kinds of evidence to support the theory of multiple intelligences. The theory has been widely used in education, and some schools, such as the Key School in Indianapolis, were based entirely on Gardner's theory. (The school is now closed.) Many teachers have found the theory useful in recognizing and appreciating the wide range of skills students bring to the classroom.

The theory is widely covered in introductory-psychology texts, but the reception of the theory by psychologists has been mixed (as is true with many new theories!). The main criticisms are threefold (see, e.g., Sternberg, 1983b).

First, some of the "intelligences" do not fit traditional conceptions of what intelligence should be. Although there is no universally agreed-upon definition of intelligence, intelligence is usually viewed as critically involving adaptation to the environment. Some of the intelligences seem critical to such adaptation (e.g., logical–mathematical, visual–spatial), whereas others do not (e.g., musical, bodily–kinesthetic). Someone could be totally tone-deaf, yet others might never know so long as the individual did not enter a musical occupation and stayed out of the church choir. Similarly, someone like Helen Keller (blind, deaf, and mute) or Stephen Hawking could have severely reduced bodily–kinesthetic intelligence, and yet function very well in the world.

Second, the evidence for the intelligences being independent appears to be weak. Visser, Ashton, and Vernon (2006) conducted an investigation of the theory and failed to find evidence for the independence of the intelligences. Psychometric evidence comparing different abilities overwhelmingly suggests that, under most circumstance, most mental abilities are at least moderately correlated with each other.

Third, current neuropsychological evidence (Haier, 2016) runs exactly counter to Gardner's theory. It suggests that various abilities are widely distributed across the brain – that rather than there being distinct areas of the brain responsible for particular skills, instead many different parts of the brain contribute to each of the variety of skills we have.

Some scholars might be inclined to minimize or even dismiss Gardner's theory of multiple intelligences because the predictive evidence has not been particularly favorable. However, there are three important things to keep in mind regarding the theory.

First, when the theory was originally published (Gardner, 1983) – and even today – there was and still is a tendency to dwell on general intelligence, sometimes to the exclusion of other abilities. Gardner made a strong statement that there is more to a person's intelligence, and indeed, to a person, than his or her general intelligence. And he even went beyond the abilities often included in hierarchical models of intelligence (e.g., Carroll, 1993). The plea to look at abilities beyond g is as important in contemporary times as in the past.

Second, Gardner emphasized the importance of converging operations – the use of multiple methods of analysis – in understanding intelligence. Prior to his work, many workers in the field had relied almost exclusively on psychometric methods. Although there is nothing wrong, per se, with psychometric methods, almost any phenomenon is best studied through a variety of methods. If all the methods yield the same results, then one can have more confidence in the findings.

Third, Gardner's theory proved to be useful to teachers in a way that general-intelligence theory probably never could be. If an educator is given merely an IQ or related score, there is not much one can do as an educator with the information. What traditionally was done was to group students by ability levels, but such groupings did not do much to suggest how to teach students in one group or another. Gardner's theory, in contrast, opened up new avenues to teachers in their efforts to support learning. If a student was not learning concepts so well verbally, perhaps the concepts could be taught in another way, such as with more emphasis on spatial or naturalistic presentation. Many teachers reacted to the theory with enthusiasm because they believed it had more practical application than previous theories.

Another systems theory is the theory of successful intelligence, described next. This theory has been subjected to a fairly extensive body of research.

The Theory of Successful Intelligence

The theory of successful intelligence views the nature of intelligence in a somewhat different way from many other theories.

The Nature of Intelligence

There are many different definitions of intelligence. Typically, however, intelligence is defined at least in part in terms of a person's ability to adapt to the environment and to learn from experience (Sternberg & Detterman, 1986). In the theory of successful intelligence, the definition of intelligence is somewhat more elaborated and complex (Sternberg, 1997a, 2003). **Successful intelligence** is (1) the ability to formulate, strive for, and, to the extent possible, achieve sensible and meaningful goals for and in one's life, given one's sociocultural context, (2) by capitalizing on strengths and correcting or compensating for weaknesses (3) in order to adapt to, shape, and select environments (4) through a combination of analytical, creative, practical, and wisdom-based skills (Sternberg, 2003). How can one unpack this definition of successful intelligence?

Although psychologists sometimes talk of a "general" factor of intelligence (Jensen, 1998; Spearman, 1904, 1927; see essays in Sternberg & Kaufman, 2011; Sternberg & Grigorenko, 2002), really, virtually no one is good at everything or bad at everything. Successfully intelligent people have identified their strengths and weaknesses and have found ways to work effectively within that pattern of strengths and weaknesses. The theory points out that there is no uniform way to succeed in life or in any career.

In adaptation to the environment, one modifies oneself to fit better into the environment. In life, adaptation is not enough, however. Adaptation needs to be balanced with shaping of the environment. In **shaping**, one modifies the environment to fit what one seeks for it, rather than modifying oneself to fit the environment (as in adaptation). Sometimes, one attempts unsuccessfully to adapt to an environment and then also fails in attempts at shaping that environment. No matter what one does to try to make the environment work out, nothing in fact seems to work. In such cases, the appropriate action may be to *select* another environment.

Successful intelligence, as defined here, involves a broader range of abilities than is typically measured by conventional tests of intellectual (e.g., IQ tests) and academic skills (e.g., achievement tests). Most of these conventional tests assess primarily or exclusively memory and analytical skills. With respect to memory, the tests assess the abilities involved in recall and recognition of information. With respect to analytical abilities, they assess the skills involved when one analyzes, evaluates, critiques, compares and contrasts, and judges. These skills are very important during the school years and remain at least somewhat important in later life. But they certainly are not the only skills that matter for success in school and life. An individual needs not only to remember and analyze ideas; one also needs to be able to generate new ideas and to apply these ideas in everyday life. Memory is fundamental to analytic, creative, and practical thinking – it is necessary for the execution of these kinds of thinking; but it is far from sufficient.

Processes Underlying Intelligence

According to the theory of successful intelligence and its development (Sternberg, 1985a, 1997a, 2003, 2004), a common set of mental processes underlies all aspects of intelligence. These mental processes are hypothesized to be universal, across cultures (Sternberg, 2004), racial and ethnic groups (Sternberg, Grigorenko, & Kidd, 2005), and other groupings. What is considered to be an intelligent solution in one culture may be different from the solutions considered to be intelligent in another culture. But the need to define problems and to translate strategies into action to solve these problems exists in any culture. Even within cultures, though, there may be differences in what different groups mean by intelligence (Grigorenko et al., 2001; Okagaki & Sternberg, 1993; Sternberg, 1985c). The theory of successful intelligence proposes that intelligence comprises three sets of processes, as described below:

Metacomponents are executive processes that, in problem solving, plan what to do, monitor solution processes as they are being executed, and evaluate the problem solving after it is completed. Examples of metacomponents are recognizing the existence of a problem (e.g., one has homework to do), defining the nature of the problem (e.g., it will be hard to get the homework done because there is a concert tonight), deciding on a strategy for solving the problem (e.g., deciding to attend only the first half of the concert), monitoring the solution of the problem (e.g., is the homework getting done?), and evaluating the solution after the problem is solved (e.g., did the homework get handed in on time?).

Performance components execute the instructions of the metacomponents – essentially, they perform the actions directed by the metacomponents. For example, inference is employed to decide how two stimuli (e.g., zebra and tiger) are related (e.g., they both have stripes) and application is used to apply what one has inferred (e.g., finding another animal with stripes) (Sternberg, 1983a).

Knowledge-acquisition components are used to learn how to solve problems or simply to acquire declarative (i.e., memory about facts, things, ideas) knowledge in the first place (Sternberg, 1985a). Selective encoding is used to decide what information in a problem is relevant in the context of one's learning (e.g., what items at a crime scene might lead a detective to a killer?). Selective comparison is used to bring old information stored in memory to bear on new problems (e.g., what does the detective know from past cases that might help solve the present one?). And selective combination is used to bring together the selectively encoded and compared information into a single and possibly even insightful solution to a problem (e.g., who committed the crime?).

According to the theory of successful intelligence, the same mental processes are used universally for all three aspects of intelligence. People apply these mental processes to different kinds of tasks in different kinds of situations. What processes they use depends on what kinds of thinking a particular problem requires. In particular, people use analytical thinking when the components of information processing are applied to fairly familiar kinds of problems that are abstracted and far removed from everyday life. People use creative thinking when the components of information processing are applied to relatively novel kinds of tasks or somewhat familiar tasks presented in the context of novel situations. People use practical thinking when the components of information processing are applied to experience

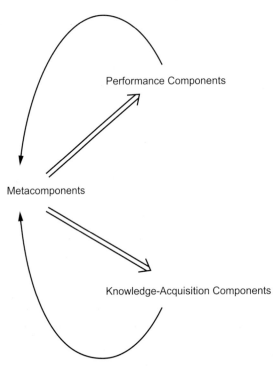

Figure 8.3 The interrelationship of processes in the theory of successful intelligence. The theory of successful intelligence includes metacomponents, performance components, and knowledge-acquisition components. Metacomponents activate performance components and knowledge-acquisition components, which in turn provide feedback to the metacomponents.

to adapt to, shape, and select environments. People need (a) creative skills and attitudes to generate ideas, (b) analytical skills and attitudes to figure out if they are good ideas, and (c) practical skills and attitudes to put one's ideas into practice and also to convince other people of the value of those ideas. Because the theory of successful intelligence as a whole comprises three subtheories – a componential subtheory dealing with the formulation and execution of components of intelligence, an experiential subtheory dealing with the importance of experience in coping with relative novelty and of automatization of information processing, and a contextual subtheory dealing with processes of adaptation, shaping, and selection to the real world, the theory has sometimes been referred to as *triarchic* (Sternberg, 1988).

Figure 8.3 shows how the three kinds of processes in the theory of successful intelligence – metacomponents, performance components, and knowledge-acquisition components – are interrelated. Metacomponents activate performance components and knowledge-acquisition components, which in turn provide feedback to the metacomponents.

The Assessment of Successful Intelligence

Assessments of successful intelligence have been organized primarily around the analytical, creative, and practical aspects of it. (Current research projects are focusing on assessments of wisdom.) We discuss those earlier assessments here, singly and collectively.

Analytical Intelligence

Analytical intelligence is involved when the information-processing components of intelligence are applied to analyze, evaluate, judge, or compare and contrast. It is typically involved when components are applied to relatively familiar kinds of problems where the judgments to be made are of a fairly abstract nature.

Some early work showed how analytical kinds of problems, such as analogies or syllogisms, can be analyzed componentially (Guyote & Sternberg, 1981; Sternberg, 1983a), with response times or error rates decomposed to yield their underlying information-processing components. The goal of this research was to understand the information-processing origins of individual differences in (the analytical aspect of) human intelligence. With componential analysis, one could specify sources of individual differences underlying a factor score such as that for "inductive reasoning" (Sternberg, 1983a), or deductive reasoning (Guyote & Sternberg, 1981).

As an example, through componential analysis, it was possible to decompose inductive-reasoning performance into a set of underlying information-processing components (Sternberg, 1983a). The analogy $A : B : C : D1, D2, D3, D4$ will be used as an example to illustrate the components. These components are (1) *encoding*, the amount of time needed to register each stimulus ($A, B, C, D1, D2, D3, D4$); (2) *inference*, the amount of time needed to discern the basic relation between given stimuli (A to B); (3) *mapping*, the amount of time needed to transfer the relation from one set of stimuli to another (needed in analogical reasoning) (A to C); (4) *application*, the amount of time needed to apply the relation as inferred (and sometimes as mapped) to a new set of stimuli (A to B to C to?); (5) *comparison*, the amount of time needed to compare the validity of the response options ($D1, D2, D3, D4$); (6) *justification*, the amount of time needed to justify one answer as the best of the bunch (e.g., $D1$); and (7) *preparation-response*, the amount of time needed to prepare for problem solution and to respond.

Research on the components of human intelligence yielded some interesting results. Consider some examples. First, in a study of the development of figural analogical reasoning, it was found that although children generally became quicker in information processing with age, not all components were executed more rapidly with age (Sternberg & Rifkin, 1979). The encoding component first showed a decrease in component time with age and then an increase. Apparently, older children realized that their best strategy was to spend more time encoding the terms of a problem so that they would be able to spend less time operating on these encodings later. A related, second finding was that better reasoners tend to spend relatively more time than do poorer reasoners in global, up-front metacomponential planning, when they solve difficult reasoning problems. Poorer reasoners, on the other hand, tend to spend relatively more time in local planning (Sternberg, 1981). Presumably, the better reasoners recognize that it is better to invest more time up front so as to be able to process a problem more efficiently later on. Third, it also was found in verbal analogical reasoning that, as children grew older, their strategies shifted so that they relied on word association less and abstract relations more (Sternberg & Nigro, 1980).

Some of the componential studies concentrated on knowledge-acquisition components rather than performance components or metacomponents. For example, in one set of studies, researchers focused on sources of individual differences in vocabulary (Sternberg, 1987). The three main sources were in knowledge-acquisition components, use of context clues, and use of mediating variables. For example, in the sentence, "The blen rises in the east and sets in the west," the knowledge-acquisition component of selective comparison is used to relate prior knowledge about a known concept, the sun, to the unknown word (neologism) in the sentence, "blen." Several context cues appear in the sentence, such as the fact that a blen rises, the fact that it sets, and the information about where it rises and sets. A mediating variable is that the information can occur after the presentation of the unknown word.

Sternberg and his colleagues carried out studies like the ones described above because they believed that conventional psychometric research sometimes incorrectly attributed individual and developmental differences. For example, a verbal analogies test that might appear on its surface to measure verbal reasoning might in fact measure primarily vocabulary and general information (Sternberg, 1983a). In fact, in some populations, reasoning might hardly be a source of individual or developmental differences at all. And if researchers then look at the sources of the individual differences in vocabulary, they would need to understand that the differences in knowledge did not come from nowhere: Some children had much more frequent and better opportunities to learn word meanings than did others.

In the componential-analysis work described above, correlations were computed between component scores of individuals and scores on tests of different kinds of psychometric abilities. First, in the studies of inductive reasoning (Sternberg, 1983a), it was found that although inference, mapping, application, comparison, and justification tended to correlate with such tests, the highest correlation typically was with the preparation-response component. This result was puzzling at first, because this component was estimated as the regression constant in the predictive regression equation. This result ended up giving birth to the concept of the metacomponents: higher order processes used to plan, monitor, and evaluate task performance. It was also found, second, that the correlations obtained for all the components showed convergent-discriminant validation: They tended to be significant with psychometric tests of reasoning but not with psychometric tests of perceptual speed (Sternberg, 1983a). Moreover, third, significant correlations with vocabulary tended to be obtained only for encoding verbal stimuli (Sternberg, 1983a).

Creative Intelligence

Intelligence tests contain a range of problems, some of them more novel than others. In some of the componential work it has been shown that when one goes beyond the range of novelty of the conventional tests of intelligence, one starts to tap sources of individual differences that are measured little or not at all by the tests. According to the theory of successful intelligence, **creative intelligence** is the ability to generate novel and potentially compelling or useful ideas. It is particularly well measured by questions assessing how well an individual can cope with relative novelty. Some examples of these types of questions appear in Figure 8.4.

Researchers presented 80 individuals with novel kinds of reasoning problems that had a single best answer. For example, they might be told that some objects are green and others blue; but still other objects might be *grue*, meaning green until the year 3000 (2000 was used in the original studies, because they were done before the year 2000) and blue thereafter, or *bleen*, meaning blue until the year 3000 and green thereafter. Or they might be told of four kinds of people on the planet Kyron: *blens*, who are born young and die young; *kwefs*, who are born old and die old; *balts*, who are born young and die old; and *prosses*, who are born old and die young (Sternberg, 1981; Tetewsky & Sternberg, 1986). Their task was to predict future states from past states, given incomplete information. In another set of studies, 60 people were given more conventional kinds of inductive reasoning problems, such as analogies, series completions, and classifications, and they were told to solve them. However, the problems had premises preceding them that were either conventional (dancers wear shoes) or novel (dancers eat shoes). The participants had to solve the problems as though the counterfactuals were true (Sternberg & Gastel, 1989a, 1989b).

In these studies, researchers found that correlations with conventional kinds of tests depended on how novel or nonentrenched the conventional tests were. The more novel the items, the higher the correlations of these tests with scores on successively more novel conventional tests. Thus, the components isolated for relatively novel items would tend to correlate more highly with more unusual tests of fluid abilities (e.g., that of Cattell & Cattell, 1973) than with tests of crystallized abilities. In addition, when response times on the relatively novel problems were componentially analyzed, some components measured the creative aspect of

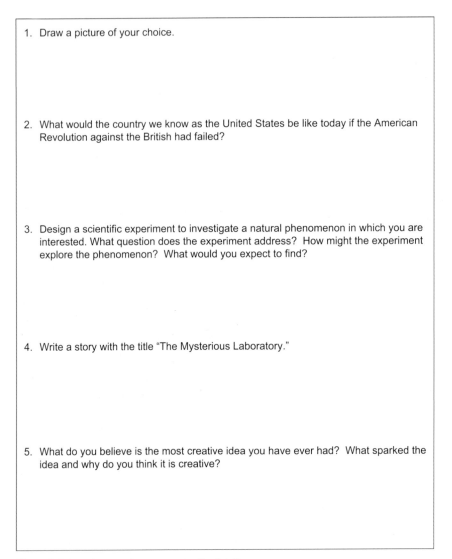

1. Draw a picture of your choice.

2. What would the country we know as the United States be like today if the American Revolution against the British had failed?

3. Design a scientific experiment to investigate a natural phenomenon in which you are interested. What question does the experiment address? How might the experiment explore the phenomenon? What would you expect to find?

4. Write a story with the title "The Mysterious Laboratory."

5. What do you believe is the most creative idea you have ever had? What sparked the idea and why do you think it is creative?

Figure 8.4 Questions used to assess creative intelligence

intelligence better than others. For example, in the "grue-bleen" task mentioned earlier, the information-processing component requiring people to switch from conventional green-blue thinking to grue-bleen thinking and then back to green-blue thinking again was a particularly good measure of the ability to cope with novelty.

Creativity goes beyond creative intelligence. It largely comprises an attitude toward life (Sternberg & Lubart, 1995). In particular, creative people are willing to defy the crowd, to defy themselves and go beyond their past ideas, and to defy the zeitgeist, not accepting conventional presuppositions just because others do.

Practical Intelligence

Practical intelligence is used when individuals apply their abilities to the kinds of problems that confront them in everyday life, such as finding a job, buying a home, or dealing with crying children. Using practical intelligence, an individual applies the information-processing components of intelligence to experiences to (1) adapt to, (2) shape, and (3) select environments. Individuals differ in how they balance adaptation, shaping, and selection. They also differ in the level of skill with which they achieve balance among the three possible kinds of action (Sternberg, 1997a, 1997b).

Much of the research regarding practical intelligence has focused on the concept of tacit knowledge. *Tacit knowledge* is defined as what one needs procedurally to know in order to work effectively in an environment that one is not explicitly taught and that often is not even verbalized (Sternberg et al., 2000; Sternberg & Hedlund, 2002; Williams et al., 2002). Tacit knowledge is presented in the form of production systems, or sequences of "if-then" statements that describe procedures one follows in various kinds of everyday situations. Figure 8.5 provides some examples of questions used to measure practical intelligence. Questions such as these have been used in assessments of successful intelligence.

Researchers have typically measured tacit knowledge using work-related situations that present problems a worker of some kind – salesperson, teacher, businessperson, etc. – might encounter on the job. Tacit knowledge we measured for both children and adults, and among adults, for people in over two dozen occupations, such as management, sales, academia, teaching, school administration, secretarial work, and the military. In a typical tacit-knowledge problem, individuals read a scenario about a problem a person faces. The individuals then are asked to rate, for each of several statements following the scenario, how good a solution the statement represents. In a paper-and-pencil measure of tacit knowledge for sales, for example, one problem deals with sales of photocopy machines. In the scenario, a relatively inexpensive machine is not selling well in the showroom and is now overstocked. The individual rates the quality of each solution for moving the particular photocopier model out of the showroom. In a separate, performance-based measure devised to be given to sales people, the individual test-taker makes a simulated phone call to a supposed customer, who, the test-taker knows, is actually the examiner. The test-taker then tries to sell advertising space over the phone to the hypothetical customer. The hypothetical customer raises various objections to buying the advertising space. The test-taker is then judged for the quality, rapidity, and fluency of the responses he or she makes on the telephone to the hypothetical customer's objections.

In the tacit-knowledge studies, investigators discovered that practical intelligence, as measured by tacit knowledge tests, tends to increase with experience. However, it is *profiting* from experience, rather than experience per se, that leads to

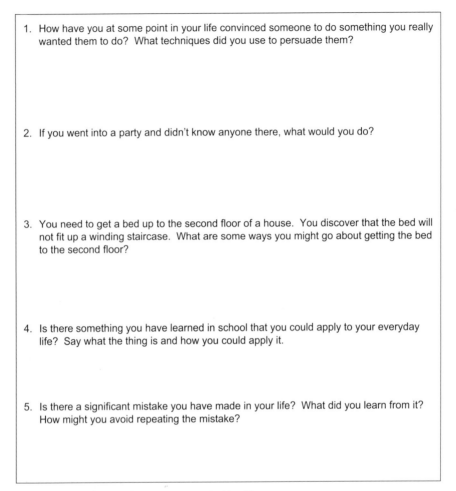

1. How have you at some point in your life convinced someone to do something you really wanted them to do? What techniques did you use to persuade them?

2. If you went into a party and didn't know anyone there, what would you do?

3. You need to get a bed up to the second floor of a house. You discover that the bed will not fit up a winding staircase. What are some ways you might go about getting the bed to the second floor?

4. Is there something you have learned in school that you could apply to your everyday life? Say what the thing is and how you could apply it.

5. Is there a significant mistake you have made in your life? What did you learn from it? How might you avoid repeating the mistake?

Figure 8.5 Questions used to measure practical intelligence

increases in scores. Some individuals can have been in a job for many years and still have gained relatively little relevant tacit knowledge about the job. Scores on a variety of tests of tacit knowledge, such as for university professors and managers, are also correlated fairly substantially with each other (at about the .5 level). Scores on tacit-knowledge tests, however, correlate only weakly or not at all with scores on conventional tests of intelligence. Despite the relative lack of correlation between practical-intellectual tests and conventional measures of intelligence, scores on tacit-knowledge tests have been found to predict job performance about as well as or even better than do conventional psychometric intelligence tests (see Hedlund et al., 2003; Sternberg & Hedlund, 2002; Sternberg et al., 2000). In research with Eskimos, Grigorenko et al. (2004) found that children who are low achievers in school nevertheless can have exceptionally high practical adaptive skills (tacit knowledge) for tasks at home.

Successful intelligence researchers have also done studies of social intelligence as measured by nonverbal communication skills (Barnes & Sternberg, 1989; Sternberg & Smith, 1985). Females were found to be superior to males on these tasks. Scores on two such tasks did not correlate with scores on conventional intelligence tests.

So far we have considered each of the aspects of intelligence separately. How do these aspects of intelligence fare when they are assessed together?

Putting Together All Three Aspects of Intelligence

The Rainbow Project

Sternberg and the Rainbow Project Collaborators (2006) used an extensive set of tests on 1,015 students at 15 different institutions (13 colleges and 2 high schools). The goal was not to replace the SAT but to devise tests that would supplement the SAT, measuring skills that this test does not measure. In addition to the multiple-choice SAT tests described earlier, they used three additional measures of creative skills and three of practical skills. The additional tests of creative skills were captioning cartoons, writing stories, and orally telling stories. The additional practical tests involved solving practical problems presented in movies, and two tests of common-sense reasoning in everyday situations.

These tests significantly and substantially improved upon the validity of the SAT for predicting first-year college grades (Sternberg & the Rainbow Project Collaborators, 2006). The test also improved equity across students: Using the test to admit a class would have resulted in greater ethnic diversity than would have using just the SAT, or using just the SAT combined with grade-point average.

The Kaleidoscope Project

The Kaleidoscope Project (Sternberg, 2010) gave college applicants a selection of essays assessing analytical, creative, practical, and also wisdom-based skills. Applicants had the option of completing one of the essays, of their choice. The analytical, creative, practical, and wisdom-based skills demonstrated through these essays and other aspects of the application were then rated.

The exact Kaleidoscope prompts varied from year to year. A question might ask a student to state his or her favorite book and why it is a favorite (analytical); or to draw a picture or write a story (creative); or to say how the student persuaded a friend of an idea (practical); or to say how the student someday might make the world a better place (wisdom).

The questions used in the Kaleidoscope Project differed in the particular skills they were designed to emphasize. But no question was a "pure" measure of any single component of successful intelligence. Scoring of the exercises by admissions officers was holistic and was done using rubrics, which are guidelines for scoring. Kaleidoscope improved prediction of both academic and extracurricular success and decreased ethnic-group differences relative to the SAT alone.

For an extension of this work into the area of graduate school admissions, see Focus on Contemporary Research box below.

FOCUS ON CONTEMPORARY RESEARCH: ROBERT J. STERNBERG'S WORK ON ALTERNATIVES TO CURRENT GRADUATE SCHOOL-ADMISSIONS TESTS

My colleagues and I designed two projects to show that ideas similar to those that motivated the research on undergraduate admissions could also be applied to graduate admissions in psychology and related disciplines (Sternberg & Sternberg, 2017; Sternberg, Sternberg, & Todhunter, 2017). The research was motivated in part by a study that showed that the GRE was not a successful predictor of performance in a graduate psychology program after the first year of course grades (Sternberg & Williams, 1997). Although that study showed that the GRE was not a great predictor, it provided no alternative or supplementary measure.

The new studies are based on the simple notion that the best predictor of future behavior of any kind is past behavior of the same kind. So we asked what it is that future psychological scientists will actually have to do – in graduate school and later when they take jobs. Well, in a way, that's an easy question to answer: The two main things psychological scientists do are research and teaching. So our new measures assess reasoning about research and teaching in the context of psychological science.

The measures require, in a psychological-scientific context, that students (a) generate hypotheses, (b) generate experiments, (c) draw conclusions, (d) review articles, and (e) evaluate teaching. For example, students might be presented with an experiment, be given a hypothesis about why the results were obtained, and then be asked to generate alternative hypotheses regarding why that result came about. Or they might be presented with a video of a professor teaching a psychology lesson and then be asked to specify what the teacher is doing sub-optimally (from a pedagogical point of view) in teaching the lesson. Performance on these measures was compared with performance on tests of fluid intelligence (number series and letter sets) and also on standardized tests (SAT/ACT). We also collected undergraduate grade-point average (GPA) data. Our subjects were undergraduates at Cornell.

The main findings of the research were that (a) the various measures of scientific reasoning and reasoning about teaching clustered together correlationally and hence factorially, (b) the inductive-reasoning tests and the standardized tests also clustered together (as they are all measures of general intelligence), and (c) our tests did *not* cluster with the inductive-reasoning or standardized tests, suggesting that they measure a different construct. Moreover, (d) our tests did *not* show the gender gap that is commonly found on many standardized tests. We thought it interesting that our measures of reasoning about research and about teaching clustered together factorially, suggesting that many of the same analytical, creative, and practical skills that investigators apply to research can be applied to teaching – if the researchers expend the effort to think about their teaching in the same way they do about their research.

Why are these results important? We believe they are important because admission to graduate school in psychological science is more competitive than ever; we need excellent scientists more than ever, and yet we may be admitting and rejecting, in some cases, the wrong people. I have argued for more than 30 years that the measures we use to assess young people focus almost entirely on memory and abstract-analytical skills, to the exclusion of the creative and practical skills students will eventually need to succeed in their work (Sternberg, 1985a). My colleagues and I believe our results are consistent with this view – that if we want to admit students who later will become excellent researchers and teachers, we should gather an early assessment of their skills for success in their future discipline in research and teaching. Our goal is not to simply criticize the Graduate Record Examination (GRE) and related tests. We recognize that students who lack sufficient levels of the kind of academic preparation measured by these tests may have trouble simply meeting the academic requirements of many graduate programs. But we believe these academic skills, while necessary for graduate success, are by no means sufficient. And moreover, they are necessary at more modest levels than many of the competitive programs require. That is, to succeed in a competitive program, what really matters ultimately is not whether one has top-tier scores on a standardized test, but rather, whether one will be able to succeed in research and ultimately in teaching. Some students applying to graduate school have had research experience, but the quantity and quality of that experience often depends on the availability of opportunities in the undergraduate institution one attended. Our assessments, in contrast, are relevant and could be potentially accessible to students in any institution.

CONCLUSION

Some psychologists believe that systems approaches enhance our understanding of intelligence by broadening the construct. Other psychologists believe that systems approaches to intelligence depart too much from the conventional theory of general intelligence proposed by Spearman (1904) and from hierarchical theories such as that of Carroll (1993).

The theory of multiple intelligences (Gardner, 2011) provided a way to view intelligence not as a single thing but rather as an entire spectrum of skills. The theory has been fairly widely applied in education. However, the theory is difficult to test, and what evidence there is does not support the idea of independent intelligences. If anything, recent neuropsychological research (see Chapter 6) has suggested the opposite – that abilities arise as a complex interaction of interrelated elements. Instead of the brain comprising separate modules, it comprises interacting systems that draw heavily on each other.

The theory of successful intelligence has been tested rather extensively and has at least some empirical support. Nevertheless, some disagree with parts or all of the theory of successful intelligence (e.g., Brody, 2003; Gottfredson, 2003). Others believe the theory does not depart from conventional g theory enough (Gardner, 1983, 2006). Still others have proposed theories that are compatible, at least in spirit, with systems theories of intelligence (Ceci, 1996). The theory of successful intelligence is relatively new and has generated, so far, much less research to support or refute it; but it may serve as a broader basis for future theories. No doubt, there will be those who wish to preserve Spearman's theory of general intelligence and related older theories, and those who will continue to do research that replicates hundreds and thousands of times that so-called general intelligence does indeed matter for success in many aspects of life. This correlation is an established fact.

CHAPTER SUMMARY

This chapter reviews two major systems approaches to intelligence: Howard Gardner's theory of multiple intelligences and Robert J. Sternberg's theory of successful intelligence. Gardner (1983, 2006) has proposed that there are eight independent multiple intelligences: linguistic, logical–mathematical, visual–spatial, bodily–kinesthetic, musical, naturalist, interpersonal, and intrapersonal. These intelligences are theorized to be modular – that is, they involve different parts of the brain. They can be recognized through a number of methods, including the presence of core operations, a separate symbol system, a distinct developmental progression, potential isolation through brain damage, a distinct evolutionary history, the existence of prodigies or savants, support from experimental psychology, and support from psychometrics. More empirical research is needed to support the elements of Gardner's theory.

Sternberg (1997a, 1997b) has proposed a theory of successful intelligence, according to which successful intelligence can be understood in terms of one's success in developing, executing, and constantly reevaluating a life plan. The theory posits that creative abilities are used to generate novel and somehow useful or effective ideas or products; analytical abilities are used to ascertain the quality of these and other ideas; practical abilities are used to implement the ideas and argue for their effectiveness; and wisdom-based abilities are used to help ensure that the ideas can be directed toward the attainment of some kind of common good. Successfully intelligent people figure out their strengths and weaknesses and then find ways to capitalize on their strengths and to compensate for or correct their weaknesses. Sternberg and his colleagues have used a variety of different methods – psychometric, experimental, developmental, cultural, educational – to test the theory. The results of empirical investigations suggest that the theory can be useful in understanding intelligence in a broad sense.

KEY TERMS

analytical intelligence • bodily–kinesthetic intelligence • creative intelligence • interpersonal intelligence • intrapersonal intelligence • knowledge-acquisition components • linguistic intelligence • logical–mathematical intelligence • metacomponents • musical intelligence • naturalist intelligence • performance components • practical intelligence • shaping • theory of successful intelligence • visual–spatial intelligence

COMPREHENSION AND REFLECTION QUESTIONS

1. How are Gardner's and Sternberg's theories similar? How are they different?
2. How have you tried to shape your environments?
3. Which of Gardner's intelligences do you believe would be most important for a mechanic? Why?
4. What might someone do to improve his or her creative skills?
5. Are practical intelligence and interpersonal intelligence the same thing? If not, how are they different?

References

Barnes, M. L., & Sternberg, R. J. (1989). Social intelligence and decoding of nonverbal cues. *Intelligence, 13*, 263–287.

Brody, N. (2003). What Sternberg should have concluded. *Intelligence, 31*(4), 339–342.

Carroll, J. B. (1993). *Human cognitive abilities: A survey of factor-analytic studies.* New York: Cambridge University Press.

Cattell, R. B., & Cattell, H. E. P. (1973). *Measuring intelligence with the Culture Fair Tests.* Champaign, IL: Institute for Personality and Ability Testing.

Ceci, S. J. (1996). *On intelligence* (rev. and exp. ed.). Cambridge, MA: Harvard University Press.

Gardner, H. (1983). *Frames of mind: The theory of multiple intelligences.* New York: Basic Books.

Gardner, H. (1995). Reflections on multiple intelligences: Myths and messages. *Phi Delta Kappan, 77*, 200-209.

Gardner, H. (2006). *Multiple intelligences: New horizons in theory and practice.* New York: Basic Books.

Gardner, H. (2011). *Frames of mind: The theory of multiple intelligences* (rev. ed.). New York: Basic Books.

Gottfredson, L. S. (2003). Discussion: On Sternberg's "Reply to Gottfredson." *Intelligence, 31*(4), 415–424.

Grigorenko, E. L., Geissler, P. W., Prince, R., Okatcha, F., Nokes, C., Kenny, D. A., Bundy, D. A., & Sternberg, R. J. (2001). The organization of Luo conceptions of intelligence: A study of implicit theories in a Kenyan village. *International Journal of Behavioral Development, 25*(4), 367–378.

Grigorenko, E. L., Jarvin, L., & Sternberg, R. J. (2002). School-based tests of the triarchic theory of intelligence: Three settings, three samples, three syllabi. *Contemporary Educational Psychology, 27*, 167–208.

Grigorenko, E. L., Meier, E., Lipka, J., Mohatt, G., Yanez, E., & Sternberg, R. J. (2004). Academic and practical intelligence: A case study of the Yup'ik in Alaska. *Learning and Individual Differences, 14*, 183–207.

Guyote, M. J., & Sternberg, R. J. (1981). A transitive-chain theory of syllogistic reasoning. *Cognitive Psychology, 13*, 461–525.

Haier, R. J. (2016). *The neuroscience of intelligence.* New York: Cambridge University Press.

Hedlund, J., Forsythe, G. B., Horvath, J. A., Williams, W. M., Snook, S., & Sternberg, R. J. (2003). Identifying and assessing tacit knowledge: Understanding the practical intelligence of military leaders. *Leadership Quarterly, 14*, 117–140.

Jensen, A. R. (1998). *The g factor: The science of mental ability.* Westport, CT: Praeger/ Greenwood.

Mayer, J. D., Salovey, P., Caruso, D. R., & Sitarenios, G. (2003). Measuring emotional intelligence with the MSCEIT V2.0. *Emotion, 3*, 97–105.

Okagaki, L., & Sternberg, R. J. (1993). Parental beliefs and children's school performance. *Child Development, 64*(1), 36–56.

Spearman, C. (1904). "General intelligence," objectively determined and measured. *American Journal of Psychology, 15*(2), 201–293.

Spearman, C. (1927). *The abilities of man.* London, UK: Macmillan.

Sternberg, R. J. (1981). Intelligence and nonentrenchment. *Journal of Educational Psychology, 73*, 1–16.

Sternberg, R. J. (1983a). Components of human intelligence. *Cognition, 15*, 1–48.

Sternberg, R. J. (1983b). How much gall is too much gall? [Review of H. Gardner, *Frames of mind: The theory of multiple intelligences*]. *Contemporary Education Review, 2,* 215–224.

Sternberg, R. J. (1985a). *Beyond IQ: A triarchic theory of human intelligence.* New York: Cambridge University Press.

Sternberg, R. J. (1985b). Human intelligence: The model is the message. *Science, 230,* 1111–1118.

Sternberg, R. J. (1985c). Implicit theories of intelligence, creativity, and wisdom. *Journal of Personality and Social Psychology, 49*(3), 607–627.

Sternberg, R. J. (1986). Inside intelligence. *American Scientist, 74,* 137–143.

Sternberg, R. J. (1987). The psychology of verbal comprehension. In R. Glaser (ed.), *Advances in instructional psychology* (vol. 3, pp. 97–151). Hillsdale, NJ: Lawrence Erlbaum Associates.

Sternberg, R. J. (1988). *The triarchic mind.* New York: Viking.

Sternberg, R. J. (1997a). *Successful intelligence.* New York: Plume.

Sternberg, R. J. (1997b). What does it mean to be smart? *Educational Leadership, 54*(6), 20–24.

Sternberg, R. J. (2003). *WICS: A theory of wisdom, intelligence, and creativity, synthesized.* New York: Cambridge University Press.

Sternberg, R. J. (2004). Culture and intelligence. *American Psychologist, 59*(5), 325–338.

Sternberg, R. J. (2010). *College admissions for the 21st century.* Cambridge, MA: Harvard University Press.

Sternberg, R. J. (2016). *What universities can be.* Ithaca, NY: Cornell University Press.

Sternberg, R. J., & Detterman, D. K. (eds.). (1986). *What is intelligence?* Norwood, NJ: Ablex.

Sternberg, R. J., Forsythe, G. B., Hedlund, J., Horvath, J., Snook, S., Williams, W. M., Wagner, R. K., & Grigorenko, E. L. (2000). *Practical intelligence in everyday life.* New York: Cambridge University Press.

Sternberg, R. J., & Gastel, J. (1989a). Coping with novelty in human intelligence: An empirical investigation. *Intelligence, 13,* 187–197.

Sternberg, R. J., & Gastel, J. (1989b). If dancers ate their shoes: Inductive reasoning with factual and counterfactual premises. *Memory and Cognition, 17,* 1–10.

Sternberg, R. J., & Grigorenko E. L. (eds.). (2002). *The general factor of intelligence: How general is it?* Mahwah, NJ: Lawrence Erlbaum Associates.

Sternberg, R. J., Grigorenko, E. L., & Kidd, K. K. (2005). Intelligence, race, and genetics. *American Psychologist, 60*(1), 46–59.

Sternberg, R. J., & Hedlund, J. (2002). Practical intelligence, *g,* and work psychology. *Human Performance 15*(1/2), 143–160.

Sternberg, R. J., & Kaufman, S. B. (eds.) (2011). *Cambridge handbook of intelligence.* New York: Cambridge University Press.

Sternberg, R. J., & Lubart, T. I. (1995). *Defying the crowd: Cultivating creativity in a culture of conformity.* New York: Free Press.

Sternberg, R. J., & Nigro, G. (1980). Developmental patterns in the solution of verbal analogies. *Child Development*, *51*, 27–38.

Sternberg, R. J., & The Rainbow Project Collaborators. (2006). The Rainbow Project: Enhancing the SAT through assessments of analytical, practical and creative skills. *Intelligence*, *34*(4), 321–350.

Sternberg, R. J., & Rifkin, B. (1979). The development of analogical reasoning processes. *Journal of Experimental Child Psychology*, *27*, 195–232.

Sternberg, R. J., & Smith, C. (1985). Social intelligence and decoding skills in nonverbal communication. *Social Cognition*, *2*, 168–192.

Sternberg, R. J., & Sternberg, K. (2017). Measuring scientific reasoning for graduate admissions in psychology and related disciplines. *Journal of Intelligence*. www.mdpi .com/2079-3200/5/3/29/pdf

Sternberg, R. J., Sternberg, K., & Todhunter, R. J. E. (2017). Measuring reasoning about teaching for graduate admissions in psychology and related disciplines. *Journal of Intelligence*. www.mdpi.com/2079-3200/5/4/34/pdf

Sternberg, R. J., & Williams, W. M. (1997). Does the Graduate Record Examination predict meaningful success in the graduate training of psychologists? A case study. *American Psychologist*, *52*, 630–641.

Tetewsky, S. J., & Sternberg, R. J. (1986). Conceptual and lexical determinants of nonentrenched thinking. *Journal of Memory and Language*, *25*, 202–225.

Visser, B. A., Ashton, M. C., & Vernon, P. A. (2006). Beyond *g*: Putting multiple intelligence theory to the test. *Intelligence*, 34, 487–502.

Williams, W. M., Blythe, T., White, N., Li, J., Gardner, H., & Sternberg, R. J. (2002). Practical intelligence for school: Developing metacognitive sources of achievement in adolescence. *Developmental Review*, *22*(2), 162–210.

PART III
Theories on the Development of Intelligence

9 Genetics/Genomics and Intelligence

MEI TAN AND ELENA L. GRIGORENKO

> People learn something every day, and a lot of times it's that what they
> learned the day before was wrong.

This observation is attributed to William E. Vaughan, an American columnist and
author who liked to be clever in his commentaries on life. Whether generally true or
not, the wry humor of his words gives us a way to graciously face the sometimes
overwhelming speed at which knowledge seems to accumulate and change. This has
certainly been the case in the rapidly evolving fields of genetics and genomics.
Genetics, refers to the general field of science that studies the composition of genes
and how they work. **Genomics** is the study of organism-specific sets of genetic
material, or chromosomes. A person's **genotype** includes all the genes a person will
have for his or her life; it is set at the moment of fertilization. It is also often referred
to as a person's *genetic make-up*. A person's phenotype is the set of observable
characteristics which result from the interaction of their genotype with the environment. **Chromosomes** are discrete bundles of DNA; they come in pairs, with one
chromosome of each pair from one parent. Every individual has his or her own set of
chromosomes, or **genome**, but genomes may be defined at any number of levels of
classification: species-specific genomes, such as the human genome (e.g., the
genome of *Homo Sapiens*) or the mammalian genome (e.g., the genome that reflects
the common features of different types of mammals – humans, mice, elephants, and
so on).

In the fields of both genetics and genomics, the discoveries of the last two
decades have resulted in a great many adjustments to what we thought we knew.
Technological developments in research, in particular, have had us constantly
pruning, tuning, differentiating, and growing our knowledge of how the genome
functions and exerts its influences on complex human traits, such as intelligence.
Complex human traits are those characteristics that are thought to result from the
influence of many genes that interact with the environment. The complex nature of

Appreciation is extended to the graduate students of the GENESIS Laboratory at the University of
Houston, whose comments on the content of this chapter were very helpful. The writing of this chapter
was supported by grant #R01 HD085836 from the National Institutes of Health (PI: Grigorenko).
Grantees undertaking such projects are encouraged to express freely their professional judgment. The
chapter does not necessarily reflect the position or policies of the NIH, and no official endorsement
should be inferred.

intelligence – how it arises, how it is exhibited in individuals, how it may be measured – has been intensely studied for centuries. Yet, armed with new tools for genetic research, we are entering a new and exciting phase of exploration into the genetic bases of intelligence.

In this chapter, we will (1) define what is meant by "intelligence" when its origins are investigated; (2) briefly outline the major methods used in investigations into the origins of intelligence; (3) sketch out the frontiers of the field of genetic studies of intelligence, which encompass these investigations; and (4) consider practical implications of this field.

The Definition of Intelligence and How We Investigate It

There are two concepts crucial to grasping how we investigate the origins of intelligence: its measurement and its distribution. First, because intelligence is defined as a trait that is observable in people, it has been assumed that it can be measured. How it is measured is one of the most important aspects of any investigation into intelligence. Second, by measuring the intelligence of individuals, we can chart the frequency of different levels of intelligence in a population; that is, how many people have low, average, or high intelligence (and all other values in-between), according to the particular measure used. How frequently different levels of intelligence occur within a population is known as its **distribution**. The characteristic distribution of intelligence, when it is measured in particular ways, has played a central role in how we have studied the genetic origins of intelligence. We discuss the measurement and distribution of intelligence in more detail here.

As we've seen in earlier chapters, researchers in the field of intelligence overwhelmingly use general cognitive ability, or the so-called g factor, to represent intelligence (Deary, Penke, & Johnson, 2010). The concept of the g factor was derived early in the twentieth century via a lengthy process of assessment development. The g factor is assumed to describe a general set of abilities that support academic achievement and other aspects of daily functioning. Although g has been referred to as "the pinnacle of the hierarchical model of cognitive abilities" (Plomin & Deary, 2015, p. 99), it is important to remember that the power of the g factor is highly dependent on the collection of tests and tasks that are used to estimate it. Yet, even when sets of such tests and tasks appear to be theoretically reliable and an accurate assessment of g, and are given to a sample of people who represent a large range of cognitive ability, the g factor estimated by these tests (Carroll, 1993; Spearman, 1904) generally accounts for or explains only approximately 40 percent of the variance in people's intelligence within the sample. Importantly, the broader the range of tasks used to assess intelligence, the smaller is the shared variance between them. Yet, for better or for worse, it is the g factor, as captured primarily by conventional standardized intelligence tests, that dominates the field of genetic studies of intelligence. There is only a limited collection of genetic studies of intelligence in which theories other than of the *g* factor have been used. For example, a literature search for studies on the genetic contributions to emotional intelligence found only a few isolated studies (Baughman et al., 2011; Kim, Kang, Namkoong, & Song, 2011; Schermer, Petrides, & Vernon, 2015; Vernon, Petrides, Bratko, & Schermer, 2008; Veselka et al., 2010). Thus, it is important to remember that when genetic studies of intelligence are discussed, what is meant by intelligence is the *g* factor, however captured, but primarily by various standardized tests of intelligence.

Despite the fact that the *g* factor construct and the tests that measure it considerably narrow conceptions of intelligence, such tests are used because they have been devised to differentiate people's intelligence according to a normal curve. That is, within a typical population, a relatively small proportion of individuals will perform very poorly; a similarly small proportion will perform at very high levels; the vast majority of individuals perform at what might be called average levels, in between the two extremes. Thus, intelligence, when measured as the *g* factor using standardized tests of intelligence, is generally described as being continuously distributed on a bell curve of normal distribution. Of additional importance is that when intelligence is measured in this way, these proportions are likely to exist in any given population, although the distribution moments (e.g., the averages) might differ.

Based on the general understanding that intelligence, as measured by standardized intelligence or *g* factor tests, is a normally distributed trait within populations, and that intelligence is at least partially determined by our genes, it is proposed that there must be a genetic system underlying this distribution. This genetic system must include specific mechanisms or variable elements that may lead to high intelligence; it must allow for a blend of advantageous, neutral, and even some risky elements that may lead to average intelligence; but then also include one or a number of certain elements that may lead to low intelligence. These variation-producing elements of the genetic system are called "alleles"; how they provide sources of individual differences is explained below. A **gene** is a functional unit of DNA. According to its classical definition, it provides the instructions for the production of a specific protein that carries out a specific role in the organism's functioning. **Alleles** are simply different versions of the same gene or its subcomponents. Every person receives two alleles of every gene (or its subcomponents), one from each parent. When these two versions are the same, it is said that the individual is **homozygous** for that allele. When these two versions are different, it is said that the individual is **heterozygous** for that allele. An individual may be heterozygous because two parents each contributed a different allele. However, alleles may also differ if a change or alteration has occurred in one *de novo*, that is, spontaneously as a mutation. The potential for these differences is one source of the incredible variation that exists between individuals. Investigations into how this genetic system contributes to various levels of intelligence, then, focus on the different combinations of alleles that people of different intelligence levels have, and how much of this variation may have been inherited from parents.

Methods of the Field: A Capsule Overview

We begin by summarizing how evidence is collected and understood in genetic studies (but see Kornilov & Grigorenko, 2016, for more detail). The realization that individual differences in intelligence are substantially related to individual differences in genomes has been supported primarily by two types of evidence: quantitative-genetic information and molecular-genetic information.

Quantitative-Genetic Methods

Quantitative-genetic methods investigate the etiology (or origins) of traits that exhibit continuous variation, or infinite variety, like height or weight. These methods are defined by the use of **genetically informative designs**. These designs rely on the availability of different types of biological relatives who share genetic material. The most well-known quantitative genetic methods, variations of what is termed the family method, rely on the existence of very specific family relationships. This method examines different types of families in which genetic relationships can be clearly defined based on the fact that an individual receives one half of their genetic material from each biological parent. For example, *twin families* include **monozygotic twins** (identical twins), whose genetic material (i.e., DNA) is basically identical because they developed from the same fertilized egg, or **dizygotic twins** (fraternal twins), who developed from two different fertilized eggs. *Nuclear families* include only parents and their biological children (i.e., children who have been neither adopted nor conceived by a surrogate). In such families, each child is assumed to have inherited approximately 50 percent of their DNA from each parent, although in different combinations, so has on average 50 percent of the same DNA as any sibling. Nonbiological (i.e., adopted) family members, in contrast, do not share any inherited DNA with any other family member. These different types of families, in other words, exhibit very specific levels of genetic relatedness: 100 percent relatedness for **monozygotic** twins, those who developed from one fertilized egg; on average ~50 percent relatedness for all siblings, including fraternal or **dizygotic** twins; and 50 percent relatedness between parents and offspring. We defined a person's genotype above as their inherited genetic make-up. A person's **phenotype** is the set of observable characteristics, such as height, weight, or intelligence, which result from the interaction of their genotype with the environment. Taking genetic relationships into account, family members are evaluated for specific physically measurable phenotypic traits which are then compared to their assumed genetic similarities.

The observed phenotypic correlation between combinations of relatives can be attributed to genetic and environmental components that they may have in common, thus reflecting potential sources of the observed similarity. The similarity between these people's genomes is considered maximal for monozygotic twins and minimal for adopted individuals; the similarity in environments is maximal for twins living together and engaged in the same school and after-school activities, and is minimal for siblings separated at birth. When studying the genetic origins of intelligence according to these methods, the phenotype of interest (e.g., intelligence) is assessed, while everything else (e.g., heritability) is estimated. For example, the twin method allows us to estimate heritability by comparing the phenotypic similarity (such as, IQ scores) found between identical twins with the phenotypic similarity found between fraternal twins. We compare this measured similarity against the similarity we expected to find based on their assumed genetic similarity. That is, we expect identical twins' scores to be closer to each other's than fraternal twins' scores, specifically, about two times closer.

As we discussed in earlier chapters, **heritability** in its broadest sense refers to the proportion of variation in a particular trait (such as differences of levels of intelligence) in the general population that can be accounted for or explained by genetic variance (differences in genetic material). The "twin sibling" of the concept of heritability is that of environmentality, which refers to the amount of variance in a particular trait in the general population that can be attributed to the environmental variance. Together with an error term to capture the various random and nonrandom factors that cannot be comprehensively explained here, heritability and environmentality should add up to 100 percent; that is, they should account for all of the variance in a trait in the general population. When a trait is said to be heritable, it is meant that its heritability estimate is statistically significantly different from zero, but it does not mean that it is significantly different from environmentality. While it cannot be claimed that they are perfectly accurate, estimates of heritability have been incredibly useful in outlining the extent to which certain traits are inherited from parents (via nature) and to what extent they are fostered by the environment (via nurturance). To date, hundreds of quantitative-genetic studies of the heritability of intelligence have indicated that intelligence is heritable to some degree (~50 percent); that is, intelligence is a heritable trait, although only moderately so (Plomin & Deary, 2015).

Molecular-Genetic Methods

While quantitative methods are based on our measurements of phenotypes (such as intelligence) and their comparison with what is known about individuals' genetic relationships, **molecular-genetic methods** capitalize on what we can now learn about each individual's DNA and its molecular composition. Each person's genetic material is composed of long, thread-like molecules of DNA (short for deoxyribonucleic acid). The basic structural unit of a single molecule of DNA consists of one sugar and one phosphate group, and one base, and is called a **nucleotide**. Each molecule of DNA looks like a twisted ladder: The two long sides of the ladder are made of the connected phosphate-sugar components, and these are connected by rungs made of two linked pieces called bases. There are four different bases found in DNA and the "rungs" are made of specific pairs: guanine always links to cytosine to make a rung; adenine always links to thymine. The total length of the human genome is estimated to consist of 6.2 billion (6.2×10^9) base pairs, or "ladder rungs," of nucleotides. While these rungs or pairings are the same in every individual's DNA, the *order* or sequence in which they occur will vary from person to person. What this means is that, while it has long been known that the human genome possesses sources of variation that do not challenge the integrity of the human species, *Homo sapiens*, these sources do differentiate individuals within the species.

The different types and extent of the genetic variation between individuals has become evident in waves, as new information is produced with new advancements in genetic research. In particular, the knowledge yielded in such efforts as the Human Genome Project (www.genome.gov/10001772/all-about-the-human-genome-project-hgp/), the 1,000 Genomes Project (www.genome.gov/27528684/1000-genomes-project/), and the 100,000 Genomes Project (www.genomicsengland.co.uk/the-100000-genomes-project/) has increased as more and more individuals' genomes are sequenced, that is, analyzed to determine their exact nucleotide sequences. In parallel with this intense growth of knowledge, technological advances have resulted in an unprecedented decrease in the costs of obtaining data on the variability in the human genome and relating these data to the information on individual differences in complex human traits. All of these advances have permitted the field to shift from predominantly quantitative-genetic to molecular-genetic studies into the etiology of intelligence. Now, instead of being estimated, the sources of genetic variance can be explicitly mapped and quantified. It is estimated that, on average, the human genome is 99 percent **monomorphic** (i.e., there are no differences between different people on these traits). Thus, only 1 percent of the genome differentiates one person from another. Although seemingly small, this 1 percent of the human genome includes 10 million (6.2×10^7) nucleotides. As molecular-genetic studies permit a precise quantification of the degree of genetic similarity between individuals, their research designs do not have to be limited to known types of relatives; even unrelated individuals can be assessed for the degree of shared and unshared variance between their genomes. Then genetic variability can be associated with the phenotypic variability of any particular behavior trait (e.g., intelligence). As the human genome harbors many instances of variation (referred to as **polymorphisms**), these can be assessed across the whole genome; such types of studies are called genome-wide studies.

There are two principal ways by which the information on polymorphisms can be evaluated. In the first approach, known as *genotyping*, only those areas of the genome that are assumed to contain known polymorphisms are assessed. In other words, genotyping is carried out with only that portion of the genome that is known to be variable between people (i.e., in aggregate, about 1 percent). The second approach, known as *sequencing*, is more exhaustive in that it accounts for every single nucleotide in the human genome, including known polymorphisms (i.e., the polymorphisms from the 1 percent of the genome discussed above) and individual-specific, previously unknown or *de novo* polymorphisms (those arising via spontaneous mutation). Although they use different modes of genomic data acquisition, both analytic approaches amount to searching for associations between variations in the genome and variations in the trait of interest (e.g., intelligence). The only major difference between the two is the amount of genomic data produced (substantially more in sequencing than in genotyping). At this time, genotyping is much cheaper than sequencing, although it should be noted that this may change. Studies that employ the genotyping approach are called **genome-wide association studies (GWAS)** (see the Focus on Contemporary Research for an example of such a study). Those that employ sequencing are called **whole-genome sequencing (WGS) studies**. Quite a few intelligence GWAS have been carried out (e.g., Davies et al., 2011; Davis et al., 2010; Marioni et al., 2014; Spain et al., 2016), as well as a limited number of WGS studies (e.g., Luciano et al., 2015). For a more detailed description of a GWAS study on aspects of intelligence in an African population, see the Focus on Contemporary Research below.

FOCUS ON CONTEMPORARY RESEARCH: SERGEY KORNILOV, MEI TAN, AND ELENA L. GRIGORENKO: THE FIRST GWAS ON ASPECTS OF INTELLIGENCE IN AN AFRICAN POPULATION

As part of an ongoing study on the etiology of reading disability in a rural Zambian population, we are focusing on establishing associations between a number of developmental traits. Some of these traits are dichotomous, such as the existence of a reading disability or an intellectual disability. Other traits are continuous, such as intelligence and reading achievement scores and a large number of single nucleotide polymorphisms (SNPs). To pinpoint the specific regions, genes, and variants that may contribute to cognitive development, we are carrying out a genome-wide association study (GWAS), in which the genomes of individuals are sampled at many specific locations or loci, evenly spaced along the DNA's length. Occurrences of known SNPs for each individual are then looked at beside occurrences of specific phenotypes, based on indicators of reading and/or intellectual disability, reading achievement, and intelligence. The phenotypic data in this study are drawn from assessments administered to all children on component reading skills, such as phonological awareness, knowledge of letter–sound correspondence, word reading, and reading comprehension, as well as assessments for cognitive skills such as reasoning and memory. Genetic data were collected via saliva samples provided by each child and selected family members.

Specifically, this GWAS involves genotyping the DNA from a total of 1,353 children using Illumina's (Illumina, Inc.) HumanCoreExome microarray panel, which identifies 550,000 SNPs known to be markers for variants within the portions of the genome that we know may have an impact on protein structure and function. The inclusion of a large number of markers allows us to simultaneously assess the contribution of rare (but impactful) as well as common (generally considered less impactful) genetic variants that affect intelligence and reading development, both individually and jointly. To this end, we will perform univariate (i.e., per-phenotype-per-marker) as well as multivariate (taking into account multiple phenotypes and multiple genetic markers at the same time) genetic-association analyses, in an attempt to identify novel candidate reading genes. By relying on the availability of dense SNP genotyping data and recent developments in statistical genetics, we are able to circumvent the issues of population stratification and unreported relatedness (e.g., two cousins who do not know they are cousins) in the data set by accounting for the relatedness directly estimated for each pair of individuals from the genetic data.

Focusing on cognitive development in this unique and diverse population using a variety of approaches to phenotyping and genetic association analysis will allow us to greatly expand our understanding of the genetic architecture of developing cognition. We may also evaluate the emerging landscape of GWAS findings from mostly European-ancestry populations from the standpoint of their generality to a particular African population.

Genetics/Genomics and Intelligence: The Frontiers of Knowledge

Here we provide a general overview of the field of genetic/genomic studies of intelligence. As a number of theoreticians in the field do not accept the exclusive use of the g factor as the best representation of intelligence, we will briefly review not only g factor studies, but also studies of processes that are considered relevant to broader definitions of intelligence, such as executive functioning and creativity.

Debates over the Origins of Intelligence

In the early years of the twentieth century, as tensions were rising in the debate concerning whether intelligence was inherited or shaped solely by the environment (the "nature–nurture debate"), intelligence was the complex human trait most commonly subjected to studies using genetically informative designs, for example, studies focusing on twins and adopted children (Burks, 1928; Freeman, Holzinger, & Mitchell, 1928; Merriman, 1924; van Senden Theis, 1924; Ignatiev, 1936). These early studies launched the field of quantitative-genetic studies of intelligence, which has grown into the largest field of studies investigating the origins of complex human behavioral traits. This field is almost a century old now and has unfailingly demonstrated the importance of genetic factors in the emergence and maintenance of the measurable individual differences in intelligence. But what else has been learned after a century of genetically informative designs? According to the latest reviews (Deary et al., 2010; Plomin & Deary, 2015; Plomin, DeFries, Knopik, & Neiderhiser, 2016), there are seven findings worth knowing about and following up on, and whose importance is agreed upon by the field. We discuss each of these below.

Genetic Factors Do Contribute to Intelligence

A voluminous body of quantitative-genetic research has consistently demonstrated that a statistically significant portion of the total variance of intelligence in the general population can be accounted for by genetic factors (Plomin, DeFries, Knopik, & Neiderhiser, 2013). Yet, although statistically significant, the heritability of intelligence is moderate, wavering at about 50 percent (Deary, Johnson, & Houlihan, 2009). It is in fact comparable to the heritability of other complex human traits, such as height and weight. Similar to studies that are now being carried out to discover the specific genes that may account for the variations in height and weight found within a population, there are studies searching for the specific genes that may account for the heritability of intelligence.

The Heritability of Intelligence Is Dynamic

It appears that the heritability of intelligence is dynamic (Haworth et al., 2010; Lee, Henry, Trollor, & Sachdev, 2010; Panizzon et al., 2014). This means that the heritability of intelligence has been found to differ at different ages across the lifespan. Its heritability seems to be at its lowest in infancy (~20 percent), gradually increase through childhood and adolescence (~40 percent) and into young adulthood (~60 percent), and then reach a maximum of about 80 percent in later adulthood with a possible decline (to ~60 percent) after age 80.

There Is No Single (or Even a Few) Intelligence Gene(s)

It seems that the genes thought to contribute to the variation in intelligence are characterized by functional **pleiotropy**, or the occurrence of a single gene contributing to two or more seemingly unrelated effects. Thus, it is unlikely that the genes that contribute to the variance in intelligence are intelligence-specific. Rather, these genes most likely affect other cognitive and noncognitive complex traits in addition to intelligence. To differentiate these influences and map them onto different complex traits, including intelligence, multiple combinations of genetic variants being expressed in different patterns should be considered.

Genetic Studies of Intelligence Must Account for the Multifaceted Nature of Intelligence

Various theories and tests of intelligence commonly acknowledge the multifaceted nature of intelligence: that it has multiple components, such as memory and processing speed; and that it changes across the lifespan. The extent to which this heterogeneity is taken into account in the different studies of intelligence, however, varies. Most intelligence researchers, even those who favor the g factor model, at least differentiate verbal and nonverbal intelligence, or crystallized and fluid intelligence (Carroll, 1993; Cattell, 1963). You may remember from Chapter 4 that we defined crystallized intelligence (g-crystallized, or Gc) as the store of previously acquired knowledge and skills that help a person reason and solve problems, and fluid intelligence (g-fluid or Gf) as the ability to reason in novel situations. Researchers (Christoforou et al., 2014) have used previously published GWAS data (Davies et al., 2011) to conduct further analyses and investigate whether Gc and Gf could be distinguished at the genetic level. Although the heritability for Gc and Gf are similar (Davies et al., 2011), they have different developmental trajectories across the lifespan. An additional difference between Gc and Gf is that, at the population level, large gains in performance have been registered over time for Gf, but not Gc (Flynn, 2012). Both types of intelligence are highly **polygenic** (generated by many interactions of multiple genes), but it appears that the sets of genes governing Gc and Gf are different. In fact, Gf has been associated with genes affecting the quantity and quality of **neurons** (the nerve cells that transmit electrical signals in response to stimuli to and from the brain) and therefore neuronal efficiency; Gc, in contrast, has been associated with genes affecting **long-term synaptic depression** (**LTD**; the long-term weakening of nerve cell connections), versus **long-term potentiation** (**LTP**; long-term strengthening of nerve cell connections), both of which are enduring changes in synaptic strength (Christoforou et al., 2014). These disparate relationships illustrate the presumed distinct nature of intelligence, and how each type of intelligence may involve a variety of different genes.

Contributions of Multiple Genes Exert Small Effects on Intelligence

According to Fisher's theory of quantitative genetics (Fisher, 1918), it is likely that the heritability of complex genetic traits such as intelligence is attributable to contributions of multiple genes exerting small effects. These many small effects combine differently in each person to result in individual differences in intelligence. However, as with any small effects, their detection requires study samples that include many individuals and precise instrumentation. These two requirements explain why the early molecular-genetic research on intelligence generated inconsistent results. In contrast, research carried out in the first quarter of the twenty-first century has had access to inexpensive, highly informative, and reliable methods for assessing the genomes of individuals, as well as access to large samples of individuals. The results of these studies are in line with Fisher's expectations. For example, in the largest GWAS of its time, in which known sources of variation across the whole genome were considered in a sample of 18,000 children, the strongest effect size registered amounted to 0.2 percent of the variance in indicators of intelligence (Benyamin et al., 2014). In other words, in this study, only 1/5th of one percent of phenotypic variation could be explained by genetic variation.

Similarly, a recent GWAS meta-analysis of intelligence in a sample of approximately 54,000 adults (Davies et al., 2015) revealed comparable effect sizes. In a study with a sample of 1,500 children, the largest registered effect accounted for 0.5 percent of the variance in indicators of intelligence (Desrivières et al., 2015). The associations of small effect sizes between specific sources of variation in the genome (i.e., DNA variants) and indicators of intelligence can be summed across multiple variants to generate a polygenic score. **Polygenic** scores (PGS) are a useful way to combine the small effects from several sources of variation – too small to explain any variation individually – to explain a single complex construct (e.g., intelligence).

Genetic Research on Intelligence Must Include Studies of Intellectual Disability

In order to truly grasp the scope of all the research on intelligence, it is important to consider not only studies on the etiology of intelligence in its typical ranges, but also studies on the etiology of intellectual disability (ID). This is because ID, while occurring on the continuum of intelligence, has etiologies that may be very distinct, some of which are genetically related and others of which are not. That is, one may be born with an ID, as in the former case; or ID may result from a stroke or some form of brain trauma (as may occur in a car accident, for example). ID's defining features are an IQ<70, age of onset before 18 years, and the impairment of at least two adaptive skills. *Adaptive skills* are those that are heavily involved in everyday activities, such as expressive communication. In the general population, ID appears to arise from a variety of causes, both from birth (congenital) and acquired after birth. It has been both theorized (Penrose, 1938) and empirically demonstrated (Reichenberg et al., 2016) that congenital ID is etiologically heterogeneous. That is, it has many possible causes.

Severe intellectual disability (lowest 0.5 percent of IQ distribution, with IQ≤35) is neither familial (observed in multiple family members) nor heritable (capable of being passed from parent to child via genetic material). In other words, severe ID, even if rooted in genetic abnormalities, is not generally transmitted from parent to child. In cases of mild ID, the genes involved differ from those that influence IQ scores in the normal range. Notably, ID is a common feature of genomic syndromes, that is, multi-symptomatic conditions, in which a genomic event affects different body tissues and is therefore associated with several atypical manifestations such as physical dysmorphologies (physical irregularities) and the malfunction of various organs, including the brain. Well-known examples of genomic syndromes are Down syndrome (trisomy of chromosome 21, in which three versions of chromosome 21 are generated in an individual's DNA, rather than the expected two versions); Smith–Magenis syndrome (a deletion of genetic material from a specific region of chromosome 17); Potocki–Lupski syndrome (an addition of genetic material from a specific region of chromosome 17); DiGeorge syndrome (a deletion of genetic material from a specific region of chromosome 21); and many other neurodevelopmental disorders. Such syndromes typically arise from an extensive genomic alteration and impact numerous aspects of physical and mental health.

There are, however, large numbers of individuals with intellectual disability (1-3 percent of the general population) who do not have any of the known and catalogued genomic events and their impairments appear to be limited to the cognitive domain. This type of ID is typically referred to as *nonsyndromic intellectual disability*. It is thought that intellectual disability is caused by genetic factors in about 50 percent of autosomal (non-sex-related) recessive conditions. These are conditions in which receiving the same recessive (nondominant) version of a gene from each parent can lead to atypical development. Such genetic conditions account for about a quarter of genetically caused nonsyndromatic ID, and this proportion might be even higher in societies that commonly practice consanguineous marriages (marriage between close relatives; Ropers et al., 2011). Thus, epidemiological data indicate a higher prevalence of nonsyndromic ID in Arab, Iranian, and Pakistani populations due to a high rate of consanguinity (Khan et al., 2016). Studies of nonsyndromic ID have resulted in the identification and localization of 100 X-linked and 51 autosomal locations where such genes may occur, the majority of which have revealed the ID-causal genes they harbor. Yet it is important to note that genetic/genomic forms of ID can be caused not only by single gene impairments, but by a variety of genetic factors (Winnepenninckx, Rooms, & Kooy, 2003), including chromosomal anomalies (e.g., Patau's syndrome, which is a trisomy of chromosome 13); mitochondrial disorders, caused by a mutation occurring within the mitochondrial DNA, or within genes directly affecting the mitochondria, the power generating organelles of the cell (e.g., Alpers syndrome); epigenetic defects (e.g., Angelman and Prader–Willi syndromes), defects in the structural and regulatory rather than protein-coding elements of the genome; and repeat extension diseases (e.g., Huntington's disease and fragile X syndrome).

Genetic Research on Intelligence Must Include Studies of Intellectual Giftedness

Just as it is important to include an understanding of the etiology of ID in genetic studies, it is also important to understand the etiology of intellectual giftedness. Recently, the field of quantitative-genetic studies of intelligence has been enriched with a number of studies having very large sample-sizes. For example, using records on the cognitive assessments administered to 3 million 18-year-old males as part of conscription into the military service in Sweden between 1968 and 2010, researchers (Shakeshaft et al., 2015) examined data from 360,000 sibling and 9,000 twin pairs. Based on the results of their quantitative-genetic analyses, they reported that high intelligence is familial, heritable, and caused by the same genetic and environmental factors responsible for the normal distribution of intelligence. In light of these findings, researchers (Spain et al., 2016) used data from four different samples – the High-intelligence cases (HiQ) Study, the Minnesota Twin Family Study (MTFS), the Twins Early Development Study (TEDS), and the Avon Longitudinal Study of Parents and Children (ALSPAC) – to perform a case–control association analysis with 1,409 individuals drawn from particular levels of IQ performance. Such analyses look for correlations between genotypes and phenotypes, but in a stratified sample. In the abovementioned study, the participants were the top 0.0003 (IQ 170) of the population distribution of intelligence (the HiQ sample), and 3,253 unselected population-based controls (the MTFS sample, all individuals had 70<IQ<150), and two replication/extension samples (n=11,533 from the TEDS and ALSPAC samples). DNA from the participants in the HiQ and MTFS samples was genotyped; the results did not identify any variants reproducibly associated with either extremely high or average intelligence. Similarly, no single or combinations of rare alleles within individual genes were statistically significant. Yet, when a genome-wide complex trait analysis was performed and the PGS were constructed, the genotyped functional protein-altering variation yielded, based on a liability model, a heritability estimate of 17.4 percent. The term "liability model" is generally used to collectively represent all of the genetic and environmental factors that might affect a particular condition or outcome, such as intelligence. Based on knowledge of the field regarding the genetic cases of low intelligence (see above) and the obtained results, the authors hypothesized that rare functional alleles are more frequently detrimental than beneficial to intelligence.

Intelligence-Related Processes

One of the reasons for this continued inquiry is that the predictive power of IQ does, in fact, have its limits, and the field is interested in going beyond these limits. During the last few decades of research in various subdomains of psychology (e.g., cognitive, developmental, clinical, educational, and organizations), inquiries into individual differences have been traditionally dominated by studies of IQ.

More recently, however, several of these fields have launched investigations into "other than" IQ constructs to capture major sources of individual differences predictive of health and disease outcomes. Some examples of these concepts are given below.

Executive Functions Research

Although multiple definitions exist, *executive functions* are commonly referred to as meta-cognitive processes that maintain, assemble, coordinate, and monitor component cognitive processes into higher-order structures needed to carry out goal-directed behavior. Executive functions form a complex multidimensional system with multiple sources of individual differences in both lower-level component processes and higher-level systemic arrangements. Although quantitative-genetic research on executive functioning is limited, it has demonstrated that individual differences in performance on various executive function tasks are marked by high, nearly 100 percent, heritability in middle childhood (Engelhardt, Briley, Mann, Harden, & Tucker-Drob, 2015) and young adulthood (Friedman et al., 2008), and they appear to be highly stable and attributable primarily to genetic factors (Friedman et al., 2015). A question of particular interest, however, both for the field and for the purposes of discussion in this chapter, is whether the correlation typically observed between executive functions and intelligence at the behavioral (phenotypic) level is driven primarily by genetic or environmental factors. If there are very few quantitative-genetic studies of executive functions, there are even fewer studies in which genetically informative designs are used so that the variation in both executive functions and intelligence can be considered simultaneously. Two studies should be mentioned here. The first estimated the genetic correlation between executive functions and full-scale IQ in young adults at .57 (Friedman et al., 2008) and the second in children at .92 (Engelhardt et al., 2016). Based on these results, researchers have concluded that the genetic influence on the *g* factor might highly overlap with the genes that influence executive functions.

Studies Combining Quantitative- and Molecular-Genetic Methods

Consider yet another illustration that utilizes both quantitative- and molecular-genetic methods. Here researchers have focused on three well-known tasks, Sentence Comprehension, N-term, and Latin Square, which are quite similar to typical tasks used in conventional tests of intelligence to access a construct referred to as cognitive complexity or relational complexity, defined as "the ability to mentally link variables relevant for goal-directed behavior" (Hansell et al., 2015, p. 2). In Sentence Comprehension, the child must sort out complex subject-verb-object relationships and answer a question, such as "What did the goats do?"; in N-term, given a set of relational rules (such as "B > A," "A < F," etc.), the child has to reason through the logical order of the terms; and in Latin Square, given a partially filled

4 × 4 grid and four shapes, the child must fill in the rest of the grid, making sure that each shape occurs only once in each row and column. These tasks were administered to individuals in five samples: (1) an Australian twin sample of adolescents and young adults deemed the Discovery sample; and (2) four large internationally known samples (the English Avon Longitudinal Study of Parents and Children; the Scottish Lothian Birth Cohort; the Dutch Netherlands Twin Registry; and the Norwegian Cognitive NeuroGenetics), deemed the Replication samples. The researchers factor-analyzed the indices on these three tasks and registered a single factor, named relational/cognitive complexity, which accounted for 63.9 percent of the variance in them. The score on this factor was subsequently subjected to conventional quantitative-genetic analyses to estimate the heritability of this trait, and to molecular-genetic analyses to identify DNA variants in the genome that are associated with the trait of cognitive complexity. The corresponding quantitative-analyses demonstrated that this factor is highly heritable (with a heritability of 67 percent) and has considerable genetic overlap with IQ (59 percent). Using molecular-genetic analyses, the researchers registered six common variants as stat-istically significant sources of variance for the trait of interest, but none of these variants sustained the replication test in four independent samples meta-analytically. While none of the independent samples were given the same three tasks used to quantify relational/cognitive complexity in the Australian sample, all were adminis-tered measures of reasoning, working memory, and/or IQ. Using these measures of reasoning as "proxies" for complexity, the researchers detected significant associ-ations at the gene-based level (in the *NPS* gene, which has also been implicated in susceptibility for schizophrenia): in two of the samples (ALSPAC and LBC1936), at the statistically significant level; and in one sample (NCNG), at the threshold level, as relevant to the variation in relational/cognitive complexity. Interpreting their results, the researchers suggested that relational complexity might be an indicator of capacity, triggering "a genetic cascade effect whereby genetic factors influencing core cognitive traits have flow-on effects to more complex cognitive behaviours" (Hansell et al., 2015, p. 14).

Testing Creativity

A cognitive function that is often considered to be etiologically related to intelli-gence is *creativity*. Creativity and its component processes appear to be both familial (e.g., Tan & Grigorenko, 2013) and heritable (e.g., Grigorenko, LaBuda, & Carter, 1992). Yet the number of quantitative-genetic studies on creativity and its various facets is limited. One review of the relevant literature (Kaufman, Kornilov, Bristol, Tan, & Grigorenko, 2010) has indicated that, at first approximation, studies confirm the importance of genetic factors as sources of individual differences for creativity and its related processes. Given the modest but consistent phenotypic correlations between creativity and intelligence, intelligence is considered to be a prerequisite for creativity (Silvia & Beaty, 2012), as well as a gatekeeper that monitors the conversion of creativity into a useful product (Jauk, Benedek, & Neubauer, 2014). As expected, although statistically significant genetic correlations between creativity and intelligence have been detected, none of the genetic variance in creativity was accounted for by the genetic variance in intelligence (Kandler et al., 2016; Tan & Grigorenko, 2013).

Educational Attainment, Life Success, and Lifespan

To conclude this section on the frontiers of the field, we consider, finally, a bundle of concepts typically perceived as being predicted by IQ: *educational attainment, life success*, and *lifespan*. We consider first a large-scale GWAS (n > 125,000 individuals and >1,000,000 genetic polymorphisms) of educational attainment, described as "the first successful genomewide association study (GWAS) of a social-science outcome, educational attainment" (Belsky et al., 2016, p. 957). The largest effect size accounted for 1 percent of the variance and was captured by a polygenic score (PGS) – a combination of genetic variants scattered across the genome that, when considered together, explain a statistically significant amount of variance in the trait of interest, in this case, years of education; yet the variance explained was only 0.02 percent in a replication sample (Rietveld et al., 2013). This study triggered a number of related studies, which capitalized on the PGS. Specifically, in one study (Belsky et al., 2016), this polygenic score was studied in association with lifespan indicators of success in a well-known longitudinal study, the Dunedin Study, which spans four decades of the participants' lives. The primary finding from this study was that the PGS predicted, even when educational attainment was controlled for, a number of life outcomes indicative of social success (e.g., social status, social mobility, economic success). Similarly, using three large samples of twins from the USA, Sweden, and Denmark, researchers have studied the etiology of the correlation between intelligence and the lifespan (Arden et al., 2016). Although the observed correlation was small, 95 percent of it in the combined sample was explained by shared genetic variance.

Are there Practical Implications for Genetic Research on Intelligence?

To conclude, we address a final question: What are the possible practical implications of the work being carried out on the genetic etiology of intelligence? As in many such quests for knowledge, the absolute value of the knowledge generated is difficult to predict or foresee in advance. Yet there are of course ongoing discussions of possible practical applications of the knowledge we currently have. We end here with brief summaries of three such discussions.

Sociogenomics: The Study of How Social Life Evolved

The rapidly developing field of **sociogenomics** – the study of social life in genetic terms – strives to understand how social life evolved, how it is guided and how it influences all aspects of the genome structure, genome activity, and how an organism functions (Robinson, Grozinger, & Whitfield, 2005). Intelligence in all of its forms and types, not only the g factor, is intimately related to the emergence of social life and the development of human civilization. Sociogenomic studies have convincingly indicated that (1) social behavior emerged with the use of evolutionary liable pathways involved in other (nonsocial) behaviors (Robinson et al., 2005); and (2) the genome is highly sensitive and responsive to social influences, such that sociability is likely to be associated, although perhaps not exclusively, with unique forms of transcription regulatory nucleotide sequences (Robinson & Ben-Shahar, 2002). The sequences of DNA that regulate how and when genes are expressed – via transcription – are called the transcriptome. Thus, one possible direction for socio-genomics would be to qualify and quantify those social influences that are needed to maximize the regulatory potential of the genome. In other words, understanding gene/genome regulation and the correlation of this process with intelligence will lead, most likely, to understanding how specific environments have to be chosen, structured, and experienced to maximize the regulatory aspects of the genome needed to support the rise, positive function, and enhancement of human intelligence. It is really important to appreciate both the content and power of these assumptions. What is assumed here is that intelligence is not so much a product of the structural variation in the genome, which is, by definition, inflexible and deterministic, but a product of the transcriptome, which is highly agile and dynamic. Thus, the task is not to find a large number of structural variants of small effect that might, even collectively, account for a modest amount of individual differences in the genome. Rather, it is to understand how to organize environmental influences to maximize the potential of a flexible transcriptome to substantiate the enhancement of intelligence.

Development of an Oligogenic System to Substantiate Intelligence

The second discussion centers on the current efforts to identify those variants in the human genome that account for the largest amount of variance in intelligence individually, or contribute to some oligo-/poly-/omnigenic system (involving from more than one to all genes per trait) that substantiates intelligence. There are numerous efforts around the world (e.g., see above and http://nautil.us/issue/34/ adaptation/super_intelligent-humans-are-coming-rp) that are devoted to such a search; the Social Science Genome Association Consortium orchestrates one of them. Questions concern what can possibly be done with this information, for example, "once the project turns up intelligence genes, ... people might begin testing embryos to find the most desirable ones" (Check Hayden, 2013, p. 26).

In fact, two of the participants and proponents of the Consortium were quoted (Check Hayden, 2013, p. 27) as saying, "I'm 100% sure that a technology will eventually exist for people to evaluate their embryos or zygotes for quantitative traits, like height or intelligence. I don't see anything wrong with that" (Dr. Stephen Hsu), and, "I'm optimistic that we will find [a genetic contribution]... I'm not going to quit until we do" (Dr. Robert Plomin). The future will determine the true practical applications of these efforts. Might it be possible that one day a direct-to-consumer company such as 23andme will add an intelligence test to its list of offerings? Given the rapid growth of this list, from the inclusion of Bloom syndrome in February 2015 to Parkinson's disease and late-onset Alzheimer's disease in April of 2017 ("The rise and fall and rise again of 23andMe," 2017), it is not beyond consideration. But what would consumers do with their reports? Where will they take them and what would they argue for themselves and their children, with whom and for what services? These questions are all unanswered and often not even raised. And the list of such questions may be even harder for testing embryos, as prenatal testing and related alterations (see below) could lead to an abolition, at least in theory, of whole groups of people, whose group identity is established through the characteristics of their genome (e.g., people with Down syndrome or other syndromes with known etiologies). Knowledge, in other words, can provide opportunities to make choices, such as the acceptance or rejection of certain fetuses based on projected intelligence, but do we want to face such choices?

Genetic Alteration of Intelligence

This subject is not complete without addressing the issue of the genetic alteration of intelligence. The first successful use of *clustered regularly interspaced short palindromic repeats* (CRISPR), CRISPR-associated protein 9 (CRISPR-Cas9) in mammalian cells took place in early 2013. It is a technique that is now recognized as the most promising tool for gene editing (www.cell.com/nucleus-CRISPR) (Cho, Kim, Kim, & Kim, 2013; Cong et al., 2013; Hwang et al., 2013; Jinek et al., 2013; Mali et al., 2013). Since then it has captured the attention of the lay public to a degree that is rather uncommon for a scientific development. The technology has been discussed in major mass media outlets under catchy titles, such as *Editing Humanity* (*The Economist*, August 22, 2015, www.economist.com/news/leaders/21661651-new-technique-manipulating-genes-holds-great-promisebut-rules-are-needed-govern-its), where the cover depicts a baby with engineered characteristics such as sprinter muscles, perfect pitch, no baldness... ever, low risk for Alzheimer's, breast cancer, and strokes, 20/20 vision, and... high IQ. So, how much of this is fad and how much of this is for real? What is the potential for genome editing to affect human development in general and the development of intelligence in particular? The CRISPR-Cas9 system is one of a number of existing genome-editing tools (e.g., zinc-finger nucleases, meganucleases, and transcription activator-like effector nucleases, TALENs) that have been developed over the last decade. CRISPR-Cas9, compared to others, is characterized by ease of use, efficacy, and target effectiveness (Musunuru, 2017). Although it is spectacularly promising, at this point there are simply not enough empirical data to appraise both the potential advantages and potential disadvantages. The most obvious disadvantage is that, as an effective cleavage tool, it might cleave the genome at some location other than the targeted site, causing off-target alterations or triggering inefficient on-target mutagenesis (i.e., unintended mutations). To appraise the long-term potential and safety of CRISPR-Cas9, it will be critical to carry out human clinical trials, monitoring the patients who receive these therapies for short-, long-, and life-long outcomes. In the absence of this knowledge, it is most likely that the first CRISPR-Cas9 therapies will be utilized in treating very ill patients, where the therapy is driven by the assumption that its potential benefits greatly outweigh the risks. Given the technical characteristics of the CRISPR-Cas9 system, its most beneficial applications are thought to be for patients whose targeted cells, having been altered, would rapidly proliferate (i.e., to infants or even in utero). According to this logic, the most effective application would be to the single cell, so that the corrected genome could proliferate. However, this would involve altering germ cells (eggs and sperm), so descendants would also have the altered genome. Germ cell engineering opens up a large number of social, ethical, moral, and legal issues. These issues are far from trivial; they have raised complex questions and have generated divided opinions among scientists (National Academies of Sciences, 2017) and laypeople (Blendon, Gorski, & Benson, 2016). In both groups, there are complex feelings about the future of genetic editing, the types of which are differentiated by one of the four specific applications (Musunuru, 2017): (1) treating or preventing severe genetic disorders that may result in early loss of life or extremely poor quality of life; (2) addressing genetic causes of infertility; (3) reducing the risk of common adult diseases (e.g., coronary heart disease and Alzheimer's disease); and (4) enhancement (selection of advantageous or otherwise desirable traits). Predictably, there is a much higher comfort level among both scientists and laypeople with the first two, compared with the last two applications. But, as is always the case, empirical science keeps developing and inevitably generating new intellectual and moral challenges for scientists and the public alike.

It is worth noting, in closing, two recent papers published in the August and September 2017 issues of *Nature* (Fogarty et al., 2017; Ma et al., 2017), respectively, that brought to the fore crucial issues concerning how this type of research should be appraised (*Nature*, September 21, 2017). The first article explored the outcomes of the correction of a specific genetic mutation, carried out by editing embryos with CRISPR-Cas9; the second described mutating a specific gene using CRISPR-Cas9 in a fertilized egg. In both instances, material from human donors was used: the egg and sperm (Ma et al., 2017) and surplus embryos from IVF (*in vitro* fertilization) treatments (Fogarty et al., 2017). These studies, once again, stirred a new wave of discussion on genetic engineering research carried out on human embryos.

Discussing these studies, *Nature* ("Ethical embryo editing," 2017) stressed the importance of fully informing and seeking the consent of all donors on the specifics of the research prior to their donations, putting forward the idea that initially researchers should perform the intended work on human pluripotent stem cells or animal model embryos to optimize and even pre-publish before working with human embryos.

CONCLUSION

The question of the etiology of intelligence has been of interest to scientific and lay minds alike since humanity began reflecting on itself and documenting such self-reflection. As science and its tools have developed, it has become less an arena for the development of theory and more a field of empirical studies. Although various theories concerning intelligence have swung between the two extremes (either nature or nurture matters), the accumulation of empirical studies settled the theoretical debate (both nature and nurture matter), yet generated many subsequent questions, some of which have been discussed above. The etiology of intelligence, for better or for worse, has always been an emotionally charged subject. It has been exaggerated, prohibited, and tabooed – and it has served as the source of endless debates. It has always been hot (Check Hayden, 2013) and it remains so today (Henig, 2015). Have we learned anything useful in 150 years – counting the year Francis Galton's book *Hereditary Genius* (1869) was published as the cornerstone of the field? Absolutely! Do we know everything there is to know, 50 percent of what there is to know, or 1 percent of what there is to know? We definitely know that we do not know everything, but where we are on the road to that knowing is unclear. The real question is whether it is worth stomping ahead on this road (Check Hayden, 2013; Henig, 2015).

It is our belief that science cannot be stopped but only questioned. Is it possible that tomorrow we will learn that everything we know about the etiology of intelligence today is wrong? Not likely, although some of our ideas might still need adjustment. So perhaps we may proceed with only half of Mr. Vaughan's conviction: to learn something new every day, fine tuning and augmenting our conclusions as we go.

CHAPTER SUMMARY

In this chapter, the still rapidly evolving field of the genetics/genomics of intelligence has been introduced, starting with the basic elements of how intelligence is defined and measured, particularly for studies investigating the genetic contributions to intelligence. How the genome might influence the underpinnings of intelligence is then discussed, and the methods that have been used to estimate genetic contributions to intelligence are described – both quantitative and the more currently employed molecular methods. A general overview of the field of genetic/genomic studies of intelligence is presented, including studies that have chosen not to focus on the *g* factor as the best representation of intelligence. Our current state of knowledge indicates the complex, interactive nature of genetic and environmental influences on human development in general, and intelligence in particular. The chapter concludes with a consideration of some possible practical uses of this research, and a glimpse of what the future might hold. New and upcoming technologies, combined with a developing understanding of the many genes likely to be involved in the expression of intelligence, represent the boundaries of our knowledge. Here, we may consider how environments may be manipulated to optimize genetic influences on intelligence, and how the manipulation of genes themselves – almost a commonplace now – may be used sometime in the future to actively shape or stimulate intelligence.

KEY TERMS

allele • chromosomes • distribution (of intelligence) • dizygotic twins • gene • genetically informative design • genetics • genome • genome-wide association study (GWAS) • genomics • genotype • heritability • heterozygous • homozygous • long-term potentiation (LTP) • long-term synaptic depression (LTD) • molecular genetic methods • monomorphic • monozygotic twins • neuron • nucleotide • oligo-/poly-/omnigenic score • phenotype • pleiotropy • polygenic • polygenic score (PGS) • polymorphism • quantitative-genetic methods • sociogenomics • whole-genome sequencing (WGS) studies

COMPREHENSION AND REFLECTION QUESTIONS

1. Why does it matter what test is used to measure children's intelligence?
2. Describe the similarities and differences between quantitative- and molecular-genetic studies.
3. Why and how does a polygenic model account for the nature of intelligence better than a single-gene model?
4. List and describe genetically informative designs.
5. Describe some of the ethical issues that might arise with new uses of CRISPR-Cas9 with regard to understanding human intelligence. Do you see any way to avoid these conflicts?

References

Arden, R., Luciano, M., Deary, I. J., Reynolds, C. A., Pedersen, N. L., Plassman, B. L., . . . &
Visscher, P. M. (2016). The association between intelligence and lifespan is mostly
genetic. *International Journal of Epidemiology, 45,* 178-185. doi: 10.1093/ije/dyv112

Baughman, H. M., Schwartz, S., Schermer, J. A., Veselka, L., Petrides, K., & Vernon, P. A.
(2011). A behavioral-genetic study of alexithymia and its relationships with trait
emotional intelligence. *Twin Research and Human Genetics, 14,* 539-543.

Belsky, D. W., Moffitt, T. E., Corcoran, D. L., Domingue, B., Harrington, H., Hogan, S., . . .
& Caspi, A. (2016). The genetics of success. *Psychological Science, 27,* 957-972.
doi: 10.1177/0956797616643070

Benyamin, B., Pourcain, B., Davis, O. S., Davies, G., Hansell, N. K., Brion, M. J., . . . &
Visscher, P. M. (2014). Childhood intelligence is heritable, highly polygenic and
associated with FNBP1L. *Molecular Psychiatry, 19,* 253-258. doi: 10.1038/mp.2012.184

Blendon, R. J., Gorski, M. T., & Benson, J. M. (2016). The public and the gene-editing
revolution. *New England Journal Medicine, 374,* 1406-1411.

Burks, B. (1928). The relative influence of nature and nurture upon mental development:
A comparative study on foster parent-foster child resemblance. In G. M. Whipple (ed.),
Yearbook of the National Society for the Study of Education. Part 1 (vol. 27,
pp. 219–316). Bloomington, IL: Public School Publishing Co.

Carroll, J. B. (1993). *Human cognitive abilities.* New York: Cambridge University Press.

Cattell, R. B. (1963). Theory of fluid and crystallized intelligence: A critical experiment.
Journal of Educational Psychology, 54(1), 1-22. doi: 10.1037/h0046743

Check Hayden, E. (2013). Ethics: Taboo genetics. *Nature, 502,* 26-28.

Cho, S. W., Kim, S., Kim, J. M., & Kim, J.-S. (2013). Targeted genome engineering in human
cells with the Cas9 RNA-guided endonuclease. *Nature Biotechnology, 31,* 230-232.
doi: 10.1038/nbt.2507

Christoforou, A., Espeseth, T., Davies, G., Fernandes, C. P. D., Giddaluru, S., Mattheisen,
M., . . . & Le Hellard, S. (2014). GWAS-based pathway analysis differentiates
between fluid and crystallized intelligence. *Genes, Brain, and Behavior, 13,* 663-674.
doi: 10.1111/gbb.12152

Cong, L., Ran, F. A., Cox, D., Lin, S., Barretto, R., Habib, N., . . . & Zhang, F. (2013).
Multiplex genome engineering using CRISPR/Cas systems. *Science, 339,* 819-823.
doi: 10.1126/science.1231143

Davies, G., Armstrong, N., Bis, J. C., Bressler, J., Chouraki, V., Giddaluru, S., . . . & Deary, I. J.
(2015). Genetic contributions to variation in general cognitive function: A meta-
analysis of genome-wide association studies in the CHARGE consortium (N=53,949).
Molecular Psychiatry, 20, 183-192. doi:10.1038/mp.2014.188

Davies, G., Tenesa, A., Payton, A., Yang, J., Harris, S. E., Liewald, D., . . . & Deary, I. J.
(2011). Genome-wide association studies establish that human intelligence is highly

heritable and polygenic. *Molecular Psychiatry, 16*, 996-1005. www.nature.com/mp/journal/v16/n10/suppinfo/mp201185s1.html

Davis, O. S., Butcher, L. M., Docherty, S. J., Meaburn, E. L., Curtis, C. J., Simpson, M. A., . . . & Plomin, R. (2010). A three-stage genome-wide association study of general cognitive ability: Hunting the small effects. *Behavior Genetics, 40*, 759–767.

Deary, I. J., Johnson, W., & Houlihan, L. (2009). Genetic foundations of human intelligence. *Human Genetics, 126*, 215-232.

Deary, I. J., Penke, L., & Johnson, W. (2010). The neuroscience of human intelligence differences. *Nature Reviews Neuroscience, 11*, 201-211.

Desrivières, S., Lourdusamy, A., Tao, C., Toro, R., Jia, T., Loth, E., . . . & IMAGEN Consortium (2015). Single nucleotide polymorphism in the neuroplastin locus associates with cortical thickness and intellectual ability in adolescents. *Molecular Psychiatry, 20*, 263-274. doi: 10.1038/mp.2013.197

Engelhardt, L. E., Briley, D. A., Mann, F. D., Harden, K. P., & Tucker-Drob, E. M. (2015). Genes unite executive functions in childhood. *Psychological Science, 26*, 1151–1163. doi: 10.1177/0956797615577209

Engelhardt, L. E., Mann, F. D., Briley, D. A., Church, J. A., Harden, K. P., & Tucker-Drob, E. M. (2016). Strong genetic overlap between executive functions and intelligence. *Journal of Experimental Psychology, 145*, 1141-1159. doi: 10.1037/xge0000195

Ethical embryo editing (2017). *Nature, 549*, 307. doi: 10.1038/549307a

Fisher, R. A. (1918). The correlation between relatives on the supposition of Mendelian inheritance. *Transactions of the Royal Society of Edinburgh, 52*, 399–433.

Flynn, J. R. (2012). *Are we getting smarter? Rising IQ in the twenty-first century.* Cambridge: Cambridge University Press.

Fogarty, N. M. E., McCarthy, A., Snijders, K. E., Powell, B. E., Kubikova, N., Blakeley, P., . . . & Niakan, K. K. (2017). Genome editing reveals a role for OCT4 in human embryogenesis. *Nature, 550*, 67-73. doi: 10.1038/nature24033

Freeman, F. N., Holzinger, K. J., & Mitchell, B. (1928). The influence of environment on the intelligence, school achievement, and conduct of foster children. In G. M. Whipple (ed.), *Yearbook of the National Society for the Study of Education. Part 1* (vol. 27, pp. 103–217). Bloomington, IL: Public School Publishing Co.

Friedman, N. P., Miyake, A., Altamirano, L. J., Corley, R. P., Young, S. E., Rhea, S. A., & Hewitt, J. K. (2015). Stability and change in executive function abilities from late adolescence to early adulthood: A longitudinal twin study. *Developmental Psychology, 52*, 326–340.

Friedman, N. P., Miyake, A., Young, S. E., DeFries, J. C., Corley, R. P., & Hewitt, J. K. (2008). Individual differences in executive functions are almost entirely genetic in origin. *Journal of Experimental Psychology, 137*, 201-225.

Galton, F. (1869). *Hereditary genius: An inquiry into its laws and consequences.* London: Macmillan and Co.

Grigorenko, E. L., LaBuda, M. C., & Carter, A. S. (1992). Similarity in general cognitive ability, creativity, and cognitive styles in a sample of adolescent Russian twins. *Acta Geneticae Medicae et Gemellologiae, 41*, 65–72.

Hansell, N. K., Halford, G. S., Andrews, G., Shum, D. H. K., Harris, S. E., Davies, G., ... & Wright, M. J. (2015). Genetic basis of a cognitive complexity metric. *PLoS ONE, 10*, e0123886. doi: 10.1371/journal.pone.0123886

Haworth, C. M. A., Wright, M. J., Luciano, M., Martin, N. G., de Geus, E. J. C., van Beijsterveldt, C. E. M., ... & Plomin, R. (2010). The heritability of general cognitive ability increases linearly from childhood to young adulthood. *Molecular Psychiatry, 15*, 1112-1120. doi:10.1038/mp.2009.55

Henig, R. M. (2015). Are there genes for intelligence – And is it racist to ask? *National Geographic.* http://news.nationalgeographic.com/2015/12/151211-genetics-intelligence-racism-science/

Hwang, W. Y., Fu, Y., Reyon, D., Maeder, M. L., Tsai, S. Q., Sander, J. D., ... & Joung, J. K. (2013). Efficient genome editing in zebrafish using a CRISPR-Cas system. *Nature Biotechnology, 31*(3), 227-229. doi:10.1038/nbt.2501

Ignatiev, M. V. (1936). On the question of the mathematical interpretation of twin correlations. *Proceedings of the Biomedical Institute M. Gorky, 4*, 284–295. [in Russian]

Jauk, E., Benedek, M., & Neubauer, A. C. (2014). The road to creative achievement: A latent variable model of ability and personality predictors. *European Journal of Personality, 28*, 95–105. doi: 10.1002/per.1941

Jinek, M., East, A., Cheng, A., Lin, S., Ma, E., & Doudna, J. (2013). RNA-programmed genome editing in human cells. *eLife, 2*, e00471. doi: 10.7554/eLife.00471

Kandler, C., Riemann, R., Angleitner, A., Spinath, F. M., Borkenau, P., & Penke, L. (2016). The nature of creativity: The roles of genetic factors, personality traits, cognitive abilities, and environmental sources. *Journal of Personality and Social Psychology, 111*, 230-249. doi: 10.1037/pspp0000087

Kaufman, A. B., Kornilov, S. A., Bristol, A. S., Tan, M., & Grigorenko, E. L. (2010). The neurobiological foundations of creative cognition. In J. C. Kaufman & R. J. Sternberg (eds.), *Cambridge handbook of creativity* (pp. 216-232). New York: Cambridge University Press.

Khan, M. A., Khan, S., Windpassinger, C., Badar, M., Nawaz, Z., & Mohammad, R. M. (2016). The molecular genetics of autosomal recessive nonsyndromic intellectual disability: A mutational continuum and future recommendations. *Annals of Human Genetics, 80*, 342-368. doi: 10.1111/ahg.12176

Kim, S. J., Kang, J. I., Namkoong, K., & Song, D. H. (2011). The effects of serotonin transporter promoter and monoamine oxidase A gene polymorphisms on trait emotional intelligence. *Neuropsychobiology, 64*, 224-230.

Kornilov, S., & Grigorenko, E. L. (2016). Molecular genetics methods for developmental scientists. In D. Cicchetti (ed.), *Developmental psychopathology* (3rd ed.), vol. 2: *Developmental neuroscience* (pp. 378-415). New York: Wiley.

Lee, T., Henry, J. D., Trollor, J. N., & Sachdev, P. S. (2010). Genetic influences on cognitive functions in the elderly: A selective review of twin studies. *Brain Research Reviews, 64*, 1-13. doi: 10.1016/j.brainresrev.2010.02.001

Luciano, M., Svinti, V., Campbell, A., Marioni, R. E., Hayward, C., Wright, A. F., ... & Deary, I. J. (2015). Exome sequencing to detect rare variants associated with general cognitive ability: A pilot study. *Twin Research and Human Genetics, 18*, 117-125. doi: 10.1017/thg.2015.10

Ma, H., Marti-Gutierrez, N., Park, S.-W., Wu, J., Lee, Y., Suzuki, K., ... & Mitalipov, S. (2017). Correction of a pathogenic gene mutation in human embryos. *Nature, 548*(7668), 413-419. doi: 10.1038/nature23305

Mali, P., Yang, L., Esvelt, K. M., Aach, J., Guell, M., DiCarlo, J. E., ... & Church, G. M. (2013). RNA-guided human genome engineering via Cas-9. *Science, 339*, 823-826. doi: 10.1126/science.1232033

Marioni, R. E., Penke, L., Davies, G., Huffman, J. E., Hayward, C., & Deary, I. J. (2014). The total burden of rare, non-synonymous exome genetic variants is not associated with childhood or late-life cognitive ability. *Proceedings of the Royal Society B: Biological Sciences, 281*, 20140117. doi: 10.1098/rspb.2014.0117

Merriman, C. (1924). The intellectual resemblance of twins. *Psychological Monographs, 33*, 1–57.

Musunuru, K. (2017). The hope and hype of crispr-cas9 genome editing: A review. *JAMA Cardiology, 2*, 914-919. doi: 10.1001/jamacardio.2017.1713

National Academies of Sciences, Engineering, and Medicine (2017). *Human genome editing: Science, ethics, and governance.* Washington, DC: National Academies Press.

Panizzon, M. S., Vuoksimaa, E., Spoon, K. M., Jacobson, K. C., Lyons, M. J., Franz, C. E., ... & Kremen, W. S. (2014). Genetic and environmental influences of general cognitive ability: Is *g* a valid latent construct? *Intelligence, 43*, 65-76. doi: 10.1016/j.intell.2014.01.008

Penrose, L. S. (1938). *A clinical and genetic study of 1,280 cases of mental defect.* London: HMSO.

Plomin, R., & Deary, I. J. (2015). Genetics and intelligence differences: Five special findings. *Molecular Psychiatry, 20*, 98-108. doi: 10.1038/mp.2014.105

Plomin, R., DeFries, J. C., Knopik, V. S., & Neiderhiser, J. M. (2013). *Behavioral genetics.* New York: Worth.

Plomin, R., DeFries, J. C., Knopik, V. S., & Neiderhiser, J. M. (2016). Top 10 Replicated Findings From Behavioral Genetics. *Perspectives on Psychological Science, 11*, 3-23. doi: 10.1177/1745691615617439

Reichenberg, A., Cederlöf, M., McMillan, A., Trzaskowski, M., Kapara, O., Fruchter, E., ... & Lichtenstein, P. (2016). Discontinuity in the genetic and environmental causes of the intellectual disability spectrum. *Proceedings of the National Academy of Science of the United States of America, 113*, 1098-1103. doi: 10.1073/pnas.1508093112

Rietveld, C. A., Medland, S. E., Derringer, J., Yang, J., Esko, T., Martin, N. W., ... & Koellinger, P. D. (2013). GWAS of 126,559 individuals identifies genetic variants associated with educational attainment. *Science, 340*, 1467-1471. doi:10.1126/science.1235488

The rise and fall and rise again of 23andMe. (2017). *Nature, 559*, 174–177. doi: 10.1038/550174a

Robinson, G. E., & Ben-Shahar, Y. (2002). Social behavior and comparative genomics: New genes or new gene regulation? *Genes, Brain, and Behavior, 4*, 197–203.

Robinson, G. E., Grozinger, C. M., & Whitfield, C. W. (2005). Sociogenomics: Social life in molecular terms. *Nature Reviews Genetics, 6*, 257-270.

Ropers, F., Derivery, E., Hu, H., Garshasbi, M., Karbasiyan, M., Herold, M., . . . & Rajab, A. (2011). Identification of a novel candidate gene for non-syndromic autosomal recessive intellectual disability: The WASH complex member SWIP. *Human Molecular Genetics, 20*, 2585-2590. doi:10.1093/hmg/ddr158

Schermer, J. A., Petrides, K. V., & Vernon, P. A. (2015). On the genetic and environmental correlations between trait emotional intelligence and vocational interest factors. *Twin Research and Human Genetics, 18*, 134-137.

Shakeshaft, N. G., Trzaskowski, M., McMillan, A., Krapohl, E., Simpson, M. A., Reichenberg, A., . . . & Plomin, R. (2015). Thinking positively: The genetics of high intelligence. *Intelligence, 48*, 123-132. doi: 10.1016/j.intell.2014.11.005

Silvia, P. J., & Beaty, R. E. (2012). Making creative metaphors: The importance of fluid intelligence for creative thought. *Intelligence, 40*, 343–351. doi: 10.1016/j.intell.2012.02.005

Spain, S. L., Pedroso, I., Kadeva, N., Miller, M. B., Iacono, W. G., McGue, M., . . . & Simpson, M. A. (2016). A genome-wide analysis of putative functional and exonic variation associated with extremely high intelligence. *Molecular Psychiatry, 21*, 1145-1151. doi:10.1038/mp.2015.108

Spearman, C. (1904). General intelligence, objectively determined and measured. *American Journal of Psychology, 15*, 201-292.

Tan, M., & Grigorenko, E. L. (2013). All in the family: Is creative writing familial and heritable? *Learning and Individual Differences, 28*, 177-180.

van Senden Theis, S. (1924). *How foster children turn out*. New York: State Charities Aid Association.

Vernon, P. A., Petrides, K., Bratko, D., & Schermer, J. A. (2008). A behavioral genetic study of trait emotional intelligence. *Emotion, 8*, 635-642.

Veselka, L., Petrides, K., Schermer, J. A., Cherkas, L. F., Spector, T. D., & Vernon, P. A. (2010). Phenotypic and genetic relations between the HEXACO dimensions and trait emotional intelligence. *Twin Research and Human Genetics, 13*, 66-71.

Winnepenninckx, B., Rooms, L., & Kooy, R. F. (2003). Mental retardation: A review of the genetic causes. *The British Journal of Development Disabilities, 49*, 29-44. doi: 10.1179/096979503799104138

10 | Environment and Intelligence

JAMES R. FLYNN AND ROBERT J. STERNBERG

Chapter 9 described in some detail the major studies investigating genetic contributions to intelligence. In this chapter, we will look at studies investigating the environmental influences on intelligence. We'll start by looking at the relationship between environment and IQ scores and a brief reconsideration of the most prominent IQ tests, the WISC (*Wechsler Intelligence Scale for Children*), the WAIS (*Wechsler Adult Intelligence Scale*), and the Stanford–Binet. Are these measures of IQ true measures of intelligence? The answer is no, but nevertheless we believe that IQ measures skills significant in advanced Western societies like the United States and Great Britain. After exploring this subject, we will explore in some depth how the environment has altered our cognitive abilities over the last 150 years; how it affects the individual competing with other individuals at a given time and place; how it allows for human autonomy; and facets of the environment that lurk in the background and have a deleterious effect on our brains (such as exposure to toxins, lead, and certain illnesses).

IQ and Intelligence

Throughout this book intelligence has been defined as the set of cognitive skills that meet the demands of a particular culture at a particular time. We've also seen that these skills vary from society to society. Our contemporary society demands the cognitive skills that help us progress through formal education and do the jobs that exist in a post-industrial world. Pre-industrial societies do not demand all of these. For instance, traditional Australian Aboriginal culture demanded primarily searching out water and game in a barren wasteland and mastering the oral traditions of a pre-literate society. It demanded, and in some places still demands, prodigious feats of map reading and memory.

Note: The introduction and the two sections, "IQ and Intelligence, Relative Roles of Genes and the Environment in the History of the Individual" and "Focus on Contemporary Research," were written by James Flynn. The section "Specific Environmental Factors Affecting Human Development" was written by Robert J. Sternberg.

Within our own society there are also subcultures that make different demands from those of the mainstream. People who live in a neighborhood that is poor and gang-organized experience demands that many of us would view as atypical: how to get enough food for the day and shelter for the night; when police are likely to be neutral or hostile; when a stranger poses a threat; and so forth. Children in this environment may develop plenty of problem-solving skills, but both their family and their schools may be less efficient in giving them the peculiar kind of skills that promote academic excellence.

Over time, the demands of even our mainstream culture have changed. In 1900, most people did not drive cars and did not need mapping skills such as how to navigate unknown parts of their city. By 1950, almost everyone drove a car and needed mapping skills. Studies found that London taxi drivers had an enlarged hippocampus, the part of the brain that helps us do mapping (Maguire, Woolet, & Spiers, 2006). Today, many of us have an automatic guidance system in our car and may not need to develop mapping skills. Over the course of 100 years, our society has gone from making heavy demands on map-reading cognition to making almost none.

And finally, as we've also stated previously, when we focus on the demands our society makes today, most conventional IQ tests are tilted more toward measuring the cognitive skills that are useful in the classroom and less toward the skills useful in the wider world (Sternberg & Hedlund, 2002). Be that as it may, IQ tests on their own still measure the skills needed for academic success or for a wide range of jobs. In contrast, each successively higher level of IQ opens up new possibilities in terms of education and jobs that require credentials. Although IQ thresholds are not set in concrete (effort also counts), an IQ of 70 is usually required to avoid special education, an IQ of 100 (the average) to get certain white-collar jobs (like computer programmer), and an IQ of 120 or so to get a PhD at a good university.

All in all, whatever the limitations of IQ, it does measure vocabulary, general information, whether you understand basic aspects of modern society, whether you can classify things using the categories formal schooling requires, how good you are at solving problems on the spot that are conceptually demanding, and whether you have a good spatial visualization. These skills are important enough, even if tilted toward formal schooling, to make many psychologists want to know how much your environment and your genes contribute to them. And the record of how generations of people performed on IQ tests over the last century gives a fascinating "cognitive history" of how the minds of different generations were altered as they adapted to a changing environment. Over time people went from a world with little formal schooling for most (in 1900 almost half of people did not go beyond the 6th grade) to 52 percent getting some post-secondary education, and from a world where most people were employed as subsistence farmers or unskilled factory workers to the galaxy of cognitively demanding jobs we have today.

Relative Roles of Genes and the Environment in the History of Our Minds

The twentieth century recorded massive IQ gains (sometimes called the Flynn effect) in societies evolving because of the Industrial Revolution. The United States and Great Britain offer the best data, but almost 30 advanced societies around the world show much the same pattern. In this regard, Flynn (2009) attempted to write a cognitive history of the twentieth century.

Scored against the average person in 2000 (who by definition was assigned an IQ of 100), the average person in 1900 had an estimated IQ of about 70 on the Wechsler and Binet tests and 50 on Raven's Progressive Matrices. The latter is a test of problems using patterns of shapes or symbols that have no counterpart in everyday life. (See Chapter 7 for more discussion of Raven's Progressive Matrices in research in different cultures.) Raven's test was supposed to test for an unchanging intelligence that was not dependent on environment or school learning (thus unlike the Wechsler and Binet tests). As these data show, the Raven Progressive Matrices was actually even more dependent on the environment of the time. The lower scores of the past do not mean that at least half of our forebears were on the verge of intellectual disability (in that the cutting line is usually 70). Rather, the lower scores simply mean that these people, unlike us, were not exposed to the modern world; as a result, they did not have a chance to profit from how much the social environment changed during the twentieth century; and therefore did not develop "advanced" conceptual skills – skills demanded in our time but not in theirs (see Figure 10.1).

How People Reasoned in the Past

As we first learned in Chapter 7, some of the best evidence of how people reasoned in the past comes from Alexander Luria, who interviewed isolated rural people in Russia in the 1920s. These were people who were like Americans in 1900, with little formal education. Here is an excerpt from the first interview:

> Fish and crows (Luria, 1976, p. 82)
> Q: What do a fish and a crow have in common?
> A: A fish lives in water. A crow flies. If the fish just lies on top of the water, the crow could peck at it. A crow can eat a fish but a fish can't eat a crow.
> Q: Could you use one word for them both?
> A: If you call them both "animals", that wouldn't be right. A fish isn't an animal and a crow isn't either. A crow can eat a fish but a fish can't eat a bird. A person can eat a fish but not a crow.

Note how differently these people classify the world from the way we do. They exploit the world to their advantage and therefore focus on what differentiates

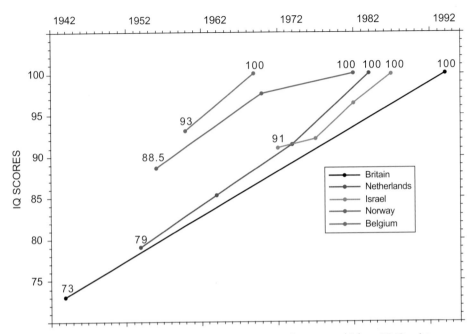

Figure 10.1 IQ gains over time. Note the huge gains on Raven's, some as high as 27 IQ points (Source: "IQ gains over time: towards finding the causes." In U. Neisser (ed.), *The rising curve: Long-term gains in IQ and related measures*, Washington, DC: American Psychological Association (1998), pp. 25–66)

things: The most important thing for them is how different fish and crows are; they are reluctant to lump the two kinds species together. We have become used to the categories modern science gives us to understand things. We have developed what we call new "habits of mind." We are ready to ignore differences and consequently lump fish and crows together as animals, dogs and ourselves as mammals, monkeys and ourselves as primates. When asked what dogs and rabbits have in common, we say they are both mammals – the rural Russian people interviewed by Luria tended to say that you use dogs to hunt rabbits. None of our modern abstract concepts can actually be perceived in the concrete world. We have a whole new pair of spectacles that they largely lacked. The Wechsler subtest called "Similarities" measures abstract classification skills. It is no mystery why IQ gains on that test have been huge.

Second interview:

Camels and German cities (Luria, 1976, p. 122)

Q: There are no camels in Germany; the city of B is in Germany; are there camels there or not?

A: I don't know, I have never seen German villages. If B is a large city, there should be camels there.

Q: But what if there aren't any in all of Germany?

A: If B is a village, there is probably no room for camels.

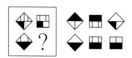

Figure 10.2 The Raven's test. This test is about using logic to order symbols that are "valued" for their own sake and that have no concrete reference. Here is an item very like those found on the Raven's Progressive Matrices test.

Note how reluctant these people once were to use logic to reason about hypothetical situations (what *if* Germany were a country without camels?). Even when the logical conclusion is suggested, this man tries to turns it into something that describes a concrete situation (perhaps the village is too small for camels). In everyday life, whether you have camels is the important question, not using logic on words or symbols that posit a possible situation that has no reference to anything you have encountered in the real world. We in the modern Western world have the kind of "habit of mind" that takes the hypothetical seriously, no matter how far it is from anything we "know." We have had plenty of practice in using logic to determine its consequences. Many of the bits of science or social science you learn at school put forward hypotheses to be tested in terms of logic and novel experiences. The Raven's test is entirely about using logic to order symbols that are "valued" for their own sake and that have no concrete reference. It is little wonder that our minds are prepared to do the test and their minds were not – and that Raven's scores have skyrocketed over the last century (see Figure 10.2).

New Habits of Mind in Practice

The adaptation of our minds to the new environment created by modernity does more, of course, than raise IQ test performance. The new habits of mind are everywhere. Every farmer who runs his farm as a small business rather than as a simple tiller of the soil, everyone who uses a computer, every computer programmer, everyone who plays the stock market, every doctor who reads articles about the long-term consequences of the operations she performs, every banker who relies on statistics, has a vocabulary and analytic skills that few people could have matched in 1900. Studies show that economic progress, schooling, and rising IQ are all interrelated. Woodley (2012) showed that the historical trend of IQ gains over the last 10 decades both parallels and predicts economic growth by Western nations.

Raising IQ through Education

Ireland is a classic case of a society that used schooling as a way of achieving rising IQ and economic growth. Between 1970 and 1985, the Irish went from educational parity with Great Britain to well above Great Britain: Ireland boosted years of education by 2.3 years, while Great Britain rose by only 0.77 years; Ireland multiplied those with tertiary education by six times, while Great Britain did so by only three times. In 1970, the dollar value per capita of the total goods and services of each nation was virtually the same. By 2005, it was $65,292 (US dollars) in Ireland and $38,149 in the United Kingdom (Nisbett, 2015). During this period Ireland went from 13 IQ points below Great Britain to IQ parity (Lynn, 2006; Lynn & Vanhanen, 2002; PISA, 2009; Flynn, in press).

Jobs are much more cognitively demanding than they were in 1900. The explosion of the number of years of schooling (from 6 years completed, on average, to about 13 years) means the existence of cognitive demands far beyond basic literacy. The very content of what is demanded in school has changed. Genovese (2002) compared the exams the State of Ohio gave to 14-year-old schoolchildren between 1902 and 1913 with those the state gave between 1997 and 1999. The former tested for in-depth knowledge of culturally valued information; the latter expected only superficial knowledge of such information and tested for understanding complex relationships between concepts. The former exams were likely to ask you to name the capitals of the (then) 46 to 48 states. The later exams tended to ask you why the largest city of a state was rarely the state capital (rural members dominated state legislatures, hated the big city, and bestowed the capital on a rural town). Genovese (2002, p. 101) concludes: "These findings suggest that there have been substantial changes in the cognitive skills valued by Ohio educators over the course of the 20th century."

Some Contradictory Trends

On average, the hours of study of the average student at a four-year university has declined from 25 hours in 1961, to 17 hours in the 1980s, to little more than 8.5 according to the most recent data. Only a lesser portion of study hours are devoted to preparing for class: 37 percent spend less than 5 hours per week (the rest goes on homework or essays); the average is not given but would not be above 6 or 7 hours. At highly selective institutions (top 100), students do spend an extra 5 hours per week studying, for a total of 17. During this period, the total time all students invested in academic pursuits has fallen from 40 hours per week to 27 (Arum & Roska, 2011, pp. 68, 70, and 97; Babcock, & Marks, 2011).

In addition, just as Americans have given up on reading at university, so too are they beginning to abandon reading throughout their adult lives. Between 1982 and 2015, the percentage of adults who read for pleasure (novels, short stories, poems, or plays) fell from 57 percent to 43 percent. Men stand at only 36 percent (National Endowment for the Arts, 2016). This is despite the fact that the percentage of adults with a bachelor's degree or higher almost doubled over that period. Reduced reading includes biography and history. George Orwell, the famous novelist who wrote *1984*, thought you had to censor history to produce people who were uncritical about their political elite and the media. All you really need is a generation that knows no history and little about the contemporary world.

When people simply do not know that things are done differently abroad, what people and their societies and their histories are like in, say, the Middle East, they feel helpless: "I can't form a really solid opinion" – "I think that getting out of wars would help, but I guess I don't know enough to say very surely what would happen." – "I don't know what direction the country should go, let alone what direction it will go" (Arum and Roska, 2010, 85-86, 99-105).

Here are a few facts about America and the rest of the world. Try these out on your friends and family. They are the sort of facts anyone would want to know to assess current US politics and foreign policy:

(1) In 2010, Cuba, a very poor country, spent $600 (US dollars) per person on health, while America spent $8,223 – life expectancy was the same in the two countries (although Cuba was a bit better on infant mortality);

(2) In the 1980s, America colluded in supplying Pol Pot with aid and arms despite knowledge that when he was in power, he had presided over the "killing fields" (Flynn, 2012b, pp. 106-107);

(3) Saddam Hussein, who was overthrown as President of Iraq in 2003, was a fierce opponent of Al-Qaeda and tried to kill its members whenever he could locate them.

Take note of the people who do not understand why these facts are significant. Rising IQ will not have much effect on better social criticism so long as it is accompanied by the willful rise of ignorance (Flynn, 2010; 2016b).

The Decline of IQ Gains in Developed Countries

Beginning about 1995, data show that 18-year-olds in Scandinavia began to show moderate IQ losses. Recent data from Britain, France, Germany, and Australia are mixed. The United States shows substantial gains up through the latest data from 2014. Perhaps typical is the Netherlands, which shows different trends at different ages. Families are furnishing a static cognitive environment for preschoolers, high school quality may be in mild decline, jobs are significantly more cognitively demanding, and the Dutch (like everyone else) have greatly enhanced the quality of life of the aged due to better health and more exercise (Flynn & Shayer, 2017).

There is nothing mysterious about a decline. The progress of the Industrial Revolution raised IQ only because it affected the social institutions that affected people. Families got smaller and more affluent and parents began to stimulate the minds of their children and plan for their university education. The years of schooling increased to the point that university was almost the norm. The indus-trializing economy generated thousands of jobs that were far more cognitively demanding. Workers got the eight-hour day so that, rather than collapsing when they got home, they could exercise their minds when at leisure: chat with people (all of them using larger vocabularies), play chess or bridge or video games.

Significant IQ Gains in Developing Countries

There is now evidence of significant IQ gains in Brazil, Kenya, Turkey, Saudi Arabia, Dominica, and the Sudan (Flynn, 2012a). Developing nations are on the way to catching up in terms of average IQ. This all assumes that economic progress continues and that a nation is not devastated by war, famine, or climate change. The first three nations listed look perhaps somewhat promising; the latter three do not. Some say that less advanced nations are crippled by having worse genes for IQ than Europeans; this thesis looks ripe for refutation.

Should we be too upset if the day of IQ increases in our nation is over? Society will be content so long as people have the cognitive skills needed to perform whatever roles it asks of them. During the twentieth century, when society escalated its demands, average IQ rose. During the twenty-first century, if society reduces its demands, average IQ will fall. It is always possible that our schools and universities will graduate more young people who read and who then become more critically astute. Such education in itself would put a limit on IQ losses on Vocabulary, Information, and most Verbal tests, and on accepting the stereotypes that cloud moral reasoning and political prudence. As we have seen, *the fate of the world in this century will be determined more by capitalizing on people's intelligence rather than by increasing their intelligence.* Ignorance cripples every generation, however high their average IQ (Flynn, 2012c).

The Case for the Environment as the Source of Intelligence

Over the twentieth century, environment has overwhelmed genes as the agent of cognitive change. This is because environmental change from generation to generation has been huge and genetic changes small. No one has been machine–gunning either the bottom half or the top half of the IQ curve before they can reproduce. Scholars like Woodley believe that there has been a gradual deterioration of genes for intelligence that began in the late nineteenth century (Woodley, te Nienhuis, & Murphy, 2013). It is possible that he is correct, at least in part, if only because higher-IQ people tend to have fewer children than lower-IQ people. This argument actually reinforces the case for the potency of environmental gains. To affect the real world, environment had to overcome genetic losses and thus provide a net gain for "intelligence" in the sense of enhanced cognitive abilities. However, if gradual genetic loss existed, and were to continue indefinitely, it would be serious. Fortunately, there are several scenarios in which it would not, but to examine these would take us far afield (Flynn, 2013). To see how one psychologist has applied what is known about intelligence and environment to some issues important to our world today, see Focus on Contemporary Research box below.

FOCUS ON CONTEMPORARY RESEARCH: JAMES R. FLYNN'S WORK APPLYING WHAT WE KNOW ABOUT ENVIRONMENT AND INTELLIGENCE TO REAL-WORLD PROBLEMS

Sometimes what we discover through social science research can confirm what we think we already know about the world. Sometimes it can be confusing, or conflict with the results of other research. Often it can't be easily explained. But when we apply the findings of social science research to larger, societal issues, we can sometimes make large breakthroughs. I have spent most of my career looking at the results of research on intelligence and trying to explain what the research uncovered. In a similar vein, I am currently looking more closely at two interesting phenomena going on in our world today involving human autonomy and critical thinking.

First, I am working on one book that will be called *Universities without Free Speech: How to Liberate the Human Mind*. It will discuss the things that hamper universities from improving the critical thinking abilities of their graduates so that they can be good citizens. I will explore the pressures that limit freedom of speech on campus: students who want to exclude speakers with whom they disagree; departments that have dogmas they want to put beyond criticism; and vocational education that has no room for giving students all the skills they need to be critical thinkers.

Moving from the world of ideas to the world of finance, I am writing a second book that will be called *Taming the Banks: We Do Not Need a Crisis Every Ten Years*. Behavioral psychology focuses on how to use incentives to alter people's behavior; in this case, the relevant question is how to keep bank executives (and others) from making private profit by behavior that causes a banking crisis. In other words, how can private profit and the public good be brought into line?

Relative Roles of Genes and the Environment in the History of the Individual

When we look at people *within* rather than *between* generations, a very different picture emerges about the relative roles of genes and environment. There is a big difference between **between-group comparisons**, which look at differences between groups over time, space, or classification, and **within-group comparisons**, which look at similarities and differences for given groups. Here, we are referring to people within a group who belong to one cohort, meaning that they are born in the same society in the same year. It is not that there are no environmental differences between people who "compete" with one another as they age. But there is a tendency for the quality of a person's genes for cognitive ability to match the quality of their environment. This result emerges most clearly when we analyze the ages from infancy to adulthood.

Ages 2–3 and the Fairness Factor

Most parents try to be fair. The **fairness factor** is parents' attempts to provide their multiple children with equally favorable environments. They may be aware that two of their children seem to differ in genetic promise, but they nevertheless may try to give both the same quality of environment (read the same number of books to them both, etc.). If both children get the same environment, the less promising child will of necessity get an environment that enhances his or her genetic capacity more than it enhances that of the more gifted child (Flynn, 2016a, pp. 73-78).

Imagine a chariot called "cognitive performance" pulled by two horses called genes and environment. At these ages, they are pulling in "opposite" directions, although actually environment is more powerful. The chariot goes along a path that makes genes a bad predictor of cognitive performance.

Age 10 and the Rising Correlation

By age 10, school and teachers and peers (the current environment) have begun to swamp the effects of family. Take mathematics performance. Before school, despite genetic differences, two siblings may be very much alike in arithmetic because the only arithmetic they get is from their parents. On the other hand, the whole thrust of their new current environment at school is to differentiate them in terms of their genetic promise (Flynn, 2016a, ch. 4). The sibling that finds math easy will seek out a better math environment: spend more time on math, ask to do extra problems, join a math club. In addition, the math teacher may be on the lookout for children who want enrichment work, and may want to recruit children for the math team. What may have been a slight genetic advantage for mathematics becomes a much greater advantage as the more gifted child enters a better math environment and the less gifted child enters a poorer math environment.

Extend this to all the school-related skills children have. The more verbally gifted child will tend to make friends with children who also have larger vocabularies and join the drama club or debate society. Add all these skills together and you have a higher or lower score on IQ tests. In sum, the child with better genes for IQ will match those genes with a better IQ-enriching environment. Go back to the chariot and two horses. Now the gene and environment horses are getting closer to pulling

Imagine two horses pulling a sleigh

Individual IQ Differences

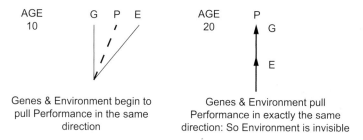

AGES
2-3
Fairness
Factor

G ◄──── P ────► E

Genes & Environment pull performance
in opposite directions

AGE
10

G   P   E

Genes & Environment begin to
pull Performance in the same
direction

AGE
20

P

G

E

Genes & Environment pull
Performance in exactly the same
direction: So Environment is invisible

IQ Gains Over Time

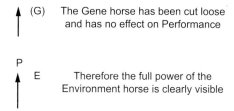

(G)   The Gene horse has been cut loose
and has no effect on Performance

P

E   Therefore the full power of the
Environment horse is clearly visible

Figure 10.3 Changes in the strength of genes versus environment at different ages. Genes for cognitive ability now predict most cognitive performance, with exceptions in the case of people living through war or prolonged natural disasters.

in the same direction. If you know the genetic differences between two people, identical twins (same genes), siblings (half their genes in common), random individuals ("none" in common except both are human), you can use their genetic similarity to predict their IQ. The environment horse is still there, but it has been "taught" to follow docilely behind the gene horse and go in the same direction. The correlation between genes and environment has become very high, which means that genes for cognitive ability now predict most of your cognitive performance (Flynn, 2016a). Of course, there are huge exceptions to these generalizations, as in the case of war or prolonged natural disasters, which can disrupt learning and other kinds of functioning in a major way. In such cases, this (possibly hellish) environment still has some influence on development (see Figure 10.3).

Age 20 and the Correlation Made Near Perfect

During your teens, your family background still influences your cognitive skills. This is most persistent for vocabulary, assuming you are still speaking to your parents. Therefore, bad luck in family can handicap you by limiting your options when entering university (you do worse than your genes would predict on the SAT-Reading Test). Eventually, by age 20, the correlation between the excellence of current common environment and genes may become almost perfect (Flynn, 2016a, pp. 64-67). You may now be matched with jobs and peers that make greater or lesser cognitive demands, and these tend to correspond to your genetic promise. Metaphorically, you are either doing a PhD at Harvard or are a career burger flipper at McDonalds.

Human Autonomy

Human autonomy refers to people's ability to choose their own actions and futures. The roles of genes and environment within a generation are entirely compatible with their role between generations. Within generations, a chariot called "cognitive performance" is pulled in the same direction by the gene and environment horses. But between generations, there are no important genetic differences, only environmental ones. Between generations, it is as if you cut the gene horse loose from the chariot and only the environment horse is left. Remember the environment horse never lost its potency. It just fell in line behind the gene horse and became largely "undetectable." IQ gains show how powerful the environmental horse is when free to act on its own.

Nonetheless, although each person can be impressed by how much cognitive progress the general population can make (over a century), this may not be much consolation to the individual living out his or her life within a cohort. It would be absurd, of course, to assume that the level of your cognitive abilities is everything. A dull person can be born with a silver spoon in his or her mouth and live out a wealthy life, or an intelligent person can be born in conditions of staggering disadvantage. What the data suggest is that it is likely that lower (or higher) genetic promise will eventually match a lower (or higher) quality cognitive environment.

From this perspective, is your cognitive quality entirely written in your genes? It is not – because we have oversimplified the relationship between genes and environment within a cohort. All lines of data, whether twin studies or the age-table method, agree on this. At all ages, there is an unshared environment that explains 20 percent of IQ variations (Flynn, 2016a, p. 22; Haworth et al., 2010). For some, IQ always remains uncorrelated with either genes or current environment or the combination of the two. No matter how excellent your genes or environment, you can be dropped on your head: at age 18, you can be drafted out of an environment commensurate with your genes and submerged into the inferior environment of cutting throats in the forest. There is also good luck: marrying a partner who lifts you into a new peer group, one that gives you an environment that is superior to one commensurate with your genes.

When we talk about how much your IQ level can be uncorrelated with genes and current environment, we refer to advanced nations. In many nations (Syria with its wars, the Sudan with its famines), life is less secure and the frequency of chance events that determine your fate is much higher. But our point is this: Even in the US, it is wrong to think of "fate" as mere luck. We do not know how to partition it, but at least half of it may reflect human autonomy. When an academic staff member volunteers for mind-numbing work, he has *chosen* an inferior environment. When someone who did poorly at school and is trapped in a humdrum environment decides to go back to university at age 35, he has *chosen* a superior environment.

Matching occurs when an environment matches an individual's genetic potential. Assume a school leaver's genetic promise would put him at an IQ of 130 were he to have a matching environment; and that he is actually stuck at the average environment. Then his current IQ would be 10 points below his "target." If university affords him a commensurate environment, he will go from an IQ of 120 to 130. His voluntary action has allowed him to leapfrog over four-fifths of the people who were above him on the IQ scale. Despite the dominant role of genes in pulling the chariot, human autonomy is alive and well (Flynn, 2016a, pp. 23-26).

Specific Environmental Factors Affecting Human Development

In advanced societies, about 97 percent of babies are born without a "major physical anomaly," meaning without a physical difference that poses cosmetic or functional problems. They "look like" their peers and do not need special treatment to cope with life. Most go from infancy to childhood to adulthood to old age with only the risks that the environment poses for everyone through common illnesses or injury or personal crises or the afflictions of old age. People in developing societies are at much greater risk. This is not to say that people in developed nations are immune. There are clinically toxic factors (dangerous drugs or lead exposure, for instance) that can affect them from conception onward. Others may suffer from "socially toxic" factors having to do with family, schooling, and wealth. Often people of low socioeconomic status (SES) suffer from a poverty that extends beyond income. Finally, just as aging affects everyone's body, it can affect the brains of a large percentage of people.

Prenatal Factors

There are many impacts on the developing baby when it is in the mother's womb. This is why there is such a big focus on prenatal health and nutrition – and why doctors are very cautious about what drugs women take while pregnant.

Teratogens are environmental agents that damage a developing baby during the time the child is in the womb. Their effects are complex, depending on (a) what the given teratogen is, (b) how strong a dose is administered to the developing child, (c) when in the prenatal period the dose is received, (d) the developing child's susceptibility to the teratogen, given his or her genetic makeup, and (e) environmental factors pertaining to the mother, such as the mother's medical care, nutrition, and general health.

Effects vary as a function of when the developing child encounters the teratogen (Moore & Persaud, 2008). During the first two weeks of a pregnancy, the zygote is generally not especially susceptible to teratogens, although it may not be totally immune either. In those rare cases where there is susceptibility, the zygote probably will die, as it has virtually no defenses at all. Teratogens affecting development during the third to eighth weeks of pregnancy are likely to result in serious structural abnormalities of the embryo, whereas teratogenic effects thereafter tend to result in specific birth defects and less serious structural abnormalities.

Medicinal Drugs

Mothers are advised to take as few drugs as possible during pregnancy because, often, the effects of the drugs on the prenatally developing child are uncertain and may vary from one baby to another. Thus it is difficult to guarantee that any drug a mother takes will not have an effect on the child.

The world learned just how serious such effects could be during the early 1960s, when an over-the-counter drug, thalidomide, proved to be a time bomb. The drug was taken by pregnant mothers as a sedative that would help the mothers sleep and also to combat symptoms of morning sickness. The drug was invented in the 1950s and passed European safety tests. The drug was used in Europe and some other parts of the world, although its use was never approved in the United States. By 1962, it was realized that the drug was a medical disaster. Over 10,000 babies were born with thalidomide-related deformities, most frequently, insufficiently developed or deformed arms and legs, but also in some cases, damage to the heart, kidneys, and other parts of the body (www.sciencemuseum.org.uk/broughttolife/themes/contro versies/thalidomide).

One might have hoped that a fiasco such as the thalidomide nightmare would have ended the use of drugs taken by pregnant mothers that proved to be teratogens. (Many teratogenic drugs have clear warning labels that they should not be taken by pregnant women.) But it happened in at least one other major instance. A drug called DES (diethylstilbestrol) was used for a long period of time (1945–1970) to forestall miscarriages. At the time, people did not well understand that miscarriages are often nature's way of preventing children from being born who would have extremely serious chromosomal or other genetic abnormalities. Instead, they were viewed as tragic all around. Unfortunately, daughters of mothers who took DES were found later to have unusually high rates of vaginal cancer, malformation of the uterus, and sterility (see Herbst et al., 1971; Troisi et al., 2007). Although these outcomes are not direct effects on intelligence, they show that one simply cannot always predict which drugs will have effects on the brain or other organs that would not have been predicted in advance.

The most notable teratogen now available for use is probably a drug called Accutane (isotretinoin) that is used to treat serious acne. Prenatal exposure to this drug during the first trimester can result in serious birth defects, including of the eyes, ears, heart, and most importantly from our point of view, brain (Honein, Paulozzi, & Erickson, 2001). Packaging of Accutane does contain clear warnings as to its risks. The problem is that many of its users are at a point in their lives when they may become pregnant. And even though the drug packaging warns women not to use the drug if they are pregnant or may become pregnant, women often believe that they will not become pregnant (perhaps because of the use of birth control), only to find that they have become pregnant after all.

Recreational Drugs: Tobacco and Alcohol

Legal recreational drugs include alcohol, tobacco (nicotine), and in some US states, marijuana. Tobacco use has been linked to shorter attention span, impulsivity, memory problems, and possibly, although not certainly, lower cognitive abilities (Braun, Daniels, Kalkbrenner, Zimmerman, & Nicholas, 2009; see review in Berk, 2013). The effects of alcohol on cognitive and other abilities are clearer. Alcohol use during pregnancy can lead to **fetal alcohol syndrome (FAS)**, which is associated with intellectual disability, among other abnormalities, primarily physical ones (such as a thin upper lip, a flattened philtrum, and malformed openings of the eyelids). Another risk is partial-FAS, which results in some but not all the abnormalities associated with the full-blown syndrome. One might ask, of course, what a sufficient dose of alcohol is to lead to FAS. Unfortunately, it is not clear, and may differ from one mother to another. In general, greater alcohol consumption is associated with poorer intellectual outcomes for the child (Burden, Jacobson, & Jacobson, 2005). As little as one drink per day by a pregnant mother-to-be can be associated with adverse alcohol-related effects in children (Jacobson et al., 2004). The current recommendation is that pregnant mothers should not drink any quantity of alcohol at all (see Ornoy & Ergaz, 2010).

Illegal Drugs

The drugs that are most likely to affect the brain in particular are illegal ones – heroin, cocaine, fentanyl, and possibly marijuana. The problem is that it often is difficult to pinpoint exactly what is an effect of such drugs (Mayes & Fahy, 2001). For one thing, because the drugs are illegal, people are reluctant to report using them. For another, people who use illegal drugs often have a number of unhealthy habits, so it is hard to know exactly which effects are due to which habits. For example, prenatal methamphetamine exposure is associated with increased problems in attention and, in general, with increased likelihood of attention deficit hyperactivity disorder (www.drugabuse.gov/news-events/nida-notes/2012/12/pre natal-methamphetamine-exposure-linked-problems).

Maternal Illness

A number of maternal illnesses, including AIDS, chickenpox, cytomegalovirus, genital herpes, mumps, rubella, chlamydia, syphilis, tuberculosis, malaria, and toxoplasmosis have been associated with intellectual deficiencies in children (Berk, 2013; Jones, Lopez, & Wilson, 2003; Mardh, 2002). Most recently, Zika virus, caused by pregnant women receiving bites from Zika-infected mosquitoes, has been associated with abnormal outcomes in children, including heads of reduced size (microcephaly) (www.scientificamerican.com/article/what-s-behind-brazil-s-alarming-surge-in-babies-born-with-small-heads/). It is not yet clear just how much children's mental abilities will be affected, but it seems almost certain that intellectual challenges will result as a result of the microcephaly caused by the disease. Pregnant women not living in areas with *Aedes aegypti* mosquitoes or other mosquitoes spreading the infection have been advised not to travel to these areas during their pregnancy or at least to take serious precautions, if they do so travel, against receiving mosquito bites (wwwnc.cdc.gov/travel/page/zika-travel-information).

Maternal Nutrition

Effects of maternal nutrition on children's subsequent cognitive abilities are not entirely clear, nor are effects of micronutrient deficiencies on the children themselves. It appears useful to give pregnant women vitamin supplements, but it may also be necessary to give the children supplements upon birth (Grantham-McGregor et al., 2001).

During the winter of 1944 to 1945, there was a severe famine in the Netherlands. The famine was man-made, caused by a Nazi embargo on the country. Stein et al. (1972) analyzed the effects of the famine and found effects on birth weight and subsequent height, but not on IQ. However, Rush et al. (1980) found that high-protein supplements for pregnant African American women increased subsequent performance of infants on infant intelligence tests. Moreover, there is evidence that iodine deficiency in children after birth can result in a later IQ difference of 12 points (Qian et al., 2005). The results for iron deficiencies are less clear.

Postnatal Factors: Growing Children and Adults

Nutritional challenges and illnesses endured at any age can have extremely detrimental effects on human intelligence. Some illnesses affect cognitive functioning directly and with others, cognitive impairment may result as a consequence of a disease or period of illness.

Childhood Nutrition

Nutrition may affect children from just after birth, but as with prenatal nutrition, the results are far from clear. Some early studies suggested that breastfeeding may be associated with higher IQ of the breastfed children (Masters, 1997). However, later research has called this hypothesis into question (Der et al., 2006), arguing that the differences between breastfed and non-breastfed children were due to differences not in ways of feeding, but rather, in maternal IQ. That is, mothers who breastfed tended to have higher IQs than mothers who did not. Still later studies suggested that only children with a certain genetic predisposition may benefit from breastfeeding, but those studies also later gave way to studies that failed to find the effect. The benefits of breastfeeding for cognitive functioning thus remain unclear.

Nutritional studies reveal a serious challenge in looking at effects of environmental variables on intelligence, namely, *multiple confoundings*. Children who grow up with one environmental challenge often grow up with many other environmental challenges. Moreover, the parents of children growing up in such environments may themselves have been challenged early in their lives, or may have ended up in such environments due in part to their own cognitive challenges. Whatever the reasons, definitive studies are very hard to do – studies that take into account all possible confoundings and then give a clear account of the effect of any single variable on intelligence. The result is that science ends up, in this area, with many uncertain results that later are subject to question. Nutritional effects are not limited to youngsters. Vitamin B-12 and folate deficiencies also maybe be risk factors for cognitive abilities in the elderly (Duthie et al., 2002).

Childhood Exposure to Toxic Chemicals

Toxins in the environment have been shown to be a major cause of intellectual challenges, including especially lead and mercury, but also arsenic, toluene, and PCBs. There are hundreds of chemicals with negative effects on cognitive skills (Grandjean & Landrigan, 2006). At one time – when both authors of this chapter were growing up – leaded gasoline was common throughout the world, and it may well have lowered the average intelligence of countless children right into their adulthood. So the good news is that leaded gasoline has been on its way out, at least in the developed world. The bad news is that there are so many chemicals now in the environment that it is simply no longer possible to estimate what their effects are, or even really what they are. The effects are not just on intelligence. In less than 40 years, sperm counts among men have gone down 50 percent in much of the developed world (http://time.com/4871540/infertility-men-sperm-count/). This is a world-changing phenomenon, clearly, and no one is quite certain how to account for it, although it seems likely that industrial substances released into the environment are a cause. Certainly, the genetic makeup of people has not changed in a 40-year period. It is clear that introducing a wide variety of potentially toxic substances into the environment, without adequate testing, places not only intelligence, but the whole future of civilization, at risk.

Childhood Diseases and Illnesses

Childhood diseases have been shown to affect cognitive functioning (Sternberg, Powell, McGrane, & McGregor, 1997). For example, in some developing countries, especially in South America, Africa, and parts of Asia, parasitic illnesses are endemic among youngsters. These include diseases such as malaria, schistosomiasis, and whipworm (Grigorenko et al., 2006). Malaria is generally contracted through the bite of an anopheles or a related mosquito. Schistosomiasis is a worm that typically enters by burrowing into the feet when a child walks through contaminated water. Whipworm is caused by ingesting dirt that contains worm eggs – the worms then hatch in the body. Although these diseases can be fatal, they usually are not, as fatality would be bad for the parasites. If the host dies, then the parasites will die too. Rather, the parasites typically weaken the individual. In the case of youngsters, with moderate to heavy rates of infection, they can become listless and have trouble with paying attention. They are likely to miss school, or else to go to school but have trouble concentrating. So they lose knowledge and cognitive skills through their inability to devote the attention that would be required to learn new information, or through their absence from school.

Alzheimer's Disease

Perhaps the most devastating disease in terms of effects on cognitive functioning is **Alzheimer's disease (AD),** an illness usually associated with older people that results in plaques and tangles in the cerebral cortex. Plaques are groupings or clumps of a particular kind of protein called *beta-amyloid. Tangles* are twisted threads forming into clumps of a protein referred to as *tau.* The brains of many older people have plaques and tangles, but for unknown reasons, these symptoms are associated with Alzheimer's disease in some cases but not others. This fact has led some scientists to suspect that plaques and tangles are symptoms rather than causes of AD. The actual cause of AD is unknown. A best guess at this point is that AD is sometimes caused by environmental factors that have an increasingly serious effect with age, and sometimes caused by genetic predisposition. In particular, AD is associated with the presence of SORLI and ApoE4 genes, which increase the risk of AD, especially early-onset forms (which begin before the age of 65). The possible environmental causes are unknown, although people in less cognitively demanding jobs are more at risk than are other people. A low-fat diet, exercise, and increased consumption of fish may help prevent AD (Grant et al., 2002). In particular, the concept of *cognitive reserve* has been introduced to account for why brighter people who are more intellectually engaged might be more protected against Alzheimer's. The idea is that their higher mental capacities provide some protection from Alzheimer's.

Unfortunately, such capacities do not provide complete protection, and once AD shows up in such individuals, it usually progresses as fast as or even faster than in people with less cognitive reserve.

Alzheimer's disease often starts out as **mild cognitive impairment**, which shows itself as a form of forgetfulness and of loss of verbal fluency. The forgetfulness is not typically of the type of "Where did I put my keys?" or "I forgot your name," but rather more threatening sorts, such as inability to find one's way home from work, forgetfulness as to how to get to the supermarket, or inability to find one's way through the building in which one works.

Non-Alzheimer's Related Dementia

Other forms of dementia adversely impact intelligence, including *vascular dementia*, caused by strokes, and dementias associated with Parkinson's disease, which come about in the latter stages of the disease. None of these diseases, in our current state of knowledge, is either clearly preventable or curable. However, there seems to be an association between exercise and retention of cognitive functioning (www.health .harvard.edu/blog/regular-exercise-changes-brain-improve-memory-thinking-skills-201404097110).

Socioeconomic Status

One of the strongest correlates of intelligence is **socioeconomic status (SES)**, which, roughly speaking, is a measure of family employment, wealth, income, and education (Seifer, 2001). Why is socioeconomic status so important to intellectual potential? For one thing, at least some people of higher SES are likely to have gotten to their higher SES through their intelligence, and they can in turn pass on their higher intelligence to their children. Part of this transmission is almost certainly genetic, but part is also almost certainly environmental. Parents of higher socioeconomic status are likely to have more books in the home, to read to their children more, to engage them in more sophisticated questioning, and to be able to provide them with more opportunities for intellectual development, such as special schools, camps, and instruction. Of course, this is not always the case; some wealthy people may use their wealth in ways other than to improve the intellectual capital of their children.

In contrast, children of low SES are more likely to grow up in environments where parents are unable to help their children as much intellectually, as a result of lower education, or as a result of time constraints. The parents may work long hours, or the children may not even live with both parents. Of course, living with a single parent can happen at any SES level; it merely is more common in lower SES households. Children of lower SES also may live in more dangerous environments, as a result of high crime rates, high rates of disease, environmental pollutants, or even war. These children thus face serious environmental disadvantages, regardless of the genetic makeup they bring into the situation.

Schooling

Most of this discussion has focused on influences that have negative impacts on intelligence. But schooling is an environmental factor that has a positive impact upon intelligence. Indeed, there may be no environmental factor that can match schooling for its positive effect on IQ (Ceci, 1996). Children who spend more time in school have higher IQs, and the effect is not merely correlational: Schooling teaches students how to do the kinds of thinking required by intelligence tests (Ceci, 1996; Sternberg, 1997b).

The effects of schooling are generally but not always associated with enhancements in cognitive abilities. Some schools, especially those that view education solely in terms of memorizing a religious or other book or doctrines can actually harm a child's cognitive skills. Children may find themselves so ill-equipped to function outside the religious or other community that educates them that their ability to explore work outside their own community may be seriously challenged. Some schools around the world also teach children to hate members of opposing religious, ideological, ethnic, or other groups, which scarcely places the children in a position to think rationally or to weigh evidence critically or insightfully. Yet critical thinking (Sternberg, 1985, 1988; Sternberg & Grigorenko, 2004) and insightful thinking (Sternberg & Davidson, 1982, 1983) are cornerstones of intelligence.

It is worth keeping in mind that although schooling is critical to the development of intelligence, it does not necessarily equally develop all aspects of intelligence. For example, it tends to neglect the creative (Niu & Sternberg, 2002; Sternberg & Lubart, 1995) and practical aspects of intelligence (Sternberg, 1997a; Sternberg & Hedlund, 2002).

CONCLUSION

It is possible, of course, to review only a brief sampling of environmental benefits and hazards in a short section in a textbook. (For a more comprehensive analysis of environmental effects on cognitive abilities, see Sternberg & Grigorenko, 2001.) But it should be clear that a wide variety of environmental causes can either increase or decrease levels of IQ, and probably, of intelligence as well. Although scholars are not in complete agreement with regard to precise environmental effects, they are in good agreement that environment can have beneficial or deleterious effects on intelligence. There is less evidence showing that environment radically changes the intelligence of most people who live in developed nations. But it almost certainly can make a large enough difference to substantially affect a person's chances for success in life.

CHAPTER SUMMARY

This chapter has reviewed some of the important issues related to environmental influences on intelligence. Our attempt to partition IQ differences into those that arise from genetic differences and environmental differences respectively refers primarily to mainstream people in developing nations. Here, as people mature within each generation, there is a strong tendency for genetic quality and environmental quality to correlate. By early adulthood, people with above average genes for IQ tend to live in the most intellectually challenging environments and those with below average genes for IQ tend to live in the least intellectually challenging environments. This may seem to indicate that environment lacks potency but what it really shows is that that two potent factors, genes and environment, tend to reinforce one another within a generation when people "compete" with one another for school credentials and jobs and even spouses, and find peers who are their intellectual equals.

Unlike the potent genetic differences that separate individuals within a generation, the genetic factors that separate one generation from another are relatively feeble. Between generations, there have been massive gains on all of the cognitive abilities our society values, and their pattern reflects the changes in what society values over time. Compared to 1900, society today values the conceptual skills that help us cope with advanced schooling, more cognitively demanding jobs and leisure, more conversationally demanding peers, and a more active old age. The huge magnitude of these conceptual gains shows how potent environment is compared to genes, when its potency is not masked by the correspondence between environmental differences and genetic differences. The history of human cognition is at the core of the history that took us from the world of our ancestors to the world of today. Whether the world has become better or worse is for each to judge, but certain trends appear beneficial: a more prosperous society and better moral reasoning about issues like race and gender. These do not guarantee that better thinking will be accompanied by more knowledge and wiser conclusions.

It is also important to note that even within a generation, there is latitude for human choice or autonomy. A considerable portion of IQ differences depends on whether an individual decides to upgrade or downgrade his or her current environment, for example, to maximize or minimize what benefit they can get from education, reading, conversation with peers, and creating a stimulating retirement environment.

The "global" effects of environment on human conceptual abilities must not blind us to the many specific environmental factors that can affect human intelligence throughout our lives. Teratogens can affect children's intelligence adversely before children are even born. Maternal exposure to substances such as alcohol or nicotine have effects on babies *in utero*. Medicines, prescribed or over the counter, also can have harmful effects, leading many physicians to suggest that pregnant mothers avoid drugs to the extent possible. Recreational drugs can be teratogens and should be avoided. Illegal drugs, such as heroin, can result in the birth of addicted babies, whose life then begins fighting their own heroin addiction. Maternal illnesses, especially rubella (German measles), can be dangerous to developing children as well.

Risk factors, of course, continue once children are born. Illnesses can impair children's ability to cope with the environment, and in later adulthood, diseases such as Parkinson's disease and Alzheimer's disease, both thought to be linked to environment but in unknown ways, can result in steep declines in cognitive functioning. Lack of schooling typically results in lesser mental abilities, as does severe nutritional deprivation and exposure to toxins.

KEY TERMS

Alzheimer's disease (AD) • between-group comparisons • fairness factor • fetal alcohol syndrome (FAS) • human autonomy • matching • mild cognitive impairment • socioeconomic status (SES) • teratogens • within-group comparisons

COMPREHENSION AND REFLECTION QUESTIONS

1. Why does the task of balancing genes versus environment pose a different problem within a generation and between generations?
2. Why do social factors like family, schooling, work, and leisure sometimes encourage and sometimes discourage IQ gains over time?
3. Why is socioeconomic status (SES) such a powerful predictor of intelligence?
4. What mechanisms lead to people's tending to match their genetic predispositions with their environments?
5. Under what kinds of conditions can genetic predispositions come to be of little importance?
6. What kinds of conditions in a society tend to (a) raise, or (b) lower IQ?
7. Why is the future of society more dependent on how people use their IQs than on the IQs themselves?

References

Arum, R., & Roska, J. (2010). *Academically adrift: Limited learning on college campuses.* Chicago: University of Chicago Press.

Babcock, P., & Marks, M. (2011). The falling time cost of college: Evidence from half a century of time use data. *Review of Economics and Statistics* 93: 468-478.

Berk, L. E. (2013). *Child Development* (9th ed.). Hoboken, NJ: Pearson.

Braun, J. M., Daniels, J. L., Kalkbrenner, A., Zimmerman, J., & Nicholas, J. S. (2009). The effect of maternal smoking during pregnancy on intellectual disabilities among 8-year-old children. *Paediatric Perinatal Epidemiology, 23*(5), 482-491.

Burden, M. J., Jacobson, S. W., & Jacobson, J. L. (2005). Relation of prenatal alcohol exposure to cognitive processing speed and efficiency in childhood. *Alcoholism: Clinical and Experimental Research, 29*, 1473-1483.

Ceci, S. J. (1996). *On intelligence...more or less.* Cambridge, MA: Harvard University Press.

Der, G., Batty, G. D., & Deary, I. J. (2006). Effect of breast feeding on intelligence in children: prospective study, sibling pairs analysis, and meta-analysis. *British Medical Journal, 333* (7575). www.bmj.com/content/333/7575/945

Duthie, S. J., Whalley, L. J., Collins, A. R., Leaper, S., Berger, K., & Deary, I. J. (2002). Homocysteine, B vitamin status, and cognitive function in the elderly. *American Journal of Clinical Nutrition, 75*, 908-913.

Flynn, J. R. (2009). *What is intelligence? Beyond the Flynn Effect.* Cambridge: Cambridge University Press (paperback edition).

Flynn, J. R. (2010). *The torchlight list: Around the world in 200 books.* Wellington, New Zealand: AWA Press.

Flynn, J. R. (2012a). *Are we getting smarter: Rising IQ in the twenty-first century.* Cambridge: Cambridge University Press.

Flynn, J. R. (2012b). *Beyond patriotism: From Truman to Obama.* Exeter, UK: Imprint Academic.

Flynn, J. R. (2012c). *How to improve your mind: Twenty keys to unlock the modern world.* London: Wiley-Blackwell.

Flynn, J. R. (2013). *Intelligence and human progress: The story of what was hidden in our genes.* London: Elsevier.

Flynn, J. R. (2016a). *Does your family make you smarter? Nature, nurture, and human autonomy.* Cambridge: Cambridge University Press.

Flynn, J. R. (2016b). *The new torchlight list: In search of the best modern authors.* Wellington, New Zealand: AWA Press.

Flynn, J. R. (in press). Reflections about intelligence over 30 years. *Perspectives on Psychological Science.*

Flynn, J. R., & Shayer, M. (2017). IQ decline and Piaget: Does the rot start at the top? *Intelligence, 66*, 112-121.

Gardner, H. (1983). *Frames of mind: The theory of multiple intelligences.* New York: Basic Books.

Gardner, H. (1993). Introduction. In H. Gardner, *Frames of mind: The theory of multiple intelligences* (10th anniversary edition). New York: Basic Books.

Gardner, H. (1999). *Intelligence reframed.* New York: Basic Books.

Genovese, J. E. (2002). Cognitive skills values by educators: Historic content analysis of testing in Ohio. *Journal of Educational Research, 96*, 101-114.

Grandjean, P., & Landrigan, P. J. (2006). Developmental neurotoxicity of industrial chemicals. *Lancet, 368*(9553), 2167–2178.

Grant, W. B., Campbell, A., Itzhaki, R. F., & Savory, J. (2002). The significance of environmental factors in the etiology of Alzheimer's disease. *Journal of Alzheimer's Disease, 4*(3), 179-189.

Grantham-McGregor, S., Ani, C., & Fernald, L. (2001). The role of nutrition in intellectual development. In R. J. Sternberg & E. L. Grigorenko (eds.), *Environmental effects on cognitive abilities* (pp. 119-156). Mahwah, NJ: Lawrence Erlbaum Associates.

Grigorenko, E. L., Sternberg, R. J., Jukes, M., Alcock, K., Lambo, J., Ngorosho, D., Nokes, C., & Bundy, D. A. (2006). Effects of antiparasitic treatment on dynamically and statically tested cognitive skills over time. *Journal of Applied Developmental Psychology, 27* (6), 499-526.

Haworth, C. M. et al., 2010. The heritability of general cognitive ability increases linearly from childhood to young adulthood. *Molecular Psychiatry, 15*, 1112-1120.

Herbst, A. L., Ulfelder, H., & Poskanzer, D. C. (1971). Adenocarcinoma of the vagina: Association of maternal stilbestrol therapy with tumor appearance in young women. *New England Journal of Medicine, 284* (15), 878–881.

Honein, M. A., Paulozzi, L. J., & Erickson, J. D. (2001). Continued occurrences of Accutane-exposed pregnancies. *Teratology, 64*, 142-147.

Jacobson, S. W., Jacobson, J. L., Sokol, R. J., Chiodo, L. M., & Corobana, R. (2004). Maternal age, alcohol abuse history, and quality of parenting as moderators of the effects of prenatal alcohol exposure on 7.5-year intellectual function. *Alcoholism: Clinical and Experimental Research, 28*, 1732-1745.

Jones, J., Lopez, A., & Wilson, M. (2003). Congenital toxoplasmosis. *American Family Physician, 67*, 2131-2137.

Lynn, R. (2006). *Race differences in intelligence.* Whitefish, MT: Washington Summit Publishers.

Lynn, R., & Vanhanen, T. (2002). *IQ and the wealth of nations.* Westport, CT: Praeger/Greenwood.

Luria, A. R. (1976). *Cognitive development: Its cultural and social foundations.* Cambridge, MA: Harvard University Press.

Maguire, E. A., Woolett, K., & Spiers, H. J. (2006). London taxi drivers and bus drivers: a structural MRI and neuropsychological analysis. *Hippocampus, 16*, 1091-1101.

Mardh, P. A. (2002). Influence of infection with *Chlamydia trachomatis* on pregnancy outcome, infant health and lifelong sequelae in infected offspring. *Best Practices in Clinical Obstetrics and Gynecology, 16*, 847-964.

Masters, R. (1997). Brain biochemistry and social status: The neurotoxicity hypothesis. In E. White (ed.), *Intelligence, political inequality, and public policy* (pp. 41–183). New York: Prager.

Mayes, L. C., & Fahy, T. (2001). Prenatal drug exposure and cognitive development. In R. J. Sternberg & E. L. Grigorenko (eds.), *Environmental effects on cognitive abilities* (pp. 189-220). Mahwah, NJ: Lawrence Erlbaum Associates.

Moore, K. L., & Persaud, T. V. N. (2008). *Before we are born* (7th ed.). Philadelphia: Saunders.

National Endowment for the Arts (2016). Arts Data Profile #10 – Results from the Annual Arts Basic Survey (AABS): 2013-2015.

Nisbett, R. (2015). *Mindware: Tools for smart thinking.* New York: Farrar, Straus, and Giroux.

Niu, W., & Sternberg, R. J. (2002). Contemporary studies on the concept of creativity: The East and the West. *Journal of Creative Behavior, 36*, 269–288.

Ornoy, A., & Ergaz, Z. (2010). Alcohol use in pregnant women: Effects on the fetus and newborn, modes of action and material treatment. *International Journal of Environmental Research and Public Health, 7*(2), 364-379.

PISA (2009). *PISA 2009 results: what students know and can do: Student performance in reading, mathematics and science* (vol. I). Paris: OECD (Organisation for Economic Co-operation and Development).

Qian, M., Wang, D., & Watkins, W. E., et al. (2005). The effects of iodine on intelligence in children: A meta-analysis of studies conducted in China. *Asia Pacific Journal of Clinical Nutrition, 14*(1), 32–42.

Rush, D., Stein, Z., & Susser, M. (1980). A randomized control trial of prenatal nutritional supplementation in New York City. *Pediatrics, 65*(4), 683-697.

Seifer, R. (2001). Socioeconomic status, multiple risks, and development of intelligence. In R. J. Sternberg & E. L. Grigorenko (eds.), *Environmental effects on cognitive abilities* (pp. 59-82). Mahwah, NJ: Lawrence Erlbaum Associates.

Stein, Z., Susser, M., Saenger, G., & Marolla, F. (1972). Nutrition and mental performance. *Science, 178*, 708-713.

Sternberg, R. J. (ed.). (1985). *Human abilities: An information-processing approach.* San Francisco: Freeman.

Sternberg, R. J. (ed.). (1988). *Advances in the psychology of human intelligence* (vol. 4). Hillsdale, NJ: Lawrence Erlbaum Associates.

Sternberg, R. J. (1997a). Managerial intelligence: Why IQ isn't enough. *Journal of Management, 23*(3), 463–475.

Sternberg, R. J. (1997b). *Successful intelligence.* New York: Plume.

Sternberg, R. J. (2007). Intelligence and culture. In S. Kitayama & D. Cohen (eds.), *Handbook of cultural psychology* (pp. 547-568). New York: Guilford Press.

Sternberg, R. J., & Davidson, J. E. (1982). The mind of the puzzler. *Psychology Today, 16*, 37–44.

Sternberg, R. J., & Davidson, J. E. (1983). Insight in the gifted. *Educational Psychologist, 18*, 51–57.

Sternberg, R. J., & Grigorenko, E. L. (eds.). (2001). *Environmental effects on cognitive abilities.* Mahwah, NJ: Lawrence Erlbaum Associates.

Sternberg, R. J., & Grigorenko, E. L. (2004). Successful intelligence in the classroom. *Theory into Practice, 43*, 274-280.

Sternberg, R. J., & Hedlund, J. (2002). Practical intelligence, *g*, and work psychology. *Human Performance, 15*(1/2), 143–160.

Sternberg, R. J., & Lubart, T. I. (1995). *Defying the crowd: Cultivating creativity in a culture of conformity.* New York: Free Press.

Sternberg, R. J., Powell, C., McGrane, P. A., & McGregor, S. (1997). Effects of a parasitic infection on cognitive functioning. *Journal of Experimental Psychology: Applied, 3*, 67–76.

Sternberg, R. J., & The Rainbow Project Collaborators (2006). The Rainbow Project: Enhancing the SAT through assessments of analytical, practical and creative skills. *Intelligence, 34* (4), 321-350.

Troisi, R., Hatch, E. E., Titus-Ernstoff, L., Hyer, M., Palmer, J. R., Robboy, S. J., Strohsnitter, W. C., Kaufman, R., Herbst, A. L., & Hoover, R. N. (2007). Cancer risk in women prenatally exposed to diethylstilbestrol. *International Journal of Cancer, 121*(2), 356–360.

Woodley, M. A. (2012). The social and scientific temporal correlates of genotypic intelligence and the Flynn effect. *Intelligence, 40*, 189-204.

Woodley, M. A., te Nienhuis, J., & Murphy, R. (2013). Were the Victorians cleverer than us? The decline in general intelligence estimated from a meta-analysis of the slowing of simple reaction time. *Intelligence, 41*, 843-850.

11 | Lifespan Development of Intelligence

CHRISTOPHER HERTZOG

Lifespan approaches to intelligence must consider several issues. How many types of intelligence should be considered? Do different types of intelligence develop in different ways? What can developmental perspectives suggest about individual differences in intelligence? What are the causes of intellectual development at different points of the lifespan? In this chapter, we'll look at each of these important questions in turn. But first we need to consider the underlying *worldviews* or metatheories about development that play a role in how people think about intelligence and how it changes over the life course.

Metatheoretical Views of Intelligence and Intellectual Development

Metatheories involve basic assumptions or viewpoints about the nature and origins of cognitive development, including explanations for how and why intelligence changes across the human lifespan and theoretical concepts about development over the human lifespan. We saw in Chapter 7 that scientists and laypeople alike hold implicit theories (folk conceptions) about the nature of development in general, and of the development of intelligence in particular. One implicit theory relevant to development concerns an entity versus skill view of cognition and cognitive development (Dweck, 2006). **Entity theorists** view intelligence in children as innate and governed by genetic endowments and biological factors; **skill theorists** view cognition and intelligence as an acquired set of dispositions and skills influenced by learning and environmental factors. People who hold these different theories prefer different types of explanations for learning disabilities, success in school, vocational aptitude, and other outcomes seen as depending on intellectual prowess. For example, skill theorists are more likely than entity theorists to believe that intellectual abilities can be modified by training.

Developmental psychologists have emphasized that different metatheoretical assumptions about development influence how psychologists think about possible explanations for developmental change (Dixon & Hertzog, 1996; Reese & Overton, 1970). **Organismic theorists** like Piaget emphasize intellectual development during childhood as a regular sequence of (largely genetically programmed) emerging cognitive traits. Likewise, organismic views of adult intellectual development from young adulthood to old age regard intellectual change as determined mostly by genetically programmed neurobiological aging. **Mechanistic theorists**, on the other hand, emphasize development across the lifespan as a process of learning and experience during childhood and into adulthood. Mechanists view intellectual development during adulthood, involving stability of learned patterns of behavior. Finally, theorists with a **contextualist worldview** emphasize the importance of environmental factors, including social niches, for determining behavioral development (Dixon & Hertzog, 1996).

In reality, almost every psychologist adopts a mixture of worldviews, recognizing a multiplicity of possible influences on intellectual development and accepting the idea that development is inherently a complex transaction of what has been characterized as "nature" and "nurture." Having said that, worldviews almost certainly operate to bias a scientist toward interpreting empirical data as consistent with their preferred metatheoretical orientations.

Theories of Intellectual Development

We start by acknowledging that any theory of intellectual development begins with a view of the nature of intelligence itself. One relevant starting point is Sternberg's (1985) triarchic theory, which differentiates three broad types or classes of intelligence: analytic (or academic), creative, and practical. This chapter will emphasize analytic intelligence. There are alternative views on taxonomies of analytic intelligence, based on psychometric research on individual differences in intelligence test performance. This chapter adopts the **Cattell/Horn/Carroll (CHC) hierarchical model** (Carroll, 1993; McGrew, 2009; Wilhelm, 2005) (introduced in Chapter 4) as a basis for discussing intelligence. Figure 11.1 illustrates Carroll's (1993) summary of the literature on psychometric intellectual abilities, based in part on work of Cattell (1971) and Horn (1985). He viewed "narrow stratum" tests as measuring different aspects of primary mental abilities (such as induction, spatial orientation, secondary [episodic] memory, and verbal comprehension.

It is now widely accepted that intellectual development during childhood involves rapid acquisition of conceptual distinctions and declarative knowledge. What may start as a relatively undifferentiated general ability in infancy evolves early in life into multiple different (or differentiated abilities), morphing into the Cattell–Horn–Carroll (CHC) taxonomy roughly between ages 5 and 7. Intellectual development is viewed by organismic theorists as involving a transition from concrete to formal operations (the various facets of analytic intelligence like numeracy, conservation, and causal logic). One can speak of broad general intelligence or aptitude even at the earliest ages, but it is possible to identify individual differences in specific primary abilities relatively early in the lifespan.

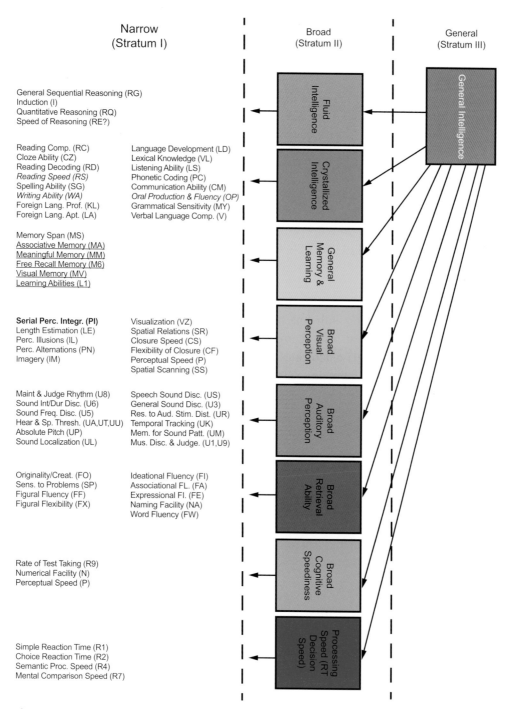

Figure 11.1 Hierarchical conception of levels of intelligence according to Carroll (1993). Conception of hierarchies of analytical (psychometric) intelligence based on the synthesized Cattell–Horn–Carroll (CHC) taxonomy of human abilities. Stratum I (Narrow) consists of primary abilities such as general knowledge. Stratum II (Broad) consists of higher-order ability factors such as fluid and crystallized intelligence. Stratum III (General) is identified as general intelligence. Horn and Cattell denied the utility of the general intelligence concept, whereas Carroll embraced it (see Gustaffson, 1989). Figure from Carroll (1993).
Copyright: Cambridge University Press. Reprinted with permission.

A study by Palejwala and Fine (2015) illustrates the consequences of maturation, in terms of the possibility of measuring more differentiated intellectual abilities. The preschool version of the Wechsler (2012) intelligence test targeting measurement of abilities in 2–3-year-olds has a limited number of abilities, in part owing to the difficulty of measuring multiple tests for children in this age range, along with the need for emerging comprehension skills to understand instructions for analytical reasoning tests. Figure 11.2a shows a structural regression model for Wechsler test scores that is similar to the hierarchy proposed by the CHC model, but weighted toward spatial visualization (the ability to imagine objects moving in space). Namely, general intelligence is measured by broad-stratum abilities that are in turn factors that account for the correlations among specific tests. Figure 11.2b shows a hierarchical model for the expanded primary school level test (Wechsler, 2012). Here it is possible to measure many additional abilities, although the tests available for the 2-year-olds are also measured at these older ages.

The interesting question is whether this differentiation reflects evolution in the structure of underlying abilities, evolution in the capability to measure different underlying abilities, or both (the answer appears to be: both). Nevertheless, the available data suggest that correlations among the broad-spectrum abilities decrease as children get older, consistent with the idea of increasing differentiation among abilities with increasing maturation. One indirect manifestion of this differentiation process is the fact that girls score better than boys on tests of spatial visualization at ages 2-3, but this sex difference reverses by age 7 to the pattern seen in adulthood: males scoring better than females (Palejwala & Fine, 2015).

An even more interesting and difficult question is whether adult development and aging alters the nature of intelligence, especially in old age. In terms of the abilities identified in the CHC model, the answer is probably no. The same abilities that can be observed in young adults can also be observed across the adult lifespan (e.g., Brickley, Keith, & Wolfe, 1995). Abilities like spatial visualization (the ability to imagine rotation of objects in space, or assembly of three-dimensional objects from two-dimensional diagrams) are manifested by adults of any age. This conclusion is at odds with the **dedifferentiation hypothesis**, which states that primary abilities that can be identified in late childhood and young adulthood become less distinct from one another due to the effects of aging. That is, the early differentiation of intelligence into multiple types, or primary abilities is regarded by the dedifferentiation hypothesis as reversing in late adulthood, with primary abilities becoming less distinct from one another. There is some evidence that different intellectual abilities may become more highly intercorrelated in old age (e.g., deFrias, Lövdén, Lindenberger, & Nilsson, 2007; Hertzog & Bleckley, 2001), perhaps as a function of broad, systemic effects of aging on the neural substrates of cognition, but not all studies find increasing ability correlations as people grow older. Others have argued that correlations among different primary abilities remain relatively constant across the

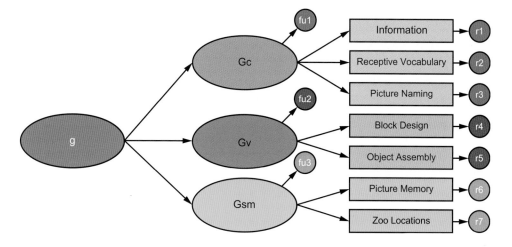

a.

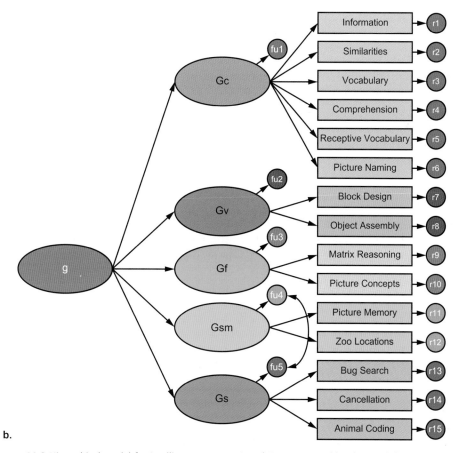

b.

Figure 11.2 Hierarchical model for intelligence at ages 2 and 7 as measured by the Wechsler Preschool and Primary Scale of Intelligence. a. Model for preschool tests. b. Model for Primary level tests. Differences between panels a and b reflect the ability to measure an expanded range of ability tests in children in early stages of elementary school, owing to both measurement factors and differentiation of intellectual abilities. Abbreviations: *g*: general intelligence; Gc – crystallized intelligence; Gf – fluid intelligence; Gs – general speed; Gv – spatial visualization; Gsm – general secondary memory. From Palejwala and Fine (2015). Copyright: Elsevier B.V. Reprinted with permission.

life course (e.g., Salthouse, 2012). It is therefore clear that primary abilities do not disappear or coalesce into an undifferentiated general intellectual ability, even when one contracts diseases that affect the brain, such as Alzheimer's disease – at least until such a disease progresses to the point where the ability to think itself is lost.

One implication of these findings is that one can probably think about intellectual abilities as being relatively invariant and identifiable across the adult lifespan. This is not to say, however, that the level of performance on intellectual ability tests is stable across the lifespan. As we shall see, levels of many intellectual abilities vary with age, and in a pattern explained in different ways by different developmental theorists.

Relevant Methodological Principles

Development can only be observed, not experimentally manipulated. This truism has important implications for understanding changes in intellectual abilities within individuals, between cultural entities (countries, societies, social classes), and across historical time. First, we can only observe intellectual change by measuring it. Second, development is by definition a within-person process of growth and change, and hence observing development implies measuring the same persons as they grow older. Third, it is absolutely impractical to measure intellectual development in the same individual from womb to tomb. The human lifespan is typically between 60 and 100 years duration (the current average life expectancy in economically advanced nations is just short of 80 years, with some people surviving past age 100, up to a maximum lifespan of about 120 years) (Crimmins, 2015). It is even relatively impractical to measure intellectual development in the same persons as they grow from childhood to maturity, say ages 2 to 18. For this reason, developmental psychologists use special sampling designs to approximate development under rather strong methodological assumptions.

Developmental Research Designs

The typical short-cut design is a **cross-sectional study** that observes people of different ages at the same point in time. Its name implies that a slice of the population varying in ages is sampled, and this can be true, although usually the cross-section includes additional decisions about a target age range to sample. Lifespan studies are rare, so one division is childhood to late adolescence or maturity (say, ages 2 to 18), and another is adulthood (say, ages 18 to 100). Practical difficulties in sampling and testing very young children (under the age of 5) and very old adults (over the age of 90, given accelerating mortality and morbidity past age 90; Crimmins, 2015) might constrain the width of the cross-sectional slice. Other practical considerations (e.g., cost savings) may dictate more limited age sampling; a popular design in aging studies is the extreme age groups design, where young adults (say, people 18-25) are compared with older adults (say, ages 65-80), a design limited in its ability to capture the shape of developmental functions but one that can provide a quick answer to the question of whether there are age differences in some aspect of cognition and intelligence (Hertzog, 1996).

Alternatively, deevelopmental research can involve a **longitudinal design** – measurement of the same people as they develop over an extended period of time. This type of study is necessary if one wishes to ask questions about critical phenomena like individual differences in change (Baltes, Reese, & Nesselroade, 1988). It is possible to use so-called **accelerated longitudinal designs**, in which a cross-sectional sample is followed for a short longitudinal timespan (say, 5-10 years) to piece together estimates of change by combining within-person data and between-person data (e.g., McArdle et al., 2002). More generally, **sequential sampling designs** (Schaie, 1965) involve repeated cross-sectional sampling from the same population on some regular testing interval (e.g., 5 years) – a cross-sectional sequence, and then, perhaps, following the same people over time – a longitudinal sequence.

Why would one bother to do so? Why not simply collect cross-sectional data, given its efficiency in collecting data in the shortest possible period of time? One answer, already mentioned, is that certain research questions require longitudinal (within-person) data (Baltes & Nesselroade, 1979). Another answer, however, is that one cannot necessarily assume that societies are stationary and that historical change does not matter for intelligence, even if an organismic metatheoretical view argues this is so.

The Flynn Effect

Previous chapters have discussed the **Flynn effect** – the recognition that levels of intelligence as measured by standardized tests have been changing, especially in the developed world, over the last century (Flynn, 2007). This phenomenon is observable when samples of children and adolescents are compared across historical time periods, so the effect emerges during early development. It probably reflects multiple sources of influence, including the nature of schooling, nutritional practices, family size, and urbanization (see Pietschnig & Voracek, 2015). The consequence of these historical changes is the creation of birth cohort effects, in which people born earlier in historical time are expected to have lower levels of cognitive performance at maturity than people born at a later point in historical time.

Methodological Challenges in Development Research

Flynn effects have consequences for the validity of inferences about age changes in intelligence, given standard research designs. Cross-sectional samples confound one's current age with one's date of birth: inevitably, at a particular year of sampling (say, 2020), one's age is determined by when one was born (20-year-olds were born in 2000, 50-year-olds in 1970, 80-year-olds in 1940). Any cross-sectional sample therefore combines (confounds) cohort and age effects, so that observed age differences are a joint function of unknown "true" age effects and unknown cohort effects. Furthermore, there is some evidence that later birth cohorts may produce different patterns of age change than earlier birth cohorts (i.e., Cohort X Age interactions; Schaie, 2012; Zelinski & Kennison, 2007). Hence the cross-sectional short-cut design can create a distorted estimate of average age-correlated change across the lifespan. Examination of both cohort differences and age changes requires a sequential sampling design and advanced statistical models to estimate the effects.

Sequential sampling designs are no panacea. They are still subject to a variety of well-known methodological issues (e.g., Shadish, Cook, & Campbell, 2002). Given individual differences in longevity or mortality (death at varying ages), adult cross-sectional samples contain people at earlier ages who will not in the future survive past a certain age. Any cross-sectional comparison of 80-year-olds to 20-year-olds includes 20-year-olds who will die before reaching age 80 (we just don't know who). Sampling procedures may also not be equally effective in recruiting people of different age groups (for example, refusal to volunteer may be greater in midlife during the working years than it is post-retirement).

Longitudinal sequences that repeatedly measure people over time risk sample attrition that is typically non-random with respect to intellectual ability (lower-performing individuals may refuse to return for further testing). Repeated testing can result in people learning how to take tests, and some longitudinal studies repeatedly use the same tests, so that people can benefit from practice on the same test items. These practice effects are a major problem for longitudinal studies, where within-person changes combine to an unknown degree actual within-person change with practice effects. There are a number of other concerns regarding the validity of inferences about lifespan developmental data as well that cannot be reviewed here (see Baltes, Reese, & Nesselroade, 1988; Schaie & Hertzog, 1982; Salthouse, 2000).

Given these complications, providing interpretations of empirical data on intellectual development turns out to be a hard problem! The problem leads to complicated designs and complex statistical models; it invites alternative sets of assumptions, governed by different theoretical viewpoints. Different scientists can draw radically different inferences about how to interpret results from the same data sets, and replication and synthesis – given qualitative differences in sampling designs and methods – are often problematic. Small wonder, then, that arguments about intellectual development, particularly in adulthood, remain contentious despite decades of empirical research on the topic.

Measurement Equivalence

One difficulty in comparing people of different ages on intellectual abilities is the requirement to have measures of the constructs that have comparable reliability and validity at different points in the lifespan (Baltes, Reese, & Nesselroade, 1988). It is extremely difficult to compare infants to adolescents, given that standard methods for assessing intelligence require comprehension of task instructions, something that infants cannot do. Developmental psychologists have created interesting methods for assessing cognitive mechanisms early in life (e.g., attentional habitu- ation) but such measures are probably best treated as early predictors of later intellectual development, not measures of intelligence itself. Likewise, intelligence tests that work well with young adults may have different measurement properties in older adults, given age changes in visual and auditory perception as well as age- related slowing in rates of information processing. A test with small font size or dense item characteristics might produce performance differences that are due to age-related perceptual, attentional, and processing-speed limitations rather than age differences in the intellectual abilities one is attempting to measure (Hertzog, 1989; Lustig, Hasher, & Tonev, 2006).

Intellectual Development Across the Lifespan

Analytic intelligence, as measured by tests of inductive and deductive reasoning, shows dramatic growth during childhood and appears to decline during adulthood, although the latter inference is more controversial than the former. On the other hand, knowledge about semantics (the study of meaning in language), culturally determined facts, and practical aspects of one's cultural setting appear to continue to increase across the lifespan, albeit with some evidence of decline in very old age. This generalization is based on literally decades of research on intellectual abilities, and has been recognized for decades (Botwinick, 1977; Horn, 1985; Salthouse, 1982). For instance, Wechsler (1939) had already classified abilities as stable versus declining – what he termed "hold" versus "don't-hold" tests – based on standard- ization data for his tests of intelligence. As you read in Chapter 4, Cattell (1971) argued that one could identify two broad classes of abilities, fluid intelligence and crystallized intelligence. The developmental argument is that growth in **fluid intelli- gence** drove realization of the latter in childhood by a process of investment of intellectual aptitude in the service of learning about one's culture, its symbol systems, its rules, and its regularities (Cattell, 1971). In adulthood, **crystallized intelligence** was argued to be maintained into old age, whereas fluid intelligence declined from maturity in young adulthood (arbitrarily, age 20-25).

Cross-sectional Studies of Fluid and Crystallized Intelligence
The empirical pattern seen in early data on intellectual ability is nicely depicted in a number of excellent reviews (e.g., Salthouse, 1982) and captured by more recent cross-sectional studies of cognition. McArdle et al. (2002) provided one of the most

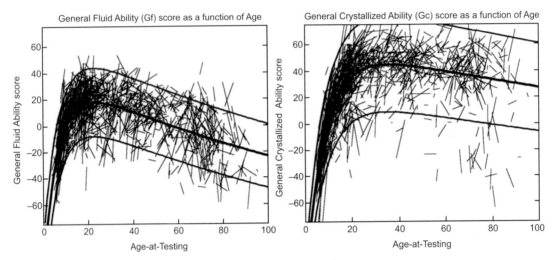

Figure 11.3 Estimated lifespan trajectories of fluid and crystallized intelligence.
Left-hand panel depicts estimated growth and decline in fluid intelligence across the human lifespan (see text). Right-hand panel depicts estimated growth and decline in crystallized intelligence across the human lifespan, with less average decline for crystallized intelligence. From McArdle et al. (2002). Copyright: American Psychological Association. Reprinted with permission.

compelling demonstrations of the similarity and differences in lifespan trajectories for fluid and crystallized intelligence. They statistically analyzed standardization data from the Woodcock–Johnson–Revised (WJ-R) test of intellectual abilities. The WJ-R has a number of important advantages for developmental assessment. Its tests were selected and constructed based on the CHC model for second-order abilities, including fluid intelligence (Gf), crystallized intelligence (Gc), spatial visualization (Gv), secondary (episodic) memory (Gm), and general speed of processing (Gs). The test includes versions that are appropriate for young children, enabling a lifespan study design. Its validation was based on an application of item-response theory (Embretson & Reise, 2000) to generate a wide range of item difficulties appropriate for heterogeneous populations. Because the WJ-R includes multiple primary abilities that can be used to define Gf and Gc, it is both consistent with the hierarchical CHC model and leverages it to obtain statistically optimal developmental curves of Gf and Gc, aggregating over multiple test scores.

McArdle et al. (2002) used cross-sectional and longitudinal sequence data to generate fitted average curves across ages for different abilities, using an advanced statistical technique known as growth-curve modeling (Duncan, Duncan, & Strycker, 2006) to capture the aggregate trends. Figure 11.3 depicts fitted lifespan curves for fluid and crystallized intelligence. Both higher-order abilities showed rapid increases in ability during childhood, followed by different patterns of change in adulthood. Fluid intelligence showed substantial age differences in performance between age 20 and age 75, whereas crystallized intelligence showed much shallower adult age differences across the same age period. This pattern captures quite nicely the different patterns of age differences for the two broad classes of intellectual abilities.

The elegance of the statistical models used by McArdle et al. (2002) should not blind us to some potential issues, several of which were explicitly acknowledged in the paper. First, the curves that are shown are fitted (nonlinear) regression lines, and to a degree the similarity of the two curves could result in part because the same class of nonlinear regression models was fit to the data. Second, these curves can mask individual differences in rates of change, or heterogeneity in the data. McArdle et al. addressed this issue in part by plotting 95 percent confidence intervals on the curves (upper and lower curves in Figure 11.3) and by randomly selecting some data points to plot underneath the fitted functions so as to visually depict individual differences in change. Third, although longitudinal data were included in the analysis, the models were probably dominated by the cross-sectional information, given the wide cross-sectional span of years combined with a limited period of longitudinal sampling. Fourth, the curves were not (and probably could not be) corrected for cohort differences, given limited replication of ages across different cohorts in the sampling design. Fifth, one should view the fitted curves as statistical averages, and little more. From a statistical point of view they represent the best guess of how a person of a given age will perform on tests of Gf and Gc. Connecting the fitted dots to form a line implies an aggregate or average developmental curve, but one should not overinterpret its meaning. These average curves are well known to distort, in principle, individual curves for specific individuals as they change over time (which could not be estimated from the limited available longitudinal data). Actual individual trajectories in Gf and Gc could vary substantially from the average in the slope of change across adulthood (e.g., Heathcote, Brown, & Mewhort, 2000). Be that as it may, the McArdle et al. (2002) estimates of the age trends in these two broad intellectual ability constructs are some of the best information we have on these patterns, and they certainly reinforce observations that there are differences in the age trend observed in Gf and Gc.

Cognitive Mechanics and Cognitive Pragmatics

The argument that fluid and crystallized intelligence differ in adult developmental patterns mirrors the arguments made by Baltes and colleagues, who chose to emphasize the distinction as one of cognitive mechanics and cognitive pragmatics (e.g., Baltes, Staudinger, & Lindenberger, 1999). **Cognitive mechanics** are assumed to be basic information-processing mechanisms and operations closely linked to analytical intelligence. The idea was possibly inspired by information processing models of reasoning and thought created by cognitive psychologists (e.g., Hunt, 1978; Sternberg, 1983; Mumaw & Pellegrino, 1984) that connect higher-order cognition to more atomistic component processes that contribute to it. For instance, working memory capacity – the ability to maintain mental representations while transforming or "working with" them (Baddeley, 1986; Chapter 5, this volume) – has been seen as critical to being able to induce complex patterns in sequences of stimuli as required by inductive reasoning tests.

Cognitive pragmatics is certainly related to the aspects of declarative knowledge about culturally embedded variables like symbols, semantics, shared myths, and facts about the world emphasized in the CHC tasks. But Baltes et al. (1999) also view pragmatics as involving knowledge about how to achieve goals in contexts, wisdom as knowledge about the world and how it operates (e.g., Baltes & Smith, 2008), and everyday behavioral procedures that would be subsumed by other theorists under concepts like practical intelligence or social intelligence (Wagner & Sternberg, 1985) and not captured by tests like the WJ-R.

Limitations of the Gf–Gc Model

Although the Gf–Gc (or mechanics–pragmatics) distinction may capture the broad-brush pattern of adult age differences in human abilities, it is limited in several respects. First, there is relatively little that the CHC theory has to say about adult intellectual development of Gf beyond (1) an empirical generalization based on the large number of cross-sectional studies that had already emerged in the first half of the twentieth century, combined with (2) a largely metatheoretical assumption that Gf declines in adulthood due to effects of neurobiological aging. This metatheoretical view is grounded in the organismic worldview outlined earlier; it posits that age-related variation is directly or indirectly due to genetically programmed development. The implicit appeal to genetic determinants of development was most likely connected to the views of Galton, Spearman, and others (e.g., Jensen, 1998) that intellectual ability is a genetically determined endowment (for a critique of early evidence cited for this claim, see Gould, 1981). The implicit assumptions argue for the following kind of inference: If one observes age differences in fluid intelligence, they are likely to be (1) due to aging more than any other factors, and (2) largely immutable and unavoidable due to their origins in genetically programmed developmental sequences. Certainly genetics and epigenetics play critical roles in cognitive development across the lifespan (Tucker-Drob & Riley, 2014). However, whether average age-related changes in intellectual ability are due to genetic or genetic X environment interactions (as opposed, say, to secondary effects of age-correlated disease and preventable factors like alcohol consumption, lack of physical activity, and cumulative stress-related physiological effects [McEwen & Gianolos, 2011; Spiro & Brady, 2008]) is unclear at present.

Second, the estimated curve for Gc is not necessarily representative of how culturally embedded knowledge grows with experience, even across adulthood. Ackerman (2000) has argued that vocabulary peaks in midlife because acquisition of new word meanings is not representative of the kinds of knowledge acquisition that occur as one continues to live into old age. Instead, he argues that individuals occupy vocational and avocational niches within society, and they continue to acquire new knowledge within those niches. Arguably, the same idea applies to acquisition of world knowledge as one lives through different historical epochs. History is formed before our very eyes, as a society changes (e.g., emergence of new technologies; outcomes of political elections, and trends in fashion and attitudes). Our knowledge encodes, processes, and assimilates these changes to the extent we actually experience them. Acquisition of new knowledge is not merely a function of investment of Gf but also of relevant dispositions such as cultural engagement and intellectual curiosity (von Stumm & Ackerman, 2013). Baltes (1997) argued that people select themselves into specific societal roles and then optimize function (and knowledge) within these roles, an idea related to arguments about tacit knowledge in practical intelligence by Wagner and Sternberg (1985). From this point of view, the curve seen in Figure 11.3 for Gc does a poor job of representing how crystallized knowledge grows during adulthood because it samples and tests knowledge that is commonly held and, more often than not, acquired early in life.

Third, and as explicitly recognized by Horn (1985; Horn & Hofer, 1992), there are probably multiple cross-sectional functions relating age to different aspects of cognitive mechanics (or different primary and secondary abilities), even if they can be construed broadly as showing decline-consistent patterns of variation with respect to age. McArdle et al. (2002) found empirical evidence for this in the WJ-R normative data. Estimated slopes of decline varied across abilities that Baltes would consider cognitive mechanics, with greater age sensitivity for speed of processing (Gs) than for Gf, and less age sensitivity for episodic memory retrieval, short-term memory, and spatial visualization. A model that allowed all cognitive mechanics related abilities to be fit by the same age curve did not fit the data as well as one with ability-specific heterogeneous age curves. This finding is consistent with other research (e.g., Hertzog & Schaie, 1988); in particular, it is widely found that speed of processing varies more by cross-sectional age than other abilities measured in the same sample (e.g., Schaie, 1989; Hertzog, 1989), consistent with the argument that slowing of information processing is a hallmark of all cognitive processes as one ages (Birren & Fisher, 1995). Hertzog (2008) has also pointed out that other aspects of cognitive mechanics not included in typical psychometric test batteries show relatively flat cross-sectional curves, including monitoring of learning new information (e.g., Hertzog, Sinclair, & Dunlosky, 2010). These patterns are inconsistent with the idea that all aspects of cognitive mechanics inevitably decline in old age.

Longitudinal Evidence about Patterns of Age Changes

What does data from long-term longitudinal sequences say about patterns of age changes in intelligence? Schaie's (2012) Seattle Longitudinal Study provides extensive evidence regarding that question, as well as data on cohort differences in intellectual abilities. Begun in 1956, the study collected cross-sectional samples of adults every seven years through 1998 (seven samples in all) from a health maintenance organization in the greater Seattle WA area, then followed these individuals longitudinally over time. The original test battery included the adolescent version of the Thurstone Primary Mental Abilities test: Letter Series (a test of induction and a marker of Gf), Verbal Meaning (a recognition vocabulary test, and a marker of Gc), Number (a test of simple arithmetic skills, related to Gc), Space (a test of mental rotation, and a marker of Gv), and Word Fluency. Letter series required induction of patterns among letters and mapping to predict the next letter (e.g., with a pattern "abacada" the next letter would be "e"). Verbal meaning required selection of a synonym (e.g., "burglar") to a target word (e.g., "thief"). Space rotated simple objects, like the capital letter F, in two-dimensional space, requesting discrimination of F from its mirror image (backwards F). Number required two-column addition, verifying whether a supplied answer was correct or incorrect. Word Fluency required one to generate as many words as possible beginning with a letter from the alphabet (e.g., S). In later samples the battery was augmented to include multiple indicators of each ability, and to sample additional abilities like secondary memory.

Evidence from the SLS Study

The SLS data show typical cross-sectional curves relating age to different primary abilities (see Figure 11.4a, taken from Schaie, 1994). These data, based on multiple indicators for each primary ability show steeper cross-sectional age curves for inductive reasoning, spatial ability, and word fluency than for verbal comprehension and numerical facility. However, estimates of cohort differences, taken from the sequential data, show major cohort differences contributing to these cross-sectional curves (see Figure 11.4b). The longitudinal data, pieced together from seven-year change information (see Figure 11.4c), suggest a much more benign pattern of age-related changes. This pattern holds even when all longitudinal data in the SLS are used (Schaie, 2012). Other longitudinal studies report similar results (e.g., Rönnlund & Nilsson, 2008; Zelinski & Kennison, 2007).

As noted earlier, a major concern regarding longitudinal studies is the potential confounding of practice effects, working against age-related changes. These effects are almost certainly present in the data shown in Figure 11.4c, but Schaie (2012) has also found reductions in estimated age changes, controlling for cohort differences, in his repeated cross-sectional sequences, in which people are only tested once. It seems evident that, at least through the historical period in which Flynn effects seem to be operating, cross-sectional data overestimate the magnitude of age-related changes in intellectual abilities in adults.

Methodological Concerns with SLS Data

Another feature of Figure 11.4c is somewhat surprising. The longitudinal trends on the primary abilities show more similarity than difference between the primary

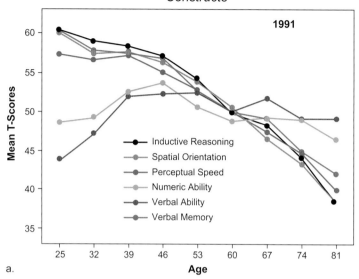

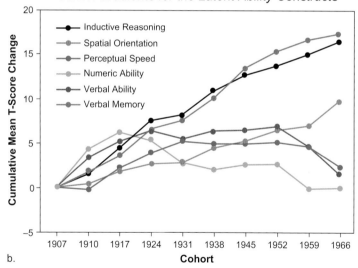

Figure 11.4 Longitudinal estimates of mean factor scores for the latent ability constructs Age-related trends on seven primary mental abilities from the Seattle Longitudinal Study. Panel a: Cross-sectional data from one wave of the study (1991) based on estimated factor scores from multiple ability tests. Panel b: Estimated differences across multiple birth cohorts for the same variables, showing generational change in intellectual abilities. Panel c: Estimated longitudinal changes in the primary abilities adjusting for cohort effects. From Schaie (1994). Copyright: American Psychological Association. Reprinted with permission.

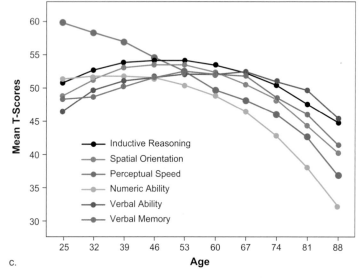

Longitudinal Estimates of Mean Factor Scores for the Latent Ability Constructs

Note. From 7-year within-subject data.

Figure 11.4 (*cont.*)

abilities assessed. Perceptual Speed shows the greatest and earliest rates of age-related decline (Schaie, 1989), consistent with cross-sectional data. However, the other abilities' longitudinal gradients are more similar than different. Does this pattern suggest that the classic hold vs. don't hold pattern encapsulated in Gf-Gc theory is an artifact of cross-sectional designs? Probably not! There is another major methodological concern regarding the SLS data that may produce this effect. The tests used in the SLS, particularly its original tests, are speeded tests of intelligence (Anastasi & Urbina, 1997), in which the rate of solving relatively easy test items plays a major role in overall test performance. The tests of numerical facility, for instance, all require generating answers to simple arithmetic problems (e.g., two-column addition) in which error rates are low and the test score is mostly a function of how many problems can be solved in a fixed time period. As noted earlier, this creates the opportunity for age changes in rates of information processing speed to influence test scores while also obscuring age differences that might be observed if the method of test administration emphasized assessing the level of problem complexity each person could reach. For example, advanced measurement using computerized adaptive testing can assess people using items of heterogeneous difficulty (Embretson & Reise, 2000). Such procedures would increase sensitivity to detect the full range of underlying ability and reduce the effects of speed of processing on ability test scores. In Schaie's longitudinal data, use of speeded ability tests could accelerate estimated age change for measures of Gc past midlife due to slowing of processing speed.

Hertzog (1989) tested the **speed-contamination hypothesis** (speed factors distorting age-based cognitive changes) by asking a cross-sectional sample of adults to complete old-style answer-marking sheets using intelligence test booklets in which the correct answers were already circled. One only needed to search for the correct answer and then mark the appropriate answer. This test of perceptual speed strongly correlated with ability test performance, inflated the cross-sectional age differences for some variables (particularly the markers of Gc), and dramatically inflated correlations among ability latent variables estimated in a confirmatory factor analysis (Hertzog & Bleckley, 2001).

Ironically, then, one can claim that despite decades of research on this problem, the issue of a valid description of aggregate age changes in human abilities is a hard problem that remains unresolved! To some degree this is inevitable and a function of limited generalizability, because we cannot assume that true age changes will remain invariant across historical periods – the available evidence suggests they do not. But charting average within-person age changes in abilities will remain controversial given the nature of the available data and the complexity of statistical models and assumptions required to unpack the age-cohort-period problem using sequential data sets.

Individual Differences in the Development of Intellectual Abilities

A critical question regarding human abilities is whether individuals differ in rates of growth and decline in human abilities. One way to assess this question is to examine longitudinal test–retest correlations of human abilities. If individual differences in rates of change are small, the stability of individual differences performance should be high. This is true independent of whether there is substantial growth or decline across a given age range. **Stability coefficients** are defined as correlations of a test with itself in a longitudinal sample. Stability coefficients should be high if individual differences in rates of change are small. How high can we expect such estimates of stability to be? Empirical test–retest correlations reflect not only stability of individual differences but also reductions in correlations due to inconsistency (unreliability) of measures in capturing underlying ability. The less reliable a measure, the smaller any test–retest correlation can be. The upper limit, assuming zero variance in rates of change, would be the reliability of the variable (Rogosa, Brandt, & Zimowski, 1982). Modern psychometric approaches adjust for unreliability by using latent variable models, which estimate stability of individual differences corrected for unreliability. When corrected for unreliability, stability coefficients will go as high as 1.0 if there is perfect stability of individual differences in the ability across the longitudinal timespan (implying, conversely, no individual differences in change).

The stability of individual differences in intellectual abilities over extended years is impressively large. A recent meta-analysis by Tucker-Drob and Briley (2014) suggested that stability of individual differences in intelligence is low early in the lifespan but rapidly increases to a stable asymptote (or maximum) in adolescence and beyond. Deary and colleagues recovered data archives on adolescent test scores in Scotland, retesting these people in old age. Corrected stability coefficients for a general intelligence over a span of 70 years were estimated to be about .6 (Deary et al., 2004). During adulthood, standardized estimates of the stability of general intelligence from latent variable models over 14 years of aging, even in older adults, were about .9 (Hertzog & Schaie, 1986; see also Salthouse, 2012). Furthermore, measures of infant cognition, such as habituation to repeated stimuli, predict intelligence test performance in adolescence and early adulthood (Bornstein, 2014), suggesting that while individual differences may not be perfectly stable, there is at least some continuity in cognitive ability even from early childhood. Thus, after early development (say, beyond about age 7), cognitive abilities are consistent traits that are relatively well preserved in rank-order consistency into adulthood, and then across the lifespan. Those individuals who have high levels of intellectual ability in adolescence are likely to remain in the upper levels of ability late in life.

Indirectly, the stability of primary abilities as well as higher-order constructs like Gf and Gc implies that profiles of ability variation within individuals should also remain stable over time, although this phenomenon is less widely studied. The term "profile" refers to a pattern of ability levels within a person, such as high in spatial visualization, low in episodic memory, about average in numerical facility (and so on). Given ideas about selection, investment, and optimization, one can certainly anticipate heterogeneous profiles across domains of crystallized intelligence and specific topic knowledge (e.g., Ackerman & Wolman, 2007), but within-person profiles of ability across the range of primary abilities might also be expected, to a degree, despite the positive correlations amongst abilities that help to define higher-order ability constructs like general intelligence. Schaie (2012) has produced evidence that decline in intellectual abilities is not universal, but often limited to a subset of the five primary abilities he has studied; however, he has not connected this phenomenon to the preservation of profiles of ability across the lifespan.

High levels of stability suggest that any individual differences in rates of intellectual growth during childhood, and possible decline across adulthood, are small relative to the overall level of ability variation in the population. That does not imply, however, that individual differences in change in abilities don't happen. They most certainly do. One way to evaluate this claim is to run a latent growth curve model on longitudinal data. Latent growth curves include a slope parameter or parameters that capture the shape of the developmental curve (Ferrer & McArdle, 2011). The shape of change could be linear, or nonlinear (as in Figure 11.3).

However, the model also makes it possible to estimate individual differences in those changes, estimated as a *variance* in slopes. Rejecting the null hypothesis of zero slope variance in favor of the alternative of a positive variance indicates that there are individual differences in change over the time period measured in the study.

There are now multiple longitudinal studies that have shown individual differences in rates of change in cognitive abilities during some phase of adulthood. For example, Hertzog et al. (2003) found reliable variance in slopes in two-occasion data spanning six years in a longitudinal sample of adults initially ages 55-85 for several abilities, including inductive reasoning, working memory, episodic memory, and perceptual speed. Furthermore, these individual differences in change were positively intercorrelated, consistent with the argument that changes in cognitive abilities can, to a degree, be general across multiple different types of ability. Perhaps more important, however, is that there was ability-specific variance in change along with general variance in change.

Tucker-Drob (2011) reported similar findings from the Virginia Cognitive Aging Study, using the WJ-R intellectual ability test to examine change in hierarchically organized abilities based on the CHC model. A wide cross-section of adults was tested twice at varying retest intervals (on average about three years). Figure 11.5 shows basic results at the level of latent changes (ignoring intercept or start-point variance). The bottom part of the figure shows the hierarchical model for slopes (or individual differences in change), not intercepts (starting points). The pie chart at the top of the figure partitions the slope variance into general (shared) change across all variables, domain-specific shared change (e.g., among the three indicators for Gf), and change specific to each ability test. Although 39 percent of the variance in intellectual change is shared in common (i.e., a common factor of individual differences in rates of change), fully 33 percent is specific to different primary abilities. This pattern establishes that the similarity in cross-sectional gradients belies the underlying heterogeneity in change found in longitudinal data (see Hertzog et al., 2003, for similar results). We would not expect to see robust individual differences in change at the primary ability level, controlling on the general factor of change, if all intellectual abilities declined in tandem late in life (Rabbitt, 1993).

Explanations for Individual Differences in Ability Change

There are a variety of explanations for differences in ability changes. We will selectively illustrate two broad classes of explanations: (1) cognitive resource theory and (2) environmental and genetic influences.

Cognitive Resource Theory

Cognitive psychologists have considered the hypothesis that age-related changes in basic information processing resources, such as attention and working memory, might account for age-related changes in higher-order cognition, including fluid

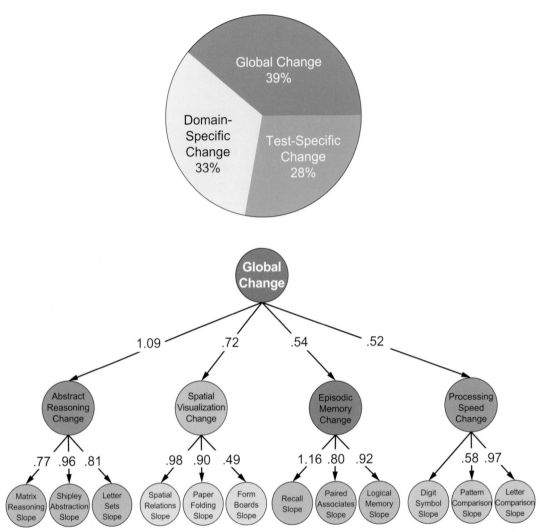

Figure 11.5 Hierarchical model of individual differences in intellectual change at levels of specific tests, second-order (domain-specific) abilities, and global (common) change. Graphical representation of latent change scores in adulthood from longitudinal data reported by Tucker-Drob (2011). At the bottom of the hierarchy, latent change factors are modeled for multiple tests from a given domain (e.g., Matrix Reasoning test changes). The second-order factors capture changes common to tests for a given domain (e.g., Abstract Reasoning). The highest level is global changes (common to all domains) determined from the correlations among the latent difference scores. Pie chart shows proportion of change-related variance that is global (shared by all tests), domain-specific (residual change variance in a domain, controlling on common or global change), or test-specific (residual change in each test, controlling on global and domain-specific changes). Copyright: American Psychological Association. Reprinted with permission.

intelligence. The hypothesis is consistent with arguments that there is a close linkage between executive control mechanisms, functional working memory capacity, and fluid intelligence (e.g., Kyllonen, 2002). Salthouse (1996; Verhaeghen & Salthouse, 1997) has argued that information processing speed should also be considered a fundamental age-sensitive cognitive resource as well, pointing out that statistical control for processing speed accounts for most of the age-related variance in intelligence in cross-sectional data (e.g., Salthouse & Ferrer-Caja, 2003). The speed-as-resource argument, as well as the ancillary claim that psychometric tests of processing speed are ideal for capturing age-related slowing of information processing speed, has met with a mixed reception (see Hartley, 2006: Lustig, Hasher, & Tonev, 2006). There is also evidence that late-life changes in working memory are connected to changes in episodic memory (perhaps due to common retrieval demands) and fluid intelligence (Hertzog et al., 2003; Tucker-Drob, 2011). However, some of the cross-sectional evidence for mediation of age differences in reasoning by processing speed and working memory may ovestimate the degree of cognitive-resource mediation. These analyses are prone to mean-induced association, in which variables sharing similar average cross-sectional patterns have inflated correlations, increasing the age-related overlap between them (Hofer et al., 2006; Lindenberger et al., 2011). There is also evidence that maintained levels of knowledge and verbal ability serve as an important resource for successful everyday cognitive behavior by older adults (e.g., Czaja et al., 2006), suggesting that resources should not be narrowly construed as aspects of cognitive mechanics that might explain intellectual decline. In any event, cognitive resource theories, useful as they may be, still leave open the question as to what variables cause age-related improvements and decline in resource variables like working memory.

Environmental and Genetic Factors

During the first 15 years of life, the most important predictors of intellectual development appear to be both genetic influences and factors related to social status and schooling (e.g., Tucker-Drob & Briley, 2014). Consider results from von Stumm & Plomin (2015), who used latent growth curve models to assess relations of socio-economic status (SES) to intellectual growth in children. Figure 11.6 shows their results on a general measure of intelligence. The scaling of the variables, an IQ score, adjusts for the average growth curve found in standardization data (and as seen in Figure 11.3). This scaling allows SES effects to be revealed as curves that deviate from the average (the flat line at 0 implied by the IQ scale). As can be seen, both boys and girls from above-average SES backgrounds show greater rates of improvement in intelligence, whereas below-average SES children show the opposite pattern.

In contrast, SES is essentially irrelevant to individual differences in cognitive development in adulthood, at least for abilities broadly classified as cognitive mechanics (e.g., Hultsch et al., 1998; Schaie, 2012). SES predicts levels of intellectual ability at early maturity, consistent with its association with intellectual growth during childhood and adolescence. However, it has rarely been found to be associated with individual differences in cognitive change (but see Schooler & Kaplan, 2009). It is also at best a distal predictor of change in cognitive pragmatics, which is more related to variables like typical intellectual engagement that are related to educational attainment, openness to experience, and other predictors (von Stumm & Ackerman, 2013).

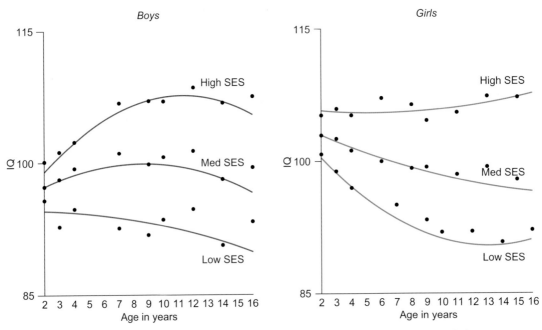

Figure 11.6 Norm-adjusted growth curves from childhood to adolescence for a general intelligence (IQ) measure as moderated by socioeconomic status. Changes in IQ (with average growth, as seen in Figure 11.1, removed by the use of age-graded norms to create IQ scores), separately for boys and girls. Fitted lines represent moderated effects due to socioeconomic status (SES), with the moderated regression equation evaluated at the mean (Med SES), + 1 SD SES (High SES), or -1 SD SES (Low SES). Maintaining the average growth pattern into adolescence would be represented by a flat line across age at IQ = 100. Instead, the regression model revealed both (a) average separation as a function of SES (higher SES is associated with better test scores at all ages) and (b) differences in developmental trends as a function of SES. Low SES is correlated with falling behind the average developmental function defined by IQ, whereas high SES is correlated with improvement relative to the average function. Data from von Stumm & Plomin (2015).

Behavior genetics studies using twin and family data indicate that a substantial proportion of variance in intelligence in adulthood and aging is heritable (Reynolds, 2008). However, research in this area also finds that nonshared environmental influences increase across the lifespan in their relation to human abilities (Tucker-Drob & Briley, 2014). That finding implicates heterogeneous environmental and behavioral influences on adult intellectual development other than genetic variation, such as chronic disease, or gene X environment interactions (including genetic risk for different types of disease). One set of possible predictors of variation in late-life cognitive outcomes is life-style and behavior. Tobacco use and alcohol consumption, to excess, have been implicated in mortality risk but may also affect cognitive changes in adulthood. Metabolic factors are related to obesity and risk for cardiovascular disease, which is known to be associated with greater rates of cognitive decline in adulthood.

Conversely, there is evidence that physical fitness in old age, as measured by vital capacity, is related to preservation of intellectual abilities in adulthood (e.g., Clarkson-Smith & Hartley, 1990; Colcombe & Kramer, 2003; Eggermont et al., 2009), although there are some contradictory findings (e.g., Sink et al. 2015). Some experts question the long-term benefits of exercise programs for moderating intellectual decline in old age (e.g., Salthouse, 2006), but at present there is little relevant data. Preventable chronic diseases like Type 2 (late onset) diabetes or adult sleep apnea may also affect adults' cognition, and chronically elevated levels of stress hormones like cortisol have been found to be a risk factor for reduced executive function and episodic memory. Such effects may also interact with genetic predispositions (e.g., patterns of single nucleic polypeptide genes, or SNPs) that create variation in how genes are expressed. For example, SNPs for the enzyme COMT affect how quickly the neurotransmitter dopamine is catabolized after it is released at the synaptic cleft (Lindenberger et al., 2008). Certain SNPs relevant to brain function can render certain individuals more vulnerable to the negative effects of workload (e.g., Nagel et al., 2008), age-related shrinkage in brain volume in specific regions (e.g., Erickson et al., 2010), risk for Alzheimer's disease (e.g., Jun et al., 2010), or risk factors for vascular disease (e.g., Raz et al., 2008, 2017). SNPs for brain-derived neurotrophic factor (related to growth of new synaptic connections) have been linked to individual differences in late-life changes in reasoning ability (e.g., Harris et al., 2006). Genetics may also affect who is more likely to benefit from changes in lifestyle targeting physical and mental fitness (e.g., Voss et al., 2013). Given the large number of genes relevant to brain development and function, variability in genetic profiles is almost certainly a major source of heterogeneity in intellectual development across the lifespan. In old age, different constellations of genetic features could, in interaction with environmental variables, produce different rates of age-related changes in cognition.

Challenges to Detecting Causes for Rates of Change

A major problem in the field for detecting causes of rates of change is that age-related changes are probably shaped by a large number of factors experienced on a probabilistic basis, including exposure to diseases. That is, these factors are not universal in their presence or impact, so individuals vary in the probability that a large number of different variables may impact their cognitive function. Hence detecting the multiplicity of effects, possibly associated with small to moderate effect sizes at the population level, may require prospective outcome studies with much larger inception samples than are typical in the field. If effect sizes of particular variables are small and dependent on unique constellations of genetic profiles and associated risk factors, large samples will be needed to detect their effects.

Plasticity of Human Abilities Across the Lifespan

No issue better illustrates the impact of metatheoretical views on the nature of aging than the question of the malleability, or **plasticity of intelligence** across the life course. When Willis, Baltes, and colleagues first provided evidence that older adults' intellectual abilities, including tests of fluid intelligence, could be trained (e.g., Plemons, Willis, & Baltes, 1978), critics argued that the studies were training the test and not the underlying ability trait (which, in the case of fluid intelligence, was regarded as immutable). At that time the dominant model of the central nervous system was a static one; individuals at maturity had a fixed number of neurons and synaptic connections that were seen as vulnerable to aging and decreasing across the lifespan. Today's view of the nervous system emphasizes continual **neural plasticity**, defined as experience-dependent changes in the morphology (form and structure) and functional connectivity of brain systems. Neural plasticity, including even the growth, migration, and functional evolution of one kind of neuron (granule cells), is now known to continue into late life. The correct model for aging may involve an age-graded reduction in the degree of neural plasticity, but plasticity is a feature of the nervous system, even an older one. This view has important theoretical consequences for how we think about human abilities and their change over the lifespan (Lindenberger, 2014).

Training Programs Targeting Cognition

It is clear at present that training programs targeting cognitive strategies (such as mnemonics for encoding new stimuli) that are relevant to some ability tests (such as a test of associative memory) improve the targeted ability test performance, even in older adults (e.g., Ball et al., 2002; see Karbach & Verhaeghen, 2014; Simons et al., 2016). However, this type of training appears to be process-specific and does not easily generalize to untrained cognitive tasks, unless the same strategy is afforded by different test contexts (Bailey et al., 2014). A second type of cognitive experience involves extensive practice at attention-demanding, high-workload cognitive tasks. There are a number of studies indicating that performance in real-time tasks can lead to improvement in other tasks, so long as the type of process required to improve (e.g., reducing susceptibility to attend to distractors (irrelevant information) in a noisy environment; Basak, Boot, Voss, & Kramer, 2008; Bherer et al., 2008) can be beneficial in other task environments (Karbach & Verhaeghen, 2014). One concern in this area is that some for-profit corporations aggressively market "brain training" games to older adults with little evidence that their training procedures actually improve task performance (let alone improve brain function; Simons et al., 2016). Extended practice can lead to cognitive task improvements in younger and older adults (Schmiedek, Lövdén, & Lindenberger, 2010; Baltes, Sowarka & Kliegl, 1989), in part because it can help individuals discover strategies that work well for them

(Hertzog et al., 2017; Flegal & Lustig, 2016). However, there is no guarantee such improvements will occur, and the magnitude of improvement probably depends on a number of factors, such as how item difficulty is maintained and used to foster continued improvement in the practice environment as the practiced skill improves.

Predicting Older Adults' Everyday Cognitive Function from Intellectual Abilities

In some instances, intellectual abilities predict everyday cognitive function in adults. For instance, Czaja et al. (2006) found that fluid and crystallized intelligence predicted use of technology, and in particular, use of computers, in everyday life. This was true at all ages, despite the large age differences in technology use. Fluid intelligence also predicts performance on some simulated everyday cognition tasks (Allaire & Marsiske, 2002). Chen, Hertzog, and Park (2017) found evidence that crystallized intelligence became a stronger predictor of simulated everyday cognition in older adults, relative to younger ages. They interpreted this finding as an increase in the importance of crystallized intelligence in determining older adults' everyday cognitive competence. Fluid intelligence remained a strong predictor of everyday cognition across the adult age range. See the Focus on Contemporary Research for more discussion of research on everyday cognition.

FOCUS ON CONTEMPORARY RESEARCH: HERTZOG ET AL.'S RESEARCH ON INTELLECTUAL ABILITY AND OTHER FACTORS AS PREDICTORS OF EVERYDAY COGNITION

Intellectual abilities may not be potent predictors of everyday cognition because factors other than intellectual ability determine performance (Phillips, Henry, & Martin, 2008). Colonia-Willner (1998) showed that age differences in inductive reasoning were not predictive of simulated banking decisions (mostly whether to grant a loan in a hypothetical application vignette) by managers currently employed by a major Brazilian bank. Instead, a measure of tacit knowledge of best practices in banking predicted evaluations of the quality of the simulated loan decisions. Hertzog, Park, Morrell, and Martin (2000) found that a latent variable of general cognition (closely related to Gf) predicted medication adherence errors assessed in the natural ecology, but did not account for age differences in adherence errors. In fact, the general ability factor acted as a suppressor that reduced a trend for older adults to do better in everyday adherence. A self-report of difficulty remembering to take the prescribed medications, taken before the assessment period for adherence, prospectively predicted later adherence errors, implying influences other than intellectual ability on managing one's medications. In other words, older adults forget to take their medications for a variety of reasons. Reductions over time in general intelligence comprise only one of those reasons.

Maintaining Intellectual Function in Old Age

Based on the available research evidence, it is at present difficult to make firm statements about how individuals should go about preserving intellectual functioning in old age. Certainly one should consider ways of preventing or mitigating disease associated with intellectual decline, such as cardiovascular disease. Maintaining healthy life practices, such as a program of physical activity, good nutrition, and early detection and treatment of diseases like diabetes or sleep apnea, is important for both longevity and continuing cognitive vitality (Crimmins, 2015). In particular, a regular program of aerobic exercise is perhaps the best means of protecting the nervous system and cognitive function. Likewise, avoiding risky behaviors such as tobacco consumption and excessive alcohol consumption reduces risk for diseases that can affect intellectual function. It is unclear at present whether an intellectually engaged lifestyle has additional protective benefits for maintaining intellectual abilities, although one can argue that it is at least valuable for maintaining a high quality of life, if not preservation of analytic intelligence. Perhaps the best means of preserving everyday competence is to focus on enhancing practical intelligence. Developing good habits for cognitive self-regulation in everyday life, a type of cognitive pragmatics, may be the best means of preserving everyday functioning even in the face of late-life decline in fluid intelligence (Hertzog et al., 2019).

CONCLUSION

Substantial progress has been made in our understanding of how intellectual abilities change over the human lifespan. The CHC model fares well in accounting for data on psychometrically measured ability tests, and the hierarchical model seems to emerge in childhood and remain qualitatively invariant across the human lifespan. The broad distinction of preservation of cognitive pragmatics as opposed to more substantial and earlier decline in cognitive mechanics continues to be supported by available data. However, a number of questions remain regarding how age correlates with different abilities, and whether these correlations will continue to change in future historical time. The biggest unanswered questions at present involve the modifiability of abilities and how to understand individual differences in intellectual development, particularly in old age. The large number of potentially relevant variables for explaining variation in intellectual decline in old age creates difficulties for evaluating the benefits and risks of different personal characteristics, including genetic profiles and lifestyle variables, that could moderate intellectual development in old age.

CHAPTER SUMMARY

This chapter considered how intellectual abilities change across the human lifespan, with an emphasis on adult development and aging. It takes as a foundation an assumption that analytical or academic intelligence can be captured by the taxonomy of abilities established in the Cattell–Horn–Carroll (CHC) model (McGrew, 2009). It is argued that this taxonomy captures a stable structure of intellectual abilities that differentiates after about age 7, is fully established at maturity, and remains in place across the adult lifespan.

The available evidence indicates there are developmental differences in rates of growth and change in intellectual abilities. In adulthood there are large cross-sectional differences indicating age-related decline in tests of fluid intelligence and other abilities such as spatial visualization. In contrast, cross-sectional studies suggest little change in crystallized intelligence until late in life. These patterns are complicated by the existence of cohort effects, or Flynn effects, in which more recently born generations score better on intellectual ability tests, including tests of fluid reasoning and spatial ability. Longitudinal studies suggest more benign magnitudes of change (that may be affected by practice effects and selective mortality). They also show individual differences in rates of intellectual change in both childhood and adulthood. Predictors of individual differences in rates of intellectual growth and decline vary across the life course, with contextual factors and lifestyle appearing to play a greater role in determining rates of intellectual decline in old age. Despite normative decline in intellectual abilities after age 60, some older adults maintain high levels of function into very old age, and there is the potential for plasticity (experience-dependent improvement) in ability performance in old age.

KEY TERMS

accelerated longitudinal designs • Cattell–Horn–Carroll (CHC) hierarchical model • cognitive mechanics • cognitive pragmatics • contextualist worldview • cross-sectional design • crystallized intelligence • dedifferentiation hypothesis • entity theorist • fluid intelligence • Flynn effect • longitudinal design • mechanistic theorist • neural plasticity • organismic theorist • plasticity of intelligence • sequential sampling design • skill theorist • speed contamination hypothesis • stability coefficients

COMPREHENSION AND REFLECTION QUESTIONS

1. What is the CHC model of intelligence? What are the different modal shapes of lifespan development of the second-order factors, fluid and crystallized intelligence?
2. Why does the Flynn effect create problems for estimating age changes in an intellectual ability from cross-sectional data? What is a cohort effect? Is there evidence that cohort effects exist that could be contributing to observed cross-sectional age differences?
3. Are there individual differences in rates of change in different cognitive abilities? How highly correlated are the changes? According to Figure 11.3, how much of overall change variance can be attributed to a general factor of change?
4. What variable has been identified that predicts individual differences in intellectual growth in childhood? What variables may predict individual differences in rates of intellectual change in adulthood and old age?
5. How is plasticity in adult cognition often assessed? Can older adults' test performance be improved through strategy training or practice? How broadly does a trained cognitive procedure transfer to other task contexts?

References

Ackerman, P. L. (2000). Domain-specific knowledge as the "dark matter" of adult intelligence: Gf/Gc personality and interest correlates. *Journal of Gerontology: Psychological Sciences, 55,* P69–P84.

Ackerman, P. L., & Wolman, S. D. (2007). Determinants and validity of self-estimates of abilities and self-concept measures. *Journal of Experimental Psychology: Applied, 13,* 57-78.

Allaire, J. C., & Marsiske, M. (2002). Well- and ill-defined measures of everyday cognition: Relationship to older adults' intellectual ability and functional status. *Psychology and Aging, 17,* 101-115. doi: 10.1037//0882-7974.17.1.101

Anastasi, A., & Urbina, S. (1997). *Psychological testing* (7th ed.). Upper Saddle River, NJ: Prentice Hall.

Baddeley, A. (1986). *Working memory.* New York: Oxford University Press.

Bailey, H. R., Dunlosky, J., & Hertzog, C. (2014). Does strategy training reduce age deficits in working memory? *Gerontology, 60,* 346-356. doi: 10.1159/000356699

Ball, K., Berch, D. B., Helmer, K. F., Jobe, J. B., Leveck, M. D., Marsiske, M., et al. (2002). Effects of cognitive training interventions with older adults: A randomized controlled trial. *Journal of the American Medical Association, 288,* 2271–2281.

Baltes, P. B. (1997). On the incomplete architecture of human ontogeny: Selection, optimization, and compensation as a foundation for developmental theory. *American Psychologist, 52*, 366–380.

Baltes, P. B., & Nesselroade, J. R. (1979). History and rationale of longitudinal research. In J. R. Nesselroade & P. B. Baltes (eds.), *Longitudinal research in the study of behavior and development.* New York: Academic Press.

Baltes, P. B., Reese, H. W., & Nesselroade, J. R. (1988). *Life-span developmental psychology: Introduction to research methods.* Hillsdale, NJ: Lawrence Erlbaum Associates.

Baltes, P. B., & Smith, J. (2008). The fascination of wisdom: Its nature, ontogeny, and function. *Perspectives on Psychological Science, 3*, 56-62.

Baltes, P. B., Sowarka, D., & Kliegl, R. (1989). Cognitive training research on fluid intelligence in old age: What can older adults achieve by themselves? *Psychology and Aging, 4*, 217-221.

Baltes, P. B., Staudinger, U. M., & Lindenberger, U. (1999). Lifespan psychology: Theory and application to intellectual functioning. *Annual Review of Psychology, 50*, 471-507.

Basak, C., Boot, W. R., Voss, M. W. & Kramer, A. F. (2008). Can training in a real-time strategy videogame attenuate cognitive decline in older adults? *Psychology & Aging, 23*, 765-777.

Bherer, L., Kramer, A. F., Peterson, M. S., Colcombe, S., Erickson, K., & Becic, E. (2008). Transfer effects in task-set cost and dual-task cost after dual-task training in older and younger adults: Further evidence for cognitive plasticity in attentional control in late adulthood. *Experimental Aging Research, 34*, 188-219. doi: 10.1080/036107730802070068

Birren, J. E., & Fisher, L. M. (1995). Aging and speed of behavior: Possible consequences for psychological functioning. *Annual Review of Psychology, 46*, 329-353.

Bornstein, M. H. (2014). Human infancy . . . and the rest of the life span. *Annual Review of Psychology, 65*, 121-128. doi: 10.1146/annurev-psych-120710-100359

Botwinick, J. (1977). Intellectual abilities. In J. E. Birren & K. W. Schaie (eds.), *Handbook of the psychology of aging* (pp. 580-605). New York: Van Nostrand Reinhold.

Brickley, P. G., Keith, T. Z., & Wolfle, L. M. (1995). The three-stratum theory of cognitive abilities: Test of the structure of intellect across the adult life span. *Intelligence, 20*, 309-328.

Buchman, A. S., Tanne, D., Boyle, P. A., Shah, R. C., Leurgans, S. E., & Bennett, D. A. (2009). Kidney function is associated with the rate of cognitive decline in the elderly. *Neurology, 73*, 920-927.

Carroll, J. B. (1993). *Human cognitive abilities: A survey of factor analytic studies.* Cambridge: Cambridge University Press.

Cattell, R. B. (1971). *Abilities: Their structure, growth, and action.* Boston: Houghton Mifflin.

Chen, X., Hertzog, C., & Park, D. C. (2017). Cognitive predictors of everyday problem solving across the lifespan. *Gerontology, 63*, 372-384. doi: 10.1159/000459622

Clarkson-Smith, L., & Hartley, A. A. (1990). Structural equation models of relationships between exercise and cognitive abilities. *Psychology and Aging, 5,* 437-446.

Colcombe, S., & Kramer, A. F. (2003). Fitness effects on the cognitive function of older adults: A meta-analytic study. *Psychological Science, 14,* 125–130.

Colonia-Willner, R. (1998). Practical intelligence at work: Relationships between aging and cognitive efficiency among managers in a bank environment. *Psychology and Aging, 13,* 45–57.

Crimmins, E. M. (2015). Lifespan and healthspan: Past, present, and promise. *Gerontologist, 55,* 901-911. doi: 10.1093/geront/gnv130

Czaja, S., Charness, N., Fisk, A. D., Hertzog, C., Nair, S., Rogers, W. A., & Sharit, J. (2006) Factors Predicting the Use of Technology: Findings from the Center for Research and Education on Aging and Technology Enhancement (CREATE). *Psychology and Aging, 21,* 333-352.

Deary, I. J., Whiteman, M. C., Starr, J. M., Whalley, L. J., & Fox, H. C. (2004). The impact of childhood intelligence on later life: Following up the Scottish Mental Surveys of 1932 and 1947. *Journal of Personality and Social Psychology, 86,* 130-147.

deFrias, C. M., Lövdén, M., Lindenberger, U., & Nilsson, L-G. (2007). Revisiting the de-differentiation hypothesis with longitudinal multi-cohort data. *Intelligence, 35,* 381-392.

Dixon, R. A., & Hertzog, C. (1996). Theoretical issues in cognitive aging. In F. Blanchard-Fields & T. Hess (eds.), *Perspectives on Cognitive Change in Adult Development and Aging* (pp. 25-65). New York: McGraw-Hill.

Duncan, T. E., Duncan, S. C., & Strycker, L. A. (2006). *An introduction to latent variable growth curve modeling: Concepts, issues, and applications.* New York and London: Routledge.

Dweck, C. S. (2006). *Mindset.* New York: Random House.

Eggermont, L. H. P., Milberg, W. P., Lipsitz, L. A., Scherder, E. J. A., & Leveille, S. G. (2009). Physical activity and executive function in aging: The MOBILIZE Boston study. *Journal of the American Geriatric Society, 57,* 1750-1756.

Embretson, S.E., & Reise, S.P. (2000). *Item response theory for psychologists.* Mahwah, NJ: Lawrence Erlbaum Associates.

Erickson, K. I., Prakash, R. S., Voss, M. W., Chaddock, L., et al. (2010). Brain-derived neurotrophic factor is associated with age-related decline in hippocampal volume. *Journal of Neuroscience, 30,* 5368-5375. doi: 10.1523/JNEUROSCI.6251-09.2010

Ferrer, E., & McArdle, J. J. (2011). Longitudinal modeling of developmental changes in psychological research. *Current Directions in Psychological Science, 19,* 149-154.

Flegal, K. E., & Lustig, C. (2016). You can go your own way: Effectiveness of participant-driven versus experimenter-driven processing strategies in memory training and transfer. *Aging, Neuropsychology, and Cognition, 23,* 389-417. doi: 10.1080/13825585.2015.1108386

Flynn, J. R. (2007). *What is intelligence? Beyond the Flynn effect.* Cambridge: Cambridge University Press.

Gould, S. J. (1981). *The mismeasure of man.* New York: Norton.

Harris, S. E., Fox, H., Wright, A. F., Hayward, C., Starr, J. M., Whalley, L. J., & Deary, I. J. (2006). The brain-derived neurotrophic factor Val66Met polymorphism is associated with age-related change in reasoning skills. *Molecular Psychiatry, 11,* 505-513.

Hartley, A. (2006). Changing role of the speed of processing construct in the cognitive psychology of human aging. In J. E. Birren & K. W. Schaie (eds.), *Handbook of the psychology of aging* (6th ed., pp. 183-207). Amsterdam: Elsevier Academic Press.

Heathcote, A. S., Brown, S., & Mewhort, D. J. K. (2000). The power law repealed: The case for an exponential law of practice. *Psychonomic Bulletin & Review, 7,* 185-207.

Hertzog, C. (1989). The influence of cognitive slowing on age differences in intelligence. *Developmental Psychology, 25,* 636–651.

Hertzog, C. (1996). Research design in studies of aging and cognition. In J. E. Birren & K. W. Schaie (eds.), *Handbook of the Psychology of Aging* (4th ed., pp. 24-37). New York: Academic Press.

Hertzog, C. (2008). Theoretical approaches to the study of cognitive aging: An individual-differences perspective. In S. M. Hofer & D. F. Alwin (eds.), *Handbook of cognitive aging: Interdisciplinary perspectives* (pp. 34-49). Thousand Oaks, CA: Sage.

Hertzog, C., & Bleckley, M. K. (2001). Age differences in the structure of intelligence: Influences of information processing speed. *Intelligence, 29,* 191-217.

Hertzog, C., Dixon, R. A., Hultsch, D. F., & MacDonald, S. W. S. (2003). Latent change models of adult cognition: Are changes in processing speed and working memory associated with changes in episodic memory? *Psychology and Aging, 18,* 755–769.

Hertzog, C., Lustig, E., Pearman, A., & Waris, A. (2019). Behaviors and strategies supporting everyday memory in older adults. *Gerontology.* doi: 10.1159/000495910.

Hertzog, C., Park, D. C., Morrell, R. W., & Martin, M. (2000). Ask and ye shall receive: Behavioral specificity in the accuracy of subjective memory complaints. *Applied Cognitive Psychology, 14,* 257-275. doi: 10.1002(SICI)1099-0720(200005/06) 14:3<257::AID-ACP651>3.0.CO;2-0

Hertzog, C., & Schaie, K. W. (1986). Stability and change in adult intelligence: 1. Analysis of longitudinal covariance structures. *Psychology and Aging, 1,* 159-171.

Hertzog, C., & Schaie, K. W. (1988). Stability and change in adult intelligence: 2. Simultaneous analysis of longitudinal means and covariance structures. *Psychology and Aging, 3,* 122-130. doi: 10.1037/0882-7974.3.2.122

Hertzog, C., Sinclair, S. M., & Dunlosky, J. (2010). Age differences in the monitoring of learning: Cross-sectional evidence of spared resolution across the adult life span. *Developmental Psychology, 46,* 939-948. doi:10.1037/a0019812

Hofer, S. M., Flaherty, B. P., & Hoffman, L. (2006). Cross-sectional analysis of time-dependent data: Mean-induced association in age-heterogeneous samples and an alternative method based on sequential narrow age-cohort samples. *Multivariate Behavioral Research, 41*, 165–187.

Horn, J. L. (1985). Remodeling old models of intelligence: Gf–Gc theory. In B B. Wolman (ed.), *Handbook of intelligence* (pp. 267-300). New York: Wiley.

Horn, J. L., & Hofer, S. M. (1992). Major abilities and development in the adult period. In R. J. Sternberg & C. A. Berg (eds.), *Intellectual development* (pp. 44-99). New York: Cambridge University Press.

Hultsch, D. F., Hertzog, C., Dixon, R. A., & Small, B. J. (1998). *Memory change in the aged.* New York: Cambridge University Press.

Hunt, E. (1978). Mechanics of verbal ability. *Psychological Review, 85*, 109-130.

Jensen, A. R. (1998). *The g factor: The science of mental ability.* New York: Praeger.

Jun, G., Naj, A. C., Beecham, G., Wang, L.-S., Buros, J., et al. (2010). Meta-analysis confirms CR1, CLU, and PICALM as Alzheimer's disease risk loci and reveals interactions with APoE genotypes. *Archives of Neurology, 67*, 1473-1484. doi: 10.1001/ archneurol.2010.201

Karbach, J., & Verhaeghen, P. (2014). Making working memory work: A meta-analysis of executive-control and working memory training in older adults. *Psychological Science, 25*, 2027-2037. doi: 10.1177/0956797614548725.

Kyllonen, P. C. (2002). G: Knowledge, speed, strategies, or working-memory capacity? A systems perspective. In R. J. Sternberg & E. L. Grigorenko (eds.), *The general factor of intelligence: How general is it?* (pp. 415-445). Mahwah, NJ: Lawrence Erlbaum Associates.

Lindenberger, U. (2014). Human cognitive aging: Corriger la fortune? *Science, 346*, 572-578.

Lindenberger, U., Ghisletta, P., von Oertzen, T., & Hertzog, C. (2011). Cross-sectional age-related variance extraction: What's change got to do with it? *Psychology and Aging, 26*, 34-47. doi: 10.1037/a0020525

Lindenberger, U., Nagel, I. E., Chicherio, C., Li, S-C., Heekeren, H. R., & Bäckman, L. (2008). Age-related decline in brain resources modulates genetic effects on cognitive functioning. *Frontiers in Neuroscience, 2*, 234-244.

Lustig, C., Hasher, L., & Tonev, S. (2006). Distraction as a determinant of processing speed. *Psychonomic Bulletin & Review, 13*, 619-623.

McArdle, J. J., Ferrer-Caja, E., Hamagami, F., & Woodcock, R. W. (2002). Comparative longitudinal structural analyses of the growth and decline of multiple intellectual abilities over the life span. *Developmental Psychology, 38*, 115-142.

McEwen, B. S., & Gianolos, P. J. (2011). Stress- and allostasis-induced brain plasticity. *Annual Review of Medicine, 62*, 431-445. doi: 10.1146/annrev-med-052209-100430

McGrew, K. S. (2009). CHC theory and the human cognitive abilities project: Standing on the shoulders of giants in psychometric intelligence research. *Intelligence, 37*, 1-10.

Mumaw, R. J., & Pellegrino, J. W. (1984). Individual differences in complex spatial processing. *Journal of Educational Psychology, 76*, 920-939.

Nagel, I. E., Chicherio, C., Li, S-C., & von Oertzen, T., et al. (2008). Human aging magnifies genetic effects on executive functioning and working memory. *Frontiers in Human Neuroscience, 2*, article 1. doi: 10.3389/neuro.09.001.2008

Palejwala, M. H., & Fine, J. G. (2015). Gender differences in latent cognitive abilities in children aged 2 to 7. *Intelligence, 48*, 96-108.

Phillips, L. H., Henry, J. D., & Martin, M. (2008). Adult aging and prospective memory: The importance of ecological validity. In M. Kliegel, M. A. McDaniel, & G. O. Einstein (eds.), *Prospective memory: Cognitive, neuroscience, developmental, and applied perspectives* (pp. 161-185). New York: Taylor and Francis/ Lawrence Erlbaum Associates.

Pietschnig, J. & Voracek, M. (2015). One century of global IQ gains: A formal meta-analysis of the Flynn effect (1909-2013). *Perspectives on Psychological Science, 10*, 282-315. doi: 10.1177/ 1745691615577701

Plemons, J. K., Willis, S. L., & Baltes, P. B. (1978). Modifiability of fluid intelligence in aging: Short-term longitudinal training approach. *Journal of Gerontology, 33*, 224-231.

Rabbitt, P. M. A. (1993). Does it all go together when it goes? The nineteenth Bartlett memorial lecture. *Quarterly Journal of Experimental Psychology, 46A*, 385-434.

Raz, N., Lindenberger, U., Ghisletta, P., Rodrigue, K. M., Kennedy, K. M., & Acker, J. M. (2008). Neuroanatomical correlates of fluid intelligence in healthy adults and persons with vascular risk factors. *Cerebral Cortex, 18*, 718-726.

Raz, N., Daugherty, A. M., Sethi, S. K., Arshad, M., & Haacke, E. M. (2017). Age differences in arterial and venous extra-cerebral blood flow in healthy adults: Contributions of vascular risk factors and genetic variants. *Brain Structure and Function, 222*, 2641-2653.

Reese, H. W., & Overton, W. F. (1970). Models of development and theories of development. In L. R. Goulet & P. B. Baltes (eds.), *Life-span developmental psychology: Theory and research*. New York: Academic Press.

Reynolds, C. A. (2008). Genetic and environmental influences on cognitive change. In S. M. Hofer & D. F. Alwin (eds.), *Handbook of cognitive aging: Interdisciplinary perspectives* (pp. 557-574). Thousand Oaks, CA: Sage.

Rogosa, D., Brandt, D., & Zimowski, M. (1982). A growth curve approach to the measurement of change. *Psychological Bulletin, 92*, 726-748.

Rönnlund, M., & Nilsson, L-G. (2008). The magnitude, generality, and determinants of Flynn effects on forms of declarative memory and visuospatial ability: Time-sequential analyses of data from a Swedish cohort study. *Intelligence, 36*, 192-209.

Salthouse, T. A. (1982). *Adult cognition: An experimental psychology of human aging.* New York: Springer-Verlag.

Salthouse, T. A. (1996). The processing-speed theory of adult age differences in cognition. *Psychological Review, 103*, 403–428.

Salthouse, T. A. (2000). Methodological assumptions in cognitive aging research. In F. I. M. Craik & T. A. Salthouse (eds.), *The handbook of aging and cognition* (2nd ed., pp. 467-498). Mahwah, NJ: Lawrence Erlbaum Associates.

Salthouse, T. A. (2006). Mental exercise and mental aging: Evaluating the validity of the "use it or lose it" hypothesis. *Perspectives on Psychological Science, 1*, 68-87.

Salthouse, T. A. (2012). Are individual differences in rates of aging greater at older ages? *Neurobiology of Aging, 33*, 2373-2381.

Salthouse, T. A., & Ferrer-Caja, E. (2003). What needs to be explained to account for age-related effects on multiple cognitive variables? *Psychology and Aging, 18*, 91-110.

Schaie, K. W. (1965). A general model for the study of developmental problems. *Psychological Bulletin, 64*, 92-107.

Schaie, K. W. (1977). Quasi-experimental designs in the psychology of aging. In J. E. Birren & K. W. Schaie (eds.), *Handbook of the psychology of aging* (pp. 39-58). New York: Van Nostrand Reinhold.

Schaie, K. W. (1989). Perceptual speed in adulthood: Cross-sectional and longitudinal studies. *Psychology and Aging, 4*, 443-453.

Schaie, K. W. (1994). The course of adult intellectual development. *American Psychologist, 49*, 304-313.

Schaie, K. W. (2012). *Developmental influences on adult intelligence: The Seattle Longitudinal Study* (2nd ed.). New York: Oxford University Press.

Schaie, K. W., & Hertzog, C. (1982). Longitudinal methods. In B. B. Wolman (ed.), *Handbook of developmental psychology* (pp. 91-115). Englewood Cliffs, NJ: Prentice Hall.

Schmiedek, F., Lövdén, M., & Lindenberger, U. (2010). Hundred days of cognitive training enhance broad cognitive abilities in adulthood: Findings from the COGITO study. *Frontiers in Aging Neuroscience, 2*, 1-10.

Schooler, C., & Kaplan, L. J. (2009). How those who have, thrive: Mechanisms underlying the well-being of the advantaged in later life. In H. B. Bosworth & C. Hertzog (eds.), *Aging and cognition: Research methodologies and empirical advances* (pp. 121-141). Washington, DC: American Psychological Association.

Shadish, W., Cook, T. D., & Campbell, D. T. (2002). *Experimental and quasi-experimental designs for generalized causal inference*. Boston, MA: Houghton Mifflin.

Simons, D. J., Boot, W. R., Charness, N., Gathercole, S. E., Chabris, C. S., Hambrick, D. Z., & Stine-Morrow, E. A. L. (2016). Do "brain-training" programs work? *Psychological Science in the Public Interest, 17*, 103-186.

Sink, K. M., Espeland, M. A., Castro, C. M., et al. (2015). Effect of a 24-month physical activity intervention vs. health education on cognitive outcomes in sedentary older adults: The LIFE Randomized Trial. *Journal of the American Medical Association, 314*, 781-790. doi: 10.1001/jama.2015.9617

Spiro, A. III, & Brady, C. B. (2008). Integrating health into cognitive aging research and theory: Quo vadis? In S. M. Hofer & D. F. Alwin (eds.), *Handbook of cognitive aging: Interdisciplinary perspectives* (pp. 260-283). Thousand Oaks, CA: Sage.

Sternberg, R. J. (1983). Components of human intelligence. *Cognition*, *15*, 1-48. doi: 10.1016/0010-0277(83)90032-X.

Sternberg, R. J. (1985). *Beyond IQ: A triarchic theory of human intelligence.* Cambridge: Cambridge University Press.

Tucker-Drob, E. M. (2011). Global and domain-specific changes in cognition throughout adulthood. *Developmental Psychology*, *47*, 331-343. doi: 10.1037/a0021361.

Tucker-Drob, E. M., & Briley, D. A. (2014). Continuity of genetic environmental influences on cognition across the life span: A meta-analysis of longitudinal twin and adoption studies. *Psychological Bulletin*, *140*, 949-979. doi: 10.1037/a0035893

Verhaeghen, P., & Salthouse, T. A. (1997). Meta-analyses of age-cognition relations in adulthood: Estimates of linear and non-linear age effects and structural models. *Psychological Bulletin*, *122*, 231-249.

von Stumm, S., & Ackerman, P. L. (2013). Investment and intellect: A review and meta-analysis. *Psychological Bulletin*, *109*, 841-869. doi: 10.1037/a0030746

von Stumm, S., & Plomin, R. (2015). Socioeconomic status and the growth of intelligence from infancy through adolescence. *Intelligence*, *48*, 30-36. doi: 10.1016/j.intell.2014.10.002

Voss, M. W., Erickson, K. I., Prakash, R. S., Chaddock, L., et al. (2013). Neurobiological markers of exercise-related brain plasticity in older adults. *Brain, Behavior, and Immunity*, 28, 90-99. doi: 10.1016/j.bbi.2012.10.021

Wagner, R. K., & Sternberg, R. J. (1985). Practical intelligence in real-world pursuits: The role of tacit knowledge. *Journal of Personality and Social Psychology*, *49*, 436-458.

Wechsler, D. (1939). *Measurement of adult intelligence.* Baltimore, MD: Williams & Wilkins.

Wechsler, D. (2012). *Wechsler Preschool and Primary Scale of Intelligence – Fourth Edition Technical and Interpretive Manual.* San Antonio, TX: Psychological Corporation.

Wilhelm, O. (2005). Measuring reasoning ability. In O. Wilhelm & R. W. Engle (eds.), *Handbook of understanding and measuring intelligence* (pp. 373-392). Thousand Oaks, CA: Sage.

Zelinski, E. M., & Kennison, R. F. (2007). Not your father's test scores: Cohort reduces psychometric aging effects. *Psychology and Aging*, *22*, 546-557.

PART IV
Applications of Intelligence Research

12 Extremes of Intelligence

JULIAN G. ELLIOTT AND WILMA C. RESING

Previous chapters have explored the dimensions of intelligence, its measurement, and various approaches to understanding it. We have seen that, for many aspects of human functioning, the distribution of human intelligence approximates to a normal distribution. This means that if we were to place a score for each person on a graph, the numbers of those at each point on the x-axis would decrease as we moved away from the mean. These numbers fall away particularly sharply as we move toward the extremes, a distribution that is often referred to as the bell curve.

IQ tests are typically designed and modified to ensure that scores fit the so-called normal distribution, with the distribution of scores greatest in the center of the curve and lower as we move to the tails. Generally, those deemed to be at the intellectual extremes are typically located more than two standard deviations from the mean. As most popular IQ tests have a standard deviation of 15, the somewhat arbitrary cut-off points will be where IQ scores are approximately lower than 70 or greater than 130. These areas represent approximately 2 percent of the population at each end of the distribution.

What adds complexity to our understanding of intelligence and the bell curve is that, unlike many measures assumed to fit a normal distribution – things like height, weight, or the time it takes to run 800 meters – there are uncertainties and disagreements as to what exactly it is that we are identifying in the distribution (and extremes). If we accept Boring's famous statement (Boring, 1923) that intelligence is what intelligence tests measure, consideration of those functioning at the intellectual extremes is seemingly a relatively easy task. We simply identify those individuals whose scores are very high or very low on appropriate measures of intelligence. Indeed, this has been the dominant practice for more than a century.

The centrality of IQ as a measure of intelligence went largely unchallenged until the second half of the twentieth century. We have considered this issue in many of the chapters of this book, and we will examine it as it pertains to the extremes, below.

Intelligence Assessed at the Higher Extreme of the IQ Distribution

Historically, a score of more than 130 on an IQ test typically resulted in a determination that an individual was "**gifted**"; a score of 160+, achieved by 1 in 10,000 people, indicating that an individual was "profoundly gifted." According to this view, giftedness equated to high intellectual ability, as measured by IQ. Obviously, there are a number of conceptual and methodological pressure points to consider here, in particular, whether giftedness should be seen as synonymous with high intelligence, whether measured by IQ or not. A second important issue concerns the extent to which current measures of intelligence/giftedness are able to accurately identify potential high achievers irrespective of social or cultural background.

Is Giftedness Synonymous with High Intelligence?

In order to say whether giftedness and intelligence are synonomous, we need to determine the meanings of the terms "intelligence" and "giftedness," both of which are now commonly used to describe a wider range of skill areas than was the case for much of the twentieth century. In a study of gifted and talented identification in various American states (NAGC, 2009), for example, the most prevalent domain cited was intellectual, followed in descending order by creative, performing/visual arts, specific academic areas, and leadership.

If high intelligence refers solely to the intellectual domain, then it would seem that this is widely seen as the most important of several different areas of giftedness – but it is not synonymous with the term "giftedness." However, if high intelligence is understood to encompass abilities in a variety of spheres (as is discussed throughout this book), the overlap between the two constructs becomes much greater. Definitions matter!

In some cases, a distinction is made between cognitive functions (the realm of the intellect) and broader areas of performance. Thus, the National Association for Gifted Children (NAGC) defines gifted individuals as those

> who demonstrate outstanding levels of aptitude (defined as an exceptional ability to reason and learn) or competence (documented performance or achievement in the top 10% or rarer) in one or more domains. Domains include any structured area of activity with its own symbol system (e.g., mathematics, music, and language) and/or set of sensorimotor skills (e.g., painting, dance, and sports). (NAGC, 2018)

Such a notion is quite different from earlier conceptions of giftedness that were almost wholly based upon an IQ score. This older view reflects a belief that individuals scoring highly on IQ tests have a generic, innate ability in reasoning and problem solving that can serve them well in school and life generally.

Terman's Contributions

An early leader in the field, Terman, recognized that factors other than general intelligence are also important for high achievement. He noted that intelligence tests are not able to:

> predict what direction the achievement will take ... both interest patterns and special aptitudes play important roles in the making of a gifted scientist, mathematician, mechanic, artist, poet, or musical composer. (Terman, 1954, p. 224)

Terman was interested to discover whether genius (typically involving greater accomplishment than significant performance-related success or eminence) is primarily a consequence of superior intelligence. In his famous study of approximately 1,500 children, all with very high IQ scores (with an average of 151), Terman and his colleagues followed the children's progress from middle childhood, in 1921, into later adulthood.

The professional achievements of many of Terman's participants, colloquially known as "termites," were certainly very impressive. In addition, they tended to have highly productive lives in several other respects – physical health, marital relationships, mental health, and social functioning were all more positive compared with their peers. However, we cannot conclude that it was their high intelligence that was the key determinant of these outcomes, as it is possible that several other factors were influential in their success. For example, while there was only a 5-point IQ difference (155 versus 150) between groups deemed to be more and less successful in adulthood, the fathers of the higher performing group were more than twice as likely to have a college degree and professional employment.

One methodological difficulty in Terman's study was that student recruitment relied upon recommendations from others, particularly teachers. Unsurprisingly, perhaps, those selected tended to come from white, middle-class homes and were likely to benefit from relative affluence, family and social support, and a range of personal contacts that could help them in their later lives. Despite the fact that such factors are highly unlikely to fully explain the impressive success of the termites, the great weakness of Terman's study is that Terman did not work with a group of children that was representative of the general population. For this reason, it is difficult to offer generalizations about the impact of very high IQ in respect of all children.

The Duke Longitudinal High IQ Study

Another large-scale, longitudinal study of the top 1 percent of children has been conducted over the past 35 years at Duke University. Here the selection criteria employed were exceptional ability in mathematical and/or verbal reasoning based upon performance in the SAT-Math and SAT-Verbal tests administered at the age of 13. Findings from the huge data set accumulated have shown that not only have this group been more academically successful than their peers, but also that there were large differences in outcomes within this sample. In reflecting upon the achieve-ments of the most able of the participants (the top 1 in 10,000 of the general population), Makel et al. (2016) comment that, "By age 38, the magnitude of their creativity, occupational success, and professional stature was astonishing" (p. 1004). These findings suggest that there is no intellectual threshold for outstanding performance although, of course, drive and opportunity will also be significant contributory factors. Interestingly, and perhaps not unexpectedly, those who were at the highest peak of achievement in the arts and humanities were more likely to have higher verbal ability scores, with math ability being more associated with accomplishments in the sciences, technology, engineering, and mathematics.

One of the advantages of using SATs, rather than measures of IQ, with young adolescents is that, because this form of assessment is usually undertaken by older students, there was unlikely to be a **ceiling effect**. This term describes a situation where a test is insufficiently demanding to enable a spread of performance; put simply, too many people find the test to be easy. A further measurement problem with commonly employed IQ tests, such as the Wechsler Scales, which have variants used with children and adults, is that at the highest levels of performance a substantial rise in an individual's score can be achieved by success on a relatively few items. As a result, discriminations between respondents may not be based upon sufficiently reliable or valid data.

Theories Related to High Intelligence and Giftedness

The perceived relationship between high intelligence and giftedness has been influ-enced by important theorists such as Renzulli, Gardner, and Sternberg. Renzulli (1978, 2005) has argued that the development of gifted behavior is driven by above-average ability, creativity, and task commitment – the three constituent elements of Renzulli's Three-Ring Conception of Giftedness (See Figure 12.1). According to Renzulli's theory, all three need to operate together for the highest levels of achievement to be realized. In relation to above-average ability, Renzulli refers to both general and specific levels of functioning. Superior functioning at a general level involves high levels of abstract thinking, the capacity to adapt to novel situations, and the ability to retrieve information both rapidly and accurately. At a specific level, highly able individuals are able to apply these general abilities to specific areas of knowledge. Task commitment concerns interest and motivation, self-confidence, and determination to succeed. Finally, creativity involves acting flexibly, showing originality, being open to new experiences, and being prepared to take risks.

Renzulli (1978, 2005) contends that there are two kinds of giftedness: school-house giftedness, as witnessed in school-related activities; and creative/productive giftedness, which is concerned with creativity and originality.

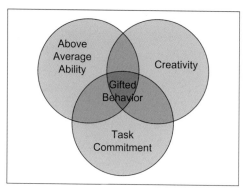

Figure 12.1 The three constituent elements of Renzulli's Three-Ring Conception of Giftedness. According to Renzulli's theory, all three need to operate together for the highest levels of achievement to be realized. (Source: Renzulli, 2005)

Theories of intelligence put forward by Sternberg and Gardner have had an important impact upon what is meant when we speak of high intelligence. Sternberg's (1988, 1996) view that "successful intelligence" should include creative and practical, alongside analytical abilities, and Gardner's conception of multiple intelligences (MI) (1983), embracing a range of different domains, have greatly influenced modern conceptions of giftedness (and talent).

Gardner argues that our society has become overly preoccupied with linguistic and logical-mathematical forms of intelligence, typically assessed by IQ tests. He contends that, instead, we should also value, and seek to develop, several other forms of intelligence: spatial, bodily–kinesthetic, musical, intrapersonal, interpersonal, and naturalist (and possibly, moral, spiritual, and existential). Rather than conceiving these intelligences as operating in isolation, Gardner considers that they rarely function independently of one another.

Application of Multiple Intelligences and Successful Intelligence Theories to the Education of Gifted Students

Gardner's theory has had wide appeal to educators who are eager to focus upon the "whole" child, rather than the narrow domains covered by high stakes tests. It is hardly surprising, therefore, that his conception sits favorably with those charged to develop and operate programs for gifted and talented students. It particularly plays to the sympathies of those who wish to nurture the particular skills and talents of children who may not thrive on traditional classroom activity, and has had the beneficial effect of helping teachers to reflect upon their practice and, in some cases, broaden their educational focus in ways that many would perceive as helpful. However, the theory has been criticized; for example, is it really meaningful to describe all of these abilities as "intelligences"? Furthermore, moving from broad theory to meaningful educational practice has often proved to be a challenge. Currently, research showing how MI theory can be utilized in gifted education has not been highly persuasive (Plucker, Callahan, & Tomchin, 1996; Visser, Ashton, & Vernon, 2006).

Sternberg and his colleagues have made greater efforts to examine the application of his theory to educational practice. In respect to high ability, he has sought to identify approaches for the selection of university students and develop tools to identify gifted school students whose abilities may not be immediately apparent in school contexts (Kornilov, Tan, Elliott, Sternberg, & Grigorenko, 2012; Sternberg, 2010, 2016; Sternberg & the Rainbow Project Collaborators, 2006).

Sternberg has subsequently extended his theory to emphasize the importance of wisdom, citizenship, and ethical behavior (Sternberg, 1998, 2005). With regard to high performance, Sternberg noted that a person may be highly able analytically (with a superior IQ) but also act foolishly or unethically – the relationship between IQ and wisdom is quite small. Sternberg has queried whether the emphasis of modern education systems upon fostering a form of academic achievement that is driven by testing has resulted in the production of "smart fools" (Sternberg, 2002): people who are high scorers on conventional measures of intelligence, but who are often not suited to help the world to become a better place (see also Wallis, 2017). The steady rise of IQ scores across the world by as many as 30 points during the past century doesn't seem to have helped us resolve many of our major problems. In his opinion, IQ tests have outserved their unique usefulness for identifying the gifted because tackling our greatest social, political and environmental challenges requires creativity, common sense, and wisdom (Sternberg, 2017). These qualities are often lacking in those with stellar IQs who, as we know from the many crises and scandals reported in the media, often engage in remarkably stupid behaviors (Sternberg, 2008).

Gardner's and Sternberg's work, moving beyond IQ, has emphasized the contributions of the social and cultural environment upon intellectual functioning. In line with such thinking, theoretical conceptions of giftedness began to emphasize multidimensional models involving ongoing reciprocal interactions between the individual, their environment, and the sociocultural context in which they developed (Heller, Mönks, Subotnik, & Sternberg, 2000). Such ideas are in tune with increasingly popular philosophical ideas and theories (e.g. situated cognition, and legitimate peripheral participation) that were influenced by the work of the Russian psychologists Vygotsky and Leont'ev in the early twentieth century. The theory of **situated cognition** argues that knowledge is inseparable from action, and is situated in activities that are closely bound to the individual's social, cultural, and physical contexts. The concept of **legitimate peripheral participation** is employed to describe the process by which the newcomer gains experience and expertise via active participation within a particular community of practice. These, and other similar, theoretical perspectives emphasized the role and development of the learner in acquiring skills in specific social contexts, and the importance of expert others in providing closely tailored assistance (sometimes known as *scaffolded instruction*), to facilitate the individual's learning process.

Such conceptualizations imply that high ability/giftedness is not simply located in the individual and uniquely revealed by intelligence tests or even by measures of personality and attainment. Rather, proficiency is dependent upon the interactions of the individual with multiple aspects of their environment. On this basis, to identify and enable the realization of the potential of highly able children, assessment and intervention should operate using real-world problems, and involve carefully tailored support and guidance.

The Continuing Debate over the Identification and Causes of Giftedness

While there is greater recognition of the need to consider special abilities, as well as general intelligence (Lubinski, 2016) in some quarters, there continues to be a disconnect between IQ-based approaches to identification and selection and the increasingly complex scientific conceptions of giftedness that now exist in the research literature. Warne (2016) notes that some specialists in gifted education seek to avoid the term "intelligence" altogether and instead refer to "above-average ability," "high ability," "aptitude," and "cognitive analytic abilities." In educational contexts, however, decisions will often be influenced by the availability of resources and political pressures. Noting the relatively high correlations typically found between IQ and academic performance (although, perhaps these correlations are often not as high as you might think – Mackintosh (2011) states that these range from 0.4 to 0.7), it is, perhaps, unsurprising that many school districts continue to use standardized intelligence tests as a key criterion for selecting students for gifted programs (Plucker & Callahan, 2014). The tests will appeal to administrators because they take relatively little time to administer and score, tend to be less expensive than more complex assessments, and because it is often difficult to overcome organizational inertia in respect to large-scale educational change (Persson, 2017). They also provide the appearance of "objectivity." It is also possible that they will be favored by socially advantaged stakeholders whose offspring are more likely to benefit from the use of such measures (Subotnik, Stoeger, & Olszewski-Kubilius, 2017).

It is interesting to note that in the United States, those considered to be intelligent are often described as "smart," although this term can have a rather more practical "street" emphasis. Within this vernacular, you can be very smart, and you can become very smart. In contrast, it is less common to find explicit reference to an individual becoming very intelligent, despite these two constructs' heavy conceptual overlap. This is a tricky area because, despite the widely held view that those who are really intelligent are born that way, a significant body of work has shown that people have wide-ranging beliefs as to whether their own intelligence is fixed or can be increased (e.g. Dweck, 2006).

In the case of giftedness, there is a widespread acceptance that you can become gifted as a result of environmental factors such as practice and opportunity (Subotnik, Olszewski-Kubilius, & Worrell, 2011). While the importance of deliberative practice over an extensive period, often more than ten years (Ericsson, Krampe, & Tesch-Römer, 1993), is widely accepted as important for the development of exceptional expertise, few would consider that the various domain-specific skills (for example, in music, sports, or chess) that result are quite what is meant by the term intelligence.

In line with broader conceptions of giftedness that reflect the interaction of the individual and their environment, Subotnik, Stoeger, and Olszewski-Kubilius (2017) provide a more nuanced developmental account that reflects changing emphases during the individual's lifespan. For these authors:

> Giftedness is the manifestation of performance or production that is clearly at the upper end of the distribution in a talent domain even relative to that of other high-functioning individuals in that domain. Further, giftedness can be viewed as developmental, in that in the beginning stages, potential is the key variable; in later stages, achievement is the measure of giftedness; and in fully developed talents, eminence is the basis on which this label is granted. Psychosocial variables play an essential role in the manifestation of giftedness at every developmental stage. Both cognitive and psychosocial variables are malleable and need to be deliberately cultivated. (p. 7)

According to their conception, important psychosocial components include self-confidence, independence, positive mindsets, resilience, motivation, and a willingness to take risks.

Are Current Measures of High Intelligence/Giftedness Able to Accurately Identify Potential High Achievers Irrespective of Social or Cultural Background?

The literature on gifted education has consistently demonstrated that children from minority backgrounds tend to perform less well than their peers on standardized assessment and, partially as a result, are typically underrepresented in gifted programs (Warne, 2016).

One of the ways proposed to reduce assessment bias is to undertake multiple measures such as teacher ratings and achievement tests. How results from these different measures are best brought together to enable a judgment about an individual is not straightforward, however. Are we searching for high performance in a range of areas or just in one? Various models have been used to identify the gifted. The *conjunctive model* requires a minimum level of performance in each of the measures. The *compensatory model* permits a poor score in one area to be offset by a high performance in another. Finally, the *disjunctive model* permits the highest score to be used to determine giftedness and enable access to a gifted program. In examining the use of such approaches, McBee, Peters, and Waterman (2014) emphasize that there is no one correct approach. Rather, different approaches should be used depending upon their particular purposes, and the extent to which any error in the measures has adverse consequences for participants. For example, if particular measures are being employed to identify those who would benefit from enrichment activities, it would not be greatly problematic if they over-identified gifted students. However, if their purpose is to select a small number of individuals for enrollment onto a highly selective, resource-intensive program, the precision of the measure is far more important. In its ability to cast a wide net (McBee, Peters, & Waterman, 2014, p. 82), the disjunctive approach is likely to increase access for those from low-income or minority backgrounds. Educators need to understand, therefore, that simply adding measures to build up a profile of ability is less important than being careful to ensure that their use corresponds with their purpose.

It is widely believed that able children from diverse backgrounds are likely to be disadvantaged by tests with high verbal content. For this reason, nonverbal ability tests such as the Raven's Progressive Matrices Test (Raven, Raven, & Court, 2003), the Naglieri Nonverbal Ability Test (Naglieri, 2008), or the nonverbal section of the Cognitive Abilities Test (Lohman, 2011) have been promoted as fairer means of assessing ability. However, the ability of such tests to identify a higher proportion of students from such backgrounds has been questioned (Giessman, Gambrell, & Stebbins, 2013). Indeed, there is some evidence that nonverbal tests may also disadvantage some minority groups (Te Nijenhuis, Willigers, Dragt, & van der Flier, 2016). It is questionable whether nonverbal tests predict academic achievement as well as tests with verbal and quantitative content and, if used alone, they may increase bias by failing to identify those minority students who currently exhibit academic prowess or who are likely to benefit from educational enrichment programs (Lohman, 2005).

Dynamic Assessment: An Alternative to Standardized Testing

An alternative approach to the use of standardized tests involving IQ or academic achievement is dynamic testing, which we discussed in earlier chapters. **Dynamic assessment** is an umbrella term that refers to a broad range of approaches and techniques which vary considerably in the nature of the help provided. During standardized testing, such as that typically operating in IQ tests, the assessor gives each set of instructions following a script in the test manual, and then tries not to influence the testee's performance, beyond maintaining necessary rapport. Any inadvertent help that improves or impairs testee performance is seen as increasing the error of the measurement. However, in dynamic assessment, helping the testee to improve performance is key to the approach. The nature of such help varies; in some types of dynamic assessment, the assistance offered follows a predetermined script of hints and prompts; in other approaches, the help is determined by the tester in the light of the particular test situation and the unique characteristics and responses of the testee (Elliott, 2003; Elliott, Resing, & Beckmann, 2018).

Dynamic assessment has primarily been employed to assess the cognitive abilities of children who struggle with their learning because of their special educational needs, or their social, economic, or cultural backgrounds (Sternberg & Grigorenko, 2002). Many of these children may underperform in formal, standardized test settings because of unfamiliarity with test processes and content. As a result, they can become easily disempowered and demotivated should they encounter difficulties. Dynamic assessment involves striking up a very different, supportive relationship between the assessor and the testee. Here, opportunities to learn before and/or during the test session(s) are offered, and the testee's response to assistance and progress over time are deemed to be an important indicator of their cognitive potential. Underpinning this approach is the belief that a child with significant potential may be identified even if their initial performance is modest.

As noted above, the approach is typically used with struggling learners, and few dynamic testing studies have been conducted to assess the cognitive abilities of gifted children. Here the focus has been primarily on the identification of giftedness in ethnic and linguistically diverse populations for participation in gifted programs (e.g., Lidz & Elliott, 2006; Lidz & Macrine, 2001). This approach would appear to be valuable as research suggests that gifted children have significant potential to improve their performance when provided with assistance, and are often good at transferring their learning from one situation to another (Calero, García-Martín, & Robles, 2011; Kanevsky, 1995, 2000).

Lidz and Macrine (2001) used dynamic assessment to assist in the identification of gifted culturally and linguistically diverse learners (first to fifth graders). They tested 473 children in first to fifth grade in one school. Approximately 60 percent of the students had an immigrant or ethnic minority background. By means of their dynamic approach, 5 percent of the children were subsequently deemed as suitable for gifted education (similar to the figures for the school district more generally), whereas, previously in this institution, fewer than 1 percent in the school had been identified.

Dynamic assessment has proven to be an attractive notion to those seeking more equitable means of assessing high ability. However, dynamic assessment approaches continue to be underresearched and underdeveloped, and claims that insights from the assessments can be used to assist in the design of individually tailored educational programs have yet to be realized.

Are Highly Intelligent People Likely to Be High Achievers?

As noted above, many studies have demonstrated that, while far from a certainty, those with high IQ tend to have more productive and successful lives (Strenze, 2015). Of course, what is deemed to be a successful life may vary. In most cases, however, the term is used to describe success in formal education, career, personal relationships, and physical and mental health. However, as Gottfredson (1997) has pointed out, the effects of high intelligence (understood in its narrower sense) only increase the probability of success in school and life more generally; they do not guarantee such outcomes. Not only do other personal characteristics such as motivation and drive, resilience, creativity, and conscientiousness play an important role, but success also will be greatly influenced by a wide range of environmental factors. Important influences will include family experience, socioeconomic status, the quality of schooling, cultural and social capital, the availability of suitable mentors, and the ability to draw upon personal connections to gain access to occupational and other opportunities. Of course, the good fortune to avoid highly adverse environmental experiences such as war, experience as a refugee, child abuse, and extreme poverty will typically be significant in achieving life success.

The Relationship Between Giftedness and Psychological Health

It has been suggested that those with high intelligence are more likely to struggle with negative emotions (Blaas, 2014), attentional difficulties (Guénolé et al., 2015), and poorer relationships (Cross & Cross, 2015). If so, would this be a feature of very young children? The evidence available does not support this suggestion. One study (Peyre et al., 2016), examining 23 French 5–6-year-olds with IQs above 130, found they did not appear to experience more emotional, social, or behavioral problems than a comparison group of 1,058 same-age peers scoring in the normal range of IQ. However, it is possible that problems may emerge later for some gifted people perhaps because, during their childhood, some highly able individuals may feel different from other participants and struggle to cope as a result (Cross, Coleman, & Stewart, 1995; Daniels & Piechowski, 2009).

There has been particular inconsistency in findings from studies that have explored whether gifted individuals are more prone to anxiety. Findings from a meta-analytic review led Martin, Burns, and Schonlau (2010) to conclude that symptoms of both anxiety and depression appear to be less common in gifted children. A similar finding is reported by Francis, Hawes, and Abbot (2016). Their systematic review of 18 studies examined children and adolescents with high IQ ($\geq$ 125) and the incidence of problems of internalizing (e.g., experiencing anxiety, depression) and externalizing (e.g., experiencing conduct disorder, delinquency). Gifted children with other diagnoses such as autism or ADHD were excluded on the grounds that any psychological problems identified may have resulted from this condition. Overall, the review found that the gifted children exhibited fewer behavior problems and superior socioemotional adjustment relative to their nongifted peers. The authors noted, however, that their review drew solely upon studies where giftedness was based upon high IQ and that the findings may not apply to those whose identification as gifted is based on other special abilities or talents.

The relationship between giftedness and psychological health has not only been muddied by differing understandings of these terms but also by methodological weaknesses in many studies (Martin, Burns, & Schonlau, 2010). One particular challenge is that studies often recruit participants from gifted programs, or from teacher recommendations. These pariticipants, correspondingly, are more likely to be functioning well. This could result in a selection bias that underestimates the prevalence of intellectually able children with social, emotional, and behavioral difficulties. Despite such caveats, the weight of research evidence suggests that those with high cognitive ability are not more likely to experience emotional difficulties than their peers. However, longitudinal research is needed to ascertain the interactive influence of age, ethnicity, and gender, and to identify whether there are particular life experiences, at certain stages of development, that are of significant importance. Furthermore, it is possible that, when problems do arise, the particular needs and abilities of gifted children may be such that tailored forms of intervention are required (Cross & Cross, 2015).

Intelligence Assessed at the Lower Extreme of the IQ Distribution

At the other extreme of the IQ distribution curve, a score of more than two standard deviations from the mean has also been employed as an important cut-off point for classification and intervention. The terms used to describe those with such scores vary across countries, and have frequently changed over time, largely because they came to be used as insults. Certainly, terms used a century ago would horrify us if employed today. In 1921, for example, the American Association of Mental Retardation suggested the use of three levels. Those with IQs in the 75-50 range were to be termed as "morons"; those scoring 25-50 were termed "imbeciles"; and those with IQs below 25 were termed "idiots." Nomenclature for those with both physical and intellectual disabilities has continuously evolved, and, indeed, "mental retardation," until recently a term used widely in the United States, was often viewed with distaste by other societies such as the UK.

The use of these labels was not problematic solely because these were employed pejoratively but also because of their contribution to a powerful eugenics movement, which sought to encourage or discourage reproduction on the basis of a person's alleged hereditary traits, including intelligence. The forcible sterilization of an individual with intellectual disabilities was perhaps easier to justify to oneself or others if the individual had been clinically branded as an "idiot" or an "imbecile."

As with giftedness, the labeling of those at the low extreme of the IQ distribution has shifted from an almost complete reliance upon IQ to the incorporation of a broader set of competencies. While historical IQ cut-off points have remained highly influential, the individual's ability to adapt to their environment – at school, at home, and in their community – is increasingly being taken into account. Such a shift was spurred by changing philosophies about the nature of schooling for children. As educational systems in developed countries increasingly included children with complex special educational needs in mainstream classrooms, what appeared to be most important for success was a determination of how well the child could function in their school environment and what assistance was required to achieve this end.

Classification Systems and Assessment Tools

This shift of thinking is reflected by changes in formal classification systems. One of the most influential of these is the *Diagnostic and Statistical Manual of Mental Disorders* (DSM) published by the American Psychiatric Association (APA) and used widely by clinicians and researchers. The fifth edition, DSM-5 (APA, 2013), introduced the term **intellectual disability** or intellectual development disorder, to replace "mental retardation," the term employed formerly. Intellectual disabilities are grouped with the larger set of neurodevelopmental disorders that originate in childhood. These include autistic spectrum disorder, attention deficit hyperactivity disorder, language and communication disorders, and motor disorders such as developmental coordination disorder. Often these disorders co-occur so that, for example, an individual may be diagnosed as having both autism and intellectual disability.

Determination of intellectual disability continues to be conditional upon evidence of poor intellectual functioning but now greater importance is also attached to the capacity of the individual to adapt to their environment. Intellectual functioning – "reasoning, problem solving, planning, abstract thinking, judgement, academic learning, and learning from experience" (APA 2013, p. 33) – is assessed by a combination of standardized IQ testing and clinical evaluation. Problems of adaptive functioning should be understood in relation to the individual's capability to act independently and to meet their social responsibilities within the developmental and sociocultural standards of their community.

The American Association on Intellectual and Developmental Disabilities (AAIDD) was influential in guiding the terminology employed in DSM-5. The AAIDD (Schalock et al., 2010) refers to intellectual disability as originating before the age of 18 and as being characterized by significant limitations in both intellectual functioning and adaptive behavior. With reference to the latter, it highlights three kinds of adaptive skills:

- Conceptual skills: language and literacy; money, time, and number concepts; and self-direction;
- Social skills: interpersonal skills, social responsibility, self-esteem, gullibility, naïveté (i.e., wariness), social problem solving, and the ability to follow rules, obey laws, and avoid being victimized;
- Practical skills: activities of daily living (personal care), occupational skills, healthcare, travel/transportation, schedules/routines, safety, use of money, use of the telephone.

The AAIDD has developed a standardized assessment tool, the Diagnostic Adaptive Behavior Scale, for individuals from 4 to 21 years of age. The scale is designed to measure the three skill domains above, focusing particularly on the "cut-off" area for the purposes of making or ruling out a diagnosis of intellectual disability or a related developmental disability. This approach ensures that clinical attention is particularly directed to those levels of adaptive functioning that are most crucial for diagnostic purposes.

The functional differences within the group scoring in the bottom 2 percent, most of whom will have some organic pathology, are, of course, considerably greater than is the case for those with high IQs. Similarly, the forms of intervention and support required will vary greatly between those with greater or lesser severity. For this reason, clear categories within this range have been established in many countries. In the United States, there are four categories of intellectual disability – mild, moderate, severe, and profound. As is the case for intellectual disability in general, while these categories were determined largely by IQ scores, the predominant emphasis is now upon the individual's daily functioning and the amount and type of support that is required, particularly in cases of extreme disability.

Mild Disability

The great majority (c. 85 percent) of those falling in these groups are classified as having mild disability. Such individuals are typically found in the 50-70 IQ score range. While they often struggle to cope academically, they may acquire basic reading, writing, and math skills, and function socially. Their ability to decode text is often likely to be superior to their capacity to comprehend its meaning, as the latter process is more intellectually demanding. Slow functioning in most aspects of their lives is a core characteristic. However, despite the challenges they face, most people with a mild intellectual disability are able to live an independent life as adults with minimal support.

Moderate Disability

Approximately 10 percent of those with intellectual disability are classified as having a moderate level of severity. Here, IQ scores are typically between 35 and 49, although as one moves to the lower level of this range, the value of such tests for assisting in understanding and supporting the individual becomes increasingly questionable. Those with moderate intellectual disability will have more noticeable developmental delays in areas such as speech and language (although they can usually engage in basic forms of communication), reasoning, social relationships, and physical activity. While they may be able to largely care for themselves, they are unlikely to be fully independent and, as adults, will usually need to reside in a supportive group-home setting.

Severe Disability

Those identified as having a severe intellectual disability (3-4 percent of those with intellectual disability) will experience very considerable developmental delay. They may understand speech but are unlikely to be able to communicate with others except at the most basic level. They will be unable to lead an independent life and will need to live in a supervised setting.

Those with a profound intellectual disability (1-2 percent of those with intellectual disability) often have congenital syndromes and will require constant care and support for all aspects of their lives. Their ability to communicate will be extremely limited and many will not be ambulant. Although it is considered that such individuals will score below 20 on IQ tests, at such a level of severity, it is unlikely that IQ can offer much to a clinical assessment.

DSM-5 is designed primarily for psychiatric diagnosis and this fact poses the question as to whether intellectual disability should be considered as a (health) disorder, rather than as a disability (Bertelli, Munir, Harris, & Salvador-Carulla, 2016). DSM-V uses both the terms "intellectual disability" and "intellectual development disorder," while the influential American Association for Intellectual and Developmental Disabilities conceives of intellectual disability as a disability rather than a health condition. While this distinction could be dismissed as an unimportant semantic issue, it is important to note that it could have profound implications for the provision of services (Bertelli et al., 2016). According to Bertelli and his colleagues, conceptualizing intellectual disability fundamentally as a disability could result in a reduction in access to health-related services, particularly, mental health care. On the other hand, if intellectual disability were held to be a health condition, its consideration as a "disability" could be undermined, potentially leading to reduced social and educational services, a change in public perception, and negative implications for future policy and practice.

Etiology of Intellectual Disabilities

Intellectual disabilities may result from both genetic and environmental factors, although the ways these interact may vary according to the severity of the disability. Reichenberg et al. (2016) studied genetic and environmental influences in more than a million adults and concluded that while milder forms of intellectual disability appeared to represent the low extreme of the normal distribution of intelligence, more severe forms of intellectual disability appeared to be a distinct and qualitatively different condition.

Of the more than one thousand genetic disorders that are associated with intellectual disability, the most common is **Down syndrome**, a condition caused by having an extra 21st chromosome that leads to varying levels of impairment in cognitive ability and physical development. **Fragile X syndrome**, an inherited genetic disease passed from parents to children, usually more damaging to boys, is the most prevalent inherited cause of intellectual disability. Environmental factors include exposure to toxic substances such as substance abuse during early pregnancy, heavy metals (e.g., chronic lead exposure), nutritional deficiencies (e.g. iodine or folic acid), child or maternal infection, brain injury (for example, asphyxia, often caused by a shortage of oxygen during birth), or complications arising from premature birth.

Intellectual Disability and Related Health Conditions

Intellectual disability is associated with a range of chronic health conditions with prevalence levels considerably higher than in the general population. On the basis of their systematic review of the literature, Oeseburg et al. (2011) reported the six most common health-related conditions in children with intellectual disability as epilepsy (22.0/100), cerebral palsy (19.8/100), any anxiety disorder (17.1/100), oppositional defiant disorder (12.4/100), Down syndrome (11.0/100), and autistic disorder (10.1/100). However, prevalence rates were found to vary significantly across the studies examined, most likely because of the characteristics of the different samples, the recruitment of the study participants, the diagnostic methods employed, and the classification framework used. In considering international differences, a further significant factor could also be differences in the accessibility of healthcare for children with intellectual disability

Intellectual disability is also associated with a high rate of mental health disorders (Einfeld, Ellis, & Emerson, 2011). Children with intellectual difficulties are up to four to five times more likely to experience diagnosable mental health problems than others (Emerson & Hatton, 2007), with a significant discrepancy also applying to adults (Cooper et al., 2007). However, as is the case for chronic health problems, prevalence rates of mental disorders vary significantly across studies, with one systematic review of the literature reporting a range from 13.9 to 75.2 percent

(Buckles, Luckasson, & Keefe, 2013). Again, as for health, much of this variation appears to result from differences in the diagnostic criteria utilized and the nature of the groups of participants examined.

It appears that mental health problems may not be greater for those with only a mild disability (Whitaker & Read, 2006), but rather, only increase in prevalence at greater levels of intellectual disability. However, it is unclear whether such risk is greater at severe and profound, rather than moderate, levels of intellectual disability, a determination that is made more difficult by a lack of sound measurement tools for these groups (Flynn et al., 2017). Some evidence suggests that there is an association, but this relationship appears not to be linear (Hove & Havik, 2010). This means that increases in the severity of disability do not directly correspond in a straightforward fashion to greater problems of mental health.

Learning Disability

While both intellectual disability and learning disability impact upon an individual's capacity for educational achievement, these terms are not synonymous. The term, "**learning disability**" was first introduced in print by Kirk (1962), who described it as referring to a disorder, or delayed development, in one or more of the processes of speech, language, reading, writing, arithmetic, or other school subject. Kirk stressed that learning disability was not a consequence of intellectual disability, sensory problems involving hearing or vision, or cultural and instructional factors.

While there has been ongoing debate about the best meaning of this term (Scanlon, 2013), the key issue for the purposes of this chapter is that, in the United States, the presence of intellectual disability effectively rules out a diagnosis of learning disability. Approximately 7 percent of school-aged children in the US are classified as having a learning disability, with this group being seen as representing about one half of all those identified as having one disability or another. Given that a diagnosis may lead to the provision of additional resources and educational accommodations, it is hardly surprising that the incidence of those identified with a learning disability or specific learning disability has increased significantly in recent years. For those whose primary goal is advocating for individual students, it may be more important to get as much assistance as possible for children struggling in school rather than be overly concerned about diagnostic precision (Kavale & Forness, 2003).

It is important to note that a determination of learning disability in the education system may not map exactly onto that of "specific learning disability" as outlined in DSM-5. Adding further to the conceptual confusion is the differing usage of these terms in other countries. In the UK, for example, the term "learning disability" typically refers to those who in the US would be considered to have an intellectual disability. Those with a particular problem with their learning but no significant intellectual difficulty would be more likely to be considered to have a specific learning difficulty.

In contrast to individuals with high IQ who perform poorly on specific domains, there are others, often referred to as **savants**, who often score poorly on general measures of intelligence but nevertheless have outstanding abilities in very specific skill areas (Heaton & Wallace, 2004). Typically, savants are located within five categories: music, art, calendar calculating, mathematics (particularly, in calculation and the ability to compute prime numbers), and mechanical or spatial skills (for example, in measuring distances very precisely without any aids, or constructing complex structures with great accuracy). However, it is important to note that while the term is strongly associated with low intelligence, some savants can score highly on IQ tests (Treffert, 2014).

A Case Study of a Savant

Kim Peek was the inspiration for a character played by Dustin Hoffman in a movie entitled *Rain Man*. Born with severe brain damage, Mr. Peek scored poorly on IQ tests (an average score of 87 which, however, is not sufficiently low to be indicative of intellectual disability), yet displayed astounding abilities. He was reputed to be able to remember everything in the more than 12,000 books he had read. He was able to read two pages in approximately three seconds, one eye reading the left page, the other reading the right, and appeared to remember every detail. He had a vast store of knowledge across a large number of subject areas. If provided with a date, he could immediately state which day of the week this fell on.

The savant phenomenon is approximately six times more common in males, perhaps because of factors involved in the early development of the male brain (Geschwind & Galaburda, 1987). However, savant skills can be acquired later in life following brain trauma or disease (Lythgoe, Pollak, Kalmas, de Hann, & Chong, 2005). It is most commonly associated with autism, with approximately one in ten autistic people showing evidence of savant abilities, although it is also associated with intellectual disability (Treffert, 2009). Interestingly, it has been suggested (Crespi, 2016) that there may be genetic links between autism and intelligence that might operate only in very specialized areas of functioning.

Can Intelligence Be Increased in Those at the Extremes?

It is highly unlikely that training people to perform better on intelligence tests will result in a meaningful gain in intelligence. However, is there merit in seeking to improve intellectual functioning by targeting specific cognitive processes? If this were so, is it helpful to focus upon such processes for those scoring at both extremes of the bell curve?

The suggestion that those scoring poorly may benefit from direct training (sometimes termed **cognitive (brain) training**) to improve particular cognitive processes that they find problematic has a certain plausibility. The underlying rationale for thinking is succinctly put by Simons et al. (2016):

> If measures of cognitive ability predict real-world performance and success, and if that success depends on those cognitive abilities, then practicing those abilities should improve outcomes – and ultimately improve people's lives. (p. 105)

It is hardly surprising that attempts to boost intellectual functioning at the extremes of intelligence have focused far more upon those who are considered to have cognitive deficiencies. For those deemed to be gifted, interventions have focused primarily upon the development of academic skills (Subotnik et al., 2011) or identified special talents such as the performing arts or sports. However, there is now greater recognition of the importance of developing leadership, character, and socioemotional skills for the highly able (Bates-Krakoff, McGrath, Graves, & Ochs, 2017; Shani-Zinovich, & Zeidner, 2013).

Interventions for Gifted Children

The primary vehicle for developing high abilities in gifted children is through some form of acceleration. Subject acceleration involves providing higher-level academic instruction in those areas where the student has demonstrated particular proficiency. Typically, they remain with same-age peers for the other aspects of their schooling. Grade-based acceleration involves the student jumping grades and receiving their education with older peers. In general, research studies suggest that acceleration has both academic and, to a somewhat lesser extent, social and emotional benefits (Assouline, Marron, & Colangelo, 2014; Steenbergen-Hu, & Moon, 2011; Zeidner, 2017).

Interventions for Children with Learning Disabilities

An early attempt to identify and improve specific cognitive functions in those with learning difficulties was designed by Reuben Feuerstein and colleagues in Israel (Feuerstein et al., 1980). Feuerstein argued that children functioning poorly in school and on measurements of intelligence, particularly those suffering from various forms of social or cultural disadvantage, often had far greater potential than was recognized. Feuerstein designed a dynamic form of assessment, the *Learning Potential Assessment Device* (LPAD) (subsequently renamed the *Learning Propensity Assessment Device*) to examine several cognitive processes – attention, perception, memory, logical reasoning, and problem solving. The information obtained from this assessment was then used to inform the operation of an individually tailored cognitive intervention program called **Instrumental Enrichment (IE)** (Feuerstein, Rand, Hoffman, Hoffman, & Miller, 1980). This intervention was principally designed to help improve performance among those with cognitive deficiencies, provide the learner with new skills for learning, teach new learning strategies and approaches, and increase learners' motivation and confidence. Despite high levels of enthusiasm for an approach that seemed to be revolutionary, and which tapped into burgeoning interest in the teaching of thinking, IE has largely failed to become established in public education systems. There are several reasons for this: The program requires a lot of offsite training and formal registration; the activities are not easily integrated into existing school curricula; the theory has not been substantially modified to reflect modern developments in cognitive psychology; high-quality, independent research evidence for its effectiveness is now somewhat dated; and studies that have been done have not proven highly persuasive (Blagg, 1991; Savell, Twohig, & Rachford, 1986).

Focus on Executive Functions

In identifying deficient areas of cognitive functioning that might be amenable to training for those with intellectual disability, modern approaches have tended to eschew more basic processes and, instead, have begun to focus upon higher-level **executive functions.** You may recall from Chapter 11 that while not wholly synonymous with intelligence (Duggan & Garcia-Barrera, 2015), executive functioning involves various cognitive and emotional processes that are employed to enable the completion of a task, rather than being used for situations which require an automatic, instinctive response. While there is no definitive list of executive functions, and operational definitions are inconsistent (Jacob & Parkinson, 2015), core executive functions include (a) the capacity to inhibit one's actions appropriately (to exercise self-control and to control one's selective attention), (b) working memory (involving the temporary storage of information in memory while we engage in processing), and (c) flexibility in shifting one's focus of one's thinking (Diamond, 2013). It is not surprising that research studies have shown a relationship between executive functions and performance in a variety of school subjects, although it is unclear whether this relationship is truly causal or, alternatively, is explained by other factors.

While some researchers (e.g., Diamond, 2013; Wass, 2015) assert that cognitive training programs are powerful means to improve executive functioning, other researchers are less persuaded (Elliott & Resing, 2015; Redick, 2015; Redick et al., 2015). One of the key reasons for this discrepancy concerns differing emphases by these authors upon subsequent **transfer,** that is, the ability to apply learning to other settings. One may improve a given cognitive process or executive function in a laboratory, but is this gain demonstrated in other settings? Furthermore, even if improved functioning appears to be maintained elsewhere, does it lead to improved performance in learning situations? (See the Focus on Contemporary Research box below for a more detailed discussion of the research in this area.)

FOCUS ON CONTEMPORARY RESEARCH: JULIAN G. ELLIOTT AND WILMA C. RESING'S WORK ON DETERMINING WHO SHOULD RECEIVE SPECIALIZED READING INSTRUCTION

The authors of this chapter have spent many years seeking to ascertain how assessment of intelligence can impact upon educational intervention. Dissatisfaction with the contribution of standard IQ tests for guiding classroom practice led us to seek to develop dynamic forms of cognitive assessment that might yield more helpful information. Sadly, we have yet to make major inroads here (Elliott & Resing, 2015; Elliott, Resing, & Beckmann, 2018).

An important development in DSM-5 was that the requirement to identify a discrepancy between academic performance and IQ as a key criterion for the preferred term, "specific learning disability," was abandoned. Similarly, there is no longer a need to assess underlying cognitive processing skills. This is a welcome development because, despite the continuing claims of advocates, approaches that seek to base a diagnosis of learning disability on patterns of cognitive strengths and weaknesses have not been found to be helpful (Fletcher & Miciak, 2017; McGill & Busse, 2017a,b). Furthermore, it is important that academically struggling children with IQs that are low, but not at a level to be considered to have an intellectual disability, are deemed eligible to receive special help for reading difficulties. Such assistance can typically be provided in mainstream schools, although in such settings, reading interventions in small groups or individualized are often necessary. In the past, and indeed, sometimes currently, children who are poor readers, but with low IQs, have not been offered the same levels of reading support and provision as those who were often diagnosed as having a specific learning disability (or dyslexia), on the basis of their relatively high IQ scores.

The performance of some children at the extremes of the bell curve can vary significantly across domains. Some highly intelligent children, for example, encounter immense difficulty in decoding text. This can be an immensely distressing situation for them and their families, particularly if their cognitive strengths are not recognized and nurtured. Historically, such children were labeled as dyslexic, although nowadays it is widely accepted that IQ and reading (decoding) skill (but not reading comprehension) are unrelated. Knowing the IQ of a poor reader does not help us determine how to help the poor reader to become a better reader, nor does it predict how well the individual will respond to structured intervention (Elliott & Resing, 2015). However, the use of high IQ scores by clinicians as a means to identify so-called dyslexics continues widely despite the wealth of evidence demonstrating its irrelevance for guiding reading (decoding) intervention (O'Donnell & Miller, 2011). Where a discrepancy between an individual's IQ and decoding skills exists, the approach is often attractive because the dyslexia diagnosis often helps to obtain additional resources and educational accommodations. In addition, it may result in more sympathetic understanding from third parties, thus reducing parental fears that their child will be underestimated intellectually (Elliott & Grigorenko, 2014; Elliott, in preparation).

The executive function that has perhaps received most attention in cognitive training programs is working memory. As with most forms of "brain training" that focus upon a broad range of cognitive processes, the literature on working-memory training is replete with claims of success. Clearly, it has been found that training, typically using computers, can result in working memory improvements in the laboratory when closely related tasks are used (Dunning, Holmes, & Gathercole, 2013; Holmes, Gathercole, & Dunning, 2009), but when reassessment takes place several months later there is little evidence that any such gains have been sustained (Melby-Lervåg, & Hulme, 2013).

It is hardly surprising that repeatedly undertaking the same, narrowly constrained task in a laboratory often results in gradual improvement, at least in the short term. Practicing any single skill intensively would normally have a positive effect. Not only is constant repetition likely to improve performance, it is likely that the individual would normally work out a more effective strategy to tackle the task, and also learn to focus their attention more appropriately. For such reasons, it is unclear whether gains observed in the laboratory merely reflect practice effects and/or the development of a more effective test strategy (Estrada et al., 2015; Hayes, Petrov, & Sederberg, 2015).

If gains in the laboratory are to be meaningful, they should be observable in related activities outside the test setting. Unfortunately, working-memory training has largely failed to demonstrate such a phenomenon and there is little evidence of transfer of improved performance to other activities such as verbal and nonverbal abilities, decoding text, reading comprehension, and arithmetic (Melby-Lervåg, Redick, & Hulme, 2016). Although some studies have appeared to offer a more successful picture, close scrutiny has indicated that the findings of many of these cannot be substantiated (Kirk et al., 2015; Redick, 2015; Simons et al., 2016). In addition, it is necessary to take into account the opportunity costs that result when valuable curricular time is diverted from academic and self-help activities for the operation of such programs.

CONCLUSION

Those who are gifted or who have some intellectual disability operate at opposite ends of the intellectual spectrum. However, in many ways, these two areas share a strong resemblance:

> the primary classification feature of both ... groups is intellectual deviance. These individuals are out of sync with more average people, simply by their difference from what is expected for their age and circumstance. This asynchrony results in highly significant consequences for them and for those who share their lives. None of the familiar norms apply, and substantial adjustments are needed in parental expectations, educational settings, and social and leisure activities. (Robinson, Zigler, & Gallagher, 2000, p. 1413)

Shifts of emphasis in the identification of both groups also demonstrate strong parallels. At each extreme, the former reliance upon an IQ score as the principal, if not sole, criterion has slowly diminished. Its place has been taken by more complex forms of assessment that are guided by deeper understandings of the nature of development and learning. At each extreme, there are concerns that the representation of minority groups is not relative to their proportions in the general population. In some cases, this imbalance largely reflects a failure to undertake valid and meaningful assessment; in others, it is primarily an unfortunate consequence of multiple socioeconomic disadvantages that, cumulatively, greatly reduce their ability to fulfill their potential. Of course, issues of equity, fairness, and untapped ability concern all children. Perhaps this should serve to remind us that when we consider the circumstances of those at the extremes, we should never lose sight of the fact that they are still fundamentally part of our larger human population that ranges along the full spectrum of intellectual ability.

CHAPTER SUMMARY

This chapter focuses on people who are deemed to be operating at the intellectual extremes. Those scoring IQs of 130 or above have traditionally been considered to be intellectually gifted, while those scoring below 70 have typically been considered to have an intellectual disability. However, in both cases, the preeminence of IQ as the key criterion has declined. In part, this reflects changing views as to the nature of intelligence and how it should be measured. This change is driven, in part, by theoretical advances that place far greater emphasis upon the individual's reciprocal relationship with their physical and social environments. A further shift from past practices is that intelligence (however assessed and understood) is now often seen as only one (albeit important) component of giftedness and intellectual disability.

The individual's broader functioning is now a key consideration in assessment. For identifying the highly able, intellectual assessment will often be complemented by a focus upon creativity, performance in the arts, academic functioning, and leadership. In the case of intellectual disability, the individual's adaptive functioning in conceptual, social, and practical areas is a key determinant, particularly in the case of those experiencing the greatest levels of difficulty.

Research findings suggest that gifted individuals tend to enjoy more successful lives both professionally and personally, and suggestions that they are more likely to encounter a higher prevalence of mental health problems have not been substantiated. In contrast, intellectual disability is associated with a greater prevalence of physical and mental health difficulties.

Learning disabilities (LD) differ from intellectual disability in that the former do not include difficulties in general intellectual functioning. Rather, they reflect specific difficulties in areas such as speech and language, literacy, and other school subjects.

KEY TERMS

ceiling effect • cognitive (brain) training • Down syndrome • dynamic assessment • executive functions • fragile X syndrome • gifted • instrumental enrichment (IE) • intellectual disability • learning disability • legitimate peripheral participation • savant • situated cognition • transfer

COMPREHENSION AND REFLECTION QUESTIONS

1. How is it reasonable to say that those at the two extremes of intelligence share similar issues and problems?
2. To what extent does the ease of IQ testing justify its continued use in the selection of the gifted?
3. Why does IQ testing become increasingly less meaningful when assessing those with greater levels of severity of intellectual deficit?

4. Should a person be considered *gifted* if they have outstanding potential, but it is never realized?
5. Why is transfer of cognitive training effects to the classroom and to other real-life settings often difficult to achieve for those struggling with learning?
6. To what extent do you believe that that those at the extremes of intellectual ability are either similar to or different from everyone else?

References

American Psychiatric Association (APA). (2013). *Diagnostic and statistical manual of mental disorders* (5th ed.). Arlington, VA: American Psychiatric Association.

Assouline, S. G., Marron, M., & Colangelo, N. (2014). Acceleration. In J. A. Plucker & C. M. Callahan (eds.), *Critical issues and practices in gifted education: What the research says* (2nd ed., pp. 15–28). Waco, TX: Prufrock Press.

Bates-Krakoff, J., McGrath, R. E., Graves, K., & Ochs, L. (2017). Beyond a deficit model of strengths training in schools: Teaching targeted strength use to gifted students. *Gifted Education International, 33*(2), 102-117.

Bertelli, M. O., Munir, K., Harris, J., & Salvador-Carulla, L. (2016). "Intellectual developmental disorders": Reflections on the international consensus document for redefining "mental retardation-intellectual disability" in ICD-11. *Advances in Mental Health and Intellectual Disabilities, 10,* 36–58.

Blaas, S. (2014). The relationship between social-emotional difficulties and underachievement of gifted students. *Journal of Psychologists and Counsellors in Schools, 24*(2), 243-255.

Blagg, N. (1991). *Can we teach intelligence? A comprehensive evaluation of Feuerstein's instrumental enrichment program.* Hillsdale, NJ: Lawrence Erlbaum Associates.

Boring, E. G. (1923). Intelligence as the tests measure it. *New Republic,* 35-37.

Buckles, J., Luckasson, R., & Keefe, E. (2013). A systematic review of the prevalence of psychiatric disorders in adults with intellectual disability, 2003–2010. *Journal of Mental Health Research in Intellectual Disabilities, 6,* 181–207.

Calero, M. D., García-Martín, M. B., & Robles, M. A. (2011). Learning potential in high IQ children: The contribution of dynamic assessment to the identification of gifted children. *Learning and Individual Differences, 21,* 176-181.

Cooper, S-A., Smiley, E., Morrison, J., Williamson, A., & Allan, L. (2007). Mental ill-health in adults with intellectual disabilities: prevalence and associated factors. *British Journal of Psychiatry, 190,* 27-35.

Crespi, B. J. (2016). Autism as a disorder of high intelligence. *Frontiers of Neuroscience, 10,* 300. doi: 10.3389/fnins.2016.00300

Cross, T. L., Coleman, L. J., & Stewart, R.A. (1995). Psychosocial diversity of gifted adolescents: An exploration of the stigma of the giftedness paradigm. *Roeper Review, 17*, 181-185.

Cross, J. R., & Cross, T. L. (2015). Clinical and mental health issues in counseling the gifted individual. *Journal of Counseling & Development, 93*(2), 163-172.

Daniels, S., & Piechowski, M. M. (2009). *Living with intensity: Understanding the sensitivity, excitability and emotional development of gifted children, adolescents, and adults.* Tucson, AZ: Great Potential Press.

Diamond, A. (2013). Executive functions. *Annual Review of Psychology, 64*, 135–168.

Duggan, E. C., & Garcia-Barrera, M. A. (2015). Executive functioning and intelligence. In I. S. Goldstein, D. Princiotta, & J. A. Naglieri (eds.), *Handbook of intelligence* (pp. 435-458). New York: Springer.

Dunning, D. L., Holmes, J., & Gathercole, S. E. (2013). Does working memory training lead to generalized improvements in children with low working memory? A randomized controlled trial. *Developmental Science, 16*(6), 915-925.

Dweck, C. S. (2006). *Mindset: How you can fulfill your potential.* New York: Random House.

Einfeld, S. L., Ellis, L. A., & Emerson, E. (2011). Comorbidity of intellectual disability and mental disorder in children and adolescents: A systematic review. *Journal of Intellectual & Developmental Disability, 36*(2), 137-143.

Elliott, J. G. (2003). Dynamic assessment in educational settings: Realising potential. *Educational Review, 55*, 15–32.

Elliott, J. G. & Grigorenko, E. L. (2014). *The dyslexia debate.* New York: Cambridge University Press.

Elliott, J. G., & Resing, W. C. M. (2015). Can intelligence testing inform educational intervention for children with reading disability? *Journal of Intelligence, 3*(4), 137-157.

Elliott, J. G., Resing, W. C., & Beckmann, J. F. (2018). Dynamic assessment: A case of unfulfilled potential? *Educational Review, 70*(1), 7-17.

Emerson, E., & Hatton, C. (2007). The mental health of children and adolescents with intellectual disabilities in Britain. *British Journal of Psychiatry,191*, 493-499.

Ericsson, K. A., Krampe, R. T., & Tesch-Römer, C. (1993). The role of deliberate practice in the acquisition of expert performance. *Psychological Review, 100*, 363–406.

Estrada, E., Ferrer, E., Abad, F. J., Román, F. J., & Colom, R. (2015). A general factor of intelligence fails to account for changes in tests' scores after cognitive practice: A longitudinal multi-group latent-variable study. *Intelligence, 50*, 93-99.

Feuerstein, R., Rand, Y., Hoffman, M., & Miller, M. (1980). *Instrumental enrichment: An intervention program for cognitive modifiability,* Baltimore, MD: University Park Press.

Fletcher, J. M., & Miciak, J. (2017). Comprehensive cognitive assessments are not necessary for the identification and treatment of learning disabilities. *Archives of Clinical Neuropsychology, 32*, 2-7.

Flynn, S., Vereenooghe, L., Hastings, R. P., Adams, D., Cooper, S. A., Gore, N., . . . & McNamara, R. (2017). Measurement tools for mental health problems and mental well-being in people with severe or profound intellectual disabilities: A systematic review. *Clinical Psychology Review, 57*, 32-44. doi: 10.1016/j.cpr.2017.08.006

Francis, R., Hawes, D. J., & Abbott, M. (2016). Intellectual giftedness and psychopathology in children and adolescents: A systematic literature review. *Exceptional Children, 82*(3), 279-302.

Gardner, H. (1983). *Frames of mind: The theory of multiple intelligences.* New York: Basic Books.

Geschwind, N., & Galaburda, A. M. (1987). *Cerebral lateralization: Biological mechanisms, associations, and pathology.* Cambridge, MA: MIT Press.

Giessman, J. A., Gambrell, J. L., & Stebbins, M. S. (2013). Minority performance on the Naglieri Nonverbal Ability Test, Second Edition, versus the Cognitive Abilities Test, Form 6: One gifted program's experience. *Gifted Child Quarterly, 57*, 101–109.

Gottfredson, L. S. (1997). Why *g* matters: The complexity of everyday life. *Intelligence, 24*(1), 79-132.

Guénolé, F., Speranza, M., Louis, J., Fourneret, P., Revol, O., & Baleyte, J. M. (2015). Wechsler profiles in referred children with intellectual giftedness: Associations with trait-anxiety, emotional dysregulation, and heterogeneity of Piaget-like reasoning processes. *European Journal of Paediatric Neurology, 19*(4), 402-410.

Hayes, T. R., Petrov, A. A., & Sederberg, P. B. (2015). Do we really become smarter when our fluid-intelligence test scores improve? *Intelligence, 48*, 1-14.

Heaton, P., & Wallace, G. L. (2004). Annotation: The savant syndrome. *Journal of Child Psychology and Psychiatry, 45*(5), 899-911.

Heller, K. A., Mönks, F. J., Subotnik, R., & Sternberg, R. J. (eds.). (2000). *International handbook of giftedness and talent.* New York: Elsevier.

Holmes, J., Gathercole, S. E., & Dunning, D. L. (2009). Adaptive training leads to sustained enhancement of poor working memory in children. *Developmental Science, 12*(4), F9–F15.

Hove, O., & Havik, O. E. (2010). Developmental level and other factors associated with symptoms of mental disorders and problem behaviour in adults with intellectual disabilities living in the community. *Social Psychiatry and Psychiatric Epidemiology, 45*, 105–113.

Jacob, R., & Parkinson, J. (2015). The potential for school-based interventions that target executive function to improve academic achievement: A review. *Review of Educational Research, 85*, 512–552.

Kanevsky, L. S. (1995). Learning potentials of gifted students. *Roeper Review, 17,* 157-163.

Kanevsky, L. S. (2000). Dynamic assessment of gifted students. In K. A. Heller, F. J. Mönks, R. J. Sternberg, & R. F. Subotnik (eds.), *International handbook of giftedness and talent* (pp. 283–296). Oxford: Elsevier.

Kavale, K. A., & Forness, S. R. (2003). Learning disability as a discipline. In H. L. Swanson, K. R. Harris, & S. Graham (eds.), *Handbook of learning disabilities* (pp. 76-93). New York: Guilford Press.

Kirk, H. E., Gray, K., Riby, D. M., & Cornish, K. M. (2015). Cognitive training as a resolution for early executive function difficulties in children with intellectual disabilities. *Research in Developmental Disabilities, 38,* 145-160.

Kirk, S. A. (1962). *Educating exceptional children.* Boston: Houghton Mifflin.

Kornilov, S., Tan, M., Elliott, J. G., Sternberg, R. J., & Grigorenko, E. L. (2012). Gifted identification with Aurora: Widening the spotlight, *Journal of Psychoeducational Assessment, 30*(1), 117-133.

Lidz, C. S., & Elliott, J. G. (2006). Use of dynamic assessment with gifted students. *Gifted Education International, 21,* 151–161.

Lidz, C. S., & Macrine, S. L. (2001). An alternative approach to the identification of gifted culturally and linguistically diverse learners: The contribution of dynamic assessment. *School Psychology International, 22*(1), 74-96.

Lohman, D. F. (2005). Review of Naglieri and Ford (2003): Does the Naglieri nonverbal ability test identify equal proportions of high-scoring White, Black, and Hispanic students? *Gifted Child Quarterly, 49,* 19-28.

Lohman, D. F. (2011). *Cognitive Abilities Test.* Rolling Meadows, IL: Riverside Publishing.

Lubinski, D. (2016). From Terman to today: A century of findings on intellectual precocity. *Review of Educational Research, 86*(4), 900-944.

Lythgoe, M., Pollak, T., Kalmas, M., de Hann, M., Chong, W. K. (2005). Obsessive, prolific artistic output following subarachnoid hemorrhage. *Neurology, 64,* 397–398.

Mackintosh, N. J. (2011). *IQ and human intelligence.* Oxford: Oxford University Press.

Makel, M. C., Kell, H. J., Lubinski, D., Putallaz, M., & Benbow, C. P. (2016). When lightning strikes twice: Profoundly gifted, profoundly accomplished. *Psychological Science, 27*(7), 1004-1018.

Martin, L. T., Burns, R. M., & Schonlau, M. (2010). Mental disorders among gifted and nongifted youth: A selected review of the epidemiologic literature. *Gifted Child Quarterly, 54*(1), 31-41.

McBee, M. T., Peters, S. J., & Waterman, C. (2014). Combining scores in multiple-criteria assessment systems: The impact of combination rule. *Gifted Child Quarterly, 58*(1), 69-89.

McGill, R. J., & Busse, R. T. (2017a). When theory trumps science: a critique of the PSW Model for SLD identification. *Contemporary School Psychology, 21,* 10-18.

McGill, R. J., & Busse, R. T. (2017b). A rejoinder on the PSW model for SLD identification: Still concerned. *Contemporary School Psychology, 21,* 23-27.

Melby-Lervåg, M., & Hulme, C. (2013). Is working memory training effective? A meta-analytic review. *Developmental Psychology, 49*(2), 270.

Melby-Lervåg, M., Redick, T., & Hulme, C. (2016). Working memory training does not improve performance on measures of intelligence or other measures of "far transfer": Evidence from a meta-analytic review. *Perspectives on Psychological Science, 11,* 512–534.

Naglieri, J. A. (2008). *Naglieri Nonverbal Ability Test* (2nd ed.). San Antonio, TX: Pearson.

National Association for Gifted Children (NAGC). (2009). *State of the states in gifted education.* Washington, DC: Author.

National Association for Gifted Children (NAGC). (2018). *What is giftedness? | National Association for Gifted Children.* [online] Available at: www.nagc.org/resources-publications/resources/what-giftedness

O'Donnell, P. S., & Miller, D. N. (2011). Identifying students with specific learning disabilities: School psychologists' acceptability of the discrepancy model versus response to intervention. *Journal of Disability Policy Studies, 22,* 83-94.

Oeseburg, B., Dijkstra, G. J., Groothoff, J. W., Reijneveld, S. A., & Jansen, D. E. C. (2011). Prevalence of chronic health conditions in children with intellectual disability: A systematic literature review. *Intellectual and developmental disabilities, 49*(2), 59-85.

Persson, R. S. (2017). Reconsidering the ambitions and position of gifted education. *Roeper Review,* 39, 183–186.

Peyre, H., Ramus, F., Melchior, M., Forhan, A., Heude, B., Gauvrit, N., & EDEN Mother–Child Cohort Study Group (2016). Emotional, behavioral and social difficulties among high-IQ children during the preschool period: Results of the EDEN mother–child cohort. *Personality and Individual Differences, 94,* 366-371.

Plucker, J. A., & Callahan, C. M. (2014). Research on giftedness and gifted education: Status of the field and considerations for the future. *Exceptional Children, 80*(4), 390-406.

Plucker, J. A., Callahan, C. M., & Tomchin, E. M. (1996). Wherefore art thou, multiple intelligences? Alternative assessments for identifying talent in ethnically diverse and economically disadvantaged students. *Gifted Child Quarterly, 40,* 81–92.

Raven, J., Raven, J. C. & Court, J. J. (2003). *Manual for Raven's Progressive Matrices and Vocabulary Scales.* Oxford: Oxford Psychologists Press.

Redick, T. S. (2015). Working memory training and interpreting interactions in intelligence interventions. *Intelligence, 50,* 14-20.

Redick, T. S., Shipstead, Z., Wiemers, E. A., Melby-Lervåg, M., & Hulme, C. (2015). What's working in working memory training? An educational perspective. *Educational Psychology Review, 27*(4), 617-633.

Reichenberg, A., Cederlöf, M., McMillan, A., Trzaskowski, M., Kapara, O., Fruchter, E., et al. (2016). Discontinuity in the genetic and environmental causes of the intellectual disability spectrum. *Proceedings of the National Academy of Science, 113*, 1098–1103.

Renzulli, J. S. (1978). What makes giftedness? Reexamination of definition. *Phi Delta Kappan, 60*, 180–184.

Renzulli, J. S. (2005). The three-ring conception of giftedness: A developmental model for promoting creative productivity. In R. J. Sternberg & J. Davidson (eds.), *Conceptions of giftedness* (2nd ed., pp. 217-245). New York: Cambridge University Press.

Robinson, N. M., Zigler, E., & Gallagher, J. J. (2000). Two tails of the normal curve: Similarities and differences in the study of mental retardation and giftedness. *American Psychologist, 55*(12), 1413-1424.

Savell, J. M., Twohig, P. T., & Rachford, D. L. (1986). Empirical status of Feuerstein's "Instrumental Enrichment" (FIE) technique as a method of teaching thinking skills. *Review of Educational Research, 56*, 381–409.

Scanlon, D. (2013). Specific learning disability and its newest definition: which is comprehensive? And which is insufficient? *Journal of Learning Disabilities, 46*(1), 26-33.

Schalock, R. L., Borthwick-Duffy, S. A., Bradley, V. J., Buntinx, W. H., Coulter, D. L., Craig, E. M., et al. (2010). *Intellectual disability: Definition, classification, and systems of supports* (11th ed.). Washington, DC: American Association on Intellectual and Developmental Disabilities.

Shani-Zinovich, S., & Zeidner, M. (2013). The elusive search for the personality of the intellectually gifted student: Some cross-cultural findings and conclusions from the Israeli educational context. *Talent Development & Excellence, 5*, 13–22.

Simons, D. J., Boot, W. R., Charness, N., Gathercole, S. E., Chabris, C. F., Hambrick, D. Z., & Stine-Morrow, E. A. (2016). Do "brain-training" programs work? *Psychological Science in the Public Interest, 17*(3), 103-186.

Steenbergen-Hu, S., & Moon, S. M. (2011). The effects of acceleration on high-ability learners: A meta-analysis. *Gifted Child Quarterly, 55*(1), 39-53.

Sternberg, R. J. (1988). *The triarchic mind: A new theory of human intelligence.* New York: Viking.

Sternberg, R. J. (1996). *Successful intelligence: How practical and creative intelligence determine success in life.* New York: Simon & Schuster.

Sternberg, R. J. (1998). A balance theory of wisdom. *Review of General Psychology, 2*, 347-365.

Sternberg, R. J. (2002). Smart people are not stupid, but they sure can be foolish: The imbalance theory of foolishness. In R. J. Sternberg (ed.), *Why smart people can be so stupid* (pp. 232-242). New Haven, CT: Yale University Press.

Sternberg, R. J. (2005). WICS: A model of positive educational leadership comprising wisdom, intelligence, and creativity synthesized. *Educational Psychology Review, 17*(3), 191-262.

Sternberg, R. J. (ed.). (2008). *Why smart people can be so stupid*. New Haven, CT: Yale University Press.

Sternberg, R. J. (2010). *College admissions for the 21st century*. Cambridge, MA: Harvard University Press.

Sternberg, R. J. (2016). *What universities can be: A new model for preparing students for active concerned citizenship and ethical leadership*. Ithaca, NY: Cornell University Press.

Sternberg, R. J. (2017). ACCEL: A new model for identifying the gifted. *Roeper Review, 39*(3).

Sternberg, R. J., & The Rainbow Project Collaborators (2006). The Rainbow Project: Enhancing the SAT through assessments of analytical, practical and creative skills. *Intelligence, 34* (4), 321-350.

Sternberg, R. J., & Grigorenko, E. L. (2002). *Dynamic testing: The nature and measurement of learning potential*. Cambridge: Cambridge University Press.

Strenze, T. (2015). Intelligence and success. In S. Goldstein, D. Princiotta, & J. A. Naglieri (eds.), *Handbook of intelligence* (pp. 403-415). New York: Springer.

Subotnik, R. F., Olszewski-Kubilius, P., & Worrell, F. C. (2011). Rethinking giftedness and gifted education: A proposed direction forward based on psychological science. *Psychological Science in the Public Interest, 12*, 3–54.

Subotnik, R. F., Stoeger, H., & Olszewski-Kubilius, P. (2017). Talent development research, policy, and practice in Europe and the United States: Outcomes from a summit of international researchers. *Gifted Child Quarterly, 6*(3), 262-269.

te Nijenhuis, J., Willigers, J., Dragt, J., & van der Flier, H. (2016). The effects of language bias and cultural bias estimated using the method of correlated vectors on a large database of IQ comparisons between native Dutch and ethnic minority immigrants from non-Western countries. *Intelligence, 54*, 117–135.

Terman, L. M. (1954). The discovery and encouragement of exceptional talent. *American Psychologist, 9*(6), 221.

Treffert, D. A. (2014). Savant syndrome: Realities, myths and misconceptions. *Journal of Autism and Developmental Disorders, 44*(3), 564-571.

Treffert, D. A. (2009). The savant syndrome: an extraordinary condition. A synopsis: Past, present, future. *Philosophical Transactions of the Royal Society B: Biological Sciences, 364*(1522), 1351–1357.

Visser, B. A., Ashton, M. C., & Vernon, P. A. (2006). Beyond *g*: Putting multiple intelligences theory to the test. *Intelligence, 34*, 487–502.

Wallis, C. (2017). Is the US education system producing a society of "smart fools"? *Scientific American Mind, 28*, 60-63.

Warne, R. T. (2016). Five reasons to put the *g* back into giftedness: An argument for applying the Cattell–Horn–Carroll theory of intelligence to gifted education research and practice. *Gifted Child Quarterly, 60*(1), 3-15.

Wass, S. V. (2015). Applying cognitive training to target executive functions during early development. *Child Neuropsychology, 21*(2), 150-166.

Whitaker, S., & Read, S. (2006). The prevalence of psychiatric disorders among people with intellectual disabilities: an analysis of the literature. *Journal of Applied Research in Intellectual Disabilities, 19,* 330–345.

Worrell, F. (2009). Myth 4: A single test score or indicator tells us all we need to know about giftedness. *Gifted Child Quarterly, 53,* 242–244.

Zeidner, M. (2017). Tentative guidelines for the development of an ability based emotional intelligence intervention program for gifted students, *High Ability Studies, 28,* 29.

13 Group Differences in Intelligence

DIANE F. HALPERN AND TOMOE KANAYA

After reading the last 12 chapters, it has probably become apparent to you that virtually everything associated with the concept of intelligence, including its conceptualization and measurement, is fraught with controversy. However, the topic of group differences in intelligence is particularly treacherous for researchers and anyone who writes about differences. Here is the one statement that scientists and others concerned with group differences in intelligence can agree on: *There are some group differences, on average, on some tests that purportedly measure intelligence.* This may be the only statement that we make in this chapter that goes unchallenged. The way we answer questions about group differences in intelligence is both personal and political. Every person belongs to many groups – racial, ethnic, language, country of origin, religious, gender, age, rural–urban, and many more. Even though we will be very careful when discussing differences to emphasize that the questions are about *average differences* among groups, these statements quickly become interpreted as statements about every member of the group, and readers may become defensive or prideful depending on their own group membership. The way we understand the extent of and reasons for these group differences has important social implications. Is there little overlap between two groups or are the group means so close together that the average difference has little or no meaning? If we think of group differences as large, then we could justify different treatment for members of different groups, perhaps in education, affirmative action, social welfare programs, parenting practices, and in other ways.

Two Fundamental Questions about Group Differences in Intelligence

Before looking at these group differences, we want to begin with two fundamental questions about group differences in intelligence.

What Does It Mean to Say that There Are (on Average) Group Differences in Intelligence?

One underlying assumption for this statement is that members of different groups have been assessed with tasks or instruments that are valid measures of intelligence.

The finding that one group scores lower or higher than another group means exactly that – no more. It may be more useful to consider what this statement does *not* mean. It does not provide any evidence for the cause of the group difference, nor does it mean that any of the differences are immutable or that they have not or will not change over time. It does not mean that the size of the difference among groups is large enough to be meaningful, although it may be. It also does not say anything about the overlap among groups (i.e., variability). There typically are members of the lowest scoring groups who are among the highest scorers on standardized measures of intelligence, and there are members of the highest-scoring groups who are among the lowest scorers on standardized measures of intelligence. Conclusions about group averages do not tell us about individuals.

Why Are Group Differences in Intelligence Among the Most Contentious Topics in Psychology?

As already mentioned, there are personal and political implications to statements about group differences in intelligence. Should we keep members of low-scoring groups out of our country (regardless of what country they are from)? Do we need separate education for members of different groups based on the average score of a group to which they belong? As these questions show, we should be concerned with statements about group differences in intelligence, because they often have real consequences, but this concern does not mean that they should not be studied. The data we generate in a scientific study of group differences can be and has been misused to justify misogyny and racism. But the misuse of data does not justify the failure to study a topic. People are prejudiced against members of certain groups in the absence of data (e.g., prejudice against Chinese, Japanese, and Jews cannot be justified by reference to group differences in intelligence, yet these prejudices continue to exist). We cannot create an equitable society if we do not know where inequities occur. There are no benefits to pretending that group differences do not exist. Censorship, even self-censorship, is not an antidote to prejudice.

Causes and Correlations of Group Differences

The first question asked when most people learn about group differences on some measures that (purportedly) measure intelligence is, "Why?" This is a deceptively simple question, whose answer is loaded with landmines. In general, there are four broad categories of responses:

Biological Explanations

There is a long history of attempts to document the "inherent inferiority of many groups" using genetic-based arguments (Anderson & Nickerson, 2005, p. 6), so it is not surprising that biological explanations are often viewed with skepticism and anger. This class of explanations includes the idea that intelligence is, at least in part, inherited, so groups that obtain lower scores on intelligence tests have less general intelligence to pass on to their offspring. This argument usually concerns g, which is a common factor that correlates with different types of intelligence measures and presumably underlies intelligence (e.g., Jensen, 1985). As Flynn (2010, p. 363) explains: "People who do better than average on one cognitive task tend to do better than average on a whole range of cognitive tasks, for example, all 10 of the Wechsler subtests." Of course, genes do not exert their effect directly on intelligence – they operate via proteins that might facilitate or retard the development of a larger brain or faster neural system that facilitates learning and reasoning.

Researchers (e.g., Jensen) who advocate biological explanations estimate the heritability of intelligence around .80. In other words, about 80 percent of the variability in intelligence scores around the world is due to genetics. Therefore, the environment can account for approximately 20 percent of the variability in intelligence. Heritability is important to understand because it allows us to prioritize the ways in which we can try to increase or decrease the trait in question. For example, a trait with low heritability means that substantial environmental manipulations can lead to wider ranges of that trait throughout the population. The same manipulations, however, would have little effect on a trait with very high heritability. Even if race were a heritable factor, it does not necessarily follow that any group differences on tests of intelligence have biological origins. There are many environmental explanations that can be used to explain average racial differences on tests of intelligence. While the pundits argue about the heritability of race, evidence for the social construction of racial differences is obvious and abundant. Thus, the concept of race surely has a social reality, even while its biological reality is in doubt.

Arguments against biological explanations of group differences in intelligence include the idea that even if intelligence were partially, or even largely, heritable, there is no reason to believe that group differences in scores on intelligence tests were not completely caused by environmental/sociocultural group differences (e.g., Nisbett, 2009). Height is commonly used as an example of a trait that is highly heritable (heritability level above .90), yet easily modified by environmental variables, which is shown by the large increase in heights in the last several generations (Sternberg, Grigorenko, & Kidd, 2005). No researchers have taken the view that group differences in intelligence are 100 percent due to heritable factors, but there are some who have argued that it is caused 100 percent by environmental factors.

Environmental/Sociocultural Explanations

There are many differences in the lives of people that vary as a function of group membership. For example, just over 27 percent of African American children (in the

United States) live in poverty. The comparable rate for white Americans is slightly under 10 percent (Economic Policy Institute, n.d.). Poverty is bad for intellectual development in many ways. For example, there are consistently high teacher-turnover rates at high-poverty schools, which harm student achievement (Ronfeldt, Loeb, & Wyckoff, 2013). The number of ways men and women of different races and ethnicities vary on average is huge. At every level of education, women earn less than men, with the smallest gap for those with less than a high school diploma (women earn 80 percent of what men earn) and the largest gap for those with an advanced degree (women earn 74 percent of what men earn; American Association of University Women, 2016). Asian American women earn more than black and Hispanic men, but less than Asian American men, who make up the highest-paid group in the United States (Bureau of Labor Statistics, 2016, table 3). Advocates of the environmental/sociocultural hypothesis posit that it is the myriad of differences in life experiences that account for group differences in intelligence.

Those in the opposing camp counter that poverty is not the cause but the result of group differences in intelligence. They argue that American women earn consistently less than men because, on average, they work fewer hours and they tend to cluster in lower-paying occupations such as social work, clerical jobs, teaching, and nursing, instead of the better-paying and more prestigious jobs in STEM (science, technology, engineering, and math) and in professions that are financed-based such as economics. Such arguments ignore the fact that women are the majority of all auditors, accountants, and investment professionals in many other countries including, for example, Canada, the United Kingdom, and many European countries – and the fact that women earn more than half of accounting degrees at the bachelor's and master's level in the United States (Catalyst, 2016). Similar arguments are used to "explain" racial and ethnic differences. For example, the success of many Asian Americans is often attributed to their work ethic, a legacy of Buddhist intellectual influence, and high achievement in advanced education. Thus, an environmentalist explanation would attribute the high success rate of Asian Americans to hard work, not greater intelligence.

Arguments pro and con for these various explanations tell more about the belief system of the person doing the arguing than the data because it is not possible to use "gold standard" research designs that allow researchers to make causal inferences. Such research designs require random assignment of people to different groups, which of course is impossible when we are talking about existing groups. No one can be randomly assigned to be either female or male or to be a particular race, so the opposing camps are likely to continue finding support and counterarguments for conclusions that are preferred or disfavored.

Biopsychosocial Explanations

The **biopsychosocial hypothesis** posits that each individual is predisposed by his or her biology to learn some skills more readily than others, and everyone selects experiences in ways that are biased by their prior learning histories, opportunities afforded in their environments, and beliefs about appropriate behaviors for females and males and what is valued by one's gender, racial, and ethnic group. Similarly, many stereotypes about male and female and racial and ethnic group differences reflect group differences; by learning and endorsing them, individuals may also be selecting environments that increase or decrease these differences. Experiences change neural structures, which in turn alter how individuals respond and so on. Learning, for example, is a biological, social, and environmental event. Brain structures reflect learning and experience and change as people age, thus blurring the nature–nurture distinction beyond usefulness for most purposes.

According to the biopsychosocial hypothesis, even simple distinctions like the division of variables into biological and environmental categories are impossible. Thus, it is not possible to provide percentages for the contribution of biology and environment to intelligence. There is no single percentage that can be attributed to heredity or environment because too many variables influence the expression of genes and the way environment shapes biology. Consider, for example, the fact that there are differences in female and male brains. The differences in brain structures could have been caused, enhanced, or decreased by environmental stimuli. Brain size and structures remain *plastic*, or able to change, throughout life. For example, it is well documented that people with less education are at a greater risk for dementia than those with higher levels of education (Jankowsky et al., 2005). But this association cannot tell us whether low levels of education caused increased risks of dementia or whether those who were at increased risk for dementia were less likely to pursue or succeed at advanced education. Recent research found that when mice who were at risk for learning and memory deficits were assigned (at random) to an enriched environment (more toys and activities), they significantly improved their performance on water maze and other tests used to determine the cognitive abilities of rats (Jankowsky et al., 2005). Although generalization from rat intelligence to human intelligence must be done with caution and caveats, these data (and many more) suggest that intelligence is influenced by life events. In Chapter 6 we read about a study with humans, in which adolescent girls spent three months practicing the popular computer game, *Tetris* (Haier, Karama, Leyba, & Jung, 2009). Neuroimaging before and after training showed increased cortical thickness and changes in regional blood flow due to this relatively small manipulation. We can only imagine how lifetimes of different experiences alter the brain. What we learn influences structures like dendritic branching and cell size; brain architectures, in turn, support certain skills and abilities, which may lead us to select additional

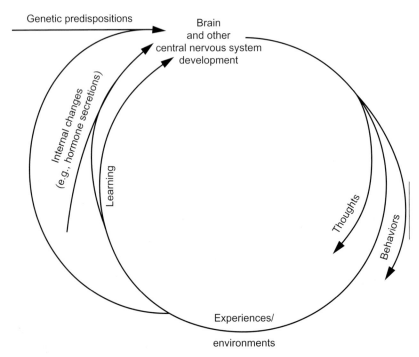

Figure 13.1 A depiction of the biopsychosocial model of intelligence in which biological factors alter life experiences and life experience, in turn, alter biological factors. (From Halpern, 2012; reproduced with permission of Taylor and Francis Publishers)

experiences. The interface between experience and biology is seamless. According to the biopsychosocial model, biology and environment are as inseparable as conjoined twins who share a common heart. It provides a framework that is a more integrated way of thinking about a holistic process (see Figure 13.1).

Explanations that Attack the Assumption of Group Differences

The fourth class of explanations attack the initial assumption that intelligence measures of any sort can be valid for different groups of people because there are no culture-free assessments. For example, researchers in Africa, Asia, and other parts of the world often have fundamentally different ideas about the nature of intelligence (Serpell, 2011). A somewhat less negative variation on this theme is the idea that although it is not possible to create any assessment that does not depend on prior learning or life experiences, culture-fair tests are possible, if the test items are based on common experiences that cut across cultures. Many so-called "culture-fair" tests are nonverbal because language is closely tied to culture. Another way of thinking about the question of culture-free testing is to ask if we really should try to remove culture from a test of intelligence. Culture refers to the collective experiences of a group of people. Raven's Progressive Matrices is commonly thought of as a "culture-fair" test, but those exposed to Western-style education will have experience with putting items in rows and columns, which may not be a common experience in non-industrialized countries. In other words, the concept of a "culture-fair" test may be impossible. Therefore, it may be more useful to think about the degree to which an intelligence measure is fair across cultures, instead of thinking about fairness as achievable or not.

One argument counter to the idea that group differences in intelligence scores reflect fundamental flaws in test construction is that scores on these tests can be used to predict many real-life events. IQ scores computed from standardized intelligence tests predict many important variables, including job performance (individuals who score higher on intelligence tests learn job-related skills more quickly and learn more of them; Hunter & Schmidt, 1996), academic performance in universities and other post-secondary institutions (Kretzschmar, Neubert, Wusternberg, & Greiff, 2016: Kuncel, Ones, & Sackett, 2010), and reduced rates of crime (Burhan, Kurniawan, Sidek, & Mohamad, 2014). For people with very high scores, IQ also predicts some kinds of exceptional creative achievements such as holding a patent, publishing scholarly articles, and achieving a doctorate (Lubinski, 2009). A strong position is taken by Ones, Viswesvaran, and Dilchert (2005), who state that "Data are resoundingly clear: [measured cognitive ability] is the most powerful individual differences trait that predicts job performance...Not relying on it for personnel selection would have serious implications for productivity. There is no getting away from or wishing away this fact" (p. 450; see also Ones, Dilchert, & Viswesvaran, 2012). Most importantly, scores on standardized tests of intelligence predict success in these various areas equally well for members of different groups (Reynolds & Suzuki, 2013). Thus, according to most experts in psychometrics (statistical properties of testing; e.g., Camilli & Shepard, 1994), a test is not biased if it predicts equally well for members of different groups, even if some groups achieve higher average scores than other groups. Although most testing associations adhere to this criterion, some individuals and groups have argued that a test is culturally biased if there is differential performance for different groups (Helms, 2010). The problem with this criterion is that it presupposes that there are no group differences and rejects any study that finds them. There are many reasons (statistical and technical) why IQ and real-life criteria such as job success have low correlations, so strong statements about predictive validity have to be taken with some cautious skepticism (Richardson & Norgate, 2015).

Standardized intelligence tests do not (generally) show **predictive bias**. In other words, they are able to predict outcomes for all groups. Despite this, the tests provide an incomplete picture of who will succeed at various tasks. There are many variables besides intelligence that are important in determining success including qualities and skills such as persistence, social skills, specialized knowledge that may be specific to a particular job, personality variables, and many more. It is also possible that IQ scores correlate with other variables because they rely on some common factor such as facility with language and it is not that intelligence is causing degrees of success at work, but both intelligence and success at work are caused by a third unidentified variable. Furthermore, any biases that are held regarding intelligence tests can also be held toward these other tasks.

Intelligence is a multifaceted concept that cannot be captured in a single number, but we have to go back to the initial question: Is intelligence testing a reasonable way of determining the relative intelligence of different people and the groups to which they belong? To answer this question, we consider two types of group differences – differences between females and males and differences among various racial and ethnic groups.

Which Is the Smarter Sex: Female or Male?

It would seem to be an easy task to answer the question about whether males or females are smarter. Theoretically, all one would have to do is see which group (on average) gets higher scores on standardized tests of intelligence. But standardized intelligence tests were originally written to show no overall sex differences. Therefore, if there was an item that one sex tended to get correct more often than the other, it was either dropped from the test or balanced with an item that favored the other sex (Brody, 1992). As Clewell and Campbell (2002, p. 264) commented: "It has long been known that it is possible to create or eliminate differences in test scores by selecting different test items." Of course, inherent in this question is the assumption that there is a smarter sex. Because the research literature on this topic is huge, we necessarily focus on a few main hypotheses and findings. For a more comprehensive review, see Halpern (2012).

If we cannot use IQ scores to answer this question, what other indicators are available? Suppose instead of scores on intelligence tests, we used grades in school as a proxy variable for intelligence. The data clearly show that girls get better grades in school, even in those areas where they score (on average) lower on standardized assessments. In a meta-analysis using data from 369 samples, Voyer and Voyer (2014) found the largest female advantage for language courses ($d = .37$) and smallest for math courses ($d = .07$). Thus, if we used school grades to assess intelligence, females would rate higher than males. But, as you might expect, a question as controversial as this one does not have such a simple answer.

Keiser, Sackett, Kuncek, and Brothen (2016) used data from college students to examine the question of whether data used to predict success in college underpredict women's performance. They examined grades on examinations and on class participation and extra credit and concluded that college entrance exams (which are similar to intelligence tests) predict equally well for men and women on test grades, but women score higher on non-cognitive components of college grades – class participation and being conscientious. They also argue that women, in general, take easier courses, so they achieve higher grades. Arguments like this one are basically about what it means to be intelligent. If intelligent people score higher on tasks that matter (in this case grades in college), does it make sense to conclude that one group really isn't smarter even though they have higher achievement on the proxy variable for intelligence?

In 1998, Arthur Jensen joined the frenzy over sex differences in intelligence. His name may be familiar to you because of his earlier writings in which he claimed that associative learning (memorizing, Level 1 Learning) was approximately the same for all races, but higher-level conceptual learning (conceptualizing, Level 2 Learning) was found more frequently among whites than non-whites (Jensen, 1969). Because IQ scores cannot be used sensibly to determine whether males or females are the smarter sex, he examined assessments that "load heavily on g." Recall that g is a generally accepted term for general intelligence, although some researchers say that it is merely a correlate of intelligence, so both could reflect a third variable that is unidentified (e.g., Gould, 1996). Jensen used five test batteries with large representative samples of test-takers that encompassed the range of ability in the population. Jensen concluded, "No evidence was found for sex differences in the mean level of g.... . Males, on average, excel on some factors; females on others" (pp. 531-532). We agree: Jensen got this one right. To learn more about the career paths of two psychologists in this area, see the Focus on Contemporary Research box below.

FOCUS ON CONTEMPORARY RESEARCH: DIANE F. HALPERN'S AND TOMOE KANAYA'S WORK ON COGNITIVE SEX DIFFERENCES

Diane Halpern started studying cognitive sex differences soon after receiving her Ph.D. and beginning her first academic job. As she was teaching courses in cognitive psychology and psychology of women, the same questions came up in both classes. Were there really any differences between women and men in their intelligence? Halpern has spent the last 37 years working on that question! Her work in this area extended to race and ethnic differences in intelligence when serving on the taskforce headed by Dick Neisser (Neisser et al., 1996) that was created by the American Psychological Association in response to the book *The Bell Curve*. That text made strong statements about the biological bases of group differences in intelligence. More recently, she worked with a group headed by Dick Nisbett (Nisbett et al., 2012), whose task was to update the earlier report, and again when asked to head a group put together by the Association for Psychological Science

(Halpern et al., 2007). Halpern also chaired a taskforce assembled by the Institute for Educational Sciences to make empirically supported recommendations to encourage girls in science and math (Halpern et al., 2007).

Halpern's major contribution to the area of group differences in intelligence has been the many editions of her textbook entitled *Sex Differences in Cognitive Abilities* (2012). Her research in this area has focused on many of the themes found in this chapter – gender stereotypes (Halpern, Straight, & Stephenson, 2011), spatial abilities (Miller & Halpern, 2013), public policy implications (Halpern et al., 2011), variability in intelligence (Turkheimer & Halpern, 2009), and recent syntheses (Miller & Halpern, 2014).

Tomoe Kanaya has always been interested in understanding why some students excel in an academic setting while others do not; she is also interested in learning how to increase the achievement of children who are underserved. Kanaya's research has focused on the impact of IQ and achievement tests on special-education diagnoses due to fluctuations that occur from the Flynn effect (e.g., Kanaya, 2016; Kanaya & Ceci, 2011). Given the established research on group differences in intelligence along with the heavy reliance on standardized tests in special-education policy, some groups are more vulnerable than others to misdiagnoses of intellectual disability (Kanaya & Ceci, 2007a; Kanaya & Ceci, 2007b) and learning disability (Kanaya & Ceci, 2012). Such misdiagnoses can have substantial and life-long consequences, including inadequate special education services, social stigmatization, social security disability funding, and death penalty eligibility (Kanaya, Ceci & Scullin, 2003).

What Are the Cognitive Tasks that Usually Show Sex Differences?

Females, on average (yes, this part is getting repetitive, but we really want to be sure that everyone understands that these are group averages that cannot be used to make judgments about individuals) score considerably higher on most assessments of reading and writing. In a review of the literature, Hedges and Nowell (1995, p. 45) wrote, "the large sex differences in writing ... are alarming." They found that "Females have consistently outperformed males in writing achievement at the 4th, 8th, and 11th grade levels between 1988 and 1996 ... The writing scores of female 8th graders were comparable with those of 11th grade males" (p. 18).

The female advantage in reading achievement is large. International data collected as part of the PIRLS project (Progress in International Reading Literacy Study; Mullis, Martin, Foy, & Drucker, 2012) showed that in 4th grade "across 45 countries ... girls have a 16-point advantage" with little reduction over the last decade in the size of the female advantage over the last decade (p. 7). The international female advantage is shown in Figure 13.2.

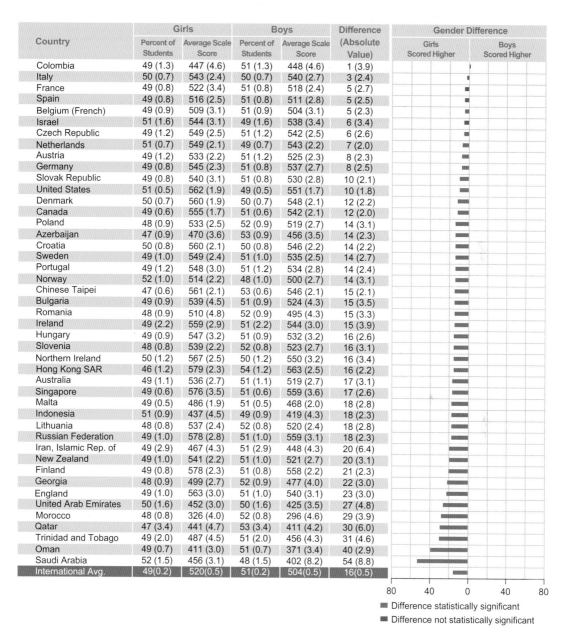

Figure 13.2 Female advantage in reading is found internationally. Data from PIRLS study of 4th graders in 2001 (Exhibit 1.5, p. 52). Source: PIRLS 2001 Assessment. Copyright © 2003 International Association for the Evaluation of Educational Achievement (IEA). TIMMS & PIRLS International Study Center, Lynch School of Education, Boston College.

Other areas where females achieve higher scores than males include memory for faces, especially female faces (Loven, Herlitz, & Rehnman, 2011); verbal retrieval tasks such as fluency (naming words that begin with a particular letter or providing a synonym for a particular word; Hirnstein, Andrews, & Hausmann, 2014); and

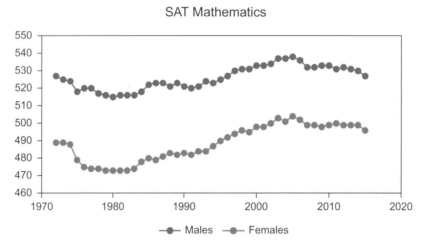

Figure 13.3 Male and female mean SAT scores for college-bound seniors 1972-2015. (data from CollegeBoard, 2015)

memory for location (Voyer, Postma, Brake, & Imperato-McGinley, 2007), which is usually thought of as a spatial skill.

Males excel on most, but not all standardized assessments of mathematics, such as the math portion of the college admissions test, the SAT (College Board).

As shown in Figure 13.3, high school boys have been outperforming girls in math at least since 1972, with little change in the size of the gap. In interpreting these data, keep in mind that more girls take the SATs than boys, so it would be expected that the greater number of female test-takers would decrease the mean score for females. Recall also that girls get better grades in (most) math courses in school at all levels. Girls are also more likely to take four years of high school math than boys are.

Although the media has made much ado about the average higher scores for males on the SATs (and other assessments that do not directly match the curriculum), one of the largest sex differences favoring males is in **mental rotation**, which is the ability to imagine what a complex shape would look like if it were rotated in space (Maeda & Yoon, 2013; Voyer, Voyer, & Bryden, 1995). These differences are found in the first few months of life (e.g., Quinn & Liben, 2008) and have been implicated as a partial cause for sex differences in those areas of math that are highly spatial.

Tails and Tales of Distributions

Throughout this chapter, we have been careful to repeat that all of the sex differences are for averages, but it is useful to think about different portions of the ability distribution if we want to gain a better understanding of what's going on. For the middle portion – where most people fall – the differences between females and males are small, but they are larger in the low-intelligence and high-intelligence ends of the distribution. Consider reading, for example. In an analysis of four independent studies, the data clearly show that the rates of reading disabilities are significantly higher for boys than for girls, as are spelling deficits, but more girls have math deficits than do boys (Moll, Kunze, Neuhoff, Bruder, & Schulte-Korne, 2014; Rutter, Caspi, & Ferguson, 2004).

Much more attention has been paid to sex differences in the high-scoring end of the distribution. The mean SAT mathematics scores show a substantial advantage for males, but a large contribution to these average scores is the large number of males scoring at the highest range. Consider how the male/female ratios have changed for the highest scorers on math-ability and science-reasoning tests. From 1981 to 1985, there were more than 13 males for every female among the top .01 percent of scores, but this ratio has fallen to approximately 3 to 4 males for every female among the scorers (Wai, Cacchio, Putallaz, & Makel, 2010).

The Why of Sex Differences in Cognition

Knowing that there are some differences on average among females and males naturally leads to the "why?" question. As readers can probably guess, there is a wide array of biological, environmental, and interactionist explanations. Let's consider the biological ones first.

Biological Explanations

There are three main categories of biological explanation for sex differences in intelligence – genetic, brain size and structure, and hormonal.

Genetic explanations are based on the fact that males have a small Y chromosome, which makes them vulnerable to recessive traits that are carried on their X chromosome. It is well established that there are more males with intellectual disabilities than females, and this disparity is caused, in part, by the genes on their X chromosome (Turkheimer & Halpern, 2009). But, genetic explanations cannot be used to explain sex differences in the mid-range of intelligence because females and males excel in different cognitive areas. They also cannot explain sex differences at the highest ranges of intelligence because there are no known intelligence genes that are linked to high intelligence.

There are many on-average sex differences in the brain, but the real questions are whether these have much effect on intelligence or whether the overlap and similarities in male and female brains are more important than their differences (Eliot, 2011). Brain size and structure have been used to explain sex differences in intelligence. It is generally agreed that male brains are larger than female brains, even after correcting for body size. There are many problems with the brain-size hypothesis, including the fact that there are no overall differences in female and male intelligence and a measure as gross as brain size cannot be linked to differences in specific components of intelligence. In addition, it is well known that life experiences alter the size of brain structures, so any differences could have been caused by differences in the everyday experiences of males and females. The general argument is that since brains are "valuable real estate," having more brain implies more intelligence (e.g., Lynn, 1994). But studies have shown that the brains of males and females are not very different – there are "mosaics" of features, some more common in females, and some more common in males, with considerable overlap (Joel et al., 2015).

A major debate in the literature on sex differences in the brain centers around the corpus callosum, which is a large tract of about 200 million neurons that connect the two hemispheres of the brain. One reason why researchers differ in their findings is that the corpus callosum has a highly irregular shape and there are several different ways to measure it. A recent study concluded that there are statistically significant, but "subtle" differences (Bjornholm et al., 2017). But a meta-analysis of research on the corpus callosum found the sex differences were eliminated when corrections were made for overall brain size (Tan, Ma, Vira, Marsha, & Eliot, 2016). Again, the important question as it relates to intelligence is whether or how much these brain differences correlate with sex differences in intelligence, and this is a much more difficult question to answer than cataloging where there are average sex differences in the brain. Research on this question is growing exponentially, as seen with an entire issue of a major neuroscience journal dedicated to sex differences in the brain, and it is likely that our understanding of the way brain structures reflect and direct intelligence will change with future research findings (*Journal of Neuroscience*, 2017).

Mention sex differences in any behavior and someone is likely to reply, "It's all in the hormones!" **Sex hormones** are chemicals that are secreted from the sex glands (testes, ovaries) and related structures. Although we tend to talk about *female* hormones – estrogen and progesterone – and *male* hormones – most notably testosterone – females and males have both types of hormones in their bodies. Females have a much greater quantity of estrogen and progesterone, and males have a much greater quantity of testosterone. To muddy the distinction even further, our bodies convert these hormones from one chemical structure to another. There are also different critical periods when hormones have their greatest effects. Prenatal hormones and those soon after birth (notably, the surge in testosterone in males in early infancy; Hines, Spencer, Kung, Browne, Constantinescu, & Noorderhaven, 2016) affect the tendency to engage in "rough and tumble play," which is more likely in boys than girls. The direct effects of hormones on cognition are difficult to study because they are confounded with other variables such as differences in the rearing of girls and boys; in addition, effects are not likely to be linear, and direct links from hormones to intelligence are difficult to create (Collaer & Hines, 1995). Because we cannot perform true experiments with humans and their exposure to hormones, researchers rely on research with other animals and on "natural experiments," such as genetic boys who are not sensitive to testosterone and genetic girls who are exposed to high levels of testosterone prenatally. But there are difficulties extrapolating about human performance from nonhuman animal studies and using abnormalities to generalize to normal functioning. There is some evidence that some abilities may vary over the menstrual cycle for cycling women, but the effects are small and the results are still controversial (e.g., Halpern & Tan, 2001).

Environmental Explanations

On average, females and males have different life experiences and expectations. The female and male **sex roles** provide a strong consensus of what males and females are like and should be like. There are powerful sex-role socialization practices throughout the lifespan. Stereotypes can be activated automatically and operate without our conscious awareness. Stereotypes are not random associations of traits with different groups of people. In fact, many stereotypes are statistically accurate (e.g., males do score higher on average on high-stakes tests of mathematics; Halpern, Straight, & Stephenson, 2011).

Stereotype threat is the idea that under some conditions, the activation of negative stereotypes about one's group (e.g., females are not as good as males in math) can depress performance in individuals because of fear of confirming the negative stereotype (Steele & Aronson, 1995). The research literature on stereotype threat is so large that it has become a cottage industry on many university campuses. There are dozens of **meta-analyses**, where researchers compile and summarize the results of multiple findings regarding one topic, that show some effect of stereotype threat, but it does not explain all of the sex differences in cognitive tests. Doyle and Voyer (2016) examined 224 effect sizes and concluded that "the effects of stereotype threat on women can be interpreted as relatively small but significant in math performance, but non-significant in spatial performance" (p. 103). They found no effect for males. Stoet and Geary (2012) have been strongly negative about the research showing stereotype threat (based in part on statistical grounds), but given the huge number of studies that document such an effect and the several meta-analyses that have been conducted, it is reasonable to conclude that fear of confirming a negative stereotype about one's group can affect performance under some conditions, but cannot explain all of the variance causing the male–female gaps.

Many of the same issues that are pertinent to sex differences in intelligence are found in research on race and ethnic differences, which is the next topic in this chapter.

Race and Ethnic Group Differences in Intelligence

Talking about sex differences is hard, but talking about racial and ethnic differences can be just as hard, if not harder. It is almost impossible to have a **"blank slate" approach**, or a completely neutral or uninformed view, to examining ethnic or racial differences in intelligence. Most people have some pre-existing belief regarding whether or not individuals of different races and ethnicities have different levels of cognitive abilities, and no amount of scientific data and analyses will be able to change the minds of those "who feel they already know the truth" (Eysenck, 1971, p. 8). Therefore, it may be useful to take some time beforehand and decide what data you would need to be convinced that racial and ethnic differences in intelligence are mostly biological or mostly environmental in their origin.

It is important to recognize that any conversation about race and ethnicity differences is a sensitive and controversial topic due to the many historical and political practices that have reduced levels of equality for many races and ethnicities. This is particularly true for blacks and African Americans,[1] who have experienced systemic and long-standing discrimination for centuries. As Neisser et al. (1996, p. 93) have pointed out, they have "the short end of nearly every stick: average income, representation in high-level occupations, health and health care, death rate, confrontations with the legal system, and so on." For these reasons, an overwhelming majority of the research and discussion on racial and ethnic differences in intelligence has focused on the black–white test score gap.

Any discussion on racial and ethnic differences requires a discussion of the definition of race and ethnicity. In its official statement, the American Anthropological Association (1998, para. 2) concluded that race is a cultural construction that is not supported by "evidence from the analysis of genetics (e.g., DNA)" and that most physical variation is within so-called racial groups. Thus, they reject the idea that there are biologically distinct racial groups. Often, the demographic information about an individual's race is based on census categories that do not allow for mixed-race and mixed-ethnicity categories. It is estimated that individuals classified as African Americans, have on average 28-30 European ancestry (Cavalli-Sforza, 1997; Nisbett, 2009). Labels based on "skin

---

[1] As used here, the term "black" refers to any person of black African descent; the term "African American" refers to anyone in the United States of black African descent.

color" are also problematic as some societies, such as apartheid South Africa, which separated their black population between "coloreds" (mixed-race individuals) and Bantu (not mixed race) do not make the same categorical divisions as others (Sternberg et al., 2005). Therefore, race and ethnic identity are separate from biological make-up, and racial categories can be considered continuous rather than discrete groups.

The Black–White Test Score Gap: Then and Now

For much of the twentieth century, the black–white test score gap was reported to be approximately 15 points, which is one standard deviation, with the average for blacks lower than that for whites (e.g., Jensen, 1980; Neisser et al., 1996). Some studies have shown that the gap was larger among adults compared with children (e.g., Thorndike, Hagen & Sattler, 1986). Recent studies show that blacks and African Americans experienced gains at different rates in IQ performance between the 1970s and early 2000s. Because of this difference, the gap has shrunk and is now 8-10 points, with adults continuing to experience a larger gap than children (Dickens & Flynn, 2001; Rindermann & Thompson, 2013).

It is common to hear that this gap is due to "biased" tests. Careful examinations of the tests, including examining the vocabulary used and specific questions included, do not support racial or ethnic bias within the test (Reynolds & Suzuki, 2013). There are statistical procedures designed to examine specific items for bias (called **differential item functioning** or **dif-analysis**), which support the idea that individual items are not biased for or against any group, although these procedures do not protect against the possibility that the entire assessment is biased. Interested readers with an advanced background in statistics can find an excellent overview in Zenisky, Hambleton, and Robin (2003). Indeed, researchers and test makers are highly motivated and have gone to great lengths to eliminate such biases, but the gap continues. Further, sociological factors that increase the likelihood that a black child will be tested by a white examiner also cannot account for the entire gap (Neisser et al., 1996). Finally, and most importantly, the tests predict achievement, such as educational attainment and grade-point averages (GPA), about equally well for all race and ethnicity groups (Jensen, 1980; Reynolds & Suzuki, 2013).

Therefore, if test bias cannot explain the black–white gap, then what can? The fact that the gap shrank during a time that blacks and African Americans experienced large gains in access and resources in order to reduce past inequalities provides strong evidence for an environmental influence. Dickens and Flynn (2001) have shown that small gains in environmental factors can multiply with each other and lead to large gains in intelligence. The wider gap seen among adults can indicate that social programs and policies that are geared toward reducing racial and ethnic disparities for children are more effective than programs and policies with similar missions that are geared for adults.

Is Race Biological or Environmental?

Research on the black–white test score gap provides a unique opportunity to examine this issue. American, biracial children with black mothers and white fathers score, on average, 9 points lower on IQ compared to biracial children with white mothers and black fathers (Willerman, Naylor & Myrianthopoulos, 1974). Although mothers and fathers play equal roles in a child's biological make-up, mothers play a larger role in a child's social upbringing compared to fathers. Therefore, these group differences within biracial children can be explained by different environmental experiences. In addition, one of the earliest studies on the intelligence of biracial children was conducted on the children of World War II soldiers who were members of US occupational forces in Germany and had children with white German women. Eyferth (1961) found that that the biracial solider-fathered children had similar IQs compared to all-white, soldier-fathered children. In other words, the biracial test gap seen among black father–white mother parents within the United States is not observed among the same parenting combination in Germany, which is opposite to what would be predicted if the gap was primarily caused by genetics. Finally, there have been several studies that have found no relationship between the "level of European ancestry" and IQ among African Americans (e.g., Scarr, Pakstis, Katz, & Barker, 1977).

These studies seem to provide strong support that the black–white gap is not a function of biological factors, given that the gap is reduced or eliminated even when the biological make-up of the individuals remains the same. But it is important to remember that these research findings are dependent on non-random selection. It is possible that black men with higher levels of intelligence are going to find biracial relationships more appealing than do black women with lower intelligence, thus increasing the intelligence of the biracial children with black fathers compared to biracial children with black mothers. Further, these studies were conducted decades ago, during a time in which policies that promoted segregation, including Jim Crow laws, were actively enforced in parts of the United States. It is possible that data on current black/white individuals would not yield the same results. Unfortunately, more current data are not available. Recent television shows that center on the surprising results of DNA/ancestry results highlight the lack of awareness that most individuals have of their biological make-up. For these reasons, the "perfect data" that would definitively prove either conclusion do not exist.

Although biracial studies provide useful biological evidence for group differences, adoption studies can provide useful environmental evidence. These studies have found that black and half-black children who were adopted by white parents experience an increase in IQ of as much as 12 points. Follow-up studies reveal, however, that these gains decrease over time and the adoptees resemble the IQs of their biological parents in adulthood (Scarr & Weinberg, 1983); but it should also be noted that everyone experienced reductions in IQ at this follow-up, and the adopted children's drop was not significantly different from the drop experienced by the biological children of the adopted parents (i.e., their siblings; Weinberg, Scarr & Waldman, 1992). Although this trend may appear to be fickle, it is seen in adoption studies of all races and ethnicities where children are adopted into a home with more resources, including higher levels of parental IQ, education, and income (Duyme, Dumaret & Tomkiewicz, 1999). This trend can also be seen on evaluations of in-depth educational interventions for at-risk and low-income children, such as **Head Start**: Initial increases in IQ seen during early childhood do not continue and are essentially eliminated by adulthood (Lazar & Darlington, 1982). Therefore, blacks and African Americans are not the only group to experience environmentally based increases during the childhood years alone, and such findings reinforce the importance of continuing intervention programs throughout the adulthood years.

Other Racial and Ethnic Groups

Similar to blacks and African Americans, studies have shown that the Hispanic-white gap, which was originally around 11 points, has been reduced to approximately 9 points (Rindermann & Thompson, 2013). Hispanic Americans, the fastest-growing minority group in the United States, represent a wide range of national origins, including Puerto Rico, Cuba, and multiple countries within Central and South America. Within that wide geographical range, there are also variations within generation and ancestry level; many Latinos have resided in the southwestern boundaries of the United States before white settlers arrived. Therefore, a clear estimate of level of European or other mixed-race ancestry for individual members of this group is extremely difficult. Hispanic Americans also face language challenges; research reveals that US-born Latinos show on average low levels of academic English and Spanish proficiency, making it difficult to perform well on standardized tests, even if translated versions are offered (Gándara & Contreras, 2009). Therefore, interpreting the intelligence findings and trends of all Hispanic Americans, and interpreting them in a manner that treats them as a solitary biological or social group is not appropriate.

Similarly, Asian Americans are a group that represents a wide range of countries and cultures. Contrary to previous race and ethnic comparisons, Asian Americans are documented to have higher achievements than whites (Nisbett et al., 2012).

Further, the Asian–white IQ gap was originally reported to be approximately 11 points, where Asians outscore whites (e.g., Lynn, 1987), but more recent accounts reveal small to no differences between the groups (e.g., Flynn, 1991). There is, however, some evidence that Asians score higher on tests of mathematical and spatial reasoning ability compared with whites (Dandy & Nettelbeck, 2002) and Asian American males are the highest-scoring group on the mathematics portion of the SATs. In addition, there is evidence that Japanese and Chinese Americans out-achieve white Americans (Neisser et al., 1996). Therefore, rather than group differences in intelligence, it appears there are group differences to the benefits yielded by intelligence: Asian Americans get "more bang for their buck" when it comes to intelligence and IQ compared to whites. Some explain this through differences in values among Asian cultures that reward achievement and education more highly than do European cultures, but an overwhelming majority of these studies have focused entirely on Chinese and Japanese Americans. Far less is known about the performance of Korean Americans, Asian-Indian Americans, or people from other regions of Southeast Asia, including Vietnamese Americans and Hmong Americans, who are not experiencing the same levels of overachievement as their Chinese and Japanese counterparts.

There is even less known about the average intelligence of other races and ethnicities. The high achievements of many Jewish professionals, particularly in the legal, medical, and academic fields, has been widely documented (Nisbett, 2009), and a few studies suggest that Jews of European descent have higher average IQs than non-Jews (e.g., Lynn, 2004). In contrast, Native Americans and Alaskan Natives have experienced poor outcomes (National Indian Education Association, 2008) and perform worse, on average, on intelligence tests (Tsethlikai, 2011) compared with other groups. But most researchers agree that these findings are preliminary and more research needs to be conducted before formal conclusions of group differences can be made.

Our Differences May Not Be Meaningful: Overlapping Populations

Another way to think about group differences is to understand that differences may not be meaningful. Consider Figure 13.4, which illustrates the entire range of possible test scores from two different groups. In this figure, Group 1 is being compared to Group 2, but you can easily substitute both of them for males versus females, or whites versus blacks or any two groups.

In Figure 13.4, Group 1 scores higher on a specific test compared with Group 2. Suppose that all the researchers agree that this difference is **statistically significant**, and therefore, this difference is not due to random chance. Some conclude that Group 1 is better than Group 2 on this particular test. Multiple studies have been conducted by different researchers covering a wide range of populations,

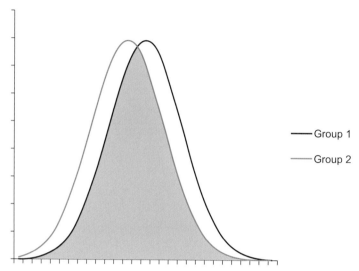

Figure 13.4 Two hypothetical distributions showing how overlap between groups calls into question the importance of a finding of "statistically significant group differences."

geographical locations, and all other factors that have been show to influence these test scores. Now, it is starting to appear that the group difference is irrefutable and scientifically **validated**, and therefore, measuring what the experts agree they should be measuring; Group 1 is better than Group 2 on this test.

Although it may not be wrong to come to this conclusion, it is important to understand that it does not represent all people from both groups. These differences are often reporting averages and *most* Group 1 and Group 2 people are *not* average. In the most basic terms, half of the population is above average and half of the population is below average. Therefore, focusing on just the individuals that receive the average score is not being inclusive of most individuals in both groups. These group differences only become meaningful when you are isolating the outer extremes of the scores, in other words, individuals who have very high or very low scores.

More specifically, using Figure 13.4 above, it is true that Group 1 is "better," on average, than Group 2 on this test. But most Group 1 *and* 2 people receive the same scores (represented in the shaded area). It is not until you isolate the highest scorers and the lowest scorers that the group difference is noticeable. As explained in the section on sex differences, if you isolate the highest scorers, you will get more Group 1 people than Group 2 people. Likewise, if you isolate the lowest scorers, you will get more Group 2 people than Group 1 people (assuming that the variability of both groups is equal, which is often not true). But you will encounter Group 1 *and* Group 2 people in both extremes.

Consider height as an analogy based on US Census (n.d.) data: If you isolate all individuals between the ages of 20-29 who are over 6'3", you will meet more males than females. Conversely, if you isolate all individuals who are below 4'11", you will meet more females than males. Regardless, while uncommon, males who are below 4'11" and females over 6'3" do exist. Therefore, just knowing that someone is male isn't enough information to make accurate assumptions of his height. And it is far more likely that a male has the same height as a female than his being over 6'3". Finally, unless there is a task that specifically requires an individual to be below 4'11" or above 6'3", there is no meaningful reason to think that males and females are different. Therefore, even if group differences are significant *on average*, you cannot assume that the groups are different *as a whole* or that these differences are meaningful.

Using What We Know about Stereotype Threat to Reduce Group Differences

We introduced stereotype threat in the previous section on sex differences, and the same concept applies in racial and ethnic differences. The original study on the impact of stereotype threat was conducted by Steele and Aronson (1995) on white and African American students at Stanford University. The students were given sample items of the Verbal GRE test. Half of the students were given instructions that the test was being used as a diagnostic tool of their intellectual ability, while the instructions for the other half called the test a problem-solving exercise. Despite the fact that all of the students had met the highly competitive standards to be enrolled in one of the most prestigious institutions in the country, the African American students received lower scores than the white students when they thought they were taking a diagnostic test. But the African American students performed just as well as the white students (when adjusting for, or controlling for, their SAT scores) when they thought they were participating in a problem-solving exercise. The underperformance has been interpreted as the result of "stereotype threat," or anxiety that is derived from knowing there is a negative stereotype about your group (in this case, the stereotype of lower intellectual performance among African Americans).

Since then, countless studies have been conducted and show that no group is immune to stereotype threat, including whites (when compared with Asians) and females (when compared with males) on math ability tests as well as Latinos (when compared with whites) on verbal ability tests (Aronson & McGlone, 2009). Eliminating the threat by saying that the test is not a measure of intelligence or that group differences do not exist on the particular test can reduce group differences in test performance, but it does not eliminate them (Spencer, Logel, & Davies, 2016). Providing reconstrual strategies (that is, strategies that help test-takers reinterpret these stereotypes), such as highlighting positive stereotypes of an individual's identity and teaching individuals that intelligence is **malleable** and can improve over time, rather than fixed and permanent, have been found to reduce the effect of stereotype threat as well (Spencer et al., 2016). Being able to misattribute the anxiety derived from stereotype threat to another environmental source can also be useful; Ben-Zeev, Fein, and Inzlicht (2005) found that the stereotype-threat condition was not effective when women were told there was an audio machine producing a "silent tone" that could not be heard by the human ear, but that reported side effects included anxiety and elevated heart rate. In other words, when the women were given another "excuse" for feeling anxiety, they were able to perform better.

Despite these results, stereotype threat cannot explain the entire black–white gap or female–male gap. Some (e.g., Sackett, Hardison & Cullen, 2004) argue that introducing stereotype threat increases the gap, while eliminating stereotype threat merely reduces it back to the original estimate. And while school-based interventions created to reduce stereotype threat have increased achievement and motivation among minority students (e.g. Aronson, Fried & Good, 2002), many of the findings on increased test performance have focused on the short-term impact on specific tests and in laboratory settings. Regardless, understanding the impact of stereotype threat is an important element to include when examining group differences, but more research must be conducted before we can determine the importance of stereotype threat among the many other environmental variables, such as test anxiety or poverty, that can lead to significant intellectual gains for any underperforming group (e.g., Dickens & Flynn, 2001).

CONCLUSION

The most important conclusion about group differences in intelligence is that these differences refer to group averages, and there are members of every group among the highest and lowest scorers on tests of intelligence. We cannot and should not make decisions about any individual based on her or his race or gender group. Racial and gender group differences in measures of intelligence have changed over time, and we expect them to continue to change along with changes in how the racial and gender groups are perceived (e.g., changing sex roles). A clear answer to questions about group differences will be possible only when cultural norms change and women and men and people of all races participate equally in society.

We began this chapter with the disclaimer that the topic of group differences is fraught with controversy. It is important to recognize that group differences, *on average,* do exist on some measures of intelligence. The ways in which these differences are interpreted, however, vary and provide the impetus for debate. The research findings included in this chapter serve as an illustration of the varying ways in which research can inform policies, attitudes, and beliefs about group differences in intelligence.

CHAPTER SUMMARY

The large body of research about group differences in intelligence is contentious because the conclusions we make as researchers and citizens have personal and political consequences. Almost everyone will agree that there are some differences in the average scores of members of different groups on some tests that purportedly measure intelligence. We conclude that it is impossible to assign a single percentage to the portion of intelligence that is "caused by" biological and environmental factors because these two types of influences influence each other and cannot be disentangled. Environmental and biological factors are not independent, so it is an essentially unanswerable controversy. Tests that purportedly assess intelligence should be evaluated along many dimensions, but tests that predict intelligence-related criteria predict variables equally well for all groups and are not biased (statistically speaking).

Although there are some cognitive areas that show on average differences for males and females, neither is the smarter sex because some tests favor females and some tests favor males. In general, females perform better on selected memory tests, writing and reading assessments, and language fluency tests. Males perform better on some visuospatial tests (especially mental rotation), and some math assessments, especially those that are not tied to the school curriculum. Females get better grades in school, even in areas when males outscore females on some standardized tests. Stereotype threat, which is the fear of confirming a negative stereotype about one's group, can explain some of these differences, but not all of them.

Racial and ethnic group differences may be even more contentious than those between males and females. The life experiences of members of different groups vary in many uncontrolled ways, making it impossible to determine the contributions of biology and environment. We conclude that both types of influences contribute to overall group differences. The excess of males in the mental disabilities portion of the intelligence distribution is due, at least in part, to X-linked recessive traits, but there is no genetic explanation for differences in the midrange or upper right-hand tail of the distribution. In understanding the many questions about group differences in intelligence it is important to consider the extent to which the distributions overlap and to remember that we cannot predict individual performance from group-level data.

KEY TERMS

"blank slate" approach • **biopsychosocial hypothesis** • **differential item functioning (dif-analysis)** • **fixed** • **Head Start** • **malleable** • **mental rotation** • **meta-analysis** • **predictive bias** • **sex hormones** • **sex roles** • **statistically significant** • **stereotype threat** • **validated**

COMPREHENSION AND REFLECTION QUESTIONS

1. Why is it so difficult to get a simple answer about the cause of group differences in intelligence?
2. Explain how the biopsychosocial hypothesis calls into question statements about the percentage contributed to intelligence by biology and environment.
3. How does stereotype threat operate in intelligence testing?
4. Why do the authors constantly repeat the phrase "on average" when they write about group differences in intelligence?
5. Given that the topic of group differences in intelligence is so contentious, why do the authors believe that it is an important topic to study?
6. Intelligence is measured as a continuum, whereas racial/ethnic groups are measured as categorical groups. But there is strong evidence that racial/ethnic categories should be measured on a continuum (e.g., mixed-race ancestry). How would your understanding and interpretation of racial/ethnic differences in intelligence change if you take this approach to race/ethnicity?
7. In what ways do females and males have the same levels of intelligence? In what ways do they have different levels of intelligence?

References

American Anthropological Association (1998). AAA statement on race. May 17. www.americananthro.org/ConnectWithAAA/Content.aspx?ItemNumber=2583

American Association of University Women (2016). *The simple truth about the gender pay gap.* Fall. www.aauw.org/resource/the-simple-truth-ppt/

Anderson, N. B., & Nickerson, K. J. (2005). Genes, race, and psychology in the genomic era: An introduction. *American Psychologist, 60*, 5-8. doi: 10.1037/0003-066X.60.1.5

Aronson, J., Fried, C. B., & Good, C. (2002). Reducing the effects of stereotype threat on African American college students by shaping theories of intelligence. *Journal of Experimental Social Psychology, 38*(2), 113-125. doi: 10.1006/jesp.2001.1491

Aronson, J., & McGlone, M. S. (2009). Stereotype and social identity threat. In T. D. Nelson (ed.), *Handbook of prejudice, stereotyping, and discrimination* (pp. 153-178). New York: Psychology Press.

Ben-Zeev, T., Fein, S., & Inzlicht, M. (2005). Arousal and stereotype threat. *Journal of Experimental Social Psychology, 41*(2), 174-181. doi: 10.1016/j.jesp.2003.11.007

Bjornholm, L., Nikkinen, J., Kiviniemi, V., Nordstrom, T., Niemela, S., . . . & Paus, T. (2017). Structural properties of the human corpus callosum: Multimodal assessment and sex differences. *Neuroimage, 152*, 108-118.

Brody, N. (1992). *Intelligence.* San Diego: Academic Press.

Bureau of Labor Statistics (2016). *Economic news releases.* Table 3. Median usual weekly earning of full-time wage and salary workers by age, race, Hispanic or Latino ethnicity, and sex, third quarter 2016 averages, not seasonally adjusted. www.bls.gov/news.release/wkyeng.t03.htm

Burhan, K. A., Kurniawan, Y., Sidek, A. H., & Mohamad, M. R. (2014). Crimes and the Bell curve: The role of people with high, average, and low intelligence. *Intelligence, 47*, 12-22. http://dx.doi.org/10.1016/j.intell.2014.08.005

Camilli, G., & Shepard, L. A. (1994). *Methods for identifying biased test items*, vol. 4. Thousand Oaks, CA: Sage Publications.

Catalyst (2016). *Women in accounting*, March 28. www.catalyst.org/knowledge/women-accounting

Cavalli-Sforza, L. (1997). Genes, peoples, and languages. *Proceedings of the National Academy of Sciences, 94*, 7719-7724.

Clewell, B. C., & Campbell, P. B. (2002). Taking stock: where we've been, where we are, where we're going. www.urban.org/url.cfm?ID=1000779

Collaer, M. L., & Hines, M. (1995). Human behavioral sex differences: A role for gonadal hormones during early development? *Psychological Bulletin, 118*, 55-107.

College Board (2015). *SAT Total group profile report, 2015 college-bound seniors.* https://secure-media.collegeboard.org/digitalServices/pdf/sat/total-group-2015.pdf

Dandy, J., & Nettelbeck, T. (2002). A cross-cultural study of parents' academic standards and educational aspirations for their children. *Educational Psychology, 22*(5), 621-627. doi: 10.1080/0144341022000023662.

Dickens, W. T., & Flynn, J. R. (2001). Heritability estimates versus large environmental effects: The IQ paradox resolved. *Psychological Review, 108*(2), 346-369. doi: 10.1037/0033-295X.108.2.346

Doyle, R. A., & Voyer, D. (2016). Stereotype manipulation effects on math and spatial test performance: A meta-analysis. *Learning and Individual Differences*, *47*, 103-116. http://dx.doi.org.ccl.idm.oclc.org/10.1016/j.lindif.2015.12.018

Duyme, M., Dumaret, A., & Tomkiewicz, S. (1999). How can we boost IQs of "dull children"? A late adoption study. *Proceedings of the National Academy of Sciences*, *96*(15), 8790-8794.

Economic Policy Institute. (n.d.). *The state of working America* (12th ed.). http://stateofworkingamerica.org/fact-sheets/poverty/

Eliot, L. (2011). The trouble with sex differences. *Neuron*, *6*, 895-898. https://doi.org/10.1016/j.neuron.2011.12.001

Eyferth, K. (1961). Leistungen verschiedener Gruppen von Besatzungskindern in Hamburg-Wechsler Intelligenztest für Kinder (HAWIK). *Archiv für die Gesamte Psychologie*, *113*, 222-241.

Eysenck, H. J. (1971). *The IQ argument: Race, intelligence and education*. Oxford: Library Press.

Fjell, A. M., Westlye, L. T., Amlien, I., Espeseth, T., Reinvang, I., Raz, N., . . . & Walhovd, K. B. (2009). Minute effects of sex on the aging brain: A multisample magnetic resonance imaging study of healthy aging and Alzheimer's disease. *Journal of Neuroscience*, *29*, 8774-8783. http://dx.doi.org/10.1523/JNEUROSCI.0115-0902009

Flynn, J. R. (1991). *Asian Americans: Achievement beyond IQ*. Hillsdale, NJ: Lawrence Erlbaum Associates.

Flynn, J. R. (2010). The spectacles through which I see the race and IQ debate. *Intelligence*, *38*, 363-366. dx.doi.org.ccl.idm.oclc.org/10.1016/j.intell.2010.05.001

Gándara, P., & Contreras, F. (2009). *The Latino education crisis: The consequences of failed social policies*. Cambridge, MA: Harvard University Press.

Gould, S. J. (1996). *The mismeasure of man*. New York: W. W. Norton.

Haier, R. J., Karama, S., Leyba, L., & Jung, R. E. (2009). MRI assessment of cortical thickness and functional activity changes in adolescent girls following three months of practice on a visual–spatial task. *BioMed Central Research Notes*, *2*, 174. doi: 10.1186/1756-0500-2-174

Halpern, D. F. (2012). *Sex Differences in Cognitive Abilities* (4th ed.). New York: Psychology Press.

Halpern, D. F., Aronson, J., Reimer, N., Simpkins, S., Star, J. R., & Wentzel, K. (2007). *Encouraging girls in math and science. Institute for Educational Sciences*, Washington, DC: United States Department of Education.

Halpern, D. F., Benbow, C., Geary, D., Gur, D., Hyde, J., & Gernsbacher, M. A. (2007). The science of sex-differences in science and mathematics. *Psychological Science in the Public Interest*, *8*, 1-52.

Halpern, D. F., Eliot, L., Bigler, R. S., Fabes, R. A., Hanish, L. D., Hyde, J. S., Liben, L., & Martin, C. L. (2011). The pseudoscience of single-sex schooling. *Science*, *333*, 1706-1707. doi: 10.1126/science.1205031

Halpern, D. F., Straight, C., & Stephenson, C. (2011). Beliefs about cognitive gender differences: Accurate for direction, underestimated for size. *Sex Roles, 64*, 336-347. doi: 10.1007/s11199-010-9891-2

Halpern, D. F., & Tan, U. (2001). Stereotypes and steroids: Using a psychobiosocial model to understand cognitive sex differences. *Brain and Cognition, 45*, 392-414.

Hedges, L. V., & Nowell, A. (1995). Sex differences in mental test scores, variability, and numbers of high-scoring individuals. *Science, 269*, 41-45. doi: 10.1126/science.7604277

Helms, J. E. (2010). Cultural bias in psychological testing. *Corsini Encyclopedia,* 1–3.

Hines, M., Spencer, D., Kung, K. F., Browne, W. V., Constantinescu, M., & Noorderhaven, R. M. (2016). The early postnatal period, mini-puberty, provides a window on the role of testosterone in human neurobehavioural development. *Current Opinion in Neurobiology,* 3869-3873. doi: 10.1016/j.conb.2016.02.008

Hirnstein, M., Andrews, L. C., & Hausmann, M. (2014). Gender-stereotyping and cognitive sex differences in mixed- and same-sex groups. *Archives of Sexual Behavior, 43*, 1663-1673. doi: 10.1007/s10508–014-0311-5

Hunter, J. E. & Schmidt, F. L. (1996). Intelligence and job performance: Economic and social implications. *Psychology, Public Policy, and Law, 2*, 447-472.

Jankowsky, J. L., Melnikova, T., Fadale, D. J., Xu, G. M., Slunt, H. H., Gonzales, V., ... & Savonenko, A. V. (2005). Environmental enrichment mitigates cognitive deficits in a mouse model of Alzheimer's disease. *Journal of Neuroscience, 25*, 5217-5224. doi: 10.1523/JNEUROSCI.5080-04.2005

Jensen, A. R. (1969). How much can we boost IQ and scholastic achievement? *Harvard Educational Review, 39*, 1–123. doi: 10.17763/haer.39.1.l3u15956627424k7

Jensen, A. R. (1980). *Bias in mental testing.* New York: Free Press.

Jensen, A. R. (1985). The nature of the black–white difference on various psychometric tests: Spearman's hypothesis. *Behavioral and Brain Sciences, 8*, 193–219.

Joel, D., Berman, Z., Tavor, I., Wexler, N., Gaber, O., Stein, Y., ... & Assaf, Y. (2015). Sex beyond the genitalia: The human brain mosaic. *Proceedings of the National Academy of Sciences, 112*, 15468-15473. doi: 10.1073/pnas.1509654112

Journal of Neuroscience Research (2017). An issue whose time has come: Sex/gender influences on nervous system function, vol. 95.

Kanaya, T. (2016). Discussing the Flynn Effect: From causes and interpretation to implications. *Measurement: Interdisciplinary Research and Perspectives, 14*, 67-69. doi: 10.1080/15366367.2016.1171607

Kanaya, T. & Ceci, S. J. (2007a). MR diagnosis and the Flynn effect: General intelligence, adaptive behavior, and context. *Child Development Perspectives, 1*, 62-63.

Kanaya, T. & Ceci, S. J. (2007b). Are all IQ scores created equal? The differential costs of IQ cut-off scores for at-risk children. *Child Development Perspectives, 1,* 52-56.

Kanaya, T. & Ceci, S. J. (2011). The Flynn effect on the WISC subtests in school children tested for special education services. *Journal of Psychoeducational Assessment, 29,* 125-136. doi: 10.1177/0734282909 370139

Kanaya, T. & Ceci, S. J. (2012). The impact of the Flynn effect on LD diagnoses in special education. *Journal of Learning Disabilities, 45,* 319-326. doi: 10.1177/ 0022219410392044

Kanaya, T., Scullin, M. H. & Ceci, S. J. (2003). The Flynn effect and US policies: The impact of rising IQ scores on American society via Mental Retardation diagnoses. *American Psychologist, 58,* 1-13.

Keiser, H. N., Sackett, P. R., Kuncel, N. R., & Brothen, T. (2016). Why women perform better in college than admissions scores would predict: Exploring the role of conscientiousness and course-taking patterns. *Journal of Applied Psychology, 101,* 569-581. http:// dx.doi.org/10.1037/apl10000069

Kretzschmar, A., Neubert, J. C., Wusternberg, S., & Greiff, S. (2016). Construct validity of complex problem-solving: A comprehensive view on different facts of intelligence and school grades. *Intelligence, 54,* 55-69. http://dx.doi.org/10.1016/ j.inell.2015.11,004

Kuncel, N. R., Ones, D. S., & Sackett, P. R. (2010). Individual differences as predictors of work, educational, and broad life outcomes. *Personality and Individual Differences, 49,* 331-336.

Lazar, I., & Darlington, R. B. (1982). Lasting effects of early education: A report from the Consortium for Longitudinal Studies. *Monographs of the Society for Research in Child Development, 47*(2-3), 1-151. doi: 10.2307/1165938

Loven, J., Herlitz, A., & Rehman, J. (2011). Women's own-gender bias in face recognition memory: The role of attention at encoding. *Experimental Psychology, 58,* 333-340. doi: 10.1027/1618-3169/a000100

Lubinski, D. (2009). Exceptional cognitive ability: The phenotype. *Behavior Genetics, 39,* 350-358.

Lynn, R. (1987). Japan: Land of the rising IQ: A reply to Flynn. *Bulletin of The British Psychological Society, 40,* 464-468.

Lynn, R. (1994). Sex differences in intelligence and brain size: A paradox resolved. *Personality and Individual Differences, 17,* 257-271. doi: 10.1016/0191-8869(94) 90030-2

Lynn, R. (2004). The intelligence of American Jews. *Personality and Individual Differences, 36*(1), 201-206. doi: 10.1016/S0191-8869(03)00079-5

Maeda, Y., & Yoon, S. Y. (2013). A meta-analysis on gender differences in mental rotation ability measured by the Purdue Spatial Visualize Test and Visualization of Rotations. *Educational Psychology Review, 25*, 69-94. doi: 10.1007/s10648-012-9215-x

Miller, D. I., & Halpern, D. F. (2013). Can spatial training improve long-term outcomes for gifted STEM undergraduates? *Learning and Individual Differences, 26*, 141-152. doi.org/10.1016/j.lindif.2012.03.012

Miller, D. I., & Halpern, D. F. (2014). The new science of cognitive sex differences. *Trends in Cognitive Sciences, 18*, 37-45. doi: 10.1016/j.tics.2013.10.011

Moll, K., Kunze, S., Neuhoff, N., Bruder, J., & Schulte-Korne, G. (2014). Specific learning disorder: Prevalence and gender differences. http://journals.plos.org/plosone/article?id=10.1371/journal.pone.0103537

Mullis, I. V. S., Martin, M. O., Foy, P., & Drucker, K. T. (2012). *PIRLS 2011 international reading results.* http://files.eric.ed.gov/fulltext/ED544362.pdf

National Indian Education Association (2008). Native Education 101: Basic facts about American Indian, Alaska Native, and Native Hawaiian education. www.niea.org/.

Neisser, U., Boodoo, G., Bouchard, T. J., Boykin, A. W., Brody, N., Ceci, S. J., ... & Urbina, S. (1996). Intelligence: Knowns and unknowns. *American Psychologist, 51*(2), 77-101. doi: 10.1037/0003-066X.51.2.77

Nisbett, R. (2009). *Intelligence and How to Get It.* New York: Norton.

Nisbett, R. E., Aronson, J., Blair, C., Dickens, W., Flynn, J., Halpern, D. F., & Turkheimer, E. (2012). Intelligence: New findings and theoretical developments. *American Psychologist, 67*(2), 130-159. doi: 10.1037/a0026699

Ones, D. S., Viswesvaran, C., & Dilchert, S. (2005). Cognitive ability in personnel selection decisions. In A. Evers, N. Anderson, & O. Voskuijl (eds.), *The Blackwell handbook of personnel selection* (pp. 331–353). Oxford: Blackwell.

Ones, D. S., Dilchert, S. & Viswesvaran, C. (2012). Cognitive ability. In N. Schmitt (ed.), *Oxford handbook of personnel assessment and selection* (pp. 179–224). Oxford: Oxford University Press.

Quinn, P. C., & Liben, L. S. (2008). A sex difference in mental rotation in young infants. *Psychological Science, 19*, 1067-1070. doi: 10.1111/j.1467-9280.2008.02201.x

Reynolds, C. R., & Suzuki, L. (2013). Bias in psychological assessment: An empirical review and recommendations. In J. R. Graham, J. A. Naglieri, & I. B. Weiner (eds.), *Handbook of psychology, vol. 10: Assessment psychology* (2nd ed., pp. 82-113). Hoboken, NJ: Wiley.

Richardson, K., & Norgate, S. H, (2015). Does IQ really predict job performance? *Applied Developmental Science, 19*, 153-169. http://dx.doi.org/10.1080/10888691.2014.983635

Rindermann, H., & Thompson, J. (2013). Ability rise in NAEP and narrowing ethnic gaps? *Intelligence, 41*(6), 821-831. doi: 10.1016/j.intell.2013.06.016

Ronfeldt, M., Loeb, S., & Wyckoff, J. (2013). How teacher turnover harms student achievement. *American Education Research Journal, 50*(1), 4-36. doi: 10.3102/0002831212463813

Rutter, M., Caspi, A., & Fergusson, D. (2004). Sex differences in developmental reading disability. *JAMA, 291*, 2007-2012.

Sackett, P. R., Hardison, C. M., & Cullen, M. J. (2004). On interpreting stereotype threat as accounting for African American–White differences on cognitive tests. *American Psychologist, 59*(1), 7-13. doi: 10.1037/0003-066X.59.1.7

Scarr, S., Pakstis, A. J., Katz, S. H., & Barker, W. B. (1977). Absence of a relationship between degree of white ancestry and intellectual skill in a black population. *Human Genetics, 39*, 69-86.

Scarr, S., & Weinberg, R. A. (1983). The Minnesota Adoption Studies: Genetic differences and malleability. *Child Development, 54*, 260–267. doi: 10.2307/1129689

Serpell, R. (2011). Social responsibility as a dimension of intelligence, and as an educational goal: Insights from programmatic research in an African society. *Child Development Perspectives, 5*, 126-133. doi: 10.1111/j.1750-8606.2011 .00167.x

Spencer, S. J., Logel, C., & Davies, P. G. (2016). Stereotype threat. *Annual Review of Psychology, 67*415-67437. doi:10.1146/annurev-psych-073115-103235

Steele, C. M., & Aronson, J. (1995). Stereotype threat and the intellectual test performance of African Americans. *Journal of Personality and Social Psychology, 69*, 797–811. http:// dx.doi.org.ccl.idm.oclc.org/10.1037/0022–3514.69.5.797

Sternberg, R. J., Grigorenko, E. L., & Kidd, K. K. (2005). Intelligence, race, and genetics. *American Psychologist, 60*, 46-59. doi: 10.1037/0003-066X.60.1.46

Stoet, G., & Geary, D. C. (2012). Can stereotype threat explain the gender gap in mathematics performance and achievement? *Review of General Psychology, 16*, 93-102. doi: 10.1037/a0026617

Tan, A., Ma, W., Vira, A., Marwha, D., & Eliot, L. (2016). The human hippocampus is not sexually-dimorphic: Meta-analysis of structural MRI volumes. *Neuroimage, 124*, 350-366. https://doi.org/10.1016/j.neuroimage.2015.08.050

Thorndike, R. L., Hagen, E. P., & Sattler, J. M. (1986). *Stanford–Binet intelligence scale: Fourth edition (Technical Manual)*. Chicago, IL: Riverside.

Tsethlikai, M. (2011). An exploratory analysis of American Indian children's cultural engagement, fluid cognitive skills, and standardized verbal IQ scores. *Developmental Psychology, 47*(1), 192-202. doi: 10.1037/a0020803

Turkheimer, E., & Halpern, D. F. (2009). Sex differences in variability for cognitive measures: Do the ends justify the genes? (Commentary on Johnson et al., 2009). *Perspectives on Psychological Science, 4*, 612-614. doi: 10.1111/j.1745-6924.2009.01169.x

US Census (nd). *Table 205. Cumulative percent distribution of population by height and sex: 2007 to 2008*. www.census.gov

Voyer, D., Postma, A., Brake, B., & Imperato-McGinley, J. (2007). Gender differences in object location memory: A meta-analysis. *Psychonomic Bulletin & Review, 14*, 23-38. doi: 10.3758/BF03194024.

Voyer, D., & Voyer, S. (2014). Gender differences in scholastic achievement: A meta-analysis. *Psychological Bulletin, 140*, 1174-1204. http://dx.doi.org/10.1037/a0036620

Voyer, D., Voyer, S., & Bryden, M. P. (1995). Magnitude of sex differences in spatial abilities: A meta-analysis and consideration of critical variables. *Psychological Bulletin, 117*, 250-270. doi: 10.1037/0033-2909.117.2.250

Wai, J., Cacchio, M., Putallaz, M., & Makel, M. C. (2010). Sex differences in the right tail of cognitive abilities: A 30 year examination. *Intelligence, 38*, 412-423. doi: 10.1016/intel.2010.04.006

Weinberg, R. A., Scarr, S., & Waldman, I. D. (1992). The Minnesota Transracial Adoption Study: A follow-up of IQ test performance at adolescence. *Intelligence, 16*(1), 117-135. doi:10.1016/0160-2896(92)90028-P

Willerman, L., Naylor, A. F., & Myrianthopoulos, N. C. (1974). Intellectual development of children from interracial matings: Performance in infancy and at 4 years. *Behavior Genetics, 4*(1), 83-90. doi: 10.1007/BF01066706

Zenisky, A. L., Hambleton, R. K., & Robin, F. (2003). DIF detection and interpretation in large-scale science assessments: Informing item writing practices. www.umass.edu/remp/docs/MCAS-RR-1.pdf

14 The Predictive Value of General Intelligence

PAUL R. SACKETT, OREN R. SHEWACH, AND JEFFREY A. DAHLKE

The chapters you have read so far have looked at various approaches for under-standing and measuring intelligence. Our focus in this chapter is on the predictive value of measures of general cognitive ability. We write as applied psychologists whose work focuses on the operational use of tests for making decisions about whom to select for admission in higher education contexts and whom to select into jobs in employment contexts. We note that work in these contexts uses the termin-ology "general cognitive ability" (GCA), rather than "intelligence," and we use that terminology throughout the chapter.

The term *general cognitive ability* or GCA is often preferred in applied fields such as industrial-organizational psychology and education for a variety of reasons. Test developers in those fields do not set out to assess intelligence. Rather, they design measures of abilities hypothesized to be relevant to success at work or in higher education, commonly including constructs such as verbal reasoning, mathematical reasoning, and writing skills, and sometimes including measures reflecting specific areas of knowledge, such as science. Researchers have discovered that while there is indeed something specific and unique about each of these constructs, there is also a general component that is common to all of them. When multiple constructs are measured and combined into an overall score, this general component becomes dominant; this is what is widely referred to as **general cognitive ability (GCA)**. GCA has been found to be highly similar to the construct of intelligence; thus, while we use different terminology than many other chapters in this book, we are still capturing the idea of intelligence when we speak of GCA. In this chapter we will examine the relationship between GCA and a variety of important life outcomes, including educational achievement and attainment, job performance, occupational attainment, engaging in delinquent and criminal behavior, and a wide variety of health outcomes (see Figure 14.1 for an overview). The overarching message is that GCA is predictive of a great many outcomes in many facets of life.

A Model of General Cognitive Ability (GCA)

A useful way of thinking about GCA comes from a framework that we adopt from Gottfredson (2002). Think of the tasks and activities making up various outcomes as

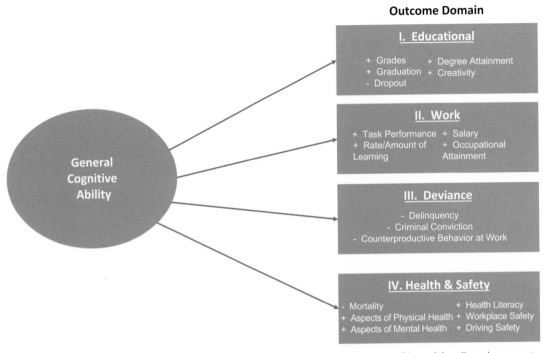

Figure 14.1 An overview of the relationship between GCA and a variety of life outcomes. This model outlines the concepts covered in the chapter, illustrating the domains and variables general cognitive ability (GCA) predicts. The "+" indicates GCA predicts this variable positively; the "-" indicates GCA predicts this variable negatively.

falling into a two-dimensional space. One dimension is cognitive vs. non-cognitive. At the cognitive end are outcomes that rely heavily on thinking, analyzing, problem solving, and drawing upon an accumulated body of knowledge. At the non-cognitive end are activities that are social, emotional, and/or motivational. The other dimension is the complexity of the tasks and activities, from simple to complex. A general finding is that GCA will be more predictive of outcomes that are near the cognitive end of the first dimension and near the complex end of the second dimension (see Table 14.1).

As an illustration, a recent study took a deep look at the relationship between a college admission test – the ACT – and grades in an introductory psychology class (Keiser, Sackett, Kuncel, & Brothen, 2016). It is common to correlate admissions tests with grades; this study had a unique twist. The course grade was made up of four components: exams, quizzes, participation, and extra-credit activities (participating in experiments), and the authors looked at the relationship between ACT scores and each separate component of the overall grade. The ACT was strongly predictive of exam scores, moderately predictive of quiz scores, and very weakly predictive of participation and extra credit. This fits into our two-dimensional framework: Exams and quizzes are largely cognitive in nature, while class participation and choosing

Table 14.1 The effects of task type and task complexity on the predictive value of general cognitive ability (GCA)

GCA becomes a better predictor of performance when the cognitive demands of the task increase and as the complexity of the task increases. In the table, "0" indicates the low-complexity non-cognitive scenario where GCA has little or no predictive power. In the other cells, the number of "+" symbols indicates the relative importance of GCA for predicting performance, where "+++" indicates that GCA is the most useful for predicting performance on tasks that are complex and highly cognitive in nature.

Type of task demands	Complexity of task	
	Low	High
Primarily non-cognitive	0	+
Primarily cognitive	++	+++

to seek extra credit are not. Participation and extra credit reflect the choice to engage in the activity, while exam and quiz scores reflect success in acquiring a body of knowledge. And among our more cognitive measures, exams are higher in complexity than quizzes, as they involve a larger body of information to be studied and retained over a longer period of time, relative to a quiz on one week's material.

Interpreting the Relationship between GCA and Outcomes

We want to add some cautionary notes as to how to interpret findings of predictive relationships between GCA and outcomes. In all cases, the correlation between GCA and the outcome is far less than perfect. If the correlation were perfect, then we could forecast a person's standing on the outcome of interest with perfect accuracy ("knowing your GCA score, we can say with certainty that you will obtain a B or better average in college"). But with imperfect correlations, we are limited to probabilistic statements ("on average, students with this GCA score have an 80 per-cent likelihood of obtaining a B or better average in college").

We've talked about correlation throughout this book, but here we offer a numerical guide to interpreting correlations between GCA (or any other measure) and an outcome. A **correlation** of 0 indicates that there is no relationship between the two: knowing a person's GCA score would tell us nothing about their likely standing on the outcome. At the other extreme is a perfect correlation of 1.0: knowing the GCA score would mean we also know the person's standing on the outcome. Many correlations between GCA and outcomes are in the .2 to .5 range: better than zero, but far from perfect. Correlations are tricky to interpret. One useful approach focuses on the average level of the outcome if the test in question is used for selection, which we illustrate below.

Imagine a large firm had 1,000 applicants for a real-estate sales job and hired them all. The firm then wanted to know what would have happened if they had instead used a particular test to select, say, 100 applicants. To answer this question, we could first put everyone's name in a hat and pull out 100 of them: This is hiring at random. We then compute the performance (measured as the annual home sales volume) of the 100 selected people; let's assume we find that the average sales volume is $1 million. Second, we compute the mean performance of the top-performing 100 people: They are the ones we'd hire if we had a test with a perfect correlation of 1.0 with performance; let's assume we find the average sales are $2 million. This sets us up to explore the value of selecting using a test with a particular correlation with performance. A test with a correlation of .5 with performance will result in mean performance that is 50 percent of the gap between random selection ($1 million) and perfect selection ($2 million), namely, mean sales of $1.5 million. A test with a .2 correlation will result in mean performance that is 20 percent of the gap between random and perfect, or $1.2 million. This illustrates a general principle: *the correlation indexes the percentage of the gap between random and perfect selection that is obtained using a test with that correlation.* Clearly, the higher the correlation, the better. But even our relatively small correlation of .2 gives a real improvement over not using the test. Figure 14.2 depicts the concepts from this example visually.

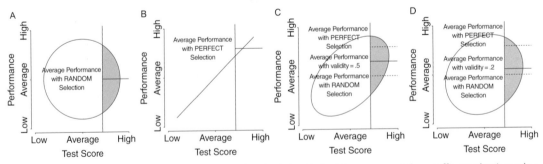

Figure 14.2 Illustration of how to interpret criterion-related validity. Vertical lines represent the cutoff score that is used to select 10 percent of applicants (selectees are indicated by the shaded sections) and the labeled horizontal lines represent mean performance among those who pass the cutoff score for the selection test. Panel A shows that selection using test scores that have no systematic relationship with performance (i.e., random selection) results in a group of selectees whose performance is the same as what the average would be if everyone had been selected. Panel B shows what average performance would be if we could predict performance perfectly. Panels C and D show that the gap between random and perfect selection is closed by 50 and 20 percent when the scores on the selection test have validities of .5 and .2, respectively.

Another common interpretation rests on the fact that squaring a correlation gives the percentage of variance in an outcome that is accounted for by the predictor variable in question. But what does "percentage of variance" mean, anyway? Well, if we know that people vary in their standing on both the predictor and the outcome in question, percentage of variance is a way of stating the extent to which differences among people on the outcome variable are systematically related to the predictor (with the remaining differences unexplained). If we could achieve perfect prediction, we would explain 100 percent of the variation among people; but, if we found a correlation of 0, we could explain none of that variation. So, continuing with our real-estate example, a correlation of .5 means that the predictor accounts for 25 percent (.5 squared equals .25) of the variance in the outcome and a correlation of .2 accounts for 4 percent (.2 squared equals .04) of the variance. This seems quite small, and people who want to be critical of or dismiss a research finding commonly point to the small value of a squared correlation as indicating the relationship is trivial. But, as we demonstrated above, even a small correlation can be useful (as in this example, where each additional percentage of variance explained is worth thousands of dollars).

Accounting for the Complexity of Human Behavior

The fact that the correlation between GCA and various life outcomes is not perfect is primarily the result of the fact that virtually all human behavior is influenced by multiple factors. Consider performance at work, for example. Performance is influenced by one's level of GCA, but also by motivation, access to needed tools and supplies, quality of job training, quality of supervision and mentoring, competing demands (e.g., child care and elder care responsibilities), peer influences, drug and alcohol use, and many more factors. It is a useful exercise to look at the items on the above list and sort them into factors potentially knowable prior to hire and factors that emerge after hire. Given that many factors emerge after hire, it follows that characteristics measureable prior to hire can only be imperfect predictors of performance. And the fact that there are multiple characteristics that are knowable prior to hire is the reason why it will virtually always be the case that organizations attempting to hire new employees will assess multiple characteristics in their hiring process. For example, most organizations try to gauge applicants' motivation and GCA – they know that greater effort can compensate for lower ability, and vice versa.

What Makes This Research Credible?

In summarizing evidence in this chapter, we focus on studies that we view as most trustworthy. These are studies that either focus on very large and representative samples (commonly thousands of people) or make use of meta-analysis. **Meta-analysis** is a technique in which the researcher locates as many studies as possible reporting the relationship of interest (e.g., the relationships between GCA and academic performance) and quantitatively combines the results. In many domains, one finds dozens or hundreds of studies reporting the same relationship. While individual studies may be small in scope, this combining of studies results in a very large sample size and a stable estimate of the relationship of interest.

Sampling Error

We note that there are studies that produce findings contrary to what we report here. We briefly outline features that can distort research findings, leading to results contrary to what we see in large-scale studies. The first is small sample size. Any sample might not be representative of the population from which it is drawn: The smaller a sample, the greater the risk of an unrepresentative draw; formally, this is called **sampling error**. It would be useful if all reported correlations were accompanied by the plus/minus margin of error that accompanies them to address the issue of sampling error. A small sample of, say, 30 has a plus/minus margin of error of about .38. Saying "my study found a correlation of .2, plus or minus .38" just isn't very impressive. With a sample of 1,000, the margin of error is down to about plus or minus .06. Be wary of anyone making claims based on small samples. Figure 14.3 shows sampling distributions of means as an example of how larger sample sizes give us much more precise estimates of the "true" mean of the population.

Range Restriction

The second feature that can distort relationships is the study of samples in which the range of scores is limited (known as **range restriction**). Imagine an employer who

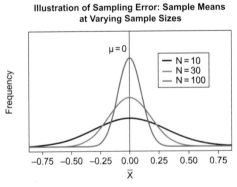

Figure 14.3 Sampling error: sample means at varying sample sizes. This graph shows the frequency distributions of sample means (X) drawn from sample sizes of 10, 30 and 100. When the sample size is larger (i.e., N = 100), the sample means are distributed much closer to the population mean (μ) of 0. This is why larger samples are desirable: with a larger sample size, your sample will more accurately represent the population. Sampling distributions of means show how larger sample sizes give us much more precise estimates of the "true" mean of the population.

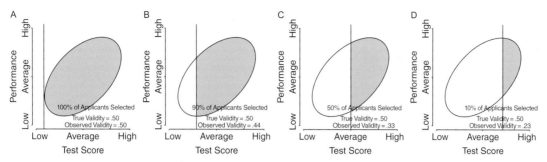

Figure 14.4 Samples with narrower ranges of scores produce small correlations. The "true validity" (i.e., the test-performance correlation when everyone is selected, as in Panel A) is .5 for all plotted scenarios. However, when the variability of test scores is reduced by using those scores to select applicants, the "observed validity" (i.e., the test-performance correlation when only performance data from selectees is available) is smaller than the true validity. In Panel B, the top 90 percent of applicants are selected and the observed validity is .44. When we are more selective in Panel C and select only the top 50 percent of applicants, the observed validity is .33. When we are very selective in Panel D and select only the top 10 percent of applicants, the observed validity is only .23 – less than half the magnitude of the true validity!

gives a test to all applicants and only hires those in the top 10 percent of the score distribution. Correlating test scores with job performance will give a very distorted picture of how well the test functions in the applicant population – which is what we really care about. Samples with narrower ranges of scores produce small correlations – often dramatically smaller than what we would find in a full-range sample (see Figure 14.4). This is a very common problem. There are quantitative techniques available for correcting for range restriction. Be wary of studies with restricted samples unless they carefully make these corrections. A good study will report both the uncorrected and corrected correlation to avoid confusion as to what is being reported.

Quality of the Outcome Measure

The third distorting feature is the quality of the outcome measure with which a test is correlated. One concern is with how reliable, stable, and repeatable the measure is. Imagine a car dealership wants to measure sales performance. Here are three options: (a) How many cars did you sell today?, (b) How many cars did you sell this week?, and (c) How many cars did you sell this year? Clearly, we get a better measure of sales performance using a longer time period to frame performance: Idiosyncratic features affect performance in the short term, such as weather or the release of a new car in our car sales example. However, these idiosyncratic features average out over time. A test that correlates well with one-year performance will produce much smaller correlations with one-week performance. Strong research studies examine and report the reliability of the outcome measure.

In short, individual studies can fall prey to issues of small samples, restricted samples, and unreliable outcome measures, and thus produce findings that are in error. In order to avoid these issues, as stated above we focus on studies with large, representative samples or meta-analyses. We now proceed to discuss substantive topics of interest, beginning with educational outcomes, followed by deviance/wrongdoing and the workplace, and finally health and safety.

Using GCA to Predict Educational Outcomes

Education is one of the life domains in which GCA displays the strongest relationships with outcomes. In fact, the first broad test of GCA was developed for the purpose of predicting differences across individuals in educational outcomes (Binet, 1905; Deary, Strand, Smith, & Gernandes, 2007). GCA predicts success in schooling across all stages of education (i.e., grade school, high school, college, and graduate school), and across a variety of different educational outcomes. We will examine educational outcomes ranging from student performance, to graduation and educational attainment, to creativity. Here we will discuss the nature of these GCA–education relationships and why GCA predicts these outcomes. While we will highlight GCA's substantial relationships with varied academic outcomes, we also note that GCA is far from the only factor that determines educational success. Study skills and non-cognitive factors such as motivation and personality also play a role, as examined below.

GCA Predicts Academic Grades across Stages of School and across Wide Time Intervals

Correlations between GCA and school grades are substantial at all levels of schooling. In a nationally representative, longitudinal study of middle school students (part of the *National Education Longitudinal Study of 1988*), Dumais (2002) found that cognitive tests displayed a strong, positive relationship with grade point average (GPA) throughout middle school. Casillas and colleagues (2012) tracked students from middle to high school across many schools, and found that those scoring higher on an academic achievement test (ACT's EXPLORE test) had higher subsequent GPAs in early high school. Similarly, Sackett and colleagues (2009) found in a large-scale nationally representative sample that the SAT (administered in high school) displayed a substantial positive relationship with college grade point average. We note that we view standardized measures of academic achievement and aptitude as **proxy variables** for GCA due to GCA's high correlation with achievement and aptitude (e.g., Frey & Detterman, 2004; Koenig, Frey, & Detterman, 2008; Marks, 2013). In other words, even though they are not exactly the same thing, standardized tests are a reasonable stand-in for a GCA assessment.

In fact, this pattern of findings even extends to grades in graduate school. In a meta-analysis of a GCA test called the Miller Analogies Test, Kuncel, Hezlett, and

Ones (2004) discovered that this test displayed sizable correlations with GPA throughout graduate school. Interestingly, GCA's prediction of academic performance is not limited to just a span of a few years. Many large-scale studies find that GCA measured early in life predicts grades or academic achievement much later in life (e.g., Fergusson & Horwood, 1995; Maani & Kalb, 2007; Schoon, 2008). For example, in a sample from New Zealand, GCA measured at age 8 predicted grades in tenth grade (Maani & Kalb, 2007). While these relationships are typically not as strong as GCA–grade relationships measured at a closer point in time, they are still sizable.

So, why does GCA predict grades across levels of school and various time intervals? One of the major explanations is learning. Specifically, GCA predicts knowledge acquisition across many contexts (Deary, Strand, Smith, & Gernandes, 2007; Ree & Earles, 1991), and academic courses are centered around acquiring knowledge on a given subject. So, the fact that those with higher GCA are likely to learn more and learn faster (Hunter, 1986; Ree & Earles, 1991) plays an important role in determining the grades received in courses.

GCA Predicts Graduation and Dropout at Many Stages of Schooling

Longitudinal studies that track students through graduation at a given schooling level indicate that GCA predicts graduation (and, conversely, dropout). The *National Longitudinal Survey of Youth* tracked students throughout high school and beyond. Students who scored higher in GCA also had substantially higher high school graduation rates (Belley & Lochner, 2007). Furthermore, almost all students scoring in the top quarter of the GCA test graduated high school, largely irrespective of family income. Family income appears to play a more important role for students who scored lower in GCA; in the bottom quarter of ability scorers, students with greater family income graduated at a higher rate than those with lower family income (Belley & Lochner, 2007). This finding could be due to the fact that among students with lower GCA, those with higher family income have advantages in terms of resources available at home, such as access to tutoring, that increase the likelihood of graduation. It could also be the case that students with lower family income may need to leave school early to supplement family income. Similarly, in a Canadian longitudinal sample, students with higher reading proficiency were much more likely to graduate, even after accounting for family income and parental education (Knighton & Bussiere, 2006). In addition to high school outcomes, high GCA also predicts graduation and lower dropout in college. In a meta-analysis, Westrick, Robbins, Radunzel, and Schmidt (2015) found that while college GPA was the best predictor of college retention, the ACT test positively predicted retention in the second and third years of college. In the same meta-analysis discussed above, Kuncel and colleagues (2004) found that GCA predicted degrees obtained in graduate school. For a deeper look at some research devoted to college admission tests and a variety of outcomes, see the Focus on Contemporary Research box.

FOCUS ON CONTEMPORARY RESEARCH: PAUL R. SACKETT'S WORK ON COLLEGE ADMISSIONS TESTS AND A VARIETY OF OUTCOMES

My research interests revolve around various aspects of testing and assessment in workplace, military, and educational settings. My co-authors, Oren Shewach and Jeff Dahlke, are advanced graduate students who have worked with me on a wide variety of projects. Much of our work together examines the relationship between a college admissions test (the SAT) and a variety of outcomes, a project that I co-direct with my colleague Nathan Kuncel. One unique aspect of our work is that we work with very large data sets: we have information on over 1.5 million students at over 200 colleges and universities, following them from the point where they register to take the SAT through completing or leaving college.

Much research on admissions tests correlates test scores with grade point average. However, GPA is an imperfect outcome variable, as each student takes a different batch of courses. Some students, whether intentionally or inadvertently, take an easier – or a harder – set of courses than the average student. Thus, a comparable GPA sometimes does not really mean comparable academic performance. In our work, we take advantage of our huge data set and examine the predictive power of the SAT separately within individual courses (students taking the same course at the same university at the same time). This way grades have the same meaning for each student. We find that the SAT, while already a strong predictor of GPA, becomes an even stronger predictor when differences in course-taking patterns are eliminated. We also find that while some prior research reports slightly lower predictive power for the SAT for black and Hispanic students than for white students, these differences in predictive power are influenced by differences in course-taking patterns. With our strategy of examining the predictive power of the SAT among students taking the same course, we find no evidence of lower predictive power for minority students (Dahlke, Sackett, & Kuncel, 2019).

Other recent work looks at how taking a test in a language other than one's best language affects the predictive power of the SAT. Many international students and immigrants seek to enter US colleges and universities, and it is important to understand whether admissions tests are equally effective for such students. We separate students into three language groups: English best, equally proficient in English and another language, and another language best. The most striking finding involves Asian students for whom another language is their best language. While the SAT Math subtest functions comparably for these students in comparison with native English speakers, the SAT Critical Reading subtest has a considerably weaker predictive relationship for these non-native speakers (Shewach, Shen, Sackett, & Kuncel, 2017). We think this is important work, as it indicates a need to weigh different aspect of the admissions process differently for different types of students.

GCA Predicts Educational Attainment

GCA also plays an important role in predicting the level of educational attainment achieved during one's schooling. Jencks and colleagues (1979) documented nine longitudinal studies that displayed positive, moderate to strong relationships between GCA and level of educational attainment achieved. In a more recent study, Strenze (2007) found via meta-analysis that GCA had a substantial positive relationship with education level (defined as the highest level of education completed or number of years in full-time education).

It is intuitive that GCA also predicts the level of education obtained (e.g., baccalaureate, master's, or doctorate) in addition to completion of a degree at a particular level, because the same mental resources that GCA provides (learning capacity, comprehension, etc.) are likely to contribute to both completing one's current level of schooling as well as pursuing subsequent education.

Tying together points 2 and 3, why, then, does GCA predict degree completion at a given level as well as educational attainment throughout one's life? As discussed above, GCA is related to learning and knowledge acquisition, which play important roles in predicting grades. In turn, grades play a large role in predicting graduation (Robbins et al., 2004), as one must have satisfactory grades in order to graduate.

Another mechanism that can explain the GCA–educational attainment relationship is found in individuals' expectations and aspirations. GCA is positively related to expectations and aspirations to reach higher levels of schooling (Ganzach, 2000; Sewell & Hauser, 1975). Regardless of whether these expectations are self-set or come from external sources (e.g., parents), they may lead to more motivation and goal-setting to achieve educational degrees.

Finally, higher GCA has also been found to increase the likelihood of successful transitions from one level of education to the next (Holm & Jaeger, 2009; Holm & Jaeger, 2011). Underlying this may be the fact that GCA becomes more important in increasingly complex and less routine situations (Hunter, 1986), as is likely to be the case with the beginning of a new level of schooling. In sum, GCA's relations with learning, aspirations and expectations, and successful transitions all play roles in explaining why ability predicts educational attainment.

GCA Predicts Creativity

While it is not directly academic success, creativity is often relevant in academic contexts. In a meta-analysis, Kim (2005) found GCA tests to have a small, positive relationship with creativity tests. Whereas Kim examined the relationship with explicit creativity tests, Kuncel, Hezlett, and Ones (2004) examined ratings of creativity made by an academic faculty member or work supervisor. In their meta-analysis, Kuncel and colleagues found that GCA tests had a moderate positive relationship with ratings of creativity. The authors posited that creativity could be primarily determined by GCA and related to specific cognitive abilities in the domain of interest, along with acquired knowledge in this domain. Although GCA's relationship with creativity does tend to be weaker than its relationships with other educational outcomes, there is some evidence to suggest that individuals who score higher on GCA are also more likely to be creative.

GCA Predicts Educational Outcomes Even After Accounting for Non-Cognitive Variables

As we have shown, GCA relates to many educational outcomes across different levels of education and across years. But do these relationships disappear after one takes into account other variables such as socioeconomic status, study skills, or other non-cognitive factors? In the context of testing programs, one of the most common critiques of admissions tests is that they measure nothing more than socioeconomic status (e.g., Biernat, 2003; Crosby, Iyer, Clayton, & Downing, 2003). Sackett and colleagues (2009) examined this claim in a large-scale, nationally representative sample of students who took the SAT. They found that controlling for socioeconomic status reduced the relationship between the SAT and college academic performance by only a very small amount. This indicates that the relationship between test and college performance is largely unrelated to socioeconomic status. Dumais (2002) and Casillas (2012) found the same pattern of results, such that GCA predicts academic performance across middle and high school even after controlling for socioeconomic factors.

Another consideration that might explain the relationship between ability and educational outcomes is that of study skills and other non-cognitive factors. Does GCA still predict educational outcomes after we control for these variables? Robbins and colleagues (2004) tested this question, examining study skills and psychosocial factors such as academic self-efficacy, academic goals, and motivation. Although these non-cognitive factors were found to predict college academic performance, cognitive tests still displayed substantial positive prediction of academic performance after controlling for these factors. In high-school students, Casillas and colleagues (2012) found similar results of a GCA test retaining sizable prediction of academic performance even after adjusting for these study skills and non-cognitive factors. Despite many attempts to identify variables that account for GCA's predictive power (and that, if found, would render GCA unpredictive of educational outcomes after one accounts for other factors), the body of large-scale and meta-analytic research that tests these claims indicates that GCA's effects pervade in predicting success in the domain of education.

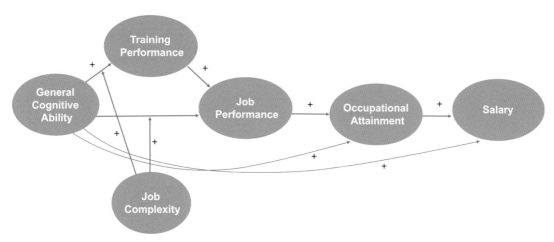

Figure 14.5 The effects of general cognitive ability on outcomes at work. All relationships are positive, such that higher GCA predicts higher training/job performance, occupational attainment, and salary. Job complexity moderates the relationship with job and training performance, such that when job complexity is higher, the GCA–performance relationship is stronger.

Applications of GCA in the Workplace

Some of the earliest applications of GCA measures were for purposes of predicting performance in work settings. Here we summarize major conclusions from research on the role of GCA in the workplace; many of these conclusions are incorporated in the diagram presented in Figure 14.5.

GCA Is the Best Predictor of Task Performance for Jobs Where People Learn the Specific Job Skills after Hire

For some jobs, individuals learn the specific skills needed prior to hire. The job of university professor is a good example: When we hire a psychology professor, we expect him/her to step into the classroom right away – we don't hire people who know nothing about psychology and teach them about it after we hire them. For other jobs, specific skills are taught after hire. When the US Army needs tank drivers, they don't put out an ad reading "experienced tank drivers wanted." Tanks are specific to the military and people don't normally learn to drive them on their own outside the military context, so new recruits go through extensive training before being put on the job driving tanks. It is in this context of hiring people who will learn specific skills after hire that GCA is of greatest value (Hunter, 1986; Schmidt & Hunter, 1998). In settings where we hire people who are expected to step onto the job right away, GCA is still positively predictive of task performance; however, measures of job-specific knowledge, skills, and abilities have somewhat greater predictive power (Hunter, 1986).

GCA Is a Stronger Predictor of Task Performance than of Other Facets of Job Performance

Job performance has a number of components. One perspective identifies three: task performance, organizational citizenship behavior (OCB), and counterproductive work behavior (CWB; Rotundo & Sackett, 2002). **Task performance** consists of behaviors formally recognized as part of the job and that contribute to the core duties of the job. **Organizational citizenship behavior** or **OCB** consists of behaviors typically outside explicit job duties and that contribute to the goals of the organization via its social and psychological environment (e.g., volunteering at work, assisting another with a task). **Counterproductive work behavior** or **CWB** consists of voluntary behaviors that harm the organization (Rotundo & Sackett, 2002).

This perspective posits that an individual's contribution to the organization can be viewed as task performance plus OCB minus CWB. These three components may be weighted differently depending on the context, which means that the relative importance of these three can vary from job to job. While GCA is a strong predictor of task performance (Hunter, 1983; Gonzalez-Mule, Mount, and Oh, 2014), it is a weaker predictor of OCB and CWB (Gonzalez-Mule, Mount, and Oh, 2014). Non-cognitive predictors, such as the personality traits of conscientiousness and agreeableness, are better predictors in those non-task domains (Berry, Ones, & Sackett, 2007; Chiaburu, Oh, Berry, Li, & Gardner, 2011).

The GCA–Performance Relationship Holds for Virtually All Jobs

One might ask whether there are some jobs for which GCA predicts performance and others for which it does not. Studies have now been done on a very large number of jobs – one US government program conducted **predictive validation studies** (i.e., studies that measure predictor measures first and obtain performance measures at a later point in time) in over 700 jobs over several decades (Hunter, 1983). The conclusion is that GCA is consistently positively predictive of performance. There may be a few exceptions: The creative work of artists is one example; the performance of professional football players is another (Kuzmits & Adams, 2008). However, GCA is predictive of performance for virtually all jobs across a striking variation in job characteristics, tasks, and levels of job complexity.

The GCA–Performance Relationship Gets Stronger as Job Complexity Increases

While GCA is consistently predictive across jobs, the strength of the relationship does vary. The key variable that explains variation in GCA's prediction across jobs is "cognitive complexity," which refers to the information processing demands of the job. Some jobs are simple and repetitive, while other jobs continually expose employees to new and unexpected problems that they may or may not have been trained to deal with. Hunter (1986) used a large database representing many occupations to demonstrate that the correlation between GCA and job performance increases in strength as cognitive complexity increases. Cognitive ability becomes more important (and becomes a better predictor of task-related job performance) as a job becomes less routine and more complex.

There Is Not a Threshold above Which Higher Levels of GCA Do Not Matter

One intuitive idea about GCA is that there is some level of GCA that is needed for a particular job and exceeding that level does not improve performance. According to this idea, as long as one reaches some threshold level of ability, higher levels of GCA do not correspond to higher levels of performance. This idea turns out to be false: Higher levels of GCA are linearly associated with higher mean levels of job performance and the relationship remains intact even for very high levels of GCA (Arneson, Sackett, & Beatty, 2011; Coward & Sackett, 1990).

It is important, however, to note that this finding of "more is better" is specific to predicting job performance and may not hold for predicting other outcomes of interest. One research finding is that, over time, people gravitate toward jobs with a level of cognitive complexity consistent with their level of GCA (Wilk, Desmarais, & Sackett, 1995; Wilk & Sackett, 1996). People who are "underplaced" (i.e., have greater GCA than required by a job's cognitive complexity) tend to move to more complex jobs, with the converse holding for people who are "overplaced" (i.e., have lower GCA than required by a job's cognitive complexity). So, an employer with an interest in limiting turnover may be wary of hiring people with a level of GCA well above job demands: Although those high-ability individuals would be expected to perform well, they would also be at risk of leaving for a more complex job.

Even though people tend to gravitate toward jobs that align with their levels of GCA, some individuals do remain in jobs that are incongruent with their ability levels. Maltarich, Nyberg, and Reilly (2010) found that low-GCA and high-GCA individuals in low-complexity jobs were more likely to leave their jobs than people with moderate levels of GCA, but that high-GCA individuals in low-complexity jobs were *less* likely to leave their jobs voluntarily than low-GCA individuals in low complexity jobs. It is important to note that these findings are not necessarily in conflict with those described above: Maltarich, Nyberg, and Reilly (2010) studied a sample of individuals who, on average, were appreciably older than the samples studied by Wilk and colleagues (1995; 1996). Thus, GCA may be a stronger factor in determining job choice for younger individuals than for older individuals; perhaps this is because younger people tend to have fewer life commitments and enjoy greater freedom to leave low-complexity jobs and seek out jobs offering adequate levels of challenge.

The GCA–Performance Relationship Holds over Time

Another intuitive idea about GCA is that GCA only matters early in one's career. This idea is based on the notion that, while GCA may matter in the early stages of employment, employees with lower GCA will catch up over time and, after that occurs, GCA will cease to predict performance. As with the idea of a GCA threshold, research does not support this. The "catch up" idea would require the performance of individuals higher in GCA to improve quite slowly (or even remain static) while individuals lower in GCA improve their performance; instead, average performance improves for individuals at all levels of GCA. Schmidt and colleagues (1988) showed that performance increases for both low-GCA and high-GCA individuals and, rather than differences in performance between the groups converging or diverging over time, the groups improve at approximately equal rates.

One way to study changes to the GCA–performance relationship over time is to take a large group of employees and examine the relationship within groups of employees with identical levels of experience (e.g., employees who have been with an organization for the same number of months). Using that strategy, Farrell and McDaniel (2001) illustrated that, although the determinants of performance seem to change over time and the strength of GCA's relationship with performance fluctuates somewhat, the relationship remains strong across all levels of tenure (including employees who have 10 years of experience). The finding that the GCA–performance relationship holds at all levels of experience is strong evidence that GCA continues to matter throughout an individual's tenure in an organization.

GCA Predicts Both Rate and Amount of Learning

One key reason why GCA is so important in the workplace is its relationship with knowledge acquisition (Hunter, 1986; Ree & Earles, 1991). High-GCA individuals learn more and learn faster, both in formal training programs and on the job. Many organizations that use GCA measures in their selection processes do so because the job involves a lengthy training program (e.g., a newly hired firefighter is commonly placed into a six-month training program prior to being put onto the job). The costs of hiring someone who fails or drops out of a training program are substantial, so it is cost-effective to screen out applicants who are unlikely to satisfactorily complete the program. Measures of GCA are highly predictive of training success and the relationship between GCA and training success is even stronger than GCA's relationship with job performance (Hunter, 1986).

GCA Predicts Salary within a Given Job and Predicts Salary Trajectories of Individuals

One common assertion is that GCA predicts grades, but does not predict anything outside the classroom. This assertion is incorrect, as is evidenced by the power of GCA in predicting salaries. However, there are two different questions that one can address when examining GCA and salary. First, what is the relationship between

GCA and salary *across* various jobs? And second, what is the relationship between GCA and salary *within* a given job? In other words, for multiple individuals in the same job, does cognitive ability predict the salary level that these individuals will achieve at a given point or over time? When the relationship between GCA and salary is examined *across* various jobs, it tends to positively predict salary only weakly (e.g., Rode, Arthaud-Day, Mooney, Near, & Baldwin, 2008). On the other hand, when looking at salaries *within* a given job, GCA positively predicts salary much more strongly (Zagorsky, 2007). These two findings suggest that although individuals at the same level of GCA may choose to go into careers with very different salaries, individuals higher in GCA are more likely to be monetarily successful in their chosen jobs. Research finds that, within individuals, those who have high GCA tend to have steeper career salary trajectories than those low in GCA (Ganzach, 2000; Judge, Klinger, & Simon, 2010). That is, individuals high in GCA tend to get salary increases more quickly and receive larger raises.

GCA Predicts Occupational Attainment

Occupational attainment has various metrics and GCA generally predicts these metrics. Salary is one occupational attainment metric, another is occupational prestige (i.e., status of careers). Judge, Klinger, and Simon (2010) found that GCA positively predicts occupational prestige over time for individuals. Similarly, GCA predicts occupation level attained (Judge, Higgins, Thoresen, & Barrick, 1999; Wilk, Desmarais, & Sackett, 1995); individuals higher in GCA are more likely to be promoted to jobs higher in the organization.

One critique of this finding is that society has created artificial barriers to occupational attainment based on GCA. For example, cut-offs have been created on standardized tests that prevent lower GCA individuals from attending top-tier colleges, which, in turn, prevents these individuals from having access to the best jobs in the hierarchy. A similar argument can be made for cut-offs on GCA tests in employment testing for selection. However, job analysis methods have found that jobs are organized in a hierarchy with respect to cognitive complexity (Hunter & Hunter, 1984), with certain jobs and job types being more complex than others. GCA has been found to predict job performance across all levels of this hierarchy (Hunter & Hunter, 1984). So, these methods of ranking jobs in a hierarchy and the predictive power of GCA across the hierarchy both function independently of the barriers imposed by GCA tests. This refutes the notion that these barriers provide the explanation for the GCA–occupational attainment relationship.

GCA as a Predictor of Deviance/Wrongdoing

There is a long history of studying the relationship between GCA and antisocial behavior. Here we discuss this relationship in three contexts: predicting delinquent behavior in adolescence, predicting conviction for criminal behavior, and predicting counterproductive behavior at work.

GCA Predicts Delinquency, but Only for Certain Forms of Delinquency

Many studies converge on the conclusion that individuals who engage in delinquent behavior in adolescence, on average, have lower GCA than those who do not (formally, a mean difference of about .5 standard deviation [SD] in GCA between delinquents and non-delinquents). However, a critical distinction needs to be drawn between "adolescence-limited" and "life-course persistent" delinquents. There is a small group (roughly 5 percent) who exhibit antisocial behavior early in childhood, which continues into adolescence and adulthood. These are the life-course persistent delinquents and they show a large mean difference in GCA compared to non-delinquents, commonly over 1 SD. There is a much larger group who begin displaying antisocial behavior in adolescence, but soon retreat from doing so. These are the adolescence-limited delinquents and they show little-to-no mean difference in GCA compared to non-delinquents (Moffitt, 1993; Raine et al., 2005).

There are different possible causal pathways for the link between GCA and delinquent behavior. We discuss three that receive considerable attention in the literature. The first is the "self-control" pathway: Individuals high in GCA have the cognitive resources to anticipate the potential consequences of deviant behavior, such as getting caught, getting imprisoned, and loss of future job opportunities. Thus they are better positioned to resist temptation and to avoid behaving impulsively. The second is the "social bond" pathway: Individuals with low GCA are more likely to experience failure in school or at work and fail to establish strong connections with school. Thus they do not develop bonds to school and do not absorb the prosocial lessons about appropriate behavior that are absorbed by students who do form bonds with school. The third is the "social learning" pathway: Individuals with low GCA who experience failure in school may be more likely to form peer networks with others who engage in and reinforce antisocial behavior. Research supports each of these pathways (McGloin, Pratt, & Maahs, 2004).

GCA also plays another role in predicting delinquent behavior. An important longitudinal study identified youth at risk for engaging in antisocial behavior based on parent and teacher ratings. Among boys identified as being at high risk for criminal behavior, those higher in GCA were less likely to actually engage in the behavior. In other words, GCA "inoculates" at-risk youth against criminal behavior (White, Moffitt, & Silva, 1989).

GCA Predicts Criminal Conviction

Given our discussion above of life-course persistent delinquency, it is not surprising that research finds a relationship between GCA and criminal conviction. The more severe the crime, the lower the mean GCA of those convicted. And GCA is further predictive of reoffending after release.

Although GCA is negatively predictive of criminal behavior, it has taken a while to understand this relationship. One worry was that the apparent relationship was simply due to low-GCA individuals being more likely to be caught, and that, in fact, GCA was not related to engaging in criminal behavior. However, studies using self-reports of engaging in wrongdoing find that those who engage in wrongdoing but are not caught also have lower mean levels of GCA. Others suggested that perhaps low GCA was a consequence, not a cause, of criminal behavior (e.g., criminals might suffer neurological damage due to being hit in fights or due to drug abuse, thus lowering their GCA), but longitudinal studies measuring GCA early in childhood show that GCA remains negatively correlated with criminal behavior many years later, thus ruling out the reverse-causality hypothesis.

GCA Is Predictive of Counterproductive Behavior at Work

There are many types of counterproductive behaviors that could be displayed by an employee. These range from the very serious (and rare), such as murder and physical assault, to the more common, such as theft, destruction of property, misuse of company resources, intentionally doing low-quality work, verbally abusing others, and voluntary absence. Research generally creates an overall measure of counterproductive behavior, rather than studying them as separate behaviors.

Research on the relationships between GCA and counterproductive behavior does not yield consistent findings. A grand average of findings across studies would, at first glance, suggest no relationship (Gonzalez-Mule, Mount, & Oh, 2014). However, when studies are separated into those that use self-reported measures vs. externally measured counterproductive behavior, a small, negative relationship is found for the objective measures. Other large-scale studies do find negative relationships between GCA and counterproductive behavior. The single study with the most carefully developed measures of counterproductive behavior examined soldiers in the US Army (McHenry, Hough, Toquam, Hanson, & Ashworth, 1990). The researchers conducting that study combined data from personnel files (e.g., being written up for various violations of military discipline rules) with supervisor ratings of soldier behavior and conducted separate analyses for each of 11 different Army jobs. They found a modest negative relationship between GCA and counterproductive behavior. Also worthy of note is a large-scale study by Dilchert, Ones, Davis, and Rostow (2007) of police officers from 143 different locations. They created a checklist of possible misbehaviors and then went through personnel files and recorded the number of times each behavior occurred (e.g., number of civilian complaints of misbehavior, number incidents of misuse of equipment); these were combined into an overall measure. This study found a stronger relationship between GCA and counterproductive behavior than the Army study.

Our overall assessment is that there is a small negative relationship between GCA and counterproductive behavior, though it is considerably weaker than GCA's positive relationship with task performance at work. It is important to note that measures of personality (e.g., dependability, achievement striving) were substantially better predictors of counterproductivity in the Army study, a finding consistent with the broader literature on personality and counterproductivity (Berry, Ones, & Sackett, 2007).

Health and Safety

We now turn our attention to outcomes concerned with mortality, health, and safety. We begin our consideration of health and safety variables with mortality, as cognitive ability's relationship with risk of death from various causes will provide a helpful context for understanding its relationships with more acute health and safety issues.

GCA Predicts Mortality

To study mortality with any degree of confidence, researchers must track large cohorts of study participants over long timeframes. There have been many longitudinal studies reporting data on GCA and mortality and their collective results reveal a robust relationship between the two. A meta-analysis of longitudinal studies reported that, on average, a 1 SD increase in GCA (as measured during youth) corresponds to a 24 percent decrease in mortality risk (Calvin et al., 2011; for reference, this is the magnitude of difference between being in the 84th percentile on GCA as opposed to the 50th percentile).

Why is it that people higher in GCA have a lower mortality rate? We can begin to understand this phenomenon by examining mortality rates by specific causes of death, rather than from all causes combined. Leon et al. (2009) used longitudinal data to determine mortality rates from different causes by level of GCA, as measured at age 7. They found that a 1 SD increase in cognitive ability corresponded to a 19 percent lower mortality rate from cancer, a 12 percent lower mortality rate from cardiovascular disease, a 26 percent lower mortality rate from external causes (e.g., injuries and violence), and a 19 percent lower mortality rate from other causes (e.g., neurological and congenital diseases). From these results, there seems to be a general relationship between GCA and mortality that spans various causes of death.

To understand why there are general differences in mortality rates as a function of ability level, it will be helpful to explore how GCA relates to specific variables such as health and safety behaviors. In the following sections, we outline evidence of GCA's role in a variety of health-related behaviors, outcomes, and aptitudes.

GCA Predicts Aspects of Physical Health

Part of the reason why GCA is correlated with mortality rates is that GCA is linked to important indicators of cardiopulmonary health, to healthy habits of living, and to health literacy. Collectively, these associations between GCA and health-related behaviors and knowledge mean that GCA can have consequential indirect effects on physical health.

Cardiopulmonary Health

Childhood GCA correlates with some important indicators of cardiopulmonary health, including blood pressure and respiratory obstructions. Analyses of longitudinal data reveal that, on average, individuals higher in GCA have slightly lower diastolic and systolic blood pressure (Hart et al., 2004; Starr et al., 2004), as well as more efficient exhalation (Deary, Whalley, Batty, & Starr, 2006; Hart et al., 2004). Hart et al. (2004) also found that individuals higher in GCA had a lower risk of hospital admission or death due to cardiovascular disease, coronary heart disease, or stroke, even after statistically adjusting for known risk factors such as blood pressure and smoking. The mechanism by which GCA is related to these health variables is still not well understood, but researchers have posited that high-GCA individuals may be more attentive or receptive to health information and may be more likely use that information to make healthier lifestyle choices, which reduces their risk of disease (e.g., Deary et al., 2006).

Smoking

In the longitudinal Scottish Mental Survey study, individuals with greater GCA had a lower risk of hospitalization or death from smoking-related causes (Taylor et al., 2005). These individuals displayed effectively no difference in the rate at which they started smoking, but higher-ability individuals were more likely to cease smoking during adulthood than were lower-ability individuals (Taylor et al., 2003). Data gathered in a more recent study of US high school students revealed that lower-ability individuals were more likely to smoke than were higher-ability individuals and that the relationship was somewhat stronger for males than for females (Sander, 1998).

Diet

If "you are what you eat," do individuals higher in GCA eat "smarter" diets? The available evidence suggests so. Using longitudinal data, Batty, Deary, Schoon, and Gale (2007) discovered that higher-GCA individuals were more likely to report eating healthy foods such as fruits, vegetables, fish, and wholegrain breads and less likely to report eating foods such as French fries and non-wholegrain breads. When it came to fried foods, higher-GCA individuals were more likely to report consuming foods fried in vegetable oil (a somewhat healthier alternative to animal-based oils), but GCA did not relate to use of other types of oils. Diet plays an important role in cumulative health over a lifetime and higher-ability people appear to make healthier dietary choices, which could be a contributor to GCA's relationships with mortality and morbidity.

Health Literacy

Functional health literacy is "the degree to which individuals have the capacity to obtain, process, and understand basic health information and services needed to make appropriate health decisions" (Ratzan & Parker, 2000, p. vi). Health literacy's inclusion of obtaining, processing, and understanding information makes it a highly cognitive construct. In fact, a narrative review of measures commonly used to assess health literacy reported correlations with cognitive measures ranging between .50 and .97 in primary studies (Paasche-Orlow, Parker, Gazmararian, Nielsen-Bohlman, & Rudd, 2005). It is also worth noting that some of the health literacy measures included in that review were actually general tests of functional literacy, verbal ability, or achievement, signaling the importance of more general cognitive abilities for health literacy.

Health literacy is an important determinant of one's ability to take proper care of one's health needs and can have a very real impact on one's health and longevity. In a large study conducted at two hospitals, individuals with lower levels of health literacy were more likely to incorrectly respond to test items about how and when to take their medication, when their next appointment was, and how to determine their financial eligibility for care (Williams et al., 1995). Among hypertension patients, those with lower health literacy were less likely to recognize levels of blood pressure that are unhealthy, know that canned foods contain high levels of sodium, and know that exercise and weight loss lower blood pressure (Williams, Baker, Parker, & Nurss, 1998). Among diabetic patients, those with lower health literacy were less able to recognize normal blood-sugar levels, know how to identify the symptoms of a low-blood-sugar episode, and know what to do when they experience low blood sugar (Williams et al., 1998). Health literacy also relates to mortality: In a large cohort study, older adults with lower levels of health literacy died at faster rates than individuals with higher levels of health literacy (Baker, Wolf, Feinglass, & Thompson, 2008).

GCA Predicts Aspects of Mental Health

In addition to its association with physical health factors, GCA has also been linked to several aspects of mental health; these include lifetime psychiatric contact, subjective well-being, and risk of schizophrenia, dementia, and suicide.

Lifetime Psychiatric Contact

One of the most general mental health criteria related to GCA is lifetime psychiatric contact, which includes consulting with a mental-health professional at any point during one's life. Walker et al.'s (2002) analysis of longitudinal data revealed that lower-GCA individuals had a higher risk of psychiatric contact (regardless of age at contact) and were also more likely to have psychiatric contact earlier in life.

Risk of Depression

Depression has a relatively well-known and robust impairing effect on mental performance (Snyder, 2013), but whether or not one's level of pre-depression GCA serves as a risk factor for depression has been less clear. A recent meta-analysis uncovered a very small negative correlation between premorbid GCA and subsequently measured levels of depression (Scult et al., 2017). One's level of GCA does not appear to be an important predictor of future depressive symptoms.

Risk of Schizophrenia

Unlike depression, premorbid levels of GCA do appear to have a meaningful association with risk of schizophrenia. Khandaker et al.'s (2011) meta-analysis found that individuals with lower levels of GCA were at greater risk of developing schizophrenia and revealed that the meta-analytic odds of developing schizophrenia were linearly related to GCA.

Risk of Dementia

Childhood GCA is not related to the development of early-onset dementia, but *is* related to the development of late-onset dementia. Longitudinal research has found that lower childhood GCA is related to an increased risk of late-onset dementia (Whalley et al., 2000). Whalley and colleagues proposed that the risk of dementia is moderated by type of dementia because age-related brain changes are more important for late-onset dementia than for early-onset dementia, which means that childhood GCA is less important for predicting early-onset dementia. Subsequent research has explored different varieties of late-onset dementia and found that lower childhood GCA predicted the development of vascular dementia, but did not predict the development of Alzheimer's disease (McGurn, Deary, & Starr, 2008). Individuals with lower cerebral blood flow appear more likely to develop vascular dementia and also tend to have lower GCA and less education. McGurn et al. posited that the effect of childhood ability on vascular dementia may be mediated by cerebral blood flow, which is affected by many lifestyle variables that are correlated with ability level, such as level of education.

Subjective Well-being

Subjective well-being is "a person's cognitive and affective evaluations of his or her life" that "includes experiencing pleasant emotions, low levels of negative moods, and high life satisfaction" (Diener, Lucas, & Shigehiro, 2001, p. 63). The available meta-analytic evidence suggests that people higher in GCA tend to report greater life satisfaction and happiness (Pinquart & Sörensen, 2000).

Suicide

Longitudinal cohort studies and other large-scale data-collection efforts have found evidence that individuals lower in GCA are more likely to commit suicide than are individuals higher in GCA. A negative relationship between GCA and suicide rate has been found in Australian Army research (O'Toole & Stankov, 1992), as well as in large studies of men conscripted into the Swedish military (Batty et al., 2009; Gunnell, Magnusson, & Rasmussen, 2005; Sörberg, Allebeck, Melin, Gunnell, & Hemmingsson, 2013).

There is an interesting phenomenon that occurs when one shifts the unit of analysis from the individual to the nation: The direction of the ability–suicide relationship reverses. Nation-level research has found that countries with higher average GCA scores tend to have higher suicide rates for both males and females, even after controlling for countries' GDPs (gross domestic products; Voracek, 2004). We note, however, that this finding is not necessarily at odds with the individual-level suicide research: It is certainly possible for suicide to be more prevalent in nations with higher average GCA and for lower-GCA individuals within a given nation being at greater risk of committing suicide.

GCA Predicts Accidents and Safety Behaviors

In the previous section, we described how individuals higher in GCA engage in healthier behaviors and have lower risk of a variety of physical and mental health concerns. Collectively, those health-related findings explain an important part of the reason why GCA is related to mortality rates. We now explore another partial reason for the GCA–mortality link: GCA is related to safety behaviors, such as those exhibited in the workplace and on the road.

Workplace Safety

GCA has not traditionally been a theoretically important predictor in safety research, as safety research tends to focus on human attributes amenable to change via interventions. Instead of GCA, workplace safety researchers tend to focus on *safety knowledge*, which is declarative knowledge about safety practices. Safety knowledge clearly has a cognitive component because it requires the acquisition and retention of information. Declarative knowledge has been identified as an important mediator of the relationship between GCA and performance (e.g., Hunter, 1986) and adhering to safety protocols is certainly a type of performance. Christian et al.'s (2009) meta-analysis reported that safety knowledge correlates positively and quite strongly with safety compliance and participation. There is insufficient data to make a confident statement about safety knowledge's relationship with objectively measured accidents/injuries, but the limited data available show a weak, negative relationship.

Although safety knowledge is typically of greater interest than GCA in safety research, there is occupation-level evidence that average ability within an occupation is associated with injuries. Ford and Wiggins (2012) found that occupation-level injury rates are strongly negatively correlated with the levels of quantitative and verbal ability required on the job. The biggest difference in injury rates between occupations requiring high and low ability levels occurs in occupations without many physical hazards; as the level of physical hazards increases, the rates of injuries for high- and low-ability occupations become more similar until becoming equal in high-hazard occupations. These findings suggest that low levels of GCA in an occupation may function as a liability, such that workers in low-ability occupations become injured at higher rates than one would predict from the levels of hazards physically present in their work environments.

Driving Safety

Data from the Australian Army have allowed interesting comparisons between individuals who died in motor vehicle accidents and those who did not, including comparisons of mean GCA. O'Toole (1990) compared service personnel who died in motor accidents to a random sample of service personnel who served during the same period but did not die. On average, those who died in accidents scored .27 standard deviations lower on the Army's cognitive test than those who did not; this is a small but non-trivial effect. Using the same Australian Army sample, O'Toole and Stankov (1992) showed that, compared to a control group of living Army personnel, those killed in motor vehicle accidents also scored significantly lower on a speed and accuracy test and on a mechanical comprehension test. However, we note that there are some confounding factors that make it difficult to draw generalizable conclusions for civilian motorists from this Army research. For example, proportionately more privates were killed in accidents than were represented in the control group. It is possible that lower-ranking service personnel simply tended to score lower on the test (after all, the test was used as a classification instrument) and also used vehicles more than higher-ranking personnel. If privates operated vehicles more frequently than higher-ranking personnel, they would naturally have more opportunities to be killed in vehicular accidents. Smaller-scale research on civilian driving has tended to find small-to-moderate negative relationships between GCA and driving errors (e.g., Aksan, Anderson, Dawson, Uc, & Rizzo, 2015; Anderson et al., 2012), but that relationship has not yet been meta-analytically summarized.

CONCLUSION

Throughout this chapter, we have illustrated how GCA is an important predictor of outcomes across many domains in life, namely, educational and workplace outcomes, deviance/wrongdoing outcomes, and health and safety outcomes. Although we know a great deal about GCA because it has been a widely researched construct,

GCA is still actively researched and there are numerous avenues for future research. For example, within the educational domain, future research investigating why family income plays a more important role for students scoring lower in GCA (than higher in GCA) would be useful, as well as research on interventions with potential to improve educational outcomes for this group. Similarly, more research is needed on the mechanisms by which GCA predicts educational attainment and drop-out. Within the domain of work, we find that GCA's average meta-analytic prediction of counterproductivity is near zero, although there is some evidence to suggest a small negative relationship between the two variables. Why does GCA predict counter-productive behavior in this set of studies, and upon which factors does the GCA–counterproductivity relationship depend? Such research holds potential to deter harmful behavior in the workplace.

CHAPTER SUMMARY

We have outlined a broad sampling of the important life outcomes of which GCA is predictive. This research has resulted in extensive operational use of GCA-related measures in settings such as personnel selection and higher-education admissions. While GCA is important, we want to emphasize a point we've made repeatedly: namely, that other factors, such as dependability and perseverance, are also import-ant (and, in some cases, more important). A common mistake is to think that only the single best predictor of an outcome should be used. For example, high school GPA is a somewhat stronger predictor of college performance than are admissions tests. Fixation on the single best predictor leads some to argue that admissions tests should not be used. However, using high school GPA and admissions test scores in conjunction results in better prediction than either one alone. Thus, we close with these two broad but critical statements: (1) GCA is a very valuable construct for predicting a host of life outcomes and (2) despite its robust relationships with important outcomes, GCA is certainly not the *only* thing that matters in education, employment, health, or any other life domain.

KEY TERMS

correlation • counterproductive work behavior (CWB) • functional health literacy • general cognitive ability • meta-analysis • organizational citizenship behavior (OCB) • predictive validation studies • proxy variable • range restriction • sampling error • task performance

COMPREHENSION AND REFLECTION QUESTIONS

1. The chapter demonstrates that general cognitive ability (GCA) is predictive of a wide array of life outcomes. Beyond the descriptive fact that GCA predicts these outcomes is the question of *why and how* GCA predicts. What have you learned from the chapter that addresses this question?

2. The opening of the chapter offers the general principle that GCA will be more strongly predictive of highly cognitive outcomes than less cognitive outcomes. How do the outcomes reviewed in the chapter differ on this cognitive-noncognitive continuum?

3. Although the chapter reviews a wide array of life outcomes, it is not an exhaustive list of outcomes. Identify several outcomes not examined in the chapter, and use the framework introduced in the chapter to offer hypotheses about whether GCA will have a strong or weak predictive relationship with each outcome you identify.

4. We have described GCA's relationships with outcomes from different life domains, but we have also highlighted the fact that GCA is seldom a direct determinant of these outcomes (i.e., there is often some mechanism between GCA and outcomes that explains why the GCA–outcome relationship exists). Think of at least two life outcomes not covered in this chapter that you expect to be related to GCA and describe mechanisms that explain why those relationships could exist (e.g., GCA relates to task performance on the job because it facilitates the acquisition of job knowledge, which helps workers to perform necessary behaviors on the job).

5. A new study in the *Journal of Specious Research* gathered data from 30 lawyers at a prestigious law firm over the course of a week and reported that there was no relationship between GCA and job performance measured during the investigation. The authors claim that their results overturn decades of research on the GCA–performance relationship. Is their claim justified? Why or why not?

References

Aksan, N., Anderson, S. W., Dawson, J., Uc, E., & Rizzo, M. (2015). Cognitive functioning differentially predicts different dimensions of older drivers' on-road safety. *Accident Analysis & Prevention, 75*, 236–244. https://doi.org/10.1016/j.aap.2014.12.00

Anderson, S. W., Aksan, N., Dawson, J. D., Uc, E. Y., Johnson, A. M., & Rizzo, M. (2012). Neuropsychological assessment of driving safety risk in older adults with and without neurologic disease. *Journal of Clinical and Experimental Neuropsychology, 34*(9), 895–905. https://doi.org/10.1080/13803395.2011.630654

Arneson, J. J., Sackett, P. R., & Beatty, A. S. (2011). Ability–performance relationships in education and employment settings: Critical tests of the more-is-better and the good-enough hypotheses. *Psychological Science, 22*(10), 1336–1342. https://doi.org/10.1177/0956797611417004

Baker, D. W., Wolf, M. S., Feinglass, J., & Thompson, J. A. (2008). Health literacy, cognitive abilities, and mortality among elderly persons. *Journal of General Internal Medicine, 23*(6), 723–726. https://doi.org/10.1007/s11606-008-0566-4

Batty, G. D., Deary, I. J., Schoon, I., & Gale, C. R. (2007). Childhood mental ability in relation to food intake and physical activity in adulthood: The 1970 British Cohort Study. *Pediatrics, 119*(1), e38–e45. https://doi.org/10.1542/peds.2006-1831

Batty, G. D., Wennerstad, K. M., Smith, G. D., Gunnell, D., Deary, I. J., Tynelius, P., & Rasmussen, F. (2009). IQ in early adulthood and mortality by middle age: Cohort study of 1 million Swedish men. *Epidemiology, 20*(1), 100–109. https://doi.org/10.1097/EDE.0b013e31818ba076

Belley, P., & Lochner, L. (2007). The changing role of family income and ability in determining educational achievement. *Journal of Human Capital, 1*, 37–89.

Berry, C. M., Ones, D. S., & Sackett, P. R. (2007). Interpersonal deviance, organizational deviance, and their common correlates: A review and meta-analysis. *Journal of Applied Psychology, 92*, 410-424.

Biernat, M. (2003). Toward a broader view of social stereotyping. *American Psychologist, 58*, 1019–1027.

Binet, A. (1905). *The development of intelligence in children (The Binet–Simon scale)* (trans. E. Kite). Baltimore: Williams and Wilkins.

Calvin, C. M., Deary, I. J., Fenton, C., Roberts, B. A., Der, G., Leckenby, N., & Batty, G. D. (2011). Intelligence in youth and all-cause-mortality: Systematic review with meta-analysis. *International Journal of Epidemiology, 40*(3), 626–644. https://doi.org/10.1093/ije/dyq190

Casillas, A., Robbins, S., Allen, J., Kuo, Y.-L., Hanson, M. A., & Schmeiser, C. (2012). Predicting early academic failure in high school from prior academic achievement, psychosocial characteristics, and behavior. *Journal of Educational Psychology, 104*, 407–420.

Chiaburu, D. S., Oh, I. S., Berry, C. M., Li, N., & Gardner, R. G. (2011). The five-factor model of personality traits and organizational citizenship behaviors: A meta-analysis. *Journal of Applied Psychology, 96*, 1140-1166.

Christian, M. S., Bradley, J. C., Wallace, J. C., & Burke, M. J. (2009). Workplace safety: A meta-analysis of the roles of person and situation factors. *Journal of Applied Psychology, 94*(5), 1103–1127. https://doi.org/10.1037/a0016172

Coward, W. M., & Sackett, P. R. (1990). Linearity of ability-performance relationships: A reconfirmation. *Journal of Applied Psychology, 75*(3), 297.

Crosby, F. J., Iyer, A., Clayton, S., & Downing, R. A. (2003). Affirmative action: Psychological data and the policy debates. *American Psychologist, 58*, 93–115.

Dahlke, J. A., Sackett, P. R., and Kuncel, N. R. (2019). Effects of range restriction and criterion contamination on the differential validity of the SAT by race, ethnicity, and sex. *Journal of Applied Psychology*. Advance on-line publication. doi: 10.1037/apl0000382

Deary, I. J., Strand, S., Smith, P., & Fernandes, C. (2007). Intelligence and educational achievement. *Intelligence, 35,* 13-21.

Deary, I. J., Whalley, L. J., Batty, G. D., & Starr, J. M. (2006). Physical fitness and lifetime cognitive change. *Neurology, 67*(7), 1195–1200. https://doi.org/10.1212/01.wnl.0000238520.06958.6a

Diener, E., Lucas, R. E., & Shigehiro, O. (2001). Subjective well-being. In C. R. Snyder & S. J. Lopez (eds.), *Handbook of Positive Psychology*. Oxford: Oxford University Press.

Dilchert, S., Ones, D. S., Davis, R. D., & Rostow, C. D. (2007). Cognitive ability predicts objectively measured counterproductive work behaviors. *Journal of Applied Psychology, 92*(3), 616.

Dumais, S. A. (2002). Cultural Capital, Gender, and School Success: The Role of Habitus. *Sociology of Education, 75,* 44.

Farrell, J. N., & McDaniel, M. A. (2001). The stability of validity coefficients over time: Ackerman's (1988) model and the General Aptitude Test Battery. *Journal of Applied Psychology, 86*(1), 60–79. https://doi.org/10.1037//0021-9010.86.1.60

Fergusson, D. M., & Horwood, L. J. (1995). Early disruptive behavior, IQ, and later school achievement and delinquent behavior. *Journal of Abnormal Child Psychology, 23,* 183–199.

Ford, M. T., & Wiggins, B. K. (2012). Occupational-level interactions between physical hazards and cognitive ability and skill requirements in predicting injury incidence rates. *Journal of Occupational Health Psychology, 17*(3), 268–278. https://doi.org/10.1037/a0028143

Frey, M. C., & Detterman, D. K. (2004). Scholastic assessment or *g*? The relationship between the scholastic assessment test and general *g*. *Psychological Science, 15,* 373–378.

Ganzach, Y. (2000). Parents' education, cognitive ability, educational expectations and educational attainment: Interactive effects. *British Journal of Educational Psychology, 70,* 419-441.

Gonzalez-Mulé, E., Mount, M. K., & Oh, I. S. (2014). A meta-analysis of the relationship between general mental ability and nontask performance. *Journal of Applied Psychology, 99,* 1222-1243.

Gottfredson, L. S. (2002). g: Highly general and highly practical. In R. J. Sternberg & E. L. Grigorenko (eds.), *The general factor of intelligence* (pp. 331-380). Mahwah, NJ: Lawrence Erlbaum Associates.

Gunnell, D., Magnusson, P. K. E., & Rasmussen, F. (2005). Low intelligence test scores in 18 year old men and risk of suicide: Cohort study. *British Medical Journal 330*(7484), 167. https://doi.org/10.1136/bmj.38310.473565.8F

Hart, C. L., Taylor, M. D., Smith, G. D., Whalley, L. J., Starr, J. M., Hole, D. J., ... Deary, I. J. (2004). Childhood IQ and cardiovascular disease in adulthood: Prospective observational study linking the Scottish Mental Survey 1932 and the Midspan studies. *Social Science & Medicine, 59*(10), 2131–2138. https://doi.org/10.1016/j.socscimed .2004.03.016

Holm, A., & Jaeger, M. M. (2009). *Selection bias in educational transition models: Theory and empirical evidence.* Copenhagen: Centre for Applied Microeconometrics, Department of Economics, University of Copenhagen.

Holm, A., & Jaeger, M. M. (2011). Dealing with selection bias in educational transition models: The bivariate probit selection model. *Research in Social Stratification and Mobility, 29,* 311-322.

Hunter, J. E. (1983). *Test validation for 12,000 jobs: An application of job classification and validity generalization analysis to the General Aptitude Test Battery.* Washington, DC: Division of Counseling and Test Development, Employment and Training Administration, US Department of Labor.

Hunter, J. E. (1986). Cognitive ability, cognitive aptitudes, job knowledge, and job performance. *Journal of Vocational Behavior, 29,* 340-362.

Hunter, J. E., & Hunter, R. F. (1984). Validity and utility of alternative predictors of job performance. *Psychological Bulletin, 96,* 72-98.

Jencks, C. (1979). *Who gets ahead? The determinants of economic success in America.* New York: Basic Books.

Judge, T. A., Higgins, C. A., Thoresen, C. J., & Barrick, M. R. (1999). The Big Five personality traits, general mental ability, and career success across the life span. *Personnel Psychology, 52,* 621-652.

Judge, T. A., Klinger, R. L., & Simon, L. S. (2010). Time is on my side: Time, general mental ability, human capital, and extrinsic career success. *Journal of Applied Psychology, 95,* 92-107.

Keiser, H. N., Sackett, P. R., Kuncel, N. R., & Brothen, T. (2016). Why women perform better in college than admission scores would predict: Exploring the roles of conscientiousness and course-taking patterns. *Journal of Applied Psychology, 101*(4), 569-581.

Khandaker, G. M., Barnett, J. H., White, I. R., & Jones, P. B. (2011). A quantitative meta-analysis of population-based studies of premorbid intelligence and schizophrenia. *Schizophrenia Research, 132*(2), 220–227. https://doi.org/10.1016/j.schres.2011.06.017

Kim, K. H. (2005). Can only intelligent people be creative? A meta-analysis. *Journal of Secondary Gifted Education, 16,* 57–66.

Knighton, T. and Bussière, P. (2006). *Educational outcomes at age 19 associated with reading ability at age 15.* Ottawa: Culture, Tourism and the Centre for Education Statistics Division, Statistics Canada.

Koenig, K. A., Frey, M. C., & Detterman, D. K. (2008). ACT and general cognitive ability. *Intelligence, 36,* 153-160.

Kuncel, N. R., Hezlett, S. A., & Ones, D. S. (2004). Academic performance, career potential, creativity, and job performance: Can one construct predict them all? *Journal of Personality and Social Psychology, 86,* 148–161.

Kuzmits, F. E., & Adams, A. J. (2008). The NFL combine: Does it predict performance in the National Football League? *Journal of Strength & Conditioning Research, 22,* 1721–1727.

Leon, D. A., Lawlor, D. A., Clark, H., Batty, G. D., & Macintyre, S. (2009). The association of childhood intelligence with mortality risk from adolescence to middle age: Findings from the Aberdeen Children of the 1950s cohort study. *Intelligence, 37*(6), 520–528. https://doi.org/10.1016/j.intell.2008.11.004

Maani, S. A., & Kalb, G. (2007). Academic performance, childhood economic resources, and the choice to leave school at age 16. *Economics of Education Review, 26,* 361–374.

Maltarich, M. A., Nyberg, A. J., & Reilly, G. (2010). A conceptual and empirical analysis of the cognitive ability–voluntary turnover relationship. *Journal of Applied Psychology, 95*(6), 1058–1070. https://doi.org/10.1037/a0020331

Marks, G. N. (2013). *Education, social background, and* g: *The decline of the social.* New York: Routledge.

McGloin, J. M., Pratt, T. C., & Maahs, J. (2004). Rethinking the IQ–delinquency relationship: A longitudinal analysis of multiple theoretical models. *Justice Quarterly, 21*(3), 603–635.

McGurn, B., Deary, I. J., & Starr, J. M. (2008). Childhood cognitive ability and risk of late-onset Alzheimer and vascular dementia. *Neurology, 71*(14), 1051–1056.

McHenry, J. J., Hough, L. M., Toquam, J. L., Hanson, M. A., & Ashworth, S. (1990). Project A validity results: The relationship between predictor and criterion domains. *Personnel Psychology, 43*(2), 335–354.

Moffitt, T. E. (1993). Adolescence-limited and life-course-persistent antisocial behavior: A developmental taxonomy. *Psychological Review, 100*(4), 674.

O'Toole, B. I. (1990). Intelligence and behaviour and motor vehicle accident mortality. *Accident Analysis & Prevention, 22*(3), 211–221. https://doi.org/10.1016/0001-4575(90)90013-B

O'Toole, B. I., & Stankov, L. (1992). Ultimate validity of psychological tests. *Personality and Individual Differences, 13*(6), 699–716. https://doi.org/10.1016/0191-8869(92)90241-G

Paasche-Orlow, M. K., Parker, R. M., Gazmararian, J. A., Nielsen-Bohlman, L. T., & Rudd, R. R. (2005). The prevalence of limited health literacy. *Journal of General Internal Medicine, 20*(2), 175–184. https://doi.org/10.1111/j.1525-1497.2005.40245.x

Pinquart, M., & Sörensen, S. (2000). Influences of socioeconomic status, social network, and competence on subjective well-being in later life: A meta-analysis. *Psychology and Aging, 15*(2), 187.

Raine, A., Moffitt, T. E., Caspi, A., Loeber, R., Stouthamer-Loeber, M., & Lynam, D. (2005). Neurocognitive impairments in boys on the life-course persistent antisocial path. *Journal of Abnormal Psychology, 114*(1), 38.

Ratzan, S. C., & Parker, R. M. (2000). Health literacy. *National Library of Medicine Current Bibliographies in Medicine.* Bethesda, MD: National Institutes of Health, US Department of Health and Human Services.

Ree, M. J., & Earles, J. A. (1991). Predicting training success: Not much more than *g*. *Personnel Psychology, 44*(2), 321–332. https://doi.org/10.1111/j.1744-6570.1991.tb00961.x

Robbins, S. B., Lauver, K., Le, H., Davis, D., Langley, R., & Carlstrom, A. (2004). Do Psychosocial and study skill factors predict college outcomes? A meta-analysis. *Psychological Bulletin, 130*, 261–288.

Rode, J. C., Arthaud-Day, M. L., Mooney, C. H., Near, J. P., & Baldwin, T. T. (2008). Ability and personality predictors of salary, perceived job success, and perceived career success in the initial career stage. *International Journal of Selection and Assessment, 16*, 292–299.

Rotundo, M., & Sackett, P. R. (2002). The relative importance of task, citizenship, and counterproductive performance to global ratings of job performance: A policy-capturing approach. *Journal of Applied Psychology, 87*, 66–80.

Sackett, P. R., Kuncel, N. R., Arneson, J. J., Cooper, S. R., & Waters, S. D. (2009). Does socioeconomic status explain the relationship between admissions tests and post-secondary academic performance? *Psychological Bulletin, 135*, 1–22.

Sander, W. (1998). The effects of schooling and cognitive ability on smoking and marijuana use by young adults. *Economics of Education Review, 17*(3), 317–324. https://doi.org/10.1016/S0272-7757(97)00051-4

Schmidt, F. L., & Hunter, J. E. (1998). The validity and utility of selection methods in personnel psychology: Practical and theoretical implications of 85 years of research findings. *Psychological Bulletin, 124*, 262–274.

Schmidt, F. L., Hunter, J. E., Outerbridge, A. N., & Goff, S. (1988). Joint relation of experience and ability with job performance: Test of three hypotheses. *Journal of Applied Psychology, 73*(1), 46.

Schoon, I. (2008). A transgenerational model of status attainment: The potential mediating role of school motivation and education. *National Institute Economic Review, 205*, 72–82.

Scult, M. A., Paulli, A. R., Mazure, E. S., Moffitt, T. E., Hariri, A. R., & Strauman, T. J. (2017). The association between cognitive function and subsequent depression: A systematic review and meta-analysis. *Psychological Medicine, 47*(1), 1–17. https://doi.org/10.1017/S0033291716002075

Sewell, W. H., & Hauser, R. M. (1975). *Education, occupation, and earnings: Achievement in the early career.* New York: Academic Press.

Shewach, O. R., Shen, W., Sackett, P. R., and Kuncel, N. R. (2017). Differential prediction in the use of the SAT and high school grades in predicting college performance: Joint effects of race and language. *Educational Measurement: Issues and Practice.* Advance online publication. https://doi.org/10.1111/emip.12150

Snyder, H. R. (2013). Major depressive disorder is associated with broad impairments on neuropsychological measures of executive function: A meta-analysis and review. *Psychological Bulletin, 139*(1), 81–132. https://doi.org/10.1037/a0028727

Sörberg, A., Allebeck, P., Melin, B., Gunnell, D., & Hemmingsson, T. (2013). Cognitive ability in early adulthood is associated with later suicide and suicide attempt: The role of risk factors over the life course. *Psychological Medicine, 43*(1), 49–60. https://doi.org/10.1017/S0033291712001043

Starr, J. M., Taylor, M. D., Hart, C. L., Smith, G. D., Whalley, L. J., Hole, D. J., . . . & Deary, I. J. (2004). Childhood mental ability and blood pressure at midlife: Linking the Scottish Mental Survey 1932 and the Midspan studies. *Journal of Hypertension, 22*(5), 893–897.

Strenze, T. (2007). Intelligence and socioeconomic success: A meta-analytic review of longitudinal research. *Intelligence, 35*, 401–426.

Taylor, M. D., Hart, C. L., Smith, G. D., Starr, J. M., Hole, D. J., Whalley, L. J., . . . Deary, I. J. (2003). Childhood mental ability and smoking cessation in adulthood: Prospective observational study linking the Scottish Mental Survey 1932 and the Midspan studies. *Journal of Epidemiology & Community Health, 57*(6), 464–465. https://doi.org/10.1136/jech.57.6.464

Taylor, M. D., Hart, C. L., Smith, G. D., Starr, J. M., Hole, D. J., Whalley, L. J., Wilson, V., & Deary, I. J. (2005). Childhood IQ and social factors on smoking behaviour, lung function and smoking-related outcomes in adulthood: Linking the Scottish Mental Survey 1932 and the Midspan studies. *British Journal of Health Psychology, 10*(3), 399–410. https://doi.org/10.1348/135910705X25075

Voracek, M. (2004). National intelligence and suicide rate: An ecological study of 85 countries. *Personality and Individual Differences, 37*(3), 543–553. https://doi.org/10.1016/j.paid.2003.09.025

Walker, N. P., McConville, P. M., Hunter, D., Deary, I. J., & Whalley, L. J. (2002). Childhood mental ability and lifetime psychiatric contact. *Intelligence, 30*(3), 233–245. https://doi.org/10.1016/S0160-2896(01)00098-8

Westrick, P. A., Le, H., Robbins, S. B., Radunzel, J. M. R., & Schmidt, F. L. (2015). College performance and retention: A meta-analysis of the predictive validities of ACT® scores, high school grades, and SES. *Educational Assessment, 20*, 23–45.

Whalley, L. J., Starr, J. M., Athawes, R., Hunter, D., Pattie, A., & Deary, I. J. (2000). Childhood mental ability and dementia. *Neurology, 55*(10), 1455–1459.

White, J. L., Moffitt, T. E., & Silva, P. A. (1989). A prospective replication of the protective effects of IQ in subjects at high risk for juvenile delinquency. *Journal of consulting and clinical psychology, 57*(6), 719.

Wilk, S. L., & Sackett, P. R. (1996). Longitudinal analysis of ability–job complexity fit and job change. *Personnel Psychology, 49*(4), 937–967. https://doi.org/10.1111/j.1744-6570.1996.tb02455.x

Wilk, S. L., Desmarais, L. B., & Sackett, P. R. (1995). Gravitation to jobs commensurate with ability: Longitudinal and cross-sectional tests. *Journal of Applied Psychology, 80*, 79–85.

Williams, M. V., Baker, D. W., Parker, R. M., & Nurss, J. R. (1998). Relationship of functional health literacy to patients' knowledge of their chronic disease: A study of patients with hypertension and diabetes. *Archives of Internal Medicine, 158*(2), 166–172. https://doi.org/10.1001/archinte.158.2.166

Williams, M. V., Parker, R. M., Baker, D. W., Parikh, N. S., Pitkin, K., Coates, W. C., & Nurss, J. R. (1995). Inadequate functional health literacy among patients at two public hospitals. *JAMA, 274*(21), 1677–1682. https://doi.org/10.1001/jama.1995.0353 0210031026

Zagorsky, J. L. (2007). Do you have to be smart to be rich? The impact of IQ on wealth, income and financial distress. *Intelligence, 35*, 489-501.

15 | The Relationship of Intelligence to Other Psychological Traits

COLIN G. DEYOUNG

People differ in intelligence, and they also differ psychologically in many other important ways. Psychologists use the term "personality" to describe all relatively stable individual differences in behavior, motivation, emotion, and cognition (McAdams & Pals, 2006). This chapter explores how intelligence is related to the rest of personality. Does knowing that someone is high or low in intelligence tell us anything else about that person? Can we make educated guesses about people's personalities if we know their IQs? The short answer to this question is *yes*. We know a lot about how intelligence is associated with personality. It turns out that there are only a few other traits with which intelligence is strongly or even moderately associated, but there are a number of others with which it is at least weakly associated. Thus, although knowing someone's IQ certainly does not allow us to be very confident about most other aspects of his or her personality, it does give us some clues about what might be likely.

One reason to study how intelligence is related to personality is to help people understand that intelligence is not the only important attribute that people have. Intelligence is highly valued in many societies, and so it can be tempting to think that smart people always have many other good qualities as well. Understanding the range of other personality traits, and the fact that intelligence is only weakly related to most of them, can help to dispel the myths that intelligence is all that matters, or that it predicts everything else that matters. Understanding the many personality traits that are largely independent of intelligence can also help us to identify other factors beyond intelligence that are important for success, happiness, and fulfillment in life. At the same time, understanding which personality traits do have some connection to intelligence can aid in the scientific exploration of the many ways that intelligence functions in human life, which in turn can enrich our understanding of intelligence as a complex and multifaceted phenomenon.

We use the term "intelligence" in this chapter to refer to *general intelligence*, defined as the so-called "*g* factor," the ability to perform well on a wide variety of challenging cognitive tasks. Intelligence thus seems to reflect a general ability to solve complex problems and generate accurate interpretations, through reasoning, learning, and the voluntary maintenance and manipulation of information in conscious attention. We will briefly discuss *emotional intelligence*, but otherwise "intelligence" will refer to the g factor that is measured well (though not perfectly) by IQ tests (Gottfredson, 1997; Neisser et al., 1996). The g factor represents the broadest form of cognitive ability because it is useful in solving virtually all difficult cognitive tasks, but we can also consider more specific types of cognitive ability. One meaningful distinction is between *verbal abilities*, which involve reasoning about the meaning and relations of words and concepts, and *nonverbal abilities*, which have been called "perceptual" or "performance" abilities and which involve reasoning about spatial, geometric, or numerical patterns (Johnson & Bouchard, 2005a, 2005b; Major, Johnson, & Deary, 2012; Wechsler, 2008); this distinction will also be important for understanding the associations of intelligence with personality.

Personality Traits and the Five-Factor Model

Although "personality" is often used to refer broadly to any reasonably persistent pattern of behavior, motivation, emotion, and cognition, including relatively specific skills, habits, beliefs, attitudes, and goals, this chapter focuses primarily on broader personality traits. **Personality traits** are dimensions of variation within the population that describe relatively stable patterns of behavior and experience that are applicable to people in any culture; they are not skills, habits, beliefs, etc., that might be specific to one cultural context or another (McAdams & Pals, 2006). Traits are qualities, like aggression or talkativeness or impulsivity, that should be applicable to human beings in any culture at any time in history (DeYoung, 2015a). In other words, anyone can be described as having some level of any given personality trait, ranging from very low to very high.

Personality psychologists have spent a lot of time attempting to determine what are the most important personality traits (John, Naumann, & Soto, 2008). In early theories of personality, various psychologists had different ideas about what traits were important, and it was difficult to make scientific progress because nearly every researcher was working with a different list of traits. This untenable situation led to a long effort to use empirical methods to identify the important traits, which was facilitated in the 1970s and 1980s as computers made complex statistical analyses easier to conduct. The major method used to identify the important personality traits was factor analysis – the same method described in Chapter 4 of this text that was used to demonstrate the existence of general intelligence through the g factor. The application of factor analysis to descriptions of personality was much more complex than its application to cognitive tests, however, because there is more than one factor at the highest level of personality organization.

Psychologists have used factor analysis to study ratings of hundreds of personality traits, identified either by poring through the dictionary to find all of the adjectives that could be used to describe a person (for example, "aggressive," "talkative," impulsive," "clever") or by collecting scales and items from many existing personality questionnaires. When people rate themselves or others on hundreds of different personality descriptors from either source, what factor analysis shows is that there are five or six major dimensions of personality that are widely replicable, meaning that they appear in study after study, in a wide variety of cultures (Ashton et al., 2004; John et al., 2008; Markon, Krueger, & Watson, 2005; Waller, DeYoung, & Bouchard, 2016). In other words, there are reliable and nearly universal ways in which personality traits tend to cluster together, such that if people have high levels of certain traits, they tend to have high levels of certain other traits as well. This means that the multitude of specific personality traits can be organized within a relatively small set of broad, overarching traits, which we can reasonably consider to be the most important traits for the purpose of much personality research – and for the purposes of this chapter.

The most widely used model for describing the major dimensions of personality that have been found using factor analysis is the **five-factor model**, also known as the "Big Five" (Goldberg, 1990; John et al., 2008; Costa & McCrae, 1992). This model became well established by the 1990s and led to a rapid advancement of scientific knowledge about personality, as many researchers were able to integrate their findings using the Big Five. The Big Five trait dimensions are typically labeled *extraversion, neuroticism, agreeableness, conscientiousness*, and *openness/intellect*. The last one has the most confusing name, but it is also the most important for understanding the relation of intelligence to personality. The awkward compound label stems from an old debate about whether this factor should be labeled "openness to experience" or "intellect." In the end, the argument has been resolved by the realization that both labels describe portions of this trait accurately. If we start with openness/intellect, we can arrange the first letters of the Big Five to spell out OCEAN, and indeed the Big Five cover the whole ocean of personality. Table 15.1 lists each of the Big Five dimensions and provides examples of the characteristics that are associated with each. Almost every specific personality trait you can think of can be categorized within one of the five dimensions, or, in some cases, described as a blend of two or more of the dimensions. Every person's personality can be reasonably well summarized by providing a score for each of the five dimensions.

Openness/Intellect

Openness/intellect is the only one of the Big Five traits that has a moderate to large association with IQ (Ackerman & Heggestad, 1997; DeYoung, 2011; Stanek, 2014), and it is also the only one that includes explicit descriptions of intelligence. Adjectives like "clever" and "intelligent" were good markers of this factor in the

Table 15.1 The five-factor model or "Big Five" personality traits and examples of associated characteristics

Openness/Intellect	Conscientiousness	Extraversion	Agreeableness	Neuroticism
artistic	careful	active	altruistic	anxious
clever	diligent	assertive	compassionate	depressive
creative	hard-working	daring	considerate	fearful
curious	industrious	energetic	cooperative	insecure
imaginative	orderly	enthusiastic	empathetic	irritable
innovative	organized	excitable	helpful	jealous
intellectual	productive	joyful	honest	moody
intelligent	reliable	loud	humble	self-pitying
original	responsible	outgoing	kind	temperamental
perceptive	self-disciplined	sociable	polite	touchy
philosophical	thorough	talkative	unaggressive	volatile

lexical research that led to the Big Five, as were adjectives like "philosophical" and "intellectual." This prompted lexical researchers to label the factor "intellect" (e.g., Goldberg, 1990). However, other researchers pointed out that the factor seemed to be broader than that label would suggest, since it also included adjectives like "artistic," "imaginative," "creative," and "perceptive." This led to the proposal that the whole factor should be called "openness to experience" (Costa & McCrae, 1992). Even in the early 1990s, however, some researchers suggested that this debate could be resolved by recognizing that there were two kinds of traits within the broader Big Five domain, some well described as "intellect" and others better described as "openness to experience" (Johnson, 1994; Saucier, 1992). More recently, this suggestion was given empirical support by the demonstration that there are two distinct major subfactors within the Big Five trait, one of which clearly reflects intellect, and one of which clearly reflects openness to experience ("openness," for short) (DeYoung, 2015b; DeYoung, Quilty, & Peterson, 2007). In this chapter we refer to the original Big Five factor as openness/intellect but use "intellect" or "openness" in isolation to mean one of the two subfactors, also known as *aspects*.

At the core of openness/intellect is the tendency to be curious about the world and innovative in one's approach to it. The main psychological function associated with openness/intellect has been described as "cognitive exploration," the tendency to find information rewarding and to try to detect patterns and make sense of the world through both cognition and perception (DeYoung, 2015b). Intellect reflects the tendency to engage with abstract information through reasoning, and it involves both confidence in one's own intellectual ability and interest in intellectual pursuits. Openness reflects the tendency to engage with sensory information, through both perception and imagination, and it is related to appreciation of aesthetics, proneness to fantasy, and the tendency to make art.

Openness/intellect as a whole is related to intelligence, as measured by IQ and similar performance tests, with a correlation (r) of about .3 (Ackerman & Heggestad, 1997; DeYoung, 2011; Stanek, 2014). This correlation can be considered to fall in the moderate to large range, because it is larger than two-thirds of all significant effects reported in psychology for variables that do not share the same method of assessment (Hemphill, 2003). Openness/intellect is more strongly related to verbal ability than it is to nonverbal ability, and this has led some researchers (who tend to equate verbal ability with crystallized intelligence) to speculate that openness/intellect may contribute to the development of greater intelligence because the trait involves curiosity and intellectual interests that lead to learning (Chamorro-Premuzic & Furnham, 2005; Ziegler, Danay, Heene, Asendorpf, & Bühner, 2012). In the context of this idea, traits related to openness/intellect are sometimes called "investment traits" because they lead people to engage time and effort in developing their intellect through education and other learning activities (von Stumm & Ackerman, 2013). It is possible that the association of openness/intellect with intelligence is partly due to the fact that those high in openness/intellect have greater curiosity and investment in learning, but other causal processes might also contribute to the association. High intelligence may cause people to be more curious and cognitively exploratory because it is rewarding to engage in activities at which one excels. Or there may be shared genetic factors that influence both intelligence and openness/intellect. The results of one large longitudinal study suggested that the latter two possibilities (intelligence leading to curiosity, or both being generated by shared mechanisms) are more likely than the possibility that openness/intellect causes change in intelligence over time. This study found no evidence that openness/intellect (measured at age 79 years) predicted change in IQ between ages 11 and 79 years, despite the fact that openness/intellect at age 79 was correlated with IQ at both ages, $r = .32$ at age 11 and $r = .22$ at age 79 (Gow, Whiteman, Pattie, & Deary, 2005).

Intellect

Separating intellect and openness helps to clarify the associations between these personality traits and intelligence. From research that measures intellect and openness separately, it is clear that questionnaire measures of intellect are more strongly associated with intelligence than openness is (DeYoung, Quilty, Peterson, & Gray, 2014; Kaufman et al., 2016; Stanek, 2014). Correlations with questionnaire measures of intellect are often around .35, whereas those with openness are closer to .20. (Note that a correlation of .20 is still larger than about one-third of all significant effects in psychology (Hemphill, 2003).) Intellect, but not openness, has been linked to the brain systems in the frontal lobes that support intelligence (DeYoung, Shamosh, Green, Braver, & Gray, 2009). (See Focus on Contemporary Research box for a discussion of the role of neuroscience in personality research.) These brain systems are crucial for working memory, the ability to maintain and manipulate information in conscious attention, even in the face of distractions. Working memory ability seems to be the largest contributor to intelligence, among underlying cognitive processes, and it is also linked to questionnaire measures of intellect (Conway, Kane, & Engle, 2003; Kaufman et al., 2010). Notably, intellect, unlike the general openness/intellect factor, is almost equally associated with both verbal and nonverbal ability. People who score higher on questionnaire measures of intellect are more intelligent and this is manifest in both verbal and nonverbal domains.

FOCUS ON CONTEMPORARY RESEARCH: COLIN G. DEYOUNG'S WORK ON PERSONALITY NEUROSCIENCE

Psychologists have made good progress in understanding what are the most important dimensions of personality and how they predict many life outcomes, but we still know relatively little about where personality traits come from. Genetically informative research shows that personality traits are influenced by both genetics and the environment, but both genes and environmental forces must have an impact on the brain if they are going to affect personality, because all behavior and experience is generated by the brain. Personality neuroscience is the area of psychology that attempts to figure out what brain systems underlie different personality traits (DeYoung, 2010). My lab uses magnetic resonance imaging (MRI) to scan people's brains and then test whether their personalities are systematically related to various aspects of brain structure and function. This research has contributed to developing a general theory of personality based on cybernetics, the study of principles that govern goal-directed systems that self-regulate via feedback (DeYoung, 2015a). This theory argues that personality traits reflect variation in the universal brain mechanisms that allow people to pursue their goals. For example, extraversion is related to brain systems that control responses to potential rewards, which may explain why people higher in extraversion tend to pursue goals more vigorously and see more exciting opportunities in various social interactions. Research on openness/intellect indicates that it is related to many complex cognitive functions, including the capacity for imagination that is controlled by a complex brain system known as the "default network" because, when we don't need to engage in an external task, by default our mind often wanders into imagining the possible future, remembering the past, or simply fantasizing (Beaty et al., 2016). Intellect is more related to intelligence, creative achievement in the sciences, and brain function associated with working memory (DeYoung et al., 2009; Kaufman et al., 2016), whereas openness is more related to creative achievement in the arts and risk for psychosis, along with patterns of brain structure that are linked to both creativity and psychosis (Grazioplene et al., 2016).

The content of intellect questionnaires can be divided into two major categories, which might be described as *intellectual engagement* and *intellectual confidence* or *perceived intelligence*. Regarding the latter characteristic, a large research literature has examined the accuracy of self-perceptions of intelligence. A meta-analysis of 41 studies found that when people estimated their own intelligence, scores were correlated with tested intelligence with a correlation of .33 (Freund & Kasten, 2012). In other words, people who describe themselves as more intelligent are on average more intelligent than people who describe themselves as less intelligent. This makes sense, but does it mean that we could stop using IQ tests and simply ask people about how smart they are? No. Although a correlation around .3 is fairly large when compared to other psychological effects, it is nowhere near strong enough to consider self-reported intelligence as a useful replacement for IQ tests (Paulhus, Lysy, & Yik, 1998). Although there is some validity to self-perceptions of intelligence, as evidenced by the fact that they predict IQ, people often have biases to claim to be more intelligent than they are (and people who lack self-confidence may be biased to claim less intelligence than they actually have), so we are better-off using performance-based tests to measure intelligence. Further, men tend to over-estimate their own intelligence, whereas women tend to underestimate it (von Stumm, Chamorro-Premuzic, & Furnham, 2009).

Interestingly, intelligence is not more strongly associated with the kind of intellectual confidence demonstrated in self-ratings of intelligence than it is with intellectual engagement, the tendency to be motivated by intellectual pursuits. The engagement side of intellect has been studied using various scales, with names like *Need for Cognition, Openness to Ideas*, and *Typical Intellectual Engagement* (DeYoung, 2015b; Mussel, 2013). These scales are also correlated with IQ at around .30–.35 (von Stumm & Ackerman, 2013). In other words, knowing that someone likes to think, to engage with philosophical questions, and to work on cognitive problems tells one as much about that person's likely intelligence as knowing that that person believes him- or herself to be highly intelligent.

To conclude this section, research on intellect indicates that the thing you can most confidently guess about people who are highly intelligent is that they will have intellectual interests and be confident in their own intellectual abilities (although even here the strength of the association leaves plenty of room to guess wrong sometimes). This is hardly surprising, so it is perhaps more interesting to think about other characteristics that also tend to go along with intelligence, but a bit more weakly, such as those related to openness.

Openness to Experience

People who are high in openness tend to enjoy and be successful in artistic creative pursuits in domains like music, painting, sculpture, writing, and acting; even those who don't create artistic products tend to appreciate art and other aesthetic qualities, such as the beauty of nature (DeYoung, 2015b; Kaufman et al., 2016). As noted above, they also tend to be more intelligent, although the trend is not as strong as for intellect. Further, unlike intellect, the association of openness with intelligence is almost entirely due to verbal ability (DeYoung et al., 2014; Stanek, 2014). People high in openness tend to be better at describing the meaning of things and reasoning about the relations among concepts, even if they are not necessarily better at nonverbal tasks involving numerical or spatial reasoning. The fact that openness is related much more strongly to verbal than nonverbal ability, whereas intellect as a personality trait is related to both verbal and nonverbal ability about equally, helps to explain why the broader openness/intellect factor from the Big Five is related more strongly to verbal than nonverbal ability. Both halves of the trait are linked to verbal ability, but only one half is also linked to nonverbal ability.

There is one trait related to openness that is negatively related to intelligence, and that is the tendency to experience **apophenia**, which means detecting patterns or connections where none in fact exist (DeYoung, Grazioplene, & Peterson, 2012). The word "apophenia" was coined by a German neurologist in the 1950s to describe the central characteristics of psychosis: hallucinations and delusions (Brugger, 2001). These are extreme forms of apophenia, but there are very common, everyday forms of apophenia as well, which just about everyone has experienced at one time or another. These include things like mistakenly thinking that one has heard one's name being called, seeing faces in inanimate objects, and holding superstitious beliefs, such as astrology. People who are high in openness are more likely to experience apophenia because they are more likely to notice patterns in general, and sometimes they detect a pattern where there isn't one. However, having high intelligence helps to avoid this potentially problematic consequence of openness. Intelligent people are better at figuring out which of the patterns they detect are real or not.

In summary, people high in openness tend to be higher in intelligence, especially where verbal ability is concerned. However, people who are high in the particular kind of openness associated with apophenia, who have a tendency to be super-stitious, engage in magical thinking, and have weird perceptual experiences, are less likely to be highly intelligent. Thus, if you know someone is highly intelligent, you can guess that they are more likely to be interested in art, aesthetics, and imagin-ation, but you can also guess that their openness will not get carried away to the point where they believe in a lot of unlikely ideas.

Creativity

The tendency to be creative is so strongly linked to openness/intellect that some researchers have suggested renaming the whole Big Five trait "creativity" (Johnson, 1994). Remember that being innovative is one of the core features of openness/intellect, and innovation is crucial for creativity. Psychologists typically define

creativity as having two parts: *novelty* and *usefulness* or *appropriateness* (Kaufman & Sternberg, 2010). Being innovative and creating something novel is an obvious requirement of creativity, but why do psychologists also specify that creative products need to be useful or appropriate? The reasoning behind this criterion is that, if a new creation does not serve some purpose effectively, it is not really creative and cannot be distinguished from a pointless or eccentric idea (like the proverbial "square wheel"). With creative products in the arts, it can sometimes be hard to see how they are "useful," which is why some researchers prefer the term "appropriate." A work of art may not have pragmatic utility, but it can still be successful in conveying some message or feeling, such that it is perceived as valuable or meaningful by an audience. In that way, it is appropriate for its role as a work of art.

Creativity can be considered as a feature of products, processes, and people (Simonton, 2003). Novel and appropriate products are creative, the psychological processes that allow people to produce creative products are creative, and people who frequently engage in creative processes and produce creative products have a creative personality. Intelligence has been linked to having a creative personality, when creativity is measured in terms of the products that people have produced or in terms of their thought processes.

Research on creative achievement in a variety of domains suggests that there are two major areas of creative achievement, which have been described as *artistic* and *scientific* (Carson, Peterson, & Higgins, 2005). People with achievements in one artistic field, like music, are more likely to have achievements in another artistic field, like creative writing, than they are to have achievements in a scientific field (and vice versa). Creative achievement is typically measured simply by asking people about their tangible accomplishments, like publishing articles or books, selling art or inventions, producing or performing in theater or film, or in other ways being publicly recognized for the quality of one's creative products. Intelligence predicts creative achievement in the scientific domain ($r = .24$), including things like publishing scientific research or patenting an invention, but does not predict achievement in art (Kaufman et al., 2016). A similar pattern is evident if we simply ask people about how creative they are in different domains, rather than asking them about concrete achievements. Intelligence is correlated ($r = .25$) with self-rated creativity in scholarly and scientific domains, but not in artistic domains (McKay, Karwowski, & Kaufman, 2017). Interestingly, this same study found that intelligence was also significantly associated with self-ratings of creativity in everyday activities (such as finding something fun to do that does not cost money or settling an argument between friends), an area in which broad public recognition for one's achievement is rarely available.

Creative cognitive processes are often measured in the laboratory using so-called divergent thinking tests, which require people to generate many solutions to a single problem, such as "What are all the uses you can think of for a brick?" (Torrance, 1972). These tests can be scored for fluency (how many ideas people generate), flexibility (how often people's answers switch categories of idea – such as from a building material to a weapon to a weight, for the brick problem), and originality (how unusual each idea is among all the people who took the test). They can also simply be rated in terms of how creative the responses are, which appears to produce the best assessment of people's creative potential (Silvia et al., 2008). No matter how these tests are scored, those scores tend to be at least moderately correlated with intelligence (Kaufman et al., 2016; Silvia, 2008). Another method for assessing creativity in the laboratory is through figural drawing tasks, which present a set of lines on paper and ask participants to complete a picture incorporating the lines. The resulting pictures are then rated for originality and elaboration to yield a creativity score. Figural creativity also appears to be positively associated with intelligence, though not as strongly as is divergent thinking (Kandler et al., 2016). In sum, we can conclude that the ability to generate creative ideas on demand, in situations that encourage thinking outside the box, is facilitated by intelligence.

One of the most influential theories about the relation between intelligence and creativity is the so-called "threshold theory," which posits that there is some level of intelligence (usually posited to be around an IQ of 120) below which intelligence is correlated with creativity, but above which it is not. In other words, intelligence is supposed to facilitate creativity up to a certain point, but above that critical level of intelligence, being more intelligent should not predict that someone will be more creative. Despite the popularity of this theory, evidence for it is not particularly promising.

Research examining people who are very high in intelligence has shown that differences in intelligence within that group still matter for creative achievement. This research has been conducted mostly in two large samples, the Study of Mathematically Precocious Youth (SMPY), which identified about 2,000 children in the 1970s and 80s who obtained high scores on the Scholastic Aptitude Test (SAT) before the age of 13, and Project Talent, a random sample of 400,000 American high school students initially assessed in 1960. Both of these groups have been followed as they grew up, and even within the top 1 percent in ability (well above an IQ of 120), intelligence continues to predict who has more creative achievements, such as patents and publications (Wai, Lubinski & Benbow, 2005; Wai, 2014; Park, Lubinski, Benbow, 2007). There seems to be no upper limit on the facilitation of creative achievement by intelligence.

One fascinating study of the SMPY sample focused on those with extremely high scores on either the math or verbal SAT or both, identifying 320 people who scored in the top .001 percent in ability – one in 10,000 – estimated to correspond to IQ > 160 (Lubinski, Webb, Morelock, & Benbow, 2001). This study found that even in this extremely intelligent group, variations in achievement depended strongly on relative ability in the mathematical versus verbal domains, with high math scorers obtaining more creative achievements in science and technology and high verbal scorers obtaining more creative achievements in humanities and the arts. This is more bad news for the threshold theory, as differences in intelligence continue to matter even within this exceptionally intelligent group.

In the domain of creative cognitive processes, even well-executed studies of the threshold hypothesis show conflicting results, with some showing that there is no change in the association of intelligence and divergent thinking performance across the range of IQ and others showing that there are indeed thresholds, though not necessarily always at an IQ of 120 (Jauk, Benedek, Dunsst, & Neubauer, 2013; Preckel, Holling, & Weise, 2006; Sligh, Conners, & Roskos-Ewoldsen, 2005). Clearly, more research is needed to determine whether there is any robust and reliable threshold effect in the relation of IQ to creative cognition in the lab.

A more promising approach to the relation of intelligence and creativity may be the theory that intelligence is necessary but not sufficient for creativity. This theory states that, to be creative, one needs a certain level of intelligence, but also that having the necessary level of intelligence still does not guarantee that one will be creative. A statistical technique called *necessary condition analysis* has been designed to test this kind of hypothesis, and it appears to confirm that intelligence is necessary but not sufficient for creativity as measured by both achievement and cognitive process measures (Karwowski et al., 2016, 2017). Thus, it is not that there is a threshold above which intelligence does not matter for creativity but rather that, for any given level of creativity, there is some level of intelligence that is necessary to enable it. This means that if we know someone is highly intelligent, we know that they have the potential to be creative, but we can't know for sure whether they have lived up to that potential.

Wisdom

Human experience suggests that to be intelligent is not necessarily to be wise, and smart people sometimes seem not to possess as much wisdom as one would like them to. What do psychologists mean by "wisdom" and how does it differ from the ability to reason and learn effectively that constitutes intelligence? Although there are disagreements about what exactly constitutes wisdom, a viable general definition is that **wisdom** is effective judgment regarding how to solve difficult and uncertain life problems (Staudinger & Glück, 2011). These "life problems" are not merely cognitive challenges about how to understand the logical structure of a situation (which requires intelligence). Rather, they are also existential or ethical problems regarding how to act in a way that balances various competing concerns effectively when taking actions that have important consequences (Sternberg, 1998, 2003).

The scientific study of wisdom is considerably less well developed than research on intelligence or any of the other traits discussed in this chapter. A number of instruments to assess wisdom have been developed recently (Glück et al., 2013). Most are self-report questionnaires, but of particular interest are those that are performance measures, actually designed to test people's ability to be wise (Staudinger, 2000; Mickler & Staudinger, 2008; Sternberg, 1998). Within these, one can differentiate between tests of general wisdom and tests of personal wisdom, where *general wisdom* refers to questions about what is wise for all people, and *personal wisdom* refers to questions about coping with difficult and uncertain matters in one's own life specifically (Mickler & Staudinger, 2008).

Openness to experience is often considered an important component of wisdom (e.g., Webster, 2007), and performance measures of wisdom have been found to correlate with openness/intellect, but not with the other Big Five traits (Mickler & Staudinger, 2008; Staudinger, Lopez, & Baltes, 1997). Thus, it is perhaps unsurprising that wisdom also tends to be correlated with intelligence, in the range of about r = .2 to .3 (Mickler & Staudinger, 2008; Staudinger et al., 1997). Although necessary condition analysis has not been applied to the relation between intelligence and wisdom, it seems possible that a similar effect might be seen as in research on creativity, such that intelligence is necessary but not sufficient for wisdom (Staudinger & Glück, 2011). Highly intelligent people are more likely to be wise, but intelligence is certainly no guarantee of wisdom.

Neuroticism

Neuroticism refers to the tendency to experience negative emotions of all kinds. People high in neuroticism are more likely to experience anxiety, depression, irritability, anger, jealousy, etc., than people low in neuroticism. Unfortunately, the tendencies to experience all of these negative emotions cluster together, such that people who are more vulnerable to one of them are likely to be more vulnerable to the others as well. Neuroticism appears to stem from the sensitivity of brain systems that respond defensively to threats and punishments (Allen & DeYoung, 2016; Shackman et al., 2016). Of course, such responses are necessary for people to avoid and defend against aversive outcomes, but being more highly sensitive in this regard than other people nonetheless leads to emotional suffering.

Relationship of Neuroticism to Intelligence

It is well established that intelligence is weakly negatively correlated with neuroticism (Ackerman & Heggestad, 1997; DeYoung, 2011; Stanek, 2014). However, the meaning of this correlation is debated. The most obvious answer would simply be that people who are less intelligent are more likely to experience negative emotions, but this answer overlooks the issue of test anxiety. Test anxiety refers to the tendency to become anxious when faced with a testing situation, such as what is encountered during an IQ test. Neuroticism is associated with test anxiety, which is not surprising since neuroticism reflects the general tendency toward negative emotion across situations (Ackerman & Heggestad, 1997). What this means, however, is that many people who are high in neuroticism might score lower on IQ tests than they should, because their test anxiety interferes with their cognitive performance. The mechanism for this interference is that anxiety disrupts the brain systems responsible for working memory (Fales et al., 2008). It is well established that test anxiety is associated with reduced test performance, and the association between test anxiety and IQ is twice as strong as the association between neuroticism and IQ (Ackerman & Heggestad, 1997). This suggests that the association between IQ and neuroticism may be due to test anxiety (Moutafi, Furnham, & Tsaousis, 2006). IQ scores are predicated on the idea that IQ tests reveal how well one can solve cognitive problems under optimal conditions (trying hard and doing one's best). If one is prevented from doing one's best by anxiety about the testing situation, then the resulting score may not accurately reflect one's intelligence in other situations.

Rather than being directly linked to lower intelligence, it may be that intelligence influences the outcomes associated with neuroticism. One study found that intelligence was positively associated with leadership performance for individuals high in neuroticism, whereas for those low in neuroticism, intelligence was unrelated to performance (Perkins & Corr, 2006). Another study found a similar effect among military conscripts (Leikas, Mäkinen, Lönnqvist, & Verkasalo, 2009). Conscripts high in neuroticism showed poor performance, physical health, and adjustment to military life only if they were also low in intelligence. Intelligence, therefore, may act as a buffer for neurotic individuals, allowing them to cope with stressors more effectively, despite their heightened sensitivity to negative emotions.

Psychopathology

Neuroticism is the personality factor that most conveys risk for mental illness or psychopathology. Neuroticism is almost indistinguishable statistically from risk for diagnosis of mood disorders like general anxiety disorder and major depression – in other words, people with higher neuroticism have a greater risk for these disorders than people with lower neuroticism (Griffiths et al., 2010). However, neuroticism is also associated, just slightly less strongly, with increased risk for drug and alcohol disorders, personality disorders, psychotic spectrum disorders like schizophrenia, and indeed, every mental disorder (Castellanos-Ryan et al., 2016; Kotov et al., 2010; Tackett et al., 2013; Wright, Hopwood, Skodol, & Morey, 2016). Unfortunately, low intelligence is also a risk factor for almost all disorders (Castellanos-Ryan et al., 2016; Gale, Batty, Tynelius, Deary, & Rasmussen, 2010; Zammit et al., 2004). This finding may reflect the fact that coping with the challenges of life is facilitated by intelligence, and better coping helps to prevent psychopathology. It may also reflect the fact that intelligence is associated with greater overall health, both mental and physical (Deary, 2012). To be intelligent is to have a brain that functions well in carrying out some of its most energetically costly operations, and this may be more difficult if there are physical flaws in the organism that lead it to function at less than optimal levels (Bates, 2007; Penke, Denissen, & Miller, 2007).

Interestingly, the only mental illness that is not associated with lower intelligence is bipolar disorder (formerly known as manic depression), in which episodes of depression alternate with episodes of mania, which involve dramatically elevated positive mood, racing thoughts, risky behavior, and pursuit of unrealistic ambitions (Zammit et al., 2004). This is particularly surprising given that, not only is bipolar disorder a form of depression, but it is also strongly genetically related to schizophrenia and often involves psychosis (Schulze et al., 2014; Song et al., 2015). Schizophrenia especially is strongly negatively related to intelligence, so why would bipolar be positively related? It may be that the underlying genetic risk for psychosis is more likely to manifest as schizophrenia among people with low intelligence and as bipolar among those with normal or high intelligence. Indeed some evidence suggests, remarkably, that intelligence might even be positively associated with risk for bipolar disorder, at least for men who do not also suffer from other mental disorders (Gale et al., 2013; MacCabe et al., 2010; Smith et al., 2015).

In short, when people are high in intelligence, they may or may not be less likely to experience negative emotions in daily life, but they are definitely at less risk for a breakdown into mental illness, with the probable exception of bipolar disorder.

Agreeableness

Agreeableness encompasses a domain of personality traits related to the tendency to be altruistic and cooperative, rather than selfish and antagonistic (DeYoung, 2015a). Human beings are intensely social creatures, so it makes sense that one of the major dimensions of personality reflects individual differences in the ways that people do (or do not) compromise and coordinate their own concerns and goals with those of others. General questionnaire measures of agreeableness typically show virtually no association with intelligence (Ackerman & Heggestad, 1997; DeYoung, 2011; Stanek, 2014). Knowing how intelligent people are tells you very little about whether they will be accommodating and helpful or pushy and uncooperative. However, there are a number of narrower traits within the domain of agreeableness that do show associations with intelligence, including compassion, emotional intelligence, and low aggression.

Compassion and Politeness
In much the same way that openness/intellect has two major subfactors, agreeableness also has two major subfactors, labeled *compassion* and *politeness*

(DeYoung et al., 2007). Compassion describes the tendency to experience and express empathy, sympathy, and concern for others – in other words, to connect with other people emotionally. (In some psychological research, the term "compassion" is used to mean something more specific, the desire to help others, explicitly differentiating this from "empathy," defined as sharing others' emotions. In personality research, however, the trait of compassion includes both of these things.) Politeness, in contrast, reflects the tendency to avoid being rude or belligerent and to refrain from manipulating or taking advantage of other people. Politeness seems to be less about connecting with people emotionally and more about following social rules and inhibiting aggressive or socially disruptive impulses.

Research that separates compassion and politeness shows that, although politeness is unrelated to intelligence, compassion is positively related to intelligence, and more strongly to verbal than nonverbal ability, just like openness (DeYoung et al., 2014; Stanek, 2014). In other words, people who are more compassionate and empathetic tend to be more intelligent, on average, than those who are callous and cold-hearted. The parallels with openness may be suggestive in trying to understand why this association exists. Openness involves the capacity for imagination, in the sense of simulating experience, such as an imagined future or a fictional world. Empathy also involves the capacity for imagination, however, because to really feel and understand what other people are experiencing, we need to be able to imagine the world from their perspective. There is a large and extensive brain system that is particularly important for imagination and understanding other people's mental experiences, and individual variation in this system has been linked both to openness and to the form of empathy known as "mentalizing ability" – the ability to make inferences about other people's mental states (Andrews-Hanna, Smallwood, & Spreng, 2014; Beaty et al., 2016). Perhaps being more intelligent helps people to take different perspectives through this kind of imagination and to draw accurate inferences about what other people are experiencing, leading to greater compassion.

Emotional Intelligence

The ability to understand other people's emotions and mental states has been described as part of "emotional intelligence," which has been defined as "the ability to engage in sophisticated information processing about one's own and others' emotions and the ability to use this information as a guide to thinking and behavior" (Mayer, Salovey, & Caruso, 2008, p. 503). To avoid confusion, we refer here to emotional intelligence as "emotional ability" and will consider only research employing ability tests rather than questionnaires to measure emotional intelligence. In these performance-based tests, emotional ability is assessed by asking people to perform a set of tasks, such as identifying emotions in facial expressions and judging how best to manage others' emotions in social situations. Consistent with the importance of the g factor for all challenging cognitive tasks, emotional ability scores are consistently associated with intelligence, with a correlation of about .3 (Mayer et al., 2004; Roberts et al., 2008). Like openness and compassion, they appear to be more strongly associated with verbal ability than with nonverbal ability. Unlike IQ scores, however, emotional ability scores are more strongly associated with agreeableness than with openness or intellect (Mayer et al., 2008; Roberts et al., 2008). At any rate, these findings indicate that people who are highly intelligent are not only more compassionate on average but also tend to be better at understanding and managing their own and others' emotions, allowing them to deploy their compassion more effectively.

Aggression

Aggression falls at the low end of the Agreeableness dimension and might be seen as one of the most severe forms of disagreeableness. Research on the relation of aggression to intelligence is somewhat confusing, with some studies indicating an association and others not (Ackerman & Heggestad, 1997; Stanek, 2014). It is possible that the resolution of this inconsistency will depend on differentiating different measures, types, or severities of aggression. Some questionnaire measures of aggression treat being rude or pushy as instances of aggression, and this way of describing aggression is very similar to politeness, which we have seen is not correlated with intelligence. If we limit our consideration to physical aggression, however, then there seems to be more consistent evidence that aggression is associated with lower intelligence (DeYoung et al., 2008; Huesmann, Eron, & Yarmel, 1987; Seguin, Boulerice, Harden, Tremblay, & Pihl, 1999).

Further, aggression is one of the so-called "externalizing" behaviors, which also includes impulsivity, antisocial behavior such as theft or vandalism, and drug abuse. The whole category of externalizing behavior has been found to be negatively correlated with intelligence, and there is some evidence that the correlation is due to genetic factors (DeYoung et al., 2008; Koenen, Caspi, Moffitt, Rijsdijk, & Taylor, 2006). In sum, people who are highly intelligent may or may not be any ruder than those low in intelligence, but at least they are probably less likely to behave violently or to engage in behavior that is harmful to others. Based on research on compassion and emotional ability, one can also assume that they are more likely to feel emotionally connected to others and to act accordingly.

Conscientiousness

Conscientiousness describes the tendency to be organized, self-disciplined, responsible, and productive, as opposed to lazy, sloppy, impulsive, and distractible. Among the Big Five, it is the best predictor of success in school and success in the workplace, not to mention health and longevity (Roberts, Lejuez, Krueger, Richards, & Hill, 2014).

In fact, the only psychological trait that seems to be as good or better at predicting these outcomes is IQ. You might expect IQ and conscientiousness to be related, then, since both seem to be important for optimal functioning and getting things done. However, they show very little relation to each other, and, if anything, it may be that conscientiousness is weakly negatively related to intelligence, although the evidence is somewhat inconsistent (Ackerman & Heggestad, 1997; DeYoung, 2011; Stanek, 2014).

Theory of Compensation

The possible association of conscientiousness with lower intelligence has been addressed by a theory of compensation (Chamorro-Premuzic & Furnham, 2005). This theory suggests that people with lower intelligence may develop higher conscientiousness in order to compensate for their lower intelligence. Being well-organized, orderly, and hard-working might make it easier to overcome the challenges posed by being less good at complex information processing. Based on a large meta-analysis, however, the most likely possibility is that traits related to being industrious and persistent are weakly positively related to intelligence, whereas traits related to organization and orderliness are weakly negatively related to intelligence (Stanek, 2014). A positive association of at least some components of conscientiousness with intelligence would be consistent with several studies that have reported that being impulsive is associated with lower intelligence (Kuntsi, et al., 2004; Lynam et al., 1993; Vigil-Colet & Morales-Vives, 2005). Perhaps, therefore, of the traits associated with conscientiousness, it is only orderliness that is sometimes a compensatory mechanism to help people avoid complexity they are not cognitively equipped to handle.

Future Discounting

As the major trait linked to planning and self-discipline, conscientiousness has a clear conceptual link to the tendency to forgo immediate rewards in favor of longer-term goals. This suggests that it might be related to the tendency not to discount the future. It is normal for human beings to discount rewards that are delayed (Frederick, Loewenstein, & O'Donoghue, 2002), meaning that they value them less than they would if they were available sooner. However, the strength of this tendency toward future discounting shows considerable variability and has the characteristics of a stable personality trait (Kirby, 2009). The major problem with having a high trait level of future discounting is that it can lead to inconsistent preferences and impulsive decisions. For example, students might value getting a good grade on a test more than going to a party, but, if they discount the future too much, they are likely to decide to go to the party anyway, instead of studying, when the party is happening now but the test is still a day or two in the future. Then the next day, they will regret their choice, reaffirming their original preference that they should have studied rather than partying. Someone who discounted the future less would be more likely to choose studying (and hence performance on the test in the future) over the party, even when the party is happening in the present.

Future discounting is typically measured through a series of choices between smaller, more immediate rewards and larger, delayed rewards. A large body of research demonstrates that the tendency to discount the future is negatively associated with intelligence, with a meta-analysis of 24 studies indicating a correlation of −.23 (Shamosh & Gray, 2008). This means that more intelligent people are more likely to be consistent in their choices in ways that avoid undermining their desires for the future. Interestingly, future discounting is more strongly associated with intelligence than it is with conscientiousness, with which its correlation is very weak, only about −.1 (Mahalingam, Stillwell, Kosinski, Rust, & Kogan, 2014). This suggests that making good choices in the lab does not necessarily translate into being responsible in daily life, and a lot of uncertainty remains regarding links between intelligence and conscientiousness.

Extraversion

The last of the Big Five, and the one that seems to have the least to do with intelligence, is extraversion. **Extraversion** reflects the tendency to be outgoing, talkative, sociable, active, and assertive, and to experience positive emotions like excitement, enthusiasm, and joy. In modern scientific parlance, the term "introversion" is simply used to label the opposite pole of the extraversion dimension and refers to the tendency to be quiet, reserved, unassertive, etc. Many people are familiar with the Jungian idea that introverts are imaginative, creative, inward-looking, and engaged with ideas, but personality research has shown that, in fact, these traits are not the opposite of extraversion, nor even negatively associated with it for the most part. Much of what Jung (1921/1971) described as part of introversion is, in fact, much more like openness/intellect, which is an entirely different factor of personality, and the modern meaning of "introversion" simply corresponds to low extraversion. At any rate, meta-analyses have found that associations of intelligence with extraversion are consistently near zero (Stanek, 2014; Wolf & Ackerman, 2005). Knowing that someone is an extravert or an introvert tells you nothing about their likely intelligence.

CONCLUSION

We have now examined the association of intelligence with personality traits associated with all of the Big Five, which map out the major dimensions of personality. Table 15.2 provides a list of all the traits discussed and how they are related to intelligence.

Table 15.2 Associations of traits with intelligence

	Strength of association	Direction of association
Openness/Intellect	Moderate to strong	Positive
Intellect	Strong	Positive
Openness to experience	Moderate	Positive
Creativity	Moderate	Positive
Creative achievement in arts	Near zero	
Creative achievement in sciences	Moderate	Positive
Apophenia	Weak	Negative
Wisdom	Moderate	Positive
Neuroticism	Weak	Negative
Test anxiety	Moderate to strong	Negative
Psychopathology (mental disorder)	Weak	Negative
Bipolar Disorder	Weak	Positive
Agreeableness	Near zero	
Compassion	Moderate	Positive
Politeness	Near zero	
Emotional intelligence	Moderate to strong	Positive
Physical aggression	Weak to moderate	Negative
Conscientiousness	Near zero	
Orderliness	Weak	Negative
Industriousness	Weak	Positive
Impulsivity	Weak	Negative
Future discounting	Moderate	Negative
Extraversion	Near Zero	

Note. The Big Five are in bold. Strength of association is based on current best estimates of correlations (r). Near zero = $|r| < .1$; weak = $|r|$ between .1–.2; moderate = $|r|$ between .2–.3; strong = $|r| > .3$

Intelligence was most strongly related to intellect, which reflects intellectual interests and intellectual confidence. However, it is also at least moderately related to a number of other traits. If people are highly intelligent, it is somewhat likely that they are also creative, wise, open to experience, compassionate, nonviolent, skilled at understanding and managing emotions, and likely to be willing to forgo smaller immediate rewards in favor of larger delayed rewards. Of course, there are many intelligent people who do not possess every one of these other characteristics, and that is because moderate correlations merely describe the trend on average; they are not deterministic. Hence, our guesses about what other traits go along with intelligence will sometimes be wrong when we apply them to individuals, but at least we can make educated guesses.

CHAPTER SUMMARY

A considerable amount of psychological research has examined which psychological traits are associated with intelligence. In this chapter, we reviewed research findings for traits with reasonably good evidence as to whether or not they are associated with intelligence and how strong those associations are. The review is organized around the five-factor model of the so-called "Big Five" personality traits, which are the major broad dimensions of personality. The Big Five can be used as a taxonomy to organize other, narrower personality traits.

The personality traits that show the strongest associations with intelligence are in the openness/intellect family of traits. This includes traits like intellectual engagement, openness to experience, and creativity. These traits all involve the tendency to engage in cognitive exploration, using reasoning and perception to understand patterns in the information that we encounter. The other one of the Big Five that is consistently related to intelligence (but in the negative direction) is neuroticism, which reflects the tendency to experience negative emotions; however, this is only a weak association and it seems to be largely due to test anxiety, as people who are nervous about taking tests underperform on IQ tests. Neuroticism is the major risk for psychopathology (mental disorders), and intelligence is at least weakly negatively associated with diagnoses of most mental disorders, except for bipolar disorder.

Traits in the agreeableness and conscientiousness families are associated with intelligence in more complicated ways. Despite showing no association with intelligence themselves, some of the narrower traits within each domain are associated with intelligence, especially for agreeableness, where compassion and emotional intelligence show at least moderate associations with intelligence. Extraversion is unrelated to intelligence.

KEY TERMS

agreeableness • apophenia • conscientiousness • creativity • extraversion • five-factor model (the Big Five) • neuroticism • openness/intellect • personality traits • wisdom

COMPREHENSION AND REFLECTION QUESTIONS

1. What are the Big Five personality traits and what characteristics are associated with each of them?
2. What traits are most strongly associated with intelligence?

3. What does it mean to say that intelligence is necessary but not sufficient for creativity?
4. If you know that someone is highly intelligent, what else can you infer about their personality?
5. Why do you think compassion might be associated with higher levels of intelligence?
6. Why might it be useful to know what other psychological traits are associated with intelligence?
7. What traits other than intelligence might contribute to success, happiness, and fulfillment in life?

References

Ackerman, P. L. & Heggestad, E. D. (1997). Intelligence, personality, and interests: Evidence for overlapping traits. *Psychological Bulletin, 121*, 219-245.

Allen, T. A., & DeYoung, C. G. (2016). Personality neuroscience and the Five Factor Model. In T. A. Widiger (ed.). *Oxford handbook of the Five Factor Model* (pp. 319-349). New York: Oxford University Press.

Andrews-Hanna, J. R., Smallwood, J., & Spreng, R. N. (2014). The default network and self-generated thought: Component processes, dynamic control, and clinical relevance. *Annals of the New York Academy of Sciences, 1316*(1), 29-52.

Ashton, M. C., Lee. K., Perugini, M., Szarota, P., de Vries, R. E., Blas, L. D., Boies, K., & De Raad, B. (2004). A six-factor structure of personality descriptive adjectives: Solutions from psycholexical studies in seven languages. *Journal of Personality and Social Psychology, 86*, 356-366.

Baltes, P. B., & Staudinger, U. M. (2000). Wisdom: A metaheuristic (pragmatic) to orchestrate mind and virtue toward excellence. *American Psychologist, 55*(1), 122-136.

Bates, T. C. (2007). Fluctuating asymmetry and intelligence. *Intelligence, 35*(1), 41-46.

Beaty, R. E., Kaufman, S. B., Benedek, M., Jung, R. E., Kenett, Y. N., Jauk, E., ... & Silvia, P. J. (2016). Personality and complex brain networks: The role of openness to experience in default network efficiency. *Human Brain Mapping, 37*(2), 773-779.

Brugger, P. (2001). From haunted brain to haunted science: A cognitive neuroscience view of paranormal and pseudoscientific thought. In J. Houran & R. Lange (eds.), *Hauntings and poltergeists: Multidisciplinary perspectives*. Jefferson, NC: McFarland & Company.

Carson, S. H., Peterson, J. B., & Higgins, D. M. (2005). Reliability, validity, and factor structure of the Creative Achievement Questionnaire. *Creativity Research Journal, 17*(1), 37-50.

Castellanos-Ryan, N., Brière, F. N., O'Leary-Barrett, M., Banaschewski, T., Bokde, A., Bromberg, U., ... & Garavan, H. (2016). The structure of psychopathology in adolescence and its common personality and cognitive correlates. *Journal of abnormal psychology*, *125*(8), 1039–1052.

Cattell, R. B. (1945). The description of personality: Principles and findings in a factor analysis. *American Journal of Psychology*, *58*, 69–90.

Chamorro-Premuzic, T., & Furnham, A. (2005). *Personality and intellectual competence*. Mahwah, NJ: Lawrence Erlbaum Associates.

Conway, A. R., Kane, M. J., & Engle, R. W. (2003). Working memory capacity and its relation to general intelligence. *Trends in Cognitive Sciences*, *7*(12), 547–552.

Costa, P. T., & McCrae, R. R. (1992). Four ways five factors are basic. *Personality and Individual Differences*, *13*(6), 653–665.

Deary, I. J. (2012). Intelligence. *Annual Review of Psychology*, *63*, 453–482.

DeYoung, C. G. (2010). Personality neuroscience and the biology of traits. *Social and Personality Psychology Compass*, *4*, 1165–1180.

DeYoung, C. G. (2011). Intelligence and personality. In R. J. Sternberg & S. B. Kaufman (eds.), *The Cambridge Handbook of Intelligence* (pp. 711–737). New York: Cambridge University Press.

DeYoung, C. G. (2015a). Cybernetic Big Five Theory. *Journal of Research in Personality*, *56*, 33–58.

DeYoung, C. G. (2015b). Openness/Intellect: A dimension of personality reflecting cognitive exploration. In M. L. Cooper & R. J. Larsen (eds.), *The APA handbook of personality and social psychology: Personality processes and individual differences* (vol. 4, pp. 369–399). Washington, DC: American Psychological Association.

DeYoung, C. G., Grazioplene, R. G., & Peterson, J. B. (2012). From madness to genius: The Openness/Intellect trait domain as a paradoxical simplex. *Journal of Research in Personality*, *46*, 63–78.

DeYoung, C. G., Peterson, J. B., Séguin, J. R., Pihl, R. O., & Tremblay, R. E. (2008). Externalizing behavior and the higher-order factors of the Big Five. *Journal of Abnormal Psychology*, *117*, 947–953.

DeYoung, C. G., Quilty, L. C., & Peterson, J. B. (2007). Between facets and domains: 10 aspects of the Big Five. *Journal of Personality and Social Psychology*, *93*, 880–896.

DeYoung, C. G., Quilty, L. C., Peterson, J. B., & Gray, J. R. (2014). Openness to Experience, Intellect, and cognitive ability. *Journal of Personality Assessment*, *96*, 46–52.

DeYoung, C. G., Shamosh, N. A., Green, A. E., Braver, T. S., & Gray, J. R. (2009). Intellect as distinct from Openness: Differences revealed by fMRI of working memory. *Journal of Personality and Social Psychology*, *97*, 883–892.

Fales, C. L., Barch, D. M., Burgess, G. C., Schaefer, A., Mennin, D. S., Braver, T. S., & Gray, J. R. (2008). Anxiety and cognitive efficiency: Differential modulation of transient and sustained neural activity during a working memory task. *Cognitive, Affective, and Behavioral Neuroscience*, *8*, 239–253.

Frederick, S., Loewenstein, G. & O'Donoghue, T. (2002). Time discounting and time preference: A critical review. *Journal of Economic Literature*, *40*, 351–401.

Freund, P. A., & Kasten, N. (2012). How smart do you think you are? A meta-analysis on the validity of self-estimates of cognitive ability. *Psychological Bulletin, 138*(2), 296–321.

Gale, C. R., Batty, G. D., McIntosh, A. M., Porteous, D. J., Deary, I. J., & Rasmussen, F. (2013). Is bipolar disorder more common in highly intelligent people? A cohort study of a million men. *Molecular Psychiatry, 18*(2), 190–194.

Gale, C. R., Batty, G. D., Tynelius, P., Deary, I. J., & Rasmussen, F. (2010). Intelligence in early adulthood and subsequent hospitalization for mental disorders. *Epidemiology, 21*, 70–77.

Glück, J., König, S., Naschenweng, K., Redzanowski, U., Dorner, L., Straßer, I., & Wiedermann, W. (2013). How to measure wisdom: Content, reliability, and validity of five measures. *Frontiers in Psychology, 4*, 1–13.

Goldberg, L. R. (1990). An alternative "description of personality": The big-five factor structure. *Journal of Personality and Social Psychology, 59*(6), 1216–1229.

Gottfredson, L. S. (1997). Mainstream science on intelligence: An editorial with 52 signatories, history, and bibliography. *Intelligence, 24*, 13–23.

Gow, A. J., Whiteman, M. C., Pattie, A., & Deary, I. J. (2005). The personality–intelligence interface: Insights from an ageing cohort. *Personality and Individual Differences, 39*, 751–761.

Grazioplene, R. G., Chavez, R. S., Rustichini, A., & DeYoung, C. G. (2016). Personality, psychosis, and connectivity: White matter correlates of psychosis-linked traits support continuity between personality and psychopathology. *Journal of Abnormal Psychology, 125*, 1135–1145.

Griffith, J. W., Zinbarg, R. E., Craske, M. G., Mineka, S., Rose, R. D., Waters, A. M., & Sutton, J. M. (2010) Neuroticism as a common dimension in the internalizing disorders. *Psychological Medicine, 40*(7), 1125-1136.

Hemphill, J. F. (2003). Interpreting the magnitudes of correlation coefficients. *American Psychologist, 58*, 78-80.

Huesmann, L. R., Eron, L. D., & Yarmel, P. W. (1987). Intellectual functioning and aggression. *Journal of Personality and Social Psychology, 52*, 232-240.

Jauk, E., Benedek, M., Dunst, B., & Neubauer, A. C. (2013). The relationship between intelligence and creativity: New support for the threshold hypothesis by means of empirical breakpoint detection. *Intelligence, 41*(4), 212-221.

John, O. P., Naumann, L. P., & Soto, C. J. (2008). Paradigm shift to the integrative Big Five trait taxonomy: History: measurement, and conceptual issue. In O. P. John, R. W. Robins, & L. A. Pervin (eds). *Handbook of personality: Theory and research* (pp. 114–158). New York: Guilford Press.

Johnson, J. A. (1994). Clarification of factor five with the help of the AB5C model. *European Journal of Personality, 8*, 311-334.

Johnson, W., & Bouchard, T. J., Jr. (2005a). The structure of human intelligence: It's verbal, perceptual, and image rotation (VPR), not fluid crystallized. *Intelligence, 33*, 393-416.

Johnson, W., & Bouchard, T. J., Jr. (2005b). Constructive replication of the visual–perceptual–image rotation model in Thurstone's (1941) battery of 60 tests of mental ability, *Intelligence, 33*, 417-430.

Johnson, W., & Bouchard, T. J., Jr. (2007). Sex differences in mental abilities: *g* masks the dimensions on which they lie. *Intelligence, 35*, 23-39.

Johnson, W., Bouchard, T. J., Jr., McGue, M., Segal, N. L., Tellegen, A., Keyes, M., & Gottesman, I. I. (2007). Genetic and environmental influences on the Verbal-Perceptual-Image Rotation (VPR) model of the structure of mental abilities in the Minnesota study of twins reared apart. *Intelligence, 35*, 542-562.

Jung, C. G. (1921/1971). *Collected works*, vol. 6: *Psychological types*. Princeton, NJ: Princeton University Press.

Kandler, C., Riemann, R., Angleitner, A., Spinath, F. M., Borkenau, P., & Penke, L. (2016). The nature of creativity: The roles of genetic factors, personality traits, cognitive abilities, and environmental sources. *Journal of Personality and Social Psychology, 111*(2), 230–249.

Karwowski, M., Kaufman, J. C., Lebuda, I., Szumski, G., & Firkowska-Mankiewicz, A. (2017). Intelligence in childhood and creative achievements in middle-age: The necessary condition approach. *Intelligence, 64*, 36-44.

Karwowski, M., Dul, J., Gralewski, J., Jauk, E., Jankowska, D. M., Gajda, A., . . . & Benedek, M. (2016). Is creativity without intelligence possible? A necessary condition analysis. *Intelligence, 57*, 105-117.

Kaufman, J. C., & Sternberg, R. J. (eds.). (2010). *The Cambridge handbook of creativity*. New York: Cambridge University Press.

Kaufman, S. B., DeYoung, C. G., Gray, J. R., Jiménez, L., Brown, J., & Mackintosh, N. J. (2010). Implicit learning as an ability. *Cognition, 116*, 321–340.

Kaufman, S. B., Quilty, L. C., Grazioplene, R. G., Hirsh, J. B., Gray, J. R., Peterson, J. B., & DeYoung, C. G. (2016). Openness to Experience and Intellect differentially predict creative achievement in the arts and sciences. *Journal of Personality, 84*, 248–258.

Kirby, K. N. (2009). One-year temporal stability of delay-discount rates. *Psychonomic Bulletin & Review, 16*, 457-462.

Koenen, K. C., Caspi, A., Moffitt, T. E., Rijsdijk, F., & Taylor, A. (2006). Genetic influences on the overlap between low IQ and antisocial behavior in young children. *Journal of Abnormal Psychology, 115*, 787–797.

Kotov, R., Gamez, W., Schmidt, F., & Watson, D. (2010). Linking "big" personality traits to anxiety, depressive, and substance use disorders: A meta-analysis. *Psychological Bulletin, 136*(5), 768–821.

Kuntsi, J., Eley, T.C., Taylor, A., Hughes, C., Asherson, P., Caspi, A., et al. (2004). Co-occurrence of ADHD and low IQ has genetic origins. *American Journal of Medical Genetics, 124*, 41-47.

Leikas, S., Mäkinen, S., Lönnqvist, J. E., & Verkasalo, M. (2009). Cognitive ability × emotional stability interactions on adjustment. *European Journal of Personality, 23*(4), 329-342.

Lubinski, D., Webb, R. M., Morelock, M. J., & Benbow, C. P. (2001). Top 1 in 10,000: A 10-year follow-up of the profoundly gifted. *Journal of Applied Psychology*, *86*(4), 718–729.

Lynam, D. R., Moffitt, T. E., & Stouthamer-Loeber, M. (1993). Explaining the relation between IQ and delinquency: Class, race, test motivation, school failure, or self-control? *Journal of Abnormal Psychology*, *102*, 187-196.

MacCabe, J. H., Lambe, M. P., Cnattingius, S., Sham, P. C., David, A. S., Reichenberg, A., Murray, R. M., & Hultman, C. M. (2010). Excellent school performance at age 16 and risk of adult bipolar disorder: National cohort study. *British Journal of Psychiatry*, *196*, 109–115.

Mahalingam, V., Stillwell, D., Kosinski, M., Rust, J., & Kogan, A. (2014). Who can wait for the future? A personality perspective. *Social Psychological and Personality Science*, *5*(5), 573-583.

Major, J. T., Johnson, W., & Deary, I. J. (2012). Comparing models of intelligence in Project TALENT: The VPR model fits better than the CHC and extended Gf–Gc models. *Intelligence*, *40*(6), 543-559.

Markon, K. E., Krueger, R. F., & Watson, D. (2005). Delineating the structure of normal and abnormal personality: An integrative hierarchical approach. *Journal of Personality and Social Psychology*, *88*, 139-157.

Mayer, J. D., Salovey, P., & Caruso, D. R. (2004). Emotional intelligence: Theory, findings, and implications. *Psychological Inquiry*, *60*, 197-215.

Mayer, J. D., Salovey, P., & Caruso, D. R. (2008). Emotional intelligence: New ability or eclectic traits? *American Psychologist*, *63*, 503-517.

McAdams, D. P., & Pals, J. L. (2006). A new Big Five: Fundamental principles for an integrative science of personality. *American Psychologist*, *61*, 204–217.

McKay, A. S., Karwowski, M., & Kaufman, J. C. (2017). Measuring the muses: validating the Kaufman domains of creativity scale (K-DOCS). *Psychology of Aesthetics, Creativity, and the Arts*, *11*(2), 216.

Mickler, C., & Staudinger, U. M. (2008). Personal wisdom: Validation and age-related differences of a performance measure. *Psychology and Aging*, *23*(4), 787-799.

Moutafi, J., Furnham, A., & Tsaousis, I. (2006). Is the relationship between intelligence and trait neuroticism mediated by test anxiety? *Personality and Individual Differences*, *40*, 587-597.

Mussel, P. (2013). Intellect: a theoretical framework for personality traits related to intellectual achievements. *Journal of Personality and Social Psychology*, *104*(5), 885-906.

Neisser, U., Boodoo, G., Bouchard Jr., T. J., Boykin, A. W., Brody, N., Ceci, S. J., ... & Urbina, S. (1996). Intelligence: Knowns and unknowns. *American Psychologist*, *51*(2), 77.

Park, G., Lubinski, D., & Benbow, C. P. (2007). Contrasting intellectual patterns predict creativity in the arts and sciences. *Psychological Science*, *18*, 948–952.

Paulhus, D. L., Lysy, D. C., & Yik, M. S. M. (1998). Self-report measures of intelligence: Are they useful as proxy IQ tests? *Journal of Personality*, *66*, 525-554.

Penke, L., Denissen, J. J., & Miller, G. F. (2007). The evolutionary genetics of personality. *European Journal of Personality*, *21*, 549-587.

Perkins, A. M., & Corr, P. J. (2006). Cognitive ability as a buffer to neuroticism: Churchill's secret weapon? *Personality and Individual Differences*, *40*, 39-51.

Preckel, F., Holling, H., & Wiese, M. (2006). Relationship of intelligence and creativity in gifted and non-gifted students: An investigation of threshold theory. *Personality and individual differences*, *40*(1), 159-170.

Roberts, B. W., Lejuez, C., Krueger, R. F., Richards, J. M., & Hill, P. L. (2014). What is conscientiousness and how can it be assessed? *Developmental Psychology*, *50*(5), 1315.

Roberts, R. D., Schulze, R., & MacCann, C. (2008). The measurement of emotional intelligence: A decade of progress? In G. Boyle, G. Matthews, & D. H. Saklofske (eds.), *The Sage handbook of personality theory and assessment*, vol. 2. Los Angeles: Sage.

Saucier, G. (1992). Openness versus intellect: Much ado about nothing? *European Journal of Personality*, *6*, 381-386.

Schulze, T. G., Akula, N., Breuer, R., Steele, J., Nalls, M. A., Singleton, A. B., . . . & Mcmahon, F. J. (2014). Molecular genetic overlap in bipolar disorder, schizophrenia, and major depressive disorder. *World Journal of Biological Psychiatry*, *15*(3), 200-208.

Séguin, J. R., Boulerice, B., Harden, P., Tremblay, R. E., & Pihl, R. O. (1999). Executive functions and physical aggression after controlling for attention deficit hyperactivity disorder, general memory, and IQ. *Journal of Child Psychology and Psychiatry*, *40*, 1197–1208.

Shackman, A. J., Tromp, D. P. M., Stockbridge, M. D., Kaplan, C. M., Tillman, R. M., & Fox, A. S. (2016). Dispositional negativity: An integrative psychological and neurobiological perspective. *Psychological Bulletin*, *142*(12), 1275–1314.

Shamosh, N. A., & Gray, J. R. (2008). Delay discounting and intelligence: A meta-analysis. *Intelligence*, *38*, 289–305.

Silvia, P. J. (2008). Another look at creativity and intelligence: Exploring higher-order models and probable confounds. *Personality and Individual Differences*, *44*(4), 1012-1021.

Silvia, P. J., Winterstein, B. P., Willse, J. T., Barona, C. M., Cram, J. T., et al. (2008). Assessing creativity with divergent thinking tasks: exploring the reliability and validity of new subjective scoring methods. *Psychology of Aesthetics, Creativity, and the Arts*, *2*(2), 68–85.

Simonton, D. K. (2003). Scientific creativity as constrained stochastic behavior: The integration of product, person, and process perspectives. *Psychological Bulletin*, *129*(4), 475.

Sligh, A. C., Conners, F. A., & Roskos-Ewoldsen, B. (2005). Relation of creativity to fluid and crystallized intelligence. *Journal of Creative Behavior*, *39*(2), 123-136.

Smith, D. J., Anderson, J., Zammit, S., Meyer, T. D., Pell, J. P., & Mackay, D. (2015). Childhood IQ and risk of bipolar disorder in adulthood: Prospective birth cohort study. *British Journal of Psychiatry Open*, *1*(1), 74-80.

Song, J., Bergen, S. E., Kuja-Halkola, R., Larsson, H., Landén, M., & Lichtenstein, P. (2015). Bipolar disorder and its relation to major psychiatric disorders: A family-based study in the Swedish population. *Bipolar Disorders, 17*(2), 184-193.

Stanek, K. C. (2014). Meta-analyses of personality and cognitive ability. Unpublished doctoral dissertation, University of Minnesota, Minneapolis.

Staudinger, U. M., & Glück, J. (2011). Psychological wisdom research: Commonalities and differences in a growing field. *Annual Review of Psychology, 62*, 215-241.

Staudinger, U. M., Lopez, D. F., & Baltes, P. B. (1997). The psychometric location of wisdom-related performance: Intelligence, personality, and more? *Personality and Social Psychology Bulletin, 23*(11), 1200-1214.

Sternberg, R. J. (1998). A balance theory of wisdom. *Review of General Psychology, 2*, 347–365.

Sternberg, R. J. (2003). *Wisdom, intelligence, and creativity synthesized.* New York: Cambridge University Press.

Tackett, J. L., Lahey, B. B., van Hulle, C., Waldman, I., Krueger, R. F., & Rathouz, P. J. (2013). Common genetic influences on negative emotionality and a general psychopathology factor in childhood and adolescence. *Journal of Abnormal Psychology, 122*(4), 1142–1153.

Torrance, E. P. (1972). Predictive validity of the Torrance Tests of Creative Thinking. *Journal of Creative Behavior, 6*, 236–252.

Vigil-Colet, A., & Morales-Vives, F. (2005). How impulsivity is related to intelligence and academic achievement. *Spanish Journal of Psychology, 8*, 199-204.

Von Stumm, S., & Ackerman, P. L. (2013). Investment and intellect: A review and meta-analysis. *Psychological Bulletin, 139*, 841–869.

von Stumm, S., Chamorro-Premuzic, T., & Furnham, A. (2009). Decomposing self-estimates of intelligence: Structure and sex differences across 12 nations. *British Journal of Psychology, 100*(2), 429-442.

Wai, J. (2014). Experts are born not made: Combining prospective and retrospective longitudinal data shows that cognitive ability matters. *Intelligence, 42*, 74-80.

Wai, J., Lubinski, D., & Benbow, C. P. (2005). Creativity and occupational accomplishments among intellectually precocious youths: An age 13 to age 33 longitudinal study. *Journal of Educational Psychology, 97*, 484–492.

Waller, N. G., DeYoung, C. G., & Bouchard, T. J. (2016). The recaptured scale technique: A method for testing the structural robustness of personality scales. *Multivariate Behavioral Research, 51*, 433–445.

Webster, J. D. (2007). Measuring the character strength of wisdom. *The International Journal of Aging and Human Development, 65*(2), 163-183.

Wechsler, D. (2008). *Wechsler Adult Intelligence Scale – Fourth edition* (WAIS–IV). San Antonio, TX: NCS Pearson.

Wolf, M. B., & Ackerman, P. L. (2005). Extraversion and intelligence: A meta-analytic investigation. *Personality and Individual Differences, 39*, 531–542.

Wright, A. G. C., Hopwood, C. J., Skodol, A. E., & Morey, L. C. (2016). Longitudinal validation of general and specific structural features of personality pathology. *Journal of Abnormal Psychology, 125*(8), 1120–1134.

Zammit, S., Allebeck, P., David, A. S., Dalman, C., Hemmingsson, T., Lundberg, I., & Lewis, G. (2004). A longitudinal study of premorbid IQ score and risk of developing schizophrenia, bipolar disorder, severe depression, and other nonaffective psychoses. *Archives of General Psychiatry, 61*, 354–360.

Ziegler, M., Danay, E., Heene, M., Asendorpf, J., & Bühner, M. (2012). Openness, fluid intelligence, and crystallized intelligence: Toward an integrative model. *Journal of Research in Personality, 46*(2), 173-183.

16 Intelligence, Education, and Society

RICHARD E. MAYER

Education is the cultivation of human intelligence. This optimistic view of intelligence has a long history in education and in society (Martinez, 2000), but how would you actually implement this idea based on research evidence and cognitive theories of how people learn? In short, to the extent that intelligence, or cognitive ability, is malleable, what role can education play in ensuring that all students reach their full intellectual potential? As summarized in Table 16.1, this chapter explores three ways of implementing this provocative proposal: (1) helping students develop learning strategies for academic learning, (2) helping learners build expertise in cognitive processing needed for academic tasks, and (3) helping students acquire transferable domain knowledge that they can use in new situations.

First, if you view intelligence as the ability to learn, consider the idea that people can learn to be better learners. The first section of this chapter explores eight learning strategies that have been shown to improve learning and understanding of academic material.

Second, if you view intelligence as the ability to engage in cognitive processing (including low-level perceptual processing, high-level thinking, and executive control of processing), consider the idea that people can develop expertise in cognitive processing needed for academic tasks through appropriate training regimens. The second section of this chapter explores the effectiveness of computer games for training of cognitive skills.

Third, if you view intelligence as knowing a lot about a subject, consider the idea that people can develop transferable knowledge about a domain through meaningful instructional methods. The third section of this chapter explores instructional methods that have been shown to foster the development of transferable knowledge in learners.

Learning Strategies

The first approach to cultivating human intelligence focuses on the teaching of strategies for how to learn. The rationale is based on the idea that intelligence is

Preparation of this chapter was supported by grant N0001416112046 from the Office of Naval Research.

Table 16.1 Three ways to improve cognitive ability

What to improve	Description
Learning strategies	Help people improve in how well they learn academic material
Cognitive processing	Help people practice cognitive processing needed for academic tasks
Transferable knowledge	Provide meaningful instruction so people acquire domain knowledge they can use in new situations

sometimes defined as the ability to learn or adapt (Sternberg, 1990). In an educational setting, intelligence may be considered the ability to learn academic material.

Is it possible to teach people to be better learners? This is an important question in education because we expect students to be effective learners, but we seldom teach them how to learn. In short, learning to learn is part of the hidden curriculum in education. In other words, although learning to learn is a fundamental goal of education it generally is not the focus of instruction. Fortunately, there is encouraging evidence that students can learn to use learning strategies that improve their understanding of academic material, effectively increasing their ability to learn (Fiorella & Mayer, 2015, 2016; Weinstein & Mayer, 1985).

What is a learning strategy? A **learning strategy** is something that learners do during learning with the intention of improving their learning. For example, if you are using a marker to highlight the key points in this chapter or a pen to underline them, you are engaging in a popular learning strategy used by 53 percent of students according to a recent analysis by Miyatsu, Nguyen, and McDaniel (2018).

Although highlighting and underlining are commonly used, they generally are not effective in improving student learning according to a recent review by Dunlosky, Rawson, Marsh, Nathan, and Willingham (2013), largely because students may not be able to distinguish between important and unimportant information or may highlight or underline too much or too little. However, when students receive training with feedback on how to highlight or underline, the effectiveness of these learning strategies becomes more effective (Miyatsu, Nguyen, & McDaniel, 2018).

Generative Learning Processes

Suppose you want to learn how to understand the material, rather than simply remember it. Table 16.2 summarizes three cognitive process involved in learning for understanding, or what can be called *generative learning*. As summarized in Table 16.2, **generative learning** occurs when the learner engages in appropriate cognitive processing during learning, including selecting the relevant incoming information, mentally organizing it into a coherent structure in working memory, and integrating it with relevant prior knowledge activated from long-term memory. The learning outcome produced by generative learning allows for *transfer* – being

Table 16.2 Three cognitive processes in generative learning

Cognitive process	Description
Selecting	Attend to relevant incoming information
Organizing	Arrange the selected information into a coherent structure
Integrating	Connect selected information with relevant prior knowledge

able to use what was learned in a new situation, such as to solve a new problem or learn something new. These outcomes – being creative in problem solving – are the hallmark of intelligent performance, so in this section we focus on learning strategies that promote understanding.

Generative Learning Strategies

What is a generative learning strategy? A **generative learning strategy** is an activity that learners engage in during learning with the intention of fostering understanding of the material. Table 16.3 lists eight generative learning strategies that have been shown to be effective in improving students' understanding of academic material, based on analyses of the research evidence (Fiorella & Mayer, 2015, 2016). Based on reviews of published experiments, we focus only on generative learning strategies that boost transfer test performance an average of at least .4 standard deviations, which has been recognized as an educationally significant effect (Hattie, 2009). Each generative learning strategy is effective when it causes students to engage in the three cognitive processes outlined in Table 16.2.

Translation Strategies

Suppose you are reading a textbook chapter such as this one. You could see your job as to read each word, which can be a called a *linear learning strategy*. The problem

Table 16.3 Eight generative learning strategies

Learning strategy	Description
Summarizing	Create a summary of the key material in the lesson
Mapping	Create a spatial arrangement of the key ideas in the lesson
Drawing	Draw an illustration to depict the key material in the lesson
Imagining	Form a mental image to depict the key material in the lesson
Self-testing	Take a practice test on the material in the lesson
Self-explaining	Create an explanation of confusing parts of the lesson
Teaching	Explain the material in the lesson to others
Enacting	Act out the key material in lesson

with this approach is that you are not likely to engage in deep processing of the material such as trying to figure out what is important (i.e., selecting), building connections between the pieces of information (i.e., organizing), and assimilating the information with what you already know (i.e., integrating). In short, you are engaging in rote learning that is unlikely to lead to good performance on transfer tests, that is, on your ability to use the material in new situations.

In contrast, what could you do to ensure that you would learn more deeply, by using a *generative learning strategy* that causes you to engage in selecting, organizing, and integrating? One approach is for you to summarize the material in your own words in either written or oral form. For example, I could ask you to write a paragraph that summarizes this section of the chapter. You would have to select the important information to put into your summary. You would have to organize your summary into a coherent paragraph. By translating from the author's words to your own words, you would have to use some of your prior knowledge and integrate it with the selected information.

Summarizing involves creating a written or oral summary of the material in a lesson in your own words. In a review of 30 published experiments, students who were asked to summarize the material in a lesson achieved higher scores on transfer tests than those who simply used their regular approach, yielding an average improvement equal to .5 standard deviations, which is a medium-sized effect (Fiorella & Mayer, 2015, 2016). The summarization effect was strongest when students were given training and guidance in how to create summaries.

Another somewhat related approach is to create a **spatial mapping** of the material, such as a concept map or graphic organizer. For example, in a concept map you pick out the key ideas and connect them with lines. In a graphic organizer, you begin with a structure such as a matrix, and you fill it in. Mapping involves creating a spatial map that contains the key ideas and relations among them. In a review of 39 published experiments, students who were asked to create maps or fill in graphic organizers achieved higher transfer test scores than those who used their regular approach, yielding an average improvement of .6 standard deviations for maps and 1.1 for graphic organizers. The mapping effect was enhanced when students received guidance in the form of partially completed maps or graphic organizers (Fiorella & Mayer, 2015).

Next consider **learning by drawing**, in which you create a drawing that depicts a process or structure described in the lesson. For example, suppose you are reading a text that describes the parts of the brain, particularly those involved in intelligent behavior. To help you understand the text, you sketch out a drawing that depicts the same areas that are described in the text. In a review of 28 published experiments, students who were asked to draw as they studied a printed lesson performed better on transfer tests than those who were told to use their regular approach, yielding a median improvement of .4 standard deviations. The drawing effect was strongest when students received support to minimize the mechanics of drawing and when they received instruction in which elements to put in their drawing (Fiorella & Mayer, 2015).

Taking this approach one step further, consider learning by imagining, in which you create a mental image that depicts a process or structure in the lesson. For example, as you read a passage about the brain and intelligence, you imagine an illustration with labels for the key parts of the brain involved in intelligent performance. In a review of 22 published experiments, students who were asked to form mental images to depict the process or structure described in the text they were reading scored higher on transfer tests than those who used their regular study approach, yielding an average improvement of .6 standard deviations. The imagination effect was strongest when students have had levels of prior knowledge and when they were given guidance in which elements to include in their image (Fiorella & Mayer, 2015).

Elaboration Strategies

So far we have explored four generative learning strategies that promote understanding by having the learner translate the presented material into another format – a summary in your own words, a spatial map, a drawing, or an image. The act of translating from one form of representation to another taps each of the three cognitive processes of selecting, organizing, and integrating. The next four generative learning strategies listed in Table 16.3 require heavier activity on the part of the learner and include taking a practice test, explaining to oneself, explaining to others, and physically acting out the lesson. In short, instead of requiring you to translate, these learning strategies require you to elaborate.

The most studied approach in Table 16.3 is learning by self-testing, in which you take a practice test on the material in the lesson. For example, I could ask you to answer some questions about this section of the chapter, such as: (1) What are the eight generative learning strategies? (2) What are the three cognitive processes in generative learning? (3) What is a generative learning strategy? In many experiments, the practice test involves trying to recall the material in the lesson, and students who learn with this activity are compared to a control group that restudies the material. In a review of 29 published experiments, students performed better on a delayed post-test if they engaged in self-testing rather than restudying after initially studying the material, yielding an average improvement of .4 standard deviations. The self-testing effect was strongest when there was a close match between the practice test and the final delayed test (Fiorella & Mayer, 2015).

Next, you could be asked to engage in self-explanation as a learning strategy, in which you explain the material to yourself, including parts that are confusing. For example, you may wish to explain to yourself how each of the eight generative learning strategies listed in Table 16.3 prime the cognitive processes of selecting, organizing, and integrating. If you can explain this to yourself, you will have activated each of those processes along the way. In a review of 45 published experiments, students performed better on transfer tests when they were required to engage in self-explanation rather than not, yielding an average improvement of .6 standard deviations. The self-explanation effect was strongest when students were given specific prompts about what to explain (Fiorella & Mayer, 2015).

In learning by teaching, the seventh learning strategy in the table, you explain the material you have studied to others. For example, you could be asked to give a short lecture on the material in this section of the chapter, which will be filmed and played for other learners. In a review of 19 published experiments, learning by teaching yielded higher transfer test scores than using one's regular approach, yielding an average improvement of .8 standard deviations. The learning by teaching effect was strongest when students study the material with the intention of teaching to others afterwards (Fiorella & Mayer, 2015).

Finally, the last strategy in Table 16.3 is learning by enacting, in which you act out the events or descriptions in the lessons using concrete objects or body movements. For example, point to the parts of your brain that correspond to the material in a text on the brain's role in intelligent behavior, such as pointing to your forehead when you read "pre-frontal cortex." In 49 published experiments, students who were told to act out the lesson scored higher on tests than those who used their regular learning strategy, yielding an average improvement of .5 standard deviations. The enacting effect was strongest with younger learners.

As you can see, using generative learning strategies that require translating (i.e., summarizing, mapping, drawing, and imagining) or elaborating (i.e., self-testing, self-explanation, teaching, and enacting) generally lead to deeper learning as measured by transfer post-tests. Research on generative learning strategies shows that people can learn to become better learners, that is, to improve their ability to learn. In this way, the teaching of learning strategies exemplifies the potential of education as a means of cultivating human intelligence. Of course, not all learning strategies are equally effective, or appropriate for all kinds of learning goals or all kinds of learners (Dunlosky, et al., 2013; Miyatsu, Nguyen, & McDaniel, 2018).

Cognitive Processing Skills

The second approach to cultivating human intelligence focuses on the teaching of cognitive processing skills. The rationale is that intelligence is sometimes defined as the ability to perform cognitive processes, including low-level (perceptual) processing, high-level (thinking) processing, and metacognitive (executive control) processing (Sternberg, 1990). In an educational setting, intelligence may be considered the ability to effectively engage in cognitive processing on academic tasks.

Is it possible to teach people how to be better at cognitive processing? Research on cognitive skill training has a long history, marked by success in the training of specific skills in specific contexts but plagued with difficulties in showing transfer to different skills or different contexts (Anderson & Bavelier, 2011; Singley & Anderson, 1989). In short, the primary challenge for cognitive process instruction is to determine whether skills learned in one context will transfer to another context that requires the same skill.

Computer Games

A recent attempt to meet this challenge involves using computer games as a platform for teaching cognitive processing skills that transfer to contexts outside the game. Many strong claims are made by visionaries concerning the potential of computer games for revolutionizing education, but in this chapter let's take a scientific approach by looking at what the evidence says about the cognitive consequences of playing off-the-shelf video games.

In *cognitive consequences research* on games for learning, we compare the pre-test-to-post-test gain in a cognitive processing skill for a group that plays a computer game that requires using the targeted skill for an extended period of time versus a group that plays an alternative game or no game at all. In particular, we are interested in identifying which kinds of games produce greater gains than a control group on which kinds of cognitive processing skills. Having an appropriate control group is a crucial feature of cognitive consequences research, so it is best to have a control group that plays a game that is similar to one in the experimental group, but that does not require exercising the targeted cognitive skill.

The theory underlying research on the cognitive consequences of playing computer games is the theory of **specific transfer of general skills** (Anderson & Bavelier, 2011: Mayer, 2014; Sims & Mayer, 2002). The main idea is that playing a game that requires repeatedly exercising a cognitive skill in a variety of contexts at increasing levels of challenge will allow the player to improve on the targeted skill in the game and in contexts outside the game that require the same target skill, such as measured by a classic cognitive processing test.

Table 16.4 summarizes the results of a recent review of cognitive consequences research based on published experiments comparing a group that was assigned to play a game for an extended period versus a group that was assigned to engage in a control activity (Mayer, 2014, 2016). As you can see, there are two bright spots in Table 16.4. The first line shows that playing a first-person shooter game such as *Unreal Tournament* or *Medal of Honor* results in greater gains on perceptual attention skills than playing a control game, yielding a net average improvement of more than 1 standard deviation based on 18 published experiments (Mayer, 2014). The second line shows that playing the spatial puzzle game *Tetris* results in greater gains on mental rotation of 2-D shapes including *Tetris*-like shapes than playing

Table 16.4 What are the cognitive consequences of playing off-the-shelf games?

Type of game	Type of test	Effect size	Number of experiments
Promising effects			
First-person shooter	Perceptual attention	1.18	17 of 18
Spatial puzzle	2-D mental rotation	0.68	11 of 11
Unpromising effects			
Spatial puzzle	Spatial cognition	0.04	9 of 15
Real-time strategy	Executive function	0.18	8 of 11
Real-time strategy	Perceptual attention	-0.10	4 of 9
Brain training	Spatial cognition	0.03	6 of 8
Spatial action	Perceptual attention	0.25	5 of 6
Brain training	Perceptual attention	0.31	4 of 5
Spatial puzzle	Perceptual attention	0.15	3 of 5

a control game, yielding a net average improvement of .7 standard deviations based on 11 published experiments (Mayer, 2014).

These two findings are consistent with the theory of specific transfer of general skill, because when students get a lot of practice in tracking moving objects in the periphery of their field of view by playing first-person shooter games, this practice allows them to develop perceptual attention skills that apply outside the game. Similarly, when students get a lot practice in rotating *Tetris* shapes by playing *Tetris*, this practice allows them to develop a skill – mental rotation of 2D shapes – that applies to tasks outside the game.

However, Table 16.4 shows that playing computer games does not foster transferable cognitive processing skills when there is not a clear match between the skills practiced in the game and the skills tested outside the game. Listed under the unpromising effects portion of Table 16.4, Mayer (2014) found seven situations in which there were at least five published experiments but none of them produced an average improvement of .4 standard deviations or greater. Although playing the spatial puzzle game *Tetris* helped improve mental rotation of 2D shapes, it did not help on other spatial skills that do not involve mental rotation or on perceptual attention skills. Playing a real-time strategy game such as *Rise of Nations* did not help players improve on perceptual attention skills or executive function skills, and playing brain-training games such as *Brain Age* did not help players improve on perceptual attention skills or executive function skills. Presumably, the unpromising effects are caused when games do not require repeated practice of the targeted skill in varying contexts at increasing levels of challenge, but rather test players on skills that were not targeted in the game. As you can see, the lesson from research on cognitive training with computer games is that the skills exercised in the game should match the skills required on tasks outside the game. (For a closer look at some research being carried out on the educational value of playing computer games, see the Focus on Contemporary Research box below.)

FOCUS ON CONTEMPORARY RESEARCH: RICHARD E. MAYER'S WORK ON COMPUTER GAMES FOR LEARNING

Homework is intended to extend learning time beyond the regular school day (Cooper, Robinson, & Patall, 2006; Xu, 2013), but sometimes students would rather do other things such as playing video games. In response, parents might say something like, "You can play video games after you finish your homework." However, suppose we could create a world in which playing video games is the homework. What has scientific research had to say about the educational value of playing video games? It may be helpful to answer this question by examining three research questions (Mayer, 2014). First, what are the features of educational computer games that foster learning? To answer this question, researchers use a value-added approach in which we compare the post-test performance of students who play the base version of the game to those who play the same game with one feature added. For example, in Design-a-Plant (as shown in the figure), you travel to a new planet that has specific environmental conditions such as periodic heavy rain and strong wind and you are asked to design a plant that will survive there by choosing appropriate roots, stem, and leaves. Then, you see what happens to your plant as Herman-the-bug explains a bit about plant growth. Students perform better on subsequent tests involving plant growth in new environments if Herman communicates by voice rather than onscreen text (which we call the modality principle) and if Herman communicates in conversational style rather than

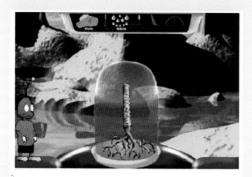

Box Figure In Design-a-Plant, a player travels to a new planet with specific environmental conditions and is asked to design a plant that will survive there by choosing appropriate roots, stem, and leaves. The player then sees what happens to the plant as Herman-the-bug explains some details about plant growth

formal style (which we call the personalization principle). In additional studies with the Circuit Game, students go through increasingly more challenging levels where they perform tasks like constructing circuits that will have equivalent rates of electron flow. We found that students learned more about electrical circuits if we added explanative feedback after their moves (which we call the feedback principle) or if we asked students to select the explanation for their moves from a menu (which we call the self-explanation principle). The Profile Game is a geology simulation in which students investigate the terrain of an unknown area. In this game, students performed better on a subsequent test if they had a brief pretraining in what each of eight major geological formations look like (which we call the pretraining principle). Overall, in an analysis of all published research, I was able to identify substantial support for these five design principles for educational games. This is encouraging news because it shows that it is possible to use computer games to help people learn and improve their minds.

Brain-Training Games

Let's take a closer look at brain-training games because they are specifically designed to improve cognitive processing outside the game. In short, brain-training games are aimed at improving your intelligence in the sense of improving your ability to process information particularly in educationally relevant contexts. *Lumosity* is a subscription-based collection of online brain-training games, intended to improve cognitive skills such as attention (e.g., keeping track of the location of moving objects on a screen) and flexibility (e.g., efficiently shifting from using one rule to another for sorting onscreen objects).

The effectiveness of *Lumosity* is a contentious issue in both the legal and scientific arenas. In the legal arena, in 2016, Lumos Labs, the company that sells *Lumosity*, agreed to settle a suit for false advertising brought by the Federal Trade Commission, without admitting or denying the allegations (Robbennolt, 2016). As part of the settlement the company agreed to stop making claims about *Lumosity*'s effects on performance or cognitive impairment without supporting scientific evidence. In the scientific arena, in 2014, a group of nearly 70 researchers signed a letter on behalf of the scientific community asserting the lack of evidence for the effectiveness of brain-training games, which was subsequently countered by a letter signed by 133 supporters of brain-training games (Simons et al., 2016).

A recent review concluded that there is evidence that people show improvements on the trained cognitive skills while playing brain-training games but there is not strong evidence of improvements on those cognitive skills when they are performed outside the game environment (Simons et al., 2016). The authors of the review criticized the existing research base and called for well-controlled experiments that clearly examine the effects of playing brain-training games with healthy participants.

In one study by Hardy et al. (2015) people who played *Lumosity* games for 50 15-minute sessions showed small improvements (of about a quarter of a standard deviation) on cognitive tests as compared to a control group, but Simons et al. (2016) point out methodological flaws and potential conflicts of interest in light of the fact that five of the seven authors are employees of the company that sells *Lumosity*. In contrast, Shute, Ventura, and Ke (2015) found no significant improvements on a battery of cognitive tests for students who trained with *Lumosity* for 8 hours.

In response to the call for well-controlled long-term research, suppose we asked a group of college students to play either five attention games (attention group) or five flexibility games (flexibility group) in *Lumosity* for 15 to 20 hours spread over 60 to 80 sessions. Would this investment in playing brain-training games pay off? When we conducted this experiment, we found that, as expected, the students showed improvement in playing the games, reaching higher levels and better scores over the course of the experiment. However, the attention group did not show better improvement on any of 7 cognitive measures of attention based on tasks performed outside the game environment than a control group, and the flexibility group showed better improvement on 2 of the 7 measures. Overall, there is not strong evidence that brain-training games such as *Lumosity* are effective for young, healthy learners.

Similar conclusions apply to the cognitive-skill-training program, *Cog Med*, which is intended to improve adaptive working memory skills (Melby-Lervag & Hulme, 2012). In a meta-analysis of 23 studies, Hulme and Melby-Lervag (2012, p. 281) concluded that "in the best designed studies, using a random allocation of participants and treated controls, even the immediate effects of training were essentially zero."

As you can see, the search for computer-based brain-training games that improve cognitive skills has been illusive, so let's consider a somewhat different approach. What would happen if we designed a game specifically aimed at one educationally important cognitive skill, such as the ability to shift from one task to another, and implemented it in a game that was fun for students to play based on extensive playtesting with students? That is what happened with the creation of *Alien Game*, as shown in Figure 16.1 (Parong et al., 2017). In this game, aliens (who are red or blue and have one or two eyes) come down from the top of screen, and your job is to shoot them up some food or water based on whether they are hungry or thirsty. The guiding rule (such as blue aliens are hungry and red aliens are thirsty) keeps changing in ever more complicated ways and in new onscreen contexts, so players get lots of practice in shifting from one rule to another. Students who play the *Alien Game* for two hours over four sessions showed greater gains in cognitive tests of shifting administered outside the game than students who played a control game. This study encourages further work on designing focused games that are fun to play and that require players to exercise a cognitive skill repeatedly in varying contexts

Figure 16.1 Screenshot from *Alien Game*. In this game, blue and red aliens come down from the top of screen, and the player's job is to shoot them up with food or water based on whether they are hungry or thirsty. The guiding rule keeps changing in ever more complicated ways and in new on-screen contexts, so players get lots of practice in shifting from one rule to another.

at an increasing level of challenge. Thus, there is some hope that games of the future will be able to make you smarter by improving general cognitive processing skills. By training targeted cognitive skills with specifically designed computer games, we can fulfill the promise of education as the cultivation of human intelligence.

Transferable Knowledge

The third approach to cultivating human intelligence focuses on the teaching of domain knowledge – including facts, concepts, procedures, strategies, and beliefs needed for mastering an academic topic. The rationale is based on the idea that intelligence is sometimes defined as knowledge (Sternberg, 1990), which is somewhat consistent with how early intelligence tests were constructed (Wolf, 1973). In an educational setting, intelligence may be considered one's knowledge of academic subjects.

Consider the following word problem:

At ARCO, gas costs $1.13 per gallon.
This is 5 cents less per gallon than gas at Chevron.
If you want to buy 5 gallons of gas, how much will you pay at Chevron?

Solving this problem could be an indication of mathematical ability (i.e., a form of intelligence), but let's consider what you need to know in order solve this problem. Table 16.5 lists five kinds of knowledge needed for solving the ARCO problem:

factual knowledge, such as knowing that there are 100 cents in a dollar; *conceptual knowledge*, such as knowing the schema for this problem is TOTAL COST = UNIT COST x NUMBER OF UNITS; *strategic knowledge*, such as knowing how to break a problem into subparts (i.e., first find the cost of a gallon of gas at Chevron, then find the total cost of

Table 16.5 Five kinds of knowledge needed for solving word problems

Type	Example
facts	Knowing there are 100 cents in a dollar, or that $ is a dollar sign.
concepts	Knowing the schema for the ARCO problem is: TOTAL COST = UNIT COST x NUMBER OF UNITS.
strategies	Knowing how to break a problem into smaller parts: in a total cost problem, first compute the unit cost and then multiply that by the number of units.
procedures	Knowing how to add, subtract, divide, and multiple numbers: 1.13 + .05 = 1.18.
beliefs	Thinking "If I persist I can solve this problem."

5 gallons); *procedural knowledge*, such as knowing how to add, subtract, multiply, and divide; and *beliefs*, such as thinking "I can get the right answer if I stick with this."

Research by Hegarty, Mayer, and Monk (1995) shows that many students get the wrong answer for this problem, usually $5.40. Instead of adding 5 cents to 1.13 to get 1.18, they subtract 5 cents from 1.13 to get 1.08 and then multiply 1.08 by 5 to get 5.40. This error indicates that they have the right procedural knowledge, but their difficulty rests in mentally representing the problem and devising a solution plan, which indicates failures in conceptual and strategic knowledge. The overall conclusion is that mathematical problem solving depends on the student's domain knowledge. This points to the central role of knowledge in problem solving.

Consider the parallelogram problem shown in the top of Figure 16.2. In this problem, your job is to find the area of the parallelogram if the height is 3 inches and the length is 5 inches. Suppose some students have learned to apply the formula: Area = Height × Length. For them, solving the problem involves plugging in 3 for Height and 5 for Length and then carrying out the multiplication: Area = 3 × 5 = 15. The Gestalt psychologist Wertheimer (1959) called this *rote learning* or *reproductive thinking*, because the learners do not understand what they are doing.

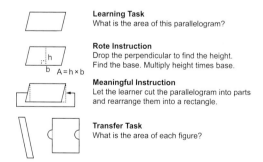

Learning Task
What is the area of this parallelogram?

Rote Instruction
Drop the perpendicular to find the height.
Find the base. Multiply height times base.

Meaningful Instruction
Let the learner cut the parallelogram into parts
and rearrange them into a rectangle.

Transfer Task
What is the area of each figure?

Figure 16.2 Parallelogram problem. In this problem, the player's job is to find the area of the parallelogram if the height is 3 inches and the length is 5 inches.

In contrast, suppose some students were given a cardboard cutout of the parallelogram and allowed to cut off a triangle on one and place it on the other end to form a rectangle. Then you can place 1 × 1 inch tiles over the rectangle to see there are 3 rows of 5 tiles, totaling 15 tiles in all. Thus, the area of 15. Wertheimer (1959) called this *meaningful learning* or *productive thinking,* because the learners understand what area of a parallelogram means.

What's the difference between rote and meaningful learning? According to Wertheimer, students who learned by rote perform well on solving similar problems (i.e., retention test as shown in the bottom left side of Figure 16.2) but not on solving different-looking problems that require the same principle (transfer test). In contrast, students who learned by understanding are able to solve both retention and transfer problems. In short, if you want to be able to use what you have learned in a new situation (which is an indication of intelligence), you need to learn by understanding rather than by rote.

These examples point to the crucial role of transferable knowledge in supporting cognitive ability. **Transferable knowledge** refers to knowledge that can be applied to new situations and has been recognized as especially important for life and work in the twenty-first century (Pellegrino & Hilton, 2012). Figure 16.3 shows how transferable knowledge works: You learn a principle or schema or model in one context (i.e. base problem) and then abstract a rule and map it onto solving problems that require the same principle or schema or model in another context (i.e. target problem).

For example, consider the oil fire problem (adapted from Gick & Holyoak, 1983):

An oil well exploded and caught fire, creating a blazing inferno. The famed firefighter Red Adair was called in to extinguish the fire. Red stationed firefighters in a circle all around the fire, each with a small hose aimed at the fire. When everyone was ready, all the hoses were turned on and a small stream of foam from each hose landed on the fire from all directions. This created a huge amount of foam landing on the fire, extinguishing it quickly.

As you can see, the context of the problem is fighting an oil fire with water hoses, and the underlying solution principle is convergence – having many small hoses around the fire all shooting a small amount of foam that converges on the location

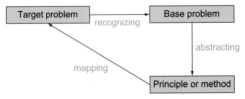

Figure 16.3 A model of transferable knowledge. A principle or schema or model is learned in one context and then applied to solving problems that require the same principle or schema or model in another context.

of the fire. Now, suppose I asked you to solve the tumor problem, which is based on Duncker's (1945) classic study of problem solving:

> Given a human being with an inoperable stomach tumor, and rays which destroy healthy tissue at sufficient intensity, by what procedure can one free him of the tumor by these rays and at the same time avoid destroying the healthy tissue which surrounds it?

The solution – sending weak rays toward the tumor from many different positions surrounding the tumor that all converge on the tumor – involves the same principle as the oil fire problem but is couched in a different context. Gick and Holyoak (1983) found that most students were not able to apply what they learned from reading about the convergence solution in one context to solving the tumor problem, which involves a different context. This indicates a failure in building transferable knowledge.

Instructional Methods for Producing Transferable Knowledge

What can be done to help students learn in ways so they can take what they have learned and apply it to solving new problems? Table 16.6 lists some instructional methods that have been shown to be effective in producing transferable knowledge, based on a review by Mayer (2008).

Explanative Feedback

Suppose elementary-school children were learning how to solve signed-arithmetic problems, such as, 3- -2 = ___. A problem is presented on the screen, the student types in an answer, and the computer responds by printing "RIGHT" or "WRONG, the answer is 5" on the screen. This is an example of **corrective feedback** because it

Table 16.6 Instructional methods for transferable knowledge

Instructional method	Description
Explanative feedback	After the learner solves a problem, providing an explanation of the principle underlying the correct solution.
Concreteness	In teaching a problem-solving principle in one context, show how it is analogous to a more familiar and concrete context.
Guided activity	Providing advice as support about the underlying principle as the learner solves a problem.
Guided examples	Provide an explanation of the reason for each step in worked-out examples.
Guided lessons	Add design features to a book, online presentation, or face-to-face lecture that guide the learner's cognitive processes of selecting, organizing, and integrating.

simply tells you whether you were right or not. In contrast, suppose the computer gave feedback by acting out the operations by showing a bunny moving along a number line – starting at space 3 on the number line, turning to face the negative side of the number line, and moving backwards 2 steps, to end up in space 5 on the number line. This is an example of **explanative feedback** because it tells you why the answer is correct. Moreno and Mayer (1999) found that students transferred to solving new problems better if they learned with explanative feedback than corrective feedback.

Overall, providing explanative feedback has been recognized as one of the most powerful influences on academic achievement (Hattie, 2009; Hattie, Gans, & Brooks, 2017). In a review of 12 meta-analyses covering 196 experiments, providing feedback boosted academic achievement by .8 standard deviations on average. However, not all forms of feedback are equally effective: Reviews (Bangert-Drowns, Kulik, Kulik, & Morgan, 1991; Johnson & Priest, 2014; Kluger & DiNisi, 1996) have repeatedly concluded that explanative feedback (i.e., feedback that provides an explanation for the correct answer) is more effective than corrective feedback (i.e., feedback that simply tells whether the answer is correct). In online learning scenarios, explanative feedback can be more effective when it is spoken rather than printed on the screen, presented after the entire problem is solved rather than step-by-step, and when learners are low in prior knowledge or ability (Johnson & Priest, 2014).

Concreteness

Suppose you wanted to help elementary school children learn how to solve two-column subtraction problems, such as:

$$\begin{array}{r} 63 \\ -28 \\ \hline \end{array}$$

For some students, the teacher goes to the board and solves the problem, step-by-step, describing what to do for each step as she writes on the board. This is the conventional method of instruction. For other students, she brings out 63 sticks and puts them into bundles of 10 by tying each set of 10 sticks into a bundle, yielding 6 bundles of 10 sticks and 3 individual sticks. If the goal is to take away 28 sticks, the teacher shows that to take away 8, you have to open one bundle so you have 13 individual sticks. When you take away 8, you have 5 individual sticks remaining (and 5 bundles of 10). Then, to take away 20, you remove two bundles of sticks, leaving 3 bundles of 10 and 5 individual sticks for a total of 35. This is the **concrete method**. In a classic set of experiments Brownell and Moser (1949) showed that students were better able to transfer what they had learned to solving three-column subtractions if they learned by the concrete method rather than the conventional method.

Using concrete objects to represent abstract mathematical concepts is a central feature of Montessori methods, and there is mounting research evidence to support their effectiveness (Lillard, 2016). In a review of research, Mayer (2008) concluded that concrete methods have been shown to be effective in improving student understanding of mathematical and scientific principles, as reflected in superior performance on transfer problems.

Guided Activity

Third, concerning guided activity, suppose that we want to help students learn to write computer programs, using a language called LOGO, in which they write commands that tell an onscreen turtle to do things like RT 90 (i.e., turn right 90 degrees) or FD 5 (i.e., move forward 5 turtle steps). We let them explore the LOGO system on their own, creating and running programs and seeing what happens. This is an example of discovery learning. Although there are many fans of discovery learning, research showed that most students did not learn much about the key ideas in programing (such as creating subroutines) and in fact often failed to learn what the LOGO commands do (Mayer, 2004). In contrast, suppose we give students specific projects for what to create with LOGO, and provide hints and advice along the way to make sure they are successful. This is guided discovery. Students who learned with guided discovery performed better on subsequent transfer tasks involving new programing problems than students who learned by discovery without guidance (Fay & Mayer, 1994).

Overall, reviews of research have repeatedly concluded that when the goal is to produce superior transfer test performance in subject areas such as mathematics or science, students learn better with guided discovery methods than pure discovery methods (Kirschner, Sweller, & Clark, 2006; Mayer, 2004). More recently, adding guided activity to educational games – such as hints and advice during playing simulation games – improved subsequent transfer test performance (Mayer, 2014).

Guided Examples

Fourth, concerning guided examples, suppose we wanted to teach students how to solve probability problems such as:

> Mister Flash is an inexperienced photographer. Independently of each other he frequently makes two errors when he takes a picture. He manages to blur the image in 30 percent of the photos and he forgets to activate the flash in 40 percent of the photos so that pictures wind up too dark. If you randomly chose one of Dr. Flash's developed pictures, what is the probability that it is flawless?

We could present the problem on a computer screen, followed by each of four steps required to solve the problems, displayed one at a time. This is a worked-out example. To help even more, in addition to this worked-out example, along with each step we could display the explanation by displaying the rule that applied to that step. This is a guided worked-out example. Renkl (2002) found that students who learned with guided examples performed substantially better on transfer problems than students who learned from worked-examples without explanations. In follow-up studies, students also benefited by being asked to generate brief explanations or for each step (Atkinson, Renkl, & Merrill, 2003) or select them from a menu (Johnson & Mayer, 2010), which can be called *self-explanations*.

Overall, recent reviews (Renkl, 2014, 2017) have confirmed that learning with worked-out examples is improved when explanations are provided, including explanations of the underlying principles or explanations of how the operations in steps are related to accomplishing specific goals. In short, guided examples can be a powerful technique for improving understanding that leads to transfer.

Guided Lessons

Finally, suppose you wanted to know how lightning storms develop so you look it up in an online encyclopedia. You find a page that explains how lightning storms develop in several paragraphs that are printed on the screen. You read the paragraphs, and you can recite it back, but you do not understand how lightning storms develop well enough to answer transfer questions, such as, "Suppose you see clouds in the sky, but no lightning. Why not?" In order to help people learn more deeply from lessons, we could add illustrations or an animation that depicts the events described in the text. This is called a multimedia lesson because it involves both words and graphics.

Adding graphics to text is a powerful technique for increasing learner understanding. In 11 out of 11 experiments reviewed by Mayer (2009), students performed better on transfer tests when they learned from a lesson containing words and graphics than from a lesson containing the identical words alone, yielding an improvement of more than 1 standard deviation on average. Mayer (2009) refers to this as the **multimedia principle**: People learn more deeply from words and graphics than from words alone. Multimedia lessons include textbooks that contain printed text and illustrations, online lessons such as narrated animations, and face-to-face lessons such as narrated slideshows.

Multimedia lessons are intended to prime the three cognitive processes needed for meaningful learning summarized in Table 16.2: selecting, organizing, and integrating. Adding graphics can help learners select the relevant material, see the connections among them, and integrate the graphics and text with each other and with prior knowledge primed by the graphics. However, all graphics are not equally effective, so researchers have developed a set of evidence-based principles for designing multimedia lessons. These principles, covered in the next section, form the basis for guided lessons – lessons that are designed to guide the learner's cognitive processing in terms selecting relevant information, mentally organizing it, and integrating it with prior knowledge.

Principles for Designing Multimedia Lessons

Extraneous processing is processing that does not serve the instructional objective, and is caused by poor instructional design. Three exemplary principles for reducing extraneous processing are:

coherence principle, which calls for eliminating extraneous material such as unneeded color and detail in graphics and unneeded facts in text;

signaling principle, which calls for highlighting essential material such as using bold font for important words or color cueing for important parts of a graphic; and

spatial contiguity principle, which calls for placing printed text next to the part of the graphic it refers to.

As you can see, each of these techniques helps guide the process of selecting essential material for further progress. In addition, signaling can guide how the learner organizes the material by including outlines and headings, and spatial contiguity can guide how the learner integrates corresponding words and images. A review of published experiments shows that implementing the coherence principle increases transfer test performance by .8 standard deviations on average, signaling results in an average improvement of .4 standard deviations, and spatial contiguity adds more than 1 standard deviation on average (Mayer & Fiorella, 2014).

Three exemplary principles for managing **essential processing** – cognitive processing of essential material that may threaten to overload the learner's processing capacity – are:

pretraining principle, which calls for teaching students about the names and characteristics of key terms before the lesson;

segmenting principle, which calls for breaking a continuous presentation into manageable parts controlled by the learner; and

modality principle, which calls for presenting words in spoken form rather than printed form.

Pretraining helps guide how learners select and organize the key elements in the lesson, segmenting gives learners a chance to select and organize the material in one part of the lesson before moving on, and modality allows learners to select and integrate corresponding words and images that can be held in working memory at the same time. A review of published experiments shows that adding pretraining improves transfer test performance by an average of .8 standard deviations on average, adding segmenting improves transfer test performance by .7 standard deviations on average, and adding modality creates an average improvement of .8 standard deviations (Mayer & Pilegard, 2014).

Two exemplary principles for fostering generative processing – making sense of the essential material – are:

personalization principle, which calls for putting words in conversational style rather than formal style, and

embodiment principle, which calls for the instructor to use human-like gesture and movements while teaching.

Both of these techniques are intended to guide the learner's cognitive processing in a way that involves deeper learning, such as organizing and integrating the material. Research on the personalization principle shows that changing from formal to conversational style improves transfer test performance by .8 standard deviations on average, whereas adding embodiment to a video or animated onscreen agent creates an average improvement of .4 standard deviations (Mayer, 2014). Overall, research on instructional design of multimedia lessons has identified ways to help learners build transferable knowledge.

CONCLUSION

Three ways that education can improve human intelligence are: (1) by helping people develop learning strategies that make them more effective learners, (2) by helping people develop cognitive processing skills such as how to focus their attention, and (3) by helping people acquire transferable knowledge, that is, domain knowledge that can be applied to new situations. This review reports on pockets of research progress on each of these approaches to improving human intelligence, but future research is needed to systematically prepare people for success in the twenty-first century.

CHAPTER SUMMARY

In this chapter, we have explored three evidence-based ways to implement the proposal that education is the cultivation of intelligence. If you are good at learning academic content, we might say you are intelligent. There is mounting evidence that you can improve how well you learn by effectively employing generative learning strategies, such as summarizing, mapping, drawing, imagining, self-testing, self-explaining, teaching, and enacting. If you are a successful problem solver on academic tasks, we might say you are intelligent. There is emerging evidence that under certain circumstances, you can improve your cognitive processing, including executive control of your cognitive processing, through practice in game-like settings. Finally, if you use what you have learned to solve new problems or more easily learn new knowledge, we might say you are intelligent. There is long-standing evidence that meaningful instructional methods can promote the development of transferable knowledge – such as explanative feedback, concreteness, guided activity, guided examples, and guided lessons. Overall, this chapter shows you examples of the progress being made in figuring out how to implement the hopeful proposal that education is the cultivation of human intelligence.

KEY TERMS

cognitive consequences research • coherence principle • concrete method • corrective feedback • embodiment principle • essential processing • explanative feedback • extraneous processing • generative learning • generative learning strategy • learning by drawing • learning strategy • modality principle • multimedia principle • personalization principle • pretraining principle • segmenting principle • signaling principle • spatial contiguity principle • spatial mapping • specific transfer of general skills • transfer • transferable knowledge

COMPREHENSION AND REFLECTION QUESTIONS

1. Based on what you have learned from this chapter, describe a change you would make in how you study for courses you are taking. Explain why that change would improve your learning.
2. Explain what is meant by "transferable knowledge" and why this is an important idea for education, intelligence, and society.
3. It is sometimes said that "practice makes perfect." Based on what you have learned about the feedback, explain why this is or is not an accurate statement.
4. Based on what you have learned about how to teach for transfer, make specific suggestions for how you would improve lectures based on slideshows. Explain why you make each change.
5. How can games be used to improve learning of cognitive skills and academic knowledge?

References

Anderson, A. F., & Bavelier, D. (2011). Action game play as a tool to enhance perception, attention, and cognition. In S. Tobias & J. D. Fletcher (eds.), *Computer games and instruction* (pp. 307-330). Charlotte, NC: Information Age Publishing.

Atkinson, R. K., Renkl, A., & Merrill, M. M. (2003). Transitioning from studying examples to solving problems: Effects of self-explanation prompts and fading worked-out steps. *Journal of Educational Psychology*, 95(4), 774-783.

Bangert-Drowns, R. L., Kulik, C. L. C., & Kulik, J. A., & Morgan, M. (1991). The instructional effect of feedback in test-like events. *Review of Educational Research*, 61(2), 213-238.

Brownell, W. A., & Moser, H. E. (1949). *Meaningful vs. mechanical learning: A study in grade III subtraction.* Duke University Research Series in Education no. 8. Durham, NC: Duke University Press.

Cooper, H., Robinson, J. C., & Patall, E. A. (2006). Does homework improve academic achievement? A synthesis of research 1987–2003. *Review of Educational Research, 76*, 1–62.

Duncker, K. (1945). *On problem-solving.* Psychological Monographs no. 270. Washington, DC: American Psychological Association.

Dunlosky, J., Rawson, K. A., Marsh, E. J., Nathan, M. J., & Willingham, D. T. (2013). Improving students' learning with effective learning techniques: Promising directions from cognitive and educational psychology. *Psychological Science in the Public Interest, 14*(1), 7-58.

Fay, A. L., & Mayer, R. E. (1994). Benefits of teaching design skills before teaching logo computer programming: Evidence for syntax-independent learning. *Journal of Educational Computing Research, 11*(3), 187-210.

Fiorella, L., & Mayer, R. E. (2015). *Learning as a generative activity: Eight learning strategies that promote understanding.* New York: Cambridge University Press.

Fiorella, L., & Mayer, R. E. (2016). Eight ways to promote generative learning. *Educational Psychology Review, 28*, 717-741.

Gick, M. L., & Holyoak, K. L. (1983). Schema induction and analogical transfer. *Cognitive Psychology, 15*, 1-38.

Hardy, J. L., Drescher, D., Sarkar, K., Kellett, G., & Scanlon, M. (2011). Enhancing visual attention and working memory with a web-based cognitive training program. *Mensa Research Journal, 42*(2), 13–20.

Hardy, J. L., Nelson, R. A., Thomason, M. E., Sternberg, D. A., Katovich, K., Farzin, F., & Scanlon, M. (2015). Enhancing cognitive abilities with comprehensive training: A large, online, randomized, active-controlled trial. *PLoS ONE, 10*(9), e0134467. doi: 10.1371/journal.pone.0134467

Hattie, J. (2009). *Visible learning.* New York: Routledge.

Hattie, J., Gan, M., & Brooks, C. (2017). Instruction based on feedback. In R. E. Mayer & P. A. Alexander (eds.), *Handbook of research on learning and instruction* (2nd ed., pp. 290-324). New York: Routledge.

Hegarty, M., Mayer, R. E., & Monk, C. A. (1995). Comprehension of arithmetic word problems: A comparison of successful and unsuccessful problem solvers. *Journal of Educational Psychology, 87*, 18-32.

Hulme, C., & Melby-Lervåg, M. (2012). Current evidence does not support the claims made for CogMed working memory training. *Journal of Applied Research in Memory and Cognition, 1*(3), 197–200.

Johnson, C. I., & Mayer, R. E. (2010). Adding the self-explanation principle to multimedia learning in a computer-based game-like environment. *Computers in Human Behavior, 26*, 1246-1252.

Johnson, C. I., & Priest, H. A. (2014). The feedback principle in multimedia learning. In R. E. Mayer (ed.), *The Cambridge handbook of multimedia learning* (2nd ed., pp. 449-463). New York: Cambridge University Press.

Kirschner, P. A., Sweller, J., & Clark, R. E. (2006). Why minimal guidance during instruction does not work: An analysis of the failure of constructivist, discovery, problem-based, experiential, and inquiry-based teaching. *Educational Psychologist*, *41*(2), 75-86.

Kluger, A. N., & DiNisi, A. (1996). The effects of feedback interventions on performance: A historical review, a meta-analysis, and a preliminary feedback intervention theory. *Psychological Bulletin*, *119*(2), 254-284.

Lillard, A. S. (2016). *Montessori: The science behind the genius* (2nd ed.). New York: Oxford University Press.

Martinez, M. E. (2000). *Education as the cultivation of intelligence*. Mahwah, NJ: Lawrence Erlbaum Associates.

Mayer, R. E. (2004). Should there be a three-strikes rule against pure discovery learning? *American Psychologist*, *59*(1), 14.

Mayer, R. E. (2008). *Learning and instruction* (2nd ed.). Upper Saddle River, NJ: Pearson.

Mayer, R. E. (2009). *Multimedia learning* (2nd ed.). New York: Cambridge University Press.

Mayer, R. E. (2014). *Computer games for learning: An evidence-based approach*. Cambridge, MA: MIT Press.

Mayer, R. E. (2016). What should be the role of computer games in education? *Policy Insights from Behavioral and Brain Sciences*, *3*(1), 20-26.

Mayer, R. E., & Fiorella, L. (2014). Principles for reducing extraneous processing in multimedia learning: Coherence, signaling, redundancy, spatial contiguity, and spatial contiguity principles. In R. E. Mayer (ed.), *The Cambridge handbook of multimedia learning* (2nd ed., pp. 279-315). New York: Cambridge University Press.

Mayer, R. E., & Pilegard, C. (2014). Principles for managing essential processing in multimedia learning: Segmenting, pre-training, and modality principles. In R. E. Mayer (ed.), *The Cambridge handbook of multimedia learning* (2nd ed., pp. 316-344). New York: Cambridge University Press.

Melby-Lervåg, M., & Hulme, C. (2012). Is working memory training effective? A meta-analytic review. *Developmental Psychology*, *49*(2), 270–291.

Miyatsu, T., Nguyen, K., & McDaniel, M. (2018). Five popular study strategies: Their pitfalls and optimal implementations. *Perspectives on Psychological Science*, *13*, 390-407.

Moreno, R., & Mayer, R. E. (1999). Multimedia-supported metaphors for meaning making in mathematics. *Cognition and instruction*, *17*(3), 215-248.

Parong, J., Mayer, R. E., Fiorella, L., MacNamara, A., Plass, J., & Homer, B. (2017). Learning executive function skills by playing focused video games. *Contemporary Educational Psychology*, *51*, 141-151.

Pellegrino, J. W., & Hilton, M. L. (2012). *Education for life and work: Developing transferable knowledge and skills in the 21st century*. Washington, DC: National Academies Press.

Renkl, A. (2002). Worked-out examples: Instructional explanations support learning by self-explanations. *Learning and instruction, 12*(5), 529-556.

Renkl, A. (2014). The worked examples principle in multimedia learning. In R. E. Mayer (ed.). *The Cambridge handbook of multimedia learning* (2nd ed., pp. 391-412). New York: Cambridge University Press.

Renkl, A. (2017). Instruction based on examples. In R. E. Mayer & P. A. Alexander (eds.), *Handbook of research on learning and instruction* (2nd ed., pp. 325-348). New York: Routledge.

Robbennolt, J. K. (2016). Brain games: Helpful tool or false promise? *Monitor on Psychology, 47*(8), 18.

Shute, V. J., Ventura, M., & Ke, F. (2015). The power of play: The effects of *Portal 2* and *Lumosity* on cognitive and noncognitive skills. *Computers & Education, 80*, 58–67.

Simons, D. J., Boot, W. R., Charbness, N., Gathercole, S. E., Chabris, C. F., Hambrick, D. Z., & Stine-Morrow, E. A. L. (2016). Do brain training programs work? *Psychological Science in the Public Interest, 17*(3), 103-186.

Sims, V. K., & Mayer, R. E. (2002). Domain specificity of spatial expertise: The case of video game players. *Applied Cognitive Psychology, 16*, 97-115.

Singley, M., & Anderson, J. R. (1989). *The transfer of cognitive skill.* Cambridge, MA: Harvard University Press.

Sternberg, R. J. (1990). *Metaphors of mind: Conceptions of the nature of intelligence.* New York: Cambridge University Press.

Weinstein, C. E., & Mayer, R. E. (1985). The teaching of learning strategies. In M. C. Wittrock (ed.), *Handbook of research on teaching* (3rd ed., pp. 315-327). New York: Macmillan.

Wertheimer, M. (1959). *Productive thinking.* New York: Harper & Row.

Wolf, T. H. (1973). *Alfred Binet.* Chicago: Chicago University Press.

Xu, J. (2013). Homework and academic achievement. In J. Hattie & E. M. Anderman (eds.), *International guide to student achievement* (pp. 199–201). New York: Routledge.

Glossary

accelerated longitudinal designs A research design in which a cross-sectional sample is followed for a short longitudinal time span to piece together estimates of change by combining within-person data and between-person data. [11]

accommodation Changing one's cognitive structures in response to the demands of the environment. [2]

agreeableness Personality trait (one of the Big Five) reflecting individual differences in behaviors related to altruism and cooperation, such as compassion, empathy, kindness, honesty, and politeness versus callousness, rudeness, manipulativeness, and aggression. [15]

Alfred Binet French psychologist who was the principal author of the first "modern" intelligence test, measuring reasoning and judgment. [3]

allele An alternative form of a gene or genetic locus, which may have occurred by mutation (de novo), or may have been inherited from a parent. [9]

Alzheimer's disease (AD) An illness usually associated with older people that results in plaques and tangles in the cerebral cortex. [10]

analytical intelligence Intelligence involved when the information-processing components of intelligence are applied to analyze, evaluate, judge, or compare and contrast. [8]

apophenia Refers to the tendency to detect patterns or causal connections where none in fact exist. Originally used to describe a central feature of symptoms of schizophrenia (delusions and hallucinations); most people sometimes experience mild forms of apophenia, such as seeing faces in random objects or mistakenly thinking they heard their name called. [15]

assimilation Adapting one's cognitive structures to the environment. [2]

auditory processing (Ga) A broad collection of abilities related to reasoning about auditory information. [3]

average evoked response (AER) Method used to identify the specific brain wave response to a specific stimulus. [6]

between-group comparisons Comparisons which look at the differences between groups. [10]

Binet–Simon Scale An intelligence test developed by Alfred Binet and Theodore Simon in the early 1900s to ensure that children with intellectual deficits received an adequate education. [3]

biopsychosocial hypothesis View emphasizing the continuous, causal interactions between biological (e.g., brains) and environmental (e.g., activities) factors. [13]

"blank slate" approach Refers to a philosophical theory by John Locke, assuming that the mind does not have preconceived ideas or beliefs. [13]

bodily–kinesthetic intelligence Intelligence that involves the control and management of one's bodily movements and the positioning of them in space. [8]

brain connectivity patterns Brain patterns assessed quantitatively using algorithms based on structural or functional imaging data in an effort to establish how brain areas are connected to other brain areas. [6]

brain efficiency hypothesis Hypothesis based on early functional imaging studies suggesting that people with higher intelligence have more efficient information flow through brain networks during problem solving. [6]

broad abilities Latent variables that influence multiple narrow abilities. [5]

Cattell–Horn–Carroll (CHC) theory of cognitive abilities Comprehensive and empirically supported model of intelligence that combines the Cattell–Horn expanded theory of fluid and crystallized intelligence and Carroll's three-stratum theory cognitive abilities. [4]

Cattell–Horn–Carroll (CHC) hierarchical model See **Cattell–Horn–Carroll (CHC) theory of cognitive abilities.** This model takes a taxonomic view of ability factor structure based on a three-level hierarchy accounting for correlations among ability tests. Level 1 is primary mental abilities, such as verbal comprehension or induction. Level 2 involves broad second-order factors, including fluid intelligence, crystallized intelligence, and spatial visualization. Level 3 is general intelligence. [11]

ceiling effect Describes a situation in which an increase in something (e.g., the amount of physical exercise undertaken each day) reaches a point where it ceases to have a further effect on an outcome (e.g., student alertness in class). [12]

change-detection task A measure of working-memory capacity in which participants are presented with a simple array of colored squares, which is replaced by a mask and then by another array; one of the elements in the new array is then identified as the target, and the participant must indicate whether the target element changed from the first array to the second. [5]

chromosomes Discrete bundle of DNA wrapped around proteins called histones; chromosomes come in pairs, with one chromosome of each pair from one parent. [9]

chronological age Physical age. [2]

cognitive (brain) training A form of training, often using computer programs, that seeks to improve performance of one or more cognitive abilities with the intention that these will improve "real-world" performance. [12]

cognitive consequences research Applied to research on games, research that compares the pretest-to-posttest gain in a cognitive processing skill for a group that plays a computer game which requires using the targeted skill for an extended period of time versus a group that plays an alternative game or no game at all. [16]

cognitive mechanics Basic mechanisms of information processing, including allocation of attention, working memory capacity, encoding and retrieval processes for episodic memory, and induction of relations and patterns, that govern intelligence and problem solving. These mechanisms are thought by some to be vulnerable to age-related decline during adulthood. [11]

cognitive pragmatics Aspects of cognition related to declarative knowledge about people and social contexts, including ideas (semantics), knowledge about societal structures, implicit theories about permissible behaviors in social situations, wisdom, and means of solving problems in everyday contexts. Cognitive pragmatics are thought to be well-maintained and even increase with experience through mid-life and into old age. [11]

cognitive psychology Branch of psychology that focuses on mental processes. [5]

coherence principle Multimedia design principle which involves eliminating extraneous material such as unneeded color and detail in graphics and unneeded facts in text. [16]

complex span tasks Laboratory tasks frequently used to measure working memory capacity; include a processing component and a memory component. [5]

concrete method Method of teaching a problem-solving principle by using familiar concrete materials. [16]

conscientiousness Personality trait (one of the Big Five) reflecting individual differences in behaviors related to prioritizing non-immediate goals and following rules, such as self-discipline, organization, industriousness, and orderliness, versus laziness, impulsivity, disorganization, and distractibility. [15]

contextualist world view Metatheory that emphasizes the importance of environmental factors, including social niches, for determining behavioral development. [11]

converging operations A variety of methods that are used in the hope of their leading to the same scientific conclusion. [7]

corrective feedback Feedback that tells the learner whether the answer to a problem is correct. Cf. **explanative feedback**. [16]

correlation A statistic that describes the strength of a linear association between two variables. Correlations can range from -1 to 1 in value; a correlation of zero indicates no relationship and an absolute-value correlation of 1 indicates a perfect relationship. [14]

counterproductive work behavior (CWB) Component of job performance that consists of voluntary behaviors that harm the organization. [14]

creative intelligence The ability to generate novel and potentially compelling or useful ideas. [8]

creativity Ability and tendency to generate ideas and products that are both novel and compelling. [1, 15]

cross-sectional design A sampling design that recruits persons of different ages taken at a single point in time. [11]

crystallized intelligence Second-order ability in the CHC model related to knowledge that is culturally embedded, including language, symbol systems, declarative knowledge about the world and how it operates. Crystallized intelligence is argued to grow to a plateau in early mid-life and to remain relatively stable into old age. [11]

culture A set of attitudes, values, beliefs and behaviors that are shared by a group of people, and that are communicated from one generation to the next. [7]

culture-fair test A test that is allegedly equally appropriate for members of all cultures and comprises items that are equally fair to everyone; it is doubtful that any truly culture-fair test of intelligence exists. [7]

culture-relevant test A test that requires skills and knowledge that are relevant to the specific cultural experiences of the test-takers. [7]

dedifferentiation hypothesis Hypothesis which states that the primary abilities that can be identified in late childhood and young adulthood become less distinct from one another due to the effects of aging, eventually collapsing into a single general factor of intelligence. [11]

deductive reasoning The ability to follow a set of assumptions to their logical conclusions. [4]

differential item functioning (dif-analysis) Statistical procedures designed to examine specific items for bias. [13]

differential research Research focused on relationships between variables that cannot be manipulated (such as intelligence or personality); typically relies on correlations and related analyses. [5]

diffusion tensor imaging (DTI) An MRI method that shows the details of white matter tracts throughout the brain based on water molecular movement and orientation. [6]

disengagement In Engle's model of working memory, the mental function that allows the removal of old, potentially interfering information from working memory or the prevention of retrieval of that information. This enables attention to focus on new, potentially relevant information. [5]

distribution (of intelligence) A measure of how frequently different levels of intelligence occur within a population. [9]

divergent production The ability to draw on memory to quickly generate many answers to an open-ended prompt. [4]

dizygotic twins Twins who developed from two different fertilized eggs; also known as fraternal twins. [9]

domain-specific knowledge Knowledge considered important for specialists to know but not necessary for all members of culture to know. [4]

Down syndrome A genetic disorder caused by the presence of all or part of a third copy of chromosome 21. It is typically associated with delayed physical development and mild to moderate intellectual disability. [12]

dynamic assessment An umbrella term that refers to a variety of assessment approaches in which test assistance is provided to the test-taker, and progress is subsequently used to make a judgment about their potential. [12]

dynamic testing Testing in which individuals are given some kind of feedback in order to help them improve their performance – that is, the individuals learn while being tested. [2, 7]

electroencephalogram The primary measure of the electrical activity produced as neurons fire on and off. Electrical brain waves are detected by electrodes placed on the scalp. The pattern of these waves changes as the brain responds to different states (e.g., arousal, attention, perception). [6]

embodiment principle One of the principles for fostering generative processing which calls for the instructor to use human-like gesture and movements while teaching. [16]

emic approach Testing method derived from within the context of the culture being studied, rather than from outside it. [7]

entity theorist Theorist who views intelligence in children as innate and governed by genetic endowments and biological factors. [6]

epigenetic research The study of how gene expression may be influenced by non-genetic factors, such as environmental ones. [6]

essential processing Cognitive processing of essential material that may threaten to overload the learner's processing capacity. [16]

etic approach Testing method derived from principles that are alleged to be general and objective in their perspective. [7]

eugenics Belief in the desirability of both positive selection of desirable traits and negative selection against undesirable traits in controlled breeding of humans. [3]

executive attention The ability to control one's attention and prevent having attention captured by internal or external distractions. [5]

executive functions Various cognitive and emotional processes that are employed to enable the completion of a task. [12]

experimental research Research that investigates the effect of an intervention by randomly assigning participants to two or more groups, exposing the groups to treatments or protocols that differ only in the independent variable(s) of interest, and comparing mean levels of the dependent variable across groups. [5]

explanative feedback Feedback that provides learners with an explanation for the correct answer to a problem. Cf. **corrective feedback**. [16]

extraneous processing Processing that does not serve the instructional objective and is caused by poor instructional design. [16]

extraversion Personality trait (one of the Big Five) reflecting individual differences in behaviors – such as talkativeness, assertiveness, sociability, and positive emotionality, versus being quiet, reserved, and submissive – related to pursuing and enjoying rewards. [15]

factor analysis Statistical technique intended for discovering underlying psychological bases of observable test scores. [2, 4]

fairness factor The tendency of parents to try to give all of their children, despite differences in giftedness, a family environment of equal quality. [10]

fetal alcohol syndrome (FAS) A syndrome which occurs when children are exposed prenatally to alcohol from their mother's drinking and which is associated with intellectual disability and distinct facial features such as a thin upper lip, a flattened philtrum, and malformed openings of the eyelids. [10]

five-factor model (the Big Five) Model that describes the five major broad dimensions of personality, based on how a wide range of personality traits tend to correlate within the population; can be used as a taxonomy to categorize more specific traits. [15]

fixed The belief that intelligence cannot change due to environmental interventions and changes. [13]

fluid intelligence Second-order ability in the CHC model related to the ability to detect patterns, to extrapolate, to synthesize and analyze information, to formulate and implement strategies, to be adaptive in novel problem situations. Fluid intelligence is argued to decline during adulthood, with the rate of decline perhaps accelerating in very old age. [11]

Flynn effect Historical pattern around the world of increasing measured IQ during the twentieth century, with each new generation tending to score higher than the previous one on tests of intelligence. Increases averaged about 3 points per decade. During the twenty-first century, some countries have continued to show increases whereas others have not. [4, 11]

focus of attention In Oberauer's model of working memory, the most highly activated chunk of information in memory, which is currently being manipulated; the capacity is a single chunk of information. [5]

Fragile X syndrome A genetic condition, more common in males, that causes a range of developmental problems including intellectual, language, and learning difficulties. [12]

Francis Galton British psychologist who proposed both that intelligence can be understood in terms of basic psychomotor skills and that intelligence is highly heritable. [3]

Full-Scale IQ (FSIQ) The overall summary of performance of an intelligence test battery. On most contemporary intelligence tests, the average score is set to 100, with a standard deviation of 15. [4]

functional health literacy The degree to which individuals have the capacity to obtain, process, and understand basic health information and services needed to make appropriate health decisions. [14]

gene A unit of heredity transmitted from a parent to offspring. [9]

general cognitive ability (GCA) Representation of the shared general component that is common to multiple cognitive constructs (i.e., verbal reasoning, mathematical reasoning, or writing skills). Specific cognitive constructs have something unique to each of them, whereas general cognitive ability represents the shared component that is common to all of these constructs. [13, 14]

general factor An ability or latent variable that crosses across all tasks requiring intelligence (or some other generalized attribute). [2, 4]

general intelligence, g An ability that pervades performance on many different tasks and kinds of tasks. [1, 2]

general knowledge Knowledge emphasized as important for all members of a culture to know. [4]

generative learning Learning that occurs when the learner engages in appropriate cognitive processing, including selecting the relevant incoming information, mentally organizing it into a coherent structure in working memory, and integrating it with relevant prior knowledge activated from long-term memory. [16]

generative learning strategy Something that learners do during learning with the intention of improving their understanding, including engaging in the cognitive processes of selecting, organizing, and integrating during learning. [16]

genetically informative design A study design in which quantitative- or molecular-genetic information can be generated and meaningfully interpreted (e.g., a family design, a twin design, a case-control design). [9]

genetics The general field of science that studies the composition of genes and how they work. [9]

genome The complete set of genetic material present in an organism, defining its biological identity. [9]

genome-wide association study (GWAS) A molecular-genetic analytic approach aimed at linking or associating specific genetic polymorphisms (markers) with specific behavioral traits. [9]

genomics The study of organism-specific sets of genetic material, or chromosomes. [9]

genotype All the genetic information that one person has inherited. [9]

gifted A term used to describe very high-performing individuals. Historically, giftedness referred to high intelligence as measured by IQ or scholastic tests but the term has since been broadened to refer to performance in a variety of spheres. [12]

glucose metabolic rate (GMR) Measure that reflects how much glucose energy is being consumed during brain activity; measured using PET scanning. [6]

group factor A latent variable that influences multiple variables, but not all variables in a domain. [4]

Head Start A government-sponsored program that provides early childhood enrichment programs to low-income, preschool children. [13]

heritability The proportion of variation in a trait (e.g. intelligence) among individuals that is due to genetic effects. [1, 2, 9]

heterozygous Description of a diploid organism when two different alleles of a gene are present. [9]

homozygous Description of a diploid organism when two identical alleles of a gene are present. [9]

human autonomy The power of the individual to determine their lives and their fate through choice. [10]

implicit theory A folk conception of a construct, such as intelligence; it is what people believe the construct to be, in contrast to what it actually is. [7]

inductive reasoning The ability to observe specific instances of a phenomenon and discover patterns or rules that allow us to predict its behavior. [4]

inspection time A laboratory task meant to measure mental speed, in which a stimulus is presented very briefly, and the participant must make a simple decision about the stimulus (e.g., which of two vertical lines was longer); the shortest presentation time for which a participant can consistently respond correctly is that person's inspection time. [5]

instrumental enrichment (IE) A cognitive training program, primarily employing non-curricular activities, that is designed to enhance an individual's learning and thinking strategies. [12]

intellectual disability A disability that is characterized by significant limitations in both intellectual functioning and adaptive behavior in conceptual, social, and practical skill areas. [12]

intelligence The ability to understand complex ideas, to adapt effectively to the environment, to learn from experience, to engage in various forms of reasoning, to make good decisions, and to solve problems. [1]

Intelligence Quotient (IQ) Originally, the ratio of mental age to chronological age multiplied by 100; today, IQs are determined by converting percentile scores into standard scores with a mean of 100 and a standard deviation typically of 15. [2]

interpersonal intelligence Intelligence used to relate to other people. [8]

intrapersonal intelligence Intelligence involved in understanding oneself. [8]

knowledge-acquisition components Components used to learn how to solve problems or simply to acquire declarative knowledge in the first place. [8]

latent factor A measure of a construct (such as a cognitive process) that cannot be directly observed, that is derived from scores on multiple tests designed to assess that construct. [5]

latent variable A variable not directly observed but hypothesized to exist because of its apparent influence on observed variables. [4]

learning by drawing Method of learning in which a person creates a drawing that depicts a process or structure described in the lesson. [16]

learning disability In the United States, this refers to a disorder that affects a wide range of academic and functional skills including language, reading, writing, and mathematics; it is not to be confused with an intellectual disability. [12]

learning efficiency (Gl) The speed and ease at which information can be committed to memory. [4]

learning strategy Something that learners do during learning with the intention of improving their learning. [16]

legitimate peripheral participation Refers to a process involving a gradual transition from novice to expert in a given area of activity by means of participation in a social context with more experienced members of one's community. [12]

linguistic intelligence intelligence involved in the use of words and language in general. [8]

logical-mathematical intelligence Intelligence used in solving logical and mathematical problems. [8]

longitudinal design A sampling design that follows the same sample of persons, measuring them repeatedly, often at a fixed time interval, to be able to assess development within persons over time. [11, 13]

long-term potentiation (LTP) The long-term strengthening of nerve-cell connections. [9]

long-term synaptic depression (LTD) The long-term weakening of nerve-cell connections. [9]

macroanalytic approach Method for studying the relationship between cognitive processes and intelligence, in which relationships between latent variables are examined. [5]

magnetic resonance imaging (MRI) A non-invasive technology that uses magnetic fields to generate images revealing structural details in the brain; brain function can be inferred from blood flow determinations (fMRI). [6]

maintenance In Engle's model of working memory, the mental function that keeps information active and prevents it from decaying. [5]

malleable The belief that intelligence can change and improve with practice and/or increased education. [13]

matching The tendency of (many) individuals to match the excellence of their performance with an environment of corresponding excellence, reinforced by society's tendency to do the same. [10]

measurement error The sum of all influences that cause a measurement to deviate from its true value. [4]

mechanistic theorist Theorist who emphasizes development across the lifespan as a process of learning and experience during childhood and into adulthood. [11]

mental age A description of a child's intelligence in terms of the age at which the average child attains the same score as the individual child, regardless of chronological age. [2, 4]

mental rotation A task that requires participants to imagine what a figure would look like if it were rotated in space. [13]

meta-analysis A technique in which the researcher locates as many studies as possible reporting the relationship of interest (e.g., sex differences in mathematics performance) and quantitatively combines the results. [13, 14]

metacomponents Executive processes, used to plan what to do, monitor things

as they are being done, and evaluate things after they are done. [8]

microanalytic approach Method for studying the relationship between cognitive processes and intelligence, in which characteristics of a cognitive task are manipulated in an attempt to identify cognitive processes that are involved in intelligence test performance. [5]

mild cognitive impairment A form of forgetfulness and of loss of verbal fluency that may lead to Alzheimer's disease or to other forms of dementia. [10]

modality principle Method for managing essential processing which calls for presenting words in spoken form rather than printed form. [16]

molecular genetic methods Research methods used in genetic studies that capitalize on what we can learn about each individual's DNA and its molecular composition. [9]

mono-/oligo-/poly-/omnigenic score A descriptor reflecting the (weighted) effects of a genetic locus (mono-) or multiple loci (oligo- for few, poly- for many, and omni- for all) on a single trait (e.g., intelligence). [9]

monomorphic Genetic traits in the human genome with no variation. [9]

monozygotic twins Twins whose genetic material is basically identical because they developed from the same fertilized egg; also referred to as identical twins. [9]

multimedia principle The idea that people learn better from words and pictures than from words alone. [16]

musical intelligence Intelligence involved in understanding and producing music. [8]

narrow abilities Latent variables that influence a narrow range of abilities. [4]

naturalist intelligence Intelligence used to recognize patterns in nature. [8]

n-back task A measure of WMC in which participants are presented an ongoing series of digits and must press a button when the current digit matches the one that was presented *n* digits ago. [5]

neural plasticity Experience-dependent changes in the morphology and functional connectivity of brain systems, including even the growth, migration, and functional evolution of new neurons that is now known to continue into late life. [11]

neuron The nerve cells that transmit electrical signals in response to stimuli to and from the brain. [9]

neuroticism personality trait (one of the Big Five) that reflects individual differences in the tendency to experience negative emotions, which are defensive responses to threats and punishments.

nucleotide The basic structural unit of a single molecule of DNA. [15]

openness/intellect Personality trait that reflects individual differences in behaviors related to cognitive exploration and the tendency to find information rewarding and to use reasoning and perception to detect patterns and meanings in what we experience. [15]

organismic theorist Theorist who emphasizes intellectual development during childhood as a regular sequence of (largely genetically programmed) emerging cognitive traits. [11]

organizational citizenship behavior (OCB) Component of job performance that consists of behaviors typically outside explicit job duties and that contribute to the goals of the organization via its social and psychological environment (e.g., volunteering at work, assisting another with a task). [14]

parieto-frontal integration theory (P-FIT) of intelligence Model proposed in 2007 based on a review of brain-imaging studies, identifying a network of brain areas related to intelligence. The network is distributed throughout the brain, contrary to previous suggestions that only the frontal lobes are involved in intelligence. [6]

path diagram A drawing showing the hypothesized influences among observed and latent variables. [4]

percentile The percentage of scores a given score exceeds; thus, the score of a person who scores in the 50th percentile exceeds the scores of 50 percent of test-takers. [2]

performance components Components that execute the instructions of the metacomponents – essentially, they perform the actions directed by the metacomponents. [8]

personality traits Dimensions of variation within the population that describe relatively stable patterns of behavior, motivation, emotion, and cognition. They are typically considered to be applicable to people in any culture, rather than referring to skills, habits, or beliefs that might be specific to one cultural context or another. [15]

personalization principle Calls for putting words in conversational style rather than formal style. [16]

phenotype The set of observable characteristics of a person that result from that person's interaction with the environment. [9]

plasticity of intelligence Experience-dependent changes in the level of intellectual ability performance, often through explicit strategy training or through extended practice with tests. [11]

pleiotropy The capability of a single gene to influence two or more seemingly unrelated phenotypes. [9]

polygenic Genetic characteristic generated by many interactions of multiple genes. [9]

polygenic score A number generated by combining the weighted effects of multiple genetic loci (gene variants or other nucleotide sequence variations, i.e., alleles) on a single trait (e.g., intelligence). [9]

polymorphism Instances of variation in the human genome. [9]

population norms Statistical characteristics of a population such as the variable's mean and standard deviation. Norms are used to compare individual scores with what is typical in a population. [4]

positron emission tomography (PET) Imaging technology based on injecting a low level radioactive tracer into a person to label brain areas active during problem solving. [6]

practical intelligence Intelligence used when individuals apply their abilities to the kinds of problems that confront them in daily life, such as on the job or in the home. [8]

predictive bias Occurs when a test has a better prediction of a criterion (e.g., success in college) for one group of people than for another. [13]

predictive validation studies Study design in which predictor measures are obtained first and then performance measures are obtained at a later point in time. This study design is ideal for employment selection contexts because selection scenarios involve obtaining measures in order to predict performance at a later point (post-hire). [14]

pretraining principle Method for managing essential processing which calls for teaching students about the names and characteristics of key terms before the lesson. [16]

processing speed (Gs) The fluency with which the spotlight of attention can be directed from task to task. [4]

proxy variable A variable used in place of another variable that proves to be immeasurable. Basically, a stand-in for another variable. [14]

psychological g A single mental process thought to cause psychometric g. [5]

psychometric approach Approach to understanding intelligence through the statistical analysis of scores on tests alleged to measure intelligence. [4]

psychometric g The positive correlation between mental tests. [5]

psychometrics The science of measuring psychological states, traits, and processes. [4]

quantitative-genetic methods Research methods used when investigating the genetic origins of traits that exhibit continuous variation, or infinite variety, like height or weight; frequently defined by the use of genetically informative designs, which draw upon types of biological relatives who share genetic material. [9]

range restriction Lower variability of scores in a selected sample (e.g., employees) relative to an unselected population (e.g., job applicants). Samples with narrower ranges of scores tend to produce small correlations – often dramatically smaller than what we would find in a full-range sample. [14]

reaction time (RT) A laboratory task meant to measure mental speed, in which a stimulus is presented and the participant must respond as quickly as possible (often by pressing a button). [5]

reasoning ability Ability to draw reasonable conclusions from data. [2]

region of direct access In Oberauer's model of working memory, the chunks of information that are activated, but are not in the focus of attention. [5]

retrieval fluency (Gr) The speed and ease at which information can be retrieved from long-term memory storage. [4]

sampling error The error in statistical analysis to account for a sample that doesn't represent the population from which it is drawn. Any sample might not be representative of its population. The smaller a sample, the greater the risk of an unrepresentative draw. [14]

savant A person who demonstrates one or more exceptional capacities or abilities in areas such as memory, music, calculation, or art while also demonstrating significant deficits in other areas of cognitive functioning. [12]

segmenting principle Method for managing essential processing which calls for breaking a continuous presentation into manageable parts controlled by the learner. [16]

sequential sampling design Design of research that involves repeated cross-sectional sampling from the same population on some regular testing interval (e.g., 5 years) – a cross-sectional sequence, and then, perhaps, following the same people over time – a longitudinal sequence. [11]

sex hormones Chemicals secreted from the sex glands (testes, ovaries) and related structures that influence sex-differentiated characteristics such as reproduction. [13]

sex roles Beliefs about the way males and females differ and how they should differ. [13]

shaping Modifying an environment to better suit one's abilities, interests, and motivations. [8]

signaling principle Multimedia design principle which calls for highlighting essential material such as using bold font for important words or color cueing for important parts of a graphic. [16]

situated cognition A theoretical position which holds that all knowledge is situated in activity that is closely bound to social, cultural, and physical contexts. [12]

skill theorist Theorist who views cognition and intelligence as an acquired set of dispositions and skills influenced by learning and environmental factors. [11]

socioeconomic status (SES) A measure of family employment, wealth, income, and education. [10]

sociogenomics The study of social life in genetic terms. [9]

spatial contiguity principle Multimedia design principle which calls for placing printed text next to the part of the graphic it refers to. [16]

spatial mapping A method of learning that involves creating a graphic organizer or concept map of the material. [16]

specific factor A latent variable that influences a single observed variable in a factor analysis. [4]

specific transfer of general skills The theory that playing a game that requires repeatedly exercising a cognitive skill in a variety of contexts at increasing levels of challenge will allow the player to improve on the targeted skill in the game and in contexts outside the game that require the same target skill, such as measured by a classic cognitive processing test. [16]

speed contamination hypothesis Hypothesis that speeded tests of intelligence overestimate late-life decline in intelligence due to age-related slowing of information processing speed, which reduces the validity of the tests in old age as measures of the target intellectual ability. [11]

stability coefficients Correlations of a test with itself in a longitudinal sample; coefficients should be high if individual differences in rates of change are small; when corrected for measurement error (unreliability), perfect stability of 1.0 would imply no individual differences (variance) in change. [11]

Stanford–Binet Intelligence Scales An Intelligence test developed by Lewis Terman of Stanford University, based on Alfred Binet's work on intelligence and intelligence testing. [3]

static testing Intelligence testing in which an examinee takes a test and later receives a test score. [2]

statistically significant A statistical threshold where it can be concluded that a relationship between variables is not due to chance. [13]

stereotype threat Being at risk of confirming a negative stereotype about one's social group. This phenomenon can often lower cognitive performance. [13]

structural equation modeling Statistical technique that allows investigators to examine relationships between latent factors. [5]

task performance Component of job performance that consists of behaviors formally recognized as part of the job and that contribute to the core duties of the job. [14]

teratogens Environmental agents that damage a developing baby during the time the child is in the womb. [10]

test norms The reference groups for determining how well children and adults score, on average, on an IQ test. [4]

theory of successful intelligence A more complex definition of intelligence that considers the ability to formulate and strive for goals in one's life given one's sociocultural context, making the best use of analytical, creative and practical strengths, while at the same time compensating for weaknesses in any of these areas. [8]

transfer The ability to use what was learned before in a new situation, such as to solve a new problem or learn something new. [12, 16]

transferable knowledge Knowledge that can be applied to new situations. [12]

validated Finding that meets the requirements of the scientific method and research process. [13]

verbal ability One's ability with words. [2]

visual–spatial intelligence Intelligence involved in mentally rotating objects in one's head, imagining how to fit suitcases into the trunk of a car, imagining what a building project will look like when it is done, solving jigsaw puzzles, making sense of maps and routes planned using maps, and finding one's way from one place to another without the use of a map.

visual–spatial processing (Gv) A broad collection of abilities related to reasoning about visual and spatial information. [8]

voxel–based morphometry (VBM) A method of brain image analysis that quantifies brain characteristics (e.g. amount of gray or white matter, GMR) in each voxel of the image. [6]

Wechsler Adult Intelligence Scale (WAIS) A general intelligence test for adults, 16 years and older, designed by David Wechsler. [3]

Wechsler Intelligence Scale for Children (WISC) A general intelligence test designed for children between the ages of 6 and 15, designed by David Wechsler. [3]

whole genome sequencing (WGS) The process of determining the exact sequence of nucleotides that make up a single genome. [9]

wisdom Effective judgment regarding how to solve difficult and uncertain life problems. [15]

within-group comparison Comparisons which look at similarities and differences in a specific group. [10]

working memory capacity (Gwm or WMC) A cognitive system responsible for holding information in a state available for deliberate processing. [4, 5]

worst performance rule Phenomenon in which an examinee's longest response times in a response time task have the strongest (negative) correlation with intelligence test performance. [5]

zone of proximal development (ZPD) The idea that learning occurs best with guidance from an experienced teacher at a level just beyond that at which an individual feels comfortable. [2]

Index

Bold type refers to tables; *italic* to figures

Abbreviations used in subheadings
CHC theory = Cattell–Horn–Carroll theory
GCA = general cognitive ability